Levons nos verres, buvons à ta promotion et à tes nouvelles responsabilités.

Puisse ce livre de l'automobile t'en distraire de temps en temps, et surtout les fins de quarter.

avec toute notre affection —

Papa

Maman

Karl

Olivier

Valérie

Poupouette

THE GREAT BOOK of AUTOMOBILES

WHITE STAR
PUBLISHERS

CONTENTS

GRAPHIC DESIGN
Patrizia Balocco Lovisetti
Maria Cucchi

THE GREAT BOOK OF AUTOMOBILES
© 2003 White Star S.r.l.
Via Candido Sassone, 22/24
13100 Vercelli, Italy
www.whitestar.it

ISBN 88-544-0012-2

REPRINTS:
2 3 4 5 6 08 07 06 05 04

Printed in China

Taken from:

CONVERTIBLES - history and evolution of dream cars
© 1998 White Star S.r.l.
ISBN 88-8095-305-2

CLASSIC CARS - from 1945 to the present
© 2001 White Star S.r.l.
ISBN 88-8095-652-3

A century of competition and human challenges
MOTOR RACING
New extended and updated edition
© 1999, 2001 White Star S.r.l.
ISBN 88-8095-643-4

CONVERTIBLES

HISTORY AND EVOLUTION OF DREAM CARS

CONTENTS

2-3 This is the front of a Mercedes Benz 770 K "Grosser Mercedes" from 1937.
4-5 1960 Cadillac Eldorado.
6-7 An Isotta Fraschini, manufactured from 1919 to 1935.
8-9 The Mercedes 300 SL, a popular model during the 1960s.

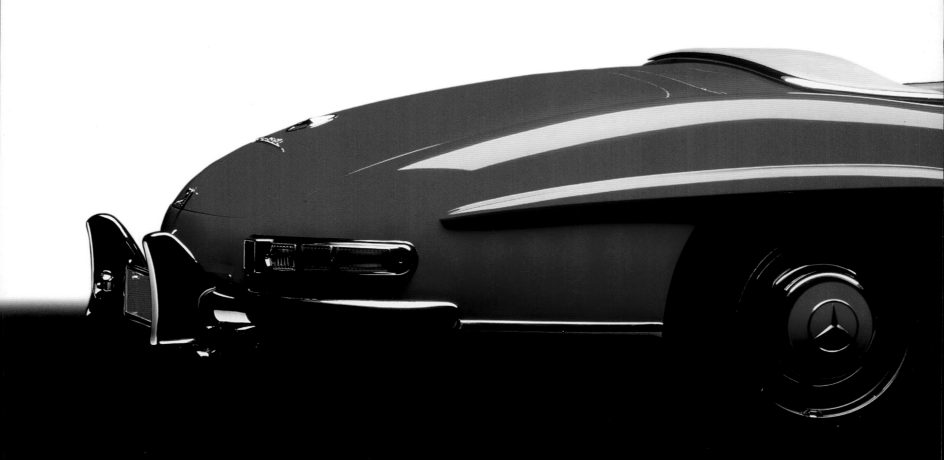

PREFACE

The convertible is to the car what the thoroughbred is to the horse. The comparison of the convertible with this most noble of animals is also valid for the spirit they share which evokes the desire for open spaces, freedom and riding at full speed with the wind in one's hair. But convertibles are much more: They are a legacy of recent world history, bearing an intrinsic message that no other type of car can and a tangible symbol of the moods, wishes and social habits of the western world. They have survived dictatorships, recessions, revolutions, reconstructions and wars, often being used as a symbol of, if not a participant in, moments of contemporary history. There have been very many books dedicated to this elite type of car: Some are monographic works on famous models, from enormous convertible sedans to small, fleet-footed sports cars; some illustrate the production of a certain type of open top while others analyze a precise period, a dominant style or perhaps production from a particular part of the world. Those that remain deal with technological, formal and production aspects. This book, "Convertibles", attempts to fill the gap created by the lack of an all-round history of the open-topped car from its origins up to the year 2000, from when cars were open-topped from necessity rather than choice up till the most recent stylistic innovations. It has been like excavating through geological strata while bouncing from one side of the globe to the other, analyzing works of designers from France, Germany, Great Britain, Italy, the United States and occasionally Japan and even China. Our research has led to the production of nine chapters, we hope sufficiently detailed, or at least enough so, to encourage other publications to deal with open-topped motoring in all its aspects. Our history is presented chronologically and the chapters are divided into design periods in the various areas of the world. The second part of the volume is dedicated to the description of models that we consider particularly significant. To have to leave out some has been a real torment. Leafing through these very best, one notices how much has changed in terms of shape and contents over ninety years, though not the desire to dream. Yesterday, as they do today, convertibles and roadsters represented a cocktail of daring, irony and status for their owners; for their designers, they were the best opportunity to experiment with new ideas or to show the best of oneself. The result is that open-topped cars have always occupied the most elite position in the world of car fashions for their nobility, elegance and imaginativeness of design.

We hope readers will excuse us for any imperfections and for the inevitable omissions.

10-11 The Chevrolet Corvette is the definitive American sports car, the Ferrari of the United States. The photograph shows the 1997 version, the fifth generation that made its debut 44 years after the first series. It maintains the original characteristics that have made Corvettes so famous: the body made from fiberglass, a long hood, a trim rear end and the famous Chevrolet Smallblock V8 engine.

11 This poster from the end of the 19th century illustrates one of the possible uses for the heir to the carriage - a Sunday outing for the family. The car in the foreground is an 1898 Peugeot and, unlike many models of that time, the seats neither face each other nor are back to back; they herald the common configuration used today.

12-13 This picture shows the looming profile of one of the most desirable English cars of all time, the Jaguar E-Type. This car has many features worthy of note; the characteristic spoked wheels, the lights protected by transparent covers, the long hood which hid first the 6 cylinder in-line engine, then the V12 in the 1970's, and the cuttlebone-shaped back end which was soon taken up by Alfa Romeo's Duetto, later known as the Spider.

14-15 The Ferrari F50 is an open top but not a convertible, as it was only produced with a hard top that made this road monster resemble the prototype sports cars of the 1960's and 70's. The mid-mounted engine was a 4698cc V12 capable of producing 520 HP. The car's top speed was 203 mph and 0-60 acceleration was an incredible 3.8 seconds.

The car is "born" open-topped

LATE 19TH CENTURY CARRIAGES

One Sunday morning towards the end of the 1800's in one of any of the large cities in the industrialized nations, a well-bred gentleman approaching what is discreetly called "middle" age is walking down the high street.

In his right hand he carries his gloves and in his left the newspaper he has just bought from the paper-boy waiting, as usual, outside the church for those who - like the gentleman above, having listened attentively to the sermon - are looking forward to the enjoyable Sunday routine of an aperitif, lunch at the club and a leisurely perusal of the paper.

Walking towards him on the other side of the road are two elegantly dressed young ladies, close enough for the gentleman to appreciate their features and fashions, one dressed in dark red and the other in bright blue and white. It is a clear, warm day that encourages thoughts of a trip into the countryside, a picnic perhaps if you like that sort of thing. On the other hand maybe a relaxing afternoon at the club would be better.

All of a sudden, a burst of noise shatters the quiet with the same effect on the man's mood as

17 bottom The subject of the drawing is a broken down vehicle being drawn by a horse. The vis-à-vis seating arrangement was the most common on open carriages and stagecoaches.

16-17 R.E. Olds, one of the main characters in the early development of the car, at the wheel of his first model, non-topped, built in 1897.

17 top The Peugeot Vis-à-vis dates from 1897. Its name indicates that the passengers sat opposite one another. In other models of the period the seats were laid out differently: The 1897 Oldsmobile had opposed seating, i.e. they sat back to back, but generally the padded seats faced one another. The configuration dictated the position and unfolding of the soft cover.

a hammer on a crystal glass, and before he has time to realize what is happening, he finds his trousers and gaiters covered in mud.

The scoundrel responsible, with less respect for good manners than for the rules of the road, has just driven by in one of those horrible motorized carriages that have been severely testing the civility of the well-to-do for some time. Annoyed, the man tries in vain to clean off the mud.

The two ladies, seeming much less fashionable to him now, hide their laughter behind their hands and turn their heads in the direction of the daredevil already hidden behind a large cloud of smelly smoke.

The gentleman is by no means conservative; on the contrary, he considers himself something of a liberal spirit. But there is a limit to everything: If these young madcaps want to play with these useless, costly contraptions, let them do it in the countryside or in areas which the authorities should have reserved for these childish pastimes some time ago. Fortunately this fashion, like all others, will pass and the reassuring clip-clop of horses' hooves will return.

Resigned but not cheered, the gentleman continues his dignified walk to the club.

But his hopes are poorly placed. The thoughtless young man of good family, with his cap pulled tight down on his head, will shortly win the battle. Only a few years hence, horse transport will remain the prerogative of the nostalgic provincial nobility who are unwaveringly tied to their coach and four despite it being obsolete, useless and dangerous. Instead, the noisy, clumsy rig that is no more than a cutdown carriage adapted to carry what is called an "internal combustion engine" will invade the world, continually improving its technologies and changing shape - first following, then creating, its own stylistic trends: the car.

16 top left Karl Friedrich Benz's 1888 tricycle was called Model 3. A seat for the third and fourth passengers was placed in front of the rider. The power given by this tricycle's motor was 1.5 HP.

16 bottom This 1894 Peugeot was powered by a Daimler engine. Peugeot and Panhard & Levassor were among Gottlieb Daimler's first enthusiastic supporters and brought the passion for motor vehicles to France.

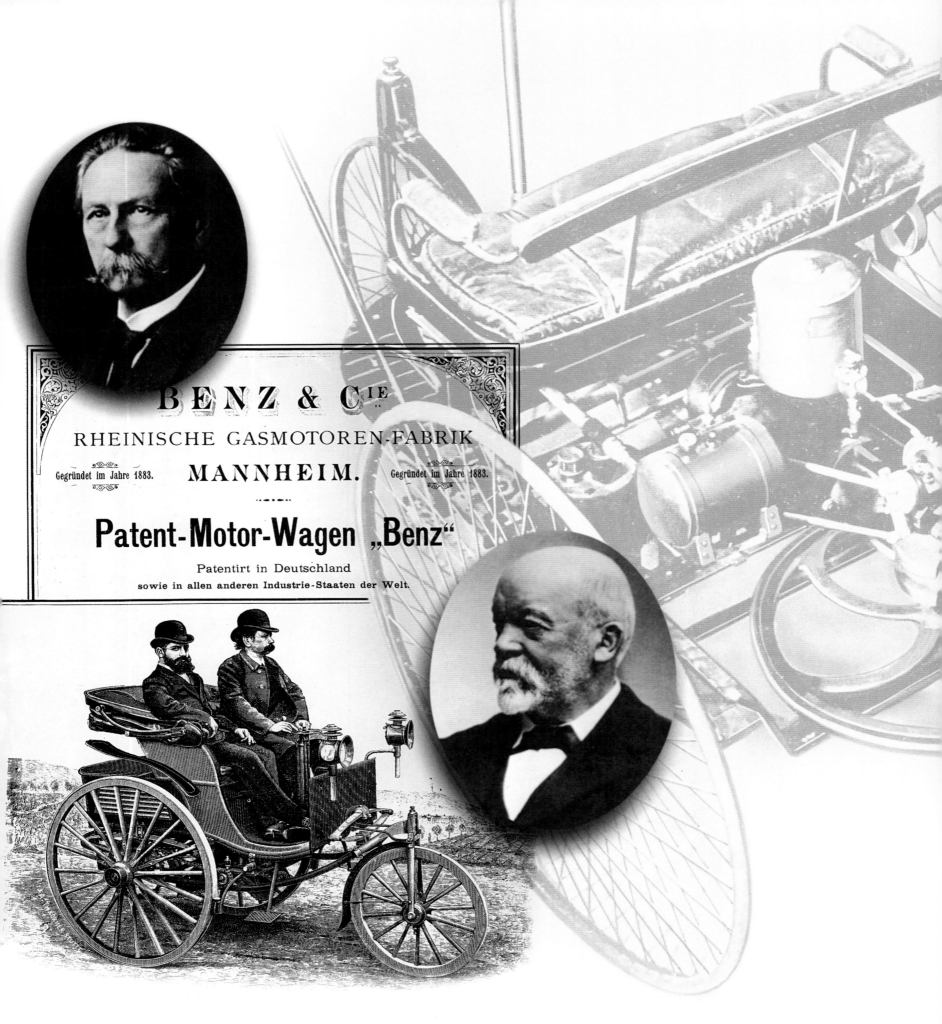

18 top left Karl Friedrich Benz (1844-1929) was one of the great figures in the history of the car.

18 bottom left The poster showing Benz's tricycle was the first advertising of a motor vehicle and dates from 1888. The cost of the Patent-Motorwagen was 2,750 marks.

18 center Gottlieb Daimler (1834-1900) built the first car, the Motorwagen, in 1886. The Daimler name was later linked with that of Benz to create one of Germany's most famous industrial brand-names.

18-19 The picture shows the motor of the first road-going automobile: the Benz Patent-Motorwagen. It was built at the end of 1885 and tested in 1886. The engine had a single 990cc cylinder capable of producing less than 1 HP. It had no fuel tank so Benz's son, Eugene, had to run after his father with a bottle to top up the motor. Karl Benz's family supported him in his obstinate wish to build internal combustion engines. In 1888, his wife, Bertha Ringer, loaded her children on one of his cars and drove from Mannheim to Pforzheim to demonstrate the reliability of her husband's vehicles!

19 top These are the drawings Benz included in his application for the patent number 37435, which was awarded to him on 2 November 1886.

19 center The Benz Velociped of 1894 shows the first attempt to rationalize the layout of the components.

19 bottom The Curved Dash Oldsmobile of 1903 can be considered one of the two most important early cars with the Ford Model T. Finally the wheels were of equal size.

Can the hero of this story really already be called a "car"? That is a controversial question.

We believe that the automobile became a car from the moment it had four wheels, an internal propulsion unit (internal combustion engine not a steam-driven motor), a steering wheel (not a lever system or handlebar) and was able to carry at least one passenger as well as the driver, seated and facing in the direction of travel.

After a long series of prototypes, sometimes ingenious, sometimes absolutely mad (like the mechanical horse with six hooves), the car began to develop in a fixed direction. The first examples, produced in 1886 by Gottlieb Daimler and Karl Benz, can be considered an excellent starting point due to the chain effects that they generated. It did not take long for Daimler's ideas to arrive in France thanks to Panhard & Levassor and Peugeot, in Italy through Giovanni Agnelli, in England through a branch of Daimler's own company and in the United States through the piano manufacturer Steinway, while Benz became the world's most important carmaker producing over 600 machines a year. Today's cars therefore descend from a German lineage. But it was in England and above all France that the motoring fever took rapid hold, finding enthusiasts in every social stratum. In Italy, too, passion for the car was not slow in arriving while the reaction of industry and America was reluctant. Once started, though, the US market was unstoppable: 4,192 cars were sold in 1900 but three times that number were sold in 1903. By 1914 there were over one and a half million cars in the world, almost all of them open-topped.

Most of today's most important manufacturers came into being during this period: Buick, Cadillac, Ford, Fiat, Mercedes, Oldsmobile, Peugeot, Rolls Royce, while others which had been important at the beginning of the century had disappeared, failed, been swallowed up by other marques or just did not have the necessary creative force to keep up with the increasingly competitive market both

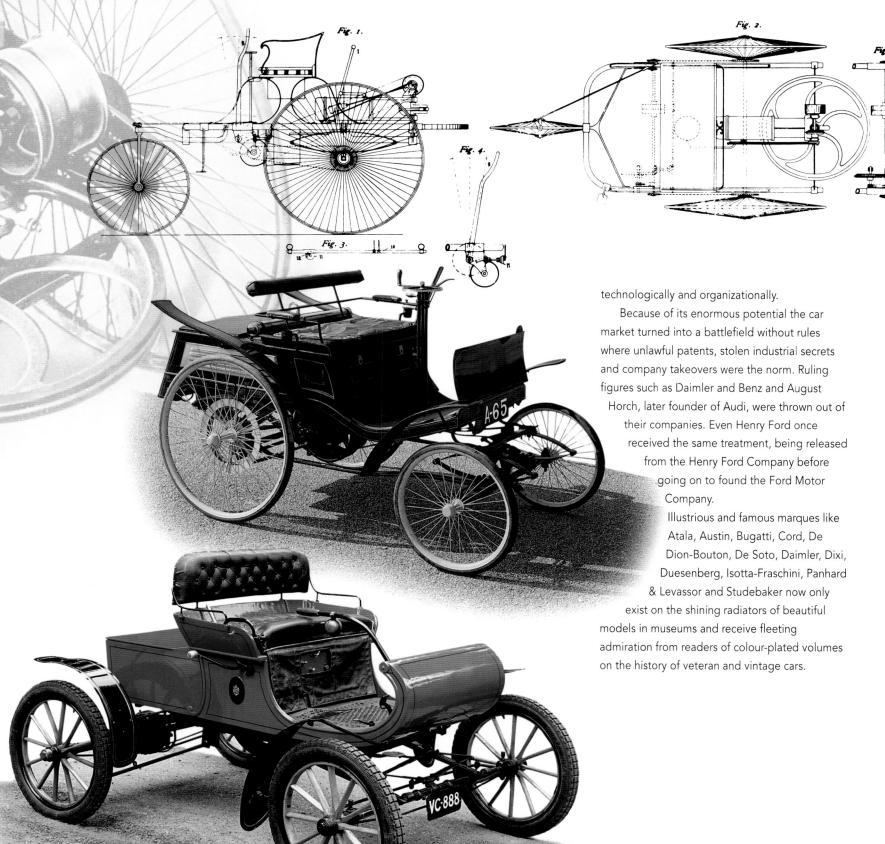

technologically and organizationally.

Because of its enormous potential the car market turned into a battlefield without rules where unlawful patents, stolen industrial secrets and company takeovers were the norm. Ruling figures such as Daimler and Benz and August Horch, later founder of Audi, were thrown out of their companies. Even Henry Ford once received the same treatment, being released from the Henry Ford Company before going on to found the Ford Motor Company.

Illustrious and famous marques like Atala, Austin, Bugatti, Cord, De Dion-Bouton, De Soto, Daimler, Dixi, Duesenberg, Isotta-Fraschini, Panhard & Levassor and Studebaker now only exist on the shining radiators of beautiful models in museums and receive fleeting admiration from readers of colour-plated volumes on the history of veteran and vintage cars.

THE VERY FIRST CARS
AT THE TURN OF THE CENTURY

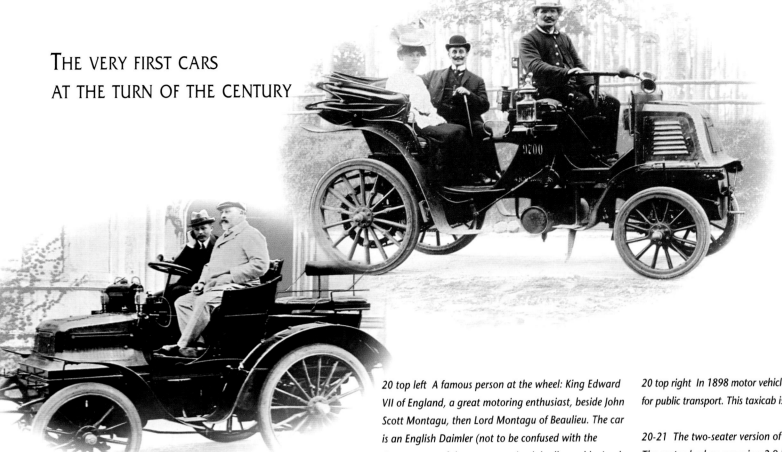

20 top left A famous person at the wheel: King Edward VII of England, a great motoring enthusiast, beside John Scott Montagu, then Lord Montagu of Beaulieu. The car is an English Daimler (not to be confused with the German cars of the same name) originally used by Lord Montagu, a key British auto booster.

20 top right In 1898 motor vehicles were already being used for public transport. This taxicab is a Daimler Phoenix-Wagen.

20-21 The two-seater version of the 1893 Benz Viktoria. The motor had an amazing 2.9 liter single cylinder to give a power of only 6 HP.

Before chassis could be designed specifically for the requirements of a car, it was necessary to wait until industrial production turned serious during the first decade of the century. In the meantime horse-drawn carriages had to satisfy the feverish activity of inventors and mechanics and were continually cannibalized. They were stripped right down to make space for the motor, radiator, auxiliary parts and control systems with the result that they no longer had anything in common with their original equestrian models. It goes without saying that the first cars had large wheels with spokes and wooden, tireless rims (or spokes and bicycle tires), large springs to absorb the unevenness of the roads, and interiors like wooden shells with seats not always padded or covered in leather, which caused easily imaginable problems to the base of the spine of the intrepid drivers.

Progress always demands some sacrifices.

The motor was huge and noisy in proportion to its power output. The internal combustion engine was almost immediately adopted, although numerous attempts used electric, steam or gas-driven propulsion units.

It was positioned indifferently at either end of the machine or under the passenger cab. The steering column was visible and topped by an almost horizontal, large diameter steering wheel, originally with a grip similar to that of a tram.

The first models were open-topped and had at most a waxed cloth hood just like the "romantic coupés", the short two-seater carriages in vogue with high society gentlemen. During this pioneering

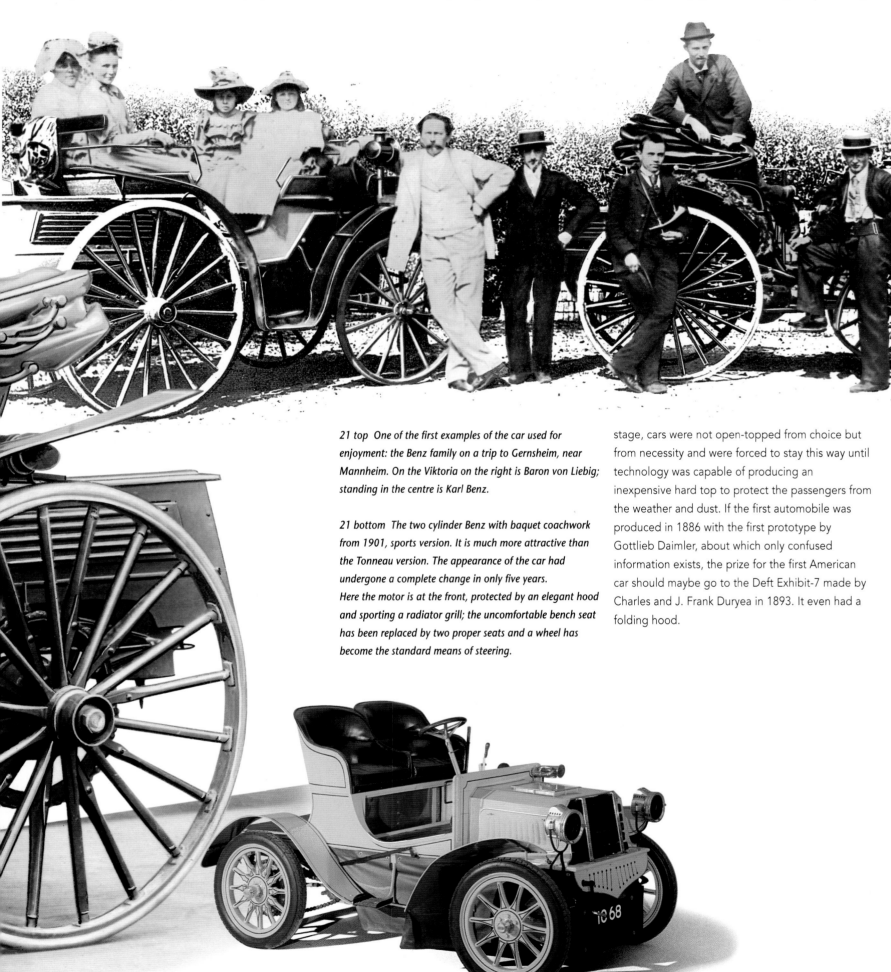

21 top One of the first examples of the car used for enjoyment: the Benz family on a trip to Gernsheim, near Mannheim. On the Viktoria on the right is Baron von Liebig; standing in the centre is Karl Benz.

21 bottom The two cylinder Benz with baquet coachwork from 1901, sports version. It is much more attractive than the Tonneau version. The appearance of the car had undergone a complete change in only five years.
Here the motor is at the front, protected by an elegant hood and sporting a radiator grill; the uncomfortable bench seat has been replaced by two proper seats and a wheel has become the standard means of steering.

stage, cars were not open-topped from choice but from necessity and were forced to stay this way until technology was capable of producing an inexpensive hard top to protect the passengers from the weather and dust. If the first automobile was produced in 1886 with the first prototype by Gottlieb Daimler, about which only confused information exists, the prize for the first American car should maybe go to the Deft Exhibit-7 made by Charles and J. Frank Duryea in 1893. It even had a folding hood.

The turn of the century was still an experimental, pioneering period but the greats of the car industry were nearly all already enrolled in the "Hall of Fame". There was Nikolas August Otto, traveling salesman and father of the four-stroke Otto cycle engine; Gottlieb Daimler, gun manufacturer, whose name will always be linked with that of Karl Benz, mechanic; Ransom E. Olds, another mechanic, who was among the first in the United States to believe in a vehicle with an internal engine and to create a marque which is still today one of the largest, Oldsmobile; Giovanni Agnelli, a founder of FIAT, who was a cavalry officer; Schmidt and Stoll, knitwear industrialists whose managerial activities were the origin of Audi; and the greatest of them all, Henry Ford, a locomotive repairman.

22 top Cavalry officer Giovanni Agnelli, key founder of Fiat, with the engineer Marchesi. They are inside the factory in Corso Dante in Turin, the first address of Italy's most important car manufacturer, founded on 11 August 1899. The photograph was taken in 1904. Agnelli was one of the first supporters of Daimler's and Benz' work and took their results to Italy.

22 bottom The picture shows the feverish activity in the Fiat factory in 1900.

22-23 top The first emblem of the "Fabbrica Italiana di Automobili Torino" (FIAT) displayed at the factory under an Art Deco floral design.

22-23 bottom The first Fiat was called the 4 HP though in reality the power was actually 3.5 HP. The body was called Duo and designed by the horse-drawn carriage builder Marcello Alessio. It could seat three passengers face to face though the customer could choose other configurations. The 679cc, two-cylinder, horizontally mounted engine was designed by Aristide Faccioli and placed in the rear.

23 top left The darker, parallel lines in the design drawings of the 4 HP show the chain-driven transmission. The fuel tank was placed under the main seat.

23 bottom left The first Fiat, the 4 HP, seen from below. The steering gear can be seen, which was controlled by a rod similar to those used on trams. At the front, the radiator coil can be seen.

23 right In Italy too the car builders discovered advertisement: This is Fiat's first. Note the colours that were used on cars, like the red on the touching spoke wheels with white tires.

23

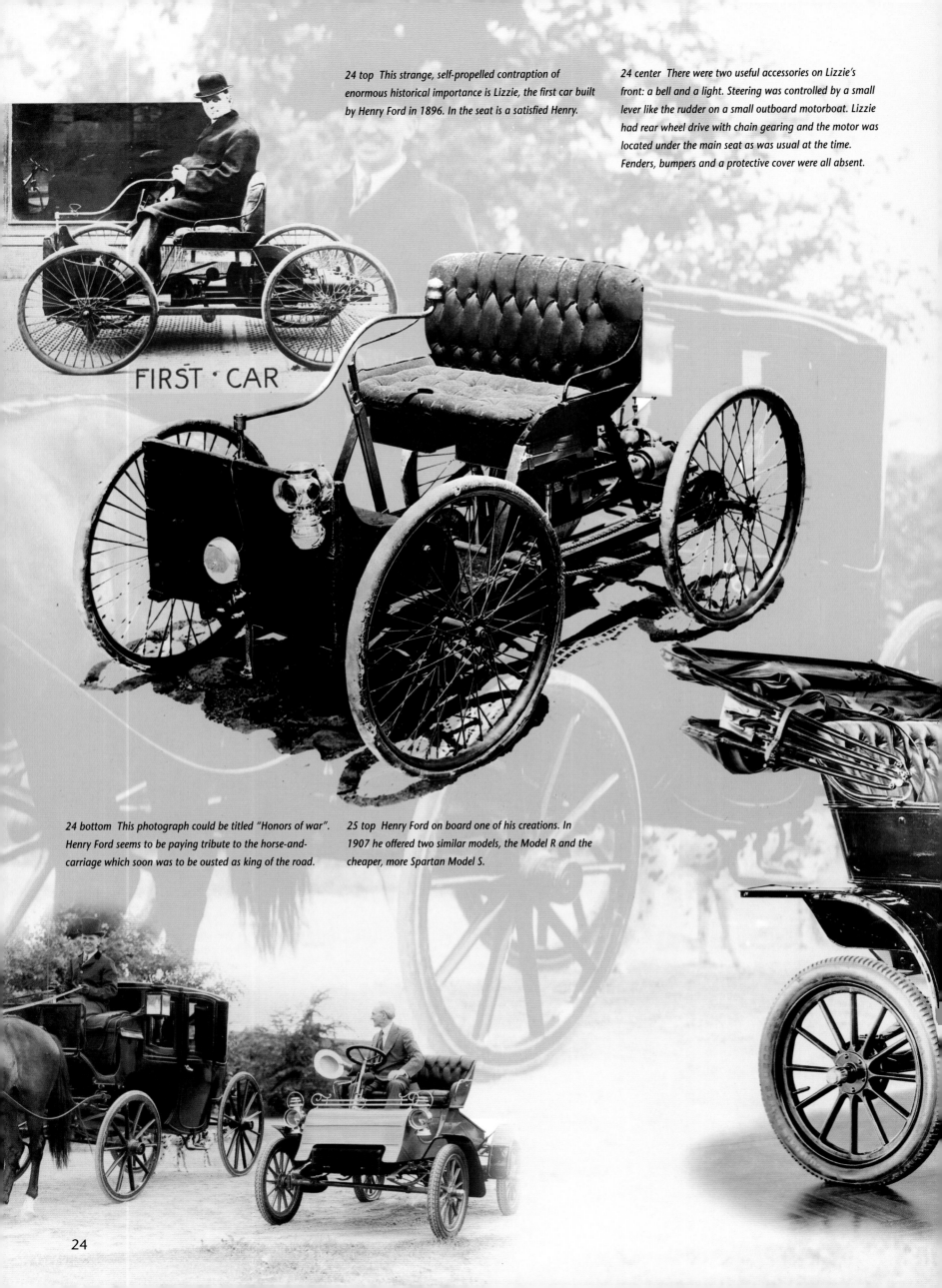

24 top This strange, self-propelled contraption of enormous historical importance is Lizzie, the first car built by Henry Ford in 1896. In the seat is a satisfied Henry.

24 center There were two useful accessories on Lizzie's front: a bell and a light. Steering was controlled by a small lever like the rudder on a small outboard motorboat. Lizzie had rear wheel drive with chain gearing and the motor was located under the main seat as was usual at the time. Fenders, bumpers and a protective cover were all absent.

FIRST · CAR

24 bottom This photograph could be titled "Honors of war". Henry Ford seems to be paying tribute to the horse-and-carriage which soon was to be ousted as king of the road.

25 top Henry Ford on board one of his creations. In 1907 he offered two similar models, the Model R and the cheaper, more Spartan Model S.

Henry Ford was very active in the automobile industry right from the start. His first model was called the Quadricycle and it is believed to have been first produced in 1896.

Olds however was already traveling around in his first four-seater, a real, working, reliable long distance car, inflicting every kind of torture on it. This open-topped car, the Curved Dash, was second in importance during the pioneering era only to the Ford Model T.

The first Quadricycle was a perfect example of the minimalism characteristic of handmade prototypes. It had large wheels, a rear-mounted two cylinder engine (later in the center under the seat), and a horizontal steering lever.

Two years later, the new model was better finished and even had a padded seat. The model produced in 1901 by the Detroit Automobile Company also had a steering wheel. The Ford Motor Company was established in 1903 and its first car was the Model A. This was replaced by the Model C and in 1906 by the Model N.

25 bottom The Ford Model T, probably the most important car in the history of the automobile, the car that motorized America. There were very many versions: two and four-seaters, tourers and roadsters, even pick-up trucks. The typical features of an efficient car are already all there plus the novelty of cross suspension. In this 1909 touring version, which cost 850 dollars, the oil lamps were standard.

Similar but more technologically advanced models were common in Europe.

They challenged each other's speed in races, reliability in trials and appearance in car beauty contests, but this was all aimed at improving overall design and perfecting experimental and revolutionary ideas.

Many technological innovations which appear in today's cars were conceived during these years. One example is the Twin Spark, the system of double ignition of the fuel mixture, which was patented by Alfa Romeo at this time.

Unfortunately we cannot dwell longer on this marvelously creative period as it belongs to the history of all cars and not just open-topped machines to which this book is dedicated. In the next chapter their paths separate and the histories of the convertible and sports car become independent and distinctive.

26 top left This Curved Dash Olds Runabout from 1902 has the top unfolded. Runabout was a frequent term at the beginning of the century and referred to short wheelbase vehicles as opposed to tourers, which were bigger and more spacious. Genetically and historically, runabouts were the forerunners of two-door convertibles, roadsters and sports cars. Tourers, on the other hand, were the precursors of torpedoes, four-door convertibles and cabriolets. The Curved Dash was the first mass-produced automobile in the US. The engine was single cylinder and produced 4 HP.

26 top right Cadillac was founded in 1902 as a result of the reorganization of the Henry Ford Company. The Model A Tourer in the picture, its first model, was presented at the 1903 New York Auto Show and found great success: 2,286 were sold. It was similar to the first Ford Model A (not to be confused with the later Ford Model A introduced in 1928).

26 bottom Compared to the Curved Dash, the Oldsmobile Touring of 1905 has a longer wheelbase.

27 top One of the first Peugeots, the 1892 Vis-à-vis. Note the mostly floral decorations on the sides and top. There are also patterns on the fenders.

27 bottom Horch was a very important marque in the first stages of the history of the car. This tonneau, built between 1900 and 1905, had a powerful 2.5 liter engine which could produce 12 HP. Maximum speed was 22 mph.

IN THE OPEN AIR WITH RUNABOUTS, ROADSTERS AND TOURING CARS

Shortly after the turn of the century, the paths of cars with and without a hard top began to separate: sedans had finally come into existence. For the purposes of this book two types of semi-open hard tops shall not be dealt with (a decision taken not without remorse). They are the partially open limousines called "landau-landaulet", which derives from the term for horse-drawn vehicles that were in part uncovered, and cars on which the rear part of the top could be rotated as though it were the lid of a trunk; these models were the antecedents of the modern "Targa" like the Porsche 911, C4 Corvette, Honda del Sol and Fiat X1/9, cars with a removable hard top.

For the most part, the motoring literature assigns the birth of the convertible and sports car such as they are to the mid 1920's, but in addition to moving this date back by at least ten years without hesitation, the authors would also like to draw attention to developments that occurred between 1900 and 1910. There were certainly many

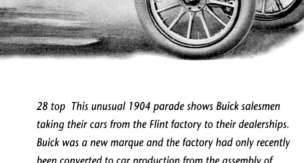

28 top This unusual 1904 parade shows Buick salesmen taking their cars from the Flint factory to their dealerships. Buick was a new marque and the factory had only recently been converted to car production from the assembly of agricultural carriages.

28 center After only three years, Buick was second in sales to Ford. The photograph shows a Model H Tourer of 1907.

28 bottom The Ford Model N; its importance lies in being the precursor of the Model T. It was a small runabout which reached the high speed of 28 mph.

significant models but, more importantly, the stylistic evolution and technological innovations were numerous.

Most of them had their origin in the design centers in the United States.

There were three types of car that had no hard top (excluding racing cars): runabouts, roadsters and touring cars.

Runabouts were tiny two-seaters with or without a top for which the body was the mainstay of the machine. The motor had either one or two cylinders though may have been electrically or even steam-driven. Their short wheelbase made them the precursors of the European and American mini-convertibles of the 1920's but they were still very much tied to the tradition of the horse-drawn carriage. They became very popular throughout the industrialized countries.

A step up from the small unpretentious runabouts were the noisy roadsters. These were only slightly longer but certainly more powerful; besides

29 top This 1907 Cadillac Model G is fitted with a top. The picture is interesting because it shows how the protective cover, called a "cape cart top", precursor of the proper top, was fitted. It had to be fixed in place each time it was used by means of three metal supports and tie rods at the side. It cost 120 dollars.

29 center Queen Margherita of Italy in a Fiat Brevetti, known as a Cabriolet Royal and built between 1905-12. It is a typical Landau with the rear part that could be open or covered with a folding hood. Two passengers could sit in front, like in a carriage, while the driver and companion were protected by a hard top without protection at the sides.

29 bottom The inclined windshield is noticeable on this 1912 Buick Model 22. It reduced the car's air resistance.

the two front seats, roadsters also often provided a highly risky and uncomfortable jump seat which, it is left to the reader to decide why, was known as the "mother-in-law's seat".

Finally touring cars, sometimes known as 'baquets' or 'phaétons', also had romantic links with horse-drawn vehicles through the shape of their body: The French name 'phaéton' was remarkably apt as it means a wooden tub. Compared to runabouts and roadsters they were large, comfortable, powerful and elegant. The 3-4 liter motor often had four cylinders and the car could carry at least four passengers seated high above the ground with those at the rear raised even further. The interior resembled a small salon with two sofas or two armchairs and a sofa or four separate armchairs. The hood was often missing, the windshield always, and depending on the level of comfort required, often the side doors too, particularly the front ones.

Production of runabouts was high on both sides of the Atlantic. Sometimes a long wheelbase version (or touring car) existed.

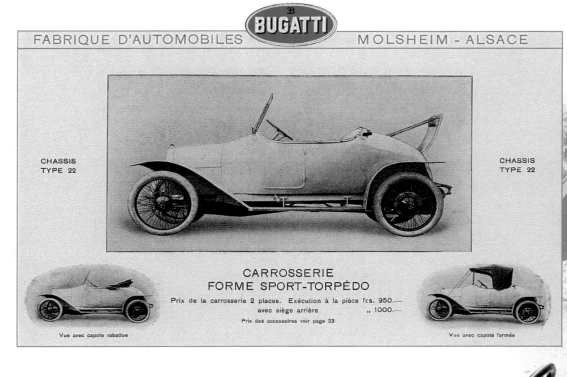

30 top The Bugatti Type 22 looked good in the company catalog. It was a simple design, far from the elegance of the Atalante Type 57, and was described as having a sport torpedo body. In truth, it resembles a runabout, precursor of the roadster. Note the jump seat ("mother-in-law's seat"), which was offered as an option at 50 francs.

30-31 The Buick Model 26 from 1911 of which 1,000 examples were sold. It is representative of the first roadsters, sporty but well-finished. There is no roof but the shapes of the fenders and footboard are interesting - they are just beginning their evolution into the soft, rounded, tapered forms representative of Futurism.

30 left This 1909 Cadillac offered a cover for the runabouts while the rear seat left the passengers to the mercy of the weather; this was why it was reserved for mothers-in-law. Right from its founding, Cadillac distinguished itself for the care it took in construction.

30 bottom The photograph was taken long after the models were produced (the dates are shown on the license plates); Augustus Horch (left), founder of the company of the same name, is sitting at the wheel of a Tonneau. These models were generally called Breaks and were more ungainly than functional. To Horch's left is Dr. Stöss at the wheel of a much more elegant Doppelphaeton.

31 top The 1912 Buick Model 24 roadster differed from the Model 26 by its sensible raincover.

31 center Louis Delage, founder of the company of the same name, together with Augustin Legros and one of his first cars. The company was established in 1905 and used components from one of the most prestigious and reliable manufacturers of the period, De Dion-Bouton.

31 bottom The flags on the windshield give a clue to the occupants: they are Franklin Delano Roosevelt and his wife, Eleanor, in a 1912 Cadillac.

An overview of these various models would start with the oldest car still running produced in Great Britain - the Daimler AD 1897. Daimler in this case was the German company's British branch, later to be taken over by Jaguar, which still uses this marque for its top-of-the-range sedans. Two years after its initial production, the Daimler AD 1897's direction bar was replaced with a steering wheel. In 1900 the Austrian diplomat Herr Emil Jellinek, whose genius and passion for motors was later to pass him into history with his daughter Mercedes, commissioned a beautiful racing Phoenix to be made entirely of steel from the German Daimler.

In 1903 the 24-32 HP Short Wheelbase Fiat went on sale (the Long Wheelbase version was a touring car) as did the Packard Model F (showing a distinct lack of imagination in name) which had an unusually modern sheet metal body. There was also the single cylinder Overland and the 1903 Rambler which was perhaps more of a touring car with its extraordinary seating arrangement; besides the usual two places in the front, two children could sit at the feet of the driver and his passenger while there were two more seats behind facing in the opposite direction, all in a very restricted space. Finally there was the De Dion-Bouton which had a well-profiled motor compartment. In 1904 came the "Colonel's car", the Pope Tribune, also single cylinder; the following year brought the Overland Model 17 with a high seat back and a radiator, and the Ford Model N, the precursor of the Model T which will be dealt with separately.

32 top Miss Mercedes Jellinek did not build cars but her name is one of those that will never be forgotten in the history of the car. Her diplomat father Emil was a devotee of motors and had a sharp commercial instinct. He commissioned increasingly powerful versions of Daimler engines which achieved brilliant racing victories and a consequent avalanche of publicity. Although Daimler were not keen on this type of exhibitionism, they could not say no to such an important customer even when he started to call his cars after his daughter. This was the origin of the name Mercedes.

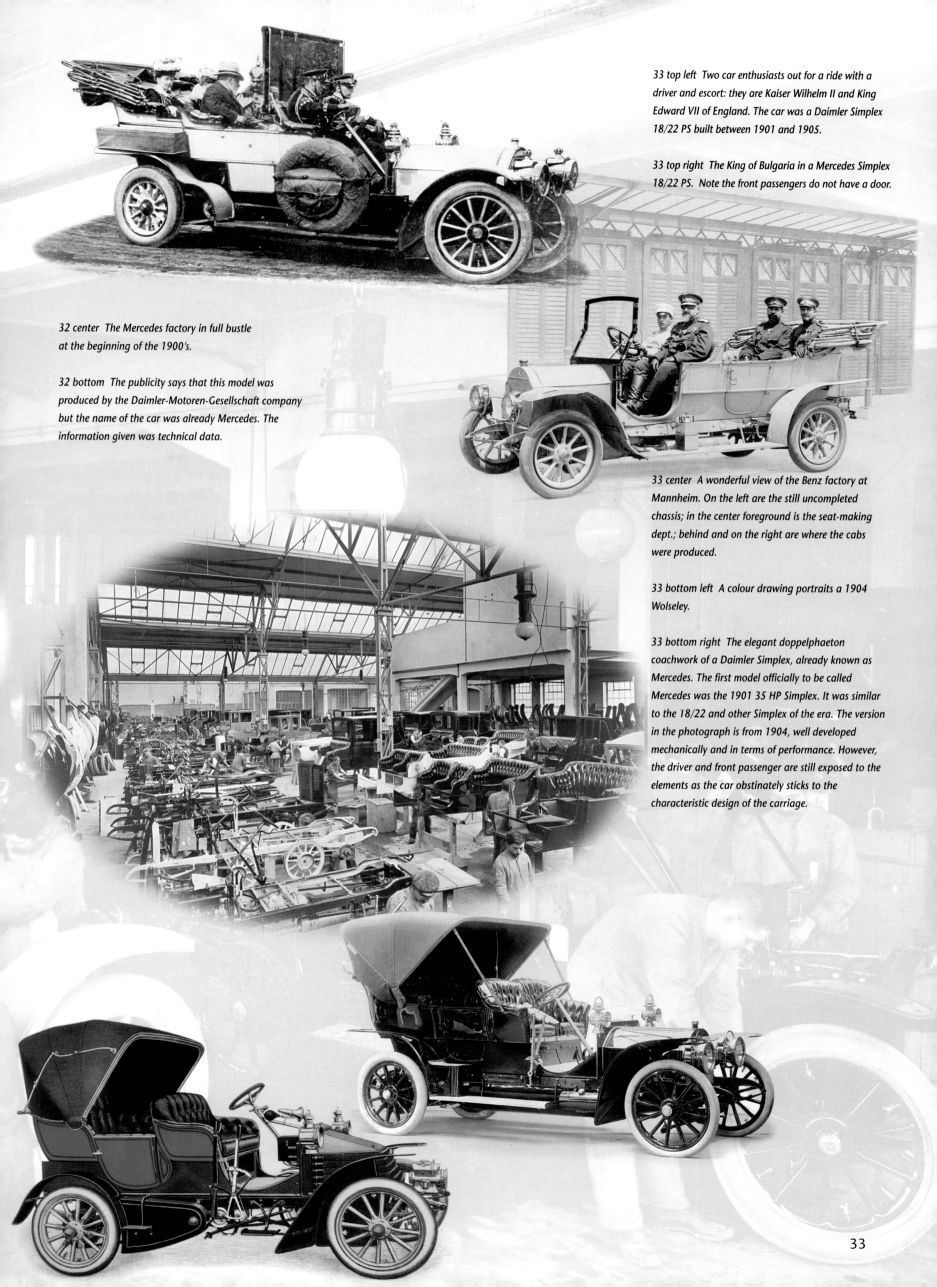

33 top left Two car enthusiasts out for a ride with a driver and escort: they are Kaiser Wilhelm II and King Edward VII of England. The car was a Daimler Simplex 18/22 PS built between 1901 and 1905.

33 top right The King of Bulgaria in a Mercedes Simplex 18/22 PS. Note the front passengers do not have a door.

32 center The Mercedes factory in full bustle at the beginning of the 1900's.

32 bottom The publicity says that this model was produced by the Daimler-Motoren-Gesellschaft company but the name of the car was already Mercedes. The information given was technical data.

33 center A wonderful view of the Benz factory at Mannheim. On the left are the still uncompleted chassis; in the center foreground is the seat-making dept.; behind and on the right are where the cabs were produced.

33 bottom left A colour drawing portraits a 1904 Wolseley.

33 bottom right The elegant doppelphaeton coachwork of a Daimler Simplex, already known as Mercedes. The first model officially to be called Mercedes was the 1901 35 HP Simplex. It was similar to the 18/22 and other Simplex of the era. The version in the photograph is from 1904, well developed mechanically and in terms of performance. However, the driver and front passenger are still exposed to the elements as the car obstinately sticks to the characteristic design of the carriage.

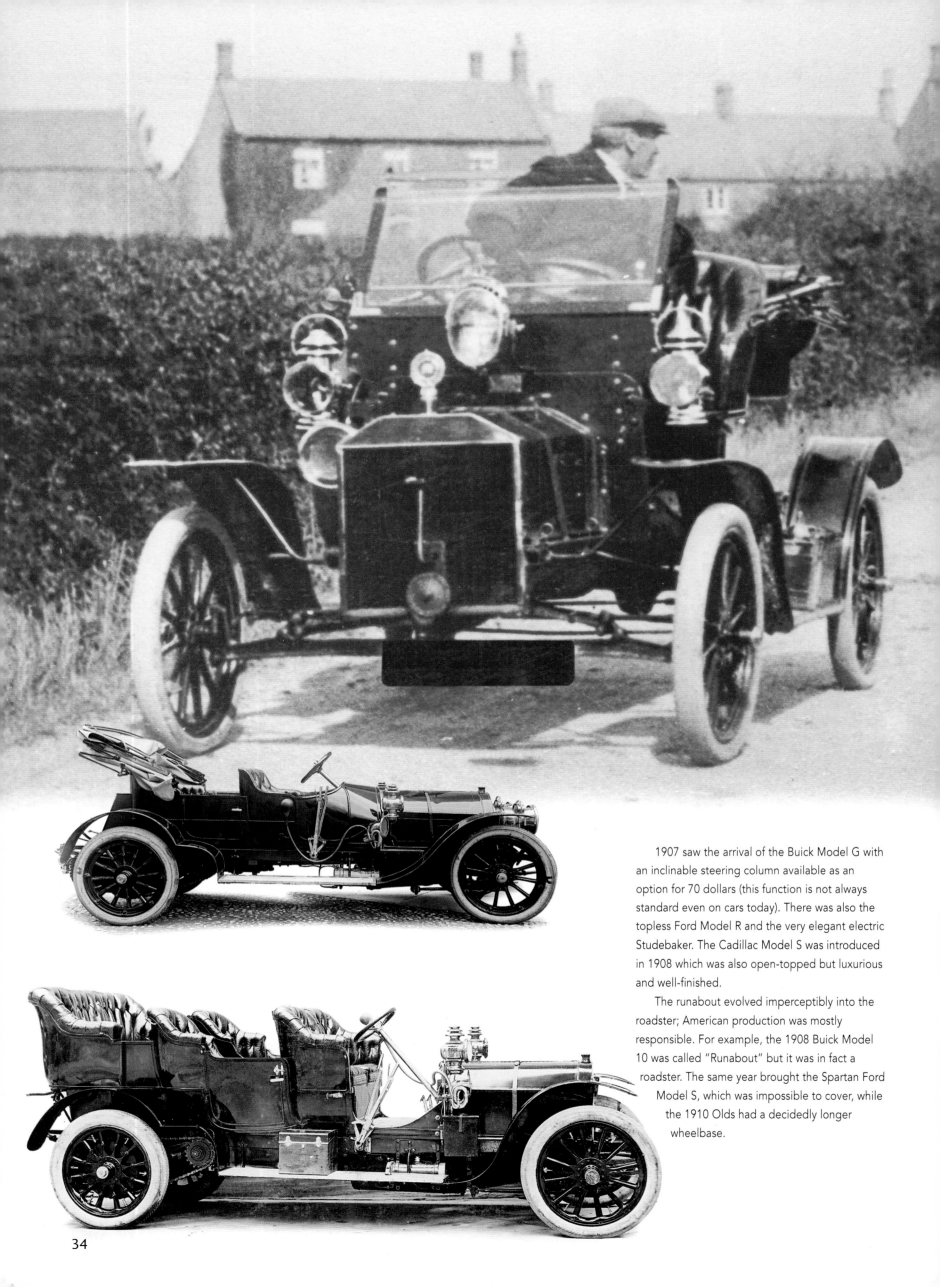

1907 saw the arrival of the Buick Model G with an inclinable steering column available as an option for 70 dollars (this function is not always standard even on cars today). There was also the topless Ford Model R and the very elegant electric Studebaker. The Cadillac Model S was introduced in 1908 which was also open-topped but luxurious and well-finished.

The runabout evolved imperceptibly into the roadster; American production was mostly responsible. For example, the 1908 Buick Model 10 was called "Runabout" but it was in fact a roadster. The same year brought the Spartan Ford Model S, which was impossible to cover, while the 1910 Olds had a decidedly longer wheelbase.

37 center This Ford T was fitted especially for desert conditions, or rather, for a Maharajah. Note the panel that hides the bay for plates and provisions and which transforms into a picnic table.

37 bottom The picture shows several stages which took place outside in the construction of a car. Here a worker is checking the forecarriage of a Ford Model T 5-seater. Note how the chassis is made from side members and how the absence of coachwork enhances the design of the wheels (known as "artillery wheels").

Meanwhile in Europe there were the clumsy baquets (touring cars), near relations of the runabouts and those horrible machines - sometimes called "breaks", sometimes "tonneaux" - which provided a high canopy as a cover. A single example is enough - the Horch 10/12 HP Tonneau from 1903.

On the subject of touring cars, reference must be made to the first Daimler to be called Mercedes (after the daughter of the brilliant Austrian consul in Nice, Emil Jellinek, whose contribution to the growth of the car market was greater than most); it was the 18/22 PS Simplex made in 1902. The top protected only the passengers behind and, although quite short, the car had a footboard which was separate from the front and rear fenders. There was also a landau version of this model with a closed body. The 5900cc engine supplied a maximum power of 35 HP.

The same year saw the Benz Phaéton Tonneau and the Parsifal (engine power varying between 8-14 HP). Both were furnished with a rear end unfortunately similar to a bath tub and certainly neither of them could escape the label "baquet".

Meanwhile the American Model K from 1906 did better as a tourer than as a roadster. In 1907, Rambler presented the Model 24 and Buick the Model H; in 1908 came the Oldsmobile Series M Touring. The Opel-Darracq 9 PS from 1909 offered only two points of access and a single sofa for passengers. The top was very wide with two metal support rods, four ribs and two tie-rods which hooked onto the forecarriage, a similar system to the torpedoes. The result was similar to a camping tent with the sides open and exposed to the wind. Due to the very short wheelbase, the footboard was no more than a curve between the front and rear fenders. There was no door. The nose of the vehicle was ugly with the radiator heavily inclined backwards.

The starting handle was very obvious. The driver's posture was still very upright as became a gentleman of the period.

Just as a curiosity, the 1910 steam-driven Stanley should be noted. Then there were two Italian cars: the 20 HP Lancia Beta from 1909 and the 15 HP Alfa from 1910. The Lancia has had a clear influence on the Gamma, Delta and Epsilon lines which have followed and its characteristics should be considered. Despite having no doors, its appearance was refined and its equipment luxurious; the fenders were large but well-proportioned; the headlights were also large and housed next to the vertical, gilded radiator in what was to become the standard position rather than next to the driver's seat. The wheels had tires and ten wooden spokes similar to artillery wheels or contemporary locomotives. The spokes were painted, often red, to reflect the fashionable color of the day.

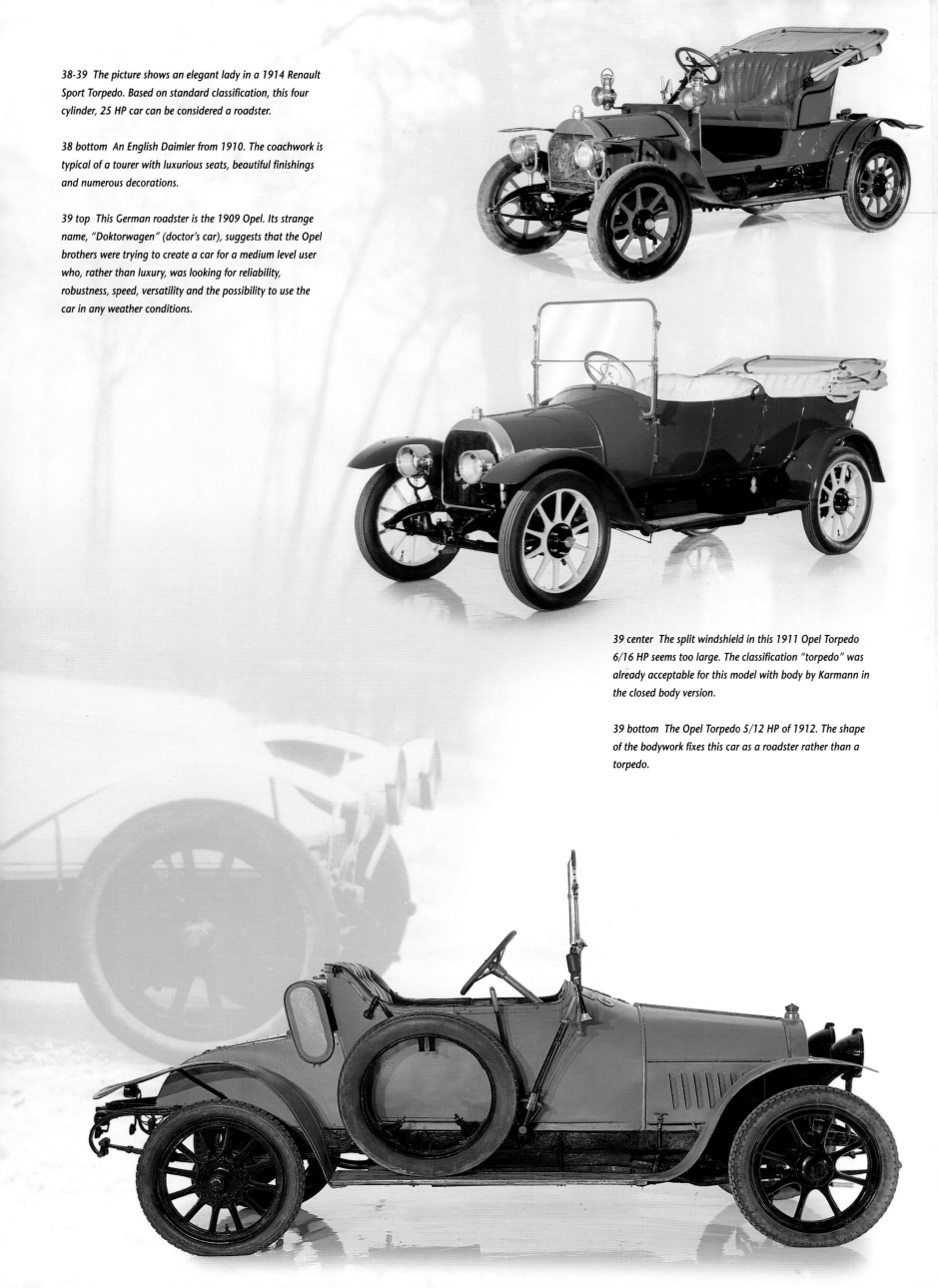

38-39 The picture shows an elegant lady in a 1914 Renault Sport Torpedo. Based on standard classification, this four cylinder, 25 HP car can be considered a roadster.

38 bottom An English Daimler from 1910. The coachwork is typical of a tourer with luxurious seats, beautiful finishings and numerous decorations.

39 top This German roadster is the 1909 Opel. Its strange name, "Doktorwagen" (doctor's car), suggests that the Opel brothers were trying to create a car for a medium level user who, rather than luxury, was looking for reliability, robustness, speed, versatility and the possibility to use the car in any weather conditions.

39 center The split windshield in this 1911 Opel Torpedo 6/16 HP seems too large. The classification "torpedo" was already acceptable for this model with body by Karmann in the closed body version.

39 bottom The Opel Torpedo 5/12 HP of 1912. The shape of the bodywork fixes this car as a roadster rather than a torpedo.

The vehicle was long with the chassis alone reaching 12 feet. Overall width was a shade over 5 feet and the footboard was indispensable for reaching the raised seats. The two front seats were real padded leather armchairs while the two behind were a proper sofa. The frame of the top had four arms.

The car had a 3120cc, four cylinder motor capable of 34 HP at 1500 rpm and for the first time there was a fixed head monobloc engine.

It had four gears, a cardan shaft transmission (chain-driven transmission was also used at the time) and mechanical brakes which acted on both the rear wheels and the transmission.

Top speed was 56 mph. One hundred and fifty examples of this model were built, one of which can be seen in the Vincenzo Lancia Museum in Turin.

A luxurious touring car was the Rolls Royce Silver Ghost from 1912. It was very long and elegant but had no top. The Chesterfield-style seats were covered with leather; the driving position was central, like horse-drawn carriages, and the cabin had no door. The running boards were connected to the fenders in an unbroken line, creating the dominant theme of the sideview.

The headlights were separate from the body as were the wheels, which were not covered by the coachwork; this was to be a feature of Rolls Royce cars for a long time.

Nearly all touring cars mentioned here were produced without front doors, which were only to arrive with the advent of the torpedo.

40 top This is one of the most elegant cars of the period, the Rolls Royce Silver Ghost 40/50 from 1907. It belonged to the Belgian royal family. The top is held taut by tie rods hooked onto the front bumpers and hides the elegance of the large baquet.

40 center The open door of the Silver Ghost shows the richness of the interior, worthy of a monarch. Besides the two jump seats, there is an intermediate windshield making this Roller a dual cowl design.

40 bottom The picture shows the detail of the motor compartment of the Rolls Royce Silver Ghost 40/50.

40-41 A 1911 Rolls Royce Landau. Landau, like landaulette, is a term which generally means very luxurious bodywork and a cab closed on all sides which can be partially or completely opened from the back. Another variable is the covering for the driver, who is sometimes left open to the elements, sometimes included in the closed cab.

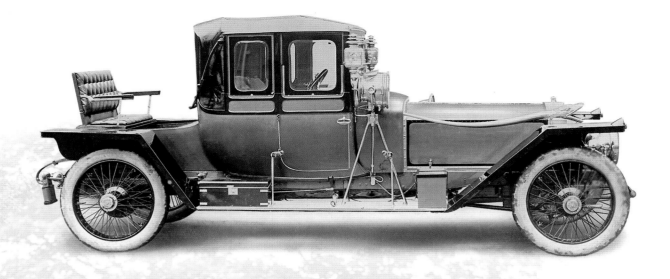

41 top This Rolls Royce was made for a Maharajah. It has features suitable for royal parades: The wheelbase is extremely long, the turret-like cab closed and the rear open. Despite the luxury of the finishings and the opulence of the materials used, the shape is awkward and clumsy.

41 bottom This 1906 Rolls Royce Silver Ghost has a steel-colored body in a classic baquet design. The huge tires for the period were justified by the enormous size of the car. The footboard hides useful storage compartments.

HEROES AND THEIR EXPLOITS

A distasteful but probably truthful cliché says that every war generates technological advances that benefit society. The same principle is said to be true about car races:

The experiences garnered from the conditions of extreme stress to which the cars are subjected are said to brings benefits to the whole automobile industry.

This is nonsense if we think of the knowledge matured over the past 100 years, but above all if we bear in mind that the design from scratch of a new car requires hundreds of millions of dollars.

For most of the history of road transport, car races have effectively been used as opportunities for experimentation and testing, particularly if the cars being raced are similar to production models as happened with the early open-topped machines.

Leaving aside the useless and ephemeral beauty contests often held in the early days of the industry, the competitive spirit found its outlet

in producing a winner over a fixed distance or within a fixed time, in finishing trials of uniform performance without incurring penalties, in overcoming demanding tests of endurance, distance, reliability and consumption, and in beating one's rivals in speed contests whether on racing circuits, paved or unpaved roads.

From 1895 the competitions became valuable for marketing purposes as advertising trumpeted the model and marque of winners. The heroic drivers, whose biographies almost always have a dramatic end, made a powerful impact on the imagination of a public in search of thrills and adventure.

Governments and monarchies considered car racing a political rather than technological fact and did not neglect to support the endeavors of these medieval knights transported into the industrial century.

France was the unrivaled home of car racing: It held the first competitions and instituted the first annual Grand Prix. From 1894 the Automobile Club of France organized demanding intercity

competitions for cars that were almost production models.

The list below gives the routes and distances.
1894, Paris-Rouen, 79 miles;
1895, Paris-Bordeaux-Paris, 732 miles;
1896, Paris-Marseilles-Paris, 1063 miles;
1897, Paris-Dieppe, 106 miles;
1898, Paris-Amsterdam-Paris, 889 miles;
1899, Paris-Bordeaux (351 miles) and Tour de France (1350 miles);
1900, Paris-Toulouse-Paris, 837 miles;
1901, Paris-Bordeaux (328 miles) and Paris-Berlin (687 miles);
1902, Paris-Vienna, 615 miles;
1903, Paris-Madrid, 342 miles (cancelled at Bordeaux due to accidents).

43 top right Vittorio Lancia, the famous Fiat engineer and driver, drives the 75 HP successor to the 60 HP at the 1904 Susa-Moncenisio race.

43 bottom right Dan Wurgis, record-breaking racing driver, at grips with a dangerous racing "cart", the Oldsmobile Pirate, with which he beat a Winton Bullet in the first organized racing event held at Daytona Beach.

42 top This picture shows a team passing through city streets in the first Grand Prix, Paris-Rouen in 1894. The passers-by do not seem to be paying attention - probably they are unaware that it is a race, and the streets are still the dominion of the horse-and-carriage. The 79 mile race was won by Count de Dion driving a de Dion, but he was disqualified because he was not accompanied by a mechanic. First place was then awarded to Lemaitre in a Peugeot.

42 bottom Giovanni Agnelli, a founder of Fiat, with Felice Nazzaro during a test run in the 1901 Tour of Italy. The car is a Fiat 8 HP.

43 top left A Fiat 45 HP in action in 1904 with Vittorio Lancia at the wheel. The 60 HP version was better known; its engine was over 10 liters! It was first in its class at the Targa Florio.

43 bottom left Fiat participating at the 1906 Winter Cup. The driver is Salmson, twice winner of this competition, and the car is the 60 HP. Notice the spikes on the spare wheel.

The many accidents during the 1903 race caused the deaths of ten drivers, mechanics and spectators and was halted at Bordeaux.

Outright winners of many early contests were the Panhards, driven by Panhard's partner Emile Levassor. The two Frenchmen are also important because they managed to import the technology and motors of Daimler into France from 1890 on. This was due to the intervention of the future wife of Levassor, the enterprising Madame Sarazin, widow of Emile Sarazin the French importer of Deutz products. Peugeot too obtained Daimler motors though was never able to beat the amazing pair. The only cars to manage that feat were Mors and Renault.

Mors is generally an unrecognized name today yet it was this company that later nurtured the creative genius of André Citroën. Average speeds for the first races were between 10 and 28 mph but these soon increased appreciably.

In 1899 James Gordon Bennet, editor of the New York Herald's European edition, established a race that bore his name and ran from 1900 to 1905. The French dominated at first, but Briton Selwyn Edge's Napier won in 1902, then Camille Jenatzy's Mercedes 60 PS (1903). Each year, the race moved to the previous victor's country.

In addition to the French races and the Gordon Bennet Trophy (which often overlapped), the newspapers reported a large number of events held throughout the industrialized world. Perhaps the list below will give the reader the sensation of competitive tension that existed between 1895 and 1905 before road racing of open-topped touring and racing cars went their separate ways. This happened soon after as countries all over the world instituted their own Grand Prix events, though they were not yet organized into a regular world championship.

1895: Oscar Mueller in a Benz vis-à-vis won the first test of reliability in the US.

1898: The first race on German soil (Berlin-Potsdam-Berlin) with Daimler's racing debut.

1900: The first racing Fiat, a 6 HP model, driven

44 top The picture shows some details of the direction bar and drip-feed oiler of the 1903 Mercedes Simplex 60 HP.

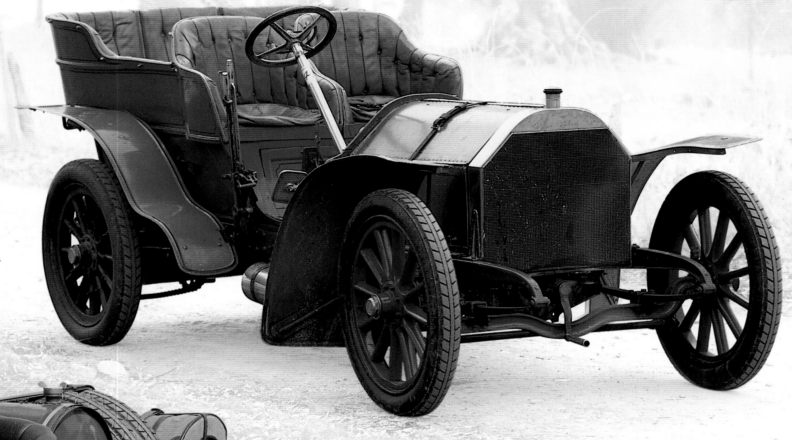

44 center The 1903 Simplex 60 HP had baquet coachwork, i.e. with four seats. Note the tub-like rear volume and the fact that there is no front door. The car's overall appearance does not impress, particularly the radiator without decoration of any kind. Several versions of this important model were available including a single-seater, 90 HP racer.

44 bottom This photo of a 1903 Mercedes Simplex 60 HP shows the enormous chain-drive crown wheel. Three tires are seen behind the fuel tank which suggests this was to be used on a long journey. This hypothesis is confirmed by the absence of a rear fender and by the trunk fixed to the rear.

by two future constructors, Felice Nazzaro and Vincenzo Lancia, won the Vicenza-Bassano-Treviso-Padova race at an average speed of 38 mph.

1901: The number of races increased enough to permit division of cars into four classes based on overall weight.

1903: The first victory of a Benz car, at Huy in Belgium, in an acceleration competition. Second was a Daimler-Mercedes. Average speed was 74.9 mph. The 60 HP Fiat tourer won a trial raced on snow, the Winter Cup.

Meanwhile there was an unending series of extraordinary long distance exploits in open-topped cars over dusty, risky courses. Sometimes these were individual undertakings, sometimes competitions. In 1897, Winton drove from Cleveland to New York in 10 days in a car of his own construction. In 1900 the first long distance

trial took place in Great Britain, the "Thousand Miles Trials", and was won by a 4 cylinder English Daimler. In 1902 a two cylinder Autocar Runabout covered the relatively rough and badly surfaced roads between Philadelphia and New York in 6 hours 10 minutes.

Another race version which held great excitement for the public was the challenge between two contestants only. In 1901 the first racing Ford beat a Winton over 10 miles at an average speed of 44 mph. In 1902 the racing circuit at Daytona Beach was inaugurated when Dan Wurgis beat a Winton Bullet driving an extremely dangerous single cylinder machine where the driver more or less clung onto a light cart like a jockey. In the same year a 12 HP Fiat Corsa beat a Panhard in a challenge over 189 miles between Villanova and Bologna at an average speed of 22 mph.

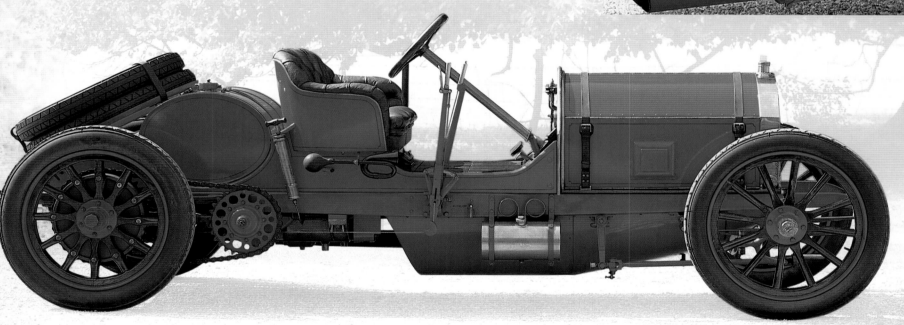

45 top The simplicity of the cockpit of the Fiat Targa Florio 28/40 HP of 1907 was determined by its racing use.

45 center The Fiat Targa Florio 28/40 HP triumphed in a hard fought Targa Florio in 1907. It won first and second places driven by Nazzaro and Lancia.

45 bottom The photograph shows the engine unit of the 1907 Fiat Targa Florio. The size of this 4 cylinder engine was 7363cc. Note the external components of the symmetrical valve timing system but more importantly the

characteristic two block architecture with two cylinders per block. The name 28/40 HP should not fool anyone - the power it produced was actually 60 HP at 1200 rpm, giving a top speed of 59 mph.

46-47 This 2-seater runabout with separate seats is a 1907 Mercedes Simplex. It was produced from 1901 in various body styles and in long and short wheelbase versions. The engine had an unusual structure: the 4 cylinders were grouped in 2 blocks cast separately. Engine size varied from 4.1 to 9.2 liters depending on the version.

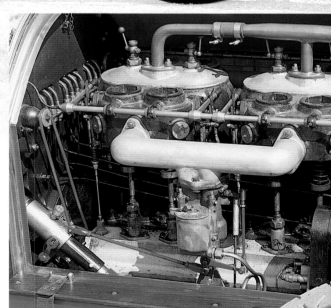

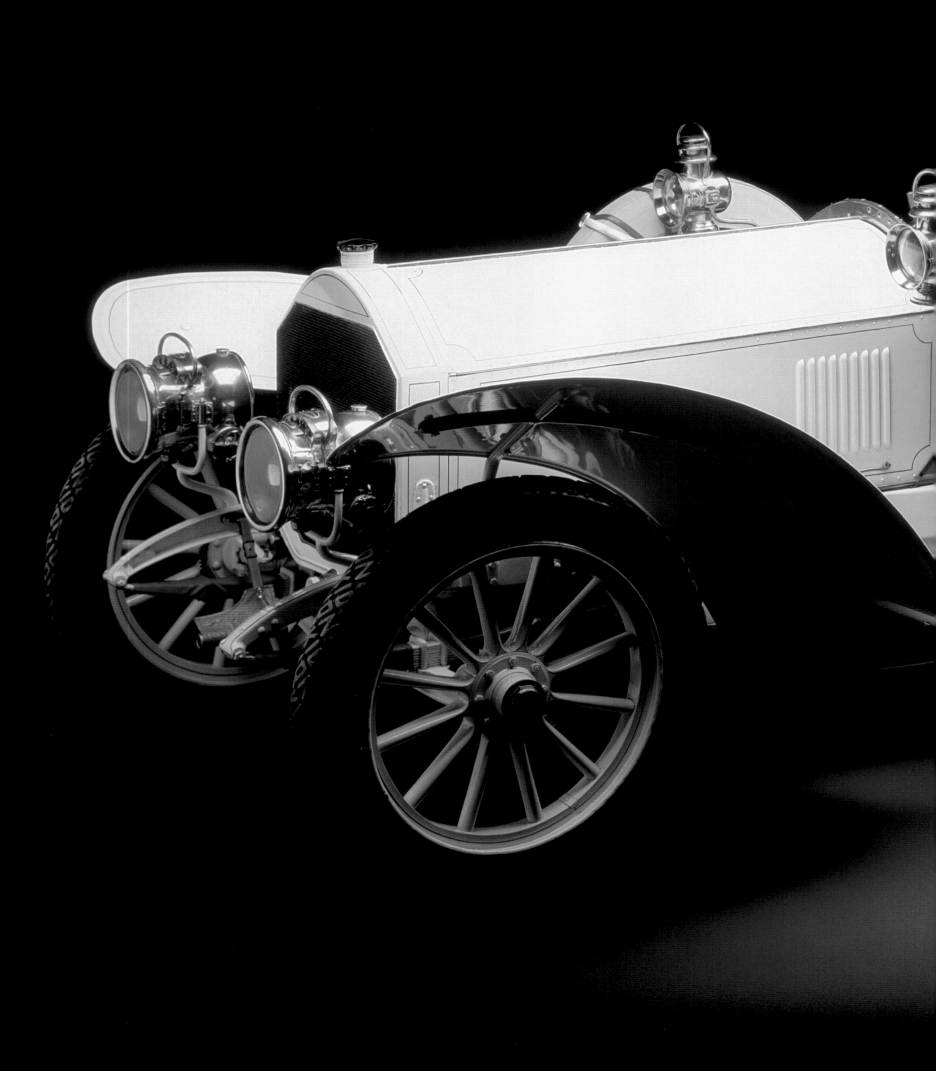

The car "turns" open-topped

THE METAMORPHOSIS: THE TORPEDO

48 top Another famous Daimler-Benz owner was Tsar Nicholas II seen here with his daughters while following military maneuvers in 1911. The car was a Daimler Knight 16/40 PS produced from 1910 to the beginning of World War I. The unusual feature of the Knight engine, whose patent was bought by Paul Daimler, was that the timing system used an internal metallic sleeve lining controlled by a lateral camshaft and roller gear. The Knight timing system was silent.

Technical development saw cars become longer, more comfortable and offer more accessories as they moved further and further away from their antecedent, the horse-drawn carriage. It was still too early though for sporting variations on closed bodywork - the forerunner of the coupé was still a long way off - but by 1910 many of the features that would be familiar until the 1940's had appeared.

The link between the "baquet", the touring car from the beginning of the century, and the cabriolet (convertible) and Gran Turismo (GT) models of the 1920's was the "torpedo".

The torpedo was long with bodywork made up mainly of flat, square metal sheets. The doors were low and above them no covering or protection was offered to the passengers. The soft top wrapped around a central rod just behind the driver's seat and was held rigid by three or four ribs; it was either held tight by tie-rods that hooked onto the front leaf springs (a very ugly arrangement) or by slender uprights close to the windshield or thereabouts (windshields were not always a feature of the torpedo). Seen from the side with the hood down, the top of the car was flat as though it had

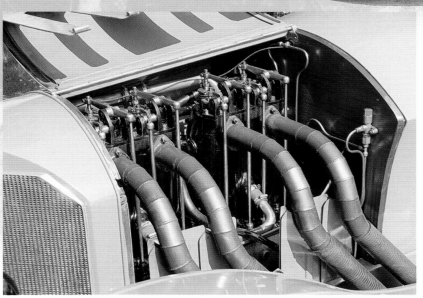

been planed; with the hood up, the large bay between the central rod and the front fastener becomes apparent.

The Benz 40-45 PS from 1910 is a good example of the transition from baquet to torpedo: The rounded lines have hardened and even the rear fender became a thin flat sheet, but the seats still stand up generously to put their passengers in good view.

48 bottom The Daimler Phaéton 22/40 PS came on the market in 1910. The car in the picture had a slightly more powerful engine and was produced in 1912. Besides the 4-seater 22/40 with the removable top, closed and tracked versions were available, the "Kolonialwagen" and the "Camp".

49 top The steering wheel of the Mercedes 37/90 PS had a pale wooden grip and four undulating steel spokes which were fixed to the steering column.

49 center The Mercedes 37/90 PS was made from the start of 1910. In the foreground the full wheels are clearly seen. Less visible are the straight rear fenders which did not last long as both manufacturers and customers preferred the traditional, curved form.

49 bottom The picture shows the motor compartment of a Mercedes 37/90 PS. Note the timing system, the pushrods and rocker arms (it had three valves, one inlet and two outlets) and the first stages of the curved and welded exhaust pipes which later were to become flexible. The motor had a cooling system for each cylinder which operated via "a welded plate envelope in which cooling water circulates" to quote the technical description of the time. In practice, each cylinder was surrounded by water.

50 top Louis Chevrolet, racing driver, shows off his prototype. The car manufacturing company was actually founded by Billy Durant who wanted to exploit the driver's fame. Louis Chevrolet designed an elegant and luxurious car, as we can see, while Durant needed a cheap model for mass-production, so Louis Chevrolet left the company to work with Frontenac while Durant continued on his way, using the Chevrolet to successfully regain control of General Motors. The black and white photograph does not do justice to the beautiful dark gray of the car which contrasted with the gold on the borders of the door, the radiator grill, the starting handle and the headlights. The wheels were cream-colored.

50 center and bottom This can be considered the first A.L.F.A., predecessor to Alfa Romeo: It is the 24 HP from 1910, here in torpedo form. This car and its early successors were designed by Giuseppe Merosi. The picture below shows the horn: Positioned on the right fender, it could be blown by the driver via a pump outside the door.

51 top This car describes itself with the name, model and first year of production written on the side. The body is a typical torpedo. The spare tire is a real curiosity.0

The Chevrolet Classic Six of 1910 is a good starting point for a roundup of the torpedo.

It had a complete and elegant body although still without a top. The frames of the doors were decorated with patterns the same color as the interior. The motor was a 6 cylinder 40 HP model housed in a long motor compartment and fronted by an attractive honeycomb grill, a design which was later to become a distinctive feature of Mercedes.

In 1911, Opel presented a model which was quite different to the 9 PS of two years earlier. It was a lovely torpedo with attractive lines.

It had a vertical radiator and headlights positioned next to the driver, a custom that was soon to disappear. A large baggage compartment appeared behind, not a trunk but a real bay in the body. The wheels had ten spokes each. The 1912 Daimler 18/60 PS boasted a laudable novelty: Its wooden wheels could be easily disassembled to make substitution of a tire less difficult.

51 center The Oldsmobile advertising for the Six and also celebrating 15 years of business.
The text describes this model as "a new car with old traditions". Given that this was still at the very start of the automobile industry, the claim seems ironic.

51 bottom This 1911 Oldsmobile Limited is a 7-seater Tourster.

52 top A Lancia with typical torpedo coachwork. This is the 1913 Theta, a luxurious version which was very successful both in Europe and the US, selling a total of 1,696 units. It was second only to the 1912 Cadillac in having a complete electric plant including starting motor as standard. Note the two halves of the windshield, which could be turned in opposite directions. The front and rear cabs were separate in a configuration known as "dual cowl"; the two rectangular elements by the doors are the backrests of the jump seats.

The term "baquet" had been synonymous with touring car up until this point but now "touring" came to mean a car with four doors, four seats and a long wheelbase; the same in fact as for production model torpedoes. The 1913 Buick Model 25 Touring was an example of the type and enjoyed great success, selling 8,000 units. Cadillac took no chances and decided to call that year's model a Torpedo Touring. Finally, the gearshift and all other controls were placed inside the body.

The Lancia Theta Torpedo (1913-1919) can be considered a standard of this type of car.

The body panels were continuous and uniformly square like the door panels. It had a windshield and a less upright driving seat with the steering column and wheel less exposed.

The technological and stylistic progress was clear, particularly compared to the Beta baquet discussed in the previous chapter and the Fiat 20-30 HP Type 3 produced from 1910-12. As a landau version of this Fiat existed, it can be considered a true convertible!

52 bottom Count von Ratibor, president of the Imperial Automobil Club, greets Kaiser Wilhelm II on board a 1913 Mercedes Knight called a "Kardanwagen".

53 top left King Alfonso XIII of Spain on a state parade to Morocco in 1919. The car is a very costly Benz Runabout 22/25 PS.

53 top right The Citroën price list in the 1920's. Besides the torpedo in the center, the top car to the right is interesting - it was the 1923 Caddy Sport used successfully in racing.

53 center This 1913 Lancia Beta Torpedo is distinguished by its long-span hood.

53 bottom This simple torpedo with full wheels is the 1928 Opel Viersitzer Kabriolet.

The First World War greatly influenced automobile production especially in Europe.

The torpedoes were used in war as ideal vehicles for fast transport of officers and their entourage. The long chassis were well suited to adoption of crawler tracks, front and rear axle drive, bullet-proof paneling and closed bodywork for ambulances. The Buick D45 from 1916 moved the spare wheel from the side of the car to the back which was to become standard. The following year the Chevrolet Series D introduced a curiosity: Two waterproof peepholes were placed at the rear of the top, along the lines of current plastic or glass-plate windows in convertible and sports soft tops.

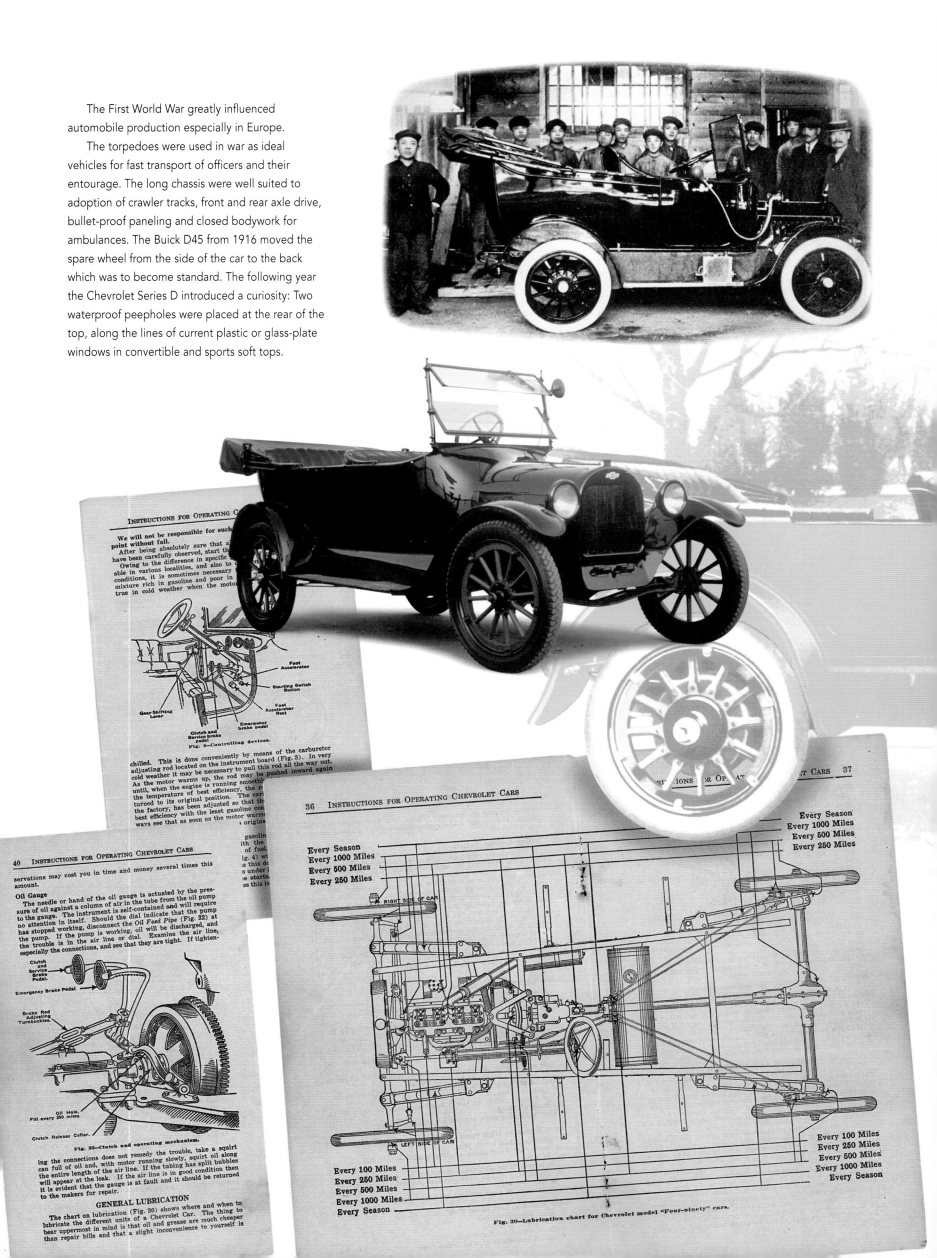

54 top This is a very special car. It is a 1915 Dat 31. Dat was the forerunner of Datsun and therefore of Nissan. For a long time, Japanese car production was almost unknown to the rest of the world, particularly of convertibles which were practically non-existent.

54 center This is a Chevrolet 4 90 Touring from 1919, a low cost and smallish torpedo.

54-55 The picture is of an Oldsmobile Model 53 from 1913. Olds was counting on this model to relaunch sales which had been disappointing with the Limited. The Model 53 had a Delco integrated ignition and lighting unit.

55 top The most popular Buick in 1916 was the Model 45. Almost 74,000 were built.

55 bottom Instead of a rectangular or lozenge rear window, the 1917 Chevrolet Series D had two portholes.

54 bottom Pages from the Chevrolet 4 90 manual. The double page shows the lubrication intervals for each element subject to friction. The motor oil had to be topped up every 100 miles and the suspension was to be checked and tightened at every change of season.

55

56 and 57 top This is the elegant 1912 Minerva which belonged to the king of Belgium. Note how the top protects only the rear passengers and only partially at that. The detail above shows the hood opening and closing system; the design of the curved, gilded lever depended on the model. It turned almost 180° around a central pin. On the next page at the top, a detail is shown of the radiator cap, which was often mounted with symbols that identified the car such as birds, cats, mythological or other figures. This one is the goddess Minerva who gave her name to the car. The symbol was also attached to the top of the grill where the goddess was shown in profile with her helmet clearly evident.

57 center The 1914 Rolls Royce Silver Ghost Alpine Eagle was very luxurious. The coachwork was that of a traditional high class torpedo. The touching spoke wheels are very attractive, especially when compared to the more solid "artillery" type design.

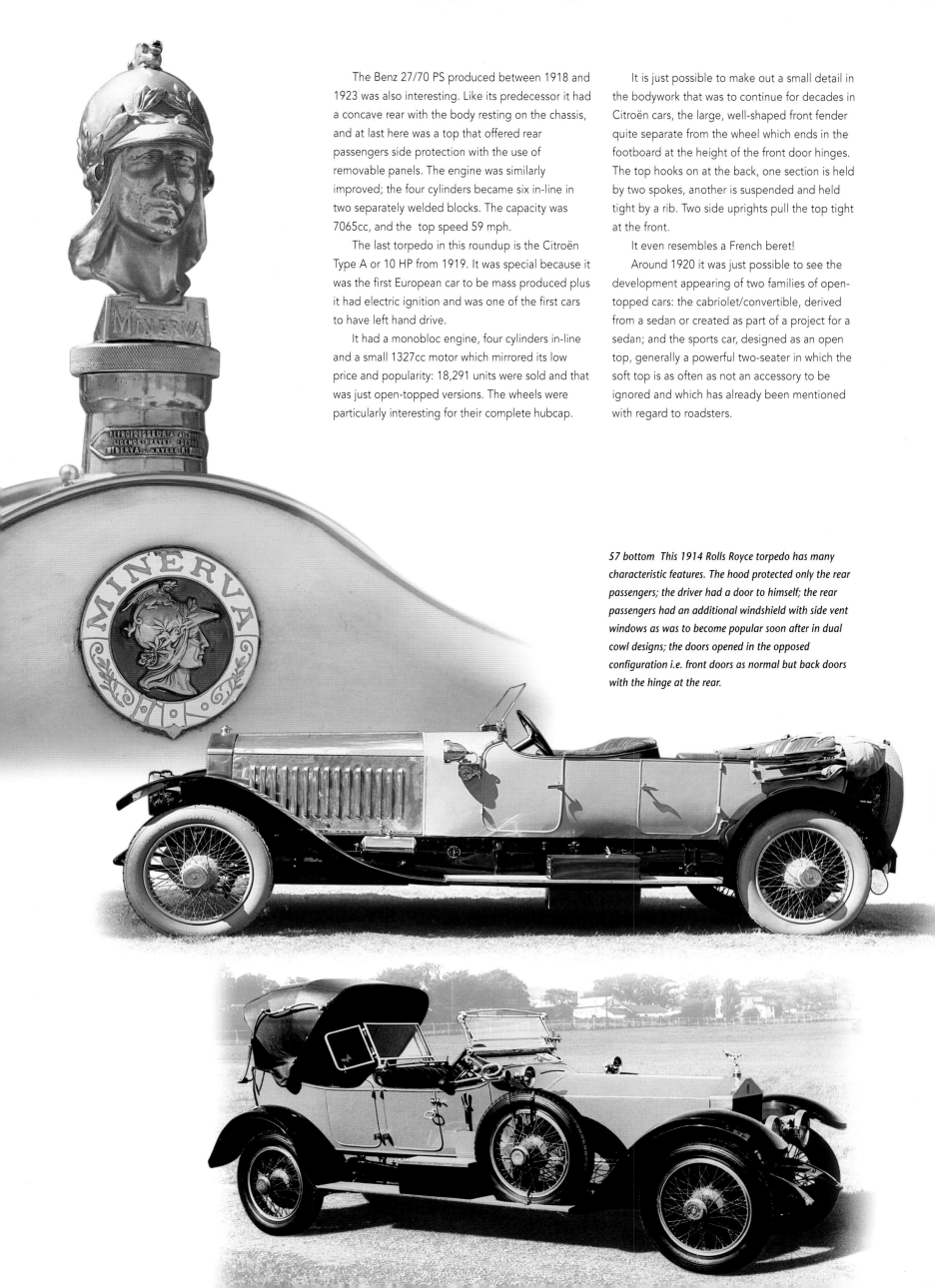

The Benz 27/70 PS produced between 1918 and 1923 was also interesting. Like its predecessor it had a concave rear with the body resting on the chassis, and at last here was a top that offered rear passengers side protection with the use of removable panels. The engine was similarly improved; the four cylinders became six in-line in two separately welded blocks. The capacity was 7065cc, and the top speed 59 mph.

The last torpedo in this roundup is the Citroën Type A or 10 HP from 1919. It was special because it was the first European car to be mass produced plus it had electric ignition and was one of the first cars to have left hand drive.

It had a monobloc engine, four cylinders in-line and a small 1327cc motor which mirrored its low price and popularity: 18,291 units were sold and that was just open-topped versions. The wheels were particularly interesting for their complete hubcap.

It is just possible to make out a small detail in the bodywork that was to continue for decades in Citroën cars, the large, well-shaped front fender quite separate from the wheel which ends in the footboard at the height of the front door hinges. The top hooks on at the back, one section is held by two spokes, another is suspended and held tight by a rib. Two side uprights pull the top tight at the front.

It even resembles a French beret!

Around 1920 it was just possible to see the development appearing of two families of open-topped cars: the cabriolet/convertible, derived from a sedan or created as part of a project for a sedan; and the sports car, designed as an open top, generally a powerful two-seater in which the soft top is as often as not an accessory to be ignored and which has already been mentioned with regard to roadsters.

57 bottom This 1914 Rolls Royce torpedo has many characteristic features. The hood protected only the rear passengers; the driver had a door to himself; the rear passengers had an additional windshield with side vent windows as was to become popular soon after in dual cowl designs; the doors opened in the opposed configuration i.e. front doors as normal but back doors with the hinge at the rear.

THE CAR IN EUROPE DURING THE 1920's

From about 1920 the car took on even more definite shapes. Following the schools of thought and philosophical trends of the day, the secular marriage of form and function took place which is still current today. In the United States basic positive values linked to lightheartedness, fun and well-being came to the fore: Why shouldn't the car be beautiful, too, and a companion to share happy times with?

At the end of the 1990's, a guru of design, Chris Bangle, who works for BMW and is the creator of the modern 3-Series, claims that beauty is functional and not an end in itself as is commonly thought. He says that the ability to "make someone happy", to cheer someone up, is as important as offering convenience and being practical. The same credo was extant in the US during the 1920's and 30's.

But the situation in Europe during the third decade of the century was very different. Dictatorships and a widespread conservative and rigid mentality

one to arrive at the Ascot races, Rue Faubourg St. Honoré for a little shopping, Rockefeller Plaza for breakfast, the start of the Targa Florio or the first night of the opera in Berlin? Which vehicle was the best combination of disguised modernism and the need to show off? One just had to have a torpedo. Industrial production was expanding, and with it the list of potential customers; so too did the range of variants and versions grow. Two events, however, had a major effect on the economic and industrial development of this period (1920-30): the carryover from the First World War and the Wall Street Crash in 1929.

The first affected both ownership structures and production strongly because German industries had made the strategic error of dedicating their efforts to the production of luxury models. The second brought ruin indiscriminately and put paid to the weakest companies or those who had not yet reached large scale production.

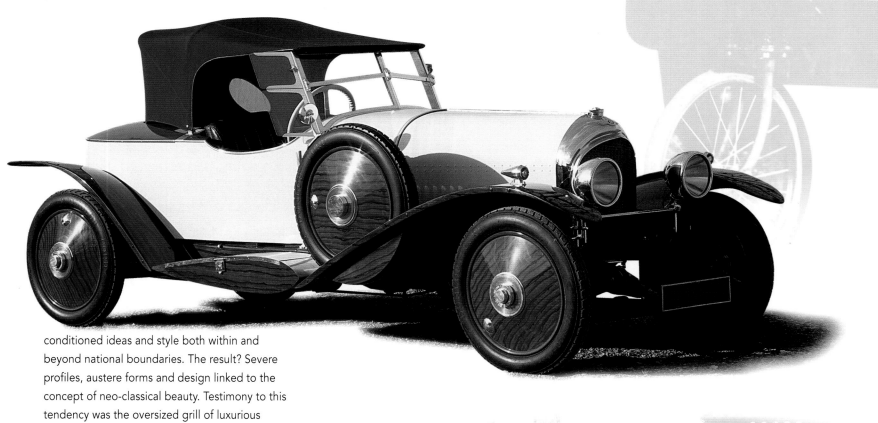

conditioned ideas and style both within and beyond national boundaries. The result? Severe profiles, austere forms and design linked to the concept of neo-classical beauty. Testimony to this tendency was the oversized grill of luxurious cabriolets and convertible limousines of the period.

It became a Greek temple in a modern form. Mercedes, Hispano Suiza, Bugatti, Rolls Royce, Delage, Alfa Romeo and others all had their important metal symbol: a woman's face, Nike of Samothrace, an eagle, a stork, a stylized propeller and a famous jaguar (that would come later). Open bodies were still the most common design and their de luxe variants were no longer the preserve of the aristocracy, VIP's, maharajahs and stars of the silent screen.

The middle classes also wanted their elegant and refined status symbols. Now that the carriage had passed out of fashion, how was

58 top The picture shows a 1926 8 liter Bentley in the long wheelbase version.

58 bottom The Berlin Automobil Club celebrates the anniversary of its founding. It is 1925 and the procession of open tops is preparing to leave the Avus race track.

59 top This Daimler Lancaster 21 dates from 1926. While car design was moving ahead in leaps and bounds in the US, in Europe the trend was towards more austere, classical shapes, particularly in countries governed by dictators like Italy and Germany. This model was fitted with comfortable cantilever suspension.

59 center Henry Royce, one of the founders of Rolls Royce, at the wheel of one of his models with its extra long motor compartment from the 1920's.

59 bottom Rolls Royces evolved too, taking on forms less and less related to the horse-drawn carriage during the 1920's. This 1928 Phantom I Open Tourer boasts a splendid chrome radiator grill topped by the famous Winged Victory. The resemblance of the grill to a Greek temple is quite evident.

58-59 Improved reliability meant that the car increasingly became a means of long-distance family transport. This family in the 1920's seems to be preparing for a long journey to judge by the amount of baggage. Note how the cases are fixed with leather straps to a special flap. Bearing in mind the quality of the roads and suspensions in use at the time, it is easy to imagine the stress imposed on the bags!

The German industrial situation was complex.

In 1926 an important financial event took place which affected the balance of the whole motoring industry, the merger of Daimler and Benz. In Germany in 1927 there was only one car per every 171 inhabitants and the total number of cars in circulation was small - 218,000, compared to 585,000 in France and 754,000 in Great Britain. There were also fewer roads, 219,000 miles as compared with 391,000 miles in France; and there were twenty active manufacturers producing forty models. When the government opened its arms to American industry, ruthless competition ensued which saw the less-organized German companies

succumb to the enormous economies of scale that the Americans enjoyed. Ford alone produced twice as many cars as all Germany. One of the most important companies was Horch, which had once belonged to August Horch. He had been ousted in 1909 and had since founded another marque, Audi. The name was the Latin version of his own name, meaning "listen". In 1923 the head of the Horch design team was Paul Daimler, son of the great Gottlieb, who had been technical manager of Mercedes from 1907 to 1922. In 1925 Paul Daimler saw his dream come true, a futuristic 8 cylinder motor with double camshafts (later replaced with a single overhead cam due to thermal problems) to power the luxury models of the 300 and later 400 Series. A representative cabriolet of the range was the 375, whose 3-3.9 liter engines produced 80 HP. The pneumatically controlled four-wheel brakes were innovative, but the design was traditional. At the front, two large headlights and the radiator with vertical bars vied for attention. The bumper was composed of three separate chromed parts and was the precursor of a style that was later to be seen on American convertibles of the Machine Age. The wheels had slender "bicycle" spokes and were

covered by large fenders on which rested two smaller lights. The spare wheel was close to the driver on a wide footboard. The top was held up by an S-shaped support (as in the majority of such cars) which allowed it to fold down easily. Running along the top of the outside of the windshield was an adjustable fin for keeping the sun off.

And Mercedes? It was second in sales volume to Opel and continued to produce beautiful, sophisticated models, especially in the gran turismo niche. Among the cabriolets, the Mannheim series is certainly worthy of note, created by Ferdinand Porsche around a new motor which was supposed to replace the admirable but thirsty supercharged 8 cylinder K Series engine. The first Mannheim was produced in 1926 with a 55 HP, 3 liter, 6 cylinder in-line engine. Soon a new style began to make itself felt based on medium sized American convertibles which had more balance between the front and rear volumes. The passenger cab was a shapeless box created by the semi-hard top. The next version maintained the same overall length but gave more room to the rear passengers and the top returned to the double support design used on the torpedo.

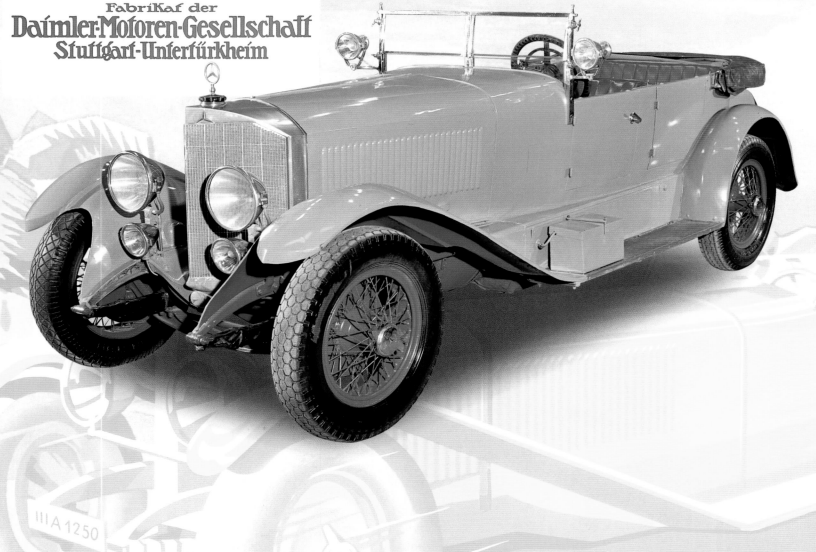

61 top The President of Germany, Hindenburg, in a statuesque 1924 Daimler Mercedes.
After the merger with Benz, the name of this model was changed from 15/70/100 PS to Mercedes Benz Type 400.

61 center The smallest open top Benz (less than 1.6 liters) before the merger with Daimler in 1926. This sports model was very popular with the young.

60 top This Mercedes advertisement is set in Egypt. As well as the three pointed star not yet inscribed in a metal circle, note that the official name was still Daimler-Motoren-Gesellschaft.

60 bottom Paul Daimler, son of Gottlieb, brilliant mechanical engineer, brought the experience gained in the first years of Grand Prix racing to bear on the 28/95 PS: overhead camshaft, overhead valves and high voltage magneto ignition (more reliable than coil ignition and long used in airplanes). The grill is not inspired by Greek temples but is a bullnose design. The finishing details, such as the choice of paint, were all of top quality: The wheels, interior, hood cover and underbody were all the same color.

61 bottom These three Mercedes Benz were produced shortly after the Benz merger. On the left is the 15/70/100 PS and on the right two 24/100/140 PS. The K model was part of this series, from which were derived the S, SK and SSK. Production of these models throughout the rest of the 1920's ranged from elegance and absolute luxury to immense power and sportiness.

In 1929 a car with an old name, the 3/15, but made by a new company, BMW, went on sale. The Bayerische Motoren Werke was a distinguished company which produced powerful airplane engines. The year before it had bought the company Fahrzeugfabrik Eisenach which already made the Dixi 3/15. The aim of both Dixi and BMW was to assemble and sell small economical cars - and preferably under license, rather than designed and produced from scratch, for the economics of the period discouraged large projects. Their choice was an English car, the 748cc Austin Seven. It was a happy choice and in 1928 alone about 6,000 were sold. This was a perfect example of pragmatism winning over patriotism.

The 3/15 (DA 1 and successive models) differed from the English car by having left hand drive and Bosch electrics. It had a four cylinder engine which produced 15 HP to give a maximum speed of 47 mph. There were cable operated brakes on the rear wheels (later on all four) and bicycle style spokes. The 74 inch wheelbase was that of a small economy car. The shape was square without any attempt at beauty. There were two-seat and four-seat versions.

The Dixi was produced in two open-topped versions, the roadster and the so-called gran turismo, and two closed, the coupé and the RM sedan. The open tops were the more economical of the four. However, there were numerous variants of the cabriolet. The roadster bodywork designed by Ihle displayed the double kidney radiator still dear to BMW designers today. Despite its tiny size, it was called a limousine and had a removable top. As the BMW Wartburg (DA 3), it had no doors and a pointed rear end; as the gran turismo model it had 4 seats, fixed uprights and fixed windows and was very popular; as a cabriolet with bodywork by Buhne, it had windows which could be opened, a sloping windshield and sidelights.

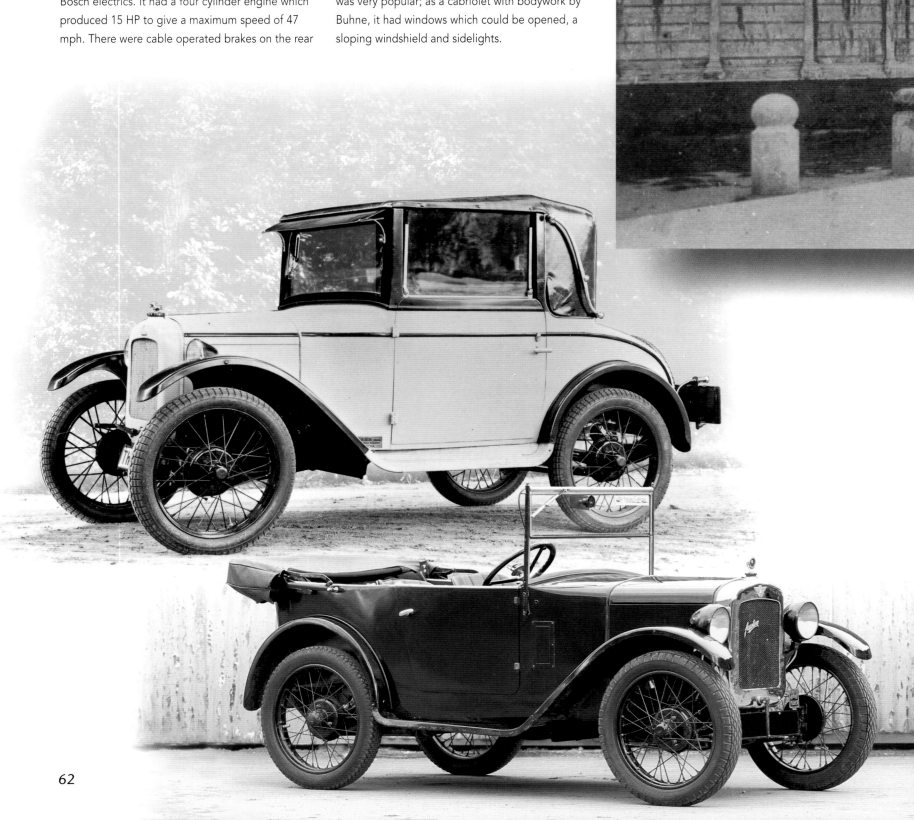

62 top The 1928 Dixi 3/15 was small and cheap and presented in a large number of versions and body types. This was the secret of the mini convertible.

62 bottom This small open top is the Austin Seven that was produced under license in Germany and sold as the Dixi 3/15. The Dixi belonged to the company Fahrzeugfabrik Eisenach which was bought in 1928 by BMW, an airplane-engine manufacturer which wanted to assemble and sell small, cheap cars without much investment.

62-63 This BMW 3/15 took its owner to the Italian city of Pisa at the end of the 1920's. The 3/15 was a small and very successful car under both the Dixi and BMW names but in fact it was a replica of the English Austin Seven. The version shown is the cabrio limousine. At this point it still had not assumed the double kidney grill which was to become the distinguishing feature of most successive BMW cars.

63 top This 1928 advertisement publicizes "a car of German quality" - quality was what the company founded by Adam Opel wanted to be known for. Opel was going through a golden period thanks to shrewd investments giving it state-of-the-art machine tools and foreign currency in a time of German financial mega-inflation.

63 bottom The small Opel 4/12 HP Laubfrosch ("Frog") from 1924 was built in the most modern German factory of the age. The curious name was given because the 2-seater was only available in green. The engine was a 951cc, four cylinder model which gave 47 mpg and the hood was made of rubberized canvas. Tens of thousands were sold.

64 top The side view of this Fiat 501 from 1921 shows a perfect example of a mid-class torpedo.

64 bottom and 64-65 center bottom This is the Fiat 509 built from 1927-29. It was called a coupé but it was in fact a convertible. Note the third seat in the back by the spare wheel in a truly uncomfortable position.

64-65 center top A Fiat 501 on the steps of the Reichstag in Berlin. This type of frequent exhibitionism was used for commercial purposes to demonstrate the strength of the car.

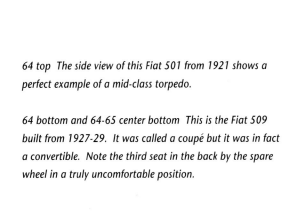

The situation in Italy was no better than in Germany due to a very punitive fiscal policy particularly regarding large engined cars. In 1921 the tax for a 50 HP Italian car was five times that for a French equivalent and fifteen times that for an English one, not to mention extremely costly fuel.

Sixteen thousand cars were produced in Italy in 1922, making 65,000 in total. Five years later Italy was still only twenty-second in the table of cars per inhabitants.

Many Italian marques were barely surviving or

had failed or were absorbed by Fiat which in those years controlled 70-80% of the market. Many of these companies had only recently been started up: Om, Ansaldo, Spa, Scat, Diatto, Itala and Bianchi for example. To maintain their position at the top of the production and sales league, Fiat had to renounce any unnecessary feature on their cars, to reduce design to its minimum and leave aside innovation and stylistic flair in favor of pragmatism. And it worked, just as it had for BMW.

A good example is the little 501, a true economy car with a 16 HP engine which sold 45,000 units between 1919 and 1926. It was 12'6" long and had a wheelbase of 8'6". Maximum speed was 44 mph and fuel consumption was claimed to be 22 miles per gallon. An important fact was that the 501 was offered both as a 4-seater torpedo with baggage compartment and as a 2-seater sports car. There is little to say about the bodywork except that it was a set of panels correctly assembled with a minimum of affectation or distinction.

65 right The sequence shows the operations to lay out the Fiat 501's hood. First it was necessary to open the long, horizontal expanse which was then laid out on the Fiat's body.

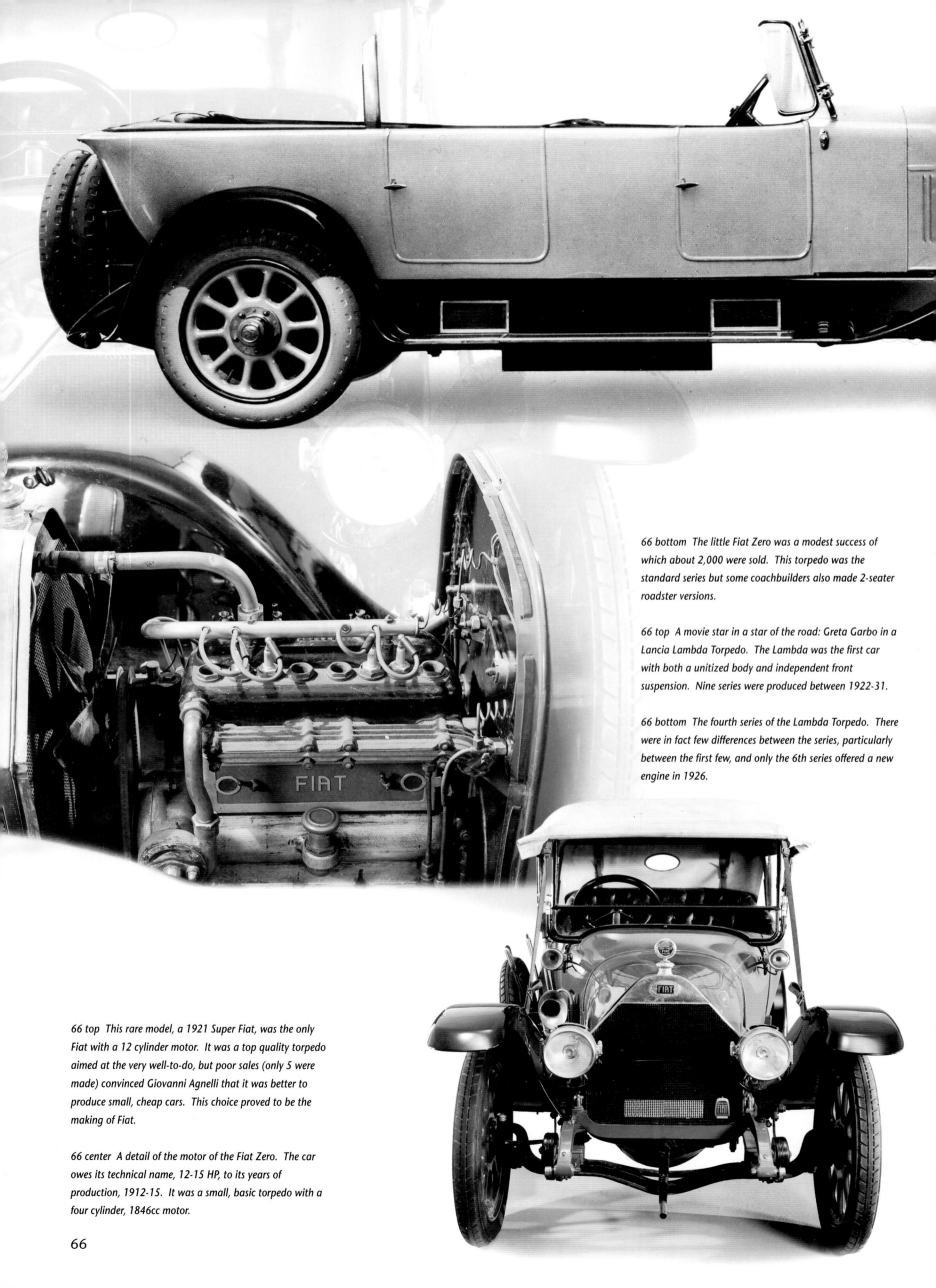

66 bottom The little Fiat Zero was a modest success of which about 2,000 were sold. This torpedo was the standard series but some coachbuilders also made 2-seater roadster versions.

66 top A movie star in a star of the road: Greta Garbo in a Lancia Lambda Torpedo. The Lambda was the first car with both a unitized body and independent front suspension. Nine series were produced between 1922-31.

66 bottom The fourth series of the Lambda Torpedo. There were in fact few differences between the series, particularly between the first few, and only the 6th series offered a new engine in 1926.

66 top This rare model, a 1921 Super Fiat, was the only Fiat with a 12 cylinder motor. It was a top quality torpedo aimed at the very well-to-do, but poor sales (only 5 were made) convinced Giovanni Agnelli that it was better to produce small, cheap cars. This choice proved to be the making of Fiat.

66 center A detail of the motor of the Fiat Zero. The car owes its technical name, 12-15 HP, to its years of production, 1912-15. It was a small, basic torpedo with a four cylinder, 1846cc motor.

The conviction of Fiat boss Agnelli to stick to producing small, economical cars was justified when their only large torpedo, the 520 Super Fiat with V12 engine produced in 1921 for export only, sold 5 units.

Apart from Alfa Romeo which was directing its efforts to producing a magnificent chassis called the RL designed by Merosi, the most active company was Lancia. Their most important car was the Lambda, produced from 1922-31 in 9 series of which, it appears, ten thousand were sold. It had many technical innovations such as a monocoque body with independent front suspension. The motor too was new, a monobloc 2120cc V4 made from aluminum and with three gears. And there were open top models galore, from the traditional Series II torpedo to the two-seater sports version of the Series VII with bodywork by Casaro, and also the lovely Mille Miglia sports.

68 top The 1921 Peugeot Quadrilette had one front seat and one back seat with a door only for the passenger. The length was just 9'5" and the tiny engine just 667cc. 11,575 were sold.

68 center This is not a carousel or a cradle factory but the assembly line for the Peugeot 5 HP cabriolet.

68 bottom The cover of the 1924 Peugeot Revue (in-house magazine) was dedicated to the 5 HP.

Production of cabriolets in France between 1922 and 1926 saw the Peugeot 17-series excel, starting with the successful chassis of the 174 on which many coachbuilders based their creative talents. Various designs were produced but in limited numbers and so were particularly sought after. Curiously, the left hand wheel hubs had a reverse thread with respect to the right hand hubs with the result that two spare wheels were necessary, one for each side.

After the 174 came the 176 and in 1924 the small 172 BC with a 5 HP engine; this car was significant because it was the first cabriolet to be mass produced by Peugeot and because it succeeded in replacing a car that had been very successful, the Quadrilette.

The 174 and 176 followed the contemporary, balanced, three volume design for a cabriolet. The engine was famous because it had sleeve valves; the 174 had a 3800cc version and the 176, 2500cc. The little 172 BC had a tiny engine, 667cc which was increased to 720cc in 1925.

The 1926 "all steel" Citroën B12 Commercial Torpedo was also a novelty. It was designed as an open-topped car but could be converted into a goods van in just a few minutes thanks to its open back and folding flap. It was strong enough to carry up to 1,100 lbs. This was indeed a rare case among European open-topped cars and was an early example of a car with a double use. In all other respects it was a torpedo.

68-69 The 1924 Peugeot cabriolet replaced the Quadrilette and repeated its success. The company firmly believed in this 5 HP 172 BC, the first mass-produced Peugeot. It was the smallest model in the 17 series and showed great reliability during the Tour de France. 7,085 were produced.

69 top The 1928 Peugeot Cabriolet 183 D had to combine the desire for prestige cars with the need to mass-produce economic models. The design of the coachwork was influenced by what was happening in the US where cars were entering a new phase. Although it was only a small open top, it was elegant, appealing and well-proportioned with a powerful 6 cylinder engine.

69 bottom The Peugeot Cabriolet 174 was built from 1922-28. Peugeot provided the chassis. This example is from 1927 in which the 174 was offered with a small cab and convex wheels. It had a 3828cc engine, top speed was 62 mph and the Peugeot lion pranced on the radiator cap.

70 top The picture shows the smile of a young woman who has discovered how maneuverable the small 5 HP Citroën Type C is.

70 center Citroën's diminutive 5 HP was also called the Little Lemon because it was colored yellow. It was mostly appreciated by women for its ease of handling and lively spirit. Note the boattail which was also seen on the Caddy Sport.

70 bottom The Renault 10 HP dates from 1923. No great effort was made to make this model look attractive—in fact quite the opposite.

71 top The small red car is the Citroën 5 HP from 1923. It was no longer a cabriolet; its appearance would classify it as a roadster or even a small torpedo. The wheels seem too large for such a small car.

71 bottom This is the Renault 45 HP seen from above. The car had a 6 cylinder, almost 10 liter engine. The body is a dual cowl design with the rear seats well protected from the wind thanks to the windshield. A second result of the rear windshield is to prevent annoying air turbulence from blowing back against the driver's and front passenger's neck and shoulders. In recent times this has been avoided by the placing of a wind-blocker just behind the front seats.

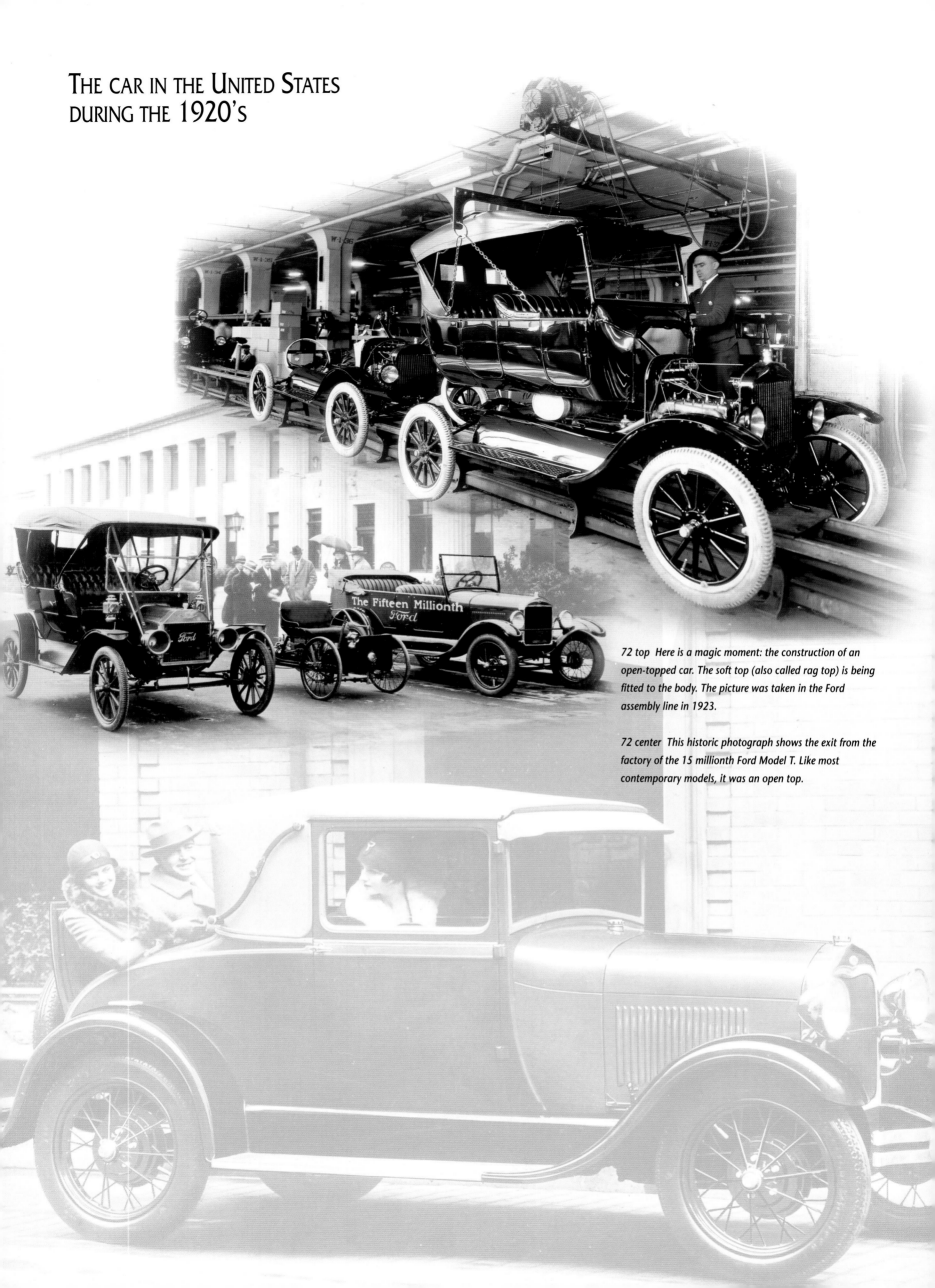

72 top Here is a magic moment: the construction of an open-topped car. The soft top (also called rag top) is being fitted to the body. The picture was taken in the Ford assembly line in 1923.

72 center This historic photograph shows the exit from the factory of the 15 millionth Ford Model T. Like most contemporary models, it was an open top.

Between 1918 and 1926 the United States became increasingly motorized and was only partially hindered by the depression of 1921-22. Industrial development during this period helped to consolidate the positive image and the confidence America had in itself, which would take the country one step too far one Friday in October 1929. The Wall Street crash was to have a strange effect on the car market; it encouraged the design and production of extremely luxurious cars - but this will be discussed later. The open-topped cars from 1927 on were quite different to those that had been available from the end of the First World War until 1926.

These were the Roaring Twenties when the desire to have fun was the motivating force behind American consumption. The car was part of the fun thanks to the increasing number of surfaced roads and freeways. It was also noticeable that the car became an outlet for the frustrations created by the 1920 Prohibition law. Consumerism and euphoria encouraged the average American not only to buy his first car but also to consider it old after just a few months. This belief in early obsolescence was cunningly exploited and fostered by marketing genius Alfred P. Sloan, President of General Motors. As regards price, the colossus of the industry, Ford, which alone accounted for more than half of American cars sold, repeatedly cut the cost of its best-seller, the Model T, a fact which could only brace the market. A description of the American car market may help to understand the mood of the public, particularly remembering that 9 out of 10 new cars were still open-topped.

72 bottom This was the convertible coupé that replaced the Model T. It was the Model A, here in roadster guise, which aroused enormous interest when, in 1928, it went on sale. In the first 36 hours, it was visited by roughly 10 million people.

73 top An ordinary day during the Roaring Twenties when consumerism and fun were the order of the day. This is Main Street in Hardesan, Texas. What is special about this picture? The majority of cars parked or passing are Model T's.

73 bottom The picture shows the tourer version of the Model T. Tourer meant a small torpedo without expensive fittings or a powerful motor. Unusually this one was blue.

In 1918 the number of cars the US produced was approximately 943,000 which rose to 1,650,000 the following year - and still the manufacturers were unable to satisfy the demand from desperate dealers due to the influence of strikes, salary increase demands and lack of components.

In 1920 the growth continued to 1,900,000 vehicles, a total which countries like Great Britain, France and Italy only reached in the 1990's, but the depression of 1920-21 reduced the market to 1.5 million. In Dallas the first drive-in appeared and in Detroit the first 3 color traffic light. After the depression, demand soared to 3.6 million in 1923, and in 1925 the 25 millionth US car was built. The volubility of users remained high, typical of immature markets, until 1929, when the record figure of 4.5 million cars were produced. Then the Great Depression smothered the consumerism of the working and lower middle classes.

To return to what happened in the world of open-topped touring vehicles during the 1920's, technological innovations made giant strides both in quantity and quality. Cars became safer, easier to drive, more comfortable, more practical and longer lasting. Safety was increased through the use of steel which progressively replaced wood; hydraulic brakes replaced mechanical brakes (and on all four wheels rather than two); wheels became stronger and more robust; and new, laminated sloping windshields were introduced. Functionality and practicality took a step forward with synchronized gears, automatic spark control, and more instrumentation on the dashboard, including the speedometer and a fuel level indicator; the horn disappeared below the hood and the radiator cap often included a thermometer for measuring water temperature. Comfort was increased by the introduction of rubber supports to reduce vibration;

74-75 The picture seems to be taken from Charlie Chaplin's "Modern Times". This is Buick's assembly line in 1923. The workers are fitting the engine unit to the chassis.

74 top Note the 6 cylinder in-line of this 4 liter Buick E/645 from 1918. The distributor cap is identical to those on modern cars.

74 bottom The official name of the 1918 Buick E/645 was Tourer according to the terminology of the period but it might be classified as one of the small torpedoes that were popular in the US among the less well-off. This type of bodywork was known in Germany as a Fetonte after the name of the son (Phaeton) of the Sun God.

75 top This was one of the cheapest cars sold at the start of the 1920's, the Chevrolet 490 which was available in 1918 for 685 dollars.

75 center Mary Pickford at the wheel of a Maxwell, a car manufacturer which did not survive the era.

75 bottom Cadillac called this model the "Standard of the World", not a modest title for this 1922 Type 61. The horn is no longer visible, being hidden under the hood.

passengers were warmed by the underfloor passage of air from the motor; and radios became a common accessory. Mechanical functionality was improved with the universal adoption of a water pump, oil and water filters, and battery operated ignition rather than a magneto; carburetors were perfected and compression ratios improved for greater efficiency and power.

Considering the boiling market and enormous speed of technological development, car design was really short of imagination, although there was no lack of great designers (Harley Earl, Ray Dietrich, etc.) and important private coachbuilders (Derham, LeBaron, etc.). Perhaps this is why the best-selling European car in the US between 1923-25 was the beautiful Isotta Fraschini Type 8.

There were still two types of open-topped car: the tourer (like a European torpedo but shorter and less elegant and well-finished) and the roadster with a short wheelbase, practically a small two-seater convertible. The touring car was the star of the market as it represented the largest percentage of open-topped cars sold - and open tops accounted for 90% of all cars.

Examples of touring cars are the 1918 Chevrolet 490 and Overland Light Four; the 1919 Buick H-45, of which 44,589 were sold; the 1921 Willys-Knight (provisionally owned by Walter Chrysler) Model 20; the 1922 Cadillac Type 61 which was rather presumptuously called the "Standard of the World"; the 1924 high-compression Chrysler 6V and the Series 60 touring phaéton of 1927.

Among smaller roadsters was the Dodge Model 30 Roadster of 1918, which had six diamond-shaped holes in the back of its top by way of a window. There was also the omnipresent Model T, in every kind of guise but always very cheap; the 1923 Buick Roadster; the 1924 Oakland "True Blue" (the first car to use fast-drying synthetic paint); and the 1927 Nash Light Six.

A novelty which was to have lasting appeal was the pointed boattail rear end, such as the one which graced the 6 cylinder Essex Speedabout of 1927.

The following year 10 million people went to look at the new Ford Model A in the first 36 hours it was in the dealers' showrooms.

A cut above the standard of popular roadsters was the 1922 Haynes (the marque did not survive beyond 1925) Model 55, the Nash Lafayette Model 134, the praised 1923 Stutz Bearcat and the 1925 Locomobile Model 48.

But this was poor stuff: For really beautiful cars, whether gran turismo or luxury convertibles, it was necessary to wait for the 1930's. Some indication of future styles was given from 1927 on and during this period American and European manufacturers marched in step in an exciting challenge to produce the most elegant, refined and desirable car in the world.

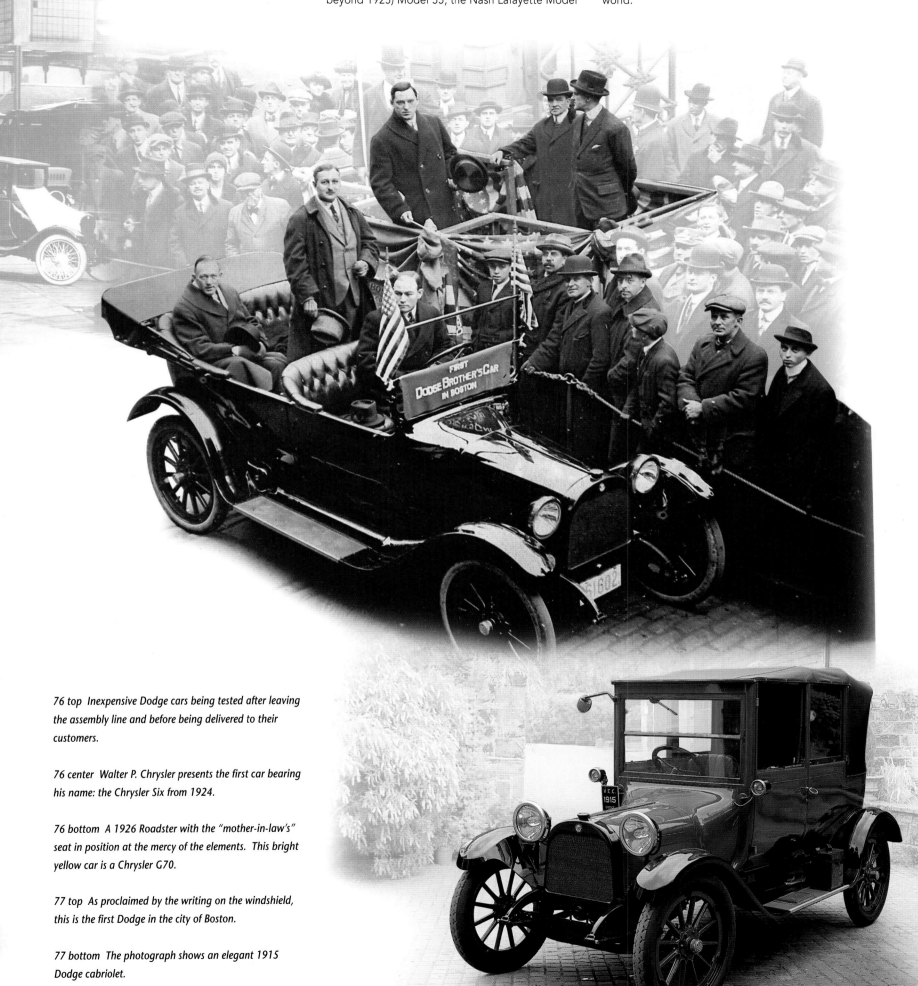

76 top Inexpensive Dodge cars being tested after leaving the assembly line and before being delivered to their customers.

76 center Walter P. Chrysler presents the first car bearing his name: the Chrysler Six from 1924.

76 bottom A 1926 Roadster with the "mother-in-law's" seat in position at the mercy of the elements. This bright yellow car is a Chrysler G70.

77 top As proclaimed by the writing on the windshield, this is the first Dodge in the city of Boston.

77 bottom The photograph shows an elegant 1915 Dodge cabriolet.

Open-Topped Racing

The races that held the fans in thrall all over the world had convinced supporters like Henry Ford, Giuseppe Merosi (first designer at Alfa Romeo) and August Horch (founder of Audi) of their worth, but had equally convinced their detractors, like Gottlieb Daimler and Karl Benz, of their worthlessness. Benz had always considered racing a distraction - simple fun for time wasters and the bored sons of the well-to-do - and he strenuously but vainly opposed the pressure to race imposed by company management. As for Daimler, nobody could refuse the rich diplomat Jellinek and his profitable orders for more powerful and competitive engines. More than anyone, it was he who instilled the competitive spirit in Mercedes.

Paradoxically, even a champion driver like Vincenzo Lancia thumbed his nose at the idea of using his cars for racing, especially if it meant making modifications to the basic model. But the commercial value of racing was confirmed, just to give one example, by the history of Alfa Romeo, which probably owed its survival to the successes of the RLs and 1750s driven by such greats as Ascari, Brilli-Peri, Nuvolari, Campari and Sivocci, in a cutthroat market that saw other glorious marques fail. After a difficult initial period, racing began to specialize. Road racing became more competitive and interesting and the number of cross country time trials (later to develop into rallying) increased. There were two important events in road and track racing in 1906: It was the first time the now-legendary Targa Florio in Sicily was held (the last would be 1977), and the first year of the French Grand Prix - the first Grand Prix to be held on an annual basis. Cagno in an Itala won the Targa Florio and a Renault won the French Grand Prix. The second time each was held Fiat won both, while at the 1908 French GP a Mercedes won with a 9 minute advantage over the second place Benz. At Brooklands in Great Britain, Felice Nazzaro in a Fiat SB 4 came home in front of Napier at an average speed of 120 mph.

In 1910 a Buick Bugs inaugurated the most famous track in the world, the Indianapolis ring at over 106 mph. The rounded and aerodynamic shape of the car reminds one of the racing cars to come. 1912 saw the first of a hat-trick of victories by Ralph de Palma in the Vanderbilt Cup in New York. An important detail was that the three

pointed star made its first appearance on the radiator of a Daimler Mercedes. At the same time Alfa made its racing debut in a 12 HP car at the Modena time trials which it finished without incurring a penalty.

Hill trials were also popular, with the thrilling ascent of Mont Ventoux near Marseilles being a classic. Today designers use this course to test the equipment and roadholding of production cars; in 1905 the racing Fiat 100 HP with a 16 liter engine won; it was driven by Cagno who finished the 13 mile race in just 19.5 minutes. The Alps were also ideal for racing: August Horch won the Alpine Cup in 1912 in an Audi C Type 14/35 HP, a success he was to repeat the following year.

A true precursor of modern day rallying was the Herkomer Race which was instituted by the Anglo-German painter Sir Hubert von Herkomer. It was held from 1905-07 on a course that started and ended in Munich taking in Baden-Baden, Stuttgart and Nuremberg.

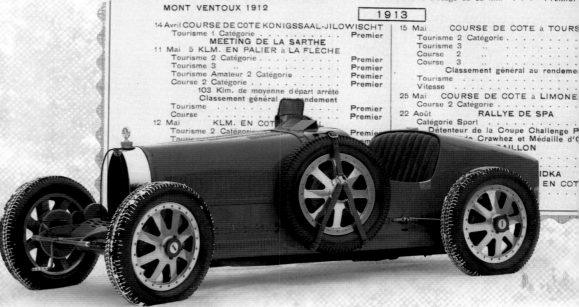

78 top A historical photograph showing the brilliant Felice Nazzaro at the 1907 Targa Florio with a Fiat 28-40 HP. Nazzaro drove car number 20B while Vincenzo Lancia, second in a similar car, drove 20A.

78 center Car racing and long distance journeys created great excitement in the western world. This is the front page of the **Seattle Daily Times** for **23 June 1909** which reports the victory of a Ford in the New York-Seattle race which took participants 23 days to complete.

78 bottom One of the greatest racing drivers of all time, Antonio Ascari, at the wheel of a Fiat S 57/14 B Corsa. This Grand Prix car could reach 94 mph thanks to its 135 HP engine. It was fitted with servo-assisted braking and Hartford mechanical shock absorbers. Together with Tazio Nuvolari, Rudolf Caracciola, Gastone Brilli-Peri, Louis Chiron and Giuseppe Campari among other great early drivers, Ascari brought the highly popular races to life after the end of the First World War. Ascari died at the wheel of an Alfa Romeo in the 1925 French Grand Prix.

79 top Manufacturers soon learned to exploit their racing triumphs to boost sales. Here Bugatti, which produced fast racing cars as well as glorious and luxurious road cars which still amaze for their quality even today, takes advantage of its win in the famous hill-climb of Mont Ventoux (France) as well as its successes in 1911, 1912 and 1913.

79 center The Bugatti Type 35 has been considered by many to be the most beautiful racing car of all time.

79 bottom In the foreground, Alessandro Cagno, driving an Itala, won the first round of the world-famous Targa Florio, held near Palermo, Sicily. The picture brings home the courage of these early drivers, who often died while racing. The fortunate Cagno was an exception, and he lived to a pleasant 78.

80 top Doctor Stoss at the wheel of a 1906 Horch in which he won the Herkomer race (as he also did the following year). August Horch, founder of the company of the same name and then Audi, is standing beside him. This model was one of the first to be shaft driven rather than have chain drive.

80 center Refueling during the 1907 French Grand Prix. The car is a Fiat and the driver, Vincenzo Lancia. His teammate, Felice Nazzaro, won the race at an average of 70.6 mph.

In 1906 the German driver Stoss won in a 18-22 HP Horch; the next year Erle won in a 50 HP Benz. More difficult were the endurance trials. Sometimes these took place as a point-to-point journey, and sometimes in the form of the modern endurance trials circling the same track repeatedly. In the latter case the aim was to demonstrate the reliability and superiority of one's car. In 1905 a Curved Dash Oldsmobile, "Old Scout", won the first transcontinental race, from New York to Portland, taking 44 days to travel 4,000 miles. The following year at Ormond Beach, a Ford K covered 1,135 miles in 24 hours at an average speed of 47.2 mph. In 1907, an Itala driven by Prince Borghese, Luigi Barzini and their mechanic Guizzardi completed the exhausting run from Peking to Paris (10,000 miles). And in 1909, an undertaking worthy of note - Mrs John R. Ramsey was the first woman to cross the United States, in a Maxwell.

To give an idea of the speed at which engines were evolving, here is a list of some records set with fairly standard technology. All were performed in open vehicles, but as some were competition cars, single seaters, prototypes or specially made record breakers, they do not all belong to the world of the convertible and sports car.

1897 - In the US, a Winton covered the mile in 1:48 at an average of 33.8 mph.

1900 - A 35 HP Daimler set a new speed record for the flying kilometer at 54 mph.

1902 - Henry Ford's "999" racer beat the record for the flying five miles, taking 5:28 for an average speed of 55.5 mph.

1903 - At Daytona Beach, Dan Wurgis' Olds Flyer does the mile in 42 seconds at 86.25 mph.

1904 - Henry Ford himself reached 91.5 mph in the Ford 999.

1909 - Fred Marriott established a new speed record of 128.4 mph in his own steam driven car.

The same year, a 21.5 liter Benz capable of producing 200 HP broke the 125 mph barrier in Europe for the first time with a speed of 126.7 mph.

1911: at Daytona, ex-Buick racing driver Bob Burman raised the record to 142 mph in a Benz with a modified body. This car and other record breaking machines came to be called "Blitzen Benz".

1919: Ralph de Palma reached 149 mph in a Packard, but at Daytona Beach a racing Duesenberg touched 165 mph.

80 bottom The picture shows a moment from one of the most outstanding achievements in the automobile world of the period: Prince Borghese, journalist Luigi Barzini and mechanic Guizzardi are passing through Berlin in an Itala during the Paris-Peking race. This team later won the exhausting event.

81 top The start of the 1908 Targa Florio from Cerda in Sicily. Vincenzo Lancia's Fiat 130 HP is about to race away. The race was won by Vittorio Trucco in an Isotta Fraschini.

81 bottom The start of a race at one of the most exciting and dangerous tracks in the world, Indianapolis. This was a 1909 event (the Indy 500 began in 1911). The light colored cars are all Buicks and the dark ones all Marmons. Bob Burman won in the Buick number 34.

82-83 This flame-red Fiat 501 SS is a sports version. The
basic model was a small but important car that sold 45,000
units. It allowed Fiat to start up postwar production in the
best possible way. The 1922 sports version shown here was
fitted with a 1.5 liter, double camshaft engine. It won its
class in several races, one of which was the 13th Targa Florio.

Styling revolutionizes the car

DESIGN STUDIOS ARE BORN IN THE UNITED STATES

In previous chapters the adjective "beautiful" and its synonyms have been used with economy. Without wishing to discuss what beauty involves - whether it is intimately linked to harmony or transgression, if it is objective or subjective, or if it owes its existence to its own organic nature or man's faculty of reason - now is the time to use with greater freedom the adjectives that express the breathtaking splendor of lines and forms that stylists and coachbuilders of open-topped cars used in the 1930's.

Why was it that this refined development did not flower during the 1920's, the decade that was so full

84 top This car belonged to Greta Garbo and can be considered a milestone in the history of the automobile. It is the Duesenberg J, loved by the wealthy for its elegance, power and uniqueness. It was produced in numerous variations and built by the best coachbuilders. Note the survival of traditional features in the J such as the shape of the radiator and the large fenders separate from the motor compartment, together with the first streamlined innovations like the drop-shaped front and rear fenders.

of intellectual and artistic fervor? Why was it that even top-of-the-range torpedoes were generally more interested in demonstrating "luxury" than "beauty"?

It is the authors' belief that the need on both sides of the Atlantic to respond to a strong requirement for motorization was responsible. Commitment to technological research, huge steps forward in reliability and functionality and a reduction in purchase price were all factors that contributed to the diffusion of the car among the public.

Beauty, too, is rarely a definable asset. Paradoxically, the best in terms of harmony, affectation and fluidity of lines and forms became prevalent in the models that immediately followed the Wall Street Crash. Fewer cars were sold, but the public admired cars in which luxury (as a byproduct of beauty) was implicit - luxury that might exorcise their underlying fear of financial suffering. Before even worse miseries were to devolve on Europe, there was a brief period in which cars were created whose "beauty" was clearly contrived as a totem against poverty and distress.

84 bottom The 1930 Cadillac Fleetwood was fitted with an enormous V16 engine. A more "economic" version was produced the following year with a "simple" V8.

85 top The 1932 Pierce-Arrow Roadster, an example of a convertible coupé.

85 bottom The Duesenberg J Convertible Coupé was an extraordinary car. Unique versions were owned by Gary Cooper, Clark Gable and Mae West, generally in a roadster design. The most popular version was produced by coachbuilders Bohman & Schwartz.

The creation of objectively "beautiful" cars was not casual. It coincided with the birth of design studios inside the large carmakers, with the maturing of new, fresh ideas spread by young architects, and with the rising sophistication of specialized coachbuilders. Often these three approaches crossed and intermingled. In general the style centers were responsible for the diffusion of new, long-lasting trends, the designers for surprising, imaginative and provocative ideas and the coachbuilders, often manual workers of humble origin, for the creation

of moving sculptures that represent beauty in the classic sense. This chapter will examine, as far as possible, the output from these three schools of thought.

The starting point came when a large auto manufacturer assigned a car body's design (and often production) to a specialized company. The difference in this respect between the Old and New Worlds was that in Europe, the coachbuilders' work was inevitably aimed at luxury sedans and tourers; in the US, it was often spread over the whole production range. The requirement was

therefore stronger in America for the creation of internal design studios which would produce a "company brand" or a corporate style, an image which the public could identify with. Furthermore, it was in the United States that young designers, including Europeans, could best express themselves. Credit for developing the concept of a "style center" is universally attributed to the boss of General Motors, Alfred P. Sloan Jr., who was among the first to understand that the interest of the public was moving away from the chassis towards the body.

86 The picture shows the glamorous lines of the Duesenberg J Dual Cowl Phaéton of 1934. The design displays the full maturity of the type of design known as the torpedo that by this stage was not far from decline, though remember this model was at the top of the market as regards power and quality of equipment, fittings and *materials. There is no modern design feature to be seen in this magisterial interpretation of the classical style. Only the very best from Cadillac and Packard (in the USA) and Rolls Royce and Mercedes (in Europe) can be compared to this sculpture in movement as Bugatti and Hispano Suiza were already out of business.*

87 top The front of the Duesenberg J Dual Cowl was enormous thanks to its huge double headlights, wave-like fenders and large radiator grill decorated with thick chrome vertical bars. The only feature that seems normal size is the bumper made from two thin rails, one slightly raised, which resembles a moustache.

87 bottom This close-up of the 1934 Duesenberg J radiator grill shows a glimpse, on the right, of the part which covers the side opening for the exhaust pipes. The decorative fender pressings also added strength.

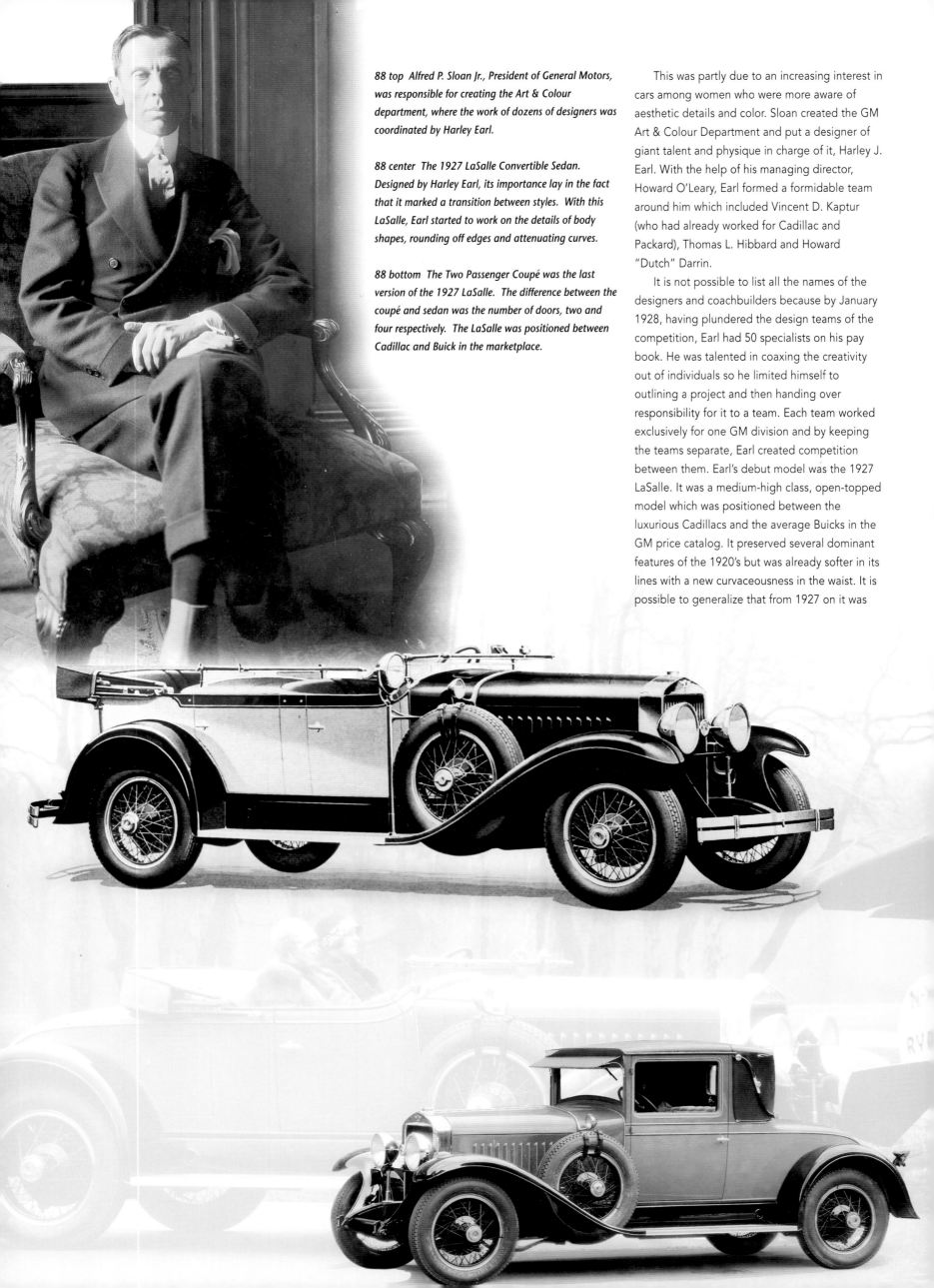

88 top Alfred P. Sloan Jr., President of General Motors, was responsible for creating the Art & Colour department, where the work of dozens of designers was coordinated by Harley Earl.

88 center The 1927 LaSalle Convertible Sedan. Designed by Harley Earl, its importance lay in the fact that it marked a transition between styles. With this LaSalle, Earl started to work on the details of body shapes, rounding off edges and attenuating curves.

88 bottom The Two Passenger Coupé was the last version of the 1927 LaSalle. The difference between the coupé and sedan was the number of doors, two and four respectively. The LaSalle was positioned between Cadillac and Buick in the marketplace.

This was partly due to an increasing interest in cars among women who were more aware of aesthetic details and color. Sloan created the GM Art & Colour Department and put a designer of giant talent and physique in charge of it, Harley J. Earl. With the help of his managing director, Howard O'Leary, Earl formed a formidable team around him which included Vincent D. Kaptur (who had already worked for Cadillac and Packard), Thomas L. Hibbard and Howard "Dutch" Darrin.

It is not possible to list all the names of the designers and coachbuilders because by January 1928, having plundered the design teams of the competition, Earl had 50 specialists on his pay book. He was talented in coaxing the creativity out of individuals so he limited himself to outlining a project and then handing over responsibility for it to a team. Each team worked exclusively for one GM division and by keeping the teams separate, Earl created competition between them. Earl's debut model was the 1927 LaSalle. It was a medium-high class, open-topped model which was positioned between the luxurious Cadillacs and the average Buicks in the GM price catalog. It preserved several dominant features of the 1920's but was already softer in its lines with a new curvaceousness in the waist. It is possible to generalize that from 1927 on it was the rear end of the car body that evolved more rapidly than the front. Roadster tails were stretched into more aerodynamic forms like the boattail and sloping backs, while the front end was still dominated by a long hood, large circular headlights on the fenders, the fenders themselves, the radiator grill and sometimes visible exhaust pipes. The round headlights of the LaSalle were positioned in front of the vertical, traditional radiator grill. The fenders did not reflect the aeronautic fashion of the period but were discreet and of a different color to the rest of the car, which sported gilded door-handles and decoration. The roof panel sloped sharply down at the back and although the top was soft, it gave the car a sense of rigidity. The windshield could be inclined forwards. This car was considered one of the first convertibles in the US, almost a standard, thanks to its vertically opening side windows and the absence of midpoint uprights. The exact term is "convertible coupé" as there were two doors rather than four (in which case it would have been a "convertible sedan"). Earl later admitted frankly that he had been inspired by one of the most luxurious European gran turismo cars, the Hispano-Suiza. Another innovative American convertible was the Cadillac V-16 of 1931.

89 top left The LaSalle advertising describes the full 1927 range of six models.

89 top right The guru of American car design from the 1920's on was Harley Earl, shown here in a prototype of a "personal car" called the Y-Job. The differences in style between this model and others on this page are clear, as this model dates from 1937.

89 bottom The similarities between airplane design and car design were to be much greater than the photographer of this historic picture could ever have guessed. The effect on the collective imagination of Charles Lindbergh's crossing of the Atlantic from New York to Paris in this ugly but strong plane, the Spirit of St. Louis, was to have long repercussions on car design on both sides of the Atlantic.

90 top This 1937 two-tone Buick Eight Drophead displays several design features that profoundly changed in the 1930's. Despite still having separate fenders and a footboard, it looks slimmer than its predecessors thanks to the new frameless "fencing mask" grill and is rounder. Note also the drop-shaped fenders, signs of the aerodynamic styling influence.

90-91 and 91 This 1931 Cadillac V16 is a typical torpedo dual cowl. This elegant model has circular instrument dials in an engine-turned panel. Note the floor type gearshift and the side-light lever clamps.

At Ford the situation was similar. Edsel Ford, Henry Ford's son, spent most of his efforts having to mediate between the unwavering traditionalism of the founder (Henry Ford's famous dictum "You can buy a Ford of any color as long as it's black" showed how interested he was in aesthetics) and his own knowledge of the necessity of moving with the times. He asked one of the first and most brilliant independent coachbuilders to Detroit, Raymond Dietrich, to create a package to rationalize prices, times and components for a design center capable of styling cars intended for series production.

Edsel used the Lincoln marque, of which he had been president since 1922, to experiment on the innovations that he wanted to see on the company's principal marque, Ford. He immediately demonstrated his qualities as a strategist and designer: the Ford Model A, which replaced the obsolete Model T, showed stylistic touches that were evident at Lincoln, while the bodies that were made for Ford by the Murray Body Corporation of America and the Briggs Manufacturing Company were examples of the general style and details prevalent at Lincoln.

92 top and center Chrysler's 1931 advertising shows some of the most popular body designs of the time: the roadster, convertible coupé (also seen in the center picture) and the limousine. The technical boasts of the 1931 Chrysler range included an 8 cylinder motor along with the existing 6 cylinder and Floating Power, a rubber support system for the engine.

92 bottom The 1930 Chrysler roadster was one of the first models to truly fulfill Chrysler's dream of luxury and speed at a reasonable price.

93 The 1940 Lincoln Continental had a grill that was reminiscent of some earlier Independents'. The Continental was in effect a rehash of the famous and important Ford Zephyr designed by Bob Gregorie and championed by Edsel Ford. The butterfly wing grill was the cause of a long dispute between Gregorie and Ford's head of engineering, who argued that the air intake would not be efficient. The picture above shows a happy Mickey Rooney taking the keys of his new Lincoln Continental.

CHRYSLER

CHRYSLER SIX ROADSTER $885

CHRYSLER EIGHT DE LUXE COUPE $1525

CHRYSLER IMPERIAL SEDAN (5-PASS.) $2945

Only Chrysler Engineering Gets Chrysler Results

CHRYSLERS at every price are *Chryslers*—and therefore joyously different from other cars. More alive, more responsive, smoother in action. All Chrysler cars are definitely related to each other by the same general design, by the same general basis of quality, by the same general excellence of engineering, by the same general spirit ... ler for practically every /value.

... big Six of sterling abil... 78-horsepower en... unch, rigid double... bodies...

Or the new Chrysler Eight De Luxe—*de luxe* in everything, inside and outside. Divided windshield. Unusually roomy bodies. Unusually deep, soft cushions. An easy-riding 124-inch wheelbase. Unusually long springs. A smooth 95-horsepower straight eight engine that gives you eighty miles an hour if you want it—with the safety of low-swung balance of weight and the positive, easy control of internal hydraulic brakes . . .

CHRYSLER SIX . . . . . $885 to $935
CHRYSLER EIGHT DE LUXE $1525 to $1585
(Five wire wheels standard; six wire wheels $35 extra)
CHRYSLER IMPERIAL EIGHT $2745 to $3145

Or the magnificent Chrysler Imperial Eight—Chrysler's very finest—a motor car for connoisseurs of motor cars. An ultra-fine car of 145-inch wheelbase and 125-horsepower—winner of 12 official A. A. A. Contest Board stock car speed records.

Both the De Luxe Eight and the Imperial Eight have the exclusive Chrysler Dual High gear transmission. TWO high gears, and you can shift from either to the other *instantly*—at any car speed—without clashing. One high gear is for flashing action in traffic. Another still higher gear gives faster car speeds at *slower* engine speeds.

Drive a Chrysler—any Chrysler—and enjoy ... difference. Enjoy the thrilling fact ...

In 1932 Ford employed a young architect, Bob Gregorie. He and Edsel designed and proposed to car body suppliers a series of ideas that were full of distinctive personality. Examples might be the 1939 Lincoln Zephyr, first designed in 1933 by John Tjaarda, a designer of Dutch origin working at Briggs, or the 1940 Ford De Luxe, a low-budget compact convertible (or convertible coupé - call it what you will). The Zephyr's story started in 1933 when it was designed as a dreamcar by Briggs in the most difficult year of the Depression. There was a battle of wills between Gregorie and Chief Engineer Frank Johnson, who strongly opposed the idea of moving the radiator fan lower down. His reason was that during summer months and in the hot states of the southwest, the engine would soon become excessively overheated. In response Gregorie proposed that the entire grill should be flattened. Edsel Ford approved the idea which was tested in the wind tunnel. It was successful, and so a new grill design ensued from a technical requirement; instead of being tall and narrow, it became low and wide. This was completely different from the Zephyr of that year with its body by LeBaron, where the grill was similar to a fencer's mask. The last of the American Big Three, Chrysler, was undergoing a similar process. Its own design department, also called Art and Color, was instituted in 1928 and put under the management of Herbert V. Henderson who had experience in industrial as well as interior design. He only had a small team, 5-6 people, which was responsible for the entire group with all its different marques: Imperial, Chrysler, De Soto, Dodge and Plymouth. Amusingly, it seems that Walter Chrysler was unable to restrain his curiosity and often liked to glance through the unfinished sketches of his (no doubt annoyed) designers.

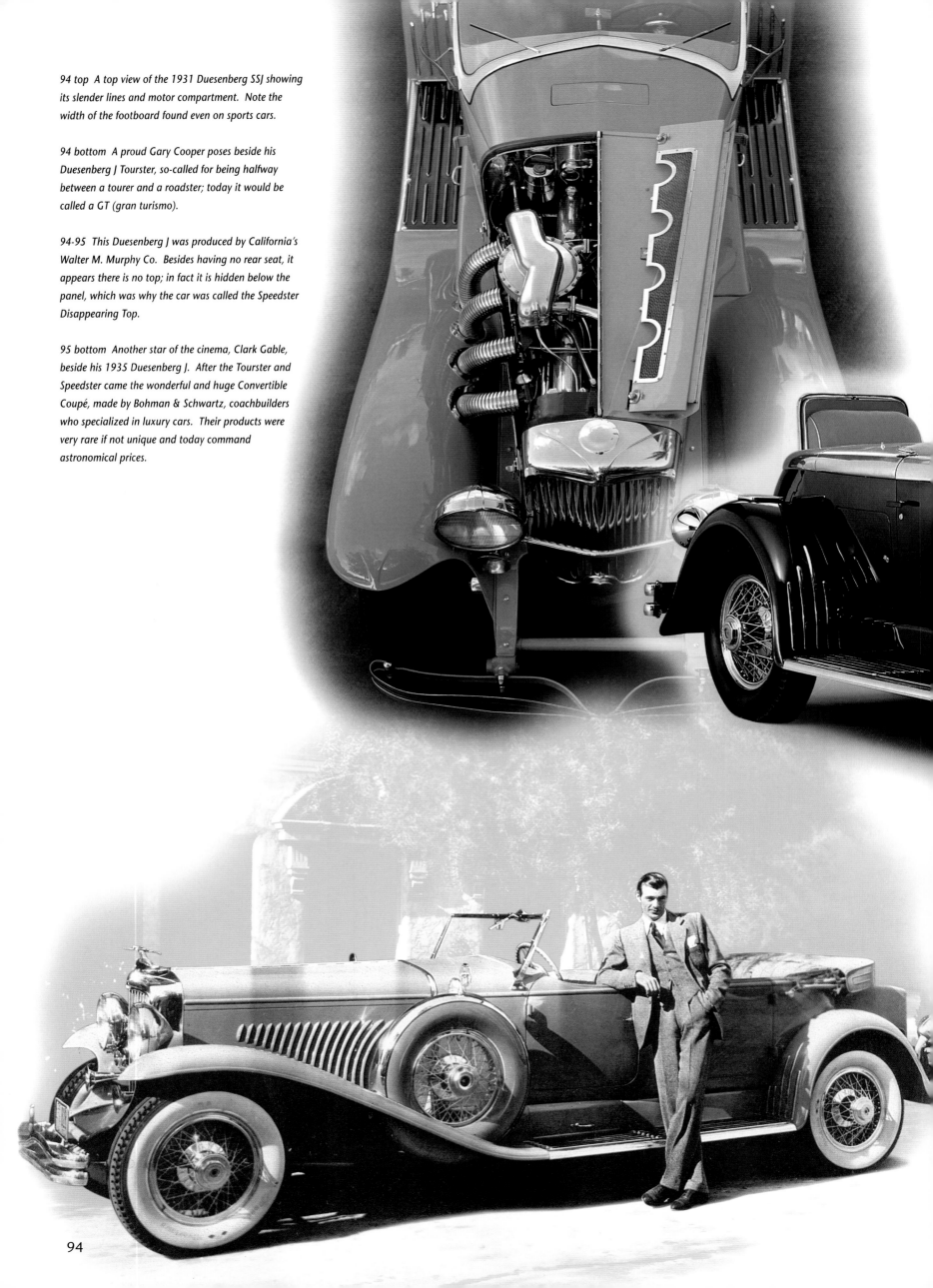

94 top A top view of the 1931 Duesenberg SSJ showing its slender lines and motor compartment. Note the width of the footboard found even on sports cars.

94 bottom A proud Gary Cooper poses beside his Duesenberg J Tourster, so-called for being halfway between a tourer and a roadster; today it would be called a GT (gran turismo).

94-95 This Duesenberg J was produced by California's Walter M. Murphy Co. Besides having no rear seat, it appears there is no top; in fact it is hidden below the panel, which was why the car was called the Speedster Disappearing Top.

95 bottom Another star of the cinema, Clark Gable, beside his 1935 Duesenberg J. After the Tourster and Speedster came the wonderful and huge Convertible Coupé, made by Bohman & Schwartz, coachbuilders who specialized in luxury cars. Their products were very rare if not unique and today command astronomical prices.

A special mention should be given to Errett Lobban Cord, the owner of Auburn, Cord and Duesenberg. His models were designed by the best stylists and designers of the age. They merit great respect and a picture in this volume.

When E.L. Cord took over Duesenberg in 1926, he asked the previous owner, Fred Duesenberg, to design him a gran turismo car. In 1928 the Model J appeared; it was produced between 1934-36 and in some special versions (SJ, SSJ Speedster, SJ Speedster-Roadster) for actors Clark Gable, Gary Cooper and Mae West and VIP's like Howard Hughes, the Maharajah of Indore and Prince Nicholas of Romania, who raced his at Le Mans twice without success. The J had a pointed tail like a traditional roadster. The SJ was largely influenced by top stylist Gordon Buehrig who had a hand in the design stage. It had a very curvaceous waist which was emphasized with a reddish-brown line of paint and a beautifully styled rear end. This car makes up a trio with the 1931 Alfa Romeo 6C 1750 S Flying Star by Italy's Carrozzeria Touring and the 1939 Mercedes 540K; all were unique in their static beauty and can only be compared to the very best customized models where no expense has been spared. The Duesenberg SJ had the most powerful engine in the world, a supercharged 6876cc Lycoming with 8 cylinders in-line capable of producing 320 HP and moving the car in excess of 125 mph (Lycoming still produces airplane engines). The motor of the Model J, if not supercharged, "only" produced 250 HP!

In 1929 another Cord model, the L-29, provoked interest mainly for its front end, which emphasized its front-wheel drive to such an extent that this styling was taken up by Chrysler in 1931. The design had come from the pen of Al Leamy, head of the Auburn design team. In addition to the very small convertible coupé there existed a long wheelbase, dual cowl version with body designed by Murphy, while Sakhnoffsky designed an elegant "short" version much loved by celebrities. The talented Ralph Roberts also worked for Duesenberg (and therefore for the whole Cord group); unfortunately, 1937 brought the final closure of the company.

96 top The Cord L-29 was very successful in its different guises from 1929 on. The picture is taken from an advertising brochure which rightly states that Cords occupied a unique place in the automobile industry. Auburn, Cord and Duesenberg were all part of the same group, founded and run by Errett Lobban Cord. Many brilliant designers produced innovative and avant-garde models for this company that unfortunately went out of business in 1937. The Cord L-29 was very popular with coachbuilders, especially in the convertible coupé version shown here.

96 bottom These two Auburn Speedsters date from 1935. The model was the result of the combined work of Gordon Buehrig and August Duesenberg who wanted to design a new version of the 1930 Auburn with supercharger at a limited price. They came up with this solid but fluid design with a deep-set grill. The extra-large fenders were so wide they seemed like a flat surface; it seems unlikely they were aerodynamically effective.

97 top left Errett Lobban Cord, founder of the Auburn-Cord-Duesenberg group.

97 top right A good example of the boattail back end that made large, powerful cars seem lighter and more slippery. This particular model is an Auburn 851 Speedster from 1935.

97 bottom A version of the Cord L-29 convertible coupé by designer Sakhnoffsky.

98 top and center Packard was probably the most conservative car manufacturer during the 1930's. This model is the 236 Touring R from 1925. The picture (center) shows inside the motor compartment with the spark plugs in view on the head. The sparking sequence of the 8 cylinder in-line is shown on the block below.

98 bottom This 1930 Packard 7-34 rivaled the Cadillac V16 and Duesenberg J as a large roadster. They were three beautiful and powerful models with similar lines and boattail rear ends.

The 1930's saw emphasis move to the appearance and the shape of the car, at least for top-of-the-range models which of course included convertibles and roadsters. Consequently, the factories welcomed a new breed of employee - painters, artists, designers, illustrators, and craftsmen who worked in wood and iron - who created a strange contrast with the workers in blue overalls of the production line. It is easy to imagine the skepticism with which they were viewed. How is it possible to design a car without knowing the mechanical components? That was the reasoning behind the reluctance of some companies (like the conservative Packard) to use designers' ideas for more than decoration or less important features. However Packard in particular made a complete turnaround where styling was concerned, passing from the highly luxurious 1929 post-torpedo 645 De Luxe Eight to the ultra-elegant, fluid curves of the 1940 Super Eight-One-Eighty Victoria designed by Howard "Dutch" Darrin.

General Motors, Ford and Chrysler continued to revolutionize the appearance of the car. The coachwork was to assume elastic and slender shapes influenced by aeronautic design and the freshness of ideas blowing in from modern graphic design centers.

99 The car at the top is yet another luxury interpretation of the convertible coupé. This is the 1933 Packard V12 designed by coachbuilder Dietrich. Compare it to the Super Eight below from the year after with its strongly emphasized and curved fenders: The tire is almost invisible.

The Great Depression of the 1930's which followed the collapse of Wall Street shook not only the economy of the whole world but also the tranquility of the American people. It was a lesson in humility that the consumer society had inflicted on itself. Poverty visited the homes of many American families while mechanical industry, until recently geared up to simply produce, produce, produce, was now running down.

In 1932 Franklin Delano Roosevelt was elected President and launched plans aimed at rousing the stunned economy. His New Deal contained the ingredients of hope and trust.

Intense intellectual activity animated the cultural debate, particularly with regard to the figurative arts, architecture, town planning and design. Intellectual energy was channeled into currents of thought that were often contradictory.

They generated peculiar trends that trod the limits of transgression (which someone claimed was a close relation of beauty) or appeared as malicious provocation.

Cars were relatively fertile ground for application of the new styles but objective limitations like functionality and fitness for use checked extravagance so that designers were forced to restrain themselves if they wanted their

ideas to take material form; function took priority over looks. The car united art and technology, form and function, and the architect Le Corbusier published a report in 1928 on the criteria on which design of comfortable passenger compartments should be based.

During the 1930's public interest in everything mechanical was strong both in the United States and Europe. The Futurist cultural

100 top and center Two interesting advertising brochures: The upper diagram summarizes the technical data of the two emerging methods of transport, the car and the airplane (the car in this case is a Studebaker). The picture (center) is taken from a brochure for the German manufacturer Adler. The American brochure offers images of the Machine Age while the continental European advertisement is based on the theme of liberty with an elegant, sporty car and a beautiful smiling woman wearing racing goggles.

100 bottom A 1928 Packard sports roadster painted bright orange - including the wheels!

101 top This advertisement photograph was taken in 1925 on the island of Malta to launch the Fiat 509.

movement started in 1909 by Marinetti exalted speed and the car as the ideal messenger of liberty and independence (concepts which are still partly valid, given that progress in the fields of transport and communications have turned the global village dream into reality) but shortly afterwards four wheels had to give way an almost unbeatable rival - the airplane.

The event which gave impetus to "air frenzy"

was perhaps exaggerated by the newspapers of the time, who were always in search of new heroes: Charles Lindbergh flew non-stop from New York to Paris in May 1927 on board the Spirit of St. Louis. All over the world records and air crossings followed one after another and fashions and styles were influenced by the search for streamlined, aerodynamic shapes.

101 bottom This is a curious experimental car, the Mercedes 500 from 1933. The aerodynamic design theme is used across the whole body. It is a pity that the designers stayed within the accepted forms of the day, for example with the front fenders that almost hide the wheels; in an experimental model they could at least have been more ambitious.

102-103 Here is a synthesis of the breaks with accepted form by emerging designers during the 1930's. The picture in the center is an Auburn Custom Twelve Speedster from 1932. Apart from the standard roadster boattail rear end, note the subtlety of the fenders made to look more streamlined by the long wheelbase and extremely long front volume and accentuated by the low, inclined windshield. In the top right there is a 1936 852 Supercharged Convertible Phaéton. A revolution in design seems to have taken place between the two Auburns: despite being less attractive, the second is smaller and has fewer parts that stick out of the overall body shape. It almost seems possible to guess what the shape of cars will be during the 1940's. The picture in the bottom left shows a car from the same group, a Cord, certainly one of the more revolutionary marques compared to other contemporary models. This is the convertible version of the Cord 810 designed by Gordon Buehrig in 1936. It is remembered as the car with the "coffin hood". Also worth noting are the headlights which disappear in the fenders.

the point where the flow is met. It should also be biconvex, i.e. convex in the central part both above and below, and taper at the tail. In other words, like a waterdrop.

In "Towards a New Architecture" Le Corbusier invokes aerodynamic lines and abolishes the rigid canons of the past. He recommends removal of everything outside the car body such as oversized headlights, elaborate fenders and side-mounted spare wheels in order to reduce the car to an outline over which the air could pass without meeting resistance. But to do so seemed to most people impractical and unthinkable. The traditionalists were not altogether wrong, certainly; long, uniform profiles without obstructions improve the coefficient of aerodynamic penetration, and therefore performance and fuel consumption, but for the cars of the 1930's that were not designed for high speeds, it was of negligible importance.

So it was not function that prompted designers to adopt rounded, sinuous forms, it was aesthetics, a little like what happened to the sports versions of compact cars during the 1980's which were dressed up in completely ineffective spoilers and miniskirts but which gave the driver the sensation of being at the wheel of a powerful sports car. This kind of decoration is applied more by the marketing department than the designer and is known as "patches". Research into streamlined profiles continued apace, and for those without expensive equipment like wind tunnels, knowledge was gained through racing.

Beautiful cars immediately attempted to adopt the slimness, fluidity and smoothness of the airplane, and what better models than sports cars and convertibles, open-topped glories, born to fly? In order to distinguish in broad outline between aesthetics and function, it is necessary to discuss briefly the basic concepts of fluid dynamics. The most efficient shape of a wing profile is the one that presents an ogival, hemispherical section at

As far as this book is concerned, the term "aeronautic" refers to shapes inspired by the passion for flight and "aerodynamic" to those involved in improving the coefficient of aerodynamic penetration and performance. Alternatively, a division between aesthetic streamlining and functional streamlining might be considered although often the line between the two gets blurred.

The 1931 Lancia Astura Cabriolet was a good example of balanced streamlining which contributed to the car's beautiful appearance to such an extent that it appeared modernized. Thanks to its length of over 14'8", the tapered fenders were absorbed into the body of the car without problem. Although classically elegant and keeping a large front end, it seemed new, slender and in a certain sense "dynamic". The cream of Italy's special-body designers and constructors, all of whom had a cautious interest in the new shapes, became involved in the design of top level models like the Astura.

Even the cab of a car could become a reproduction of a pilot's cockpit as happened to the 1931 Lincoln Aero Phaéton with body design by LeBaron. It was a dual cowl model with rear seats separated from the front ones, not by a windshield as in the production series of 1929, but by a small spoiler and, cherry on the cake, a fake ornamental rudder. Naturally there was a small fuselage on the radiator cap.

The 1932 Chrysler Imperial CH claimed to be a speedster and with good reason. Much could be written about this car which summarized the characteristic features of the gran turismo, perhaps the most important class of vehicle during the 1930's. The headlights were the complete antithesis of Le Corbusier's recommendations, being larger than ever. The fenders were still wide and rounded but behind, despite being large, the Imperial Speedster was smooth and slim. The rear volume and fenders were distinct, but in perfect harmony.

104 top One of Pinin Farina's many interpretations of the Lancia Astura. Vincenzo Lancia, ex-Fiat official racing driver, was known for the care he expended on the details of his cars and his stylistic intuition. Study of this Farina design shows that this came from the end of the 1940's: the vertical seams, previously horizontal, on the hood are the clue.

104-105 The car below is the cheaper, 1934, version of the two LaSalle roadsters available during the mid-1930's.

104 bottom Jack Dempsey, world heavyweight boxing champion, is sitting at the wheel of the Chrysler Imperial Custom Roadster.

105 top The austere forms and imposing dimensions belong to a 1938 Packard Super 8, dual cowl version. The picture shows the side windows to good effect but above all the coherence of the curves; perhaps the only fault in the Super 8 is the excessive length of the wheelbase.

105 bottom The chassis of this open top crossed the ocean to be built. It is the 1939 Buick Special Albemarle designed by the English master craftsman, Carlton.

106 top This little open top is the Frazer-Nash Tourer of 1927 which three people could squeeze into. Note the two-tone coloring which highlights the motor compartment.

106 center The picture represents a step towards the past: this is the Isotta Fraschini, one of the motoring symbols of the Belle Epoque together with Bugatti and Hispano Suiza.The car in the picture was designed by the Italian coachbuilder Castagna, known for its interpretations of Alfa Romeo GT's and the Isotta Fraschini Type 8A, the best-selling European car in the US during the late 1920's.

With regard to new, fluid shapes, a figure worthy of note was the Italian Count Mario Revelli of Beaumont. Considering that coachbuilders are usually manual workers who have opened their own workshop, the presence of an aristocrat in the lineup is a trifle odd. Actually the Count liked nothing better than to design one-off machines for his friends and produce them with the help of his colleagues Giacinto Ghia and Vittorino Viotti, two professional coachbuilders. He loved mechanical things and especially motorcycles (he was World Champion in 1925 on a motorbike of his own devising). He was a friend of Vincenzo Lancia and Battista "Pinin" Farina and he created, among others, splendid variants of the Isotta Fraschini (for the Duke of Bergamo), the Fiat 525 (for the Princess of Pistoia-Aremberg), the Lancia Aprilia Viotti (for Mussolini) and the Lancia Lambda VIII sports, the Itala 65 torpedo, and the two-tone

Chrysler 75 coupé de ville. Revelli was one of the most acute designers of the streamlining trend and took a hand in the design of the production Fiat 1500 of 1936. Analogies with aerodynamic research were even more evident in the 1941 convertible presented by Lincoln designers. This was the monumental Continental, one of the links between research, the introduction of aeronautic concepts and the rounded shapes of convertibles from the 1940's and 50's. Streamlining, future gazing, new trends: The aesthetics of the luxury cars of the 1930's became a melting pot of Art Deco, the wish to fly, novelty and daring. What a tangle of styles, ideas and shapes! In these years there was a little bit of everything present and to classify them would be impossible. The stylistic earthquake did not influence just design of the car; even Coco Chanel was struck by Art Deco and its development. The car was more practical and widespread than the airplane and it was a splendid subject for the experimental whims of young designers and the avant-garde filled with inspiration from the Bauhaus and the daring of Art Deco.

One of the most brilliant designers was Raymond Loewy, a Frenchman who had moved to the US in the 1920's. He was the creator of the Esso and Shell trademarks and the Coca Cola bottle. When it came to cars, he threw off two quick sketches, one a Hupmobile and the other a Studebaker. One of these, maybe a 1947 Studebaker Champion, appeared like a vision to a child along the streets of Tarvisio in Italy who was so awestruck that he dedicated his life to car design and became the head of the Mercedes design team: Bruno Sacco.

The new designers embraced functional objects, too, provided they made life easier, more fun or slightly outré; objects like these were a tangible demonstration of re-found material optimism. The US had been starved of this and welcomed the new ideas with open arms. In Europe the increasingly dictatorial political situation made it difficult for those unwilling to tread the approved paths, with the result that many American design projects were created by European architects, engineers and stylists who had emigrated if not fled their homelands. Loewy was only one example of those who helped to change the shape of consumer items like wardrobes, bicycles, glasses, houses, bridges or cars, etc.

106-107 and 107 top This Frazer-Nash TT from 1933 is a typical European roadster with its barrel-type rear end (in the US, the boattail was all the rage). The front end was aggressive but attractive and could be thought to resemble a customized motorbike with a little imagination; it almost looks as though it is about to rear up. The Frazer is in fact very "American" being mid-sized with a sloping tail and square cab, characteristic features of convertible coupés.

Among those cars which created a real sensation was the 1936 Cord 810, a classic of the new style. It was designed by Gordon Buehrig and the staff of the Auburn motor company. The brilliant design reduced the car to its fundamentals and then developed each element separately. The most obvious result is the nose which worryingly resembles the giant statues on Easter Island. "Coffin" was the name many maliciously gave to the engine compartment, a huge uniform nose in which the grill was replaced by thick, striking chrome horizontal frames. The headlights, apart from two foglights, were housed inside bays in the fenders while the exhaust pipes, often more ornamental than functional, became flexible tubes, though this was not an original idea. The lower part of the front half of the rear fenders was chromed, a detail which would be repeated often in the future.

108-109 The open-topped version of an important and revolutionary car from the 1930's, the 1936 Cord 810. The designer, Gordon Buehrig, was one of the most famous of his time and he surprised the world with this model that altered the accepted vision of car design on several points. For example, the lights had almost always been an important element attached externally to the car body; in the Cord they were hidden in the fenders and introduced the streamlining concept of pop-up headlights (the idea was reintroduced in sports cars during the 1960's & 70's). But the Cord will be remembered more for its very unusual nose, blown up in the picture to the left, which maligners likened to a coffin and that anticipated the themes of anthropomorphism and zoomorphism. Grills and front end design of convertibles from the end of the 1940's and the 1950's sometimes explicitly resembled faces.

109 bottom One of the countless configurations of the Cord L-29. This is an elegant two-seat, two-tone roadster, but the dual cowl and phaeton were also very successful with VIP's and movie stars.

The car was unusual for its time and for what was to follow but it represented the maturity of the work that had been carried out over the years with greater or lesser success by open-minded coachbuilders.

For example, the Auburn 8-100A Custom Eight from four years earlier had a split personality. The production model could happily be considered a convertible coupé but the Speedster version showed influences of the style to come: angular shapes in the radiator and the grill, which drops at a strange angle towards the protruding crosspiece. The headlights resemble lanterns while the chromed fender follows the angle of the radiator and takes the shape of an arrow in the center. The fenders are very obvious, designed to look like the shoulder-pieces of a suit of armor and are, as much as possible, placed further from the wheels.

Studebaker brought out 3 models in 1935 with names as worrying as the shapes: the Dictator Six, Commander Eight and President Eight. It is interesting to note how in this case, as in others, and particularly with regard to four door convertibles, the new ideas tended to give a slightly rigid appearance to the car rather than create imaginative curves and shapes. This was the opposite effect to that hoped for by the standard-bearers of Futurism. As usual, the character of 1930's cars was most defined by the radiator grill and the huge fenders which tended to fold inward. Other industrial designers who distinguished themselves in American car styling in the 1930's were Norman Bel Geddes, who worked with the short-lived firm Graham-Paige and whose ideas for the Chrysler Airflow will be seen later, and Walter Dorwin Teague, designer of the 1933 Marmon Sixteen, halfway between a convertible coupé and a roadster. This design found no success either; Marmon was absorbed by the American Automotive Corporation and closed down in 1937. In Europe too models with streamlining and Art Deco designs found an enthusiastic following. There were Voisins, Bugattis (from both Ettore and Jean Bugatti) and the rare and elite Delage, which sported a Lalique figure in glass paste on the radiator (Lalique was a famous artist noted for his glass crystal figures but he was also responsible for designing the large bronze plate presented to the winner of the Targa Florio in Sicily). Before discussing the model that more than any other represented the synthesis of Art Deco design in the car world, the Bugatti Type 57, it is worth remembering some open-topped cars that led up to it. Combining some of their elements with those of the Coupé Type 50, designed in 1932 by Ettore's son Jean, gave us the Type 57.

110 top and bottom The pictures effectively demonstrate why Bugattis have always attracted such attention. The roadster in question shows great plasticity of form both from the side and from above. The side view in particular shows the beauty of the fender-footboard-fender feature which may be the most beautiful of all time: There is no interruption between the front and rear fender, and the whole forms a soft, undulating double curve. Such dynamism of design reached its culmination in the Bugatti Type 57, a perfect interpretation of the Art Deco style.

110-111 A unique means of advertising was used to present the Studebaker President Eight. The figures in the picture give an idea of the size of the wooden silhouette used to launch this important model, which made up a trio with the Commander Six and Dictator at the start of the 1930's.

111 top and bottom The small Type 55 Roadster has all the characteristic style of a Bugatti. The picture below shows a Type 50 with coachwork of a three-seater convertible coupé. The supercharged engine could be as large as 4.9 liters.

111 center A model from another important marque from the early days of the automobile industry, the Studebaker President Roadster of 1932.

A strange car appeared in France in 1934, the Peugeot Cabriolet 301 Eclipse; its astronomical name was continued with the 402 in 1937. The two cars had in common a patent by dentist Georges Paulin who used to work on chassis sheets in his spare time in the workshop of his friend Marcel Pourtout. Paulin had invented a metal roof which slid into the baggage compartment electrically and which came to be used on the Peugeot. (In 1930, however, B.B. Ellerbach had already patented a retractable hard top in the US).

The Peugeot's body represented the best amalgamation so far of the various characteristics of the new trends. The sinuous forms were most clearly seen in the fender and along the car's waistline which both reflected the contemporary fascination with aeronautic design. The radiator was not flat like the austere, luxurious Rolls-Royces, Hispano-Suizas and Mercedes but more resembled that of the Auburn A100 being concave, tall and narrow. Another aeronautic touch was the closed case that held the spare wheel. The door was wide with a slight curve along the edge towards the bottom, a form that would be repeated time after time in English old-fashioneds.

The 402 was much more interesting. Five years of experiments had allowed Paulin to improve the roof mechanism so that it was not just reliable but also more in harmony with the car body. What had been an experiment in 1932 was now a reality as long as the owner did not mind having to open and shut the roof manually - there was no battery

powerful enough to do it electrically! With the hard top up the central volume of the car balanced the front and back ends perfectly; the nose on the 402 was shorter and the tail longer. The wheels were almost enclosed in the body with the rear wheels protected by side panels very much influenced by undercarriage fairings on airplanes. The front had a backwards sloping grill which was an intuitive foretaste of the designs to come. The door had been straightened. Other important reference points in the history of style in the 1930's were the BMW 315/1 and 319/1 roadsters made in 1935-36 and used successfully in racing. Both models had 6 cylinder engines, respectively 1490cc and 1911cc, which produced 40 and 55 HP. Maximum speed did not exceed 81 mph. The next year, 1937, saw the arrival of the Bugatti Type 57. It was compact, completely rounded, with a two-tone livery that helped to create the impression that this little sports car was nothing but a combination of curves

and ellipses with filled and empty spaces. The prominence of the front of the fenders was typical and their length towards the central section of the car made use of a footboard impossible. The Type 57 was not confined to the 1930's: in 1980 a replica called L'Atalante was produced and sold to enthusiasts by a Frenchman called de la Chappelle. Shapes like this were to return in numbers after the Second World War and remain popular until the 1960's, then to return once more during the late 20th century.

112 top and bottom The 1934 Peugeot Cabriolet 301 was called the "Eclipse" for its mechanism designed by Georges Paulin, a dentist who tinkered in his spare time, for electrically raising and lowering a hard top. His efforts were long from meeting with success because of the lack of a small battery strong enough to do the job. Paulin's dream was realized in 1937 as shown by the car below - the Peugeot 402 Eclipse - though the electrical operation was abandoned. Note the stylistic feature used by all design schools - the rear wheel almost completely covered like on airplane fairings.

112-113 This 1938 Peugeot was slightly modified with respect to the standard production version. The most evident feature is the convex radiator cover with a grill made up of thin, closely placed strips. On some models of the time, the headlights were placed inside the grill for protection but the Peugeot has them located between the fender and the hood.

113 top The rear outline of a huge 1934 cabriolet, the Hispano Suiza Type 68 which was famed for its V12 engine.

THE GENIUS OF EUROPEAN COACHBUILDERS

Having given a broad brush description of the emergence of design studios and the first enthusiastic attempts to apply the clichés of modern industrial design, attention should be turned to the master coachbuilders which sprung up all over Europe to convert, refit and improve production model cars.

Their main purpose was to create one-off versions of a particular model to satisfy the whims of the bored rich who wanted to be seen in a unique and striking status symbol regardless of the cost.

Open-topped gran turismo models and cabriolets were excellent candidates for this treatment and car manufacturers in France, Germany, Italy and sometimes the US often supplied their upmarket customers with just the chassis, motor, transmission etc. leaving the coachbuilders to create a unique custom-built car.

We do not believe that the work in general produced by private coachbuilding workshops during the 1920's and 30's is to be decried in any way, particularly as this period is considered one of great creativity and imagination; indeed, there are many descriptions that use superlatives when referring to the exceptional beauty and uniqueness of this or that model, but these are values that the authors believe would be better used to describe the truly exceptional cars of the time, of which there was no lack.

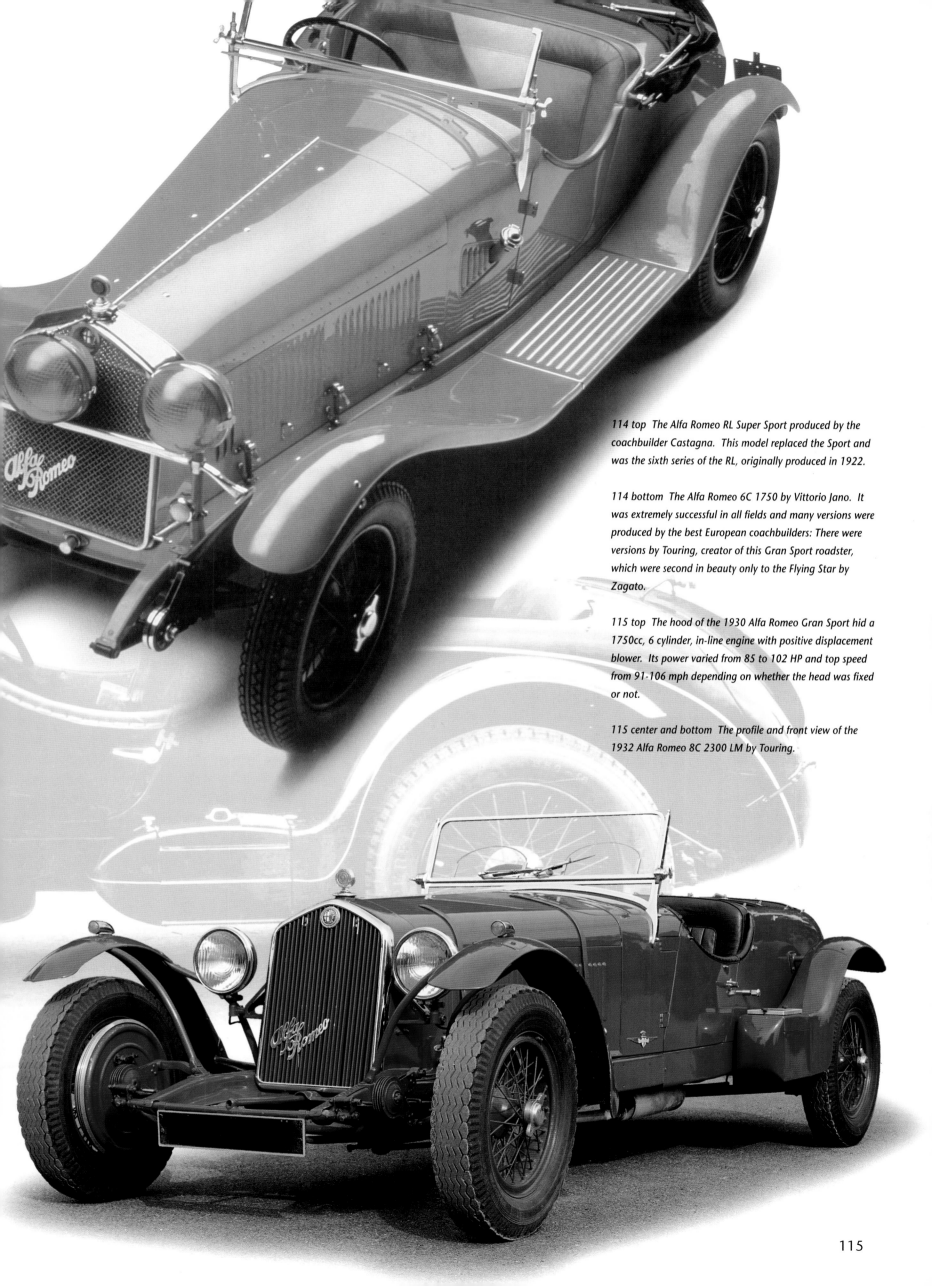

114 top The Alfa Romeo RL Super Sport produced by the coachbuilder Castagna. This model replaced the Sport and was the sixth series of the RL, originally produced in 1922.

114 bottom The Alfa Romeo 6C 1750 by Vittorio Jano. It was extremely successful in all fields and many versions were produced by the best European coachbuilders: There were versions by Touring, creator of this Gran Sport roadster, which were second in beauty only to the Flying Star by Zagato.

115 top The hood of the 1930 Alfa Romeo Gran Sport hid a 1750cc, 6 cylinder, in-line engine with positive displacement blower. Its power varied from 85 to 102 HP and top speed from 91-106 mph depending on whether the head was fixed or not.

115 center and bottom The profile and front view of the 1932 Alfa Romeo 8C 2300 LM by Touring.

*116 and 117 bottom The Alfa Romeo 6C 1750 Gran
Turismo with bodywork by Castagna. The aerial view of
the rear (left) clearly shows the dual cowl design
elements in which configuration of the cab is divided
into two compartments with a mobile windshield to
protect the rear passengers. Note how the doors opened:
the front doors opened from the front while the rear
doors opened normally so that they are hinged at a
single point. Very attractive were the layout of the pedals
and the gated shifter, which Ferrari lovers now consider
a characteristic of the cars from Maranello.*

*117 top A 1933 Alfa Romeo 8C 2300 (the prestigious
GT was built from 1931-34). In the fashion of the time,
it was a bigger version of an earlier car, the 6C 1750.
The company produced eight chassis types - short and
long wheelbase (each in three series) and Spider Corsa
short wheelbase (in two series) - but there were countless
different bodies.*

To enter the designers' Hall of Fame it is not
enough simply to create luxurious, striking and self-
important models. Genius resides in the ability to
fuse beauty and function, art and rationality, using
innovative shapes yet remaining within the limits
dictated by the safety and handling requirements
that a car must possess. Thoughtlessly following the
fashions of the time and embellishing the exterior
and interior as though it were the drawing room of
a home was often a temptation that even top-class
coachbuilders fell victim to. Having said that, it
should not be thought that the work of master
coachbuilders in those contradictory years
(characterized by widespread poverty side by side
with an opulence that went beyond the boundary
of simple riches) was negligible. On the contrary,
they were responsible for shaping the world's most
exciting automobiles and it is worth considering
what they might have achieved with modern
materials and technologies. Generally of humble
background, their success was not due to particular
artistic or aesthetic gifts, which of course have their

own importance, but to their ability to stamp
metal sheets and panels into fluent,
homogeneous and accurately gauged forms and
to resolve tedious technical problems
linked to comfort. The most bothersome
of these was probably the system required
for joining the body onto the chassis in
order to ensure the bodywork the
maximum flexibility and tolerance to
the stresses generated by the
unevenness of the roads. A widespread
system was that employed by French pilot
Charles T. Weymann. He used a wooden
framework positioned on rubber supports and
lined with a special type of fake leather, a system
often copied by the Italian coachbuilder Touring.
Other experimental techniques used with
success were the French Clairalpax (used by
Viotti), the German Kellener, the Italian
Plumelastica used by Eusebio Garavini who
was associated with the manufacturer Diatto for a
time, and Triplex by Ghia, which could be
recognized by its lining of fake crocodile skin.
Later, the increasing number of design studios,
the ever-more urgent requirement for technology
in the design of the exterior (especially for
finding a lower coefficient of aerodynamic
penetration) and more and more restrictive safety
standards slowly reduced the creative margin for
coachbuilders.

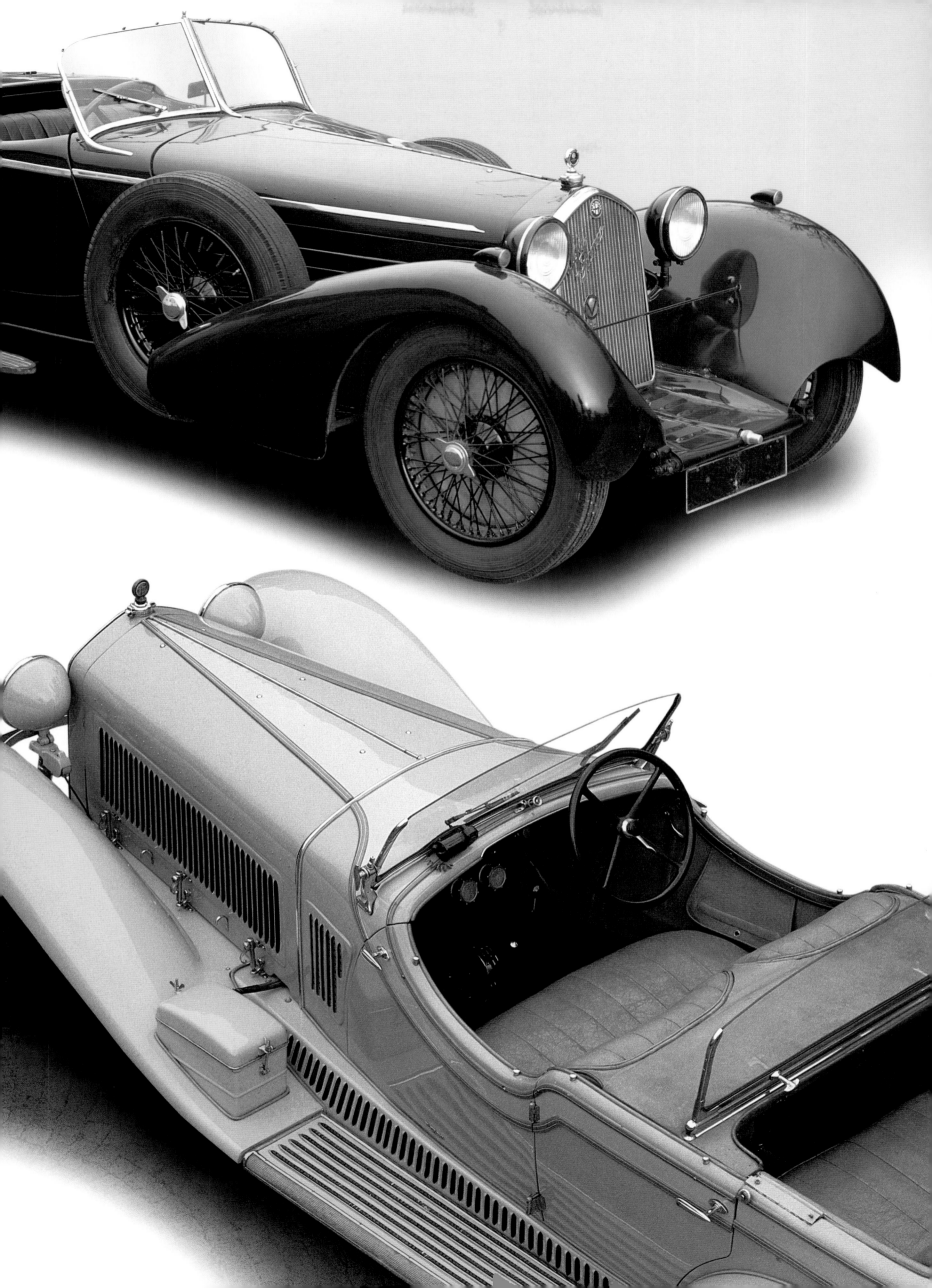

Some of them owed their fortune (or survival) by specializing in the open-top sector, others managed to transform themselves into industrial companies by following the moods of the market. The majority however went under for lack of ideas, of genius or of capital.

For reasons of chronology, this chapter will not deal with coachbuilders who came later like Michelotti, Vignale or the great Giorgetto Giugiaro, and for reasons of space it is obliged to pass over those workshops which are considered to be only medium-sized stars in the galaxy of coachbuilders of this period. It is hoped the reader will understand and make allowances.

Many of the coachbuilding practitioners of the 1930's had started as carriage builders for horsedrawn vehicles such as Giovanni Bertone, Carlo Castagna, Cesare Sala and Alessio, Assmann, Belloni, Fontana, Studebaker, Young and Vereinigte Werkstätten.

Today Bertone is still one of the world's most well-known design centers despite the death of Nuccio Bertone, never a designer but a genius at talent spotting. Giovanni Bertone, father of Nuccio, was building

118 top The side view of this small Fiat 1500 convertible is a good example of how the aeronautic theme was applied to car design in the second half of the 1930's. This 1937 version by Viotti has streamlined fenders and a flat, inclined rear end which together suggest, correctly, that the car also has a heavily inclined front end for a low coefficient of aerodynamic penetration, or Cx.

118 center The front end of a 1934 Renault Straight 8. Note the attractive windshield and vent windows.

118 bottom The name of this 1933 Fiat, the Ardita, was an obvious tribute to the Fascist regime in power in Italy; the car was more prosaically known as the 518. The version in the picture is a Double Phaéton by Pinin Farina following the American fashion.

118-119 This 6 cylinder 1938 Fiat 1500 was designed by Balbo in an aeronautical style. Most evident are the exaggerated, quite overly rounded fenders.

119 The rear end of the 1938, 6 cylinder Fiat 1500 by Balbo. Observe the splendid roadster back end with a nod in the direction of the boattail.

carriage bodies in 1912 but from 1921 moved into assembling bodies for Lancia. It was anonymous, boring work. Bertone put up with it for too long and it was only in the mid-30's that he transformed his workshop into a coachbuilder for production of custom-built cars. He worked mostly on the Alfa Romeo 6C 2300 and 2500 as did many of his colleagues like Castagna, Pinin Farina, Touring and Viotti. Castagna is also a celebrated name in the history of coachbuilding for his work on Alfas. One in particular must be mentioned but at the expense of others equally praiseworthy: The 6C 1500 was deserving of comparison both as a cabriolet and roadster with the works of Pinin Farina, Touring and Zagato. Castagna was guilty of one excusable error: In 1937 he produced the 6C 2300B Pescara Cabriolet which was a shameless copy of the previous year's Cord 810 by Gordon Buehrig. Castagna shut up shop in 1954. Sala was to close down in 1933 but his Isotta Fraschini 8A Super Sport torpedo of 1927 was a car to remember. Cesare Sala spent most of his time on large and luxurious models but on this occasion he turned his attention to a sports car. It was not an easy task as the starting model weighed three tons. The result

he came up with was a torpedo without a top. The rear passenger section was separate from the front one and so it was necessary to incorporate two small, hidden doors so that the design might more correctly be called a bateau than a torpedo. The door frames and cab were made from treated wood. The engine was a powerful 8 cylinder, larger than the 8A, and supposedly capable of pushing the car to 100 mph.

Mention has been made of coachbuilders who specialized in cabriolets and sports cars. Many are still in business and keep their handbuilt tradition alive like, for example, the Swiss Worblaufen, while others have disappeared from the scene, such as the Italian Montescani and the German Reutter. During the 1930's some companies were already in existence that have since become famous for sports car designs: for instance, there is the German Karmann, the American LeBaron and the French Chapron. Wilhelm Karmann was producing car bodies made entirely from steel as early as the 1920's. Two of his projects were the 1939 Ford Eiffel, made by the American company's European subsidiary, and the Adler Trumpf Junior, which had a strong aeronautical

influence. Later the company was to design the Beetle cabriolet and the Golf Cabrio as well as other models in which there were often two swellings on the body similar to a hunchback. Of all coachbuilders, Karmann can be considered as one which has produced the best selling models. No less important has been the American LeBaron, which was referred to in the previous chapter with regard to the curious Lincoln dual cowl "Aero Phaéton". The LeBaron studio was part of the Briggs industrial group which supplied bodies to companies such as Chrysler and Ford during this period. In 1932 the company produced the Chrysler CH Imperial dual cowl phaéton which was identical in the front to the speedster version whose aerodynamic appearance has previously been discussed. This version was less engaging but also less extreme. Similar to versions produced by Murphy and Derham, it was particularly luxurious and sophisticated. The name of the already-defunct LeBaron concern was sold to Chrysler in 1953; embarrassingly, it was post-humously applied to a line of plebian production cars and is now most associated with the small Chrysler LeBaron convertibles of the 1980's.

The obstinate but quick-witted Chapron was to become famous for the cabriolet of the Citroën DS, but other of their notable designs were the 1938 Talbot-Lago and the 1947 Delahaye 135M which, despite its postwar production date, displayed prewar styling.

A compulsory mention must be given to Touring, one of the few companies not to be called by the name of its founders, Felice Bianchi Anderloni and Gaetano Ponzoni. Touring was active between 1926 and 1966 and from 1930 produced steel bodies for Alfa Romeo, BMW, Lancia and Talbot. Among their very many excellent designs, the one that most deserves close attention is their interpretation, the umpteenth, of the Alfa Romeo 6C 1750, which they called the Flying Star after the decorations in the shape of a comet on the sides of the motor compartment. Another feature of this design, which might well be considered one of the most beautiful cars of all time, was the absence of join between the front and rear fenders which in general created the footboard in cars of the period. On the Flying Star, the front fender tapered inward and downward to end somewhere on the same line as the windshield while the rear fender was similarly designed but tapered upwards, creating a convenient step. The car's back end is proportionally small and constrained by the two spare wheels. The wheels with touching spokes and chrome wheel guards give the car the air of a competition vehicle while underlining its dynamic and elegant lines at the same time.

Touring was to repeat the excellence of the Flying Star on the large Hispano Suiza and another Alfa, the rare and costly 1938 8C 2900B Spider. Although seven years later than the 6C 1750, Touring kept the same front to rear proportions but the curves followed the aeronautical fashion much more. The radiator grill again resembles a fencer's mask while the headlights are similar to, but slightly higher than, those of the version prepared by Pinin Farina. Farina's version also had concentric disk hubcaps which were more modern but less sporty than Touring's spokes.

Another company that flourished belonged to the young and enterprising mechanic Giacinto Ghia. The story of Ghia has followed the events of the history of the car like no other and would merit its own television series. The company worked with and for Alfa, Lancia, Fiat, Chrysler (together with two famous stylists, Virgil Exner Sr. and Jr.), Karmann, Duesenberg, Bugatti and De Tomaso. Those who worked for Ghia included Rovelli, Boano Sr. and Jr. (who once owned it but who were ousted by Luigi Segre), Frua, Michelotti, Savonuzzi, Sartorelli, Coggiola, Tjaarda, Sapino, Giugiaro etc. - indeed, most of the coachbuilders' Hall of Fame. In the 1970's Ghia ended up as part of Ford, for which it designed prototypes and special production series. During the 1930's it produced the Itala 65 and the 1933 Fiat Balilla sports.

Another famous name is Ugo Zagato. He founded his workshop in 1919 and became the official coachbuilder for Alfa Romeo particularly for sports models.

In 1927 he produced the Spider Super Sport based on the RL chassis which was as exceptional as that of the 6C 1750. While Montescani envisioned the RL as a dual cowl model, Zagato saw it as a roadster with a highly profiled tail. Comparing Zagato's sports version, Montescani's elite dual cowl model, Castagna's luxury interpretation and Weymann's official landaulet, it is possible to understand the freedom of maneuver the chassis of the 1920's and 30's offered to coachbuilders. Still based on the RL chassis, Zagato had designed a classic torpedo, the Coloniale, some years before.

120 top The characteristic emblem of Pinin Farina, a blue "f" on a white background, has remained the mark of the firm's designs.

120-121 top This model is an example of how well Pinin Farina was able to combine sculptural forms with the aeronautic style. This is a 1937 Alfa Romeo 2900B Convertible, a balanced, versatile car which was popular with coachbuilders for its choice of long or short wheelbase. The flat, uniform rear end absorbs the curves of the wheelhouses.

120-121 bottom The nose and tail of the 1935 Lancia Astura Roadster Pininfarina. Note the decoration on the side in the style of a flying star (also used by Touring), the shield-shaped radiator, the split windshield and the visible sills, though without a footboard. The doors open from the front.

A praiseworthy company of the same period was Autenrieth Darmstadt which designed numerous open-topped cars. With the collaboration of Baur Stuttgart they produced the 320, 326 and 327 models using BMW chassis. Erdmann & Rossi, founded in 1898, produced a version of the Audi 225 reminiscent of the Art Deco style of the Bugatti Atalante, and also a highly profiled roadster based on a BMW 326 chassis. All Erdmann & Rossi productions were slightly extravagant but their uniqueness was well received by their customers of Bugatti, Cadillac, Horch, Mercedes Benz, Packard and Rolls Royce chassis. Lack of space makes further description impossible but here are the names of some famous coachbuilders linked with the marque they are most associated with: Mulliner with Bentley, Boneschi with Alfa Romeo, Guilloré with Delage, Pourtout and Pennock with Delahaye, Figoni and Falaschi with Talbot, Viotti with Lancia, Kellener with Hispano-Suiza, Letourneur and Marchand with Delage. One name, the most famous of all coachbuilders, has not been discussed: Pinin Farina, the dynasty of designers that more than any other has left its mark on car designs. The dynasty began when Battista Farina, nicknamed "Pinin" (Piedmontese for "small"), began to work at the age of 12 for his coachbuilder brother Giovanni. Giovanni produced fine cars until his company, Stabilimenti Farina, was forced to close in 1953. Pinin Farina had meanwhile started up on his own in 1930 and began to make progress in a business sector already filled with legendary names. In 1961, the office of the Italian President decreed that "Pinin" Farina might be unified to a single surname, Pininfarina, which would now be valid for Battista's son Sergio and the firm at large. Sergio, in turn, did not know how to design at first, but this only served to increase his applications. Fortunately for Sergio, the esteem he was held in by Enzo Ferrari was his road to greatness; it was the Ferrari marque for which he created true masterpieces,

both sports cars and GT coupes. Designs from Pinin Farina include the 1931 topless Cadillac two-seater sports in the bateau style thanks to the tapered rear end. The surprising shape of the rear fender, curved in the front, was an illusion designed to give length to the back. The front fender was also short which seemed to leave the spare wheel hanging in midair. The sill panel was a striking, engraved metal strip. The following year brought the Fiat 518 A Ardita which showed Pinin's interest for aerodynamics, or anyway for sinuous curves later associated by historians with the shape of the female body. The same year saw a typical cabriolet, a powerful Mercedes 500 SS in which references to the mother of all convertible coupés, the 1927 LaSalle, could be seen. There were also numerous versions of the Lancia Astura and Alfa Romeo 8C 2300 characterized by a classical, sculptural design. In the following years the streamlining of his designs for the Astura became sharper including the fairing for the rear wheelhouses, which was a feature of French cabriolets and based on airplane undercarriage fairings. Work from the Pininfarina studio has continued uninterrupted throughout the century. Finally, attention is passed back to the US to admire the work of Bohman & Schwartz, designers of the 1940 Cadillac Series Sixty-Two. A chromed line ran along the length of the side, dropping slightly along the doors and clipping the rear fender. It creates a mirror surface that was to become common in this position, almost a signature of the period. The front end was not raised as was common in other cars at this time but fluid with a low, narrow grill that had an abundant covering of horizontal chromework. The bumper had similar decoration, was flat on top and did not end in a point like the contemporary aerodynamic styles. The engine was a traditional 135 HP, 5.7 liter V8.

122 top This luxurious cabriolet is the 1934 Bentley with coachwork by Vanden Plas. Despite a 6 cylinder, 3.7 liter engine, top speed was only 91 mph.

122-123 bottom A Mercedes Benz 500K with bodywork by Windover. A Mercedes tradition, often annoying, was to use abbreviations in the name. In the 1930's the letter K stood for "Kurz", meaning short wheelbase, but it was changed to "Kompressor" (supercharged) as in this model.

122-123 top and 123 A Bohman & Schwartz Cadillac produced on a Series Sixty-Two chassis from 1940. Apart from the quality of materials and finishing, note the wheels with their 3 colors (black tread, white walls and red shoulders) not to mention the chrome hubcaps. Chrome was used everywhere including in the Cadillac name on the fender. This trend was to be taken to the limit in 1950's convertibles.

124 top Although they both resisted pressure to take part in racing and to build record-breaking speed cars, both Daimler and Benz were forced to give in eventually to the demands of customers and management. The results were prototypes such as the Tropfenwagen (in the picture) used to study aerodynamic effects, speed machines like the Blitzen, and production cars like the Daimler 16/45 PS Knight and Benz 6/18 PS.

124 center The photograph immortalized a frantic refueling stop for a DKW P600 Sport of 1930.

Having acknowledged the importance of style and design, attention should be paid to other directions in which the evolution of the car, whose sports models both with and without a top traditionally represent the state of the art, produced technically connected advances:

1) Improvement of mechanical performance as measured by the power-to-weight ratio (the weight one horsepower must move).

2) Optimization of body design so that the coefficient of aerodynamic penetration is minimized, giving better performance for the same power and a reduction in noise, vibration and fuel consumption plus increased comfort.

So let technology measure the development of a car as long as it is not forgotten that aesthetics, especially in roadsters and convertibles, plays a functional role which is fundamental to successful sales. A small sedan may be able to get away with sacrificing form for exciting performance but an open-topped car must satisfy aesthetic requirements in order to balance its simpler functionality and lack of creature comforts. Nor should it be forgotten that an open-topped car with its roof up or down will never have a Cd (coefficient of aerodynamic drag) less than or equal to a similar car with a hard top. Extremely common, open-topped cars were still the protagonists in racing and it was logical that they should be the basis for fluid dynamics experimentation. This was serious research carried out in the first wind tunnels and supported by competition results, and it was the racing circuit, tinged with political implications that were particularly strong in Europe during the 1920's

and 30's, that became the test bed for innovations.

The distinction must be born in mind, however, between these mobile laboratories and the stylistic exaggerations based on the fashion for flying - the "false aeronautics" also prevalent in racing, though road-based rather than track.

Road racers were often enormous, heavy machines that were rigid, very dangerous and extremely difficult to drive in which tapered profiles and slim shapes were as pleasing to the eye as they were useless. One example was the highly admired Delage D8 S driven by Renée Friedrich, daughter of the Bugatti driver of the same name. In a women-only race from Paris - St. Raphael in 1932, the young and beautiful driver smashed into a tree and died when she lost control of her four-wheeled dinosaur.

124-125 Unlike nearly all racing cars, this 1930's racing Mercedes has fenders.

125 The rear and front ends of one of the Benz Tropfenwagen prototypes, almost a single seater. Note the large central headlight and visible suspension.

126 top This strange car was known as the "Petite Rosalie". It is a 1933 racing Citroën which beat the long-distance record in March of that year on the Monthléry race track: 188,000 miles at an average speed of 58 mph. In all it established 106 world records and 193 international records.

126 bottom and 126-127 The Aerodinamica version of the Alfa Romeo Type B, better known as the P3. Modifications were made to it in 1934 by the Ferrari Racing Team that managed Alfa's racing department. Besides the obvious profile behind the cab, note the fairings behind the wheels which enabled the air passing over to be left behind without creating turbulence and therefore without creating resistance.

127 top The brochure publicizes the achievements of the production version of the Citroën Petite Rosalie, which covered 188,000 miles in 134 days.

127 bottom These three single-seater Bugattis are lined up for the official racing photograph for the French Grand Prix on 28 June 1936 at Monthléry. The drivers are Robert Benoist (car no. 82), Wimille (84) and Veyron (86).

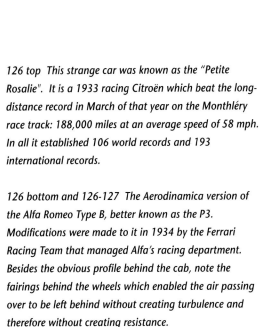

Manufacturers most involved in advanced research were, unsurprisingly, those most heavily involved in racing: Alfa Romeo (whose survival as a company probably depended on the successes of its gran turismo cars like the RL and 6C driven by exceptional talents like Ascari, Brilli-Peri, Nuvolari and Sivocci), Auto Union (created by the merger in 1932 of Audi, DKW, Horch and Wanderer, the four companies represented by the four ring Audi symbol today) and, most important, Daimler-Benz.

As early as 1914 Daimler had presented a development of the 28/95 which anticipated the

UNE **8** CV
CITROËN
DE SERIE "PETITE ROSALIE"
A PARCOURU
300000 KMS
EN 134 JOURS A 93 DE MOYENNE
AVEC UTILISATION CONSTANTE D'HUILE YACCO DU COMMERCE
LE CHASSIS DE PETITE ROSALIE EST STRICTEMENT IDENTIQUE
A CELUI DES VOITURES LIVREES QUOTIDIENNEMENT A LA CLIENTELE

boattail forms of a decade later, for example, in the 1923 Citroën Caddy Sport. The 28/95, which in all other versions had a racing streak running through it, was completely lined with strips of mahogany; the tail was tapered like the nose of a rocket, an indication of things to come, and the wheel coverings were full and convex. Benz cars were similar in vein, like the 1921 10/30 - as Futurist and ugly as it was longed-for by enthusiasts. Descendant of the Blitzen Benzes, the record-breaking tapered cars of the second decade of the century, the 10/30 opened the way for the Tropfenwagen. The Tropfenwagen is not relevant so much for being a streamlined, open-topped car but because it was an obligatory passage on the evolution of the car shape although it was never

sold. It was produced from 1923 in different versions having originally appeared as a single-seater torpedo able to reach 100 mph (the 6 cylinder engine was capable of producing 80 HP with short bursts of 90 HP). It then became a two-seater in which the fenders were turned into fins which gave the car a rather comical appearance.

The "Tropfel" was raced on several occasions with reasonably successful results. Mention should also be made in passing of the 1933 Citroën "Petite Rosalie", the 1934 Alfa Romeo Type B Aerodinamica and the 1937 Fiat 508 C MM, but the list could be extended at length. Chrysler's determined efforts in the "airstream" category of car designs were of no relevance to racing but influenced road cars for years to come.

128 top These photos demonstrate either courage or folly depending on your point of view. The photo was taken in 1937, when Auto Union and Mercedes battled to show Hitler their technological superiority. What better demonstration of power and invincibility was there than to beat speed records in front of their Italian allies and continental enemies? This aerodynamic Auto Union driven by Bernd Rosemeyer reached 253.7 mph. Above, we see it on the banking of the Avus circuit near Berlin, which was finally bisected by the construction of the Berlin Wall. Rudi Caracciola broke the record again in 1938: 273 mph (one way) which worked out at an average of 270.5 mph (both ways). A few hours later the famous driver Rosemeyer tried to beat the new record, but his car literally took off and the driver was flung into the woods where he died. As for the shape of the cars, in 1937 ideas regarding streamlining and low coefficients of drag, known as Cd, were already clear.

128 bottom This enormous French "boat", with bodywork by Figoni et Falaschi based on the Delahaye 135 chassis, was first shown at the end of the 1930's. Despite its originality, this production was one of the French coachbuilders' more sober designs.

129 A model as revolutionary as it was unsuccessful: the 1940 Chrysler Newport. The company presented the Newport as the car of the future for its total dedication to streamlined styling, which meant every part sticking out beyond the car body was removed. Unfortunately the public did not generally accept Chrysler's courageous effort.

The 1935 Airflow was too futuristic for its time and nor did its convertible version, the C7 Airstream Six, do any better despite the six years of experimentation that went into its production. Finally Chrysler hit the jackpot with the 1941 Newport and Thunderbolt Convertible models.

In the authors' opinion, the Newport merits the designer, Ralph Roberts, a place in the Hall of Fame for creative car designers. The line was definitely aerodynamic or "airstream". All the elements which stuck out further than necessary on contemporary cars were absorbed into the body, so that it appeared almost like a boat. The shape was rectangular and the central section of the front end resembled the loudspeaker of an old radio. The car was certainly very striking, even excessive, but no single part of it seemed disproportionate to

the rest, which was pure emotion. The actress Lana Turner had a flame-red dual cowl Newport. As a true dual cowl model, the front and back seats were separated not just by a metal structure but also by an elegant windshield. The doors opened from the inside and were almost invisible as they had no exterior handles. The rear of the car was an example of how convertibles were to appear in the years to follow. It seems incredible that car design was able to undergo such a radical transformation and look to the future in such a short space of time. With regard to the years to come, the publicity for the Thunderbolt Convertible concept car called it the "car of the future". Its shape seemed smoothed by the wind, the aluminum body was uniform in every detail and without edges. The hard top looked like a turret and was electrically controlled.

This chapter, which links open-topped cars to aerodynamic design, ends with mentions of two record-breaking cars, both totally streamlined. The first is the 616 HP Mercedes used by Rudi Caracciola to break the 228 mph speed record in October 1936. The driver was seated centrally and the body was completely smooth with a single shark's mouth aperture at the front. The second is the Auto Union Aerodinamica, in which Bernd Rosemeyer was killed trying to increase his own 253.7 mph record. The same Caracciola took up the challenge the following year, reaching the incredible speed of 270 mph. But these cars are not truly relevant to the history of open-tops, being no more than Grand Prix-based record rockets designed for maximum speed. Still, one wonders what it must feel like to have one's head enveloped in a rush of 270-mph air....

The era of the convertibles begins
GRAN TURISMO: FROM ROAD TO RACING AND BACK

The preceding chapter explained how the appearance of open-topped cars in the 1930's was characterized by the emergence of design for design's sake, or at least closer attention to shape. However the case was actually wider ranging than that; there was another element which had a greater influence on the personality, appearance and social symbolism of the open tops - the percentage they represented of the total number of cars sold.

During the 1920's, 90% of cars on the roads were open-topped because of their lower design and production costs. Ten years later they were only 10% of the total and falling until, at the end of the 20th century, they represent between 1-5% depending on the relative wealth of the country. This inversion has turned the open-topped car into a luxury item more dependent for success on the fact that it is unusual than on its design.

At the end of the 1930's the car had conquered people's hearts. Although still not widely diffuse, it could be considered as a social macro-phenomenon, crisis or no crisis.

The total number of cars in the US was approximately 25 million, in Great Britain and France 2 million each, in Germany 1.3 million while in Italy it was only 291 thousand. These figures represented a density of roughly 115 cars per thousand inhabitants in the US, 45 in Britain, 44 in France, 18 in Germany and 7 in Italy.

It is worth remembering that the large motoring corporations had been consolidated for some time: in 1929 in America, General Motors, Ford and Chrysler accounted for 90% of the market; in France, Citroën, Renault and Peugeot had tied up 68% of sales; in Great Britain where Bentley had been taken over by Rolls Royce, Austin, Singer and Morris represented 76% of the total; in Germany, Opel was top of the sales list; and in Italy Fiat produced 75% of all new models sold.

Despite the change in market positioning of open tops both in terms of quantity and price, their traditional classification had not altered much and now they could be categorized into three rather than two types. Previously they had been either mainly sports or mainly luxury cars, on the one hand in the form of runabout, speedster or roadster and on the other, touring car, phaéton or torpedo. This categorization excludes hybrids or customized cars.

Development of the runabout and roadster produced what shall be referred to here as gran turismo (GT) models which were the link between the dynasty of English sporting open-tops and European sports cars in general. A link also exists between the gran turismo models and the American convertibles of the 1960's, although these latter cars inherited a great deal from the convertible coupés of the 1930's, 40's and 50's, and it is these (described below) which form the second of the three classifications. The third is the convertible sedan, which differs from the convertible coupé in having four doors rather than two. Of the three categories, the last two (convertible coupés and convertible sedans) are prevalently American while the GT's, thanks to their frequent participation in sports car races and smaller size, were European.

130 top This photograph demonstrates better than any other the clarity of Bugatti's design philosophy. The harmonious whole of this cabriolet show Bugatti to have been a car manufacturer without equal, even greater perhaps in design of individual details than the Rolls Royce grill topped by the graceful winged Victory. From this perspective, the fenders, which enclose double headlights and two-tone horns, seem like enormous folded leaves. The cab seems small, indistinct and far away.

130 bottom The race has just finished and the winner, Meo Costantini, is being feted. The track is Monthléry where the French Grand Prix were held. The car is a Bugatti T39 1.5 in a torpedo or touring design. The man in the colonial hat behind the car is Ettore Bugatti.

131 top Adolf Hitler in one of the most beautiful and luxurious cabriolets of the 1930's, the Mercedes 770K. Dictators of the period did not hesitate to display themselves in convertibles which were ideal for parades.

131 bottom This little car with the racing appearance is the Fiat 508 Balilla built from 1933-37. Many variants of this model were produced including racing and street roadsters, torpedoes and closed body versions. This is the famous Balilla Sport Coppa d'Oro which can be recognized by its fenders that continue behind the wheel to meet the footboard.

132 top This 6 cylinder Renault Vivasport enjoyed a certain success at the start of the 1930's. The Vivasport was one of the early gran turismo models, successors to the runabouts and roadsters that were so popular in Europe during the 1930's.

132 center The 1931 Lincoln Model K was available as a Sport Phaéton and roadster. The former developed out of the torpedo style and was the link between the torpedo and the four door convertibles to come: The latter was the equivalent of what was beginning in Europe to be called gran turismo models and in the US convertible coupés. Both had rather poorer performance than the rival GT's.

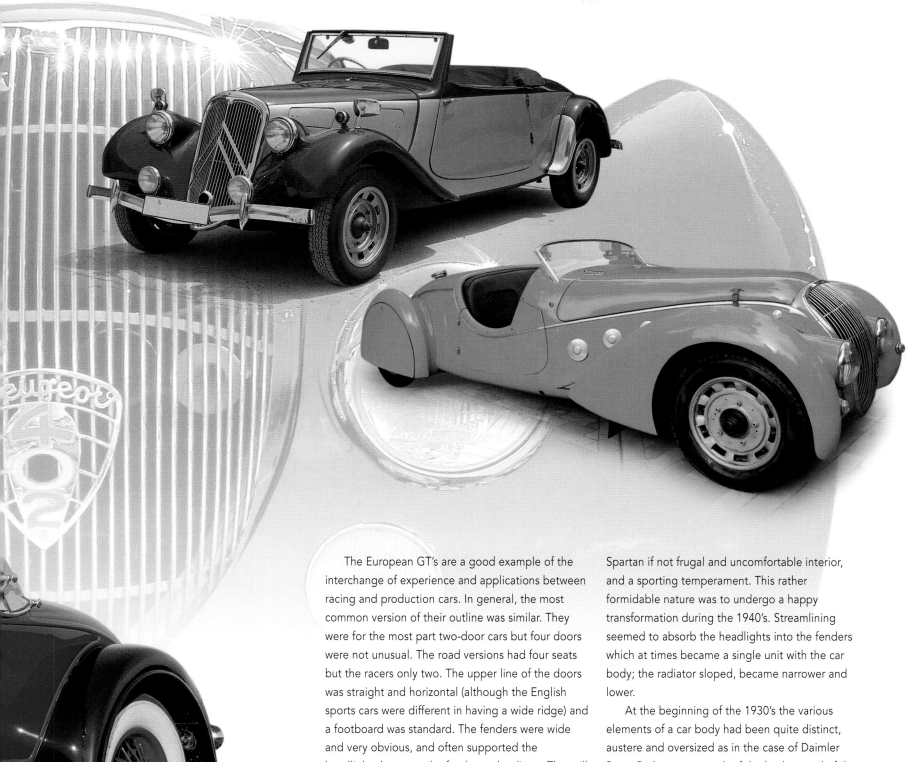

The European GT's are a good example of the interchange of experience and applications between racing and production cars. In general, the most common version of their outline was similar. They were for the most part two-door cars but four doors were not unusual. The road versions had four seats but the racers only two. The upper line of the doors was straight and horizontal (although the English sports cars were different in having a wide ridge) and a footboard was standard. The fenders were wide and very obvious, and often supported the headlights between the fender and radiator. The grill was either classically flat or bullnose and had a vertical or grid design, though occasionally honeycombed. With the top up the vehicle was less interesting and resembled the old torpedoes. Besides being known as GT's, sports or super sports models, the term Fetonte (from the name Phaetone, the son of the Greek sun god) was sometimes used in Germany.

The term "gran turismo" signified a car that was powerful, costly, sometimes customized, with a Spartan if not frugal and uncomfortable interior, and a sporting temperament. This rather formidable nature was to undergo a happy transformation during the 1940's. Streamlining seemed to absorb the headlights into the fenders which at times became a single unit with the car body; the radiator sloped, became narrower and lower.

At the beginning of the 1930's the various elements of a car body had been quite distinct, austere and oversized as in the case of Daimler Benz. Perhaps as a result of the background of the people in charge it was the engineers' designs rather than the architects' designs that were adopted (as opposed to what was happening in the US). Remember that the design head of Daimler Benz in the early 1920's was mechanic Paul Daimler, who was succeeded by another true genius, Ferdinand Porsche, from 1923-28 (later to design the extraordinary Volkswagen Beetle and Porsche 356).

132 bottom The Horch 853 was sold from 1937-40. Auto Union, the group made up of four important German companies including the one started by August Horch, called this two-door model the Cabriolet Sport to distinguish it from the more aggressive 855 Spider.

132-133 top and 133 bottom Another interpretation of a roadster on a 1938 Peugeot chassis. The car's profile seems very influenced by the English trends with a low driving position and inclined waist.

133 top Only two examples of this French gran turismo, the Citroën 15 Cabriolet, were built, one of which was destined to be owned by the Michelin family.

134 top The front of the 1930 Mercedes Benz 38/250 SS. The 'SS' was used to distinguish particularly powerful, sporting models but the whole series of S, SS and SSK versions at the beginning of the 1930's was impressive and important in terms of engines, racing and design.

134 bottom The legendary Mercedes SSK racing around a bend with the famous and fearless Rudolf Caracciola at the wheel.

An example of a typical top-of-the-range gran turismo model was the Daimler Benz SSK which was very successful in terms of sales as well as racing.

The SSK was one of the very powerful sports cars produced by Daimler Benz during the second half of the 1920's. In principle there was the 600 K series from 1924, six cylinders in-line with a total of 6240cc producing 140 HP with a supercharger (100 without) and popular among private individuals who used it for racing. Then came the 'S' series in 1926, even more powerful and more sporty looking. For example, the 680 version had a 6720cc motor which produced 180 HP to reach a maximum speed of 111 mph. The 'SS' was the sports version of the 'S': the footboard was replaced by a drop-shaped silhouette which was mirrored in the design of the front and rear fenders. There were two large headlights next to the radiator and two more by the windshield. The 1928 'SSK' was a synthesis of the two previous models though lighter and better finished. The footboard was reintroduced for both the sports and road version. The latter had a tapered rear end and the spare wheel was moved into the space between the front fender and motor compartment. The wheelcovers were full and very elegant (if it was possible to keep them clean and shiny). The sports version hid the three large exhaust pipes under the hood and the door faded into a grooving in the side panel. The rear end was flat to allow the spare wheels to be attached.

The engine size was increased to 7065cc so that the car could take part in the 7 liter category races. The result was 225 HP giving a maximum speed of 119 mph. Yet this was not the most powerful version of all; there was the 'SSKL' which developed 300 HP and reached 147 mph! The supercharging on this model was by Ferdinand Porsche and the most powerful that he achieved during his time with Daimler Benz.

The K, S and SSK racked up many victories in endurance races and hill climbs. Rudolf Caracciola's win in the 1931 Mille Miglia was the car's most celebrated result.

134-135 This three-quarters shot of the 680 SS shows the splendor of Mercedes production between 1927 and 1935. Remember that the technical director during this period was Ferdinand Porsche. It is easy to imagine the attraction that this powerful car exerted on "gentleman drivers" of the period. The SSK was the best synthesis of top-of-the-market gran turismo cars, i.e. cars with large engines. It is difficult to explain the range of motors and car versions briefly but the road versions of the S and SS were produced from 1926-30 with 6.8, 7.0 and 7.1 liter engines, while the sports versions of the S, SS and SSK were produced from 1927-34 (including the SSKL) with 6.8, 7.0 and 7.2 liter engines. All could be supercharged, and power ranged from 180-300 HP.

135 top This unusual picture shows a version of the SSK chassis shortened by 18" to make it more manageable.

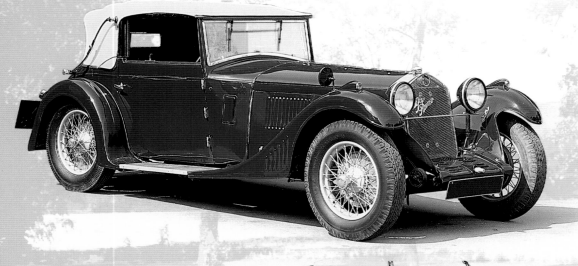

136 top The stupendous lines of the Alfa Romeo 6C 1750 Super Sport. If the S, SS and SSK Mercedes represent the most significant large-engined GT's, the various versions of the 6C 1500 and 1750 at the start of the 1930's guaranteed the survival of Alfa Romeo. It is widely thought that the racing successes of Nuvolari and Campari kept the Milan company's prestige high.

The series of six cylinder motors from Alfa Romeo may be considered as a parallel to the Mercedes 'S' series. The original engine was the rather rough RL produced as early as 1922 for a torpedo body. Six other series in innumerable versions followed up until 1927. The sports versions were very successful on the track and even the Italian leader, Benito Mussolini, liked to ride around in an RL SS.

Alfa Romeo's jewel in the crown was the 6C, the 1500 and later the 1750. Maybe the Arese (next to Milan) based company owes its very survival to the successes of this car during a period when many manufacturers of large, luxurious sports cars were suffering seriously from the economic crisis. The first 6C was produced in 1927 from a design from the genius of Vittorio Jano. The engine size was 1487cc and so it was called the 1500. The car was certainly Spartan if compared to the Mercedes S but versatile and reliable. A simple cabriolet version from Carrozzeria Touring can be considered the European equivalent of the American convertible coupés like the 1927 LaSalle.

1929 saw the arrival of the first 6C 1750's. They were beautiful, balanced and dazzling. Of this model, too - understated because it was considered the evolution of the 1500 - there were six series and countless versions (Touring's Flying Star has already been discussed in the chapter on European coachbuilders). Racing versions were driven to success by many, including Nuvolari, Campari and Benoist. Some of its major triumphs were two Mille Miglias, two 24 hour races at Spa and a Tourist Trophy.

The 6C evolved in 1931 into the 8C (8 cylinders) 2300 in the road version, and the 2300 Le Mans, 2300 Monza and 2600 Monza. The traditional shape was dominated by the design of the fenders and a front grill like a Greek temple.

136 center Zagato's interpretation of the Alfa Romeo 6C 1750 Sport chassis. The waistline was straight and the forms basic without concessions to the aeronautical trend of the period. The sinuous line of the front fender merged into the footboard which lay at the feet of the rear fender. The front end was still dominated by the upright chrome grill. The headlights, sometimes three in line, were held by supports fixed to the fenders.

136 bottom The Alfa Romeo 6C 1750 engine was developed into the 8C 2300 and produced in two versions, the Le Mans (shown) and the Monza. It was one of the most successful prewar racing GT's.

137 top The Alfa Romeo 6C 1750 Tourer from 1932; the name indicates that the version was more docile than the Sport or Super Sport.

137 bottom left An important person who does not hide his admiration for the 6 cylinder Alfa Romeo: Benito Mussolini. The photograph was taken in 1934.

137 bottom right The back of the 1932 Alfa Romeo Tourer.

138 top The 328 was the model which brought most European public attention to BMW. It was introduced to racing in 1936 and achieved so much notoriety that the Munich company decided to market it the following year. The 328 was built from 1936-40. Note the double kidney grill, vestiges of which are still seen on today's BMW's, and the absence of door handles.

138 bottom The 328 Mille Miglia at the beginning of a race. This excellent BMW dominated the 2 liter class in all races during the second half of the 1930's. Among its more important victories were the Mille Miglia of 1938 and 1940, the first won at an average speed of 75 mph and the second, 104 mph.

139 The front and rear of the BMW 328 Mille Miglia Touring. Although it was a racing car, it should be noted that the motor compartment and fenders had finally been joined. The lights were now housed in the new, more compact, single volume and the gap that previously separated the wheels from the body was now a shallow hollow. The BMW double kidney grill is clearly seen.

Similar in shape and sporting success, though at a lesser level, was the DKW Sport which collected 12 consecutive class records in 1930 on the Monthléry race track where the French Grand Prix was held. Horch (which merged with Audi, DKW and Wanderer in 1932 as the Auto Union Group) offered an elegant and refined machine, the Sport 670 produced between 1931-34. Given its design, it might better have been considered a convertible coupé but its 12 cylinder engine gave it outstanding performance. There were very many open-topped racing cars: to name just a few, from the United States there were the 1929 Stutz Model M, the 1929 Chrysler 75, and the 1930 Cadillac 8 while from Britain came the 1934 Jaguar SS2 Tourer. But it is better to look further ahead in time to see the final European car developments before the start of the Second World War canceled all traces of pleasure in design.

A German classic from 1935 was the 1.5 liter BMW 315/1 also available in a 2 liter version named the 319/1. It evolved from the production 315 but it was a smaller, sensitive machine. The headlights and fenders were still separate from the car body but there was a slight move in the direction of streamlining with the flat rear volume which hid the spare wheel. The rear wheels were half covered, like many French cabriolets. The grill had a distinctive double bean (also called double kidney) design.

The 315/1 was the testing ground for a great success, the 328. This car was produced from 1936 for sports use but was also manufactured for the road after receiving general approbation despite being uncomfortable and having little baggage space. The 328 was lined with leather, was well-finished and had a functional glove box. The lines of the car were very modern with the lights housed inside the compact form produced by the fenders and radiator (beginning to become a single unit). The BMW beans on the radiator grill were long and narrow and belts appeared over the hood to prevent the panels from rattling. The doors were tiny and useless and the rear wheels were hidden under a wheelhouse. Being a sports model, the spare wheel was brought back into view though half hidden in a cavity. The chassis was tubular with box cross-members. The six cylinder, 2 liter engine could produce 80 HP to give a maximum speed of 94 mph.

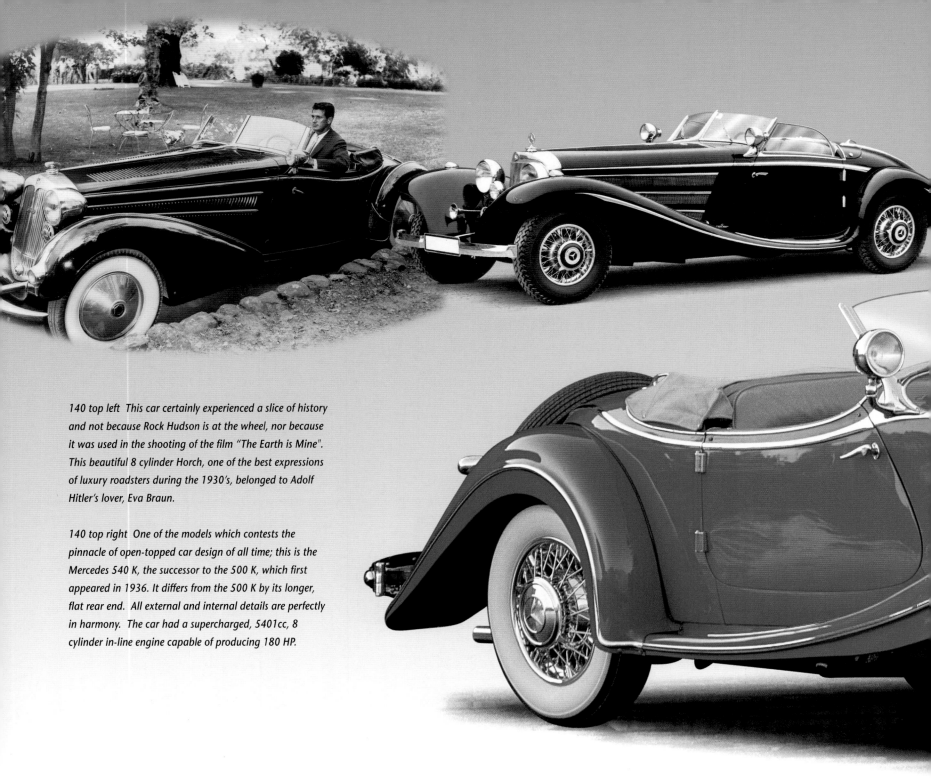

140 top left This car certainly experienced a slice of history and not because Rock Hudson is at the wheel, nor because it was used in the shooting of the film "The Earth is Mine". This beautiful 8 cylinder Horch, one of the best expressions of luxury roadsters during the 1930's, belonged to Adolf Hitler's lover, Eva Braun.

140 top right One of the models which contests the pinnacle of open-topped car design of all time; this is the Mercedes 540 K, the successor to the 500 K, which first appeared in 1936. It differs from the 500 K by its longer, flat rear end. All external and internal details are perfectly in harmony. The car had a supercharged, 5401cc, 8 cylinder in-line engine capable of producing 180 HP.

This was the era of the Third Reich when Hitler wanted a return to classical, imperial, sculptural forms and Daimler Benz obliged with two austere models: the 500 K Spezial Roadster of 1934 and the 540 K of 1936. Both had a supercharged 8 cylinder motor but differed in length, the 500 roadster had a wheelbase of 9'8" as opposed the 540's 10'8" and an overall length of 16'11" against 17'1". The shorter length of the 500 affected the design of the side of the car and made it appear more contained than its brother. The Spezial Roadster version however was given a much more luxurious appearance by the different curvature of the fenders which seemed like two waves. The door was wonderfully concave while the 540's was convex, making both a playful series of wide, sinuous curves.

Another distinctive element of the 540 K, one of the most beautiful automobiles ever produced, was the extra long rear end which was made less heavy by a light chromed fin running around the hood dock and spare wheel cover. Everything in this car gives the sensation of movement, especially the inclined windshield and side windows, both with a chromed frame.

What was happening across the ocean? The open-topped cars of the period had quieter lines and those of the true convertibles and the roadsters were less and less in evidence. American design was in a sense more advanced with more uniform lines, perhaps to the detriment of the sporting style. One independent example was the wonderful Duesenberg SJ roadster which was similar to the 540 K and a favorite of the rich and important of the time.

140-141 and 141 A unique gran turismo model, the Mercedes 500 K. It was one of the last examples produced and dates from 1936. These pictures are a perfect example of what the term "gran turismo" signifies in this book which crosses the boundaries that separate the definitions of roadster, sports car and convertible. Gran turismo models were elegant and luxurious but maintained all the power and performance of a roadster. It is as if the manufacturer wanted to state clearly that the dignity of a convertible could reside equally well in its sporting temperament.

CONVERTIBLE COUPES

Convention has it that American open-topped cars (and the European models they inspired) from 1927 on are called convertibles, though the authors follow this convention with reserve. These convertibles may be described as cars with a soft, folding top permanently attached at many points around the car body. The windows opened and closed vertically and in general there were no uprights or similar structures which rose above the waistline except of course for the windshield. The commonest version was the two-door, called a "convertible coupé", while the four-door version is known as a "convertible sedan". Both designs seat four or five people. Without wishing to lay down semantic rules, the terminology may be defined further: The European equivalent of the convertible was "cabriolet", especially when referring to an open-topped model of a closed body car, but not everywhere. The term "drophead coupé" was used in Great Britain for two-door versions and "cabriolet" was used for the four-door ones.

The cabriolet was curvaceous, sleek and had a striking profile. The cab, if covered, was like a turret placed in the center of the body. In Europe the open-topped car was endowed with the dignity of an elite car not just because of its superior performance and fittings, but also because of the growing number of hard top sedans which took the place of the open-tops as the car of the masses. Although there was no shortage of design ideas, throughout the 1930's and 40's the European public preferred the traditional styles with the car body components well separated from one another. The formal variables that differentiated the marques were minimal, aesthetic and non-structural. Combined with the heavy and powerful influence of Nazi and Fascist architectural principles, allusions to the

142 top *A German interpretation of the cabriolet, or even convertible coupé. This is a 1932 Horch 670 V12 - an atypical example from the company (which became a partner in the Auto Union group), as Horch specialized in 8 cylinder engines during this period.*

142 bottom *The 1936 Bentley 4-1/4 liters. In Great Britain the expression "drophead coupé" was used instead of "convertible coupé," while "cabriolet" meant 4-door open tops.*

143 top *This elegant BMW was a typical example of a convertible sedan though the term cabriolet was preferred in continental Europe. The position of the raised glass side windows shows off the configuration of the doors; the front doors open from the front and the rear doors from the back.*

143 bottom *The 1932 Peugeot 301, here shown in one of countless interpretations by French coachbuilders, was characterized by an unusual, slightly concave nose bearing a shield. Note the lack of a footboard which highlights the sill. Traditionally French, the car's dimensions and engine size were limited.*

Machine Age, Art Deco and airstream designs remained sadly just that.

The recommendations by Le Corbusier on the need to integrate the car's projecting elements into the body (radiator grill, headlights, rear lights, secondary lights, fenders, bumpers, exhaust pipes, footboard, spare wheel, license plate holder, etc.) were ignored. The European equivalents of the convertible coupés were the cabriolets. Their shapes differed from those of GT's but were still very much tied to neo-classical styles.

Models like the 1934 Mercedes 500 K Cabriolet B and 1940 Lancia Aprilia Cabriolet Aerodinamica Pininfarina were objectively much more beautiful than their American counterparts but added little to what had already been tried and tested by coachbuilders and designers.

In the United States the story was quite different. The stylistic hangover from the age of the carriage was still in evidence but open-topped cars took on forms and characteristics that were more typical of modern design (though certainly not typical of modern functionality). From 1930 on, the shape that was so redolent of the carriage was left behind and the car began to assume its own distinct character. This was very evident among the open tops which displayed a functional compromise between artistic expression and industrial design. The resulting style was adaptable and was variously interpreted, as can be seen by leafing through any book on the history of the convertible.

All of a sudden it became obvious that the car was somehow different. When did it lose the resemblance to the carriage? When did it assume the compact, all-of-a-piece shape that is still common today? It is difficult to give an exact date, as the transition was gradual and its application to either prototypes or production models could be cited.

Around 1934 the fencer's mask style began to replace vertical radiator grills, as was seen on the Buick Series 60 or the Ford De Luxe. This one variation freed the front end of static, imposing

and often inadequate forms.

But for the development to be more evident it was necessary to wait for the fenders to be sacrificed on the altar of modernity. This process began with their streamlining even at the sides like on the LaSalle, Pontiac and Cadillac of 1935. Even the design of the lights helped to give a sleeker, smoother appearance thanks to the streamlining at the rear. Car length increased with respect to the wheelbase and so, therefore, did the overhangs, the distance between the wheel axles and the ends of the body. Height was reduced and the coefficient of aerodynamic penetration began to take on some significance, as in the 1937 LaSalle.

Mention has already been made of the 1938

Ford Zephyr which showed startling stylistic innovations that might be considered to herald the birth of the New Car, enclosed or open top. The Zephyr had front lights integrated in the bumper (like the 1936 Cord but without the peak) and therefore right at the end of the car, no longer in the central mass. The gap between the bumper and engine compartment became a shallow cavity and was later to disappear altogether. The radiator was lowered and the hood flourished a comet which was considered a sexual reference or at least biomorphic, and at the rear end the wheelhouses were less apparent, hardly protruding from the body. One aspect of the past remained, the footboard; but that too was destined to disappear.

144 top This picture shows how modernization of the front volume made it flatter. This example is a Packard Darrin Coupé, Darrin being the name of the designer. The model was first produced in 1940, but still shows partial separation of the fenders from the hood plus a temple-like radiator that resembled those of Rolls Royce and Mercedes. On the other hand, Packard was one of the most conservative and traditionalist American manufacturers.

144 bottom A Buick 2-door convertible. Note the straight hood and narrow, curved nose. It was not unusual for cars from the 1940's and 50's to have anthropomorphic, zoomorphic or sexual connotations in the design of their front ends. This 1938 model is a Special Albemarle with bodywork by Carlton.

145 top This convertible coupé belonged to the Chrysler group; it is a 1940 DeSoto Custom S7. The low grill resembles that of the Ford Zephyr. Similarity can be seen between the rounded, pronounced hood and a nose, while the radiator grill resembles a mouth; the headlights are moved right away from the center to give the overall impression of a face.

145 bottom This photo depicts the 1938 Oldsmobile which features a curved grill and two shiny meshes at either end.

146-147 This 1939 Cadillac clearly shows the typical design features of a convertible coupé but also the renewal that open-topped cars underwent from the mid-1930's. The fenders are more wrapped around and less extreme; now they are integrated into the sides and front. A fencing-mask grill has replaced the vertical radiator shell. The lights with streamlined houses make the lines of the car lighter, while the spare wheels between the door and fender are no longer visible but hidden in what seems a more rounded third fender.

Other examples from the same period and of the same ilk were the Ford De Luxe and the Mercury. Both had an 8 cylinder engine though the Mercury had 10 HP more to offer (95 vs. 85). Further examples are the sedan and coupé versions of the Plymouth Convertible.

From the 1940's on it was no longer unusual to find lowered motor compartments with the car sides only slightly lower than the central mass. The design studios led, and the manufacturers followed, towards final liberation from the structure of the carriage.

But what was received in return? Modernity, yes. Streamlining too. But the result was disappointing. The elegant, nervous stallion that was difficult to master had been transformed into a massive ox! The power was certainly there but the brute was heavy and somnolent. It seems

incredible, but again it was the Ford Zephyr which offered a step forward. The 1940 version removed the footboard and replaced it with a light ribbing which was only a reminder of the original part.

The economic crisis was now almost past (the worst year had been 1933) but other dark clouds were massing on the horizon. The bombs that were exploding in Europe began to echo louder in the United States and only a short time was to pass before heavy industry turned its attention to the production of weapons, airplanes and munitions. For the moment however, the war was distant and life in America went on almost as normal. New cars were built like the 1942 Buick Roadmaster with its elegant chromework down the side which somehow connected with the bumpers. The design of the front wheelhouse was attractive; it ran like an elegant pleat from the front lights to the edge

of the rear fender.

Despite construction being interrupted by the war, the Roadmaster returned with a motor capable of developing 165 HP. In the meantime, the young marque Mercury seemed to take a step backwards when it reintroduced the footboard and, alas, a horrendous front end which was very wide and covered with heavy, ugly and useless chromework (especially when compared to the new Chryslers which had eliminated everything unnecessary to give the Newport and Thunderbolt the maximum in terms of modernity and streamlining). Chrysler went on to produce the New Yorker the next year, which was still heavy with chrome but at least more fluid in shape. The war intervened until 1946 when the manufacturers had to gear themselves up to produce something new, fresh and innovative to make the public forget the horrors just lived

through. The wheel had come full circle and the car was once again the means to enjoyment and fun as it had been in the 1920's. While the manufacturers were emptying the stores of the old hand-beaten metal panels, car shapes became more tapered and flat panels slowly returned to fashion; in turn this led to the immense horizontal and vertical expanses of the 1950's and 60's convertibles covered in lights, fins and chrome. Indications of the road that was being trod were given by the 1947 Fords and Mercury Sportsman, the Cadillac Series 62, the Studebaker Commander Regal De Luxe and the 1948 Pontiac (with its trademark Silver-Streak hood trim). Finally came the 1949 Buick, which introduced four small, rather curious-looking portholes on the side of the car - from the aeronautic to the marine!

148 top This large Cadillac, the Series 62, can boast a prestigious line of classic, luxury convertibles as descendants, including the Eldorado. The nose was characteristic with the grill crossed with thick, chrome horizontal strips and the bulbous hood topped by more chrome. The aeronautic theme was still popular.

148 bottom The 1952 Muntz Jet Convertible R was free from any type of extraneous decoration or parts that stick out from the main body. An inspiration was the Chrysler Thunderbolt of 1941, a convertible presented as the car of the future but which unfortunately was short-lived.

148-149 Gary Cooper in tennis clothes poses beside his Buick Convertible Cabriolet.

149 top The grill of this Cadillac Series 62 seems lighter than those of previous models.

149 bottom The motif is taken from contemporary jet engine air intakes - a stylistic fillip also toyed with by the Italian Pinin Farina. The famous car in the picture is the 1947 Studebaker Regal De Luxe designed by Raymond Loewy, creator of the Coca Cola bottle.

151 This is Chrysler's successful interpretation of the convertible sedan. The design of this 6 cylinder Royal shows it to be later than most of the other models in this section - it dates from 1937.

150 top This Mercedes set the standard for convertible sedans; it was a Type 770 Cabriolet F and part of the Grosser series. It was predominantly popular in the United States but discreetly so in Europe.

150 center This is the American equivalent of the Mercedes, the Cadillac. This interpretation of the 4-door convertible had a large front volume with a neo-classic grill design. Note the jointed castelletto which supports the lights and horns. The model was known as the All Weather and was first produced in 1931.

150 bottom The body of this 1933 Rolls Royce Torpedo Tourer literally dazzles the eye. This car was custom built for the rajah Sahib of Hathawar.

CONVERTIBLE SEDANS

Before the advent of the enormous, finned and brilliantly shiny open-topped cars of the 1950's, American car manufacturers offered not only two-door convertible coupés but four-door convertible sedans (sometimes called a convertible phaéton). Sales of these latter models were modest, partly because open tops had an increasingly small share of the market but, in addition, because they were ugly.

For this reason, little space will be devoted to them here, enough to understand that their relationship with convertible coupés was very close, and that they were if anything even more "middle-class".

They had no particular stylistic feature except the variable layout of the doors. There were three variations: The traditional one where both front and rear doors opened normally with the hinge placed at the front; opposing, where the front door opens as normal but the rear door has the hinge at the back; and butterfly, where the rear door opens as normal but the front one has the hinge at the back. With both doors open in the "opposing" configuration, the car seems cut open lengthwise and entry and exit are certainly easy. The butterfly option though makes access more uncomfortable and awkward.

Examples of cars with the traditional door layout were the Ford Flathead V8, De Soto Convertible Sedan and Cadillac Series 70 from 1936, the 1939 Packard 120, Cadillac Series 62, Oldsmobile Custom Cruiser 8 and Buick Roadmaster from 1941 and the Frazer Manhattan from 1949.

Cars with opposing doors were the 1937 Pontiac Deluxe Eight and the Cadillac Series 75 and 90 from 1938 and 1939.

As for the butterfly variation, there was the 1931 Cadillac All Weather Phaéton, the 1932 Packard Model 32 and the Cadillac V8 and Buick Series 60 from 1934. It can be seen that the models produced with the unusual butterfly door layout were prevalent in the early 1930's when cars were still linked to the design of the carriage, whereas the layout that we find normal today became standardized during the 1940's.

Four door convertibles have played an important role in history, however. They are ideal for parades, being used by US Presidents including Roosevelt, Truman, and certainly John Fitzgerald Kennedy, who died while traveling in a presidential Lincoln convertible. They were just as popular with European leaders such as Hitler and Mussolini, and with many royal families around the world - except those who, for reasons of ceremony, may not have anyone show his back to the monarch!

In Europe development of four door cabriolets was parallel but not similar to those of the United States, as cabriolet design during the 1940's was still traditional. Mercedes and Rolls Royces were classic examples of luxury open-topped cars reserved for VIP's and parades.

There is little else to say about four door convertibles and novelty in terms of design, but it should be noted that, despite the lack of change, the period they covered lasted from the beautiful torpedoes right up to the sparkling convertibles of the 1950's and 60's.

THE ENGLISH OLD-FASHIONED ROADSTERS

So far the story of automobile development in terms of creativity and design seems to have centered on the French, Germans, Americans and Italians. To attempt to grade their contributions would be both meaningless and impertinent.

And the British? They were no less involved - on the contrary. Britain can claim the parentage of a small sports roadster which uniquely has remained almost the same for sixty years or more. Unfortunately the British perhaps claim a little too much when they say that the two seater sports cars from the 1960's on are the direct descendants of

cultural stew in which ideas surrounding open tops fertilized and prospered. A great love of nature and outdoor pursuits, an irresistible attraction to a unique, exclusive and handmade product and a touch of exhibitionism mixed with humor all combined to create the cult of small, glamorous, lovable MG's, Morgans, Triumphs, Jaguars, Bentleys, Aston Martins, Lagondas, Alvis', Lotus' and all the other copies and similar makes of the past and present. This English style had an infallible effect on the American pilots stationed in Britain during the Second World War.

the old-fashioned models designed in Great Britain from as far back as the 1930's. The authors do not share this opinion as sports cars, like all other types of automobiles, are developed from constant evolution and crossover that has no geographical boundary. It is also just as clear that the classic English sports cars were influenced by the experiences accumulated in Europe and the US in the design of runabouts, roadsters and racing GT's.

What was special in Britain, however, was the

There can be no doubt that they were in serious need of fun and distraction when off duty. What better than an open-topped MG? On returning to the States, the young pilots took their cars with them so helping to spread a contagious passion; a passion not just for the beauty of the designs but also for the fun of driving. Low and with the driving position set back, these cars imparted strong sensations to the driver. The response of the cars to longitudinal and lateral acceleration was immediate

and tangible and the driver might feel he was at the wheel of a single seater. And what fun when the back-end started to slide out on a bend - as long as it could be controlled, of course! When sitting in an English roadster with the top down, the driver is low to the ground and everything seems immediate: the rumble of the motor, the road rushing past to the side and the heavily sloping windshield to give the effect of being on a motorcycle.

152 top Rolls Royce contributed significantly to English design styles in the 1930's. This Springfield Roadster was designed in 1925 and shows the first hints of the old-fashioned style to come.

152 bottom A page from an advertising brochure for the MG Midget, not the most attractive but certainly the most popular of the English cars. The slogan tells us that the Midget has sporting blood in its veins and that it is the first car with a 750cc engine to exceed 100 mph.

152-153 The rear end of a 1939 Alvis with coachwork by Vanden Plas. It was in fact similar to other continental roadsters and it can be compared to the 1936 Mercedes 540 K. Another point to be noticed that was borrowed from French cabriolets is the drop-shaped front fender.

153 top The MG Model VA from 1937. Morris Garages (MG) was one of the most faithful interpreters of the old-fashioned style and offered traditional convertibles like this one, large and heavy.

153

154 top The MG 15/100 MK III Tigress had bodywork typical of small racing GT's, including the boattail. The fenders seem to have been taken from a motorcycle.

154 center Workers on the MG 18/80 assembly line at the Abingdon factory in 1930. MG had transferred here just one year before.

154 bottom and 155 bottom Square lines for the MG 18/100 MK III Tigress with its lights pushed forward of the radiator grill. Note the "U"-shaped access to the seats. The steering wheel had four crossed spokes and the dials were set on a white background - a pure sporting thoroughbred. Note the concave, rectangular shape of the outside mirror.

No wonder the drivers had such fun as they whizzed around semi-deserted country roads. In such conditions the old-fashioned English sports cars are irresistible and unbeatable in the picture they offer of the car as fun (the very reason that young Americans were so taken by them). It was this excitement and driving experience that was continued (and not just in Britain) in the development of sports cars to come by making them low, compact and basic.

The history of the English sports cars generally began in workshops and garages out in the country or suburbs. Perfect examples of this genre of car are MG and Morgan, and although there are many other marques with similar stories, these two may be the most significant.

MG came into existence in 1922 when Cecil Kimber wanted to put together a racing car based on a Morris Cowley. His success encouraged the creation of the MG company (which stood for Morris Garages, owned by William Morris, Lord Nuffield, who provided sales outlets and assistance). In 1929

the two-seater MG Midget was produced based on a Morris Minor which had an 847cc motor developing 8 HP. This was not yet a typical English open-topped sports car but it provided a chassis for the Midget J2 which is considered the originator of all MG models built up until the 1960's and an archetype of the old-fashioned English sports car. It was presented in 1932 with the same engine as the original Midget but power had been increased to 36 HP which gave it a top speed of 69 mph.

The Midget's external appearance was truly interesting in its lack of embellishment. The fenders were beautiful in their simplicity, taken literally from a motorcycle. The driving position was set well back to give space to the disproportionately long motor compartment for the small four cylinder engine it housed. Overall length was extremely short, 7 feet, and the width just over 3 feet. The door was characteristic with the oblique angle of the top of the door similar to the F1 Magna of the preceding year.

154-155 A parade of MG's ready for delivery exits the Abingdon plant. Abingdon was the home of MG from 1929-1980.

155 top right Note the spectacles-type windows that functioned as windshield in this MG J2 from 1932. This model was an important roadster in the creation of the English old-fashioned style. In particular, note the irregularity of the waistline which cuts the door to follow the slope of the wheelhouse.

156 top   The picture shows one of the best-selling MG's, the TF, which went on sale in 1953.   Although presented decades later than Morris Garages' first models, the TF maintained all the features of typical English roadsters and even emphasized them, for example, the front fender-footboard combination.

156 center   A parade of MG J2's crossing a ford during an outing in the English countryside.

156 bottom and 157   The pictures show the backs of the MG PA and ND.   Note the curious design of the dash on both cars.   Like other, similar small roadsters, the PA had a small 4 cylinder engine, 847cc, capable of producing 36 HP.   The ND was produced on an "N"-type chassis and was known as the Magnette.

The body panels were rather crudely manufactured with slits in the side to cool the motor. The radiator was covered by a rectangular bullnose grill and the headlights sat alongside on horizontal pins. On the J2, this grill seemed an ironic comment on the imposing Greek temple design grills of the gran turismo and torpedo models of the day.

The evolution of this early sports car was seen in the similar but better finished models which followed: the 6 cylinder L-Type Magna and the PA of 1934; the '35 PB which was very successful and one of the most representative cars of the English genre; the 1936 TA, the 1939 TB and the 1945 TC, the first postwar model.

To end this glorious series was the compliant TF 1250 sold in 1953-54. In twenty two years almost nothing had been altered; the length had increased by 9 inches to give a more shapely look, top speed had increased by only 12 mph though this was significant for these cars, and engine power had been raised from 36 to 58 HP in the now 1250cc engine (which gave the car its name). In line with the fashion of the time, the hood sported two chromed grooves. Then the shape of the open-topped MG's changed radically with the MGA and MGB, adopting the design that was typical of 1960 sports cars. Both models were very successful commercially.

158 top The 1948 Morgan 4/4; it is very difficult to identify from pictures exactly the year any Morgan was produced as the company is the most faithful of all English roadster manufacturers to the traditional style established at the end of the 1920's.

158 center A very elegant and elite 1953 Lagonda from Aston Martin. The retro style had been superseded by the more modern one used by Italian and French producers.

158 bottom One of the most celebrated actors of the time: Clark Gable in a beautiful Jaguar XK 120.

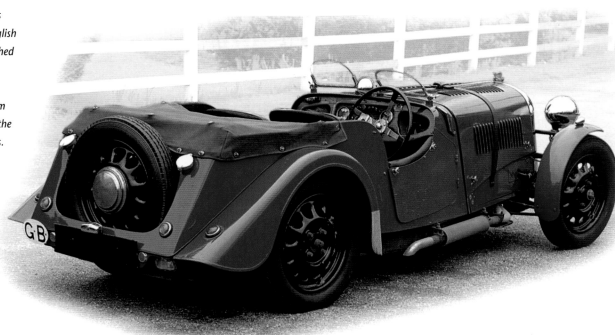

159 top Only 15 examples were ever produced of this refined car: it is the first model of Aston Martin's DB series and it is interesting because it marries the traditional style of the English GT's with that of sports cars of the 1950's. It was brought out in 1948.

Morgan was founded by H.F.M. Morgan who began to assemble three wheeled vehicles back in 1909. The first four wheeler was produced in 1936 with a waterproofed ashwood frame attached to steel side struts, a structure which has hardly changed even now. The model was called the 4/4 (four wheels, four cylinders) and is still in production today. In 1950 it was joined by the Plus 4 and in 1968 by the Plus 8. As representations of English style, the Plus 4 is more indicative with its diagonally cut door as opposed to the vertical edge of the 4/4.

Construction was and still is by hand and consequently slow, meaning production is limited. This is the great difference between Morgan and the other English sports car manufacturers which have developed into semi-industrial companies that adapt their car designs as the market develops.

But Morgan has remained faithful to the form, construction and driving techniques of the classic English sports cars. This has been the key to their success, particularly during periods when the desire to travel with the top down without fear of

159 bottom The enormous front of the Jaguar SS 100 in a splendid interpretation of the roadster theme that disregarded both the size and power attributes of small old-fashioned models and the lines that were strictly linked to the neo-classical style seen on contemporary Mercedes. This Jaguar dates from 1936.

being thought to show off was strongest. During the 1970's, when youthful dissent was loud and appearance was strongly criticized, companies such as Morgan suffered badly but made a strong comeback in the 1990's thanks to a return to fashion of old-styled roadsters in modern makeup. A point of interest regarding Morgan was that when the British air force, the RAF, wanted to test their first inflight refueling system during the Second World War, they asked Morgan to be the prime contractor.

Returning to English roadsters, it is impossible not to mention Triumph, which produced the lovely prewar Southern Cross and Dolomite, the TR 1800 from 1945, and then the snappy TR2 in 1953 and perfected TR3 in 1955. The latter were very aerodynamic and represented a distinct technological evolution of the old-fashioned English sports car - if such a thing was allowed. The hoods were wider and the lights were almost integrated. The fenders were long and shaped into a single unit with the body; there was no footboard.

The list could go on and on and we have not even mentioned Jaguar (the 1935 SS 100 and the 1948 XK120) or Aston Martin, nor, and why not, even some continental marque such as Fiat and BMW.

Postwar Europe

CABRIOLETS, A LOT OF SHOW BUT LITTLE SUBSTANCE

After the war, the European car industry had one main objective: to reconvert itself. More or less all the large scale manufacturers had had the production of military vehicles and munitions as their main activity and frequently their factories, especially the Italian and German ones, had been bombed. In addition, there was a strong need for cheap, functional cars to move people and goods. Large scale motorization was required to put the destroyed industrial, commercial and social systems back in operation. Naturally the need for functionality meant that the more elite vehicles suffered. That said, there was still no lack of interesting and attractive cabriolets or sports models.

The term cabriolet will be used more often so it is best to define it. In current terms it means a topless sedan or, more rarely, a two-seater sports car. From a design point of view and to ensure the continuity of terminology that has been used up to now, the authors believe a cabriolet should be defined as a convertible devoted to comfort and even luxury (though not always), sometimes with four doors but always with four or five seats. The ride is soft and performance dignified. Often there is a roll-bar behind the main seats and a reinforced windshield frame to protect the passengers in case the car turns over.

On the other hand, sports cars are generally open-topped, low two-seaters or maybe 2+2's.

From a formal viewpoint, cabriolets are descendants of the torpedo, touring car and baquet and of the American convertible coupé and convertible sedan of the 1940's. Sports cars continue the genealogical line of the roadster, speedster, runabout and GT.

Production of cabriolets immediately after the war was limited although all the motorized countries, Britain, France, Germany and Italy, had interesting cars on offer both for their intrinsic quality and because they ensured continuation of the line of open-topped cars. More generally, it can be stated that the generational leap from wheels in view to fenders as part of the motor compartment took place slowly thanks to the black-out during the war. European cabriolets very much resembled American convertible sedans and coupés but they were more elegant and balanced being slightly smaller and having less swollen, more linear profiles. This might have been translated into austere, rigorous, unexciting shapes but it did not happen that way - quite the opposite.

The wish for fun was strong too in Europe and this took form in "La Dolce Vita" by Fellini. There was a curious parallel at this time between the American passion for glitter and European flamboyance, not in the sense of color or use of chrome but in the design of form itself rather than additions to it. This phenomenon was less intense, evident or widespread than American glitter but it did not lack attractiveness as interpreted by European coachbuilders. Take for example some French cabriolets. There were very many interesting versions based on the Delahaye Type 135 chassis: by Antem, Chapron, De Levallois,

Ghia, Faget-Varnet, Figoni & Falaschi, Franay, Graber, Guilloré, Letourneur & Marchand, Pininfarina, Pennock, Pourtout, Saoutchik and Worblaufen. This long list gives an idea of how much this car, from a now non-existent manufacturer, was suitable for participation in the numerous beauty competitions during this period, but it also confirms the renaissance of the coachbuilders' craft which was, however, to show itself to greater effect on sports cars.

The Delahaye 135 was a large cabriolet which had been presented at the 1934 French Motor Show. In 1936 it won the Monte Carlo Rally and even after the war it kept the same 3.5 liter, 6 cylinder engine. Despite not having a high profile in the history of the car, it is worth describing some of the interpretations of the Delahaye created by the great coachbuilders' between 1946-51.

Antem's 1946 version retained the footboard and the headlights low down near the tall, narrow radiator.

160-161 and 161 top The elegance of the 1954 Jaguar XK 140. The XK series started with the 120 and was one of the most outstanding achievements of the 1950's; it took up the Art Deco stylistic themes expressed in cars like the Bugatti Type 57, particularly in the closed body version. This example, the Drophead Coupé, had softer lines. The roadster version was an original and glamorous interpretation of the postwar desire for speed, luxury and fun. Note the folded, split windshield.

160 bottom This is a luxury convertible, the Bentley MK6 from 1951. The classic version had enormous drop-shaped fenders; the front ones were painted a different color to the rest of the body and slowly faded away towards the rear axle. In this version, the features are more discreet.

161 bottom A moment from the most glamorous wedding of the 20th century: Prince Rainier of Monaco and the actress Grace Kelly pass through the streets in an enormous Rolls Royce after the wedding ceremony on 19 April 1956.

It did not use chromework heavily but brought attention to the car through the soft curves of the wheelhouses; on the other hand, the wheelhouses were less obvious in the 1947 versions by Chapron and De Levallois. Three extraordinary versions were created in 1950. The first was by Franay which replaced the grill with horizontal chromework and inflated the curves of the fenders, though not as much as Saoutchik, and certainly not as much as the narwhal constructed by Figoni & Falaschi. These last two were usually neo-classical designers

very similar to the cabriolet version of the Bugatti 101 of which only 2 examples were ever made, so similar in fact that it produced open comments. Versions of the Delahaye by Ghia and Pininfarina were very similar to Pourtout's ideas. At the other end of the scale from all points of view was the pragmatic production model, the 1951 Peugeot Cabriolet 203. The small, unpretentious, no frills car with a small but sufficient engine allowed many Frenchmen to indulge in their own "American Dream". In Britain the fortunes of the cabriolet

the only cabriolet worthy of inclusion was the 1949 Mercedes 170 S, one of the first German postwar cabriolets. In Italy Ghia and Pininfarina designed many models, for example, the Alfa Romeo 6C 2500, the Lancia Aprilia and Aurelia, and the Fiat 6C 1500. These designs shared points in common: the desire to join the front and rear wheelhouses and fill the space between, elimination of the footboard, the occasional enhancement of the sill (the element under the door often lined with chrome), and the addition of features to enliven the

but on this project they were clearly either struck by incipient madness or an excessive degree of irony. The wheelhouses were drawn over the wheels so far that they were almost convex as in record breaking cars a few decades later. They hid roughly 70% of the wheels and it is pointless to ask how the front ones were capable of being steered. In comparison, American convertibles with fins and chrome seem positively retiring.

Certainly they were stylistic exercises but often open-topped production cars are close to custom-built vehicles, a little like the relationship in the clothing industry between catwalk clothes and haute couture.

Pourtout's 1949 design was more compact but no less surprising. It was completely free of any edges or element that stood out on the smooth bodywork like the Chrysler Thunderbolt. In comparison with the profusion of sheet metal used on the hood, the grill and lights seem small. It was

rested safely in the hands of Bentley, Daimler and Jaguar. In 1949 Bentley produced the Mark VI with body design by Pininfarina. Daimler produced the classic Conquest Drophead in 1953, compact, very powerful and destined to widen the market of the exclusive English marque. There was also a roadster version but this was no beauty. Jaguar's 1957 XK 150 Drophead Coupé was a beautiful wild beast with a six cylinder engine producing 253 HP which would take the car to 140 mph (assuming anyone would want to in an open-topped car). It could be argued that the XK 150 was close on being a sports car but the presence of a Roadster version, meaner looking but less powerful, brings it within the bounds of a cabriolet.

In Germany and Italy, the two countries that lost the war, starting up again was a slow process. Whereas both were to sparkle in the design of sports cars in the years to come, the production of cabriolets was sparse and uninspired. In Germany

expanse of the sides of the car. Many comments were made in northern Europe about the wheelhouse "gaiters" which still resembled undercarriage fairings. Ghia and Pininfarina's design studios had one other point in common: The "flamboyant" style produced by the Ghia workshop. This style was propounded by their designer Capalbi, who had formerly worked for the Farina brothers and it was while working for them that the basis of the style probably originated. Synthesis of the style was the work of Mario Felice Boano. The flamboyant style tended to make cars large and gaudy by replacing the radiator grill with a chrome frame with wide vertical elements in the design of the mouth and teeth like some exotic animal. There was also an excess of chrome around the front lights. The lines as a whole were heavy and did nothing to lighten the plasticity and uniformity of the body panels. The flamboyant style was short-lived and it is unlikely anyone mourned its passing.

162 top This car is one of the countless versions of the 135M chassis produced by the French company Delahaye from 1938 on. One wonders how the front wheels were able to be steered. Actually, the majority of the versions built were produced to impress spectators at car beauty contests. Arguably, in terms of excess, such contests were one of the worst developments in the history of the automobile.

162 bottom This is the DB2 MK 1 Convertible built by one of Britain's most elite marques, Aston Martin.

163 top The drawing shows an open-topped Mercedes used in 1950 to publicize the Type 170, an important cabriolet during the period of reconstruction after World War II.

163 bottom President J.F. Kennedy passing in a Mercedes 300, called Landaulette, during an official visit to Mexico in 1960.

SPORTS CARS, THE RENAISSANCE OF THE OPEN-TOPPED CAR

Postwar European cabriolets may not have been very exciting, though more graceful than their American counterparts, but this was not the case with sports cars. The wide variety of sports models included many beautiful examples, true cult objects which matched functionality with their ability to give pleasure. Sports cars and roadsters from the 1950's were balanced and competitive thanks to strides forward in technology which allowed metal to be treated like a malleable elastic mass according to the whim of the stylist.

More importantly, greater attention was paid to the torsional resistance of the car's structure. If we think of an open-topped car as a cardboard box with the top cut off, it is clear how necessary it is to create strengthening to give back the rigidity that is lost when the top is removed. If not, the chassis is likely to twist the first time torsional stress is imposed. Reinforced chassis give greater drive comfort, better roadholding and considerable passive safety.

Body shapes were studied in wind tunnels, which resulted in designs that tended to an athletic type of beauty rather than beauty simply for appearance's sake. Motors were more refined and the power they developed could be exploited to the full because of reliable transmissions and sophisticated suspension. Thanks to this wave of technological progress and a strong desire for freedom and the open air, during the 1950's sports cars experienced perhaps the best period in their history on both sides of the Atlantic.

With reference to the design and not the product, the sports car is here defined as a two-seater car (or a 2+2) without a roof panel though with a soft or hard top (allowing targas to be included), designed as an original car and not simply a version of a sedan or coupé, and above all where performance is more important than comfort or luxury. This is, in other words, a return to the concept of the GT and roadster but with a new design. Which?

164-165 top *The picture shows the rear end of a Ferrari 166 Mille Miglia Barchetta from 1949-50. Note the right hand drive. The small engine, 2 liters, was already in the classic V12 configuration. The coachwork was designed by Touring. The car was raced by Clemente Biondetti, Felice Bonetto and Piero Taruffi.*

164-165 center *The 1958 Testa Rossa, often used for racing, was one of the most famous Ferraris of the 1950's. There were two V12 versions, which could only be told apart by the shape of the fender. The name came from the color of the cylinder head, and was used again in the 1980's on a roadgoing, mid-engined GT.*

165 bottom *The 1953 Ferrari 375 MM Spider Le Mans was designed by Pinin Farina. Note the two vertical elements on the ends of the grill that function as bumpers. The 375 MM Spider Le Mans differs from the 375 MM Spider Competizione by doing without the hollow behind the fender.*

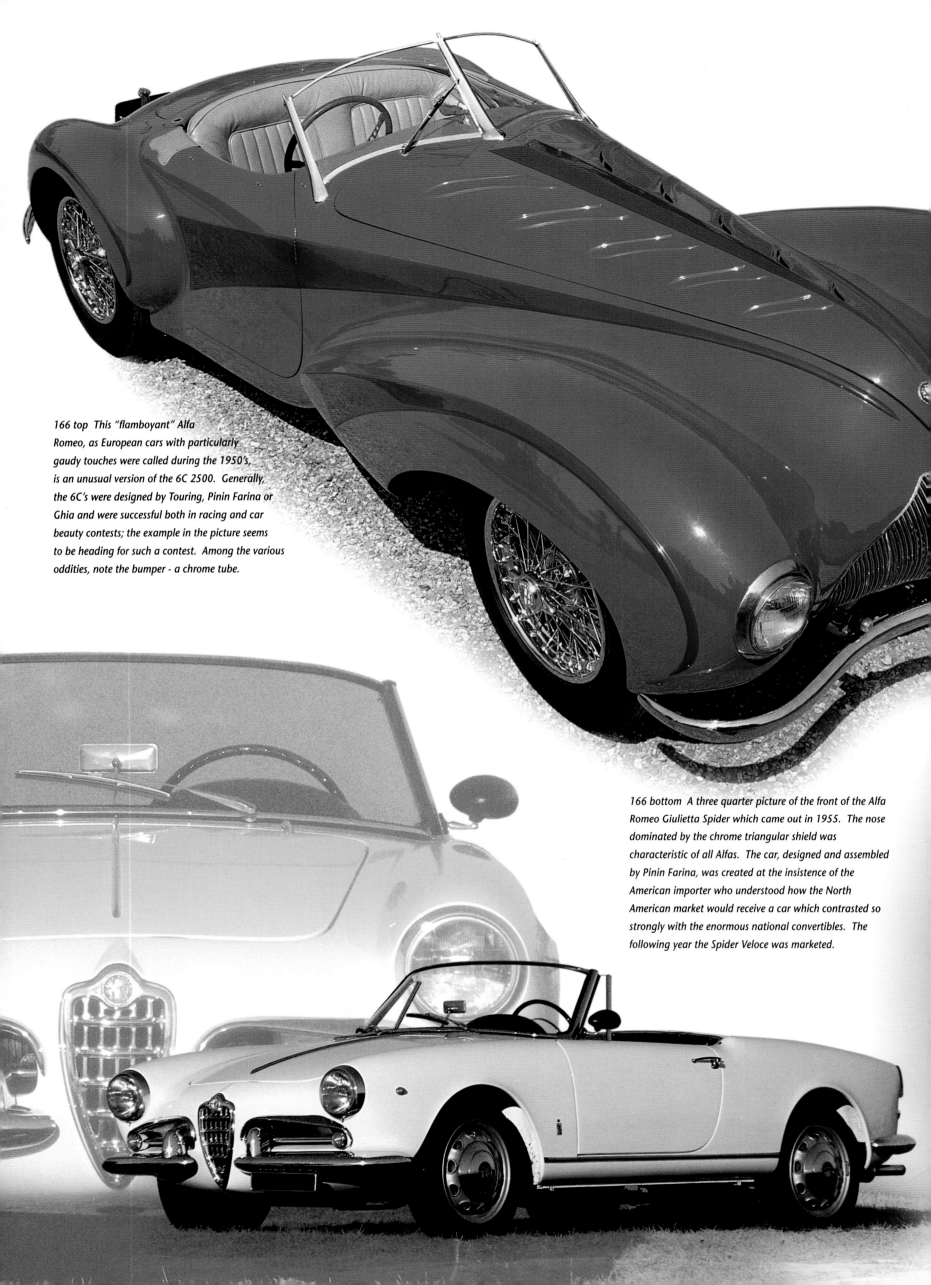

166 top This "flamboyant" Alfa Romeo, as European cars with particularly gaudy touches were called during the 1950's, is an unusual version of the 6C 2500. Generally, the 6C's were designed by Touring, Pinin Farina or Ghia and were successful both in racing and car beauty contests; the example in the picture seems to be heading for such a contest. Among the various oddities, note the bumper - a chrome tube.

166 bottom A three quarter picture of the front of the Alfa Romeo Giulietta Spider which came out in 1955. The nose dominated by the chrome triangular shield was characteristic of all Alfas. The car, designed and assembled by Pinin Farina, was created at the insistence of the American importer who understood how the North American market would receive a car which contrasted so strongly with the enormous national convertibles. The following year the Spider Veloce was marketed.

167 The singular lines of this 1952 Alfa Romeo gave it the name Disco Volante (flying saucer) which was no doubt influenced by the amount of talk dedicated to Martians and spaceships at the time. The first version did not have, like this one, the windshield which crossed the whole of the cab. The official name of this race car was the 1900 C52; another version existed which was called "tight sides" whose overall appearance can probably be guessed at. The picture shows the unusualness of the openings.

Sports cars in Europe from the 1950's on have shared many common elements. They are small or, rather, they are contained and proportioned; this has contrasted strongly with American convertibles where length was generally disproportionately more important than width. European sports cars are powerful, even the smallest, and their overall shape is square. The grill is generally still their main feature but it has lost a degree of importance and the lights have finally found their place at the extreme sides of the front end, giving a larger expanse of lighted surface.

The number of new models during the 1950's was so great that for the first time it is possible to try and group the most important models in terms of market positioning. Let's start from the bottom of the market, remembering that this is a discussion of sports cars and that therefore it is not possible to include the mini open tops that buzzed around the streets, symbols of youthful

folly and joy.

There were two very popular and desirable fast sports cars which were clear rivals: the MGA and the Alfa Romeo Giulietta Spider. Both went on sale in 1955 and boasted an enviable aesthetic and technological lineage.

The Giulietta followed on from similar models such as the 1954 1900 Convertible but the MG was revolutionary, a complete turnaround from what had till then been considered orthodox old-fashioned design in Britain. Although the Giulietta had a smaller engine (1290cc vs. 1489cc), it was declared to have a faster top speed but acceleration away from the red light was so similar that they were truly competitive. In terms of rivalry, the owners of the cabriolet and roadster versions of the Porsche 356 were still in the picture; the design of the Porsche was out of date but its performance was still competitive (all three models could reach between 97-100 mph).

In the same category but certainly less attractive were the 1953 Renault Ondine and the two Peugeots, the 403 and 404, respectively produced in 1957 and 1962. Mention should also be made of the 1959 Renault Floride and 1962 Caravelle and of course the MG Midget, which were all smaller with an engine of around 1000cc allowing the young and less well-off to have their own sports model.

The Lancia Appia Convertible and Cabriolet of 1959 had a small engine (1089cc) which could only produce 60 HP but they offered reasonably good performance and were extremely well equipped. They abandoned the fencer's mask type of grill and replaced it with a wide grill covered with a flat rectangular grate with large, right-angled weave. This feature had become frequent; it was seen in several Cadillacs and especially in the 1950's Ferraris from Pininfarina. Both the Appia and the Alfa Romeo Giulietta had modest fins in recognition of what was happening in the US.

At the next level up where the cars were more powerful and aggressive; the body shapes remained the same but engines of two liters or more required more space. Hoods were thus longer, details and fittings more refined.

Lancia, BMW and Mercedes must all be cited but Triumph is the name that stands out. Unlike MG, Triumph remained faithful to the design of the traditional British roadster until the early 1960's, particularly with the TR2 and TR3. Then after a failed experiment with the small Herald came the TR4 in 1961 and the immensely popular Spitfire 4 in 1962.

The traditional and sporty TR3 was the last model that could truly be considered as "old-fashioned". The top of the door sloped sharply down at a diagonal so seeming to divide the car into two parts. The profile rose sharply towards the front where it created the frame of the dashboard, and towards the rear where it became the edge where the tonneau cover was fixed. The windshield seemed very high for the low driving position. The front end was characterized by the curve of the

wheelhouse and the slight swelling of the motor compartment. Underneath there was a four cylinder, in-line 1991cc engine capable of 88 HP that gave a top speed of 111 mph and meant the Giulietta and company could be left behind.

It would have been harder for the Triumph to do so if it had come up against the Lancia Aurelia B24 sports which could reach 112 mph thanks to its V6 motor. Unlike the Appia Convertible, the Aurelia still had the old style radiator grill. The B24 Aurelia is dealt with in detail in the section on the most beautiful open-topped cars of all time which leaves space here to mention the Mercedes 190 SL as another representative of the medium-high bracket of the market.

This was a lovely, no frills model with little but striking chromework and balanced lines. This 1955 SL did not seem to have any competition among the luxury sports cars of the time. The performance was not exceptional as it had only a small 4 cylinder, 105 HP motor but what impressed was the freshness, lightness and loveliness that the car

exhibited. The 190 was not the only example to sport the glorious SL badge; the year before the most sought after car ever produced by Mercedes appeared, the Gullwing 300 SL, which took its name from the unique way the doors opened, upwards like the trunk, making it look like the wings of a seagull in flight. Unfortunately the original 300 SL was a coupé, so this work of art in movement has therefore been excluded from examination.

168 top A moment for pride: The 100,000th MG built, an MGA model from 1956.

168-169 This example is from the second series of the MGA produced between 1959 and 1962. Performance was slightly better than for the first series.

169 top This MG Midget MK III is from 1969. The little English sports car had a 1275cc engine and was nearly as popular as the MGA, selling 103,700 units in all.

169 bottom The Renault 4 HP prepared by Louis Rosier was a successful racing car.

The 190 SL could be considered one of the typical open tops from Stuttgart. However two years later brought the arrival of a gem that would leave even those most accustomed to expensive and elegant cars with their mouths open: the 300 SL Roadster, the open-topped version of the Gullwing. The motor compartment and side panels of the 190 were flat and straight. The hood sported a central ridge which made the surface less monotonous while the same function was performed on the sides of the car by two slight grooves at the top of the wheelhouses. This idea was to be repeated in different forms many times on successive models. The rear end was elegant and the luggage compartment occupied the volume in the tail. 1,853 examples of the Roadster were produced in the years 1957-63 (as opposed to 1,400 Gullwings) despite the car's high price -

32,500 German marks. The heart of the Roadster was a 6 cylinder, 3 liter engine. It produced 215 HP and gave a top speed of 162 mph; it was truly a performer.

Its appearance was dazzling and the details beautifully finished. The Roadster was the synthesis of the relatively modest 190 and the luxurious 300 SL sedan of 1954, from which it retained all the characteristics both inside and out except, of course, for the roof. The windshield did not seem to slope as much as the performance of the car merited.

The 190 and 300 were golden links in the SL chain which has had no equal in the history of the automobile. In stylistic terms, the SL's have almost represented perfection. They are recognizable by the absence of the Mercedes star traditionally placed on the top of the radiator; instead the star is centered in the face of the grill and accompanied by a horizontal chrome line. This positioning is aimed at rendering the radiator's air intake less imposing.

Another German open top of the period was the BMW 507 Roadster. It cost 5000 marks less than the Mercedes 300 SL but had a powerful engine, a 3168cc V8 giving 150 HP for a top speed of 137 mph. The 507 was the first postwar BMW not to show the double bean radiator grill. It was designed by Albrecht Graf Goertz and is often considered the most beautiful of BMW's.

170 top A hymn to all sports cars sung by the Aston Martin DB2/4 MK II. Actually the conventional design of this car was very different, more rounded and more like the typical English sports car styles. The car was built between 1950-59 but Touring designer Michelotti proposed this version in 1956.

170 bottom The BMW 507 - together with the modern roadsters Z1, Z3 and Z07 and the previous 328 - was certainly one of the queens of BMW's open-topped production. The 1956 model did not have the vertical double kidney grill, which was sacrificed in favor of a shark's mouth that had been squashed down and broken up by a token flange. The 3168cc V8 produced 150 HP and could take the car to 137 mph. The 507 had no immediate successor.

171 top The Volkswagen Karmann-Ghia Convertible (here from 1973) achieved moderate fame and popularity. The name combined the names of two designers and therefore two designs, both famous in the world of open-topped cars: Karmann for the Beetle and Golf, and Ghia for a succession of Fords. VW, Ghia and Karmann cooperated in the production of convertibles as early as 1960.

171 center The 1955 BMW 503 came several years before the 507. The sporting theme was right on target with a basic, nervous and overall square design which was also very popular among small but lively Italian 2-seaters.

171 bottom The 1956 Austin Healey, like other Austins, was copied and reproduced many times. Here one can see combined the rounded fairings of English inspiration together with squarish panels more of continental origin.

This exciting roundup cannot end without discussing, for the first time, the open-topped Ferraris of the time: the 1952 212 Inter Pinin Farina and 1960 250 GT California.

The 212 Inter was the first Ferrari to be designed by Pinin Farina. Noticeable was the use, or abuse, of thick chromework on the sills, the rims around the windshield, the air intakes on the hood and the lights, and most of all in the huge radiator grill and its frame. The rear lights were small, pointed and ugly. It was called a cabriolet but really it was just a straight out sports car. The motor was a 60° V12 displacing only 2.5 liters but producing 150 HP and giving a maximum speed of 122 mph. In 1961 it was the turn of the short

wheelbase 250 GT California, also designed by Pininfarina (now one word) but assembled by Scaglietti. It is considered to be one of Ferrari's most representative sports cars. Its appearance was more menacing than the 212 as the car was set lower down and the position of the headlights, higher than the shark's mouth grill, fostered the aggressive image. The impression was one of nose-heavy dynamism. Another point to notice was the transparent and streamlined covering over the headlights. Besides the rearing horse emblem, the grill accommodated the two fog lights. There was no holder for a license plate, which would have to be screwed directly onto the body.

172 left This picture is of the Porsche production line in 1951. The coachwork is of the first series, the "pre-A", of the Porsche 356 produced from 1948-55. There were three engines available for this car: all were four cylinder boxer designs of 1.1, 1.3 and 1.5 liters that produced between 40-70 HP. Performance, naturally, was not overwhelming.

172-173 This aerial view shows a Porsche 356 ready for the American market. Note the rear-mounted boxer motor.

173 top This red Porsche is the Super 90 version of the 356 B with a 1.6 liter engine, on sale from 1959-63.

173 bottom This might be considered a holy place by sports car lovers - it is the Porsche production line putting the final touches to the 356 A Cabriolet (also seen are closed body versions). In the foreground is Ferry Porsche, Ferdinand's son.

The sides of the car were characterized by a ridge which ran from one wheelhouse to the other and by a chromed air outlet with three vertical slits, a common ornamental motif in sports cars of the period. The tail was surprisingly short and the two exhausts, chromed on the outside and painted red inside, stuck out like an affectation. The V12 engine displaced almost 3 liters and this time more power was there: 280 HP, which gave a declared top speed of 156 mph.

This chapter should have made it clear that the period from 1955 to 1961 was truly exciting for lovers of sports cars. It is not accidental that, considering only Europe, three of the sports cars from this period have been selected for entry in the section on the most representative models of all time (Lancia Aurelia B 24, Mercedes 300 SL and the Ferrari 250 GT California). And this does not include the E-type Jaguar, to be described later, or the American evergreens like the Cadillac Eldorado and Ford Thunderbird.

In particular, the authors consider 1955 to be the most bountiful year for production of top quality models.

174 top and 175 bottom One of the most beautiful and desired open tops of all time, the Mercedes 300 SL, created as a spin-off from the Gullwing coupé. Evolution of the SL roadster has been continuously influenced by two factors. The first is stylistic - all SLs are slim in profile and have a strong personality (emphasized by the unusual placement of the three-pointed star not on the hood, but right in the grill). The second factor is technological - the SL range always tries to boast of the most sophisticated and

advanced mechanical equipment. The original 300 SL Gullwing pioneered automotive fuel injection, for example. VIP's and movie stars soon adopted Mercedes' sports-car series as their own; in the photograph, actor Glenn Ford can be seen with his 300 SL roadster.

175 top The SL series boasted another roadster, the 190 SL, with body characteristics more linked to forms from previous models and with performance decidedly inferior to the 300 SL.

176 top A historic picture that shows the prototype Beetle cabriolet as it leaves the house of its "father", Ferdinand Porsche.

176 bottom Defining the Beetle created difficulties for its designers who could find nothing better than "closed body soft top". On the other hand, "cabrio limousine" seemed a little over the top. The semi-elliptic split window was

rather strange. This configuration was the origin of other small-engined open tops like the Citroën 2CV, Renault 4, Fiat Topolino and Fiat 500.

177 left The very first Beetle convertible from coachbuilder Hebmüller can be recognized by the fact it was a 2-seater. When a fire destroyed the Hebmüller plant, the job passed to Karmann.

177 right Hitler's dream of a popular and cheap German car came true with the Volkswagen Beetle designed by Ferdinand Porsche. It cost just 990 marks, approximately half the price of the next cheapest car on sale in Germany.

The era of the Beetle

Unusual, clumsy, slow and with archaic lines, the definitive design of the open Volkswagen Beetle in 1948 seemed to have little chance of success with the lovers of top down motoring. Its expected public was those who had always wanted to drive with the wind in their hair but who did not have the means to buy themselves an elegant cabriolet or sporty two-seater. Overturning every prediction, the open-topped version of the Beetle was just as popular as the closed version and 331,847 units were sold. This amazing success of the Beetle Convertible was a pleasant surprise for Volkswagen and subcontractor Karmann.

The car was designed by one of the greats of the automobile industry, Ferdinand Porsche. Porsche had worked for Mercedes and Auto Union but left to form his own company. Before doing so, he was asked by Adolf Hitler to design a cheap, reliable and functional car ("Volkswagen" means "people's car"). The war interrupted production but the chassis continued to be used for military purposes. At the end of

to coachbuilder Hebmüller who produced a two-seater. When a fire at the factory interrupted production, Karmann took over in 1949 and produced the definitive four-seater version. The body of both two and four-seater versions was identical to that of the sedan; it was as though a saw had simply taken off the part above the waist. It was a triumph for roundness! The funny little car was like an overturned oval cup with a snail shell at each corner (the fenders). The handle of the cup was the enormous roof which stuck out not just a little above the waist when folded.

There is little point in describing a model which is still fresh in the minds of all drivers and which is still not infrequently seen on the road. With regard to technical details however, when the Beetle first came out, it had a modest four cylinder boxer engine mounted in the rear.

The size was 1131cc which produced a simple 25 HP. Both size and power increased as the years passed while most of the rest remained unchanged except, of course, for

the war, the Beetle was involved in an amazing blunder. A British commission was specially set up to assess the car's potential and judged it to have no future, but Volkswagen's new manager, Heinz Nordhoff, was not prepared to give in and reduce production. Sales continued to grow and the Beetle became one of the most loved symbols of the young during the 1960's.

The Beetle ("Kafer" in German) was designed during the late 1930's when there were already open-topped models in similar shapes on sale, for example, the 1936 Mercedes 170 H and the 1939 Adler 2.5. When production was restarted in 1948, responsibility for the curious cabriolet was given

equipment relating to safety and comfort.

There were restylings but nothing which took away from the car's overall appeal.

The second series (if we discount the original two-seater) appeared in 1954 and remained in production until 1960. The quantity of chrome was increased, quality of finishing was improved, the body grew in length by 3 inches and the motor slightly increased in power.

Successive versions appeared every five years or so until 1979 when the Golf Cabrio made its triumphal entry on the back of a rich genetic inheritance from the Beetle, which regretfully went into retirement.

Large American convertibles

Is there a parallel between the European sports cars of the 1950's and the large American convertibles? What did the fast, sporty, elegant but basic open tops of Europe have in common with the flashy, self-propelled juke-boxes, the core business of American style of the 1950's and 1960's? On one side of the Atlantic "La Dolce Vita", and on the other "American Graffiti". It seems there was a huge divide. But there is a parallel and a strong one: an easy-going hymn to joy, pleasure, and, perhaps, irresponsibility, sung with the wind in one's hair and the sun or stars over one's head in a determined attempt to return to childhood.

To brand these large convertibles together as gaudy, useless, childish barges is not just wrong but shows a symptom of ignorance greater only than the superficiality which generated it. Were these cars so very vulgar? In our opinion, as will already be clear, decidedly not.

Certainly, if beauty is considered as an interpretation of the classical, sculptural and anthropomorphic inheritance handed down from the history of the car we have so far seen, the Cadillac Eldorado et al had little to say. If, however, we consider beauty in the light of transgression, as a desire for novelty, surprise, excitement and freedom of thought etc., the finned wonders take

on a regal dignity. Then, too, there is the taste of excess, the desire to show off, the knowledge of being over-the-top. This is surely just plain tongue-in-cheek, a need not to be taken seriously rather than youthful swaggering. It should not be forgotten that during the 1950's the United States was struggling with the Korean War, McCarthyism, civil rights, the Cold War, and the recession of 1958. There would be little to crow about in a society that continuously criticized and attacked itself. To imagine young American boys as interested simply in creating the perfect quiff, dancing to rock'n'roll and slipping out with Pop's car keys for wild nights, or riding around on Harley Davidsons in Easy Rider style, would be to accept blindly empty stereotypes created for us by TV and the cinema. Decades on, these enormous witnesses of an era, the last in which

fun was an option for youngsters, still travel the roads of the world. Consider for a moment; what is your first reaction when you see a large American convertible on the street? Most probably a smile in recognition of a past which is only available to most of us through the small and large screens. Then perhaps common sense spurs our critical reasoning, if not a veil of sanctimonious respectability, to ask, "What is that ostentatious sky-blue Buick Limited/Ford Skyliner/Cadillac Series 62 doing in a world that takes everything so seriously?" But we are talking about open-topped cars, about dreams and abstraction, the wish to smile, to explore and to imagine the road as an infinite ocean all to ourselves. These cars, half fish, half ship, allowed their drivers to surf on the crest of fantasy. They were a world apart.

178-179 This page shows three pictures of a car made in 1959, when the shiny, glittery era was almost at an end. This was a special-bodied Sedanca built on perhaps the 1950's most representative convertible, Cadillac's Eldorado. In the picture to the left note the shape of the roof, which resembles the limousine designs at the start of the century. ("Sedanca" refers to a car in which the folding roof only partly covers the passengers, though in fact this Eldorado is really a hard top with a central insert - in other words, a classic targa.) The closeup of the back end gives an excellent view of the most important design feature of 1950's convertibles, the fins. The idea of fins came from the most powerful designer in American auto history, Harley J. Earl, and was inspired by Lockheed's P-38 fighter. The rear lights were nearly always placed right at the tip of the tail, and sometimes they were used to conceal the fuel cap.

180 top This Nash Metropolitan was an American model built with English mechanicals that was sold between 1954-62. It definitely ran counter to the times, being absolutely tiny and having only a 4 cylinder engine.

180 center and bottom This elegant convertible, the Chrysler Town & Country, was sold from 1946-48. After the Crown Imperials it was the most expensive model in the Group.

181 top The front end of the 1951 Frazer Manhattan. The amount of chrome applied had started to increase inexorably.

There is an enormous jump between the rather awkward convertibles that existed throughout the 1940's and the sparkling models from about 1952 on. Let's consider their development chronologically. At the start of this period the car manufacturers started to lengthen the outline of their open-topped cars, the angle between the upper half and the side panels became cleaner and the edges more accentuated, in contrast to the curved and swollen surfaces of a few years before. Assimilation of the hood and fenders, elimination of the footboard, resizing of the grill and integration of the lights into the car body were

difficulties which had been overcome. The body was now unified and heavy, and the grill was used to give identity to the car as had happened so often before. Two examples are the 1949 Packards, the Convertible and the Custom Eight. The first had a strange, large weave grill, round and rectangular lights and a "rail" type of bumper. The second seemed a composition formed from a curved rail-type bumper, three large pieces of chrome of equal length and a kind of long, chromed metallic protective chestpiece worn by knights in the Middle Ages, all topped by further decoration. It was horrendous. The 1950 Dodge Convertible limited itself to three very large chrome strips bent to resemble the front of a boat while the Mercury convertible of the same year had a long, narrow mouth without lips but with innumerable teeth (or even better, baleen, the cartilaginous bones in the mouth of a whale which trap the plankton). It resembled the grills of the flamboyant style designs in Italy and France. The list could go on and on, some more and some less bizarre. As for the rear, the only outstanding difference was the choice by the designer whether to cover part of the rear wheelhouse with a side panel or not.

But then came the first signs of the style that was to explode on the scene like a battery of fireworks.

Of particular importance was the evolution of details which were to characterize all models in the decades to come: the sides at the back of the car that were to be transformed into fins. Responsibility was once again due to aeronautical design and to one airplane in particular: a prototype of the Lockheed P-38 twin-boom fighter. The incorrigible Harley Earl, famous GM design head, was impressed by the oval shape of the plane's vertical stabilizers during a trip to California. The form buzzed in his head for five years until it was time to create the postwar generation of designs. A sensational model was the 1950 Buick LeSabre, the details of which were to resound like a refrain throughout all the following decade. They can be summarized as visual indications of opulence, transgression and neo-futurism.

Chrome was everywhere replacing the totemic forms of the stereotyped temple radiator shapes. There were a number of air-intakes which cooled nothing; sparkling, shiny paintwork; aeronautical reminders to celebrate the new frontier of jet propulsion including the debatable and abnormal central air-intake which unhappily tempted Pininfarina in his first American experience. The rear fins finally swallowed up the lights and became hypertrophic appendages which competed with the front as the most zoomorphic element given that both ends unquestionably resembled the body of a dangerous, aggressive shark.

Apart from the appearance of the fins, there was another sign of what was unavoidably changing, the position of the driver and the front row of seats.

In the past and especially in sporting designs, the driver sat well back while in the convertibles he tended to sit in the center of the car. At the beginning of the 1950's this trend was emphasized and the driver found himself further and further forward towards his ever-larger V8 engine. The tail grew further away to the limits of the known horizon until the rear volume was so large you could play a game of ping-pong on it. One model which suggested this trend was the 1952 Lincoln Capri. It had a large back end, fins, as much chrome as you could shake a stick at and a rather square shape.

182 The 1953 Buick Skylark was a classic model characterized by the chrome strip which ran down the side towards the rear fender. The dimensions of this model are definitely worth noting: the length was 17'10", width 6'7" and wheelbase 10'6". The V8 engine displaced 5276cc to give 157 HP and a maximum speed of 97 mph (which was increased to 103 mph in 1954). The most important detail was the shape of the grill; it was decidedly zoomorphic with the vertical bars resembling the baleen plates in the mouth of a whale. A parallel was the "flamboyant" style in Europe where the extravagant finishing touches seemed rather over the top.

182-183 This is the Buick engine control department at General Motors workshops.

183 top The front of a very popular car in the mid-50's, the Packard Caribbean. Note the two-tone coloring at the back that matches the interior. The front seems unexciting, probably because of the ugly design of the lights set against the rest of the body. It seems clear to the authors that Packard was unable to make up its mind whether to stick with the older styles or to adopt the new, extreme design themes.

183 bottom This customized Oldsmobile 98 seems to have a nautical inspiration. The similarity between the rear of the car and the stern of an average-sized yacht appears striking. The excuse is evidently the need to house the spare wheel, but what is more apparent is a simple taste for excessive display.

To empty the pockets of convertible enthusiasts there was already the Cadillac Series 62 with a whole range of state-of-the-art versions. In 1949 it was already 17'9" long, a monster, and 6'7" wide, but the following year it grew a further four inches, which it was to maintain in its first appearance as an Eldorado in 1953. Then in 1954 it spurted again to reach 18'9"! The honor of propelling all this was given to a powerful 5.4 liter V8, but let's not get ahead of ourselves and go back to 1953.

There were still many "normal" models like the Ford Crestline Sunliner at only 17'4" long, but here too the trends were clear and it boasted sparkling chrome all over the body. An important feature was the lengthening of the wheelbase which had two effects: first, the rear overhang was proportionally shortened and second, less emphasis was given to the rear volume. Less conventional were the Buick Super and Skylark of 1954 with some original chromework that widened towards the base; it resembled a wave to some extent and the marine theme was strengthened by the inclusion of three portholes taken from the previously mentioned Buick LeSabre.

And other makes? Hanging on to the older styles were Oldsmobile with the Fiesta, Packard with the Caribbean, and Plymouth with the Cranbrook, all dating from 1953. Dodge's 1954 Royal 500 and Hudson's Hornet of the same year moderated the new design ideas although the chrome was already running in rivers along the

bodywork; however, it only took one more year for those rivers to turn to torrents. At the other end of the spectrum, following the sports car Pininfarina was commissioned to design, Nash brought the Metropolitan to a market sated with excess. It was a tiny (12'5") three-seater open top which when placed next to the Cadillac Eldorado seemed like a Piper Cub next to a 747. The Metropolitan had an engine made by Austin in Great Britain.

Nash owed its name to Charles Nash, who had briefly been president of GM. His successor, George W. Mason, greatly admired the Cisitalia 202 SC designed by Battista "Pinin" Farina, and commissioned a design from him. This was a

historic event, being the first time an Italian coachbuilder had received such a major US production commission. The agreement was that the body would be mounted in Italy on an American frame, while the American designed engine would be tuned and installed in England by Healey. The resulting model was restrained and rather anonymous, distinguished only by the unusual, completely chromed grill which enclosed the circular headlights.

There were other important debuts in this period. In addition to the Eldorado in 1953 which grew out of the Series 62, the first appearance was made of America's most important sports car of all time, the Chevrolet Corvette.

184 top A moment from the General Motors Automobile Show in the Waldorf Astoria Hotel in New York. The car seems right at home in this famous hotel: note the leopard skin interior. The car is a Cadillac.

184 bottom One of the very many Cadillac Eldorados produced during the 1950's. The car belonged to President Eisenhower as can be surmised by the flags on the front bumper.

185 top The front of a 1954 Cadillac Eldorado. Note the thick weave grill. The front part of the hood can just be made out. This version was 18'5" long but this was not a record; the Cadillac Series 62 of the same year, closely related to the Eldorado, was 18'10" long.

185 bottom This 1959 Cadillac convertible is an Eldorado. Almost certainly, these were the most striking fins of the period.

186-187 top A classic shot from the cinema: a smiling Grace Kelly at the wheel looks at Cary Grant. The film, "To Catch a Thief", was directed by Alfred Hitchcock in 1955.

both the Series 62 and the Series 62 Eldorado in 1954. In both cases the designers took their cue from the aeronautical industry in their hunt for reaction. The two models were very similar, though the Eldorado was 4 inches shorter and lower. The nose was dominated by two enormous bumper guards but then everything was large including the Cadillac coat of arms over a golden "V". In the top-of-the-range model, the rear end was embellished with a metallic lining with fine horizontal lines. There was a transparent reflector which revolved on a pin in the rear lights. There were also decorations and friezes at the back, in this case small strips arranged vertically along the whole of the bumper. What were they made of? Chrome of course. And future versions of the Eldorado continued to offer sumptuous innovative extras to its well-to-do fans.

Nineteen fifty-five was an exceptional year for the market as a whole with 8 million cars registered, a new American record. The car manufacturers launched into a wave of new models with convertibles in particular giving designers the opportunity to arouse the enthusiasm of younger generations. It was a heady period which lasted until the recession of 1958. Remember too that in Europe 1955 was a year of outstanding creativity with regard to open-topped cars.

186 top The Ford Thunderbird was a car of great power and ambition sacrificed on the altar of sales figures. Successive cuts in its power and a softening of its appearance destroyed the sporting image of the car - but sales rose. The picture shows the second version of the Thunderbird from 1958.

186 bottom In 1958 the Thunderbird was still quite aggressive. The honeycomb grill sometimes held foglights.

187 top The T-bird in 1959 with its four headlights remaining. Note the silhouette of a rocket on the side which cited the start of the space age.

187 bottom A careful look at this car enables one to understand the mechanisms required to fold this roof into the T-bird's trunk (the short name of this Ford model).

And only two years later came the Ford Thunderbird, another model of major significance.

The Thunderbird was Ford's answer to GM's Corvette. It was originally just a two-seater with an aluminum body (the Corvette was in glass-fiber) and a hard top available. The motor was a large V8, which compared favorably with the earlier 6 cylinder Chevy. The original design was of a fairly athletic sports car whose power was rather toned down by its pastel colors though these were fashionable at the time. The fins and front bumper guards were still modest. Features of the T-bird gave the car a strong resemblance to an elegant motorboat: the windshield was wide and curved, the interior was compact, the back end was long and smooth; the chromework and the air intake in the center of the motor compartment only added to the similarity. Indeed, designs of the two means of transport often appeared to have borrowed freely from one another.

The market decreed that the T-bird initially won out over the Corvette - 17,500 1955 units sold compared to 700 - but while the Chevrolet was being steered towards a true sports personality, the Ford was aimed at performance and luxury accessories (electric seats and windows, power steering and braking), so much so that at the end of the 1950's the new four-seater outsold the two-seater 7 times. With the help of this success, Ford was Number One in sales overall between 1950-57. With regard to top range models, Cadillac offered

188 top This set of rear lights belonged to a 1957 Chrysler New Yorker. Here the lights are set in the hollow of the upper part of the fin. Observe the decorations on the side, seven chrome shells.

188 bottom A convertible which had a much larger public than the elite Buicks, Packards and Cadillacs; this is the 1954 Chevrolet Bel Air. It cost little more than 2,000 dollars while the cheaper hard top version was called the Sport Coupé.

One of the successful convertibles was the 1955 Bel Air, Chevy's top model, which revolutionized the whole fleet presenting the celebrated and still current Smallblock V8. Something was stirring at Chrysler too. It is strange that one of the most courageous and purposeful companies should have been idle at the start of this turbulent period. Maybe its marketing managers were so caught on the hop by Harley J. Earl's creative innovations that it was only 1955 (when Chrysler too created completely new production lines with the exception of the New Yorker) before they had models to offer in line with contemporary trends. The Chrysler Windsor showed many similarities to the DeSoto Fireflite though their use of chrome and two-tone paintwork smacked of lack of practice when compared to the artistic details and the consistent design offered by Cadillac. The decisive reawakening was that of the DeSoto range which

produced the Fireflite, Firesweep, Firedome and Adventure models between 1954-59. The Dodge Custom Royal Lancer had a more defined personality. The hood had two-tone coloring, the grill was separated into two symmetrical horizontal elements and, being a five-seater, the rear volume was contained. Big fins were to arrive the following year.

Innovative coloring was the Oldsmobile Starfire and Super 88's first claim to fame: Their fronts were painted white that ended in a sort of arrow just above the wheelhouse. A piece of chrome separated the white half from the red or sky-blue of the other half which covered most of the sides and the rear end. 1956 continued the overwhelming success of the car industry, which continued to churn out new models and multiple versions. The market bubbled and Ford and GM battled it out at the top with continual price wars. Those who suffered were the smaller companies one of which

seemed to fail every time you opened a newspaper. Consequently, the Big Three just got bigger. One of the illustrious names to fall by the wayside was the traditionalist Packard, which was always the last to adapt to new design ideas. Its collapse was aided by its rash joining to another longstanding (and troubled) American marque, Studebaker. Packard's last new convertible was the 1955 Caribbean. In the meantime, an important development concerned the Eldorado which had acquired the additional name Biarritz to contrast with that of the coupé, the Seville. From a mechanical point of view, gas suspension was introduced for the first time. The Ford Thunderbird decided to store its spare wheel on the outside, a throwback to the roadsters of 20 years before (how things had changed! It seems a century had passed to judge by the differences between the T-bird and the Duesenberg J). The Ford's engine was made slightly more powerful which enabled it to reach 125 mph.

189 bottom The 1958 Buick Roadmaster. The name was old but the creativity in terms of chromework was very modern. Note the low grill made up of dozens of cubes looking like an echo chamber. The design of the lights was classic with headlights of equal size enclosed below a rectangular brow.

189 top The front profile of the Chrysler New Yorker from 1957. Although it may be considered a classic today and it included all the extreme concepts of the convertible of the day, it sold poorly - only a few more than a thousand examples were produced.

The Thunderbird's stablemate, the Skyliner, now offered a retractable hard top which entered the trunk electrically. Imagine the enormity of the task with the dampers, hydraulic jacks and motors necessary to ensure the functionality of the whole.

There seemed to be no end to the exaggeration of the rear end in 1957, to the point where it took over from the grill as the most distinctive element of the car.

The motors continued to grow more powerful which suited the youngsters just fine for their dangerous drag races.

Towards the end of the decade there were so many convertibles on the market that certainly we are bound to err in trying to make a list of the most representative models by leaving some out. However, we shall deal with the major events of the important models that soared through the 1950's and 60's like comets through space.

At the tip of the pyramid there was of course the most luxurious model, the Cadillac Eldorado Biarritz which was supplied to 1,800 rich customers. The rear lights became smaller and were moved to the end of the curve of the rear volume. This alteration underlined the presence of the fins which seemed actually to be detached from the car body.

Meanwhile, the Thunderbird changed its nose design, got flatter and wider, and grew fins - but these were not fins in the traditional sense at the back of the car; the Thunderbird fins started out from the back of the cab. At the time of purchase the buyer also had the choice of a version with a positive displacement blower.

A model of interest was the Chrysler 300 C with its robust 341 HP motor, which pushed this strangely light vehicle (under 2 tons, compared to the Eldorado's 2.3 tons) to 144 mph. The grill was unusual for its shape (having only two sides parallel) and massive size filled with a large weave mesh. The lights were modern in design, small and with double headlights. The 300 C was certainly a very emphatic model and representative of its era.

Fortunately there were convertibles available at

the cheaper end of the market like the Chevrolet Bel Air. This striking 17'3" long model cost only 2,611 dollars against the 7,286 of the Biarritz with the result that it sold 47,562 units. The Ford Sunliner 500, contemporary of the Skyliner and Fairlane, did even better: it cost 2,505 dollars and sold 77,726 units.

The 1958 Buick Limited, perhaps the most excessive design of all, was known as the "Glitter King". Its most distinctive feature was the side decoration that ran along beneath the fin. The fin was not especially large, but its importance was emphasized by thick chromework. Decoration was provided by a long curve which came to a point with three series of five vertical chrome lines and, as if that was not enough, the characteristic wave on previous models was still present. Behind there were two large bumper guards and a host of chrome bezels.

190 top This rare and exclusive convertible is the Chrysler Imperial Crown Southampton, completely redesigned in 1957.

190 bottom The front profile of the Pontiac Star Chief from 1957. At 17'1" long it was an average size convertible and sold at an average price. Note the curves of the windshield in the corners, the two-tone coloring and the trim panel on the sides, which further lengthened the profile. The use of wide whitewall tires was common during this period.

191 top The top of the Ford Skyliner in action; imagine the power needed to raise and lower it. Attempts had been made since the 1930's to create an electric motor for this job, but the batteries available were never powerful enough. Ford used electric motors which in turn operated hydraulic rams. Note the rear fender, which almost entirely covers the wheel.

191 bottom A three quarter shot of a car which, together with the Pacer of the same series, did not enjoy much success. This is the Edsel Citation Convertible Coupé from 1958 which was much appreciated but not bought. The characteristic front of the Edsels had an oval grill, vertically set . Performance was impressive thanks to its 320 HP engine - top speed was 119 mph.

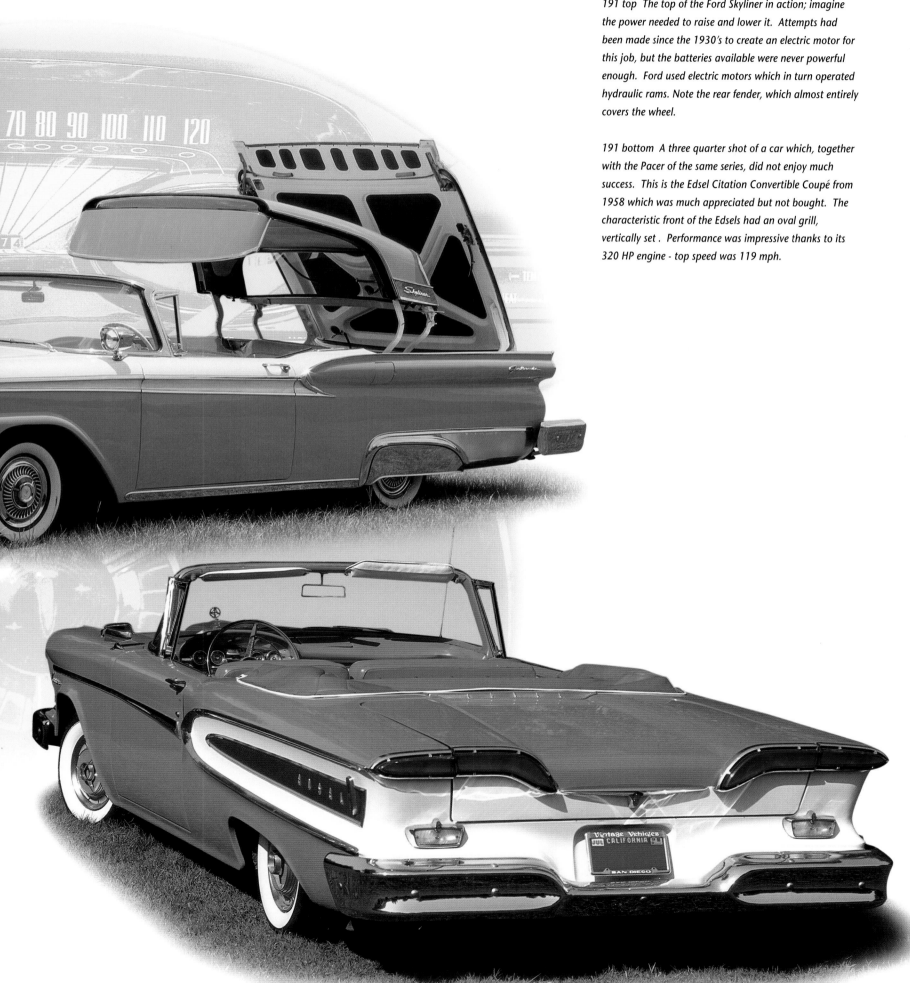

1958 was a period of profound economic crisis but convertibles represented 5% of the market. One car which cost more than the Cadillac Series 62 (but naturally less than the Eldorado) was the Imperial Crown. This was another monumental machine distinguished by its grill made up of 4 very fine, narrow and serpentine coils like a refrigerator tray. The bumper was huge and thick and the double headlights were surmounted by chrome trappings. The spare wheel sat between the rear fins. Similar in terms of expanse of metal was the gaudy Lincoln Continental Mark III.

The 1958 Pontiac Bonneville boasted the same design of the rear sides as the Buick Limited, but more accentuated to become a deep hollow lined with chromed and grained metal. Another novelty was to be found on the 1959 Dynamic 88, the cheapest and best selling Oldsmobile of the year. Instead of fins, this car had two tubes with a "stopper" formed by the rear lights. These descriptions could go on and on, but they soon become boring.

Something new was needed once more, perhaps something less ostentatious after the

excesses of the body and the competition to provide the most powerful engine.

One theme that was to prevail during the early 1960's was that the rear end tended to resemble an open tank or, more prosaically, a shovel. The fins curved outside the silhouette of the main body and the use of chrome diminished somewhat. Examples were Plymouth's Sport Fury and Buick's LeSabre and Electra 222. Going against the tide of course was the Cadillac Eldorado Biarritz which kept its huge fins vertical and with the rear lights set right in the center. In the same category, the Dodge Custom Royal seemed bandaged up by a multitude of chrome strips while the fins, rather than curving out of the body shape, seemed stuck on afterwards. The result was one of rare ugliness.

The Chevrolet Corvette, however, continued on its way deserving of every honor it received. After its timid debut, the great American sports car took on its golden existence with the introduction of the Smallblock V8 engine. Between 1953 and 1955, the small roadster defied the design trends of the

192 top The picture shows one of the queens of the open-topped sports car world, the 1960 Chevrolet Corvette. The Corvette had been launched some years before but still no one imagined the successful future this powerful car with its Smallblock engine would enjoy. Note the toothy, mean-looking grill like the Packards of a decade before, the ovals beneath the lights and the simple, sporting windshield.

192 bottom A 1953 parade of Corvettes. Great emphasis was placed by Chevrolet on its new sports model destined to represent the classic American muscle car.

193 The front end of the 1953 Corvette. Note the single rather than double headlight (as was to appear in the 1958 model). The design in 1956 created a hollow in the side.

193

"La dolce vita" - style in the 60's and 70's
ITALIAN DESIGN - THE TRIUMPHS OF PININFARINA

A chapter has not yet been dedicated to open-topped cars designed in Italy, the country that has been most prolific in terms of creativity, design and expert coachbuilders. This seems the right moment to consider the achievements of the country which has given birth to Bertone, Castagna, Ghia, Giugiaro, Pininfarina and Zagato to mention only a few. From the second half of the 1960's until well into the 1970's it was the Italians who dictated how sports cars should be styled, and the greatest Italian designer of them all was Pininfarina. From a stylistic point of view, the first example of the glories to follow was the direct descendant of the Alfa Romeo Giulietta from the decade before, the Giulia Spider

("spider" is the Italian term for sports car). It was nearly identical to its predecessor except for the engine, which grew from 1.3 to 1.6 liters. The only external detail to distinguish the two models was that the Giulia had an air intake on the hood. The Giulia and Giulietta were therefore the forerunners of the magnificent Alfa Spider of the 1960's which was to make history and be the first in a long line of beautiful models. All these Alfas bore the mark of Pininfarina. A contemporary model of the Giulia was the Alfa Romeo 2600 Spider which was produced between 1962-65. This was designed by Touring and was derived from the 2000 which in turn had evolved from the 1900. Being a step up from the Giulia, it cost about 50% more.

Stylistically, the Giulia Spider and 2600 Spider had a lot in common: the nose was made up of 3 parts, two chromed halves of a "moustache" and Alfa's characteristic triangle, in this case very narrow. The 2600 had double headlights, one positioned more centrally than the other. Both had high doors and a large sill. The wheelhouses were well shaped, circular and hid no part of the wheel which generally had a chromed and decorated hubcap. The rear volume sloped gently down towards the bumper which was chopped short at the ends. The slope of the back meant that small fins were created from the taller sides and these fins encompassed the rear lights, perhaps the weakest feature in the design of these two exciting sports

cars. The dimensions were quite different. The Giulia was 12'7" long while the 2600 was 14'7"; the wheelbases were similarly proportioned, 7'4" against 8'1"; and the first was 5' wide while the second 5'6". The weight difference was proportional to everything else with the Giulia at 2470 lbs and the 2600 at 3640 lbs. There were notable differences in the motors: the Giulia had four cylinders in-line producing 91 HP which was later raised to 113 in the faster version of the car. Top speed was therefore increased from 107 to 113 mph. The 2600 had six cylinders in-line which produced 145 HP to give a top speed of 123 mph. The two models sold pretty well in the first three years of production - roughly 10,300 Giulias and

194 top Dustin Hoffman jumps out of his Alfa Romeo Spider in the film "The Graduate". The low height of the car allowed for easy entry and exit; doors were often optional in roadsters.

194-195 Pinin Farina's interest in streamlining was always apparent. Note the homogeneity of the bodywork that resembles a hood fitted onto the chassis. The silver paint enhances the smooth surfaces and helps to soften the apparent overall solidity. This Alfa Romeo, immediately recognizable from the shield-shaped grill on the front, is the 6C 2500 SS from 1947.

195 top In the family of Italian open tops of the 1960's and 70's, the Giulia Spider came after the Giulietta and before the Duetto.

195 center At the start of the 1960's, Fiat brought out a small but finely detailed sports car, the 1500. In 1961 it was made slightly more powerful and the name was changed to the 1600 S. The power was raised from 80 to 100 HP and top speed increased from 106 to 109 mph.

195 bottom One thousand Alfa Romeo GTC cabriolets were built between 1966-67 but it was overshadowed by the launch of the Spider.

2,250 examples of the 2600.

Nineteen sixty-three brought the Fiat 1500 Cabriolet, an upgrade of the 1959 Fiat 1200 sports car. Its lines were spare and square even in the later 1600S version. As was typical of the time, the grill consisted of rectangular elements which covered the whole of the nose only leaving the lights at the side.

This too was designed by Pininfarina and analogies with the Giulia Spider were to be seen; for instance, the rear lights were also housed in small fins though in the Fiat they were less obvious as the car's back end was flatter and squarer than the Alfa's. The Fiat also went out of production in 1965.

1966 was a year full of brilliant models and commercial successes. The first group comprised the Iso Grifo by Bertone, the Fiat Dino Spider and the Ferrari 365 California; the second group included the Fiat 124 Sport Spider and the Alfa Romeo Spider better known in Italy as the Duetto (and later in the US as the Graduate, from the film of the same name in which Dustin Hoffman drove one up the coast of California).

With the exception of Bertone's Iso Grifo, the rest were designed by Pininfarina and his collaborators.

The Ferrari 365 California seems a bridge between the past and the future, and between Europe and the US. The rear, for example, had a flat and slightly sloping rear panel while the sides sloped outward to create a very wide "V" like the flat of a shovel. This is the same design seen in

American convertibles once the vertical fins from the 1950's were altered to form smooth, wide and flat surfaces. The Ferrari's door handles were unusual too in that they were made of thin metal strips laid over a deep futuristic hollow scooped partly out of the door and partly out of the rear volume. The nose was characterized by a flattened elliptical grill and the motor compartment was very short so leaving room to

the pop-up secondary lights.

The main beam lights were protected by a transparent streamlined cover. Under the hood lurked a 60° V12 capable of producing 320 HP. Maximum speed was 153 mph but only 14 were ever made.

Pininfarina's Fiat 124 Sport Spider was one the most elegant, balanced and mechanically valid sports cars of the decade

196-197 top Design of this Ferrari 275 GTS started out without the emphasis that was usually placed on non-mass produced models. It was built to compete in the growing market of small sports cars but it should be remembered that under the hood there was the usual 12 cylinder motor. Despite the efforts of the designer, the body seems a little uninspired in some details but overall it can be considered a pleasing and balanced car. The 275 GTS was introduced in 1964 and 200 were produced.

196 bottom and 197 bottom This is one of the most exciting and stylistically rich Ferraris, the Daytona. Cabriolet and closed body versions were produced by the coachbuilder Scaglietti based on designs by Pininfarina. This page shows the first, 1969, series with the lights visible though protected by a Plexiglas cover (left) and the later version with pop-up lights. This excellent and elegant car managed to combine sobriety and aggressiveness in its design. The shape of the front is strongly innovative, dominated by a narrow strip of lights just above the slender bumper. Only 121 examples of the 365 GTS/4 Daytona Spyder were produced which gives them a very high value today.

It made its debut at the 1966 Turin Motor Show beside the Fiat Dino Spider (close relation of the Ferrari Dino). It enjoyed great commercial and racing success, coming on as strongly as any other sports car in modern times. Although the World Rally Championship was held out of the Fiat's reach by the unbeatable Lancia Stratos, the 124 SS Abarth was runner up three times (1973, '74 and '75), it won two European titles (1972 and '75) and two Italian titles (1970 and '75). The Abarth version of the 124 was also available with an uprated 1.8 liter engine which offered 128 HP.

important car as the Duetto, that the design of the rear volume had already been seen on the 1961 E-type Jaguar, another truly wonderful open-topped car; nor must it be forgotten that the 1900 Disco Volante from 1952 designed by Touring more or less presented the same flattened oval shape.

The first version of the Duetto was produced from 1966-68. Stylistically descended from the 1957 Superflow Disco Volante, it is considered the last production car conceived by Battista Pininfarina before

198-199 *The Alfa Romeo 2600 Spider was extremely fast, reaching 125 mph with the top down. It was developed from the 2000 Spider and appeared for the first time in 1962. The elegant coachwork of this 2-seater was designed by Touring though the coupé was by Bertone. The picture shows actors Rossano Brazzi e Maureen O'Hara.*

Racing success apart, its simple and rational lines were a synopsis of Italian styling, perhaps even more so than the Alfa Romeo Duetto. Its back end was similar in shape to the Ferrari 275 GTS, though naturally with fewer details and poorer trim. Its tail, too, was chopped off. It is a pity that Fiat did not exploit the technological returns or commercial success of this wonderful model more, the only exception being the 850 mini sports car. The third great car to appear in 1966 was the Alfa Romeo Spider. As this model is discussed at length in the monographic section, only the basic points will be dealt with here and the reader is invited to consult the detailed section later on the most famous Italian open-topped car of all time. The first version of the Spider was distinguished by its general clam-like shape. The join between the upper and lower parts of the car were just like the valves of a clam both at the front and behind. The zoological metaphor which stuck, however, was that of "cuttlebone" because of the particular shape of the rear. It must be said, though with all the respect due to such an

198 top *The 1.6 liter version of the Fiat 124 which appeared in 1969 was characterized, as it can be clearly seen in the image, by a honeycomb grill and two swellings on the hood to make space for the new engine.*

198 bottom *The open top version of the 1.4 liter Fiat 124 convertible by Pininfarina was called the Sport Spider. Its first appearance was at the Turin Motor Show in 1966. It had a 4 cylinder, double overhead cam engine and 5 speed gearbox.*

the 1300 Junior 1,796,000 liras. The 1300 had no transparent plastic covering over the front lights. Between 1968 and 1977 it sold 7,237 units. In 1969 both versions were given new looks which were to remain untouched until 1972. The most important innovation once again concerned the tail which was now chopped short by 5 inches though the rear volume increased its baggage carrying capacity. The windshield became more inclined on both versions and the 1300 still had no light covers. The 2 liter version arrived in 1971, which was really designed for the American market; the US absorbed 60% of total production (38,379 units). Environmental pollution regulations meant that the car had to have mechanical fuel injection to meet the targets. The new engine took the new 2000 Veloce (name of the European version) to 124 mph. This basic version stayed in production until 1982 and the body design fortunately underwent no serious changes. Other versions were produced, but they were only different configurations of the existing motors and fittings.

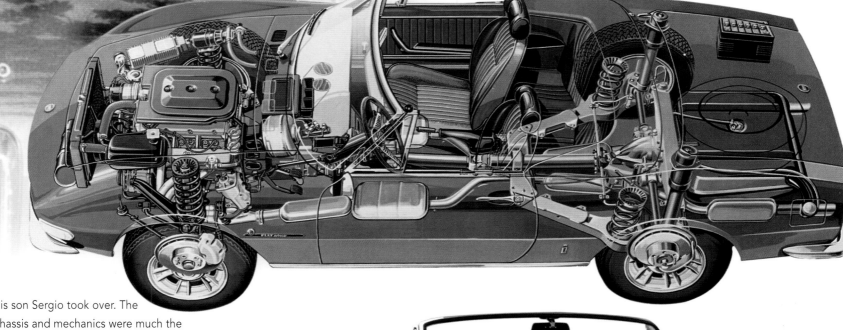

his son Sergio took over. The chassis and mechanics were much the same as the Giulia it replaced. The 1750 Veloce came out in 1967, offering more refined lines and an even livelier motor. As the Alfa Romeo Spider had rear wheel drive, rigid suspension and a small cockpit, the driving experience was similar to that of a small racing car and the more vigorous engine was therefore in keeping with the spirit of the car. The Duetto-based models are all distinguished by a horizontal groove that stretches from the front wheelhouse, through the door and rear bumper, right around to the tail. The 1750's famous "cuttlebone" tail was even more tapered than that of the first series, and these were bought by 8,701 customers. 1968 brought the Duetto a younger brother, a 1.3 liter version called the 1300 Junior. Alfa's marketing department had suggested producing two versions of the 1.6 model, one with an upbeat motor, the other with a less powerful, less "race-like" engine which would also cost less: the 1750 Veloce cost 2,312,000 liras at the time,

199 The 1969 Fiat Dino 2400 Spider was developed from the 2000 Spider presented three years before. The engine was originally developed by Ferrari for racing, but was later built by Fiat and used in the Dino 206 and 246 GT's.

The Fiat 2400 mainly differed from the previous model by its mask-like grill with double chrome thread, by the absence of the wing nuts on the wheel hubs and by several alterations which were made to instrumentation.

200 top This model comes from a marque which, unfortunately, is mentioned rarely in this book, Maserati. The reason is that the company reduced marketing of open-topped cars to a minimum to be able to direct money towards racing. This is the A6GCS 2000 Sport Spider from 1955 designed by Pinin Farina. Note the curved and pronounced fairings and the slim windshield that was reduced to a small bell shape in the single seater version. It had no top of course.

200 center Here is one of the most controversial models in Ferrari's history, the Dino GTS. The car was designed at Pininfarina's urging, who insisted Ferrari build a mid-engined car. The Dino was a modest success and this 246 GTS could be considered the standard for small contemporary and future sporting GTs. Enzo Ferrari gave strict orders that the car should not bear the Ferrari badge.

The list of brilliant Italian sports cars certainly does not end here but there is no space to list the achievements of other great coachbuilders such as Vignale; just enough, though, to mention one of the great geniuses of automobile history, Giorgetto Giugiaro, whose functional interpretation of the car means he has been little involved with the design of convertibles.

Discussion of the 1960's will end with two superb Maseratis, the Ghibli by Ghia and the Mistral by Frua, and with another successful Ferrari convertible, the Daytona GTS/4 Pininfarina. These three all gave great performance. The Ghibli could touch 175 mph, an unforgettable experience in an open-topped car!

Following the Daytona, Ferrari offered the Dino 246 GTS with a heavy roll bar which categorizes it as a targa, i.e. a car with no soft top but with a removable hard top.

This was an epic time for GT's and Pininfarina's style infected many of his colleagues. Their splendid interpretations using the simple, square, sculptural lines that truly belong to open sports cars were certainly no less worthy than those of Pininfarina himself. The cars produced were very costly, gave great performance, had aggressive lines and were sporting to their marrow. They willingly sacrificed comfort and accessories to emphasize their racing aspirations.

After the end of the Second World War, the schools of car truly deserving of celebration are the old-fashioned English sports cars of the 1950's whose designs were evolutions of the prewar models based on the English interpretation of Art Deco and Baroque themes; the American styles of the 1950's for which appearance was everything, with enormous aerodynamic shapes and excessive chromework; and the Italian philosophy of sports car design in the 1960's and 70's which lasted until the second oil crisis.

The outstanding interpreter in this last school of design, as has been made clear simply by the arithmetic involved, was Pininfarina. It was during this period that Battista "Pinin" Farina died, on 3 April 1966, the importance of whom can be compared with that of Enzo Ferrari. Their repeated collaborations, with Battista's son Sergio, attest the great respect and esteem they held for each other. The death of the great coachbuilder and handover to Sergio created no crises for the company as Sergio had practically lived in the factory for years learning his trade as an apprentice. In 1961, the President of Italy decreed that the name "Pinin" Farina could be altered permanently to Pininfarina.

200-201 bottom Another representative Italian sports car, the 1978 Lamborghini Silhouette. Its particular feature is the convex shape of the upper part of the car interrupted only by the absence of a hard top. Starting with this prototype (the most recent model on this page), compare the development of details in the bodywork of GT's during the 1960's and 70's.

201 right This was one of the models that brought public attention closer to Maserati during the 1970's thanks to attractive design, top level performance and limited prices - all qualities that particularly interested the North American market. The model is the Ghibli Spyder, which followed Maserati tradition by being named after a famous wind.

SMALL SPORTS CARS THAT GENERATED GREAT EXCITEMENT

The English and Italian schools have just been championed as the European leaders in open-topped car design but it must also be stated plainly that in Germany, and particularly in the Mercedes design studio, models of historical importance and absolute prestige have continued to be produced with at least one "jewel" in every era. Moreover, Mercedes has always been a reference point for other manufacturers regarding stylistic and technological development.

Mercedes Benz's great talent has been to emphasize the factor that more than any other characterizes the car: functionality. They have shown how functionality can serve to highlight the beauty of a car's form or how it can be an object of admiration in itself. More simply, a car can be as functional as it is beautiful (the aesthetic aspect as a source of pleasure) or as beautiful as it is functional (practicality as a source of well-being). With regard to this last aspect, and outside the context of Mercedes, the world of automobiles in modern times has had its greatest seer in Giorgetto Giugiaro. It would be very interesting to see the results of a collaboration between the Mercedes design studio of Bruno Sacco and Giugiaro's Italdesign but that is just wishful thinking as this book goes to press. Returning to the 1960's, the Pininfarina star was at its apex just as Battista Farina, known as "Pinin", died. In the United States, as shall be described in

the next chapter, the fairytale creations with their glittering chrome disappeared. But in Europe as a whole and particularly in Great Britain there was a wave of original sports cars, roadsters and cabriolets, big and small, economical and luxurious, powerful and less so.

The cabriolets were represented by the unique 1961 Citroën DS and the plethora of elegant, luxurious Mercedes but this chapter is more concerned with the production of roadsters and

sports cars between 1960 and 1977 in Germany, Great Britain and France.

The principal German manufacturers were of course BMW and Mercedes, to which can be added Porsche with the 356 and the unfortunate 914; Volkswagen with the Beetle (at its peak throughout this period in its various guises); Opel with the ephemeral GT Cabrio; and DKW with the F12 roadster.

BMW had not considered the demand for open-topped cars as something incidental or sporadic, but their models were not an unbroken line. In the 1970's, however, their philosophy changed and their line of completely open cars ceased. The cause was an amazing stubbornness on the part of BMW and their trusty coachbuilder Baur who together created a series of open tops with rigid uprights that made the cockpit look like an aquarium. It is better to pass straight on.

202 bottom This picture proves how sight of a small part is often enough for a great car to be recognized. This is the Jaguar E-type's first series, here a 4.2 liter from 1964.

203 top This 4 cylinder Porsche 914 found little success with the public, maybe because it was so atypical of the Stuttgart (Germany) company. It was rather square with a targa top, i.e. a removable hard top.

202 top This model was a development of the Mercedes SL line that started with the 190 and 300 SL Roadster in the mid-50's. It is the 280 which went on sale in 1968. The engine was another 6 cylinder, in-line model that was able to produce 170 HP. Top speed was 125 mph.

203 bottom This Jensen Healey was sold from 1972-76. It had a smaller engine than Jensen usually used, a four cylinder, 1973cc model. Maximum speed was 122 mph. The best known model from Jensen was probably the V8 powered Interceptor.

The open-topped Mercedes were divided into two ranges: the SL's, pure sports cars with above average performance, two sofa-like front seats and modern lines with a long, low grill decorated with the 3 pointed star; and the SE series, luxurious convertibles with soft lines and a traditional, large, square, temple-like grill. In both cases the forms are elegant without extravagance but with emphasis on driver and passenger comfort. There is no doubting the impression the SL's and Pagodas (the nickname given to the versions whose concave hard tops resembled the oriental building) made on drivers of all other types of car.

In Great Britain the strong presence of small marques specializing in the production of roadsters created a wide choice of models. The classic English style based on the designs of the 1930's continued to have its admirers but during the 1970's and 80's demand dropped as the oil crisis took its toll and consumers looked to more modern, equally exciting and certainly more comfortable models. Leaving aside the classic Morgan, here is a short list of the more important English models of this period.

Winning a prize for being one of the ugliest cars of the decade, or longer, is the Daimler SP 250 of 1960 of which 2,648 examples were produced. Right from the shape of its nose, this open top declared its lack of appeal. The flattened oval grill stuck out and was decorated with an ugly metal frame; the headlights extended from two large pipes projecting from the fenders (like in the Porsche 911 but with the opposite effect); at the bottom of the front wheelhouse, the rim was continued towards the door thus creating an unnecessary curve which was copied at the back end (itself crowned with small fins). Only the spoked wheels saved the car with the traditional Jaguar wheel guards.

While on the subject of Jaguar, an exciting racing model well worthy of inclusion - and probably more a precursor of the immortal E-type than even the C and D-types - was the XK SS from 1957. Only 16 were ever made which has sent its

value to the stars. Its shape can best be described by separating the front from the back. The front returned fenders to importance with large, well-shaped and very tapered models; the hood was unusually short (overall length was only 12'20", 18 inches shorter than the E-type) and ended at the base of the windshield that was so curved as to resemble a crash helmet visor. The doors were very square but curved in section. The rear of the XK SS was shaped in the form that was to be known in the 1966 Alfa Romeo Duetto as "cuttlebone". The transverse section has often been described as convex but seems more of an ellipse. The bumper was a subtle chrome half-moon. The performance was remarkable thanks to the 3.5 liter, 6 cylinders in-line which produced 253 HP and gave a top speed of 147 mph. Shortly after, Roadster and Drophead Coupé (convertible) versions were produced.

Aston Martin brought out the DB4 and DB5

models in 1961 and 1963 respectively. The latter was made famous by James Bond in the film "Goldfinger" with a model that had revolving license plates, cutting wheel guards, an oil spray, a bullet-proof shield, machine guns in the headlights and ejector seats. In reality, the DB5 was a very costly GT with ferocious power hidden under a sober exterior. Another top-of-the-range model was the Jensen Interceptor Mk III which was unusual for the size of its 8 cylinder Chrysler engine, 7.2 liters.

Among the more reasonably priced models there was the 1961 Triumph TR4, the 1962 Lotus Elan and Austin Healey Mk II, the 1963 MGB and later the 1975 Triumph TR7.

Besides the Citroën DS 19 (see the section of monographs) the French also produced two Peugeots, the 404 Pininfarina from 1966 and the 1968 504; Renault brought out the Caravelle in 1962 which sold alongside the Floride already on the market.

204 and 204-205 This 1957 Jaguar XK SS was produced four years before the original and fascinating E-type. The rear is practically the same as the flying saucer shape of the E-type except for the shape and position of the lights and the curved fenders. Note the chrome double exhaust with baffle on the left side near the door.

205 top James Bond's most famous car, the Aston Martin DB5, produced from 1963-65. The front was slightly different from that of its predecessor, the DB4 - the headlights were protected by a sloping transparent cover - but the chrome weave of the trapezoid grill remained unchanged. The DB5 had a six cylinder, 3995cc engine that powered the car to 150 mph.

205 bottom The Austin Healey 3000 was produced in three series called the MK I, MK II and MK III between 1959-68. All had a 2.9 liter engine but they were gradually increased in power until the last developed 149 HP. There were minimal differences aesthetically: the MK II differed from the MK I (shown) by having a hood that remained in sight when folded down while the MKIII was larger overall.

206 left Brigitte Bardot relaxes on her Renault Caravelle S Spider. The picture was taken in 1962 at her villa in St. Tropez.

206 right An elegant blue example of the 1965 Citroën DS 21, known as the "shark" or the "iron" for its unusual body shape. Its real name, Désirée Speciale, was shortened to DS as the abbreviation sounds like the French word for goddess. This French cabriolet offered many technological novelties, such as an automatic clutch, steering-controlled headlight direction and hydropneumatic suspension.

Both Renaults were tiny sports cars with small engines; the first series of the Floride was a great commercial success selling 177,122 units in 3 years. Both the Caravelle and the Floride had unpretentious simple lines; they were square like the BMW 700 but more pleasing. The two models were very similar and it was not easy to distinguish them. Their dimensions were almost identical as were the fins, the wheelhouses and the ridges down the sides. The motors grew progressively in size: the 1959 Floride's 845cc increased to 956cc in the 1962 version and 1108cc in the 1962 Caravelle.

The two Peugeots were more powerful, more refined and in step with the trends of the time. Pininfarina and Peugeot often collaborated and in

the case of the 404 this could be seen in the long, wide grill with its five horizontal chrome bars and in the clean lines of the side profile emphasized by a chrome strip the length of the body. The motor was a 1618cc, 4 cylinder, 70 HP unit. The 1969 504 was more aggressive and modern and in its three years of production, 7,803 examples were sold. Although common in the US, the 504's double headlights were still unusual for Europe. The car was as small as the 404 but the wheelhouses were wider and the nose narrower but heavy. This last feature was indicative of the styling of Peugeot convertibles to come in the 1970's, for example, the elegant, restyled 504 that appeared in 1971; in that model the double headlights were replaced

207 top right Advertising for the Targa version of the Porsche 911 from 1967. This is actually a hybrid: there is no glass rear window and the roll bar is clearly seen. The upper section of the illustration shows the various configurations possible, from the completely open to the completely closed version. The 911 Targa soon acquired a fixed glass rear window, however, for improved sealing and visibility.

206-207 The Renault Caravelle S. The 'S' stands for the second series made between 1962-63 and fitted with a slightly more powerful engine, 956cc instead of the original 845cc.

by a single, large and rectangular light and a lovely V6 engine was introduced in 1974.

The attentive reader may now be harboring the thought that something has been left out: very little, actually: the Porsche 911, Jaguar E-type, Lotus Seven and Triumph Spitfire. These open-topped beauties have been left till last to be the proverbial cherries on the cake. Unfortunately, there is only space for a superficial examination. The Porsche 911 was not Ferdinand Porsche's creation, but he was its spiritual father. The brilliant engineer's honored place in the history of the car is principally due to the Volkswagen Beetle and the Porsche 356 which descended from it. But the 911 was clearly the next evolutionary step

from the 356, so in truth every rear-engined Porsche is a logical descendant of Dr. Porsche's work.

The two open-topped versions of the 911 were the Targa and the Cabriolet. The latter will be discussed in the section on open-topped cars from the 1980's. The 911 Targa, on the other hand, has a fixed rear window and C-pillar as in a coupé. The space between the pillar and the windshield can be filled with a removable hard top. The widespread distribution of this version has made it natural to extend the name "targa" to models with similar characteristics, a practice that is not at all welcomed by Porsche.

The Jaguar E-type was a thoroughbred open

top and merits a place of honor on anybody's list. Its story began in 1961.

The E-type had many distinctive features, all noteworthy, which were combined with a generous motor and an overall line which married the development of several styling philosophies: the evolution of the old-fashioned 1930 styles, the search for balance between the front and rear volumes, the experience matured in Jaguar's many racing successes and the return to rounded forms in the design of the fender. Which of the three versions is more correct one cannot know.

The first series of E-type appeared in 1961 and without doubt had the most attractive rear end of all the production models. It appeared the sober maturation of the XK SS spoken of at the start of the chapter. The car had a remarkable overhang and the distance between the axles seemed a bridge over eternity. Such a long wheelbase emphasized the car's amazingly slender, lovely and fragile profile even more.

The second series appeared in 1968; it was largely identical to the first and supplanted not the 3.8 liter version (1961-64) but the 4.2 (1964-68). It kept the same engine but added a little zest (increased from 259 HP to 268); very little else was altered. The two series could only be differentiated externally by the different layout of the secondary lights. The dimensions of the third series (1971-75) were completely altered. The car was longer (15'4"), taller (4'0") and wider (5'5") but, more importantly, powered by the infinitely capable V12.

The engine size was 5343cc which developed 272 HP to give a maximum speed of 151 mph.

The wheelbase grew proportional to the increase in length to reach 8'8".

In the authors' opinion, the E-type is one of the five most beautiful open-topped cars of all time.

Still in Great Britain, the eclectic and inexhaustible genius of Colin Chapman was responsible for the Lotus Seven. Chapman was a passionate racer and managed to bolt together the Lotus Seven nearly, but not quite, infringing the racing regulations with his engineering contrivances. The Lotus Seven was an open top as ugly as it was exciting to drive. It had no doors, no top and no concession to comfort of any kind. In front it was almost a single seater racing car. The view from the front was mainly of the open suspension and an enormous radiator

mouth that didn't cease growing over the years. The front fenders were taken from a motorcycle; those at the back were partly integrated into the bodywork. In 1961 the front fenders grew in length to resemble the old-fashioned classics which preceded it; in 1963 the relationship grew even closer when the car became almost comfortable with the addition of an inch or two in length. Over the years the engine size increased: from 1172cc in 1957 to 1498 in 1961 (the Super Seven) and to 1599 in 1963.

The Lotus Seven is one of the models that can

boast the largest number of imitations and replicas. First of all there is the licensee, Caterham Motors, then the Dutch Donkervoort D8, the English Panther Kallista and the American Dakota F1 Roadster.

The MGB appeared in 1962 and was produced in three series until 1980. It was a commercial smash selling over 500,000 units which places it in the Olympus of best-selling open-topped cars of all time. Its English rival, the Triumph Spitfire (1962-81) sold 245,000 and was produced in four series.

208 top This man, Colin Chapman, made automobile history as the creator of Lotus cars. Half expert technician and half successful salesman, his stubbornness helped him produce a small, powerful and easily handled racing car which enjoyed great success in its class. It was the Lotus Seven, seen here with its creator.

208 center and 208-209 top The Lotus Seven was practically a go kart that drove like a Formula 1 single seater. English convertible lovers saw in this car a continuation of the roadster style of the 1930's, 40's and 50's which was enough to bring the model success in a

road version as well as on the track. The car's continued success was ensured by the company Caterham and others which still create more or less faithful replicas. The picture on the left shows the nose of the first, 1959, series. On the right, a Series 3 from 1965 which was fitted with an 85 HP Ford Cosworth engine. Note the rear trunk, a timid concession to functionality. The Lotus Seven was made in four series plus a Super Seven.

208-209 bottom This Jaguar E-type has its top up but nothing detracts from its aggressiveness. This 1964 example was fitted with a 4.2 liter engine which gave 259 HP.

Triumph was also responsible for the TR series, which was begun in the 1950's and ended in 1981 with the TR7 and TR8.

A comparison of the characteristics of the two models shows that the MGB had a 1.8 liter block that remained through all the years. The Spitfire's started much smaller at 1.1 liters. The power developed was naturally proportional to the engine size with the MGB giving 95 HP and the Spitfire 62 HP. The difference in top speed was 13 mph, 107 vs. 94. The differences in size were less marked with the Spitfire (11'11") giving away 12" to the larger MGB which was also taller and wider and with a greater track. The wheelbase, on the other hand, was more differentiated, with the MGB's being considerably longer, 7'6" vs. 6'6". This gave it a much sleeker appearance.

As regards shape, the MGB had greater authority with its subdued, fundamental lines; the Spitfire however was admired for its brash and cheeky image which, despite having no claims to superiority, let the owner believe himself the equal of any MG.

210 top This famous English sports car from the 1960's is the TR4 from the even more famous Triumph company. The lines are very similar to the French and Italian style; the motor was more than acceptable with its 2138cc producing 100 HP for a top speed of 113 mph. All the TR series were very popular, particularly this model of which 40,000 were sold. The round headlights were its most characteristic feature with the two bumps they created in the hood.

210 center The English model MGB had the difficult job of replacing the successful MGA and it outdid its predecessor by far: 512,733 were sold to make it a standard among sports cars. It was quite able to match the lower-echelon Alfa Romeos and Porsches in performance. This small, lively and relatively cheap car with very sharp handling was very popular and even today there are many who value it highly. It had a 4 cylinder engine and was 12'8" long and 4'11" wide.

210 bottom Comparison of the 1960's models on this page against this Triumph TR6 from the 1970's gives an indication of how sports car styles changed. The friendly curves and rounded designs were replaced, especially at the rear, by squarer and more angular shapes.

211 The nose of one of the last MGAs - from 1962 - with its rectangular grill, in the center of which the trademark MG Octagon appears. The first MGA appeared in 1955.

ANYTHING GOES IN THE USA

After the splendid, unbridled 1950's when the attempt to maintain the ideals of fun and playfulness was becoming harder and harder in the face of reality, the 1960's saw the reshaping of American cars and a decrease in their decorative features. It is difficult to point to a trend in this decade that was to last and at the same time be common to all manufacturers.

The watchword for the 1950's had been "sparkle"; now it was "anything goes". A few examples are enough to demonstrate the most important stylisms that car design underwent, but it should not be forgotten that while engine sizes increased, the occasional technological innovation - the Corvair's rear engine, GM's early use of turbocharging, and Pontiac's fiberglass OHC drive belt - went largely unrewarded. The 1957 agreement between manufacturers that performance not be mentioned in car advertising had broken down by the mid 1960's, and a war to find brute power and acceleration was now on.

The development and events the country was living through were also of great relevance.

America experienced constant economic acceleration after the recession of 1958 but the Cold War threatened and the nation placed its hopes on the youngest (and the first Catholic) president in its history, John F. Kennedy, whose personal impact on style, thought and interethnic and social relations was notable. Kennedy was attributed with being the true catalyst behind the space program which put a man on the moon in 1969 (like aeronautics, the space industry was also to influence car design).

During the 1960's, the overall dimensions of cars were reduced only slowly but the extravagant features at the rear end shrank much faster. Sometimes they changed shape, sometimes they folded over towards the outside of the body and then, faster and faster, they disappeared completely having been consigned to a style that was part of the past. Here are some examples of those three categories. The first group comprises models whose fins persisted though in a smaller format: most prominent was the Cadillac Eldorado Biarritz, the model most compromised by its own style of ostentation, then there was the Buick LeSabre and Chrysler 300F, all three from 1960. In 1961, the Chrysler New Yorker and Imperial Crown still maintained noticeable fins. The second group preferred to lay their fins flat like a paper aeroplane; examples were the 1959 Chevrolet Impala and the Edsel Ranger and Oldsmobile Super 88 from 1960. The Dodge Polara was a curious case as its fins were transformed into light convex sections that resembled stabilizers on a boat keel. Functionally, all these styling tricks would have little if any effect on vehicle stability.

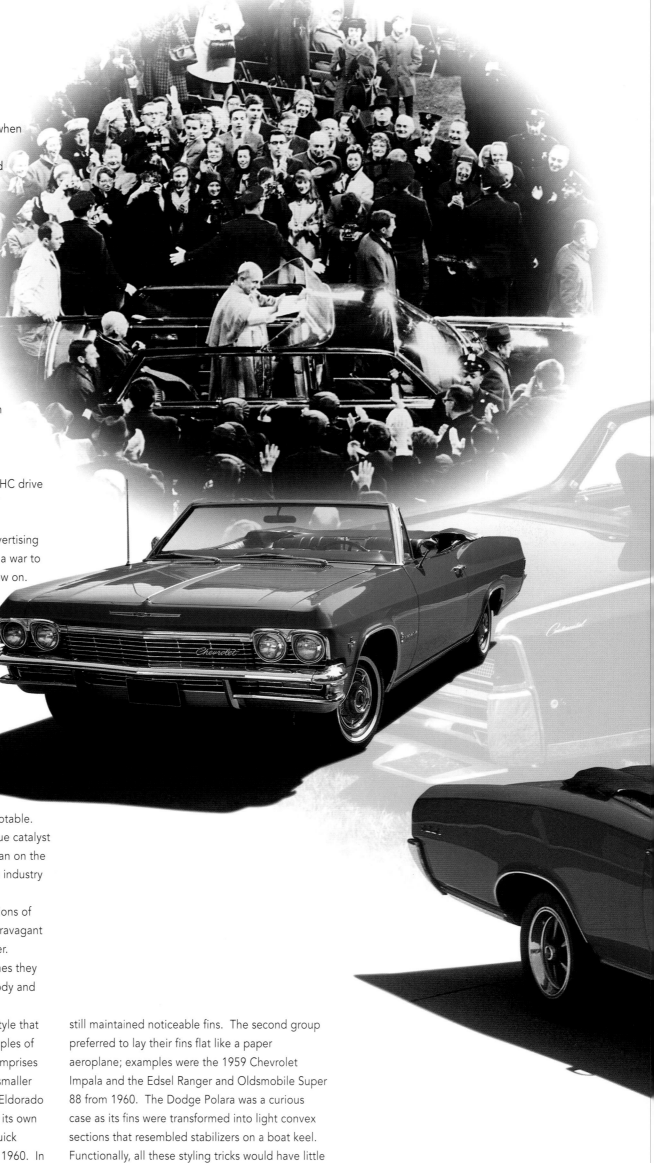

212 top and 212-213 center The Lincoln Continental Limousine, an amazing 21'6" long, in which Pope Paul VI visited the United States and took part in the Eucharist Congress in Bogotà, Colombia.

212 bottom This 1965 Chevrolet Impala has a tapered tail, light years away from the exaggerated rear fins of the 1950's and early 1960's.

213 top The 1964 Continental from Lincoln, a company that is part of the Ford group. It seems the car did not want to forget the fins of the previous decade and discreetly offered them once more on both front and rear fenders.

212-213 bottom The Pontiac GTO was produced from 1964-74. It started as no more than a sports version of the Pontiac Tempest with a 6.4 liter V8 engine producing 300 HP. Characteristic features of the early years were the double headlights arranged vertically and the supplementary lights integrated into the grill with telescopic sights.

The third group comprised nearly all other models. These designs dispensed with the fins altogether and had back ends that were square and flat with rounded edges. In the following 15 years there was a generally clean sophistication of line. The features were common to all the open-topped models and it is odd that in a period of great stylistic freedom (and particularly during a period that was very favorable to the sales of open-topped cars), the only models that refused to follow the herd were the Corvette and Mustang. Maybe it was the extreme popularity of convertibles which discouraged stylistic oddity or experiment.

Among the first models of the new style was the popular 1961 convertible, the Chevrolet Impala, and the luxurious 1962 Ford 500XL Sunliner with its powerful V8 engine. The year that DeSoto went under, 1963, saw the arrival of a new Lincoln Continental, Oldsmobile Starfire, Pontiac Tempest and Ford Falcon Futura. A year later it was the turn of the Pontiac GTO and the Studebaker Daytona.

Thunderbird was still in progress. Over the years it was transformed into a sedan, and though this did nothing to harm sales, the car lost its aggressive, fiery character. It was a little like castrating a stud bull.

Meanwhile the Mustang brought a smile to Ford management, having been sold to a record 418,000+ owners in its first (extra-long) model year. The slender Ford was very much like the European sports cars of the period. In all versions it looked like a proportionally short sports car at only 15 feet long (10 inches more than the Corvette but two feet shorter than the 1955 Thunderbird, the convertible of the older generation) and with a wheelbase of 107 inches. The design was spare with little chrome. A galloping mustang was placed in the center of the grill and the sides had only the air intakes near the rear wheelhouses for decoration. This tautness was the Mustang's trump card after a decade of excess.

Its other key to success was an endless option

At a time when many front end designs were similar (long and narrow with a large weave chrome grill and double headlights), the Studebaker's enormous, square and ugly nose resembled a luxurious English sedan. The Daytona was available as a station wagon, coupé or convertible but was not by any means the company's most beautiful model. Studebaker closed down in 1966.

Nineteen sixty-four was an important year because it celebrated the arrival of the Mustang. When it appeared in the Ford dealers' windows it was clear the Mustang was to be a success, but that it would be one of the largest selling convertibles of all time was a real surprise.

At the time, the work of destroying the lovely

214

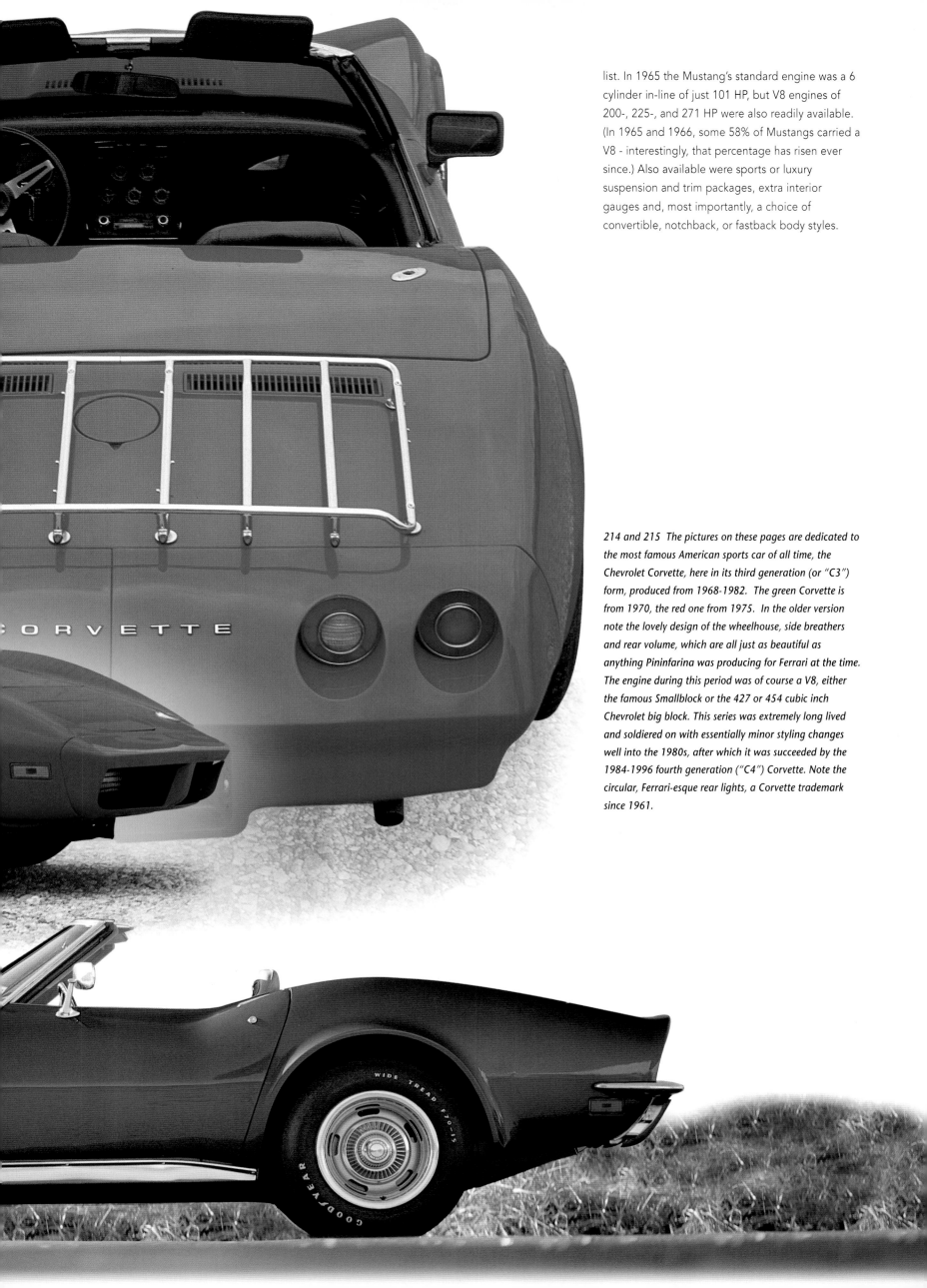

list. In 1965 the Mustang's standard engine was a 6 cylinder in-line of just 101 HP, but V8 engines of 200-, 225-, and 271 HP were also readily available. (In 1965 and 1966, some 58% of Mustangs carried a V8 - interestingly, that percentage has risen ever since.) Also available were sports or luxury suspension and trim packages, extra interior gauges and, most importantly, a choice of convertible, notchback, or fastback body styles.

214 and 215 The pictures on these pages are dedicated to the most famous American sports car of all time, the Chevrolet Corvette, here in its third generation (or "C3") form, produced from 1968-1982. The green Corvette is from 1970, the red one from 1975. In the older version note the lovely design of the wheelhouse, side breathers and rear volume, which are all just as beautiful as anything Pininfarina was producing for Ferrari at the time. The engine during this period was of course a V8, either the famous Smallblock or the 427 or 454 cubic inch Chevrolet big block. This series was extremely long lived and soldiered on with essentially minor styling changes well into the 1980s, after which it was succeeded by the 1984-1996 fourth generation ("C4") Corvette. Note the circular, Ferrari-esque rear lights, a Corvette trademark since 1961.

In 1967 Chevrolet decided to bring out another model that, like the Mustang, Corvette and Mercury Cougar, was to stay in production for many years to come - the Camaro. When fit with one of a number of optional V8s, the lightweight Camaro was among the world's fastest cars.

These small cars dominated the scene in the 1970's; their Mustang-like size earned them the nickname 'ponycars', and made them the American equivalent of the cheaper, smaller cabriolets in vogue in Europe. The European models would not have been popular in the US and would have been considered 'untrendy'.

The extraordinary 1968 Mercury Park Lane stood out from the standardized packaging of other models - it was completely lined with wood-grained panels. By the middle 1960's, a move away from flat, bare sides started to appear; a gentle swelling grew just behind the doors, as seen on the Chevrolet Impala and Mercury Cougar of 1969, the Buick LeSabre of 1970 and even more evident in the Oldsmobile Cutlass Supreme of the same year.

Taken all in all, the 1960s saw American design reach perhaps its highest postwar form; shapes became taut, clean, and elegant, whether oversized or not. These harmonious, tension-filled shapes went far toward hiding excessive length. 1976 brought the end of an era when the Eldorado Convertible went out of production. It had been the most extreme representative of luxury, though luxury of a sparkling, outmoded and gaudy kind. The day the Eldo died, 21 April 1976, has been considered by some as the day American convertibles died. That is certainly wrong, as the Cadillac Eldorado had not represented the era of huge, splendid models for some time - not since it had bowed to the adoption of clean, essential and minimalist lines (as much as a Cadillac convertible is capable of doing). Therefore, either the era of the convertible had already ended or it was just undergoing a change. Not liking epilogues we prefer the second version, although open-topped cars did see an enormous drop in availability, falling from 5.5% of total sales in 1965 to just 0.5% in

1974. After the early 1970's, Chrysler did not make another convertible until the K-cars of the 1980s, and an open Mustang was not available until 1982. 1975 was the end of the road for another prestigious open top, the Buick LeSabre, which had represented a fixed point for convertible lovers since the end of the 1940's. This twenty year period was marked by two distinct spells: The first saw record sales but little true innovation, while the second brought a crisis in sales but a certain development towards more modern and compact forms.

How did the Chevrolet Corvette cope during these two decades? For 1963, the muscular Corvette was an all-new car. Previously available only as an open top, the clean new model was now available as a coupe or convertible. The back was designed in the shape of an ellipse to give a strongly streamlined look to the tail and to balance the modern, pointed nose. The large, rounded wheelhouses were very fluid in their design. As previously mentioned, the standard Smallblock V8

216-217 The sweeping side of the 1969 Cadillac Convertible De Ville. US open cars were not limited to just the Corvette and Thunderbird but also included luxurious and desirable models as in the 1950's. The rear

seems an unending table top (note the streamlining spats on the rear wheels). The engine was an 8 cylinder, 7.7 liter monster. Total length was almost identical to the Cadillac Eldorado Biarritz from the 1950's at 18'5".

engine gave impressive power and speed, which was combined with excellent balance. Then, in 1965, a big block was made optional, first at 396 cubic inches and later with 427 and finally 454 inches. The Corvette can be considered the model which most influenced the style and design of two-door sports cars throughout the decade, and its echo even reached Europe. In 1968 the car was redesigned again, its wheelhouses becoming even more accentuated to emphasize the longer, steeply sloping nose. Where the previous version of the Corvette had a tapered tail, the 1968 model's was cut short and swept into a vertical spoiler. In front, the headlights hid beneath pop-up lids. Still, the 1968 model was longer, heavier, and less pure than before.

217 top This Oldsmobile 4-4-2 is from 1968 and offered two basic motors, 260 and 300 HP. Special editions abounded.

217 center This elegant model, the 1970 Buick LeSabre, occupied the mid-high range of the convertible market. Although it was not as long as the Cadillac Convertible De Ville, it was still longer than average at 18'2".

217 bottom This 1973 Ford Mustang seems slightly tame in a white top and with whitewall tires. The completely redone, Pinto-based 1974 Mustang II was markedly smaller.

217

The recession: small, no-frills convertibles

CONVERTIBLES AND SPORTS CARS IN EUROPE

A couple of petrol crises were more than enough to rock the automobile industry. And if they were not enough alone, there were also economic crises and recessions throughout the western world plus wars, coups d'état, secessions and new geopolitical alignments which revolutionized the modes of thought, living and movement of Europeans and North Americans.

If we add to this backdrop a greater, more pressing attention to devices aimed at increasing active and passive safety (seat belts, airbags, impact bars, progressive and programmed crumple zones, roll-bars, ABS and electronic traction control), ably exploited by marketing experts to convince us to buy new and costly cars, in addition

to the pressing need to build less polluting and more recyclable vehicles which share an increasing number of components, we find ourselves in an extensive and sad panorama of sameness, a widespread poverty of ideas and a lack of interest in convertibles and sports cars in general.

On average, the open-topped cars of the 1980's were uglier, more anonymous and more devoid of ideas than during any other period in the history of the car.

Is it coincidence that an analogous situation was occurring in other industries where the creativity of designers and stylists was required? Certainly not, and it is not surprising that exciting convertibles were not produced in a period in which art, fashion

and design were tired and unexciting. Those who thumb their noses at a gaudy 1950's convertible should humble themselves: Audacity, humor, a desire to amaze and the need to communicate through symbols and fetishes are preferable to boredom, uniformity and standardization - better bright colors than gray. Careful scrutiny of the ranges reveals, however, something interesting underneath. Starting with convertibles, there was nothing new at the top of the heap - the same old Rolls Royces, Bentleys and Mercedes.

But it was the arrival of the mini-convertibles which comprised the huge majority of open-topped cars sold. They were small and cheeky, cheap to buy and cheap to run; these little cars took away

the magic of the concept of the convertible with their lack of grace.

Among these were the Volkswagen Golf Cabrio (among the best-selling convertibles of all time), the Fiat Ritmo Bertone, the Ford Escort and the Peugeot 205. Sports cars offered a little more, but it was simply that being a step up the ladder they could offer a little more in terms of design and singleness of form.

Bear in mind that the terms sports car and roadster here also include models actually called cabriolets or convertibles in that they were open-topped versions of sedans or coupés, but which were closer in nature to sports cars with their dashing performance and line.

218 top This low, athletic sports car is a customized Turbo Esprit. The Esprit renewed the public's love affair with Lotus.

218 bottom The Maserati Spyder was very popular throughout Europe and the United States thanks to its name and low price. The Spyder in the picture was one of the first series sold from 1985-89 and had a 2.5 liter engine with double turbo. This model was followed by the 2.8 which was available until 1994.

219 top This model, the TR8, closed the glorious Triumph TR series and should go down in the history books for that reason alone. It had a 135 HP, V8 engine (the TR7 had only a four cylinder motor) that powered the car to 122 mph.

219 bottom This is a concrete example of how the style of square sports car bodies had become general. This is the Jaguar XJS Convertible which replaced the rounded E-type and was destined for a long, successful career.

220 top and 220-221 The rear and side view of a Ferrari 348 Spider, designed by Pininfarina. It differed from the GTS in that the latter was a targa with a removable hard top. Both versions had a 320 HP (310 for the US) engine able to take the cars to 171 mph. The first series was presented in 1989 but this model is from 1994.

220 bottom This Alfa Romeo Duetto belongs to the fourth and final series but by the mid-1990's this small and famous sports car had lost its magic after its thirty year career. It was replaced by the beautiful, front wheel drive car of the same name.

221 bottom The Ferrari Mondial Cabriolet can be recognized even by non-specialists by the central grill just behind the cab close to the engine.

In general, roadsters began to demonstrate softer shapes than the angled models from the 1970's even if the sides and hood and trunk stayed flat. The search for the perfectly streamlined form went ahead in small steps so as not to upset profiles which, anyway, rarely excited the imagination.

As far as price goes, the Aston Martin DBS V8 and Lagonda were unbeatable. They were sold around the end of the decade and their discreet, fluid beauty was enhanced by their rarity.

There were several Ferraris: the 308 GTS, the Mondial 8 and the Testarossa all in different versions and with different engine configurations. Ferrari fans will no doubt understand if the authors consider these, and those to come in the early 1990's, as among the worst Pininfarina products designed for mass production (relative to the capabilities of the manufacturer, that is). Until then, the intuitions of the designer had always struck gold but from this point on, he seemed stuck in a series of dry, angled forms without the elegance and

simplicity that could turn the most extreme design into a jewel that would shine in any setting. These three GT's - the 308 GTS, more targa than sports car; the dissatisfying Mondial 8 with its unrefined pop-up headlights and decoration along the hood; and the 1985 Testarossa coupe - were all clumsy, show-off designs adding nothing key to the history of open-topped cars. They were exhibitionist but without the self-parody needed that had been seen in models from the past with equally extravagant forms. The Testarossa should have been produced in a limited series to justify the furious infighting between collectors who offered ever larger sums of money, not for the car but just for the sales contract. Used cars were worth more than new ones so that anyone wanting to own one quickly had to pay thousands of dollars over the price. But in the cases of the Testarossa and 512 TR, this turned out to be unnecessary as more than enough of each were produced.

Even the fourth and last generation of the Alfa

Romeo Spider, also by Pininfarina and which had won so many laurels on its first appearance, was certainly not exciting. It looked bulky and had nothing to say for itself.

At a lower price than the Ferraris but still in the luxury class was the Jaguar XJS-C. This had the unenviable task of replacing the E-type. Other English sports cars of the period were the TVR, Reliant Scimitar, Triumph TR7 and TR8 and the MG Midget; all were small, low, square and bursting with verve, if not perhaps speed.

The BMW 3-Series in its various engine sizes was more common. With elegant design and good performance, it marked the German carmaker's return to the production of a high quality open top. Then there was the popular Saab 900, the fast and cheap (but mechanically untrustworthy) Maserati Biturbo Spyder, and the Maserati-assembled Chrysler TC. The TC offered American styling with Italian construction - in other words, combining the worst of both worlds.

The most important model of the 1980's on both sides of the Atlantic was the Porsche 911 Cabrio. However, this model was simply no more than the 911 Coupé devoid of any element above the waistline, windshield apart. The decision not to include it in the list of élite models, despite its fame, was not due to lack of space. Although nothing prohibits the inclusion of the Targa version (already referred to in the chapter of 1970's European open tops) from being defined as an open-topped car due to its removable hard top, it seems to us it is a bit of an impostor compared to sports cars, roadsters, cabriolets and convertibles. Targas try to be coupés but aren't, and due to their excellent qualities and versatility, they deserve a full but separate treatise.

The 911 Cabriolet had an unfortunate top which, when unfolded, deprived the car of the fluidity and rotundity which gave the closed version its wonderful character. At high speed it suffered from ballooning when low pressure created just above the car sucked the top up: the result was very noticeable and ugly. Although requested all over the world, the Cabrio was only a version of the 911 and seemed to have less personality than other open-topped cars included in the section of monographs. We hope the reader understands, if not agrees with, this choice.

In 1989 the Speedster version was produced. The name referred to the 1950's model with which it shared a high and aggressive rear end, more so than its reference model, the 911. The Speedster was also 1 inch lower.

The 1980's were overall a depressing decade though in 1986 a wonderful model was produced almost by chance, the BMW Z1 Roadster. It was small with many technological innovations which were then used in successive models, sedans and sports. The Z1 had a curious system for getting in: the doors did not open but slid down vertically to hide in the car body below. The welcome for this fun car was enthusiastic and the number of requests far outweighed expectations. It was the only true open top from BMW in this period that did not stint on functionality or investment. It was a real two-seater built for pure fun.

222 bottom The streamlined rear end of this 1989 Porsche 911 Speedster makes it look particularly aggressive. The name evoked the memory of the 356 Speedster of 1955 but the modern version did not have a long life. The most popular versions were the Targa and the Carreras 2 and 4.

222-223 The BMW Z1 originated as a styling exercise but was so enthusiastically received that it was put into production. It was a real roadster, predecessor of the magnificent Z3 and its successor, the evocative Z07 showcar. The most important feature of the Z1 was the electrically operated door which opened by sliding down into a bay under the body. The car's mechanical systems and geometry of the wheels contained innovations that were later adopted on more popular mass production models, sedans in particular. Only 8,000 examples of the Z1 were produced between 1988-91, making it very popular with collectors. Top speed was 143 mph.

223 top Before launching the MGF, which put the BMW-Rover group at the top of the roadster market around the world in the late 1990's, Rover brought MG out of hibernation with this model based on the MGB called the MG RV8. It was produced from 1992-95.

223 bottom The picture seems out of place but the car is actually contemporary to those on the same pages. It is the 1990 version of the Morgan Plus 8, which remains faithful to its original early postwar design except for certain modifications required to meet safety standards.

Too many targas in the USA

224-225 top The 1991 Mercury Capri XR2 shows how similar 1980-90 American and European open tops were in their flat, square and fairly impersonal designs before the "renaissance" of the mid-90's. The Capri's dimensions were typical of European cars as was the lively 4 cylinder engine.

224-225 bottom This 1992 Pontiac Trans Am demonstrates the recent North American style of bare, functional lines; it might almost be a study in minimalism, despite its sporting character. Not to be missed are the small tail fillips.

The grayness of the 1980's spread its pallor over the whole of the automobile industry. It was barren of ideas but, more importantly, it had only limited desire to produce open-topped cars. If it is any comfort, the decade was also devoid of closed sports cars, known in Europe as coupés and in the US as two-door sports.

The American sports cars that were produced were largely the same, with only the Corvette standing out as a car with great personality. But by now the Corvette was a niche product for a small specialist market, and no longer able to affect the creativity of designers in a positive manner. It was not, however, entirely the fault of the designers that this trough existed: It was the pragmatic and rational public which no longer expected great cars - or particularly fun cars. Even the glorious Mustang

had lived through humiliating moments. One of the most famous models in the history of the American convertible, it had spent much of the 1970s as a spinoff of the economical, much-reviled Pinto model. Then, in 1979, it was totally revised with a new, squarish body based on the "sheer look" of the 1970's and placed on Ford's ubiquitous Fox platform (which also supported the Fairmont, LTD, and other cars). During the 1960's the Mustang had been a nervous, exciting open top which brought excitement to the lives of two generations; during the 1980s, this heritage would slowly be re-captured by a long succession of Mustang GT and Mustang LX models carrying Ford's powerful 4.9 liter V8. Called the "5 Liter" for marketing reasons, this powerplant grew ever stronger through the decade, and on the lightweight Fox platform, the

225 top right This Cadillac Allanté was designed and assembled in the US before being shipped to the Pininfarina workshops in Italy where the electric top was installed and fittings were finished off.

Mustang V8's easily kept pace with the Chevy Smallblock powered Camaro and Firebird.

Some saw the square shape of the 1979-1994 Mustang as vulgar; others considered it taut and aggressive. Either way, in T-top and convertible (debuted 1981) form, the Mustang spent the decade as America's most popular performance car - even though its base engines were always 4 or 6 cylinder cooking motors.

Meanwhile the Corvette, totally redesigned and released as the first 1984 model of the year (there were no 1983 Corvettes) put American sports cars once again on par with Europe's finest. With its Cross-Fire Injected Smallblock V8 and world-leading .90g cornering grip, the new Corvette leapfrogged its aging predecessor and once again competed head-on with Porsche and Ferrari, in

performance if not price and status.

In mid 1986 the Corvette Convertible made its reappearance after an 11-year hiatus, with an optional plastic hardtop and strategic chassis reinforcements to combat cowl shake. The decade ended for the Corvette with the announcement of the ultra-mean, ultra-powerful ZR1 option. Featuring a 4-cam, 32-valve, 385 HP all-aluminum

V8 engine designed by Lotus and manufactured by Mercury Marine, the ZR1 was the fastest Corvette ever (180+ mph). Like all hardtop Corvettes of this generation, the ZR1's roof panel was fully removable, making it a true targa. No ZR1 convertibles were made for public consumption.

Cadillac had been a pilot fish during the 1950's and 1960's, charting the waters of open-air

opulence. During the 1980's it produced more modest versions of the Eldorado and Biarritz, but the most interesting product from the firm in years was the Allante (designed and assembled by Pininfarina), a 2 seat luxury convertible based on a shortened front-wheel-drive Seville platform with a transversely mounted V8.

But perhaps the most representative American model of all during the 1980's was the trim, stylish LeBaron Convertible from Chrysler. Very cheaply priced with a host of standard accessories, the LeBaron Convertible grew from modest beginnings (88 HP from a transverse 4 cylinder engine driving the front wheels) to an impressive 152 turbocharged HP. The wasp-waist styling recalled American designs of the 1960's.

THE FIRST JAPANESE OPEN TOPS

226 top *The Mazda MX-5 debuted as a 1990 model, though Mazda began toying with the idea of a small, rear-drive, traditional open sports car in 1983. It went on sale in mid-1989.*

The Japanese had made a name for themselves with technological ability, mechanical reliability and low prices during the 1970s, and during the early and middle 1980s they turned their attention to sports cars in a big way. Only one example - the Mazda RX7 Convertible - was a true open top, but the Nissan Z-car, Toyota Supra, Toyota MR2 and Mitsubishi Starion all offered T-top roofs as a widely ordered option.

Japan's sports car history was not nearly as bereft as many Westerners imagined. From the early 1960s, Honda (Sports 360 through 800),

Nissan (Fairlady 1200 through 2000) and Toyota (Publica Sport, 800 Sports) had all gained valuable experience with 2 seat open tops. Japan's history with closed GT models was even richer, including the radical rotary engined Mazda Cosmo L10A (1967), the Yamaha designed Toyota 2000 GT from the same year, and of course the now-legendary 6 cylinder Nissan 240Z, first revealed in 1969.

In the end, the most important open top of the 1980s would also be Japanese: the Mazda MX-5 Miata. Intentionally modeled on the best

British and Italian offerings of the 1960s, it was small, fun to handle and the first true interpretation of a roadster since the bleak days of the 1970's. Blessed with a huge pent-up market for inexpensive, high quality, traditionally designed sports cars, the Miata was successful even against the the reborn Lotus Elan, the aging but classic Alfa Romeo Spider, and the admittedly uninspired Mercury Capri XR2. Introduced in mid 1989 as a 1990 model, more than 450,000 Miatas were sold before the redesigned 1999 model was debuted in January of 1998.

226 center The Honda SSM was a prototype roadster made to commemorate the 1963 S500 Sport, Honda's first volume-built car.

226 bottom and 227 bottom The Honda del Sol is only 13' long, 5'6" wide and 4'1" high. It has an optional system for stowing the rigid hard top in the luggage compartment which operates either electrically or manually. This Japanese targa was introduced in 1992 to replace the coupe-only Honda CRX.

227 top The Toyota Celica cabrio is the open-topped version of the company's most famous coupé. The picture shows the profile of the latest version, which can be recognized by the four fixed round headlights in place of the pop-ups of its predecessor.

Convertibles heading for the 21st century

CONVERTIBLES AND SPORTS CARS ONCE MORE ON COURSE

228 top This model marked Rover's return to the small sports car and roadster market. The mid-mounted engine of this MGF gives excellent handling that makes it a joy to drive on twisting roads.

228 bottom and 229 bottom The Mercedes SLK is distinguished among late-1990 convertibles for its top. As seen in the image on the left, the rigid metal roof is automatically retracted by an electrohydraulic mechanism.

The 20th century, like this history, is coming to a close. Convertibles are now heading for the 21st century in a confident mood, having overturned the trend of falling sales during 1996-97. Now it is sports cars and roadsters which are leading the field. During the second half of the 1990's there have been many new models to awake the interest of motorists fed up with the same old anonymous boxes on wheels, and trend-setters are once again seen in powerful open tops.

Some events were clear signs of the renaissance of open-topped cars: for example, the opening of the first BMW factory in the United States in South Carolina for the production of their successful Z3 roadster, and the debut of a low-priced Mercedes convertible, the SLK, which reinterprets the concept of the electric retractable hard top.

At the same time, a quick look at social behavior around the western world shows that after decades of containment there has been a sudden reawakening of the desire to overstep the limits, to feel liberated in a car and less guilty of atmospheric pollution. The car producers are willing, as always, to welcome new trends and here all of a sudden is a flow of new convertibles to suit all tastes and pockets. The marketing departments understood that the average price of an open top had to be relatively lower without the result, as in the 1960's, that all one got in return was a silly little bath-tub verging on the ridiculous. Now design even of the smallest is smart and innovative and engine performance is exciting even in the tiniest motors.

229 top The exciting BMW Z3 roadster, which is based on the firm's 3-Series Sedan. Note the letter M in the inset picture, which signifies that the car was prepared by BMW M GmbH, the motorsport division of BMW. This makes it a top-of-the-range version in terms of power.

230 top This Porsche Boxster was long awaited after being promoted as a prototype in one Motor Show after another. It finally saw the light in 1996. The Boxster has a longitudinal, 6 cylinder, 2.5 liter boxer engine. It produces 204 HP for a top speed of 150 mph.

230 center and bottom This is Renault's unusual interpretation of the sports car. It seems that this model was inspired by cars created by Colin Chapman like the Lotus Seven though it is less extreme. This Spider was actually designed for single marque racing but was then developed into a road version. It has a 150 HP engine which gives a top speed of 134 mph with 0-60 acceleration in 6.9 seconds. Note the side air intakes.

231 This semi-handmade Lotus Elise is an interpretation of the roadster theme. It is compact, aggressive and lively. Its 1.8 liter engine produces 118 HP. Note the design feature on the sides, the hollows which look like tracks made by landing meteorites.

These factors are enough to have given open-topped cars a boost although they are still confined to a niche market in Europe, the US and Japan. Fortunately the 1980's are long past and open top lovers sincerely hope they do not return. So what is available in the 1990's? For greater clarity, we have divided the most important models into arbitrary categories of market classification and given the year of presentation, entry into the market or restyling. The major creative impetus came in the middle of the decade so that we have excluded some cars that were not available after 1995.

Middle - high range roadsters and sports cars: these are statements of success by the drivers, vehicles for showing off and being seen in. The BMW Z3 (1995) and Mercedes SLK (1996) are leaders in the category, both with features that remind one of the 1930's grand prix racers but with covered wheels; their hoods are proportionally long, the driving position low and the sensitiveness of the driver to vehicle response high. The 1995 MGF was mid-engined, like the 1996 Porsche Boxster and the Honda NSX, thanks to which the cars' trim and driveability are like small 1960's racing sedans. Renault's sports car offering is certainly curious, half way between a dune buggy and a modern interpretation of the Lotus Seven. It is called the Sport Spider and appeared in 1995.

232 The front and dashboard of the Jaguar XK8, the car which continues the glorious story of the E-type and XJS. It combines internal luxury with true sports car performance, the latter produced by an excellent engine and responsive driver controls.

233 top The Pontiac Firebird Trans Am from 1994. This is an interesting example of a modern, comfortable and sporting American convertible. The fuel injected 5.7 liter Smallblock V8 engine gives excellent acceleration, despite the chassis' considerable weight.

233 bottom Aston Martin is perhaps the world's best example of sporting luxury. This DB7 continues the tradition of prestigious, exclusive GT's. The 340 HP, 3.2 liter motor gives a top speed of 161 mph. There are several resemblances to the Jaguar XK8.

Middle market sports cars: these are more or less pure sports cars but at a more affordable cost which are aimed at those who wish to have a second car purely for fun. Certainly they are less attractive than those above but they are important in terms of the market; often they are simply convertible versions of Japanese or American liftback coupés. This category includes the extremely popular 1994 Alfa Romeo Spider, completely different to the previous series of the same name. The following models have no particular aesthetic characteristics and even their standard motors often coincide with those of their own previous series: the Chevrolet Camaro (1993), the Japanese Toyota Celica (1993) and Mitsubishi Eclipse (1994), the Fiat Barchetta (1995) and the Audi TT (1998).

Power houses: some sports cars distinguish themselves for their engine and the performance it generates, often being revised versions of less than amazing convertibles. Their appearance does not appear much influenced by their new sporting nature and thankfully there are no extreme or grotesque designs. Falling into this classification are the BMW M3, the classic American Pontiac Firebird and Porsche 911 Carrera all from 1994, and the very elegant Jaguar XK8 (1996).

Gran turismo: real GT's, open-topped by chance, with powerful performance and reserved for the most able drivers. Some of these models are rare, like the TVR Griffith 500 (1990) and the Aston Martin DB7 Volante (1993); some are more well-known, like the Chevrolet Corvette (edition dates 1986 and 1998), the Ferrari F355 Spider and the Honda NSX Targa, both from 1995.

234 top This largely handbuilt Dodge Viper RT/10 has gone against the grain of traditional open top design during the 1990's. It is uncomfortable and flashy but may be the only car apart from the Ferrari F40 or F50 able to give the lucky driver the sensation of driving a Formula 1 car. The massive 8 liter engine is capable of producing 400 HP which enables the car to accelerate from 0-60 in 4.3 seconds and reach 169 mph.

234 bottom This is a real and rare road monster, the Lamborghini Diablo Roadster, in which it is possible to touch 201 mph, given the right conditions of course. It even beats the Viper on acceleration reaching 60 mph in just 4 seconds. Despite the name Roadster, it is more in line with a targa.

235 This is the front of a car that is difficult to consider as a road model given its seating arrangement and handling characteristics. It is the Ferrari F50, a 2-seater Formula 1 machine, which for top speed (203 mph) and 0-60 acceleration (3.7 seconds) cannot be beaten.

Road monsters: expensive, uncomfortable, totally non-functional and with truly monstrous fuel consumption, these are the cars longed for by those who believe pure speed is the maximum of human aspiration. Traveling at 180 mph is one thing but if you can do it with the top down, like being in a dark tunnel with a violent and mean roar coming from the engine, so much the better. But really these cars are nothing but toys and they do not last long. The best known among them are the Chrysler/Dodge Viper RT/10 (1992), the Ferrari F50 (1995), the Lamborghini Diablo (1995) and the Maserati Barchetta (1991).

The ever-present: these are cars that were conceived years ago but which have modern lines, fittings and performance. Generally they are subject to regular restylings, as in the case of the Porsche 911 which dates from 1980, or were brought to the market during the 1980's and left unchanged, as with the Mazda Miata (1989). The Morgan Plus 8 is still identical to past versions but it had a slight touch-up in 1988, the same year the Maserati Spyder was presented. Other similar models are the reborn Lotus Elan (1989), the Honda del Sol (1992) and the Volkswagen Golf Cabrio (1993).

Convertibles: open-topped vehicles but very functional, seating 4-5 people and furnishing driver comfort and plenty of luggage space. These characteristics mean they can be used as first cars without having to make do with a hard top as, once the soft top is up, they are as functional as a sedan. They are to us particularly refined, elegant, comfortable, well-finished and with all the power one could wish for. Their design is generally sober and, windshield apart, nothing rises above the waist of the body. Typical examples in terms of commercial success and design balance are the Saab 900 (1993) and the BMW series 3 (1992); the former is curiously oyster-shaped when looked at from the side, i.e. its ends are very tapered compared to the rounded central volume. The American representatives are also very fine: there is our old friend, the Ford Mustang (1993) which ends the century halfway between the exciting creature it was devised as and the square, coarse and ugly machine of the 1980's. There are many others which are part of this list - the elegant Audi Cabriolet (1991), the Mercedes E Class (1993), the Chevrolet Cavalier and Pontiac Sunfire (1994), the Chrysler Stratus/Sebring (1995), the Renault Mégane (1996) and the Volvo C70 (1997).

The babies: these are generally preferred by women and by the young in preference to off-road vehicles. They allow drivers to show a certain statement of non-conformity and to show off without any excessive economic investment and without creating any difficulty in terms of driving or parking. It is easily the largest group in terms of sales but the least interesting visually. In comparison to other open tops they are nothing but bath tubs with four wheels, a motor, a roll-bar, and a top which balloons at 60 mph. But they are popular and deserve a mention: there is the Ford Escort (1990), the Opel Astra (1991) in Europe, the Suzuki Cappuccino and Toyota Paseo (1991) in Japan, the Rover 200 Cabriolet (1992) and the Peugeot 306 and Fiat Punto (1994).

Luxury models: at the other end of the world from the above are these luxurious convertibles at the very pinnacle of quality and beauty. Their prices, naturally, are stratospheric and inaccessible to common mortals, their engines guarantee power to spare at any speed, and their drive comfort is such that you might think you were parked. The major jewels in this range are the Mercedes SL

236 top right This Alfa Romeo replaced the Spider or Duetto. It has the same name and several of its features are similar but it has not received the same enthusiastic response from lovers of its noble predecessor.

236 top left The Audi TTS Roadster is the German company's follow-up to the modest success of the Audi 80 Cabriolet. This model is also available in a closed body version and will be remembered for its extensive use of aluminum.

236 center The rear end of the Fiat Barchetta. The Barchetta marks a return to the sports car market for Fiat which, with the exception of cabriolets, has been absent for some time.

236 bottom Chrysler has cut out a niche in the European market with the Stratus. In dimensions, price and engine size (also available is a 2 liter version), the Stratus matches European needs.

(updated 1989), the Aston Martin Virage Volante (1990) and the glorious Bentley Azure (1994). Overall the choice of open-topped cars is very rich but, we repeat, the return to interest in convertibles is due, we believe, most of all to those in the first category, in which appear suggestions of the design themes to come. It is as if these roadsters were repositories for innovations which will later be applied to all other cars.

The world of open-topped vehicles is also a world for people who like to demonstrate they are different; some of them are old-fashioned gentlemen, some jesters, and a few are nostalgic motorcyclists. All of them, however, dislike being considered as one of the masses. For them there exist many, almost unknown, makes of open tops, many of which are built to order. In Great Britain especially there is a strong following for such cars. Here is a short list, some of which may be familiar: Ginetta G27 (1992), AC Ace (1993), Caterham 21 and Reliant Scimitar (1994), Rinspeed Roadster (1995) and the Panoz AIV (1996), but the list could go on and on.

At last there is an open-topped car available for every taste like there used to be in the 1950's. On both sides of the Atlantic, with Japan a little behind, sports cars and convertibles (together with their semantic and stylistic variants which we have attempted to illustrate without going into learned and unnecessary lessons of style) seem to have survived economic crises and recessions, but more importantly they appear to be on equal terms with their natural and most dangerous enemy: raggedness.

237 top The Mercedes SL 300 (since the mid-1990's, the numbers follow the letters) is a roadster with a great lineage; its roots go back to 1957. The series shown has a choice of three different motors (6, 8 and 12 cylinders) in four sizes (2.8, 3.2, 5 and 6 liters).

237 center The Azure is Rolls and Bentley's offering in the very narrow band at the top of the market for ultra-luxurious cabriolets at the end of the 1990's.

237 bottom This elegant car with classic lines is the 1992 Rolls Royce Corniche Anniversary.s

Who will be the next design genius?

This book has been written during a period when waves of fluid curves and streamlined forms have been applied to sporting cars, particularly if open-topped. Beautiful, stunning designs are to be seen that have given new life and vigor to the range of open tops across the world, cars that reflect the correct evolution of forms, details and proportions matured in 100 years of the history of the automobile.

But, too, there are some cases where their features seem weighed down, repetitive, afraid to take chances.

We have already dwelled on the role of open-topped cars: besides bringing pride to the owner, they stimulate the imagination of the designer and herald unusual and innovative designs for the cars of the future.

They are like top models in fashion shows, "dressed" by designers to surprise and signal the emerging trends.

Just now, apart from a few cases in the second half of the 1990's, the convertibles of the decade are undergoing a crisis of identity despite being available in great numbers and looking good.

Often they are clones of coupés or, if they are designed as independent models, they do not take chances. Overall, they are too pedantic.

Our feeling, backed up by the work of outstanding designers like Philippe Starck who created the Aprilia Motò and the Ford Ka and Escort, is that new and exciting paths are about to be trod. It seems that we are moving towards a car that is prepared to take risks, have a strong individuality and sense of irony, that is able to anticipate trends and which is free of similarities and conformity.

The designs of Starck, described as a "politician of forms", seem generated by intersections of curves. The forms seem to result, not from the union of concepts with three dimensional forms, but from sections of lines that start and finish outside the car itself. These line sections are generated by each feature Starck has made visible (lights, bumpers, grill, roof panel, door etc.) but it could equally be argued that the shape of each feature is only the result of the crossing of two, sometimes three, curves.

This creative chaos is wonderfully dynamic and the eye of the beholder does not tire from running along the lines of the whole car body, searching for the primary thread from which all the forms evolve and without ever understanding whether the cuts in the bodywork are responsible for "creating" the objects or vice versa.

Starck's ideas have been taken and adapted on many prototypes, more or less functional, and exhibited at international shows, in particular Detroit, Frankfurt, Geneva and Tokyo from 1995 on. But Starck's ideas are not the only ones: even more in evidence is a strong return to more elaborate styles such as Art Déco, and the creation of vertical and rectangular sets of lights like prisms which were seen hanging from lamps during the 1920's.

A tangible example was the extraordinary Plymouth Prowler, of which only 5,000 examples were planned and which earned immediate attention. It was a real 1950's hot rod design, with wheels separate from the car body, motorcycle type fenders, visible suspension, a large and biomorphic motor compartment (with a nod in the direction of

238-239 Chrysler conceived the Plymouth Prowler as a showcar, but it entered production in 1997. The lines are a clear reference to the hot rods of America's past, especially at the front, where we see the modern version of a fencing-mask grill. Note also the motorcycle type fenders separate from the body and the curious,

government-mandated hammer-shaped bumpers with turn indicators incorporated. A two-wheeled mini trailer was also presented in the exact same color and overall formula of the rear of the car; it functioned as a supplementary luggage compartment.

the "coffin hood" of Gordon Buehrig's Cord), bumpers like mini rails, false footboards and a boattail rear end rounded like the top of a trunk. The design was a great success even without the curious revival of functionality in the form of a trailer in the same color and style. At the end of the century, here is an opportunity that convertibles cannot allow to go begging: what type of car can best embody the idea of "Differentiation"?

We may be mistaken but we are convinced that from the start of the 21st century, strange, postmodern forms will be seen, perhaps childish, exaggerated and also disquieting.

We really need a wind of change in all schools of industrial design with a brilliant designer of strong personality and charm at center stage. Maybe it will be Starck when he is allowed to design a sports car; maybe Alfa Romeo's De Silva if he is able to develop the beautiful new Nivola coupé; maybe BMW's Chris Bangle, currently the most successful and courageous modernizer of convertibles; or maybe the successors to Pininfarina and Giugiaro who are already pawing the ground

with a wave of new ideas backed up by an enormous technological patrimony; or then again maybe a young, unknown designer who, still ignored by the car manufacturers and media, works the midnight hours in some Californian or Japanese design studio trying to bring his ideas to reality. We like to think of him still working with a pencil and paper rather than computer aided design programs.

The design genius of the 21st century will be part architect, part child, part poet, part standard-bearer of hyper-technology; he will have a passion for cars but not be a slave to them; he will welcome new discoveries and try to exploit them to the maximum and in an original manner; he will abhor sameness but will not attempt to achieve effects at any cost; he will love speed but not aggression or excess; he will be flexible with materials, generous with colors, miserly with gadgets. A prodigy, no less. We like to think of him, for reasons of historical balance, as a descendant of the gentleman at the beginning of the story who was left powerless and indignant as one of the first

mechanical contraptions spattered him with mud. It is unnecessary to continue with further descriptions of abstruse models filled to the brim with electronic gadgets and original ideas, sometimes ingenious and sometimes just plain vulgar.

The reader who has come with us this far will be tired of reading, he will want a breath of fresh air, perhaps in an open-topped car. He can at least dream if he doesn't have one, and enjoy it if he already does. Very probably he will see direct descendants of the cars described in this volume, perhaps the spirited Argento Vivo by Pininfarina, the Formula by Giugiaro, the legendary Audi TT Roadster, the ambiguous De Tomaso Bigua, the small Ghia Focus, the technological Honda SSM or the modern replica of the Volkswagen Beetle.

As for us, we love this romantic world filled with incorrigible dreamers, regretful motorcyclists and adults who refuse to grow up. A world where vanity, if moderated, is not a failing and a sense of irony, if unconditioned, is a quality. A world where everyone is convinced that convertibles have a soul.

CLASSIC CARS
FROM 1945 TO THE PRESENT

CONTENTS

241 Top classic sedan - 1957 Jaguar 3.4 Mk.1.
242-243 King of the Cobras - 1967 427 CSX.

An Introduction to the World of Classic Cars

244-245 top A rare 1950 Aston Martin, one of 13 DB1 drop head coupes.

244-245 bottom The best-looking model of the T-series was the TF, a 1953 1250 here.

What is a classic car? Must it be old and rare? Must it be beautiful and expensive? Or is it just a car with class? 'Classic' in the world of art, whether architecture, painting or music, implies exceptional quality, but, in the world of cars, 'classic' means different things to different people. Any model of old Ferrari is a classic car in anyone's judgment. Some people would also call an old Vauxhall Victor a classic - there is an owners' club in the UK - but not everyone would agree. Why? It was just an ordinary car when it was new; the passing of time should not change that perception just because a few examples have been preserved. Unfortunately, the term has no standard definition, no constraint of age or price, type or style.

Broadly speaking, a classic car is a post-1945 car with some feature which set it apart from its peers, and not just the mere fact of its survival. A Ford Cortina Mk.1 is not really a classic, but the Cortina GT appeals to more than just owners of old Cortinas and it inspired the even more sporting Lotus Cortina. However if someone forms a club, even for a basic model, there are necessarily some enthusiasts who believe in the car, so it gets embraced into the general classic world whatever the purists may think.

But there are some mass-production peoples' cars that contradict the general rule. Volkswagen Beetle, Morris Minor, Citroen 2CV, Fiat 500 were technically interesting cars that generated a cult-following and have readily been accepted as classic cars, even by Ferrari owners.

An Introduction to the World of Classic Cars

CLASSIC CAR HISTORY AMERICA

If you live in America, you will have a different view. The Classic Car Club of America (CCCA) has its own definition of 'classic': "... fine or unusual cars which were built between and including the years 1925 and 1948. These very special cars are distinguished by their respective fine design, high engineering standards and superior workmanship." The CCCA have a list of acceptable cars from around the world, cars that were not mass-produced and were generally more expensive than the rest. Perhaps in response to the universal misuse of the term 'classic', these cars are now referred to as 'Full Classic', a registered CCCA trademark. The CCCA was founded in 1951 because owners of these Full Classics got fed up with being just a small class within the Antique Automobile Club of America (AACA); this had been founded in 1935 and would eventually cater for all vehicles more than 25 years old. There are over 50,000 AACA members, but only 5600 CCCA members. America is also home to the Horseless Carriage Club, a name that dates back to the turn of the last century when motor cars were built around the concept of horse-drawn carriages with a motor substituted for the horse - the dark ages. Their coverage ends at 1916, so need not concern us. Of more interest to the classic enthusiast might have been the American-based Milestone Car Society. This was

formed "to promote the preservation, and restoration of domestic and foreign automobiles made between 1945 and the end of the 1964 model year, which are distinctive because of design, engineering, performance, innovation and/or craftsmanship relative to their contemporaries." In this, a panel of judges selected cars that made a particular contribution to the history of the automobile. Covering cars from the post-war period, it was almost a chronological extension to the CCCA, except that price and rarity were not part of the decision making process. While it was a laudable attempt to separate out the more worthwhile cars, it was engulfed in the rising tide of make clubs, leaving only the name 'Milestone' behind; there is however a Milestone Car Society of California but it has no connection with the original other than the choice of name.

246-247 top Mercedes 190SL (1955) was the little brother to the 300SL supercar.

246-247 bottom First of the pony cars was the Ford Mustang in 1964.

CLASSIC CAR HISTORY
REST OF WORLD

Outside America, cars built before the 1939-45 war generally have precise age-related definitions. The first such definition came from the Veteran Car Club (VCC) which was founded in 1930 and catered for cars built before 1905; these Veterans are the cars that take part in the world-renowned London-Brighton run. Then came the Vintage Sports-Car Club, founded in 1934, which looked after the cars from 1905-1930. The date of 1930 was chosen because the General Depression brought the end of many manufacturers of expensive hand-made cars. The Thirties would see mass production take over in volume terms, although some of the hand-built cars of the previous decade were able to continue.

In time, both clubs extended their ranges. The VCC began to accept cars up to 1918 and called the 1905-1918 cars Edwardians, which was a little misleading as the English King Edward VII died in 1910. The VSCC moved its end-date to 1940 but only accepted sporting cars from the Thirties and called them Post-Vintage Thoroughbreds - cars for sporting use, but excluding such mass production sports cars as MG Midgets. The VSCC Thirties car had to be hand-built in the traditional way; more recently they have accepted certain competition cars up to 1960 which they call 'Historic'. Given such broad coverage within the two national old car clubs in England, there were some older cars that were left out. The make clubs soon followed to take care of this - Bugatti, Aston Martin, MG were all founded in the Thirties. That much is purely English history, but it was the English who were the first to appreciate the older car as a hobby rather than a cheap means of transport; English terminology and dating has led the way. As this appreciation of the older car spread to other countries, it was inevitable that an International body would be formed to try and coordinate the movement. The Federation Internationale des Voitures Anciennes (FIVA) was formed in 1966 as the world-wide extension of a previous European-only equivalent. FIVA took note of all that had been set up before and preserved the various cut-off dates, but not necessarily the names and they accepted all cars of a given date whatever the original quality.

For FIVA, the cars built before 1905 are called 'Ancetre' (Ancestors or Forefathers), while 'Veteran' referred to the 1905-1918 group. FIVA's Vintage period conformed with the VSCC and covered 1919-1930. Initially FIVA used the term 'Classic' to describe the cars of the Thirties, but, as they expanded their interests to cater for all cars more than 20 years old, this decade became simply 'Post-Vintage'. As time went on FIVA had to find new definitions for the cars that came into their range. 'Post-war' was the name given to the 1945-60 period. After which, semantic skills ran out. The Sixties became Group F and the Seventies are Group G It was the British magazine Classic Cars, launched in 1973, which took the whole old car movement under its wing. No definition. Just a proven ability

for the car to attract a following, usually demonstrated by the formation of a club of like-minded enthusiasts for the model. Where there wasn't a club, the magazine usually inspired some owner to start one. That obviously also embraced the pre-war specialist cars of the VSCC, but it was particularly the cars excluded by that club's rules that would be called classic, the new Vintage.

While organizations such as FIVA and the Antique Automobile Club of America still require cars to be 20-25 years old to qualify for membership, classic car magazines take a broader view. Any car that is out of production has the potential to be featured and, by implication, to be considered a classic. Classic cannot be new. A new car can have classic lines - often called Retro - but it can only be called a future classic. History has shown that sporting cars earn classic status sooner than standard sedans. Almost by definition sports cars are not everyday cars. Sedan cars stay in the general transport market for much longer, getting ever cheaper until they finish in the scrap yard or someone rescues them - they gradually lose any

class they had. Sporting cars are usually more expensive, they probably cover lower mileages and are better maintained by keener owners. One might say that a car becomes a classic when it ceases to depreciate in value - the market has recognized that it is worth preserving. Well maintained sporting cars stop depreciating at a younger age than less interesting sedans. This book will also recognize a few of these future classics. Just to confuse the reader, a car might well be considered a classic in one country but not in its native country. This is particularly true of American cars where such as Ford Mustangs and Chevrolet Camaros were produced in very large numbers; but in Europe they have always stood out as something different and have achieved general classic recognition much earlier. The Citroen 2CV is just an old family run-about to the French, but it has achieved classic status in countries where it is a rarity. This is also true of the Mini, but at least that had a competition variant, the Cooper S, which merits classic recognition, even in England.

248-249 top The 1961 Jaguar E-type had world-wide appeal

248-249 bottom By the time of this 1986 example, the Chevrolet Corvette had recovered the performance lost in the Seventies

An Introduction to the World of Classic Cars

CLASSIC CAR EVENTS

Part of the joy of owning a classic car is to take it to events and compete against others. As with modern motor cars, this competition takes many forms. Classic car owners can take part in anything from a static concours through touring events, rallies, trials, hill-climbs to flat-out racing; such events will be organised by make or national clubs and commercial organizations. The Concours falls into two main categories. Most are called Concours d'Elegance which recalls the events that used to take place at the end of major rallies; this was a 'beauty contest' where judges decided on what they thought was the nicest-looking car. In the Thirties this was a good chance for coachbuilders to display their special bodies. Judging nowadays is based on how closely cars conform to the condition in which they might have left the factory - the Concours d'Etat. Pebble Beach in California is the most Internationally-known annual event and their system of marking every aspect of the car has spread around the world. A 100-point car is perfect, and many classic car dealers use such terminology in advertisements, with perhaps less attention to detail than would be given by a truly impartial jury. Over the last 20 years there have been many regularity runs where durability of car and driver is more of a deciding factor than speed. These frequently follow the pattern of former classic competitions like the Monte Carlo Rally, the London-Sydney Marathon, the Peking-Paris or the Mille Miglia, but take somewhat longer than did the original competitors. While these are all for cars that were either built for such competitions originally or have been improved to the same period specification, there are many more events for those who wish to drive through nice scenery in original cars in the company of fellow enthusiasts without the pressure of competition. For those classic owners who want to drive against the clock, there are rallies, hill-climbs and races; these come under the overall control of the Federation Internationale de l'Automobile (FIA). The 'Historic Commission' was formed in 1974 under the presidency of Count "Johnny" Lurani, a well-known Italian competitor from the Thirties and Fifties. His committee came partly from FIVA and partly from the national clubs. All competition cars, from the

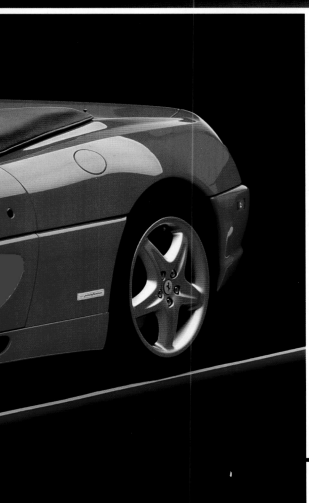

beginning to the only recently obsolete, are covered in rules for which the criteria are period originality and a continuous history for that car. The rules, which are used to control modification, are based on those of the period of the car; every entrant will have a vehicle passport to show that his car has been inspected and conforms to these rules. Most European countries, Australia and America, have many race meetings, frequently attracting entries from worldwide.

While the VSCC was probably the first club to run a race meeting solely for the older car in 1937, the first truly International old-car race meeting took place in 1973 at the Nurburgring in Germany - the first of many Oldtimer Grand Prix.

Certainly, there were many competition cars which generally fall outside the coverage of this book, but there were also many of the sports and grand touring road cars.

Touring cars (sedans) would join in later years. From 1973 onwards, the classic car competition world has expanded rapidly and there are European championships for rallying, hill-climbs and racing. Whatever classic car you own or decide to buy, be assured that you can do much more with it than just look at it in the garage or drive it down to the golf club. Welcome to the world of the mobile museum that is classic motoring. Long may we have the freedom to exercise our cars on the open road.

250-251 top McLaren F1 achieved 231 mph

250-251 bottom Pininfarina style adds to Ferrari appeal on the 355 Spyder

252-253 Cadillac's 1960 Eldorado saw a reduction in chrome plate

1946 - 1950

While the classic period is generally reckoned to start after the 1939-45 war, many of Europe's volume produced cars were only minor facelifts from 1938/9 models, their tooling costs as yet unamortised while the production machinery had sat in moth-balls for the duration of hostilities. While America did not start fighting in the war until after the attack on Pearl Harbor in December 1941, their factories had been supplying the anti-Hitler forces from 1939 with commercial vehicles and armaments. Despite this over 4 million cars were produced in 1940 and 1941. From mid 1942 all American vehicle production facilities were involved in the war effort, one of Ford's contributions being production of the Jeep – itself something of a post-war classic.

The lack of direct attack on America allowed their factories to return to vehicle production relatively quickly after the war. England was not far behind, but France, Italy and Germany all suffered major bomb damage to former car production centers.

Japan too, but their pre-war cars had made no impact outside Japan. Smaller companies could more readily consider producing new models and such new makes as Bristol and Saab emerged from airplane manufacturers.

But the return of motoring freedom was to be a slow process. Rubber and steel were hard to get.

All industries were looking for materials and governments were slow to let the automobile industries have what they needed. Nor was there the manpower to work in the factories as armies were slow to demobilize the troops. All countries had fuel rationing except the US. And then there was a shortage of dollars as America had operated the Lease-Lend system and many allied countries were in debt – they had to export goods to America to recover. Much of Britain's early post-war production went to America and other countries before the home market could be supplied, and high national taxes were brought in to encourage exports.

Not all the cars from this, or any other, distant decade can be regarded as classics, but it was an era when many small companies started up and they necessarily produced near hand-made cars in limited numbers. So this particular five-year period saw an unusual quantity of future classics; not all of these entrepreneurial manufacturers survived through to the Sixties though.

254-255 Riley RM sedan, 1950.

THE NEW SEDANS

From America, there was little to attract future classic enthusiasts. The cars got bigger and V-8s more widespread albeit that some were still flat-heads (side-valves).

The Studebaker Champion, like most of the early post-war American cars, was a revised version of the successful 1942 car, but introduced a new short nose-long tail style with a much lowered roof-line in 1946. In mechanical design there was little to separate the American cars, it was style that sold them.

In 1947, Ford separated out the top end of their range by giving the new Lincoln-Mercury division some autonomy. The 1949 Mercury was a good looking car despite its heavily chromium-plated grille; with its flat-head V-8, it was popular with the hot-rodders of the day. Lincoln, which had been directed by Edsel Ford, was the top model built in European-sized numbers. The Lincoln Zephyr of the late Thirties was one of America's more striking cars, the most popular model being an elegant fast-back with a V-12 engine. The longer hand-made Continental grew out of this in 1938, continuing through to 1942. Only a few changes were made for the 1946-1948 model years, but the cars stood out as being relatively restrained in their use of the brightwork – and a V-12 was pretty rare in those days.

Cadillac was the top of the General Motors tree. While early post-war Cadillacs were the same as those of 1941, the 1948 series were rebodied and the 'tail fin' was born. Harley Earl had set up the first in-house automotive styling studio for General Motors in 1937; impressed by the twin-boom tail plane of the Lockheed Lightning fighter, he transferred the idea to motor cars and the Cadillac was the first recipient. The 1948 cars continued with the 347 cu.in flat-head V-8s but, in 1949, Cadillac introduced the overhead valve version.

American manufacturers were relatively fortunate. There was only a four-year gap in automobile production and tastes didn't change very much over that period. But the Continentals had a much longer period of motoring stagnation. So what influenced designers when it came to starting on a new car with a clean sheet of paper? It was clear that American passenger cars were superior in comfort, performance and style to those that had provided ordinary transport on their home markets in the Thirties. However, the American cars were just too thirsty for European fuel prices and too big for most European roads although Germany had their autobahnen and Italy too had autostrade.

So the post-war British passenger car designers adopted American styling but scaled it down. Thus running boards and separate wings (fenders) disappeared and headlights were integrated into front panels. Radiators disappeared behind false grilles. Some of the styles followed the Airline, or fastback, theme which America had adopted in the late Thirties and some of the UK designers had followed, notably Rover and Talbot. On the technical side, Britain retained their four and six-cylinder engines rather than V-8s, but took on independent front suspension and hydraulic brakes which were by no means universal in the late Thirties. Unitary construction of body and chassis was another lesson learned as essential for cheaper volume production; up-market models like Rolls-Royce and Bentley, which still used coachbuilders for bodywork, retained separate chassis.

Typical of the downsized American cars launched in 1948 was Standard's new Vanguard. In style it was quite obviously based on the 1942 Plymouth with a rounded fast-back and the adoption of fared in rear wheels. It used a new 128 cu.in 'four' that would go on to power tractors, Morgans and the Triumph TR2/3/4; the gearbox was a three-speed unit with steering column change adopted from America. Standard took over Triumph in 1944. While early post-war Standards were just continuations of the pre-war cars, the Vanguard was the sole model they produced from 1947; however Triumph was allowed to proceed a little faster and had new razor-edged sedans from 1946 using pre-war Standard engines converted to overhead valves.

They also produced the striking 1800 Roadster, a two-seater with a separate compartment behind for two more passengers in a 'dickey-seat'. The Roadster adopted the Vanguard engine in late 1948.

Another to follow the American fast-back line was the Jowett Javelin, launched in 1946 having been built in prototype form in 1944. Although British factories were very much involved in the war effort, many were planning their post-war return to car production at the same time as producing, in Jowett's case, armaments and aero-engine water pumps. In style, the Jowett followed the looks of the Lincoln-Zephyr, and the rest of the car was well-conceived. Pre-war experience with a flat twin engine prompted the use of a water-cooled flat four engine, which was mounted ahead of the front

wheels. Torsion bars were used for the suspension with wishbones at the front. With a long wheelbase, the four-door sedan was very comfortable but still agile on the road; however the small company was not able to build in the vital reliability and they ceased producing cars in 1953. Like Standard, they also produced a sporting version – the Jupiter – which used the Javelin engine in a tubular chassis under two-seater bodywork; only 850 were produced.

Jaguar were a little slow to produce an all-new sedan. Initial post-war products were uprated pre-war cars but the 1950 advent of the Mark VII saw Jaguar start their long run of success. Using the twin-cam six-cylinder 207 cu.in engine which had been conceived during the war years, and first used in the XK120, the new generation Jaguar was a large and comfortable car styled in a European mold.

In avoiding American style, Jaguar produced a car that was instantly well received in the United States.

In Sweden, Volvo introduced the fast-back PV444 with a four-cylinder engine to replace their pre-war sixes. Germany, under allied control and with a number of its factories scheduled to finish up in the Russian zone, produced the Borgward Hansa in 1949 and, of course, the Beetle and Porsche. Mercedes and BMW produced nothing new until 1951, although Mercedes made uprated 170 models from 1949.

Of the French manufacturers, Citroen retained the Traction Avant Light 15 (Onze Legere in France) through the Forties and beyond the 1955 launch of the DS19. Originally designed in 1934 it was the first effective front-wheel-drive car; it used independent wishbone front suspension with torsion bars and a dead rear axle to give renowned fwd cornering with remarkable comfort for the period. Performance came from an overhead valve four-cylinder which would be stretched from 80 to the 116 cu.in, the size used post-war. A six-cylinder derivative was launched in 1938 and this too continued after the war. Peugeot continued with the pre-war 202, but introduced the 203 in 1947, another to follow the scaled down Plymouth theme of Standard and Volvo; it had a new 80 cu.in overhead-valve engine and all-coil suspension. It was a strong, well-built car that would sell until 1960; from 1949-53 it was the only Peugeot made. And finally, Panhard changed direction from large to small cars and produced their own brand of idiosyncratic Dynas from 1945 using designs from J.A.Gregoire. With powerful air-cooled flat twin

37.2 cu.in engines in aerodynamic shapes, they were quick and comfortable. The engine was increased to 45.7 cu.in in 1950 and 51.8 cu.in in 1952. Other specialists like DB and the German Veritas also used these for road and competition use.

In Italy, Alfa Romeo were still producing expensive cars, the 6C2500 in various forms including a competition coupe. The 1900 range was to start in 1950 to take the company into volume production with unitary construction and a new four-cylinder engine. Lancia continued with pre-war designs, the Aprilia with all-round independent suspension and its overhead camshaft narrow V-4 engine at 91 cu.in, and the smaller Ardea. Lancia too would introduce their new range in 1950 with the Aurelia, covered in the next chapter. Maserati were mostly building racing cars but a handful of road cars were built on the A6-1500 chassis.

Apart from those above, there were a number of old respected British names that continued with new looks but old engines after the war; although they are rightly regarded as classics within the UK, they made less impact on the International scene. In 1945, Riley, which had been taken over by Morris in 1938, brought in the sports sedan RM with styling reminiscent of the BMW 327 coupe; this used the pre-war 91 cu.in 'four' in a new chassis; a year later the 146 cu.in version was added. Alvis produced the TA series in 1946 and followed it up with the TB14 2-seater. AC's new sedan arrived in 1947. Lea-Francis had new sedans and brought out a 2-seater sports in 1948. Sunbeam-Talbot, part of the Rootes group, had a range of medium sedans with sporting performance. Armstrong-Siddeley's elegant sedans and convertibles were named after the fighter aircraft produced by the group in the war. But within a decade most of these British names would be gone or merged within larger organizations.

THE BABY CLASSICS

The Austin 7 of the Twenties had been an inspirational small car in its time; it had a separate chassis, a four-cylinder water-cooled 45.7 cu.in engine and it could carry four adults. It was the first scaled down cheap car for the people, as opposed to the cyclecar which had been little better than a four-wheeled motor cycle combination. It was also produced under licence by BMW as the Dixi, Rosengart in France, Bantam in America and Datsun in Japan. In Germany Hanomag's equivalent was the 2/10 commonly called the Kommissbrot because it looked like an army loaf of bread; it only

had a single cylinder engine and was limited to two people. DKW responded with a 2-cylinder two-stroke and produced the first front-wheel-drive baby-car in 1931.

The Austin 7 was still in production when Fiat conceived the first 500 – the Topolino. Giacosa had started in 1934, intending to make it a front-wheel-drive car but the constant velocity joints of the day were not good enough. He did, however, assemble the engine, transmission and independent front suspension into a single removable package – a very effective design; putting the radiator behind the 34.7 cu.in four-cylinder engine allowed a stylish sloping front. Brakes were hydraulic but the car was only a two-seater. It was, however, the logical successor to the Austin 7 and was widely exported – a small car with exceptional comfort and roadholding for its day. Production started in 1936 and was to continue after the war, with overhead valves replacing the original side valves, until 1955 when it was replaced by the rear engined 600 and then the Nuova Cinquecento (new 500) which came with an air-cooled twin-cylinder engine.

In Germany, the Beetle project was also started in 1934. While there had been a rival claimant to the first German Volkswagen in the form of the Standard 500 designed by Austrian Josef Ganz and launched in 1932, Dr.Porsche was given the contract to build the true Volkswagen after the Third Reich came to power in 1933. Both used rear engines – the Standard a transverse twin-cylinder – swing axles and a form of central backbone chassis. Dr Porsche used an air-cooled flat four and torsion bar springing instead of transverse leaf springs.

Development of the prototypes took place over 1936-39, but by the time that the cars and the new factory at Wolfsburg were ready for production, war was almost under way. During the war it had been adapted to serve as a cross-country vehicle (52,000 Kubelwagens were built between 1940-45) and as an amphibious vehicle (14,263 were produced from 1940-44). Production of the road car finally started in 1945; by March 1950 100,000 had been built. The five million came up in 1961 and in February 1972 Beetle production surpassed that of the model T Ford.

There is no doubt that Dr Porsche's German peoples' car and Giacosa's Fiat 500 inspired a lot of thought among European car producers during the war. While they were all manufacturing contributions to the various war efforts, the industry leaders were thinking ahead to the end of the conflict. They knew that ,whatever the outcome, people would be poor but they would need transport – cheap transport.

To keep the price down, production costs had to be kept to a minimum; therefore machinery should do as much work as possible to keep the labor costs low. Henry Ford had already shown the world the advantages of the production line with the Model T. In France, and inspired by the pre-war Beetle prototypes, Renault had been working on the 4CV from 1940 and prototypes were running during the war. In 1945 the company was nationalized. By 1947 a new factory was running with modern transfer machinery and the 4CV emerged at the 1947 Paris Show. Like the VW, this used a platform chassis and rear-mounted engine/gearbox but the 45.7 cu.in engine was water-cooled. It was also a four-door car. The design saved Renault and it was to be developed into the Dauphine and the R8 of later years. Somehow, though, it never inspired the same fanaticism as did the Beetle. However, there was another French car which would become just as much loved as the Volkswagen – the Citroen 2CV.

Like the Beetle, work had started on the 2CV well before the war in 1936. While this was designed for the people, thinking was heavily slanted towards the French agricultural community. It had to carry four farmers wearing hats, be capable of taking a basket of eggs over a ploughed field and be able to carry a pig to the market. It also had to be cheap hard wearing and easy to repair. The result was the uncompromising shape with simply curved panels, a roll-back canvas roof and hinged windows. Following the theme of Citroen's Traction Avant, it too had front wheel drive and was powered by an air-cooled flat twin with 22.8 cu.in developing just 9 bhp, enough for 38 mph. Independent suspension used interconnected leading and trailing arms with central coil springs. The springing was remarkably soft yet it was impossible to overturn the car. Prototypes were built in 1937 and production would have started in 1939 had war not intervened. Citroen destroyed all but one prototype to prevent the design being stolen. Finally it was launched in 1948. The engine was enlarged to 26 cu.in in 1954. Despite its looks, the 2CV remained in demand for many years and the final car was produced in Portugal in 1990 by which time over 5 million had been made.

In England, much of the volume production was devoted to updated pre-war designs until the Morris Minor arrived in 1948. Another wartime gestation, the Minor was conceived in 1942 by Alec Issigonis who would go on to create the Mini. With conventional front engine-rear drive and a unitary chassis, the Minor was launched in 1948 using the pre-war Morris 8 side-valve engine. What set it apart from many of its rivals was that it was the first family sedan to handle like a sports car, thanks to its wide stance and rack-and-pinion steering. In 1952 it received the overhead valve engine from the new Austin A30, following the Austin-Morris merger which created BMC. The A30 was never as popular in classic terms, although its A35 derivative developed a competition following.

The last of our small classics would be the Saab 92, the first automotive product of Sweden's wartime aircraft manufacturer. In simple terms it was a much improved DKW in a unitary body/chassis unit whose engineering and styling obviously owed much to aircraft influence. Front wheel drive and two-stroke power were retained from the DKW but the engine was a 2-cylinder 45.7 cu.in unit. Design work started in 1945 and the first prototype ran a year later. Production finally started in 1949 – the first truly aerodynamic small car.

256-257 Alfa Romeo 6C-2500 sedan

1946 - 1950

The Sporting Classics

Where touring car designers looked to America for their inspiration and small car designers chose the most innovative solutions of the past, would-be sports car designers looked back to the pre-war competition era. Few single events were more influential than the 1940 Brescia GP, that year's Mille Miglia held before Italy joined the Axis powers. Le Mans too made its share of contribution.

The two major landmarks from the Brescia event were the success of the streamlined BMW 328s (coupes and roadsters) and the arrival of Ferrari as a constructor, although the car was actually entered as an 815 by Auto-Avio Costruzioni; the Ferrari story will be told in the special cars at the end of this chapter. The BMW coupe that won the event at over 100 mph had already won its 122 cu.in class and finished 5th overall at Le Mans in 1939.

It was one of the few coupes that had been built for racing. It was only in the late Thirties that the benefits of aerodynamic designs were beginning to be appreciated for racing machinery, particularly in such high speed events as Le Mans and the Mille Miglia. Many aerodynamic sedan Lancias and Fiats, with coachbuilt bodies, had also taken part in the Italian classic race.

At Le Mans streamlined sedan Adlers had finished sixth overall in 1937 and in 1938. Alfa Romeo had fielded a single Touring-bodied 2900B coupe in 1938

and led for most of the race. It was Touring who designed the body for the BMW and for the 1939 2500SS Alfa Romeos. While much of those aerodynamic studies took place in Germany, it was the Italians that put them into the most attractive effect.

Despite Touring's major contribution to the breed it was Pinin Farina who was credited with the creation of the Gran Turismo fast-back shape. The Cisitalia 202 Gran Sport was the product of Dante Giacosa's Fiat brain, Savonuzzi's wind-tunnel studies and Pinin Farina's styling; it was launched in 1947. It only had a tuned Fiat 1100 engine but the car could reach 100 mph. Cisitalia's Piero Dusio then became involved in a Grand Prix car project – together with Porsche – and left the country in 1948 but the car continued in production until 1952 by which time only 170 cars had been built.

A further product of the 1940 Brescia race came from the open BMWs which had finished 3rd, 5th and 6th – Alfa Romeo 2500SS had finished 2nd and 4th. The open BMW bodies had been created in Germany, again following wind-tunnel theories, with smooth all-enveloping upper shapes and a flat underside – they were also very attractive. One of these cars was brought back to England after the war and became the prototype of the post-war Frazer Nash. Pre-war this company had built chain-drive sports cars but had imported BMWs from 1934 onwards.

Meanwhile the Bristol Aeroplane Company were, like Saab, wanting to make motor cars. Through a Frazer Nash association they acquired a useful amount of BMW knowledge which will be seen in the story of the Bristol 400 in the next chapter. Part of that knowledge was the design of the BMW 328 engine which was Anglicized and made available to Frazer Nash. While the most popular Frazer Nash was the Le Mans Replica – named after any early car finished 3rd in the French race in 1949, with a cigar-shaped body and cycle wings, the next model was the Mille Miglia, shaped very much like the Brescia race car. The Bristol engine was also used by AC and Arnolt (USA) in road cars and by such as Cooper, Lotus and Lister in racing cars.

When the original open Brescia BMW came to England it was viewed by all the manufacturers. Its style would eventually be seen on the MGA but the most obvious lesson was put into effect by Jaguar for the XK120, launched in 1948. The lines, including the rear wheel spats, were pure BMW.

Porsche may not have been in the 1940 race but a development of the early Beetle prototypes nearly took part in a similar long-distance event before the war, but the 1939 Berlin-Rome race was cancelled. Porsche engineers had designed a coupe around VW components, but put the engine ahead of the rear axle. This coupe body was then adapted around

a standard Beetle chassis for the race. After the war, Porsche started again and produced a mid-engined roadster on a tubular chassis with Beetle engine and gearbox. This single prototype, built in Austria, was sold to finance the move to Stuttgart and the production of the 356 on a Beetle chassis. Once more racing had established the breed.

It was to be the same for Aston Martin too. While the company restarted after the war with a 122 cu.in sports car based on pre-war thinking, the DB2 coupe was the first product of the merger of Aston Martin and Lagonda and this was demonstrated at Le Mans in 1949 – a fuller story comes at the end of this chapter. Lagonda too was to continue with new luxury cars based on designs by W.O. Bentley.

While they were both successful in amateur club events, neither the MG TC nor the Morgan 4/4 owed their existence to a background of International racing.

The TC was a direct continuation of the pre-war TB; the TC story is told later. Morgan had made its name with three-wheelers from 1910 but in 1936 they added the first four-wheeler using a side valve 68.5 cu.in Coventry Climax engine – some were made in France as Sandfords. At that time it was a modern-looking car but the style has never changed since then. After the war production continued

using a Standard overhead valve engine of 77.3 cu.in. Both that and the TC were traditional British sports cars; they looked faster than they were, but they handled well and provided fun in lesser motor sport events. For the Morgan, though, this changed when the Plus 4 came out in 1950 using the 127.4 cu.in Standard Vanguard engine; suddenly Morgan had arrived as a true sports car.

Britain was the home of the small volume sports car. In the early post-war years, a lot of these British enthusiasts cleared the first hurdle from special builder to manufacturer rather more easily than did their counterparts overseas. In Italy, Moretti succeeded over the next decade but reverted to making special Fiats.

Porsche had a similar start but expanded rapidly. In France, taxation soon killed off Delage, Delahaye and Talbot and it was some years before such as Alpine could start. Component suppliers in Britain were keen to expand their business even in small numbers and manufacturers were certainly willing to make engines and transmissions available to others. And there was still a coachbuilding industry.

Another new manufacturing name to profit from this attitude was Healey. Donald Healey, who had been an active motor sport competitor and was Technical Director of Triumph before the war, decided to make his own 4-seater cars. A welded

box section chassis with trailing arm front suspension was equipped with the effective Riley 146 cu.in four-cylinder engine which developed 104 bhp; in 1947, a closed coupe with standard Elliott bodywork achieved 110.8 mph at Jabbeke, Belgium and claimed to be the fastest production car in the world. Healey also produced the cycle-winged two-seater Silverstone on the same chassis for just two years, 1949 and 1950, as British taxation slowed demand for more expensive cars. Healey would go on to become the second half of the better known Austin-Healey.

Allard had produced Ford V-8 powered trials specials before the war, but produced a small number of open tourers from 1947 using the flat-head Ford V-8 and the two-seater sports K-type with the same engine increased to 238 cu.in and with Ardun overhead valve conversion. The cycle-winged J2 was added in 1950 and was well received in America; mostly it used a big Cadillac engine but others could easily be fitted.

By the end of the first post-war decade, the world's industry had just about recovered from the war, although German output was still restricted apart from the Volkswagen. In 1950 the UK had made 522,000 cars of which 398,000 were exported and only 1375 were imported – a useful contribution to the balance of payments.

258-259 Aston Martin DB2 with Bertone bodywork.

260-261 MG TC, left and lower, was a slightly wider version of the pre-war TB. The TF added post-war elegance but not performance in the 76.2 cu.in shown below.

MG TC e TF

Before the classic period, MG was little known outside the United Kingdom. The company had started as Morris Garages, the retail outlet near the Oxford factory. The manager, Cecil Kimber, started to produce sporting versions of the Morris Cowley from 1925. By 1930, MG was producing small sports two-seaters using Morris components – the MG Midgets with small four-cylinder engines. Six-cylinder Magnas and Magnettes followed. The Midgets were never very fast, but they had style and many owners enjoyed using them for light competition – autotests and trials.

The T-type, later called the TA, Midget arrived in 1936 with its customary twin-channel chassis suspended on leaf springs and powered by a 78.8 cu.in 52 bhp engine from Wolseley, which

Morris had owned from 1927. This engine was replaced by the stronger 76.2 cu.in Morris unit for the TB which was announced just before the 1939-45 war, so only 379 were built before production ceased.

When production restarted, MG abandoned their multi-model policy and concentrated on the new two-seater TC, which was a TB with a wider cockpit and a rear spring mounting system revised for greater reliability. Development had to be kept to a minimum to get the car into production quickly; that mattered little as there were no rivals other than pre-war cars.

The TC looked like everyone's ideal of a sports car with a strong radiator shape, a long bonnet, sweeping front wings, wire wheels and a slab petrol tank across the rear. The British motor industry wanted to export as much as possible and had a ready audience in the number of

TECHNICAL DESCRIPTION OF THE MG TF	
YEARS OF PRODUCTION	1953-1955
ENGINE	FRONT MOUNTED IN-LINE 4-CYLINDER
BORE X STROKE, CAPACITY	2.6 X 3.5 INCHES, 76.2 CU.IN
VALVEGEAR	PUSHROD OHV
FUEL SYSTEM	TWIN SU CARBURETORS
POWER	57 BHP AT 5500 RPM
TRANSMISSION	4-SPEED, REAR DRIVE
BODY/CHASSIS	STEEL PANELS ON ASH FRAME, STEEL CHANNEL CHASSIS
SUSPENSION	SEMI-ELLIPTIC LEAF SPRINGS
TIRES/WHEELS	15 X 5.50 ON WIRE WHEELS
WHEELBASE, TRACK (F), TRACK(R)	94 X 47 X 50 INCHES
LENGTH, WIDTH, HEIGHT	147 X 60 X 53 INCHES
MAX SPEED	80 MPH
WHERE BUILT	ABINGDON-ON-THAMES, ENGLAND

Allied troops still stationed in Britain. It appealed particularly to the Americans for whom it was a natural peace-time successor to the Jeep which had given many of them a taste for sporting motoring.

Of the 10,000 produced, only a third stayed in the UK and 2000 were sold in America.

By 1949, though, its pre-war design was painfully evident in the hard ride; it looked fast but its cramped cockpit and bouncy suspension was no longer fun. Even when the TB was launched in 1936 many small family sedans had independent front suspension.

So the TD came along in late 1949 using a shortened version of the chassis that had been used for the Y-type sedan from 1947. A wider front track gave added roadholding benefits, enhanced by lower fatter tires – 5.50 x 15, new rack and pinion steering and better brakes. Old-fashioned purists did not like the pressed steel wheels but they were stronger and allowed the car to sit lower. The engine, though, remained the same 76.2 cu.in unit so the TD was slower in acceleration than the TC due to the extra weight of the suspension and bumpers. However the TD looked more modern and was notably more comfortable. In its four-year life nearly 30,000 were made, including a Mk.II version with slightly more power from bigger carburetors; over 75 per cent of TDs went to America where it was as popular on the race-track as on the road. Many racing stars like Phil Hill and Richie Ginther started their track careers with an MG TD.

By 1953, such genuine post-war models as the Austin Healey 100,

from the same group following the 1952 Austin-Morris merger, and the Triumph TR2 were on the way. The TD looked old and was 20 mph slower. At that time MG were not allowed to produce an Austin-Healey rival, so the TD was just restyled with a sloping radiator grille and more flowing wing line, although still with running boards. The engine remained the same, so the TF accelerated no faster than the TC. Increasing the engine size to 89.4 cu.in in 1954 improved the performance but production stopped after a year and a half to make way for the MGA; some 9600 TFs were built, of which 3200 were the Mk.II version. The TC put the MG name on the world map and the TD strengthened the image. Although the TF was the most attractive of all, and is now the most desirable, it was too dated by 1953.

262-263 With the screen lowered to reveal the optional aero-screens, the TC looked an ideal sports car and found many American buyers.

TECHNICAL DESCRIPTION OF THE MG TC	
YEARS OF PRODUCTION	1945-1949
ENGINE	FRONT MOUNTEDIN-LINE 4-CYLINDER
BORE X STROKE, CAPACITY	2.6 x 3.5 INCHES, 76.2 CU.IN
VALVEGEAR	PUSHROD OHV
FUEL SYSTEM	TWIN SU CARBURETORS
POWER	54 BHP AT 5200 RPM
TRANSMISSION	4-SPEED, REAR DRIVE
BODY/CHASSIS	STEEL PANELS ON ASH FRAME, STEEL CHANNEL CHASSIS
SUSPENSION	SEMI-ELLIPTIC LEAF SPRINGS
TIRES/WHEELS	19 x 4.50 ON WIRE WHEELS
WHEELBASE, TRACK (F), TRACK(R)	94 x 45 x 45 INCHES
LENGTH, WIDTH, HEIGHT	140 x 56 x 53
MAX SPEED	75 MPH
WHERE BUILT	ABINGDON-ON-THAMES, ENGLAND

Alfa Romeo 6C2500

When Carrozzeria Touring won the Grand Prix at the 1949 Villa d'Este Concours with their latest bodywork on an Alfa Romeo 6C 2500 Super Sport chassis, it was the start of a new line. It didn't matter that the model was a pre-war design; the style was what counted. It was and has remained a rare beauty.

The origins of the 6C 2500 lay in Alfa Romeo's new design of 1934, undertaken by Jano who had taken time out from race-car design to create the 6C-2300. It had a new 6-cylinder engine with a cast-iron 7-bearing cylinder block and a detachable aluminium cylinder head carrying the customary twin overhead camshafts driven by chain rather than gears or a vertical shaft. A new gearbox had synchromesh on 3rd and top gears with a freewheel. The box section frame had semi-elliptic springs all round. Alfa Romeo built the majority of the 76 bhp Gran Turismo models on a 115-inch wheelbase, while Castagna used a 126-inch chassis to make 6-seater limousines. To launch the new model, Alfa Romeo entered three Touring-bodied Gran Turismo models in the 1934

264-265 *With this Touring Superleggera bodywork, an Alfa Romeo 6C 2500SS won the Grand Prix at the 1949 Villa d'Este Concours.*

Pescara 24-hours and took the first three places, giving rise to a new model name.

Around 760 of the 2300 were built, before the 6C-2300B came along in 1935 with an all independently sprung chassis and hydraulic brakes. The design used twin trailing arms with the Alfa Romeo combined coil spring and damper system at the front, and a swing axle at the rear with longitudinal torsion bars, a system very similar to that of Dr.Porsche's Auto-Union GP car. Turismo, Gran Turismo and Pescara continued but less than 300 were built over the three years as the company was required to build military trucks and air engines during 1935-6.

A 2nd series saw a few refinements in 1938 and the models renamed Lungo (128 inches wheelbase), with Corto and Touring's Miglia Miglia coupe on the 118 inch chassis; over 500 of these were built. Then came the 2500 in 1939 with the cylinder bores enlarged by 0.07 inch. The range continued with five and six-seater models on the 128 inch chassis and 4-seaters from Touring on the 118 inch. Sport chassis, but a 106 inch wheelbase chassis was

introduced for the 110 bhp Super Sports. These mostly went to Touring for open two-seaters, coupes and cabriolets – only 61 SS chassis were made from 1939-43. Six SS Corsa were also made by Touring; with 125 bhp, these won the 1939 Tobruk-Tripoli race but were beaten by BMW in the 1940 Mille Miglia (Brescia GP). Alfa Romeo also made almost 250 of the 6-7 seater limousines which would have been used by senior wartime officials, and a further 150 6C 2500 Coloniale open 4-seater staff-cars.

Production of the 2500 ceased in 1943. Although work had started on a prototype for the post-war period and it ultimately performed well, the facilities at the war-torn factory were not suited to the introduction of a new model, so post-war production continued with the existing 6C 2500; the only novelties were a steering column gear-change and the

welding of the steel bodywork to the chassis, creating an early form of unitary construction.

Body styling had more significant changes though and the traditional Alfa grille was made much narrower. Alfa Romeo used the 118 inch Sport chassis for a 5-6-seater which they called the Freccia d'oro (Golden Arrow) to set it apart from the pre-war models. Both 118 inch Sport and 106 inch Super Sport chassis were made available to coachbuilders; Stabilimenti Farina produced large sedan cars, Touring used the short chassis for some superb coupes while Pinin Farina produced many convertibles. Touring's shapes gradually evolved over 1947-8. Still smooth and aerodynamic in shape, they retained the separate outline of the wings but brought in tight creases curving back from the top of the

wheel arch. They made the rear cabin broader too. Then came the Villa d'Este line. Taking a 6C-2500SS chassis, they removed the rearward sweep of the front wing and just allowed the crease to give a hint of the shape; they curved the body sides under the chassis; they flattened the roof section and added rear quarter lights; and finally they integrated the grille with the wings with a raised section starting alongside the engine cover, sweeping down to include the fog lights before fading away under the headlights. It was a complicated piece of coachbuilding but it had the desired effect. While Alfa Romeo built nearly 700 Freccia d'oro models, over 400 SS chassis were sent out to coachbuilders from 1947-51; Touring built a number of coupes before the Villa d'Este line came in, so the coupe shown is indeed a rare and beautiful model.

266-267 Not all the 6C 2500SS chassis had wire wheels.

TECHNICAL DESCRIPTION OF THE ALFA-ROMEO 6C-2500SS

YEARS OF PRODUCTION	1947-51
MODELS	2-SEATER COUPE
ENGINE	IN-LINE 6-CYLINDER
BORE X STROKE, CAPACITY	2.8 x 3.9 INCHES, 149 CU.IN
VALVEGEAR	TWIN OVERHEAD CAMSHAFT
FUEL SYSTEM	THREE SOLEX CARBURETORS
POWER	110 BHP AT 4800 RPM
TRANSMISSION	4-SPEED MANUAL
BODY/CHASSIS	STEEL PANELS ON STEEL FRAME
FRONT SUSPENSION	TRAILING ARMS AND COIL SPRINGS
REAR SUSPENSION	SWING AXLE WITH TORSION BARS
TIRES/WHEELS	6.50 x 17 ON STEEL
	OR WIRE WHEELS
WHEELBASE x TRACK (F x R)	106.3 x 57 x 58 INCHES
LENGTH, WIDTH, HEIGHT	177 x 69.5 x 57 INCHES
MAX SPEED	100 MPH
WHERE BUILT	MILAN, ITALY

Morgan 4/4

The Morgan is an unashamedly British sports car. Conceived in the Mid-thirties, the style has hardly changed over the years until the recent launch of the Aero 8. The traditional Morgan may be too uncomfortable for some, but it always provides enjoyable motoring. From its foundation in 1910, Morgan spent the next 25 years producing three-wheeled cars. They were powered by air-cooled motor-cycle engines until 1933, when the water-cooled Ford 8 engine was added to the range. Apart from generally sound engineering, Morgan had pioneered independent front suspension, a sliding pillar system that would later be used by Lancia. The first four-wheeler arrived in 1936; four wheels and four cylinders justified the name 4/4. The engine came from Coventry-Climax; with overhead inlet and side-exhaust valves, this 68.4 cu.in engine produced 34 bhp and gave a maximum speed of 77 mph. The 4-speed Moss gearbox was separated from the engine by a short tube so that the gear lever could operate directly on the gear selectors, while the new rear axle was mounted on leaf springs set inside the chassis rails, features which stayed with the car for many years after. Additional coachwork saw steel panels laid on ash frames; the styling then was very contemporary with front wings sweeping into running boards and a long louvred bonnet going forward to a chromed radiator. A four-seater version was offered in 1937 and a new overhead valve engine of 77.3 cu.in came from the Standard Flying Ten in 1939 with 39 bhp.

268-269 This 1947 Morgan 4/4 has the longer body to provide four seats.

TECHNICAL DESCRIPTION OF THE MORGAN 4/4 (STANDARD ENGINE)

YEARS OF PRODUCTION	1939-1950
MODELS	2-SEATER, 4-SEATER
ENGINE	IN-LINE 4-CYLINDER
BORE X STROKE, CAPACITY	2.5 x 3.9 INCHES, 77.3 CU.IN
VALVEGEAR	PUSHROD OHV
FUEL SYSTEM	SOLEX CARBURETOR
POWER	40 BHP AT 4300 RPM
TRANSMISSION	4-SPEED MANUAL
BODY/CHASSIS	Z-SECTION STEEL FRAME WITH STEEL BODY PANELS ON ASH FRAME
FRONT SUSPENSION	SLIDING PILLARS AND COIL SPRINGS
REAR SUSPENSION	LIVE AXLE WITH LEAF SPRINGS
TIRES/WHEELS	5.00 x 16 ON STEEL WHEELS
WHEELBASE x TRACK (F x R)	92 x 45 x 45 INCHES
LENGHT, WIDT, HEIGHT	139 x 55 x 50 INCHES
MAX SPEED	77 MPH
WHERE BUILT	MALVERN, WORCESTERSHIRE

The post-war 4/4 used the same Standard engine in both two and four-seater models. Meanwhile Standard dropped all their pre-war engines in favor of a single 122 cu.in four-cylinder unit designed for the Vanguard. Morgan adopted this 68 bhp engine in 1950 for the Plus 4, and dropped the 4/4. By 1953, the only styling change had been the headlights blended into the front wings and the chrome grille replaced with the curved version. When the TR2 also began to use the Vanguard engine, in 90 bhp 121.4 cu.in form, Standard could not provide enough engines. Morgan brought back the 4/4 range using the side-valve 71.5 cu. in. Ford engine as the 4/4 Series 2 with the same power as the Standard. Ford continued to provide power for the 4/4 with the 60.8 cu.in Series 3 (1961), the 81.7 cu.in Series 4 (1962) and the 91.4 cu.in Series 5 (1963). The 4/4 was always more of an open tourer than a sports car, but it was just as exclusive, because Morgan never built more than 500 cars a year.

Cisitalia Gran Sport

270-271 *The Cisitalia Gran Sport by Pinin Farina was one of the world's style icons. Left, a roadster version finished second in the 1947 Mille Miglia.*

Although the Cisitalia Gran Sport was not fast, it earned its place in history as the first of the Gran Turismo line, the practical sports coupe. An example has been in the New York Museum of Modern Art since 1951 and credited to Pinin Farina who had shown the first model in October 1947 at the Milan Coachbuilders' Fair. It was a successful car, too, on the Italian race-tracks in the early post-war years thanks to light weight and good roadholding.

Cisitalia was a Turin-based industrial company established by Piero Dusio. He had been a successful racing driver before the war and, in 1934, was the Italian amateur champion; he was also a regular Mille Miglia competitor. After the war he started to build Fiat-powered single-seaters. The little D46 used the 67.1 cu.in Fiat four-cylinder engine in a tubular space-frame chassis with Fiat

independent front suspension; many Italian stars drove them.

The racer had been designed by Fiat's Dante Giacosa. Giacosa also started the design for a coupe version, based on the Savio-bodied Fiat 508C MM that was developed for the 1938 Mille Miglia. When Fiat recalled Giacosa, the work was taken on by a former Fiat engineer, Giovanni Savonuzzi. From wind tunnel studies he evolved an effective shape that would allow a tuned Fiat engine to produce 100 mph performance.

Dusio took the design to Pinin Farina. While such coupes had been built for the high speed events before the war – notably with Superleggera bodies by Touring – these all had the cabin fared into a narrow tail for better streamlining. This gave a very small rear window and no luggage space. Pinin Farina made the back of the cabin much broader, and added that subsequently familiar bulge around the rear wheels, like an animal poised to leap; the headlights were also moved outwards to the front end of the wings. In fact the cabin was too wide, resulting in a rather heavy appearance from the front, but, from the side, the proportions were perfect.

A roadster version (illustrated) was built for the 1947 Mille Miglia with rear fins similar to those that Savonuzzi had originally defined for his coupe. Driven by Tazio Nuvolari it finished second, beating the new Ferrari 125 and Maserati A6CGS, and only losing the lead to a big pre-war Alfa sedan due to heavy rain. Dusio himself entered but didn't finish, although two other Cisitalias took third and fourth places ahead of the new 1100S Fiat coupes – Giacosa's response to the Cisitalia was to produce 400 of these sporting machines. Bernabei's third-placed car recorded the fastest time from Turin to Brescia at 95 mph.

By then Dusio was involved with a Grand Prix car project. He had approached Porsche to design this in 1946, at which time Professor Porsche was interned by the French. Dusio's contract was largely responsible for providing the funds to secure Porsche's release. While the design of the four-wheel-drive supercharged 91.5 cu.in GP car was very advanced, the project consumed more money than was available and Cisitalia went into liquidation. Dusio took the project to Argentina; despite the backing of General Peron under the name of Autoar the car never raced. Although Dusio came back to Italy to re-establish Cisitalia in late 1952, he was unsuccessful; the promising start for a new manufacturer was wasted on the altar of Grand Prix aspirations.

Meanwhile Pinin Farina had built the first 100 GS using aluminium body panels. A further 70 were made with steel body panels by Vignale and Stabilimenti Farina who had also made some 25 examples of the Roadster (Tipo Nuvolari). Some of the Gran Sports were cabriolets. Fiat then followed up their 1100S with the 1950 Fiat 1100ES, using Pinin Farina to create a shape very close to that of the Cisitalia. Pinin Farina used the same lines for the Lancia Aurelia B20 in 1951. In automotive history, the Cisitalia GS was much more than just a Fiat-based special.

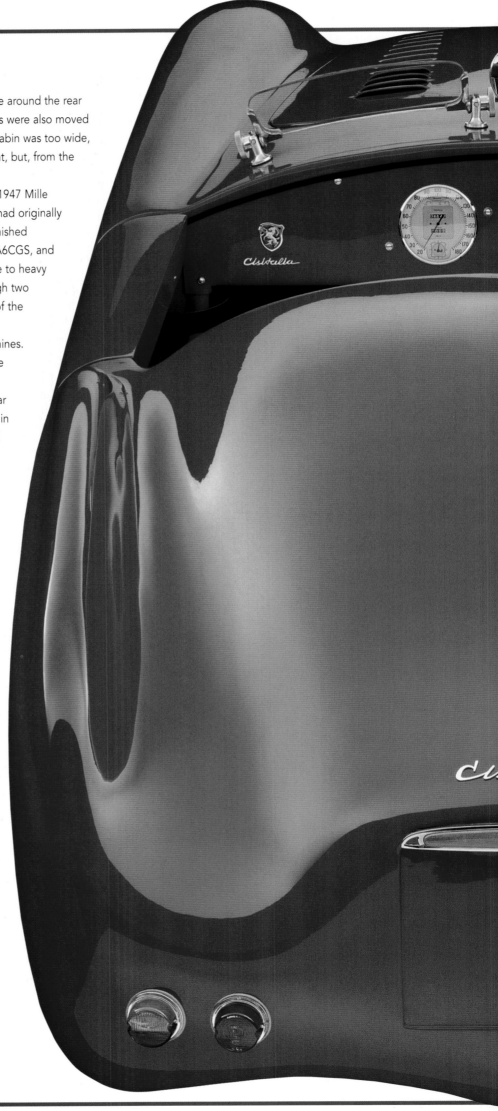

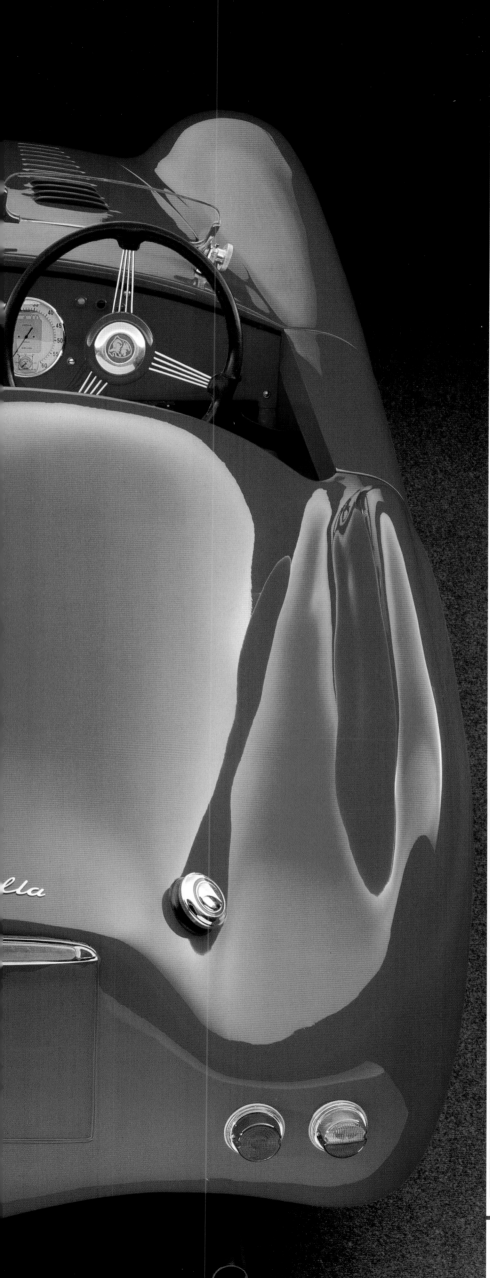

272-273 *Cisitalia Tipo Nuvolari was named after the car in which Tazio Nuvolari finished second in the 1947 Mille Miglia*

TECHNICAL DESCRIPTION OF THE CISITALIA GRAN SPORT

YEARS OF PRODUCTION	1947-52
MODELS	2-SEATER COUPE
ENGINE	IN-LINE 4-CYLINDER
BORE X STROKE, CAPACITY	2.6 X 2.9 INCHES, 66.4 CU.IN
VALVEGEAR	PUSHROD OHV
FUEL SYSTEM	TWIN SOLEX CARBURETORS
POWER	55 BHP AT 5500 RPM
TRANSMISSION	4-SPEED MANUAL
BODY/CHASSIS	ALUMINIUM OR STEEL PANELS ON SPACE FRAME
FRONT SUSPENSION	WISHBONES AND TRANSVERSE LEAF SPRINGS
REAR SUSPENSION	LIVE AXLE WITH LEAF SPRINGS
TIRES/WHEELS	5.00 X 15 ON WIRE WHEELS
WHEELBASE X TRACK (F X R)	94 X 49.5 X 49 INCHES
LENGTH, WIDTH, HEIGHT	134 X 57 X 49 INCHES
MAX SPEED	100 MPH
WHERE BUILT	TURIN, ITALY

273

Ferrari 166

No other make in the world generates the same universal respect as Ferrari. Whatever classic cars enthusiasts might revere, they accept that all Ferraris are classics. They represent all that is best in the Italian style from dashing good looks to competition success. While the 125 was used by many on road and track, the 166 was the first Ferrari to be offered for sale as a road car.

Through most of the Thirties, former racing driver Enzo Ferrari had run his own Scuderia Ferrari with Alfa Romeo racing cars. Following a spell as Alfa Romeo race team manager at the time of the birth of the immortal 158, Ferrari was not allowed to use the Scuderia name on cars for four years after he left in 1938. As a result the first Ferraris were the three AAC (Auto-Avio Costruzioni) 815s built out of Fiat parts, including two Fiat cylinder blocks to make a straight-8 1.91 cu.in engine, which took part in the 1940 Mille Miglia.

After the 1939-45 war, Ferrari set out to build his own cars, initially for competition. The first arrived in 1947 as the two-seater 125 either with all-enveloping bodywork or as a two-seater racing car with removable cycle-wings. Ferrari chose to use V-12 engines simply because he liked the idea, regardless of the complexity for a new manufacturer, but Modena was full of enterprising machine shops. The type number represented the capacity of a single cylinder as it would do for many years. Its chassis was a simple cross-braced tubular frame carrying wishbone front suspension and a live rear axle on leaf springs; a 5-speed gearbox was probably unique at the time.

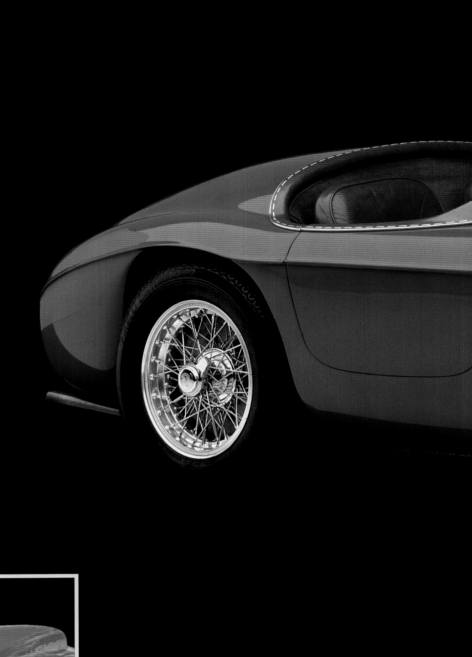

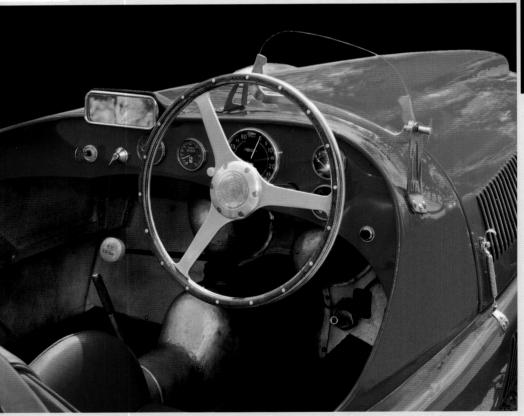

For 1948 the introduction of a 122 cu.in formula 2 led to the Tipo 166 with the Colombo-designed engine increased to 121.7 cu.in. In competition form it developed 150 bhp at 7000 rpm, impressive statistics for 1948. Meanwhile Ferrari had supercharged the original 91.5 cu.in engine from the 125 for the first Grand Prix Ferrari.

The 166 Spyder Corsa was doing well in F2 races and in Sport form had won the 1948 Targa Florio and the Mille Miglia, for which the winning car had a coupe body. Some 11 of these competition chassis were built in 1948.

At the end of 1948, there were two Ferrari 166 models at the Turin Motor Show, the sports 166MM and the coupe 166 Inter, both with bodies designed by Touring and equipped with Superleggera coachwork construction. The 166MM was the first to feature the body style that was christened Barchetta, and was to be copied by AC via Tojeiro for the first post-war Ace; MM stood for Mille Miglia in honour of the 1948 victory. The 166MM earned its own place in Mille Miglia

274-275 Ferrari 166MM, upper, and 166 Spyder Corsa 1948 (bottom left and bottom right).

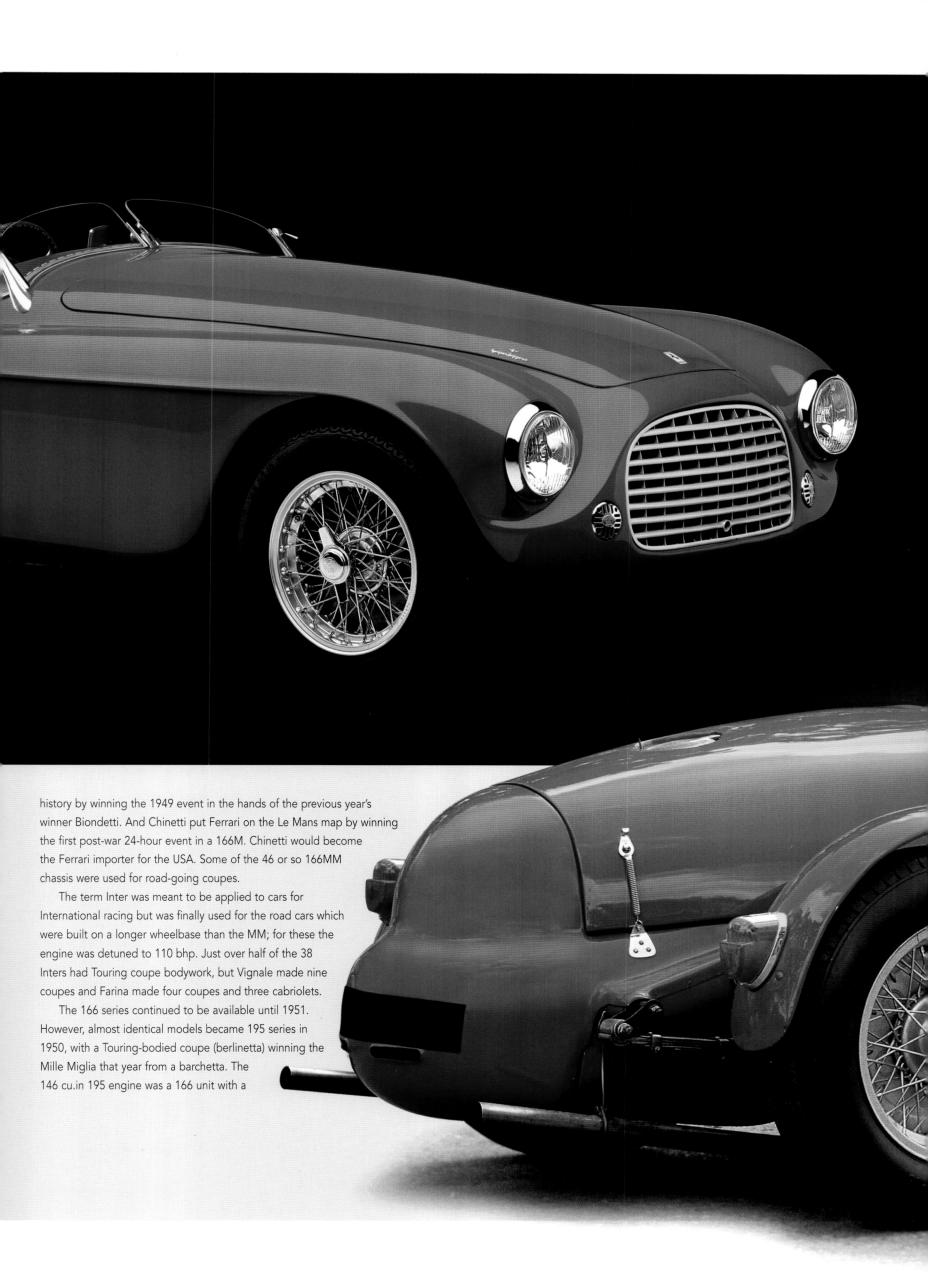

history by winning the 1949 event in the hands of the previous year's winner Biondetti. And Chinetti put Ferrari on the Le Mans map by winning the first post-war 24-hour event in a 166M. Chinetti would become the Ferrari importer for the USA. Some of the 46 or so 166MM chassis were used for road-going coupes.

The term Inter was meant to be applied to cars for International racing but was finally used for the road cars which were built on a longer wheelbase than the MM; for these the engine was detuned to 110 bhp. Just over half of the 38 Inters had Touring coupe bodywork, but Vignale made nine coupes and Farina made four coupes and three cabriolets.

The 166 series continued to be available until 1951. However, almost identical models became 195 series in 1950, with a Touring-bodied coupe (berlinetta) winning the Mille Miglia that year from a barchetta. The 146 cu.in 195 engine was a 166 unit with a

bigger cylinder bore. As before the 195 Inter used a longer wheelbase for coupes by Vignale, Ghia and Touring.

A further cylinder bore increase produced the 156 cu.in 212 series over 1951-2. Long and short chassis were called Inter and Export, with the Export intended for competition use. Some 110 chassis were built for the 212 series. Touring and Vignale built most of the 26 Export bodies in open or closed forms, while the Inters used a bigger variety of coachbuilders. Among the Inters, a number came from Pinin Farina, the first of a collaboration that has lasted through to the present day.

The 166 was Ferrari's first road car but the 212 confirmed that the Ferrari name had gained world-wide acceptance.

They may not have been the quietest or most comfortable road cars, but they had race-winning performance with Italian style.

276-277 Left, Ferrari 166 Inter by Touring. Right, 166 Inter by Stabilimenti Farina.

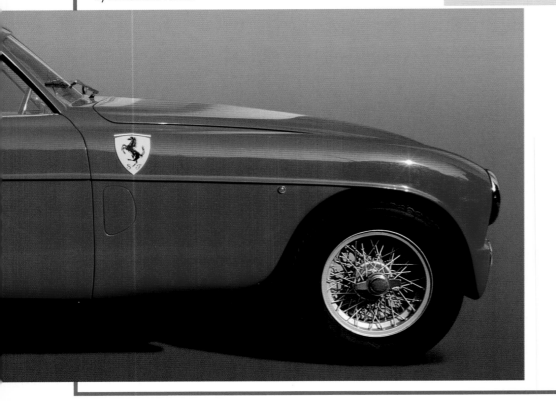

TECHNICAL DESCRIPTION OF THE FERRARI SPYDER CORSA	
YEARS OF PRODUCTION	1948-50
MODELS	SPYDER, SPORT, MM AND INTER
ENGINE	FRONT-MOUNTED V-12
BORE X STROKE, CAPACITY	2.36 X 2.31 INCHES, 121.5 CU.IN
VALVEGEAR	SINGLE OHC PER BANK
FUEL SYSTEM	THREE 30 DCF WEBERS
POWER	150 BHP AT 7000 RPM
TRANSMISSION	5-SPEED
BODY/CHASSIS	TWIN-TUBE STEEL CHASSIS WITH ALUMINIUM BODY PANELS
SUSPENSION	FRONT, WISHBONE AND TRANSVERSE LEAF SPRING; REAR, LIVE AXLE ON SEMI-ELLIPTIC LEAF SPRINGS
TIRES/WHEELS	5.50/6.00 X 15 TIRES; WIRE WHEELS
WHEELBASE, TRACK (F), TRACK(R)	90 X 47 X 47 INCHES
MAX SPEED	120 MPH
WHERE BUILT	MARANELLO, ITALY

Jaguar XK120 to XK150

For those who saw the unveiling at the Earls Court Motor Show in 1948, there was never any doubt that the Jaguar XK120 would become one of the great sporting cars in the history of motoring. In an age when most sports cars on the road still had separate wings, its all-enveloping bodywork was instantly modern, and its proportions were perfect. And it had a new 207 cu.in six-cylinder engine with twin overhead camshafts, a system previously considered as more appropriate to racing machinery. The figure 120 was chosen to represent the maximum speed the car could

reach; a demonstration run in Belgium saw a standard car achieve 126 mph complete with hood and windscreen. At £988 ($3300), without the British purchase tax, it was still twice the price of an MG TC, but it was half the cost of a Frazer Nash; it was exceptional value for its performance.

Before the war, Jaguar had used engines from Standard with their own overhead-valve cylinder heads, but the twin-cam XK engine was entirely new; conceived during the latter stages of the war it was designed to give 100 mph performance to the first new sedan. In fact, the Mk.VII did not arrive until 1951. The engine would go on to serve the company for many years in 146, 231 and 256 cu.in forms, and earned them five victories in the Le Mans 24-hour race with XK120C and D-type Jaguars.

The separate chassis used deep boxed side members with cross bracing and carried wishbone front suspension with torsion bars, while the rear suspension just used leaf springs. Jaguar did not expect a big demand for the car and used traditional methods for the body with aluminium panels laid on wooden frames.

When the orders flooded in, they changed the panels to pressed steel after 240 cars had been built. Most of the production from the first 18 months were exported and the car did not reach its home market until early 1950.

The striking style of the body owed much to the influence of the Italian coachbuilder Touring whose work was seen on the Alfa Romeos and BMWs in the final pre-war Mille Miglia events. A year later, a fixed head coupe became available and in 1953, a drop head coupe. The same body styles were carried through to the XK140 which arrived in 1954. For this the engine was uprated to the 190 bhp specification that had been offered as a Special Equipment option for the XK120 and it was moved forward three inches to give more space in the cockpit; for

278

278-279 *Graceful lines of the XK120 roadster set new standards of elegance in 1948.*

TECHNICAL DESCRIPTION OF THE JAGUAR XK120

YEARS OF PRODUCTION	1948 - 1954
MODELS	ROADSTER AND FIXED HEAD COUPE
ENGINE	FRONT-MOUNTED IN-LINE SIX-CYLINDER
BORE X STROKE, CAPACITY	3.2 X 4.1 INCHES, 210 CU.IN
VALVEGEAR	TWIN OVERHEAD CAMSHAFT
FUEL SYSTEM	TWO SU CARBURETORS
POWER	160 BHP AT 5000 RPM
TRANSMISSION	4-SPEED
BODY/CHASSIS	BOXED STEEL CHASSIS WITH ALUMINIUM OR STEEL BODY PANELS
SUSPENSION	FRONT, WISHBONES AND TORSION BARS. REAR, LIVE AXLE WITH LEAF SPRINGS
TIRES/WHEELS	6.00 X 16 ON STEEL WHEELS
WHEELBASE, TRACK (F), TRACK(R)	102 X 54 X 53 INCHES
LENGHT, WIDT, HEIGHT	162 X 62 X 52 INCHES
MAX SPEED	120 MPH
WHERE BUILT	COVENTRY, ENGLAND

TECHNICAL DESCRIPTION OF THE JAGUAR XK150 3.4

YEARS OF PRODUCTION	1957-1961
MODELS	XK150, XK150S FHC AND DHC
ENGINE	FRONT-MOUNTED IN-LINE SIX-CYLINDER
BORE X STROKE, CAPACITY	3.2 x 4.1 INCHES, 210 CU.IN
VALVEGEAR	TWIN OVERHEAD CAMSHAFT
FUEL SYSTEM	TWO SU CARBURETORS
POWER	190 BHP AT 5500 RPM
TRANSMISSION	4-SPEED AND O/D OR AUTO
BODY/CHASSIS	BOXED STEEL CHASSIS WITH STEEL BODY PANELS OR STEEL BODY PANELS
FRONT SUSPENSION	FRONT, WISHBONES AND TORSION BARS
REAR SUSPENSION	LIVE AXLE WITH LEAF SPRINGS
TIRES/WHEELS	6.00 x 16 STEEL OR WIRE WHEELS
WHEELBASE, TRACK (F), TRACK(R)	102 x 51 x 51 INCHES
LENGHT, WIDT, HEIGHT	177 x 64 x 55 INCHES
MAX SPEED	124 MPH
WHERE BUILT	COVENTRY, ENGLAND

the fixed head and drophead coupes, the front seats were moved even further forward by altering the bulkhead to allow space for occasional rear seats. An overdrive was also available while an option on Special Equipment XK140s was the C-type cylinder head which would increase the power to 210 bhp. Stiffer springing and rack and pinion steering improved the handling. Heavier bumpers and fewer strips in the grille made the new model instantly recognizable. While the XK140 did not have the refreshing purity of the XK120's appearance, it was a better car for everyday use.

The steady improvement in practicality was taken several stages further when the XK150 replaced the XK140 in 1957. Restyled in the fashion of the medium sedans – 2.7 and 3.4 – the XK150 had a curved windscreen and was usefully wider inside. The adoption of disc brakes

280-281 *XK150 was a more comfortable car but lost the purity of the XK120 line.*

was a major step forward, but in other respects the specification was similar to that of the XK140. Most cars had the 210 bhp Special Equipment cylinder heads but then the S version came out with 250 bhp with triple carburetors and a higher compression ratio in 1958. A year later the engine was increased to 230.7 cu.in and the S model produced 265 bhp, the same that would power the E-type in 1961.

Of the 30,000 cars made over 12 years, the XK120 was the most popular at 12,078 followed by the XK150 at 9395 and the XK140 at 8884. The XK120 was almost the fastest car on the road in its day, but by the time of the XK150, there were many faster. But none could match the sheer value of the XK range.

Aston Martin DB2 and DB2/4

Aston Martin were one of several British companies to challenge the Italian lead in the new Grand Touring market. While traditionalists retained the belief that a sports car had to be an open two-seater with the option of a folding hood, others recognized that higher cruising speeds demanded a closed roof for long distance comfort. Aston Martin was founded in 1913 and had long made small sports cars with efficient 91.5 or 122 cu.in engines; some models were open four-seaters, and a few sedans were made in the Thirties.

Lagonda were also in the sporting market but their cars and engines were bigger; the company had won the Le Mans 24-hour race in 1935 with a 274. cu.in engine and finished third and fourth in 1939 with a 274. cu.in V-12.

In 1947 industrialist David Brown took over both companies. Both had prepared post-war designs but it was Aston Martin's prototype Atom sports sedan which provided the basis for the first production Aston Martins. The 122 cu.in Sports, later called the DB1, was launched in October 1948, together with a stark 2-seater replica of the car that had won the 1948 Spa 24-hour race; a 122 cu.in coupe was announced at the same time but not shown. However three coupes were entered for the 1949 Le Mans 24-hour race; two used the existing pushrod four-cylinder 122 cu.in engine, but a third had the 158 cu.in twin overhead camshaft six-cylinder engine that had been designed under W.O.Bentley for Lagonda. The first post-war Lagonda was announced in 1949.

While none of the three cars finished Le Mans in 1949, two went to the Spa 24-hour race two weeks later. Chinetti repeated his Le Mans victory in a Ferrari 166 and Louveau's pre-war Delage was second but the 158 cu.in Aston finished third and the 122 cu.in was fifth. British cars did well at that event as a Jowett Javelin won the touring category and HRG took the team award in the 91.5 cu.in sports class.

The success of the six-cylinder Aston Martin was enough to convince David Brown that this was his engine of the future and the DB2 was first

exhibited at the New York Show in April 1950, with the engine in 105 bhp tune. The design followed the Le Mans cars closely; Lagonda's Frank Feeley had created a winning fast-back shape. Early cars had three separate grilles but this soon changed to the one-piece Omega shape. Underneath, the rectangular tube steel chassis carried Porsche-style trailing arms with coil springing at the front, and a well-located live rear axle.

A drophead coupe was available later in 1950, and in 1951 came the first use of the Vantage name for a high performance version with 125 bhp. The engine continued to be used in the competition DB3 and DB3S throughout the Fifties and was further developed to power the DBR1 to win the World Sports Car Championship in 1959. While the DB2 was highly rated as a GT car, it suffered from only having two seats with limited luggage space behind. This was rectified in 1953 with the introduction of the DB2/4; the DB2 body was lengthened and the rear roof line raised to give two small rear seats and more luggage space to which access was gained through an opening rear window.

Initially the engine was the Vantage 158 cu.in, but a 183 cu.in version was used from April 1954 with 140 bhp. This raised the maximum speed

282 Aston Martin DB2 1952 with Vantage engine.

283 Aston Martin DB2/4 1953 with 158 cu.in engine.

TECHNICAL DESCRIPTION OF THE ASTON MARTIN DB2 VANTAGE AND (DB2/4)	
YEARS OF PRODUCTION	1950-1954
MODELS	FIXED HEAD COUPE
ENGINE	FRONT-MOUNTED IN-LINE SIX-CYLINDER
BORE X STROKE, CAPACITY	3 x 3.5 INCHES, 157.4 CU. IN.
VALVEGEAR	TWIN OVERHEAD CAMSHAFT
FUEL SYSTEM	TWO SU CARBURETORS
POWER	125 BHP AT 5000 RPM
TRANSMISSION	4-SPEED
BODY/CHASSIS	BOXED STEEL CHASSIS WITH ALUMINIUM BODY PANELS
SUSPENSION	FRONT, TRAILING ARMS AND COILS
	REAR, LIVE AXLE, MULTI-LINK, COILS
TIRES/WHEELS	6.00 x 16 ON WIRE WHEELS
WHEELBASE, TRACK (F), TRACK(R)	99 x 54 x 54 INCHES
LENGHT, WIDT, HEIGHT	162 (169) x 65 x 54 INCHES
MAX SPEED	115 MPH
WHERE BUILT	FELTHAM, ENGLAND

to around 115 mph.

The DB2-4 Mk.11 came in 1955 with minor body changes; in addition to the existing 3-door sedan and drop-head coupe styles, a 2-door fixed head coupe was available using what was effectively a hard-top on the drop-head. The body was built at the future home of Aston Martin in Newport Pagnell by Tickford, which had been bought by David Brown in 1953.

With the 1957 announcement of the DB Mk.III came the final version of the DB2; the three body styles continued to be available but the front grille adopted the revised shape of the DB3S. Disc front brakes and a redesigned engine with 162 bhp (up to 195 bhp with options) helped to make this the best of all the Atom-based models. Some 1726 were built over the ten years to 1959 when the DB Mk.III was replaced by the DB4.

Bristol 400, 402, 404

With a background in the aircraft industry extending back to 1910, Bristol chose to move into car construction after the 1939-45 war. War-time experiments with their own design proved unsuccessful, so they decided to develop an existing one. The basis of their first car was the pre-war BMW 327/80 coupe built around a 326 chassis as a result of the Thirties association between Frazer Nash and BMW. H.J.Aldington, who had acquired the Frazer Nash car company in 1928, imported BMWs which were marketed as Frazer Nash-BMWs. After the war, he acquired the rights to BMW drawings and brought BMW designer Fritz Fiedler to England to assist. Knowing that Bristol wanted to make cars, he arranged a joint venture with a view to

284-285 Bristol 400 of 1947, the first car from the airplane manufacturer.

selling the products as Frazer Nash-Bristols.

In the end, Bristol made their own BMW-based cars but allowed Frazer Nash to use the Bristol engines and other components in their own sports cars which were modelled around war-time developments of the tubular-framed BMW 328. The new Bristol 400 chassis followed the design of that for the 4-door 326 – boxed steel ladder frame with sheet steel flooring. A transverse leaf spring gave independent suspension at the front, while the rear had a well-located live rear axle with torsion bars.

The body was a close copy of the one built by Autenreith for the 327; as the 326 wheelbase was 6 inches longer, the rear side window was lengthened. This also increased the rear seat space, aided further by the wider rear track of the 326 rear axle design.

For the engine, Bristol started from the 80 bhp version that was used in the sportier BMW 327 as well as in the BMW 328. A straight-6 122 cu.in, it used a side-mounted camshaft which operated valves in a hemispherical combustion chamber through

TECHNICAL DESCRIPTION OF THE BRISTOL 400	
YEARS OF PRODUCTION	1946-1949
MODELS	4-SEATER SEDAN
ENGINE	IN-LINE 6-CYLINDER
BORE X STROKE, CAPACITY	2.6 X 3.7 INCHES, 120 CU.IN
VALVEGEAR	TWIN PUSH-ROD SYSTEM WITH INCLINED OHV
FUEL SYSTEM	3 SU CARBURETORS
POWER	80 BHP AT 4200 RPM
TRANSMISSION	4-SPEED MANUAL
BODY/CHASSIS	BOXED GIRDER STEEL CHASSIS WITH ALUMINIUM PANELS
SUSPENSION, FRONT	UPPER WISHBONE, TRANSVERSE LEAF SPRING
SUSPENSION, REAR	LIVE AXLE, TRANSVERSE LINKS, A-BRACKET, TORSION BARS
TIRES/WHEELS	5.50 X 16 ON STEEL WHEELS
WHEELBASE, TRACK (F), TRACK(R)	114 X 52 X 54 INCHES
LENGHT, WIDT, HEIGHT	183 X 64 X 59 INCHES
MAX SPEED	95 MPH
WHERE BUILT	FILTON, BRISTOL, ENGLAND

cross-over pushrods and rockers; a smooth engine that was very efficient. The gearbox was a Bristol design.

What Bristol did was to take the best of BMW's sporting designs and apply their aircraft expertise to build the car to the highest possible standards. Every aspect was studied and improved in design and, frequently, material specification. The result was a car that had remarkable performance when it was launched in 1947 with a maximum speed of 90 mph and new standards of ride and roadholding. Hand built, it was inevitably expensive but the company never intended to enter volume production. Only 470 were built between 1947 and 1950.

Meanwhile the 401 had been launched in 1949, a 400 with an aerodynamic body that had been proposed by Touring, Milan and refined by Bristol who used the Touring Superleggera principle of small body frame tubes around which the aluminium panels were wrapped. The improved shape with the same 85 bhp brought the maximum speed up to 95 mph. Some 600 were built from 1949 to 1952. Additionally there were just 21 of the convertible 402. Outwardly the 403 was almost identical to the 401 but the engine was increased to 100 bhp and improvements were made to the gearbox, suspension and brakes. From 1953-55, around 275 were made.

Also launched in 1953 was the 404, a fastback 2-seater coupe on a shortened 403 chassis. Where the early cars had respected their BMW origins with a version of the German company's grille, the 404 looked to Bristol's own origins by using a front intake shaped like that for a jet engine. And the rear of the car featured small fins; being based on those of the Bristol 450 Le Mans racer, these were more aerodynamic in origin than the stylistic devices of the American sedans. For the 404, the 122 cu.in engine was given 105 bhp, enough for 110 mph; it was a fast car for its day and earned the title of Businessman's Express. Unfortunately only 50 of them could afford it.

TECHNICAL DESCRIPTION OF THE BRISTOL 402

YEARS OF PRODUCTION	1949-1953
MODELS	4-SEATER CONVERTIBLE
ENGINE	IN-LINE 6-CYLINDER
BORE X STROKE, CAPACITY	2.6 X 3.7 INCHES, 120 CU.IN
VALVEGEAR	TWIN PUSH-ROD SYSTEM WITH INCLINED OHV
FUEL SYSTEM	3 DOWNDRAFT SOLEX
POWER	85 BHP AT 4500 RPM
TRANSMISSION	4-SPEED MANUAL
BODY/CHASSIS	BOXED GIRDER STEEL CHASSIS WITH ALUMINIUM PANELS
SUSPENSION, FRONT	UPPER WISHBONE, TRANSVERSE LEAF SPRING
SUSPENSION, REAR	LIVE AXLE, TRANSVERSE LINKS, A-BRACKET, TORSION BARS
TIRES/WHEELS	5.50 X 16 ON STEEL WHEELS
WHEELBASE, TRACK (F), TRACK(R)	114 X 52 X 54 INCHES
LENGHT, WIDT, HEIGHT	192 X 67 X 60 INCHES
MAX SPEED	100 MPH
WHERE BUILT	FILTON, BRISTOL, ENGLAND

For the 405, Bristol stretched the 404 shape back to the standard wheelbase size and, for the only time, produced a 4-door model to replace the 403. After 340 of the 405, including 43 two-door convertibles by Abbotts of Farnham, the 406 emerged as a more conventional-looking sedan with two doors; by now comfort was beginning to add weight, so the engine was increased to 134 cu.in, but the performance was no longer class-leading. A 311 cu.in Chrysler V-8 was installed in the 406 to create the 407 from 1962, and all succeeding Bristols have used Chrysler engines.

288-289 *The 404 Businessman's Express, a shortened 405.*

TECHNICAL DESCRIPTION OF THE BRISTOL 404

YEARS OF PRODUCTION	1953-1955
MODELS	2+2 COUPE
ENGINE	IN-LINE 6-CYLINDER
BORE X STROKE, CAPACITY	2.6 x 3.7 INCHES, 120 CU.IN
VALVEGEAR	TWIN PUSH-ROD SYSTEM WITH INCLINED OHV
FUEL SYSTEM	3 DOWNDRAFT SOLEX
POWER	105 BHP AT 5000 RPM
TRANSMISSION	4-SPEED MANUAL
BODY/CHASSIS	BOXED GIRDER STEEL CHASSIS WITH ALUMINIUM PANELS
SUSPENSION, FRONT	UPPER WISHBONE WITH TRANSVERSE LEAF SPRING
SUSPENSION, REAR	LIVE AXLE, TRANSVERSE LINKS, A-BRACKET, TORSION BARS
TIRES/WHEELS	5.50 x 16 ON STEEL WHEELS
WHEELBASE, TRACK (F), TRACK(R)	96 x 52 x 54 INCHES
LENGHT, WIDT, HEIGHT	159 x 68 x 56 INCHES
MAX SPEED	110 MPH
WHERE BUILT	FILTON, BRISTOL, ENGLAND

1951 - 1960

CLASSIC SEDANS

Although most of the car producing nations were well under way by the end of the previous decade, there was still a far greater demand than supply. Waiting lists were common, even in the USA. As a result there was not the pressure on manufacturers to make frequent changes to models, although Americans still expected it to be obvious that they had the latest car, so minor changes had to be made at minimal investment to differentiate the model years. By the middle of the Fifties, basic transport was generally available and manufacturers had time to enhance their ranges with more specialist models, the ones that would become future classics. In America it was the period of the high performance V-8 when ever larger engines were inserted to satisfy the demand for rubber-burning acceleration at the local drag-strip or even

just at the traffic lights. Technological progress saw the introduction of disc brakes and more general use of radial ply tires in Europe. Curiously, America lagged behind in such primary safety features, but concerned themselves more with driving comfort aids like automatic transmission, power steering, air-conditioning and large spacious interiors.

In styling, America remained the most influential center; ever-larger tail fins were a memorable feature of the Fifties. Around the world, the old coachbuilding firms were suffering as the separate chassis was replaced by the high volume unitary construction. France had all but lost its coachbuilding industry with the demise of the Grandes Makes like Delage and Talbot. English coachbuilders were more artisan than original but there were enough makes around still using a

separate chassis. It was the Italians who saw the way ahead. They could see that their future lay in providing a styling service and in building smaller runs of specialist cars that would not be economical for major manufacturers. By working with the manufacturers they were able to have the cars taken off the production line before they were finished; they then completed the bodywork themselves. Bertone's production of the Alfa Romeo Giulietta Sprint was a notable example – Spider and SS versions also came from Bertone. At the top end of the scale Aston Martin went to Touring to generate the shape for the new DB4 and built the cars under Touring's Superleggera licence.

Italian coachbuilders were very much involved in the styling, and frequently body building, of most of the Italian cars apart from those within Fiat. The first

290-291 Lancia Flaminia 2500 Zagato 1959-1961.

Lancia was the Aurelia which arrived in 1950 to be followed, a year later, by the coupe version with fast-back styling by Pinin Farina – an enlarged Cisitalia with four seats. Pinin Farina went on to design the open Spider version too.

It was a Pinin Farina design that was to lead to the R-type Bentley Continental of 1952 using the same basic fast-back shape. The Torinese coachbuilder had made a special body for Jean Daninos who would head the Facel Vega firm; this was shown at Paris in 1948. Before the war Bentley had experimented with similar shapes. The new Continental followed these overall lines but gave them added grace with twin sweeping wing lines tailing into restrained fins. With an uprated version of the old six-cylinder 274 cu.in R-type engine, it was good for 115 mph. The style continued into the S-type. By 1959, HJ Mulliner had built 193 Continentals on the R-type chassis and over 400 on the next model, the S-type. This was introduced in 1955 when Rolls-Royce brought out the matching Silver Cloud in 1955, the first Rolls to be available with standard bodywork, something that the company had already done with the first post-war Bentley, the Mk.VI. Underneath was a new but still separate chassis which allowed continued freedom for coachbuilders. With the 1959 S2 and Silver Cloud II came a new engine, the 378 cu.in V8. The S3 and Cloud III came with twin headlamp style in 1962 and both were replaced by the first unitary-construction T-type and Silver Shadow in 1965.

Other old-established English firms like Alvis and Rover continued to develop their big sedans and Alvis used the Swiss coachbuilder Graber to provide the basis of their new TD21 in 1958; Graber had been building special bodies on the TC21 from the Mid-fifties. Rover's single shape policy had started in 1949 with the Rover 75 with a six-cylinder 128 cu.in engine; in 1953 came the 90 and the 60, the latter with a four-cylinder engine. The range was to continue through 80, 95, 100, 105 and 110 versions until 1964 by which time over 130,000 of these middle-class P4 sedans had been built. The larger 183 cu.in P5 appeared in 1959.

Although post-war MG production was initially taken up with the TC, MG launched the Y-type Magnette sedan in 1947. This had been designed pre-war with independent front suspension on its box-section chassis. Using a single carburetor version of the TC engine, it was a lively performer; it was uprated in 1951 to YB specification.

This was followed by the ZA Magnette which used the 1952 Wolseley 4/44 body – which had been powered by the 76.2 cu.in MG sports engine – fitted with an MG grille and the BMC B-series 91.5 cu.in engine, which gave it very good performance. Badge-engineering had arrived in the British Motor Corporation and would be seen at its worst with the next generation Austin, Morris, Riley and MG sedans all using the same bodies and engines – not classics.

1951 - 1960

In classic terms, however the most notable British sedan arrival was that of the Jaguar 2.4 in 1955. The Mk.VII had been in production from 1950 and would be replaced by the similar Mk.VIII in 1957. The 2.4 was the 'little Jaguar', a compact 4-door sports sedan using a short-stroke version of the famous XK 207 cu.in from the bigger car; it was also Jaguar's first unitary-bodied sedan.

The 207 cu.in engine was added to the range in 1957 making a fast car very fast for its day. The Mk.II arrived in 1959 with a wider rear track and deeper side windows; there was also the option of a 231 cu.in engine which gave genuine 125 mph performance. A 152 cu.in Daimler V-8 version was added to the range in 1963. The 'softer' S-type came in 1964 but the Mk.II cars continued on till 1968. Almost 130,000 of the Mk.I and II were built.

Big Fiat sedans of the period were sturdy but hardly classics. However Alfa Romeo's 1900 was notable for the being the first volume production sedan for the nationalized company. Announced in 1950 it had a unitary construction, independent wishbone front suspension and a well-located live axle. The new 116 cu.in four-cylinder engine retained the Alfa hallmark of twin overhead camshafts but these were chain driven. It wasn't the quietest or most comfortable car but it was certainly sporting with 100 mph performance from the basic 90 bhp engine. Later TI and TI Super versions had 100 and 115 bhp respectively and these engines were used in the Sprint and Super Sprint versions which were produced as rolling platforms for the coachbuilders. Over 17,000 4-door sedans and 1800 Sprint chassis were produced in the 1950-1958 period. It was an important classic for Alfa Romeo. The Giulietta which came out in 1955 was preceded by the sporting versions in 1954 and is covered in more detail later in the chapter.

In Sweden, Saab continued to produce the two-stroke 92, changing to the 93 in 1955 with the introduction of a 45.7 cu.in 3-cylinder engine and dead axle rear suspension; the 95 estate followed in 1959 with the engine up to 51.8 cu.in, which the 96 used in 1960. Volvo added the 4-door Amazon or B120 in 1956 using the PV444 engine increased to 97 cu.in. The 1958 PV544 continued the PV444's hump-backed shape in a thoroughly revised model which earned the 109 cu.in engine in 1961. The Amazon Sport (B 122S) came in 1958 with 4-speeds and 88 bhp, with the two-door 121 following in 1961. Although these cars were made in fairly high volumes (PV444 196,000; PV544 440,000; B120-122 564,000), the production runs were spread over long periods and the cars were very well built.

In France, Citroen produced the epochal DS19 in 1955 with many advanced features which were to justify keeping it in production for 20 years with few changes. The chassis was a steel structure to which the body panels were bolted; the style was exceptionally aerodynamic. Although the engine was initially the old long-stroke 122 cu.in, this was replaced in 1966 by short stroke 'fours' of 122 and 140 cu.in. It was unique in using hydraulic power to

operate its variable height all-independent suspension, the clutch for its semi-automatic transmission, the brakes and steering servo. Over the 20 years, 1.4 million were built including a number at their English assembly plant. The hydraulic circuitry may not make it the easiest of classic cars to maintain, but it was a true milestone design.

American classics of the period are generally regarded as those from the top end of the manufacturers' ranges. In the Fifties these were the high performance models or those produced in more limited numbers. As one of the smaller manufacturers, Studebaker set out to impress by style for which Raymond Loewy was responsible. The early post-war range was uplifted in 1950 with the circular radiator intake theme and clean lines uncluttered by chromework, quite unlike any other. The 1953 coupe designs – Starliner and Starlight – were even more remarkable.

The Cadillac Eldorado and the Lincoln

Continental were the major contenders in the luxury car market. The Cadillac used excessive chrome and styling gimmicks but the Lincoln was more restrained, more European. At the other end of the market, Chevrolet launched the Corvair compact in 1959 as a response to the success of the imported Volkswagen. Like the Beetle it used a rear-mounted air-cooled 'boxer' engine, but, being American, it was somewhat larger and had six cylinders; it was also very European in style. Unfortunately the design also adopted the Beetle's swing-axle rear suspension, which could make the car very unstable in cornering; American safety crusader Ralph Nader effectively killed the car and even a revised rear suspension system couldn't overcome the market resistance – there were some nice-looking models in the range.

In performance terms, though, the 1955 Chrysler 300 was the real classic. It was Chrysler's answer to the Ford Thunderbird, itself a response to Chevrolet's Corvette. Chrysler, though, gave sports car performance in sedan style and the hemi-headed 329 cu.in V8 produced 300 bhp, making the 300 the most powerful production car in the world at the time. For 1956 the engine was increased to 354 cu.in and 355 bhp for the 300B, and for the 1957 300C there was a 390 cu.in 390 bhp option. Chevrolet's reply to this was the Bel Air, restyled for 1957, using the new 280 cu.in small-block V-8 with fuel injection and 283 bhp for the top range model. This too was destined to become an American classic.

MINI CLASSICS

The Suez fuel crises of the Mid-fifties was responsible for the near success of another breed, the bubble-car or microcar, a latter-day evolution of the Twenties cyclecars. Like their forerunners they were powered by motor cycle engines but these were three-wheelers taking advantage of tax concessions for motor cycles and sidecars – some produced four-wheel versions as well. In Britain, there were Bond, Reliant and Berkeley of whom Reliant went on to make a proper car – the Scimitar – and Berkeleys were sports cars. In Germany, Messerschmitt took over production

of the Fend invalid car while BMW acquired the rights of the Italian Iso bubble car, and used BMW single cylinder motor cycle units. This Isetta became the twin-cylinder 600 4-wheeler, which then grew into the successful 700 in sedan and coupe forms from 1959. By the end of the decade, though, the bubble car had died as mini cars were almost as small but did everything so much more comfortably.

One was the new Fiat 500. The Fiat 500 Topolino had effectively been replaced by the rear-engined 600 in 1955 but the Nuova 500 came in 1957 as the Italian 'peoples' car'. With its air-cooled 29.2 cu.in 13 bhp twin-cylinder engine also rear-mounted, it was a neat and attractive little 2-door minicar which could just take four adults.

A 30.4 cu.in version arrived in 1958 and the model continued on through various forms until the 500R came out in 1972 using an 18 bhp version of the new 36.2 cu.in twin from the 126. Although Fiat did not produce tuned versions, Carlo Abarth sold ready-modified 500 and 600 models as Fiat-Abarths, such as the 695SS or the OT1000.By the end of its production in 1977, over 4 million new 500s had been built.

Like the Topolino it lasted twenty years. In France the 2CV continued, but Renault added the Dauphine to the range in 1956 and brought in the Dauphine Gordini in 1960. It used the same basic layout as the 4CV which continued on into 1962.

The trend-setting Mini arrived in 1959. With a 34 bhp 51.7 cu. in. version of the Morris Minor A-series engine mounted transversely on top of the gearbox, it was carefully packaged to seat four people in reasonable comfort and provide some luggage space. Front-wheel-drive and firm rubber cone suspension gave it remarkable roadholding too. The Mini-Cooper arrived in 1961 with 60.8 cu.in and 55 bhp, followed in 1963 by the various Cooper S models (59.1 cu.in - 65 bhp, 65.3 cu.in - 68 bhp, 77.8 cu.in - 75 bhp); they were extremely successful in all forms of motor sport too. Along the way came more luxurious Riley and Wolseley versions too. In its various forms the Mini was to continue until 2000, over 30 years and still an example to many. Maybe the basic Mini is hardly a collectable classic but genuine Cooper versions are much sought after.

292-293 Jaguar XK140 roadster 1954-1957.

1951 - 1960

GRAND TOURERS

Following the birth of the Grand Touring breed, exemplified by the Cisitalia, Aston Martin and Porsche 356 of the late Forties, the Fifties saw a rapid growth in this niche market. The Grand Tourer was for those who wanted to travel long distances at high speed with enough luggage for a week-end in a sporting car, but without the drawbacks of open air motoring or the noise of soft-tops. Some manufacturers just made fixed head coupe versions of their open sports cars, like the MGA or Jaguar XK120. Others offered detachable hard-tops, or Targa-tops like the Triumph TR4.

But many built proper GTs. As most of these cars were in limited volumes they retained separate chassis which allowed the remaining coachbuilders to build special bodies. The Ferrari name was established in racing and the early Ferrari GTs were built for such long distance races as the Mille Miglia or Carrera Panamericana, usually with Touring or Vignale bodywork. Pinin Farina's first work on a Ferrari was a 212 Inter roadster in 1952. Ferrari's first series of cars were all based on the smaller Colombo-designed V-12, but as Grand Prix racing had shown that large normally aspirated engines were better than small supercharged ones, the bigger Lampredi-designed V-12 was used for the road cars as well. The first genuine road-going Ferrari with no racing aspirations was the 342 America of 1952 with a 200 bhp 250 cu.in V-12; only six were built and Pinin Farina built the three coupes. The earlier 340 America had used the same engine in 220 bhp form but was also used for sports-car racing as MM or Mexico versions; Ghia, Touring and Vignale had provided the bodywork. The 375 America with 300 bhp came in 1953 and Pinin Farina produced most of the twelve cars that were built using a variety of different styles.

All GTs are classics. All Ferraris are classics. It is not possible to include every Ferrari in a general work. Although these three models were produced in very small numbers, they represent the start of the big fast road-going Ferraris. Once Ferrari had established an agreement with Pinin Farina, production numbers began to grow. The 250GT Europa of 1954 was the first of these – around 40 were built. This was followed by 77 of the 250GT Berlinetta Tour de France from 1956-59 before the arrival of the 250GT short wheelbase (SWB) Berlinetta – the classic racing GT. Ferrari called his racing GTs Berlinettas while his road cars were referred to as coupes. Coupes, cabriolets and Spyders on the longer 250GT chassis were all in production before the end of the decade.

Ferrari did not have a monopoly in Italy, though. Fiat then made a tentative foray into the GT market with the Otto-Vu (V8). Fiat engineers had designed a 122 cu.in 70 degree V-8 as a possible engine for touring cars. When this idea was shelved they created a small GT coupe around a tubular and sheet steel chassis with all-independent suspension and showed it at Geneva in 1952. Fiat built around 115 cars from 1952-54. At that point Zagato, who had already re-bodied five or six cars, acquired a further 25 units, some as complete cars, some as rolling chassis. Over the years to 1959 Zagato converted these to lightweight coupes, mostly for national competition; Elio Zagato won the Italian 2000GT championship in 1955 and 1959. Siata used their own chassis and installed Otto-Vu running gear; they built 56 Siata 208s. Fiat's little coupe did not have a big following outside Italy but it was an effective little car capable of 120 mph.

Of greater significance though was the Maserati 3500GT which arrived in 1957. The Maserati brothers had been producing competition cars since 1926 and sold many of them to private customers, but this was not enough to keep the company going so the firm was sold to the Orsi family in 1938. After the war the brothers set up OSCA. Initially they concentrated on small competition sports cars using their own engines. Formula Junior single-seaters were added in 1959. Twin-cam OSCA engines were built by Fiat for the 1500S and 1600S sports cars from 1959-66 and OSCA used them in their own GT cars using local coachbuilders.

Meanwhile Maserati continued to produce such successful competition cars as the 250F GP car and the 300S and 450S sports-cars. They hand-built a few road cars too, but it wasn't until they withdrew from racing in 1957 that they took road cars seriously and produced the 3500GT. The engine followed the design principles of the six-cylinder racing units but used chain-drive for the camshafts rather than gears; the road-going 213 cu.in engine was also used in the 350S sports-racing cars. With a tubular chassis frame, bodies were built by Touring (2+2) and Vignale (open Spider on a shortened chassis). The 213 cu.in engine was further refined and fuel injection was added in 1962 for the 3500GTI – the first car to use the GTI name. In 1959 road-going versions of the 450S V-8 power unit were used in a limited run of 32 5000GT coupes. Maserati had arrived on the road car scene.

In Germany, Porsche continued to produce their Beetle-based coupes as well as competition RS sports cars. BMW didn't start post-war production until 1952 and then produced large comfortable sedans and tourers in their new 500 series – developments of the last of the pre-war 300 series. However the launch of the 502 with a new V-8 engine in 1954 marked progress. Coupe and cabriolet versions of this arrived with the 503 in 1956 when BMW also launched the two-seater 507; although only 253 of this were produced, it was one of the finest designs of the Mid-fifties with handsome Goertz bodywork and the V-8

engine increased to 195 cu.in with 150 bhp. It was available with a factory hard-top, hence its inclusion in this GT section. Mercedes were also slow to start post-war production with a new version of the 170 sedan. The memorable 300SL arrived in 1954 as the road-going version of the 1952 Le Mans winner – more later – but the similarly-styled sporting 190SL was more affordable; with a 4-cylinder ohc 105 bhp 116 cu.in engine, it would reach 118 mph.

French taxation had all but killed the established grandes makes of Delage and Delahaye – a few were produced before they died in 1954 – but Darracq (now Talbot) continued to produce fast road-going GTs in small numbers until 1960, using successively their own 152 cu.in 4-cylinder engine, a Ford V-8 side valve and the 152 cu.in version of BMW's V-8. However a new grande make arrived in 1954; Facel emerged from the Forges et Ateliers de Construction d'Eure et Loire which produced body panels for Panhard, Simca and Ford. Using a 275 cu.in 180 bhp Chrysler V-8, the Facel Vega was a luxury GT in the old tradition. With ever larger Chrysler engines, the Vega was developed through to the FVS (1957) into the HK500 with up to 360 bhp from 384 cu.in in 1962. A four-door Excellence had been available from 1957 but the line came to an end in 1964 after 1270 V-8s

had been built. Reason for the failure was an attempt to enter the small sports-car market with the Facellia, initially with their own 4-cylinder twin-cam 97 cu.in; when this proved unreliable some were produced with the 110 cu.in Volvo engine and a few were fitted with the Austin-Healey 3000 engine. But by then the company had lost too much money and production ceased after 1250 Facellias had been built.

Somewhat in the same mold was the Spanish Pegaso as the product of a nationalized company that was and still is producing commercial vehicles.

It was designed by Wilfredo Ricart who had worked with Alfa Romeo for ten years. The Z102 used a separate chassis with wishbone and de Dion suspension; the in-house V-8 was used in a variety of sizes over the 1951-8 production period with a minor redesign in 1955 to change from gear to chain cam-drive for the Z103. Bodies were built by Touring and Saoutchik as well as in Spain. It was an expensive way of advertising Pegaso lorries.

The English had their Aston Martin DB2 in its various 2/4 and drop-head variations as the only serious challenger to Ferrari's GT reputation in the Mid-fifties. Their products came even closer in 1958 when Aston Martin unveiled the DB4 as a direct rival to the Ferrari 250GT. Meanwhile, like Facel, the Jensen company

emerged from making bodies for others to establish their own make. Pre-war they had built a few attractive sedans and tourers using the Ford V-8, Nash straight-8 and even Lagonda V-12 engines and continued post-war using Austin's 244 cu.in straight-6. Jensen built 2573 examples of the Austin A40 sports and would go on to make the big Austin-Healeys but in 1954 they showed their own 4-seater GT, the 541, retaining the big Austin engine and a number of other Austin components. It was a striking design and was technically interesting in that it used a fiberglass body on top of a substantial twin-tube chassis. The de Luxe version in 1956 saw Jensen as the first manufacturer to use four-wheel disc brakes. In 1957 the 541R brought in rack and pinion steering and a more powerful engine; the final revision was the 1960 541S, four inches wider and with the option of a GM Hydramatic automatic transmission. While the engine was hardly a thoroughbred, the 541 series was a welcome addition to the classic scene.

Fiberglass provided the basis for two more English GT cars, the TVR and Lotus Elite, both aimed at the younger enthusiast. TVR had produced some 20 2-seater coupes with proprietary fiberglass bodywork on a tubular chassis using A40 components but, in 1958, they produced the first Grantura using Coventry Climax, Ford or MGA engines. A new space-frame

294-295 1957 Porsche Speedster with Carrera engine.

chassis carried Beetle front suspension at both ends and, with a neat and very short two-seater coupe, began a production run of around 100 cars; the Mk.II (1960-1) continued with the same chassis but rack-and-pinion steering and the IIA (1961-2) had disc brakes with the later MGA engine, the production total of these second series cars being around 400. Lotus had grown from special builders to small producers of competition sports cars, but 1957 saw them established as road-car manufacturers. The low, stark Lotus 7 was the ultimate enthusiast's road car for competition use and has continued through without a break into the somewhat faster Caterham 7 of today. With the Elite they broke new ground, using a monocoque body/chassis unit of fiberglass; the suspension used Colin Chapman's racing designs and the engine was the lightweight 74.4 cu.in Coventry Climax FWE. With attractive aerodynamic styling, the Elite made a big impression at its 1957 launch; 112 mph from just 75 bhp was a significant pointer to the way ahead. By 1963 over 1000 had been produced. Both TVR and Lotus were, of course, considerably outnumbered by Alfa Romeo's successful Giulietta Sprint GT which had emerged in 1954.

SPORTS CARS

In the Fifties, England was the center stage of affordable sports car production. Following the worldwide acceptance of the MG TC and the Jaguar XK120, other manufacturers, large and small, joined in to provide America in particular with a type of motoring which their own companies were unable to produce.

MG went on to produce the 2-seater TD in 1950, using independent front suspension from the Y-type sedan, still with the same 76.2 cu.in engine. When the slightly more modern looking TF arrived in 1953, it was already outdated by a rival product from within the same newly merged Austin-Morris (BMC) company – the Austin-Healey 100 which came out the same year. Increasing the MG TF's capacity to 89.4 cu.in did not offset the decline of the make's appeal; it still had the pre-war running-board style, where the Austin-Healey had all-enveloping bodywork. It was to be 1955 before the MGA appeared to broaden MG appeal once more.

Meanwhile, the Triumph TR2 had also arrived in

1953, another with the integrated wing-line. While this used the same basic engine as the Standard Vanguard and the Morgan Plus 4, the Triumph's engine capacity was reduced to 121.4 cu.in to make it more suitable for competition. Competition inspired the creation of the AC Ace in 1954 and led to the birth of the Cobra in 1961. More detailed studies of the MGA, big Healeys, Triumph TR2 and AC Cobra appear later.

Jaguar continued to produce the XK120 until the very similar XK140 appeared in 1954. The XK150 came in 1957 bringing more space and comfort under a considerably revised shape.

The XK120 had performed well in national competitions in England and America, but Jaguar wanted to promote their name on the International racing scene, targeting the Le Mans 24-hour race as the most famous. The XK120C (competition) was ready for Le Mans 1951; it used a tubular frame chassis with XK120 front suspension but the live rear

axle was better located and the body was more streamlined.

The C-type, as it was soon called, duly won its first Le Mans and repeated this in 1953. Seeking even more speed for Le Mans, Jaguar developed the D-type with even less drag; the engine was still basically the same famous XK unit but had dry-sump lubrication; the chassis used a monocoque center section with aircraft-style rivets. Le Mans victories were repeated in 1955, 1956 and 1957. The D-type was to lead directly to the famous E-type in the next decade.

But there was still more to come from Britain. By 1956, BMC were producing the successful MGA and Austin-Healey, but these were quick cars. There was a gap at the bottom of the market for a cheap and economical two-seater, which was where the original MG Midget had come in. The Austin-Healey Sprite arrived in 1958 with the BMC A-series engine in an all-new monocoque chassis and the famous frog-eye

headlights on the bonnet-top – nearly 50,000 were built before the Mk.II came in 1961 together with the MG Midget equivalent. Although the Sprite name came to an end with the Mk.IV in 1971, the MG Midget continued through further development until 1979. Some 225,000 Midgets and 130,000 Sprites were built.

While Daimler would join Jaguar in 1960, they were independent at this stage. The company had generally produced fairly luxurious cars but made a handful of the Barker Special Sports Coupes from 1949-52. They returned to the sports car market in 1959 with the SP250 (originally Dart) using a fiberglass body and a new small 152 cu.in V-8 with a conventional steel chassis.

From 1961 chassis and body were strengthened but the SP250 ceased production in 1963 after 2645 had been built. It was an interesting sporting machine and Jaguar used that engine in Daimler versions of the Mk.II sedan. Last of the British

sporting cars to appear in this decade was the Sunbeam Alpine. The name first appeared on an open two-seater version of the Sunbeam-Talbot 90; introduced in 1953, it had some rallying success but production stopped in 1955 for the building of a new range of sedans of which the 68 bhp 91.5 cu.in Sunbeam Rapier was the most notable and had considerable competition success. The Alpine used the Hillman Husky platform and uprated Rapier running gear with 2+2 sports-car bodywork. By 1968 it had gone through five development series and 70,000 cars were produced. Along the way, an American 256 cu.in Ford V-8 had been inserted into the Mark IV to create the Tiger in 1964. Nearly 6500 were built before the 286 cu.in Ford was used for the Tiger II which added a further 571 cars to the production run. The V-8 power made a real sports car out of the rather tame Alpine.

In Italy, Fiat made some attempt to stem the all-British tide. The early post-war Fiat 1100S was a

rounded GT based on the pre-war 1100 chassis; after only 400 models, this was replaced by the 1100ES with Pinin Farina bodywork very similar to that of the Cisitalia – only 50 models were made during 1950/1. Fiat followed this up with the 1100TV Trasformabile in 1955, an open two-seater based on the unitary construction 1100TV (Turismo Veloce) sedan, but only 1030 were built in two years. The bigger-engined 1200 convertible took them through to the end of 1959 after a low run of 2363 cars. Fiat took their next little sports car more seriously using the then new 1100 as a base clothed in Pinin Farina bodywork.

Early 1959 saw the new 1200 cabriolet which was joined by the 1500 using the OSCA 91.5 cu.in twin-cam engine in the same basic car for 38% more power. In 1963, the 1200 was replaced by the 1500 from the new 1500 sedan and given front disc brakes, and the 1500 OSCA (called 1500S in hindsight) became the 1600S with discs all round and a 5-speed gearbox from March 1965. Over 7 years, Pinin Farina built some 37,500 of which 3000 were coupes, and of this total around 4000 were OSCA-powered. Local rivals Alfa Romeo had changed from the 1300 Giulietta Spider to the 1600 in 1962.

While all of Europe was flooding their market with sports cars, the Americans had not been totally idle. However the two comparable cars that were produced – the Chevrolet Corvette and the Ford Thunderbird – were hardly in the same mold as the nimble European sports cars.

The Corvette was notable for the first volume use of fiberglass for bodywork when it came out in 1953. The Thunderbird might have been aimed at the Corvette but the company changed direction to create a new niche market, the two-seater personal car; it was more of a two-door Lincoln when it arrived in 1955. Both these cars are covered in greater detail later. As the Fifties closed, world production had increased immeasurably and car design had marched on towards new levels of comfort and performance. Not every one has been proved to be a classic though.

296-297 Mercedes 300SL with the famous 'gullwing' doors.

Porsche 356

All makes have to start somewhere but Porsche's rise from the humble origins of a modified Volkswagen Beetle to the supercars of today has been a major transformation. In fact, the Beetle was just one design project for Professor Ferdinand Porsche who had earlier worked on the powerful Mercedes sports cars of the late Twenties and went on to design the Auto Union Grand Prix cars of the Thirties. The Volkswagen project started in 1934 and by 1936 the first prototypes were running. When a Berlin-Rome race was announced for September 1939, Porsche was given permission to produce three streamlined VWs; being Porsche, the company had already sketched a sporting coupe using the VW engine ahead of the rear axle. The Berlin-Rome cars used this body but on a Beetle chassis with the engine tuned to 40 bhp. War caused the race to be cancelled, but the idea lived on.

The Porsche engineering consultancy had been moved to Gmund in Austria in 1944. After the war, shortage of parts and other projects delayed a return to the sporting VW. But finally it was the Professor's son, Ferry, who ordered the work to start. The first and only prototype was completed in May 1948, an open roadster with the VW engine ahead of the rear axle, but production of the rear-mounted Porsche started immediately; all the mechanical parts were well proven as Beetle production had been under way for three years.
The first coupe was finished in September 1948.

While the concept of putting the engine and transmission package at one end of the car was well suited to carrying people and luggage in a compact sedan car, and is now the universal system, it is not ideal for a sports car where a near-equal weight

298-299 Speedster fitted with 1600 Super engine.

distribution gives fundamentally safer handling. Putting the package behind the rear wheels is even less safe than is the modern system of front wheel drive. With the Volkswagen, and hence the Porsche, the rear suspension with swing axles was inferior to the trailing arm front suspension. While all round independent suspension was good for the ride quality, the unbalanced suspension and weight distribution combined to make it easy to spin a Porsche if you take a corner too fast. Ever since the first car, Porsche have had to develop the cars around this problem. To a large extent they have succeeded but a rear-engined Porsche always demands respect from its driver.

For the new car Porsche made their own steel platform chassis, almost a foot shorter than the Beetle's. On this was mounted the Beetle front suspension, the Porsche-patented trailing arms, and the complete engine, gearbox and rear suspension package from the Beetle.

In Beetle form, the 69 cu.in flat-four air-cooled engine gave 25 bhp at 3300 rpm. With an eye to racing in the 67.1 cu.in class, Porsche reduced the capacity to 66.2 cu.in but increased the compression ratio and installed twin carburetors to reach 40 bhp at 4200 rpm.

TECHNICAL DESCRIPTION OF THE OF PORSCHE SPEEDSTER

YEARS OF PRODUCTION	1956-1962
MODELS	ROADSTER
ENGINE	REAR-MOUNTED FLAT-FOUR
BORE X STROKE, CAPACITY	3.2 X 2.9 INCHES, 96.5 CU.IN
VALVEGEAR	PUSHROD OHV
FUEL SYSTEM	TWO SOLEX 32PBI CARBURETORS
POWER	75 BHP AT 5000 RPM
TRANSMISSION	4-SPEED
BODY/CHASSIS	STEEL PLATFORM CHASSIS WITH STEEL BODY PANELS
FRONT SUSPENSION	TRAILING ARMS AND TORSION BARS
REAR SUSPENSION	SWING AXLES AND TORSION BARS
TIRES/WHEELS	5.60 X 15 ON STEEL WHEELS
WHEELBASE, TRACK (F), TRACK(R)	83 X 51 X 49 INCHES
LENGTH, WIDTH, HEIGHT	156 X 65 X 48 INCHES
MAX SPEED	110 MPH
WHERE BUILT	STUTTGART, GERMANY

This was clothed in a hand-beaten aluminium body designed by Erwin Kommenda. Conditions and supplies in that part of Austria were not good for the production of cars and only 50 were made in two years before the company negotiated a return to Porsche's old premises in Stuttgart. From 1950, all the cars had steel bodies and production started at 60 cars a month. Porsche had arrived and the cars were quickly recognized for their ability to cruise quietly and comfortably at speeds very close to their maximum of 80 mph.

For a sporting machine, more power was obviously needed. Early in 1951 the engine was bored out to 78.4 cu.in which added another 10 per cent to the power, and in October that year came a 90.7 cu.in version using roller bearings to give 60 bhp at 5000 rpm. For this a long-stroke crankshaft was made which would last the life of the 356 series. A plain-bearing 1500 came in 1953 with 55 bhp, while the roller-bearing 1500S continued with 70 bhp; the equivalent 1300S had 60 bhp.

The first cabriolet was offered in 1951 but the American market wanted a sleeker model. The 1952 America was followed in 1954 by the famous Speedster, a cabriolet with a cut-down windscreen.

When the 356A arrived in 1956, the V-screen had been replaced with a curved one, quarter-lights had been added, wider 15-inch wheels were fitted, the handling was improved and the bigger engine were increased to 97.6 cu.in Minor styling and engineering changes denoted the 356B in 1960 and 356C in 1963. The final 1600SC with 95 bhp was the ultimate 356, very far removed from its Beetle ancestry.

TECHNICAL DESCRIPTION OF THE PORSCHE CARRERA 2000GS

YEARS OF PRODUCTION	1960-1964
MODELS	COUPE
ENGINE	REAR-MOUNTED FLAT-FOUR
BORE X STROKE, CAPACITY	3.2 x 2.9 INCHES, 119.9 CU.IN
VALVEGEAR	FOUR OHC
FUEL SYSTEM	TWO TWIN-CHOKE SOLEX 40P11
POWER	140 BHP AT 6200 RPM
TRANSMISSION	4-SPEED
BODY/CHASSIS	STEEL PLATFORM CHASSIS WITH STEEL BODY PANELS
FRONT SUSPENSION	TRAILING ARMS AND TORSION BARS
REAR SUSPENSION	SWING AXLES AND TORSION BARS
TIRES/WHEELS	6.5 x 18 INCHES ON STEEL WHEELS
WHEELBASE, TRACK (F), TRACK(R)	83 x 51 x 49 INCHES
LENGHT, WIDT, HEIGHT	156 x 65 x 51 INCHES
MAX SPEED	135 MPH
WHERE BUILT	STUTTGART, GERMANY

300-301 Top, Speedster with Carrera engine. Lower, 356 Carreras used 91.5, 97.6 and 122 cu.in engines with 4-cam heads.

Lancia Aurelia B20

The Lancia B20 is one of the few cars that have gone down in history as a motoring landmark. It had that rare combination of advanced design and a shape that would also start a new fashion. And its performance was as strong as its visual appeal.

Since their foundation in 1906 Lancia have had a long history of producing cars that set trends. The 1922 Lambda pioneered unitary body/chassis construction and featured a narrow V-4 engine with a single cylinder head. The Aprilia was the first popular sedan to have all-independent suspension and a streamlined body when it arrived in 1937. Despite the death of the founder, Vicenzo Lancia, that year, innovation continued after the war.

The new Aurelia B10 sedan, announced in 1950, was mostly the work of Vittorio Jano, who had joined Lancia in 1938 after many years in charge of Alfa Romeo engineering. The Aurelia's specification included a V-6 engine, independent rear suspension using semi-trailing arms with coil springs and a 4-speed gearbox in unit with the differential; this transaxle helps to keep the weight evenly distributed between the front and rear of the car. The front suspension retained the familiar sliding pillar and coil spring system that had been introduced on the Lambda. The engine was actually the work of one of Jano's engineers, De Virgilio, who extended the V-4 philosophy to produce the world's first production V-6, a 107 cu.in unit producing 56 bhp. As this had its cylinder banks set at 60 degrees, the heads were separate and the valves were operated by a central camshaft and pushrods.

For 1951, Lancia decided to add the coupe B20 to the range using a chassis some 8 inches shorter. This was assigned to Pinin Farina – he would become Pininfarina in 1961. Drawing upon the lines of his 1947 Cisitalia GT, he created the fastback B20 which was a masterpiece of clean and effective

302-303 *The 1954 Lancia Aurelia 2500GT had a de Dion rear axle.*

design. For this, and as an option for the B21 sedan, the engine size was increased to 121.4 cu.in with 75 bhp for the B20 (70 bhp for B21). For the 1952 2nd series, Farina added four inches to the rear to improve its lines and the engine output was increased to 80 bhp; the 3rd series in 1953 included the B20 2500GT with its capacity increased to 149.5 cu.in and 118 bhp. For the final 4th series in 1954, the rear suspension was changed to use a de Dion tube on leaf springs, a design proven on the sports-racing D24 to improve stability.

Even in tuned 122 cu.in form, the B20 had already established itself in competition with a 2nd overall in the 1951 Mille Miglia; in 1952 an Aurelia was 3rd and three Aurelias finished 1,2,3 in the Targa Florio. Meanwhile the factory had started to make special competition coupes

called D20 to match the B20. Using a 183 cu.in V-6 with twin overhead camshafts they won the Targa Florio again for Lancia in 1953. The victory was repeated in 1954 with the open D24.

The final version of the Aurelia took the sports-racing car design number and became the B24 Spyder, another elegant Farina creation; as this was strictly a 2-seater, the wheelbase was shortened by a further 8 inches. In fact it was also available in cabriolet form with a windscreen more suited to a soft top. The sedan Aurelia became the Series II in 1954 with a 140 cu.in engine and also adopted the de Dion rear axle. However production ceased in 1955 after some 30,000 Aurelias had been produced and the Flaminia took over. The coupe continued until 1958 by which time 3600 examples had been assembled by Pinin Farina. It was a superb example of Lancia engineering and also helped to establish Farina as a designer for volume production road cars.

The B20 may have had its origins in the sedan Aurelia, but its design was so well executed that it became a GT car in its own right. In England the price for the 2500GT was the same as that for an Aston Martin and its performance was very similar. It certainly had as much appeal to the motoring cognoscenti of the day.

304-305 The Spyder is seen here in cabriolet form. Wire wheels are a later addition.

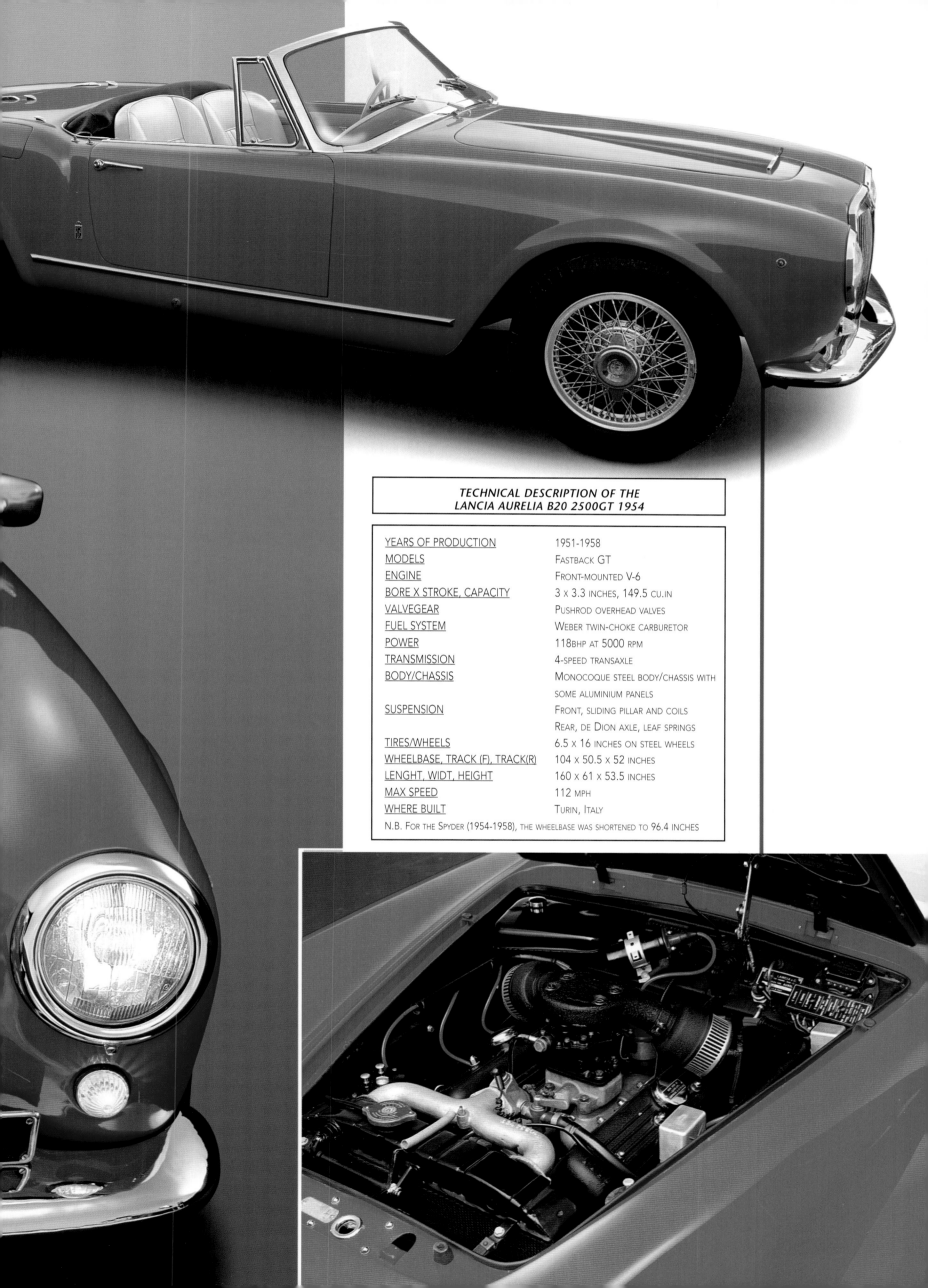

TECHNICAL DESCRIPTION OF THE
LANCIA AURELIA B20 2500GT 1954

YEARS OF PRODUCTION	1951-1958
MODELS	Fastback GT
ENGINE	Front-mounted V-6
BORE X STROKE, CAPACITY	3 x 3.3 inches, 149.5 cu.in
VALVEGEAR	Pushrod overhead valves
FUEL SYSTEM	Weber twin-choke carburetor
POWER	118bhp at 5000 rpm
TRANSMISSION	4-speed transaxle
BODY/CHASSIS	Monocoque steel body/chassis with some aluminium panels
SUSPENSION	Front, sliding pillar and coils Rear, de Dion axle, leaf springs
TIRES/WHEELS	6.5 x 16 inches on steel wheels
WHEELBASE, TRACK (F), TRACK(R)	104 x 50.5 x 52 inches
LENGHT, WIDT, HEIGHT	160 x 61 x 53.5 inches
MAX SPEED	112 mph
WHERE BUILT	Turin, Italy

N.B. For the Spyder (1954-1958), the wheelbase was shortened to 96.4 inches

Austin-Healey 100

After the failure of the A90 Atlantic to appeal to appeal to the export market, Austin's Leonard Lord invited Jensen, Frazer Nash and Healey to produce design proposals using Austin A90 components. The Healey 100 used most of the A90 running gear, including steering, brakes and suspension, and made an instant impact at the 1952 British Motor Show.

Before the end of the show, Lord and Donald Healey agreed terms and the Austin-Healey 100 became a belated star of that 1952 show. Healey would help to develop the cars, produce special variants and receive royalties, Jensen would make the body/chassis units and final assembly would take place at the Austin factory in Longbridge, Birmingham.

The long stroke A90 engine (3.4 x 4.3 inches, 162.3 cu.in) was really more suited to commercial vehicles than to sports cars, but 90

bhp at 4000 rpm was enough to make the Austin-Healey a genuine 100 mph car. The A90 with the same engine could only reach 92 mph.

As the gearbox also came from the heavier A90 it had a very low first gear ratio.

The Healey solution was to remove the first gear selector and use an overdrive for the upper two ratios, an added benefit being that the three gearbox ratios all had synchromesh. When Austin introduced the A90 Six, the Healey adopted its 4-speed gearbox and retained the overdrive for third and top.

Where the Healey scored particularly was in its appearance. Healey's Gerry Coker had designed a body with just the right mixture of long bonnet and muscular rear haunches. Another appealing feature was the clever adjustment for the angle of the windscreen. The soft top was straightforward and removable side-screens were to remain a

feature until the Convertible of 1962.

The first big Healey (BN1) went into production in 1953. As Austin Healeys had finished 12th and 14th at Le Mans in 1953, special Le Mans kits were offered with bigger carburetors and a new camshaft for 100 bhp or, with high compression pistons, 110 bhp. After 10,688 cars the BN2 came in mid-1955 with the new gearbox; cars fitted when new with the Le Mans kit became 100M, which included a louvred bonnet and a stiffer anti-roll bar. And then there were 50 100S models produced in 1955 by Donald Healey with a cut-down windscreen and aluminium body panels; underneath were a close-ratio gearbox and four-wheel disc brakes while a new aluminium cylinder head contributed to 132 bhp. The S stood for Sebring where a Healey had averaged 132.29 mph for 24 hours. Including some 1160 100Ms, only 3924 BN2s were built before the 100-Six (BN4) arrived in 1956.

306-307 The factory-built 100M was based on the BN2 with 4-speed gearbox.

308-309 The BN2 had rear reflectors above the lights.
Engine air-box has a badge to show that the Le Mans kit is fitted.

The major feature of this was the adoption of the Austin C-series 158 cu.in six-cylinder engine from the A90; initially this had the standard Austin cylinder head with siamesed inlet ports and 102 bhp but a new cylinder head with six inlet ports, bigger valves and a higher compression ratio was used from October 1957 with 117 bhp. The original chassis was lengthened by two inches to allow two occasional child seats and the windscreen became fixed. Of the 15,400 100-Sixes, 4150 were BN6 two-seaters, introduced in 1958, with the child seats removed and the battery repositioned.

First of the Healey 3000s came in 1959 with the C-series engine at 177.6 cu.in and 124 bhp; front disc brakes were fitted. By now, BN7 were two-seaters and BT7 were the 2+2 variety. These classifications continued into the 3000 Mk.II (1961-62) with triple SU carburetors and 131 bhp, but a Mk.IIA (BJ7) took over from 1962-64 which reverted to twin larger carburetors and 129 bhp. However the main feature of the

BJ7 was that it was a Convertible with curved windscreen, quarter lights and wind-up windows; the soft top used three, not two, hoops and sat in its own well behind the child seats. The rear seat back could fold down to create a luggage platform – the big Healey had finally become civilized.

The last version was the Mk.III (BJ8) which were all Convertibles and had 150 bhp from even larger carburetors and a new camshaft. Just 1390 Phase I cars were built in early 1964 before the Phase II came out with the rear suspension revised to provide more ground clearance; radius arms replaced the old Panhard rod and the leaf springs were reset.

The Phase II was the most popular of all the big Healeys with 16,322 produced out of a total 42,926 of the 3000. At the end of 1967 new safety and emissions legislation brought an end to one of England's finest post-war sports cars.

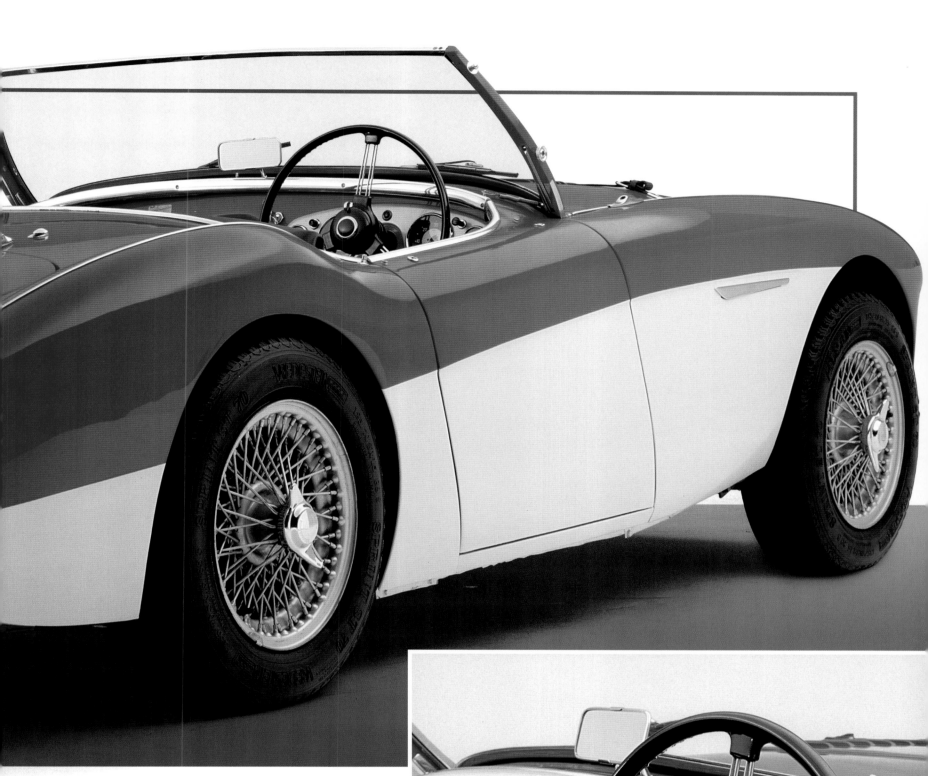

TECHNICAL DESCRIPTION OF THE AUSTIN-HEALEY 100M

YEARS OF PRODUCTION	1955-56
MODELS	SPORTS 2-SEATER
ENGINE	FRONT-MOUNTED IN-LINE 4
BORE X STROKE, CAPACITY	3.4 X 4.3 INCHES, 162.3
VALVEGEAR	PUSHROD OVERHEAD VALVES
FUEL SYSTEM	TWIN SU CARBURETORS
POWER	110 BHP AT 4500 RPM
TRANSMISSION	4-SPEED AND OVERDRIVE
BODY/CHASSIS	STEEL CHASSIS, INTEGRAL BULKHEADS
	AND DETACHABLE BODYPANELS
SUSPENSION	FRONT, WISHBONES AND COILS
	REAR, LIVE AXLE WITH LEAF SPRINGS
TIRES/WHEELS	5.90 X 15 ON STEEL WHEELS
WHEELBASE, TRACK (F), TRACK(R)	90 X 49 X 51 INCHES
LENGHT, WIDT, HEIGHT	151 X 60.5 X 49.2 INCHES
MAX SPEED	110 MPH
WHERE BUILT	LONGBRIDGE AND WARWICK, ENGLAND

Chevrolet Corvette 1956 - 1962

In the aftermath of the war, the British motor industry spearheaded the export drive to America, providing sports cars to a country whose major manufacturers had yet to appreciate the values of this niche market; the American industry was accustomed to working in larger numbers, although, as in England, there were some enthusiasts building specials around such as the Kaiser-Frazer Henry J chassis. General Motors started to rectify the situation in 1951, planning the Corvette around a low-volume facility away from Detroit but making full use of the mass production hardware.

Styled under the legendary Harley Earl by Bob McLean, the body was to be built in the new medium of fiberglass which had the benefit of much lower tooling costs than the normal metal pressing system. A new box-section chassis was designed in the Chevrolet R&D department under suspension specialist Maurice Olley and used stock steering, braking and suspension units. The best available engine was the existing Chevrolet 235 cu.in 'six' which produced 115 bhp at 3600 rpm in standard form; as they wanted to match Jaguar's 160 bhp for the Jaguar XK120, this had to be uprated in the usual speed-shop fashion – higher compression, new camshaft with solid lifters, triple carburetors – to reach 150 bhp. This engine was normally attached to the two-speed Powerglide automatic transmission, so this was chosen despite its unsporting character.

The Corvette was originally shown at the GM Motorama in early 1953. It was mid-1953 before development was completed and GM began a pilot production run of 300 cars at Flint in Michigan; production moved to a new facility in St.Louis, Missouri for 1954. While the Corvette could exceed 100 mph, and accelerate as well as an Austin-Healey 100, it was not a sports car when it came to the corners. However, performance took a step in the right direction with the 1955 model; the new 265 cu.in small block V-8 became a 195 bhp option and a 3-speed manual transmission was offered towards the end of 1955. By the end of this first generation of the Corvette, only 4640 had been built – it was just enough to keep the model alive and moving towards the new generation.

310-311 Chevrolet Corvette 1959 retained the 1958 change to 4 headlights.

Regarded as the father of the true Corvette, Zora Arkus-Duntov had arrived at Chevrolet in 1953 and had little influence on the first model, but he improved the handling with minor suspension changes to make it more track-friendly for the new generation in 1956. The V-8 engine output was increased to 210 bhp with the option of 225 bhp with a second 4-barrel carburetor, and the 3-speed manual transmission became standard.

With the restyling the second generation Corvette had a much more positive air. The tail lost its little fins and became more rounded with its profile matching concave side sculptures behind the front wheels and the headlights moved to the front of the wings.

Wind-up side windows and an optional hard-top broadened its appeal. Revealed at the January 1956 Motorama, the new car suddenly achieved instant sporting credibility when it was revealed that Duntov had recorded 150 mph at Daytona Beach with a virtually standard car. Annual production for 1956 at 3467 cars was the start of a steady growth that would reach 14,531 by the end of the model in 1962.

The story of 1957-62 was one of ever-increasing performance with a few minor body changes. For 1957, the V-8 was increased in capacity from 265 to 283 cu.in and offered in four states of tune from 245 to 283 bhp. The latter was achieved with the temperamental Rochester fuel injection which was only fitted to 240 cars that year. A four-speed manual gearbox came in too. The 283 continued to be used until it was increased again to 327 cu.in in the final year with 250-340 bhp available, or 360 bhp with an improved version of the fuel injection.

Body changes during the period covered twin headlights which increased the width and the front overhang, plus new bumpers and restyled interior (1958), mesh grille and duck-tail (1961) and removal of the chrome trims around the side sculpture (1962).

Meanwhile, Duntov continued work on the car's road behavior. The live axle suffered wind-up with the ever-increasing power, so radius arms were added to it in 1959. The ride had become less comfortable, so springs were softened in 1960 and anti-roll bars were fitted to restore the roll stiffness.

Regular Performance Options (RPO) were always available for those who wanted to adjust their cars.

By the end of its ninth year, the Corvette had become a strong muscular sports car, faster than most European products and Chevrolet could sell all they were able to make.

TECHNICAL DESCRIPTION OF THE CHEVROLET CORVETTE 1959

YEARS OF PRODUCTION	1956-1962
MODELS	SPORTS 2-SEATER
ENGINE	FRONT-MOUNTED V-8
BORE X STROKE, CAPACITY	3.8 X 2.9 INCHES, 283 CU.IN
VALVEGEAR	PUSHROD OVERHEAD VALVES
FUEL SYSTEM	ROCHESTER 4-CHOKE CARBURETOR
POWER	245 BHP AT 5000 RPM
TRANSMISSION	3-SPEED (4-SPEED OPTION)
BODY/CHASSIS	STEEL CHASSIS, FIBERGLASS BODYWORK
SUSPENSION	FRONT, WISHBONES AND COILS
	REAR, LIVE AXLE WITH LEAF SPRINGS
TIRES/WHEELS	6.70 x 15 ON STEEL WHEELS
WHEELBASE, TRACK (F), TRACK(R)	102 x 57 x 59 INCHES
LENGHT, WIDT, HEIGHT	177 x 72.8 x 50 INCHES
MAX SPEED	125 MPH
WHERE BUILT	MISSOURI, USA

312-313 *Two-tone paint was an option.*
Alloy wheels are later addition.

Triumph TR2 and TR3A

Standard bought Triumph in 1944. Before the war, neither make had produced sporting machinery in any volume, although Standard had supplied Jaguar with engines and chassis. After the war, Standard brought out the Vanguard sedan with a 128 cu.in engine which was quickly adopted by Morgan for the Plus Four in 1950; Morgan had used a Standard engine in the 1939 4/4 but side-valve Ford engines after the war.

Standard-Triumph's first sporting attempt after the war was with the 1800 Roadster which came out in 1946 based on the pre-war Standard 14 engine and chassis. After 2500 were made, the engine was replaced by the Vanguard 128 cu.in in 1948 as the 2000 Roadster. After 2000 of these, production stopped in 1949 as a new sports car, based on the Vanguard chassis, was to be launched in 1950. When it was shown in October, nobody liked it, so plans were cancelled.

Two years later, what was later called the TR1 was shown with a modified pre-war chassis and a 75 bhp version of the Vanguard engine, under a body best described as short-tail TR2. By March 1953, after considerable engine and chassis development the definitive 90 bhp TR2 was shown at Geneva, its engine reduced to under 128 cu.in for competition classes.

314 A prototype Triumph TR2 with covered rear wheels reached 114 mph at Jabbeke in 1953.

315 In the 1954 Alpine Rally, Triumph took the team prize

Sporting credibility was acquired in May with a 115 mph run at Jabbeke and production started slowly in July. Development had been rather too short and in autumn 1954 the chassis was strengthened by raising the bottom of the door and widening the sills.

Successes in rallies and races did much to promote the strength and performance of the TR2; in 1954 they won the RAC rally and took the Manufacturers Team Prize in the Alpine Rally. At Le Mans one finished 15th in 1954, and three finished 14th, 15th and 19th in 1955.

While the TR2 was destined for American sales these did not really build up until the TR3 was launched in October 1955; this was basically a TR2 with an egg-box grille, sliding panel side-screens and 95 bhp from bigger carburetors. A year later a new cylinder head had taken this to 100 bhp while disc brakes were fitted at the end of 1956.

A new full-width grille, doors and trunk lid with external handles, denoted the TR3A which arrived in early 1958. By mid-1958 the 130.4 cu.in engine became an option, although few were actually fitted at the factory. By the end of the decade, the TR3A was losing its appeal; rivals offered more comfort and more performance. Only 405 were delivered in 1961, the year Leyland took over, but by then the TR4 was on the way, being announced in September 1961.

While the 130.4 cu.in engine and chassis were basically unchanged, the front and rear tracks were widened to allow the body width to be increased by 2.5 inches, the gearbox had synchromesh on all ratios and the steering used rack-and-pinion gearing. Italian Michelotti designed the new body with a uniquely versatile roof and considerably more space for occupants and luggage. The top was a two-piece hard-top with a fixed rear window frame and a removable metal top panel which could be replaced by a soft top – the Surrey top. Passengers also had wind-up windows, a better heater and fresh air vents. The TR4 was a very big improvement over the earlier cars and gained a considerable increase in sales.

During his work for Triumph, Michelotti also designed a new body for the TR3A chassis and a number were produced by Vignale as the Triumph Italia. There was also a TR3B available on the American market; uncertain of the reception which the TR4 would get, American dealers asked for the TR3A shape to be continued in 1962 using the all-synchromesh gearbox – over 3300 were built before the more practical TR4 was appreciated.

It was 1965 before the Triumph chassis gained independent rear suspension with the TR4A, still using the 130.4 cu.in engine to carry the semi-trailing arm rear suspension that had been used on the Triumph 2000. Once again some American customers wanted to retain the old design, so a number went to America with the new chassis adapted to take the old live axle.

TR5 followed in 1967 with the 152.5 cu.in six-cylinder engine from the Triumph sedan and this was rebodied to Karmann's design for the TR6 in 1969.

TECHNICAL DESCRIPTION OF THE TRIUMPH TR2 and (TR3A)

YEARS OF PRODUCTION	1953-55 (1958-61)
MODELS	Sports 2-seater
ENGINE	Front-mounted in-line 4
BORE X STROKE, CAPACITY	3.2 x 3.6 inches, 121.4 cu.in
VALVEGEAR	Pushrod overhead valves
FUEL SYSTEM	Twin SU carburetors
POWER	90 (100) bhp at 4800 (5000) rpm
TRANSMISSION	4-speed and overdrive
BODY/CHASSIS	Steel chassis, integral bulkheads and detachable bodypanels
SUSPENSION	Front, wishbones and coils Rear, live axle with leaf springs
TIRES/WHEELS	5.50 x 15 on steel wheels
WHEELBASE, TRACK (F), TRACK(R)	88 x 45 x 45.5 inches
LENGHT, WIDT, HEIGHT	151 x 55 x 50 inches
MAX SPEED	104 (110) mph
WHERE BUILT	Coventry, England

316-317 *TR3A brought in full-width grille.*
Wire wheels were an option.

Alfa Romeo Giulietta Sprint and Spider

Stretching back to 1910, the Alfa Romeo heritage was one of fast cars and competition success until the all-conquering Tipo 159 became ineligible for Grand Prix racing at the end of 1951.

While the company continued to race sports cars during the Fifties, the future was to be sedan cars with coupe and spider derivatives produced in large numbers. The heritage ensured that even the sedan cars had good sporting characteristics.

First of these had been the medium-size 1900 series which ran from 1950-58; Touring produced a 2-door coupe and Pinin Farina made the cabriolet – only 1800 of these short-chassis variants were built out of a total of 19,000. Work started on the smaller Giulietta in 1952.

Like the 1900, this had a monocoque chassis, a twin-cam engine (79.3 cu.in), a well-located live axle and sporting performance.

As Alfa Romeo were owned by the Italian state, IRI (Institute for Industrial Reconstruction) decided to raise money for Alfa Romeo in 1953 with a bond issue; they offered new Giuliettas as prizes. Alfa Romeo had completed work on the platform but was still developing the rest of the car, so they arranged for Bertone to have platforms to build a two-door version; planned for low numbers, the Sprint did not require the same level of tooling and the early ones were produced in the traditional handbuilt way. So the Sprint came out in 1954, almost a year before the sedan Giulietta. It was an instant success. No-one had

expected the demand to be so great, so Bertone had to build a new production factory in Grugliasco outside Turin.

While the Giulietta used a single carburetor and a 7.5:1 compression ratio to give a conservative 53 bhp, the Sprint had 80 bhp due to a higher compression ratio at 8.5:1 and a twin-choke downdraft carburetor. When the Veloce version was added in 1956, the compression ratio was further increased and twin double-choke Weber carburetors were fitted to give 90 bhp. Over the six years, Bertone built more than 25,000 of which 3058 were Sprint Veloces.

Pinin Farina was given the task of producing the open sports car – the Spider. For this, an all-new body was designed for which the Giulietta chassis was shortened by 5 inches; the new car was introduced just three

318-319 Bertone's Giulietta Sprint, left, was the first of the line in 1954. The Spider followed a year later.

months after the sedan. Some 14,300 Giulietta Spiders were built with a further 2900 Veloce versions with more power.

Bertone added to the range in 1959 with the dramatic Sprint Speciale, modelled on his BAT concept cars (Berlina Aerodinamica Tecnica); although the prototype had been shown as a concept car in 1957, the decision to produce it took another two years. The first 153 Giulietta SS were built in Bertone's Turin factory using aluminium bodywork, but the rest of the 1460 total were built in Grugliasco with steel bodywork. Sprint, Spider and SS were much used in Italian racing, but the SS was no lighter than the Sprint. This was rectified by Zagato who brought out the most successful Giulietta of all at the end of 1959; the SZ was much lighter than the others and 200 were built to conform to the rules for competition GT cars. Both SS and SZ used the shorter Spider platform with 100 bhp engines and 5-speed gearboxes.

In 1962, Alfa Romeo replaced the Giulietta with the Giulia, using a 95.8 cu.in version of the superb little engine with bigger pistons and a longer stroke crankshaft. At that time, no other manufacturer offered a twin overhead camshaft engine in a small family sedan. The new square-looking body was mounted on a Giulietta chassis lengthened by 5 inches and fitted with 4-wheel disc brakes and a 5-speed gearbox. Bertone and Pinin Farina continued to build their Giulietta bodies – Sprint (7083-off), Spider (6961-off) and SS (620-off) – but used the new engine with disc brakes on the front and called them Giulias. In fact, the Sprint reappeared with a 1300 engine in 1964 together with a Giulia Spider Veloce with 112 bhp.

While the Giulietta and Giulia sedans may become classics, the models made by the coachbuilders Bertone, Pinin Farina and Zagato are already appreciated as classics.

320-321 Spider, by Pinin Farina, displays the typical twin-cam engine.

TECHNICAL DESCRIPTION OF THE ALFA ROMEO GIULIETTA SPRINT

YEARS OF PRODUCTION	1954-61
MODELS	COUPE 2 + 2
ENGINE	FRONT-MOUNTED IN-LINE 4
BORE X STROKE, CAPACITY	2.91 X 2.95 INCHES, 78.7 CU.IN
VALVEGEAR	TWIN OVERHEAD CAMSHAFTS
FUEL SYSTEM	WEBER TWIN-CHOKE CARBURETOR
POWER	80 BHP AT 6300 RPM
TRANSMISSION	4-SPEED
BODY/CHASSIS	STEEL MONOCOQUE
SUSPENSION	FRONT, WISHBONES AND COILS
	REAR, LIVE AXLE WITH RADIUS ARMS AND
	A-BRACKET, COIL SPRINGS
TIRES/WHEELS	61 X 6 INCHES ON STEEL WHEELS
WHEELBASE, TRACK (F), TRACK(R)	94 X 50.5 X 50 INCHES
LENGHT, WIDT, HEIGHT	157 X 60 X 52 INCHES
MAX SPEED	100 MPH
WHERE BUILT	MILAN, ITALY

NB THE WHEELBASE FOR THE GIULIETTA SPIDER AND SS/SZ IS 88.6 IN. FOR THE SS AND SZ, THE POWER WAS INCREASED TO 100 BHP

One of the most desirable cars of the Fifties, the Mercedes 300SL was directly derived from the racing coupe that won Le Mans in 1952. Having been one of the dominant duo of pre-war Grand Prix racing, Mercedes began to plan a return in 1951. They started to design a car for 1952 but the formula changed and they had to wait until the rules changed again for 1954. Meanwhile there was sports car racing. Jaguar had won the 1951 Le Mans 24-hour race with the C-type; this used a tubular chassis frame with running gear from the production XK120.

Like Jaguar, Mercedes could only use running gear from the production line as there was no time to design new components. So the new car was based around the six-cylinder 300 series which had been launched in 1951. As the engine potential was necessarily limited, the car had to be as light and streamlined as possible. To keep the overall

Mercedes Benz 300SL

weight down, Mercedes' previous race design work was put to good use and they made a new space-frame chassis to take the front and rear suspension of the production 300S, as well as the engine and 4-speed manual gearbox. Drum brakes were improved by using the Alfin system of ribbed aluminium drums with steel liners.

Others had shown the aerodynamic benefits of using closed coupes for long-distance sports car racing, particularly in the Mille Miglia and at Le Mans, so the new 300SL – Super Light – had closed bodywork. The drag factor of 0.25 was lower than any other coupe and much lower than that of open cars. The frontal area was kept low by inclining the six-cylinder 183 cu.in engine at 50 degrees to the vertical. As small tube space frames lose a lot of their strength if they have big spaces for door ways, the engineers evolved the gull-wing doors hinged in the center of the roof. Initially the lower edge of the doors was the bottom of the window frame; it was only when it came to Le Mans and the prospect of quick driver changes, that the doors were deepened.

In its standard form, the 300 engine produced 115 bhp at 4500 rpm using a compression ratio of 6.4:1. With a new camshaft, 8:1 compression and 3 downdraft Solex carburetors, the output was improved to 171 bhp at 5200 rpm. The new car was shown to the press in March 1952, only nine months after the Mercedes board approved the project. In May, three 300SLs ran in the Mille Miglia and finished second and fourth; the leading Ferrari 250S, also a coupe, had 230 bhp. Factory 300SLs finished 1-2-3 at Bern, also in May; new ones with modified doors went to Le Mans and finished 1-2.

For a 10-lap race over the twisty Nurburgring where low drag was

322-323 Always known as the Gullwing, the Mercedes 300SL was developed from the racing cars.

less important than light weight and more power, the coupes became roadsters and finished 1,2,3. The final 1952 event for the 300SLs was the Carrera Panamericana, two coupes and a roadster; as at Le Mans they defeated the Ferraris and finished 1,2. It had been an impressive debut year. Although development continued after the season, the proposed 1953 campaign was cancelled in favor of preparation for the Grand Prix cars.

Instead, the factory responded to the request of the American importer Max Hoffman to produce road-going replicas of the 300SLs; he also instigated the production of the similar-looking 190SL based on the floorpan of the 180/220 series with a 4-cylinder engine developing 105 bhp. The new 300SL used very much the same design as had the earlier racing versions, although, inevitably the weight was increased from the competition 1914 lb to 2557 lb – the Jaguar E-type coupe would be 2513 lb in 1961. The major change was for the engine with a power increase from around 175 bhp to 220 bhp with the sports camshaft and direct fuel injection. The 300SL was first shown at New York show in February 1954 and production started that autumn. By 1957, 1371 road-

going cars had been produced with a further 29 lightweights for competition use.

In 1957, the 300SL coupe was replaced by the Roadster, still using a space-frame chassis. Its major change was the adoption of the low-pivot swing axle which would have been used on the 1953 competition cars, and was used for the GP car. With a compensating spring to reduce rear roll stiffness, this considerably improved the handling. When disc brakes were adopted in 1961, the 300SL Roadster was a match for the E-type but more than twice the price. By 1962, 1858 had been built.

TECHNICAL DESCRIPTION OF THE MERCEDES-BENZ 300SL

YEARS OF PRODUCTION	1954-1957
MODELS	2-DOOR COUPE
ENGINE	FRONT-MOUNTED IN-LINE SIX
BORE X STROKE, CAPACITY	3.3 X 3.4 INCHES, 182.8 CU.IN
VALVEGEAR	SINGLE OVERHEAD CAMSHAFT
FUEL SYSTEM	BOSCH FUEL INJECTION
POWER	220 BHP AT 5800 RPM
TRANSMISSION	4-SPEED
BODY/CHASSIS	TUBULAR SPACE FRAME
SUSPENSION	FRONT, WISHBONES AND COIL SPRINGS
	REAR, SWING AXLE WITH COIL SPRINGS
TIRES/WHEELS	6.50 X 15 ON 5.5K STEEL WHEELS
WHEELBASE, TRACK (F), TRACK(R)	94.5 X 54 X 56 INCHES
LENGHT, WIDT, HEIGHT	178 X 70 X 51 INCHES
MAX SPEED	155 MPH
WHERE BUILT	STUTTGART, GERMANY

324-325 Low frontal area and low drag gave a 155 mph top speed from 220 bhp.

Bentley Continental S-type

Bentley is one England's more illustrious makes; the Bentley was the archetypal Vintage sports car, big, powerful and well engineered to last. After five victories at Le Mans, they were taken over by Rolls-Royce in 1931, but their sporting reputation has never been forgotten. From 1931, Rolls-Royce and Bentley cars have shared components even though the models looked very different through the Thirties. After the war, most Rolls models had a matching Bentley with just a radiator change, but there have been a number of models that have been uniquely Bentley.

The R-type Continental was the first of these. The 10-foot chassis, shared by the Bentley R-type and the Rolls-Royce Silver Dawn, was available to individual coachbuilders, but it was H.J.Mulliner who was given

326-327 The S-type Continental, a 1957 example here, continued the line established by the R-type in 1952.

YEARS OF PRODUCTION	1956-59
MODELS	FIXED HEAD COUPE, CONVERTIBLE
ENGINE	IN-LINE 6-CYLINDER
BORE X STROKE, CAPACITY	3.7 x 4.4 INCHES, 298.2 CU.IN
VALVEGEAR	INLET OVER EXHAUST
FUEL SYSTEM	TWIN SU CARBURETORS
POWER	NOT PUBLISHED
TRANSMISSION	4-SPEED OR AUTO
BODY/CHASSIS	STEEL FRAME, STEEL BODY PANELS
FRONT SUSPENSION	WISHBONES AND COIL SPRINGS
REAR SUSPENSION	LIVE AXLE AND LEAF SPRINGS
TIRES/WHEELS	8.00 x 15 ON STEEL WHEELS
WHEELBASE, TRACK (F), TRACK(R)	123 x 58 x 60 INCHES
LENGTH, WIDTH, HEIGHT	212 x 72 x 62 INCHES
MAX SPEED	120 MPH
WHERE BUILT	CREWE, ENGLAND

the more powerful version for the new Continental. Its aerodynamic body had origins in pre-war work by van Vooren. After the war, Bentley's Paris distributor commissioned Pinin Farina to produce a 2-door fast-back sedan along the same lines. What appeared at the 1948 Paris Motor Show was an enlarged Cisitalia GT of rather cleaner proportions with the belt-line running from headlight to tail-light in a single integrated sweep, a line that was recognizable in the 1951 Lancia Aurelia. The factory moved the headlights inwards towards a narrower vertical radiator and created separate sweeps around each wheel arch, running into small fins at the tail. As the chassis was still the same length as the sedans, it could still take four people in comfort. The 278.6 cu.in engine was mildly tuned, the gearbox was given close ratios and a higher back axle ratio was fitted; the prototype had been taken round Montlhery's banked track at 118 mph. When the Continental was launched in 1952, it was called the fastest four-seater in the world. After Bentley had made 208 Continental chassis, of which only 15 had not received H.J.Mulliner bodies, the company introduced the Bentley S-type and Rolls-Royce Silver Cloud in 1956 with the 299 cu.in engine that had been used in later R-types. Although the new chassis was 3 inches longer, Mulliner continued to produce the fast-back shape, and others, until the V-8 powered S2 arrived in 1959. From 1957, the S-type Continental chassis had been made available to other coachbuilders including Rolls' own Park Ward. So not every Continental is a Mulliner fast-back.

Ford Thunderbird

General Motors were the first to react to the rising tide of imported British sports cars when they launched the Corvette in 1953. In fact, Ford had reacted in 1951 but were slower to convert the project from paper to metal; it was the Corvette launch that prompted them to reopen the file. And having watched the Corvette's slow sales due to poor straight line performance, Ford chose to use V-8 power from the start in 1955 but also provided a higher level of comfort. This may have made the Thunderbird slower round the corners, but it was faster on the drag-strip and sold in much greater numbers. Although the Corvette gained a V-8 option in the same year that the Thunderbird was launched, Ford had obviously found a better interpretation of what the American buyer wanted from his home-grown personal two-seater. The Thunderbird was styled within Ford by Frank Hershey. Based on a new chassis frame with the same wheelbase as the Corvette, the T-bird had a slender elegance that was as attractive as anything from Europe. No trace of Jaguar, Ferrari or Triumph marred its lines. Underneath, the suspension was just standard Ford with wishbone independent front suspension and a simple live axle at the rear. Sporting performance came from the drive-train. Where the Corvette started with a six-cylinder engine coupled to a 2-speed automatic transmission, Ford chose a V-8 and fitted a manual 3-speed gearbox with overdrive, offering a 3-speed automatic as an option; they had finally replaced the old flat-head V-8 in 1954. In fact the top option was the 292 cu.in from the Mercury range with 193 bhp, but 239 cu.in and 256 cu.in versions were also available in some markets. For 1956, the smaller unit was increased to 272 cu.in with 200 bhp and the Mercury engine increased to 312 cu.in and 245 bhp. The horsepower race was on and Ford took the lead from GM when the big engine was also offered with a Paxton supercharger to give around 300 bhp. Despite the T-bird's long tail, there was still not enough luggage space, so for 1956 the spare wheel was taken out and mounted under a cover with its own bumper extension, like the Lincolns. The optional hard-top came with a choice of the famous port-holes in its sail panel for 1956 and appealed to 80 per cent of the 15,000 buyers. The 1957 cars were distinguished by the

arrival of more pronounced flared fins at the rear.

Although 1957 sales reached 21,380 cars, against the Corvette's 6340, this was not enough to justify the extra production lines, so Ford responded by making the T-bird into a 4-seater for 1958 – Big Bird. This added 11 inches to the wheelbase and 20 inches to the overall length; the extra 815 lb was overcome by using Ford's new big-block V-8 with 332 cu.in or, as the top option, at 352 cu.in and 300 bhp. The new style reflected the fins and chrome era with a massive plated grille at the front, four headlights and the spare wheel still carried outside the bodywork.

Although the Big Bird had lost the slim elegance of the previous car, the sales almost doubled in the first year to nearly 38,000 units, so Ford's market research had paid off.

The 1959 cars had a few changes with a horizontal bar grille replacing the honeycomb but, of greater significance was the arrival of the power-operated hood, placing the T-bird more firmly in the luxury market. However the hard-top was preferred by the majority of buyers. Performance was still a strong selling point, though, as the top engine option was increased yet again to 430 cu.in using an engine from the

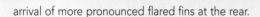

YEARS OF PRODUCTION	1955-57
MODELS	2-SEATER ROADSTER
ENGINE	FRONT-MOUNTED V-8
BORE X STROKE, CAPACITY	3.6 x 3.3 INCHES, 271.9 CU.IN
VALVEGEAR	PUSHROD OVERHEAD VALVES
FUEL SYSTEM	SINGLE FORD CARBURETOR
POWER	200 BHP AT 4400 RPM
TRANSMISSION	3-SPEED AND O/D
BODY/CHASSIS	STEEL BOX-SECTION FRAME
SUSPENSION	FRONT, WISHBONES AND COILS
	REAR, LIVE AXLE WITH LEAF SPRING
TIRES/WHEELS	7.10 x 15 ON STEEL WHEELS
WHEELBASE, TRACK (F), TRACK(R)	102 x 56 x 56 INCHES
LENGTH, WIDTH, HEIGHT	163.5 x 69 x 51.5 INCHES
MAX SPEED	115 MPH
WHERE BUILT	DETROIT, USA

328-329 Marilyn Monroe's T-bird carries the 1956 Model Year hallmarks of the external spare wheel and the port-hole hardtop.

Lincoln range. For the 1961 face-lift, the T-bird reverted to elegance with a mildly pointed front end and less chromium plate, and there was only one engine option – the 390 cu.in. Although four seats appealed to the majority of buyers, there were still some who wanted a two-seater Ford, so an option was created by covering the rear seats with a fiberglass tonneau cover complete with fared head-rests, just like a Fifties sports-racing car.

The spare wheel disappeared inside the trunk again. Successive face-lifts in 1964 and 1967 brought more luxurious fittings but the Mustang had arrived in 1964 so the T-bird gradually became just another sports sedan. Chevrolet had won the battle to produce the sports car that America lacked.

330-331 Restrained fins denoted the 1957 model. The 1959 Big Bird, left, has the optional tonneau cover covering the rear seats.

TECHNICAL DESCRIPTION OF 1959 FORD THUNDERBIRD

YEARS OF PRODUCTION	1958-59
MODELS	4-SEATER ROADSTER
ENGINE	FRONT-MOUNTED V-8
BORE X STROKE, CAPACITY	3.9 X 3.4 INCHES, 352 CU.IN
VALVEGEAR	PUSHROD OVERHEAD VALVES
FUEL SYSTEM	SINGLE FORD CARBURETOR
POWER	300 BHP AT 4600 RPM
TRANSMISSION	3-SPEEDS
BODY/CHASSIS	STEEL BOX-SECTION FRAME
SUSPENSION	FRONT, WISHBONES AND COILS
	REAR, LIVE AXLE WITH LEAF SPRING
TIRES/WHEELS	8.00 X 14 ON STEEL WHEELS
WHEELBASE, TRACK (F), TRACK(R)	113 X 60 X 57 INCHES
LENGTH, WIDTH, HEIGHT	205 X 77 X 53 INCHES
MAX SPEED	125 MPH
WHERE BUILT	DETROIT, USA

MGA 1600

The MGA was the sports car that the Abingdon factory wanted to build instead of the TF for 1953. When Austin and Morris merged in 1952 to form BMC, Austin was given the sports-car responsibility and allowed to continue with the external development which would become the Austin Healey in October 1952. MG had to continue with a further improvement to the TD to make the TF which, even with the 89.4 cu.in XPEG engine in 1954 was too old-fashioned and slow to make any impact against the Austin-Healey and TR2.

It could all have been so different. MG's Syd Enever had produced a special-bodied MG TD for privateer George Phillips to race at Le Mans in 1951. Although it retired with engine problems that year, it was the shape of the MGA to come. With a widened chassis to lower the seating, it was presented as EX175 to BMC management in late 1952, after the launch of the Austin-Healey. It was turned down. TD sales had begun to decline and the TF did little to boost MG sports car production.

However, alongside the TF on the 1953 Motor Show stand was an MG sedan, the ZA Magnette; although this looked like a Wolseley 4/44 with an MG radiator, it was fitted with a 60 bhp 90.8 cu.in version of the B-series engine which had been used by the Austin A40 in 73.2 cu.in form from 1949; the Wolseley equivalent was fitted with the 76.2 cu.in XPAG MG engine. EX175 with the bigger B-series engine could easily have been ready for 1953. As it was, the poor reception for the TF eventually forced the BMC management to re-establish an MG design office and the prototype MGA (EX182) was finally shown to the public in June 1955 – a team of three were about to run at Le Mans that year.

The car was finally launched in September 1955 and during the London Show, a near-standard MGA put over 100 miles into an hour round Montlhery. For the MGA the ZA engine was given bigger carburetors to increase the output to 68 bhp, a modification later used for the ZB Magnette. It was a straightforward but effective open sports car with the typical English curves, the long sweep over the front wheels blending into a separate sweep over the rear ones – actually, like the XK120, these were based on the pre-war Touring designs for BMW. With a 91.5 cu.in engine it wasn't intended to be as fast as the Austin-Healey,

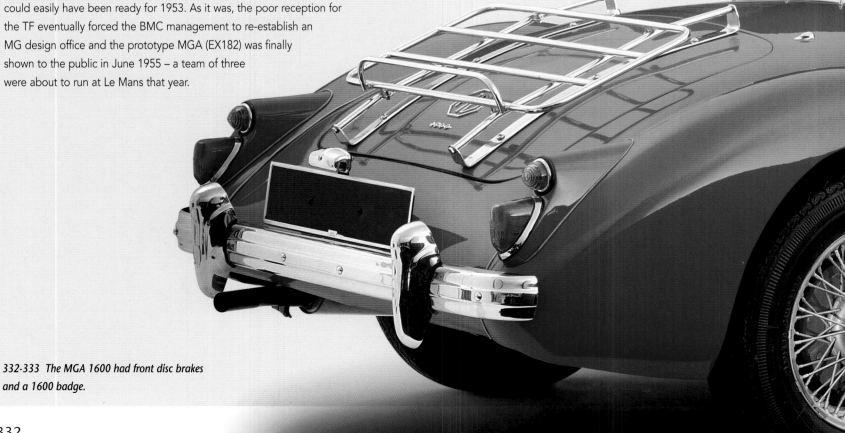

332-333 The MGA 1600 had front disc brakes and a 1600 badge.

Triumph or Jaguar but 95 mph was enough for most people.

In the USA the new MG soon achieved wider acclaim than did the TC and established a new level of production at Abingdon. In the first full year (1956) more than 13,000 were built, more than four years of the TC. When the fixed head coupe was shown in late 1956, its better aerodynamics took the maximum speed to 100 mph.

The factory competition department continued to be active in racing and rallying with the MGA and the Magnette. And they were still involved in record breaking with special streamlined bodies powered by modified production engines.

One of these experimental power units was used for a new model, the MGA Twin-Cam which was launched in 1958 in open and coupe forms; basically a B-series enlarged to 96.8 cu.in and fitted with a new twin-cam cylinder head, this gave 108 bhp which took the maximum

TECHNICAL DESCRIPTION OF THE MGA 1600

YEARS OF PRODUCTION	1959-61
MODELS	SPORTS 2-SEATER
ENGINE	FRONT-MOUNTED IN-LINE 4
BORE X STROKE, CAPACITY	2.9 x 3.5 INCHES, 96.8 CU.IN
VALVEGEAR	PUSHROD OVERHEAD VALVES
FUEL SYSTEM	TWIN SU CARBURETORS
POWER	80 BHP AT 5500 RPM
TRANSMISSION	4-SPEED
BODY/CHASSIS	STEEL CHASSIS, SEPARATE BODY
SUSPENSION	FRONT, WISHBONES AND COILS
	REAR, LIVE AXLE WITH LEAF SPRINGS
TIRES/WHEELS	5.60 x 15 ON WIRE WHEELS
WHEELBASE, TRACK (F), TRACK(R)	94 x 47.5 x 49 INCHES
LENGTH, WIDTH, HEIGHT	156 x 58 x 50 INCHES
MAX SPEED	100 MPH
WHERE BUILT	ABINGDON-ON-THAMES, ENGLAND

TECHNICAL DESCRIPTION OF THE MGA 1600 MK.11

YEARS OF PRODUCTION	1961-62
MODELS	SPORTS 2-SEATER
ENGINE	FRONT-MOUNTED IN-LINE 4
BORE X STROKE, CAPACITY	2.9 x 3.5 INCHES, 98.9 CU.IN
VALVEGEAR	PUSHROD OVERHEAD VALVES
FUEL SYSTEM	TWIN SU CARBURETORS
POWER	86 BHP AT 5500 RPM
TRANSMISSION	4-SPEED
BODY/CHASSIS	STEEL CHASSIS, SEPARATE BODY
SUSPENSION	FRONT, WISHBONES AND COILS
	REAR, LIVE AXLE WITH LEAF SPRINGS
TIRES/WHEELS	5.60 x 15 ON WIRE WHEELS
WHEELBASE, TRACK (F), TRACK(R)	94 x 47.5 x 49 INCHES
LENGTH, WIDTH, HEIGHT	156 x 58 x 50 INCHES
MAX SPEED	104 MPH
WHERE BUILT	ABINGDON-ON-THAMES, ENGLAND

speed through 110 mph. Center lock wheels hiding all-round disc brakes ensured that the Twin-Cam was easily distinguished from the normal MGA. Although the car performed well in racing, the engine was not as reliable in service as the push-rod unit and the model was discontinued in 1960 after only 2111 had been built – the problems were mostly due to the engine's need for 100-octane fuel which wasn't always available and early engines used too much oil.

For 1959 the bore of the ordinary push-rod B-series engine was

increased to that of the Twin-Cam to make the MGA 1600 with 80 bhp and front disc brakes were fitted.

The final version came in 1961 with the bore increased still further to give 98.9 cu.in and 86 bhp while a modified grille gave the Mark II a distinctive appearance. By mid-1962, 101,081 MGAs had rolled off the Abingdon production line, a record then for a single model of sports car. Over half these were the 1500, while the 1600 Mk.II was the rarest, excluding the Twin-Cam, with only 8719 built. Declining sales reflected customer demand for a new car with a little more performance and comfort – the MGB came in late 1962.

Cadillac Eldorado

Cadillac is one of the oldest American car companies having been founded in 1902 by Henry Leland; the name had come from a Frenchman who had established Detroit in 1701 and it is his coat of arms that is still used by Cadillac. The company became a part of William Durant's General Motors (GM) when that was set up in 1909, along with Buick, Cadillac, Oldsmobile and Oakland – Chevrolet became a part of GM in 1918. Cadillac was chosen as the engineering center of GM and was making the finest American cars before the 1914-18 war. It was Leland who established the Cadillac motto which still adorns the factory entrance gates – Craftsmanship a creed, accuracy a law.

Cadillac has continued to make fine cars in the traditional way; there is much more manual work on the Cadillac lines than anywhere else in GM. Although much of the basic chassis and the running gear come from GM stock, many body panels and the interior design are unique to Cadillac and production numbers are much smaller than those of Chevrolet. Cadillac, though, continued to have its own engines and, even today, the all-aluminium Northstar V-8 is unique to Cadillac and a variant of that engine was used to power the Cadillac sports racing cars at Le Mans 2000, 50 years after Cadillac had finished 10th there with a standard coupe. That

336-337 The Eldorado was always exclusive but the Brougham was very rare and only 700 were built in two years.

Fifties engine, first shown in 1949, was a new 331 cu.in V-8 which was also made available for the English Allard sports car.

The same year, Cadillac launched the tail fin which would grow in size throughout the Fifties. GM's head of styling, Harley Earl, had been impressed by the design of the Lockheed Lightning P38 fighter airplane with its twin-boom tail. The new style for 1949 featured small fins on the tail and bomb-shaped bumper guards at the front and rear.

The Eldorado convertible was added in 1953 to celebrate the 50th anniversary of the launch of the first car, so the model used a special gold chevron. It was the height of luxury with leather upholstery, two-way power seats, power steering, automatic transmission, seeker radio, power windows, concealed soft-top, wrap-round windscreen and wire wheels; many of these features heralded the future. It was expensive and exclusive; only 532 were produced in 1953, 2150 in 1954 and 3950 (with bigger tail fins) in 1955.

Emphasising their tradition of craftsmanship, Cadillac began to use such coachbuilding names for their models as Sedanca de Ville, Coupe de Ville and Brougham, even if they didn't always match the early motoring definitions. De Ville used to imply open front seats with a closed rear section, coupe being a shorter version of the Sedanca. The Brougham, after Lord Brougham's nineteenth century one-horse close

carriage, was similar to a Coupe de Ville but usually shorter and with razor-edged styling for the closed compartment. Cadillac chose to use Coupe de Ville on the 2-door coupe from which the Eldorado was derived, and used Brougham for the four-door Fleetwood and Eldorado. Both had the pillarless construction, opening the side window area completely between quarter lights.

The Eldorado Brougham grew out of one of Harley Earl's 1953 show cars. Its external novelties included a brushed stainless steel roof, tinted glass and four headlights, while the chassis was the shortest of all Cadillacs.

Power steering, automatic transmission and power assisted brakes were regular Cadillac features, but the Brougham was the first car to use air suspension with an electrically driven compressor pressurizing air in rubber domes – a short-term feature as the system leaked. Power was provided by the Cadillac V-8 increased to 365 cu.in with 325 bhp, a necessary output given a weight of over 2.75 tons.

For interior comfort, the Brougham had air conditioning, separate front and rear heating, powered front seat for driver adjustment and easier access, power door locks, power trunk lid, vanity case and a perfume atomiser in the rear armrest. The Eldorado Brougham was Cadillac's flagship to match the Lincoln Continental, but sold just 704 cars in the two years of its production.

As such small numbers could not justify the assembly space, newly styled 1959 cars were built by Pinin Farina in Italy but only 200 of these were made in two years. The true successor to the 1958 Eldorado Brougham was the less lavishly equipped Fleetwood Brougham displaying the biggest vertical fins of all, but the near-horizontal fins on the 1959 Chevrolet Biscayne are actually more attractive.

TECHNICAL DESCRIPTION OF THE CADILLAC ELDORADO	
YEARS OF PRODUCTION	1957-1958
MODELS	4-DOOR SEDAN
ENGINE	FRONT-MOUNTED V-8
BORE X STROKE, CAPACITY	3.9 X 3.5 INCHES, 364.4
VALVEGEAR	PUSHROD OVERHEAD VALVES
FUEL SYSTEM	SINGLE CARBURETOR
POWER	325 BHP AT 4800 RPM
TRANSMISSION	4-SPEED AUTOMATIC
BODY/CHASSIS	STEEL BOX-SECTION FRAME
SUSPENSION	FRONT, WISHBONES AND AIR SPRINGS
	REAR, LIVE AXLE WITH AIR SPRINGS
TIRES/WHEELS	6.70 X 15 ON STEEL WHEELS
WHEELBASE, TRACK (F), TRACK(R)	129.5 X 61 X 61 INCHES
LENGTH, WIDT, HEIGHT	210 X 80 X 55 INCHES
MAX SPEED	110 MPH
WHERE BUILT	DETROIT, USA

Aston Martin DB4 and DB4GT

The arrival of the Aston Martin DB4 at the 1958 London Motor Show put Britain back near the top of the high performance Grand Tourer league, alongside the Ferrari 250GT and the Mercedes 300SL. Styled by Touring of Milan, the DB4 looked like a proper GT and it was a genuine 140 mph four-seater, too.

Following a pre-war range of small sporting cars, the DB2/4 had successfully established Aston Martin as a high performance car manufacturer but, by the Mid-fifties, the 120 mph maximum speed

was no longer fast. Aston Martin had begun work on the DB2/4 replacement in 1954. Initially this was a perimeter frame with wishbone front suspension and a de Dion axle, but when the project was taken to Touring, they asked for a conventional platform as a better base on which to mount their tubular steel body frame – the superleggera system. By the time the first prototype was completed in mid-1957, it had a steel platform chassis and the de Dion axle had been replaced with a well located live axle. Disc brakes were used on all four wheels

340-341 The standard DB4 had five different series, here a series 4 (1961-62)

TECHNICAL DESCRIPTION OF THE ASTON MARTIN DB4

YEARS OF PRODUCTION	1958-1963
MODELS	4-SEATER COUPE
ENGINE	FRONT-MOUNTED IN-LINE 6
BORE X STROKE, CAPACITY	3.6 X 3.6 INCHES, 223.9 CU.IN
VALVEGEAR	TWIN OVERHEAD CAMSHAFTS
FUEL SYSTEM	TWIN SU CARBURETORSS
POWER	220 BHP AT 5500 RPM
TRANSMISSION	4-SPEED
BODY/CHASSIS	STEEL CHASSIS, ALUMINIUM BODY
	PANELS WRAPPED ROUND STEEL TUBING
SUSPENSION	FRONT, WISHBONES AND COILS
	REAR, LIVE AXLE WITH COIL SPRINGS
TIRES/WHEELS	6.00 x 16 ON WIRE WHEELS
WHEELBASE, TRACK (F), TRACK(R)	98 x 54 x 53 INCHES
LENGTH, WIDTH, HEIGHT	176 x 66 x 51 INCHES
MAX SPEED	140 MPH
WHERE BUILT	NEWPORT PAGNELL, ENGLAND

and a 4-speed David Brown gearbox was fitted with overdrive a later option.

Tadek Marek designed the new engine in 1955, a twin-cam six of 225 cu.in with removable wet cylinder liners; the cylinder block was intended to be made of cast iron but, at the time, only an aluminium foundry would take the task, so both head and block were in aluminium. It was a particularly appropriate engine for Aston Martin to develop in racing and the DBR2 sports-racing car performed well in 1957 and 1958, for which the capacity was increased to 238 cu.in The later DB5 would use a 244 cu.in version.

Production was slow to get under way due to a factory strike resulting from the move from Feltham to the former Tickford coachbuilding premises at Newport Pagnell; while this allowed time for further development, it limited the production rate to just 150 cars

342-343 *Giugiaro designed this unique Aston Martin Jet on a DB4GT chassis when he was working for Bertone.*

before the improved Series 2 arrived at the beginning of 1960. Series 3 and 4 followed over the next two years with minor changes. When the series 5 arrived in September 1962 with more headroom, a longer body and, for some cars, fared in headlights, the car was almost a DB5; it became a DB5 in July 1963 when the engine capacity was increased to 244 cu.in and a 5-speed ZF gearbox was offered. It was one of the DB5 prototypes that James Bond used in Goldfinger and other films.

Meanwhile the DB4GT had been launched in October 1959, after the prototype had already been raced. With 5 inches removed from the wheelbase and thinner aluminium bodywork, it was usefully lighter and considerably more powerful with new camshafts, twin-plug cylinder head and triple Weber carburetors, changes that took the output to 272 bhp. A year later this formed the basis of the beautiful version built by Zagato which was even lighter and more suitable for GT racing. Only 19 Zagato-bodied cars were built at the time but, over 1990-1, another four were built with the cooperation of the two

TECHNICAL DESCRIPTION OF THE ASTON MARTIN DB4GT

YEARS OF PRODUCTION	1959-1963
MODELS	4-SEATER COUPE
ENGINE	FRONT-MOUNTED IN-LINE 6
BORE X STROKE, CAPACITY	3.6 X 3.6 INCHES, 223.9 CU.IN
VALVEGEAR	TWIN OVERHEAD CAMSHAFTS
FUEL SYSTEM	TRIPLE WEBER CARBURETORS
POWER	272 BHP AT 6000 RPM
TRANSMISSION	4-SPEED
BODY/CHASSIS	STEEL CHASSIS, ALUMINIUM BODY PANELS WRAPPED ROUND STEEL TUBING
SUSPENSION	FRONT, WISHBONES AND COILS REAR, LIVE AXLE WITH COIL SPRINGS
TIRES/WHEELS	6.00 X 16 ON WIRE WHEELS
WHEELBASE, TRACK (F), TRACK(R)	93 X 54 X 53 INCHES
LENGTH, WIDTH, HEIGHT	171 X 66 X 51 INCHES
MAX SPEED	152 MPH
WHERE BUILT	NEWPORT PAGNELL, ENGLAND

344-345 *One of the 19 original DB4GT with body by Zagato.*

companies; outwardly identical, they had 256 cu.in engines and the 15-inch wheels that the DB5 adopted.

There had been 75 standard DB4GTs and a single car had been bodied by Bertone. Over the four and a half years of production, 1110 DB4s were built of which some 70 were convertibles introduced with the series 4 in 1961. Engine options after this date also included the 252 bhp Vantage with triple SU carburetors or the 272 bhp GT unit. For the DB5 production was a little faster and over two years, 1021 were built including 123 convertibles.

For this, the triple SUs were standard giving 282 bhp (gross), but a 314 bhp (gross) triple Weber version was offered half-way through.

The DB6 came along in 1965 with two notable changes. The chassis had been lengthened by 4 inches to improve the rear seat space and the body frame was no longer to Touring principles. Bending and welding small tubes was not really suited to the production line, so a similar frame was built up using steel pressings.

The basic body shape was much the same as before but a Kamm tail had been added as a result of Aston Martin's GT racing. The DB5 convertible continued for another year as the Volante before this changed over to the DB6 Volante. Again, engines came in two versions 282 or 325 bhp, figures somewhat inflated to keep up with the American claims – 240 and 270 bhp were the net figures.

Over the 1965-70 period 1745 DB6 were built in two series of which 178 were Volantes.

Ferrari 250GT

After the competition successes of the late Forties and early Fifties, the name of Ferrari had become synonymous with performance. As well as the factory Grand Prix team, Ferrari was building a large variety of sports cars with four, six or twelve cylinder engines for the factory or private owners to race. As GT racing was also becoming popular, Ferrari built sports cars with fully enclosed bodywork and a number of these were used as road cars, but pure road cars were a secondary consideration.

These early chassis did not use the most up-to-date technology, but their engines were superb and they were visually exciting thanks to the skills of the Italian coachbuilders who have created all their shapes. However, the early cars were made in such small quantities that many people never saw them; the 250GT SWB was to become the first Internationally recognized shape in 1959 due to its competition successes.

TECHNICAL DESCRIPTION OF THE FERRARI 250GT SPYDER

YEARS OF PRODUCTION	1960-1963
MODELS	2-Seater Spyder
ENGINE	Front-mounted V-12
BORE X STROKE, CAPACITY	2.8 x 2.1 inches, 180.1 cu.in
VALVEGEAR	Single overhead camshaft per bank
FUEL SYSTEM	3 Weber twin-choke carburetors
POWER	270 bhp at 7000 rpm
TRANSMISSION	4-speed
BODY/CHASSIS	Steel tube with aluminium or steel bodywork
SUSPENSION	Front, wishbones and coils Rear, live axle with leaf springs and radius arms
TIRES/WHEELS	6.00 x 16 on wire wheels
WHEELBASE, TRACK (F), TRACK(R)	94.5 x 53.3 x 53.1 inches
LENGHT, WIDT, HEIGHT	163.5 x 66 x 50 inches
MAX SPEED	145 mph
WHERE BUILT	Modena, Italy

346-347 Short wheelbase 250GT California Spyder had the same specification as the 250GT SWB. Engine, inset, develops 270 bhp.

TECHNICAL DESCRIPTION OF THE FERRARI 250GT SWB

YEARS OF PRODUCTION	1959-1962
MODELS	2-SEATER COUPE
ENGINE	FRONT-MOUNTED V-12
BORE X STROKE, CAPACITY	2.8 X 2.3 INCHES, 108.1 CU.IN
VALVEGEAR	SINGLE OVERHEAD CAMSHAFT PER BANK
FUEL SYSTEM	3 WEBER TWIN-CHOKE CARBURETORS
POWER	270 BHP AT 7000 RPM
TRANSMISSION	4-SPEED
BODY/CHASSIS	STEEL TUBE WITH ALUMINIUM OR STEEL BODYWORK
SUSPENSION	FRONT, WISHBONES AND COILS
	REAR, LIVE AXLE WITH LEAF SPRINGS AND RADIUS ARMS
TIRES/WHEELS	6.00/7.00 X 16 ON WIRE WHEELS
WHEELBASE, TRACK (F), TRACK(R)	94.5 X 53.3 X 53.1 INCHES
LENGHT, WIDT, HEIGHT	163.5 X 66 X 50 INCHES
MAX SPEED	155 MPH
WHERE BUILT	MODENA, ITALY

For early GT racing, the models just had to come from a recognized manufacturer. But by 1957, FIA rules stated that it was necessary to build 100 similar GT cars in 12 months in order to qualify for International GT racing; the chassis and running gear had to be identical on all of them but the body style could be closed or convertible. After the first 100, individual bodies could be used provided they weighed the same and internal measurements matched the regulations. Ferrari qualified by combining all models on the same chassis.

The 250 series was a steady evolution from the original Colombo-designed 166 V-12. This became the 225 by increasing the bore from 2.67 to 2.7 inches, 165.6 cu.in for some 20 cars in 1952, mostly for competition use. One of these coupes used a 250 engine – 2.8 inch bore – to win the 1952 Mille Miglia; it was the basis of the 250MM that followed in 1953, but only 35 or so of these were built.

First of the real road cars bearing the 250 number was the 1953 Europa, the majority of the small run being with Pinin Farina coupe bodywork; although this was still a 12 x 15.2 cu.in, it was based on the longer (Lampredi) design which was used for the larger capacity engines.

The short-block (Colombo) 250 was used for the next 250GT Europa for 1955; they were the first of the 2-seater Ferraris to use coil springs in the front suspension as all had previously used a transverse leaf spring. Most of the 36 were Pinin Farina coupes.

The arrival of the 1956 250GT (Boano), styled by Pinin Farina but built by Boano, saw the first Ferrari to be produced in any quantity; around 130 were built up to 1958. Although the engine produced 220 bhp at 7000 rpm, it was very much a road car. As the GT competition cars became more specialized, road cars were no longer dual-purpose machines.

A 250GT cabriolet came in 1957 as an open version of the Boano-bodied cars. A similar, but faster, open version of the Berlinettas was called a 250GT California Spyder from 1958. The 250GT (Boano) was replaced by the 250GT Coupe in 1958 (350 over 3 years) . This gave way in 1960 to the 250 GT 2+2 also known as the 250GTE. This was Ferrari's first family car built to attack the Aston Martin and Maserati market – despite the extra seats it still used the 102-inch wheelbase. Over 950 of these were built in three series over 1960-63; they may not have the sporting appeal of the Tour de France and SWB cars but they are an affordable classic Ferrari built in exactly the same way.

For competition Ferrari had turned the 250GT Boano into the 250GT Berlinetta, often referred to as the Tour de France model; this had the same 102-inch wheelbase twin-tube chassis with a revised version of the short-block engine. Some 90 of these were built with minor body variations from 1956-59 and mostly with headlights behind plexiglass. However a final seven were built with the headlights exposed at the front of the wings and two of these were run at Le Mans in 1959; one finished 4th behind the earlier version, the GT category winner. With the shape thus proven, Ferrari then launched the 250GT Short Wheelbase (SWB), on the same chassis shortened to a 94-inch wheelbase and fitted with Dunlop disc brakes. The live rear axle was still carried on leaf springs but radius arms improved its location. Competition versions had aluminium bodywork, but over half the 160 produced were steel-bodied road cars. The 250GT SWB certainly lived up to expectation on the track providing many victories in 1960 and 1961.

350-351 Short Wheelbase Berlinetta had many victories in GT races.

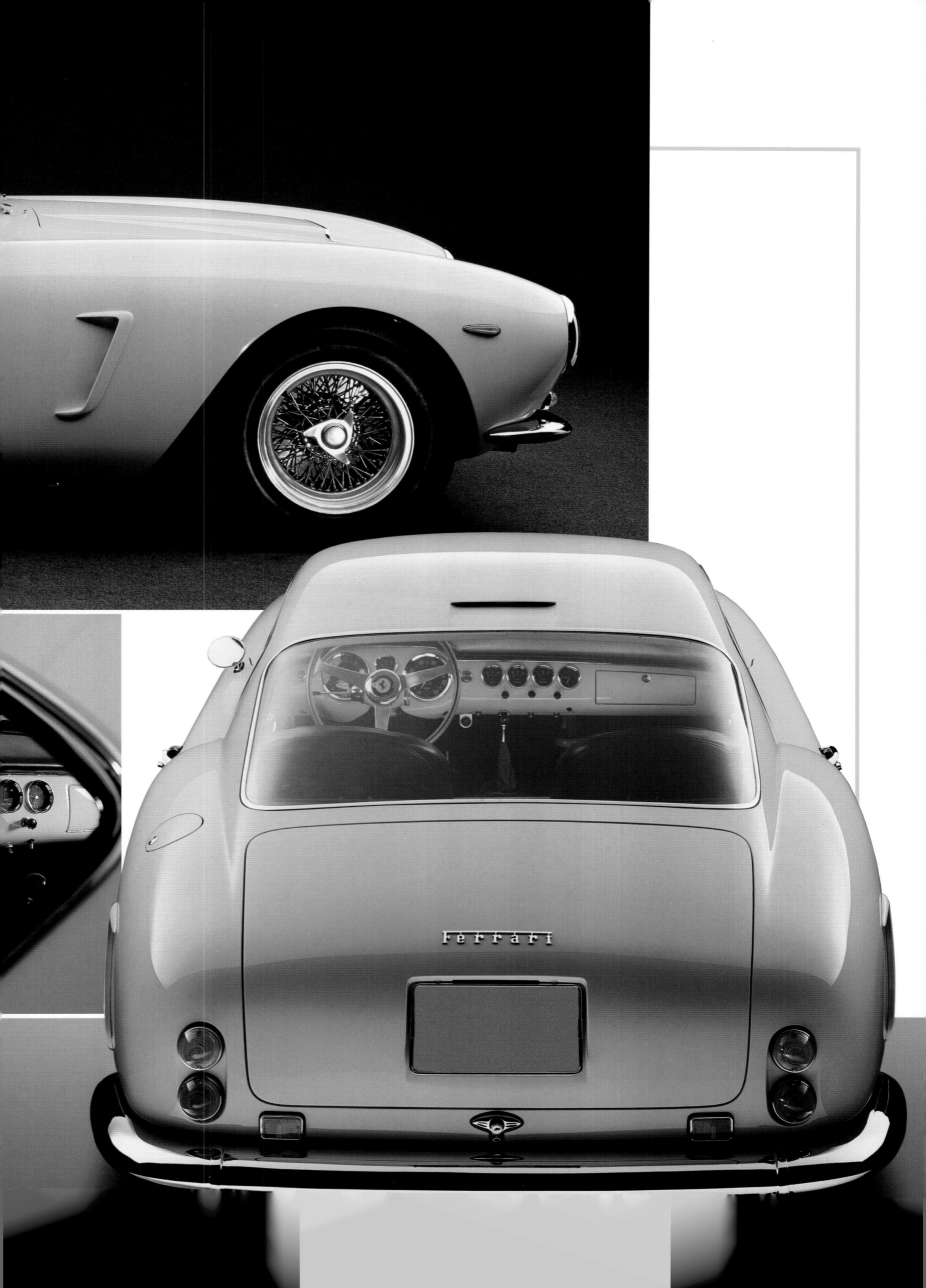

1961 - 1970

THE ARRIVAL OF THE JAPANESE

With the Sixties came European rationalization as lesser manufacturers found it difficult to compete with the majors, although very small makers like Morgan, Alpine and TVR still retained autonomy, thanks to the those majors who were keen to supply components. The decade also saw the rapid expansion of Japanese car production with exports to America as their first major target.

At the start of this decade Japan was still an emergent car producing nation. The Fifties saw co-operation with western companies to import production technology quickly. Nissan produced the Austin A40, followed by the A50; Mitsubishi made Kaiser-Frazer Jeeps; Isuzu made Hillman Minxes and Hino made Renault 4CVs – no classics there.

By 1960 production had reached 308,000 of which over half were sub-22 cu.in economy cars; imports were minimal, mostly through taxation, partly because the roads were still in a rough state. Even by 1970 very few out-of-town roads were metalled, but by then production had grown to 3.2 million and a few classics had emerged; Italian styling companies helped many on the way.

Nissan's first sports car was the 1959 Datsun Fairlady S211. Fairlady sports models and their equivalent Silvia coupes continued through the Sixties; the 1962 97 cu.in Fairlady grew to 122 cu.in. Already Nissan was making an impression on the International rally scene, finishing the decade with victory for 1600SSS sedans in the 1970 East African Safari – a tribute to the lessons learnt on their own country's poor roads. The 240Z, arriving in 1969, would continue in the same vein; with its six-cylinder engine and independent suspension all round it was the natural successor to the big Austin-Healey 3000, particularly on the American market.

Honda had made considerable impact in the motor cycle world during the Fifties and only produced their first car in 1962; this S500 two-seater used such motor cycle technology as an 8000 rpm roller-bearing four-cylinder engine and chain drive to the rear wheels. Just two years later, Honda became

352-353 Marcos produced the 1800 in 1964 with a wooden chassis and a Volvo 109 cu.in engine.

the first Japanese manufacturer to enter Formula One racing. By 1966, the S500 two-seater had grown to become the exportable S800.

Mazda too were late into car production; their first car – a 22 cu.in 2-seater coupe – came in 1960, but they were soon into larger cars and the Bertone-styled 1500 sedan was being exported from 1967. They had also taken out a Wankel licence from NSU and produced the Cosmo or 110S sports coupe from 1967, followed by the R100 coupe both using the nominally 122 cu.in twin-rotor unit. Toyota used Yamaha to build just 351 examples of the striking Toyota 2000GT as a slightly scaled down Jaguar E-type between 1966-8. The Celica came in 1969 as the

first of Toyota's own sporting machines.

In Britain Ford USA created Ford of Europe and took over the reins of Ford UK, General Motors had long controlled Vauxhall (and Opel), and Chrysler invested in the Rootes group (Humber, Hillman, Sunbeam, Singer) from 1964 before the final take-over came in 1973. So half the British motor industry was controlled from America. That left the British Motor Corporation (Austin, Morris, MG, Riley, Wolseley) and Leyland Motor Corporation (Standard, Triumph) still as major players. BMC took over Jaguar in 1966, Leyland took over Rover in 1967 and the two corporations merged in 1968. Many of these names would die, while others increasingly shared components.

While there many notable British launches in the decade, the arrival of the Jaguar E-type in 1961 was the highlight, an instant performance icon at a very reasonable price. In the small car world, the Mini was still supreme, but Rootes tried hard to challenge with the Hillman Imp using a lightweight 53 cu.in Coventry-Climax engine in the back, but it was not a commercial success, although it performed well in racing and rallying; from 1963-76 over 440,000 were built of which the fast-back versions – Singer Chamois coupe and Sunbeam Stiletto – still have some appeal.

Italy saw some change too. Fiat continued to supply most of the Italian market and Alfa Romeo remained under state control. Lancia survived most of the decade but finally became a part of Fiat in 1969. Maserati came to a technical agreement with Citroen from 1968, and in 1969 Fiat took a 50% shareholding in Ferrari. Of more lasting influence was the arrival of two new manufacturers; both de Tomaso and Lamborghini started making road cars in 1965.

In Germany, Mercedes had been the majority shareholder in the Audi group from 1956 but Volkswagen took this over in 1964. NSU joined Audi in 1969. While the Isetta, 600 and 700 had kept BMW going during the latter half of the Fifties, the Sixties saw BMW establish themselves as makers of real cars from 1962.

French production combined the utilitarian with the sophisticated as exemplified by Citroen's range from 2CV to the SM, the latter fruit of the Maserati alliance arriving in 1970; the DS19 became a DS21 in 1965 including a new short-stroke 134 cu.in engine to replace the 122 cu.in which had been designed in 1934. Peugeot brought in the 4-series, which included the nicely styled 122 cu.in 504 Coupe and the Safari-winning 404 sedan. Renault launched their 2CV rival with the fwd R4 in 1961, and the rear-engined R8 gradually replaced the Dauphine, whose sporting Floride derivative then became the Caravelle. Gordini continued his tuning association with the R8 Gordini which became a rallying success. Alpine took over the Renault competition mantle towards the end of the decade using the R8-engined A110 coupe, which was to have considerable rallying success. It was even more successful when it used the 1600 engine from the new Renault 16 which emerged in 1965 as the first real hatchback.

There was no corporate change in America, but it

1961 - 1970

was the decade that saw the publication in 1965 of Ralph Nader's safety crusading book 'Unsafe at any Speed'. Although this had little major effect until the Seventies, sales of the Chevrolet Corvair and the VW Beetle were badly affected – both rear-engined cars with swing axle suspension. Meanwhile the Sixties saw the best of the American muscle cars with ever larger engines dropped into the 'compacts' – slightly down-sized versions of the regular sedans.

Then came the 'pony' car revolution headed by the Ford Mustang in 1964, pony being a small horse like a mustang. Chevrolet continued to produce the Corvette two-seater, which became a genuine high-performance car with the big 427 cu.in V-8 engines, and also introduced the largest-engined front-wheel-drive car in the Oldsmobile Toronado.

Ford took its motor sport aspirations onto the International scene with the GT40, which won Le Mans from 1966-69 in its various guises.

The Sixties was really the last decade in which the average enthusiast could reasonably service and subsequently restore his own car. By the Seventies, emission legislation required so much hardware to be added that even simple engines became complicated to work on. And fuel injection systems were much harder to look after than carburetors.

CLASSIC SEDANS

If you wanted ultimate straight-line performance from a sedan, it had to come from America. Even if European cars could mostly outhandle them and outbrake them on the touring car race tracks, Ford's Falcons, Galaxies and Mustangs could win by brute power and the Chevrolet Camaro was just as effective.

America had two major performance outlets, NASCAR racing around the oval tracks and the drag-strip, official or unofficial. Both were all about flat out maximum power. Arguably Chrysler started the hot-rod ball rolling with the 300 in the late Fifties and Chevrolet responded with the Bel Air. Big engines meant big cars. However the arrival of the 'compacts'

brought new opportunities to get a better power/weight ratio.

When General Motors dropped their biggest V-8 with 390 cu.in and 325 bhp into the 1964 Pontiac Tempest and called it the GTO, the muscle car era had arrived. Oldsmobile replied with the 4-4-2, an F85 compact with the 330 cu.in. engine; a year later it had a 400 cu.in and in 1970 came the 455.

Chrysler further developed the 'hemi-head' V-8 to 427 cu.in for the Dodge Charger and Plymouth Belvedere. Most striking of all was the 1970 Plymouth Superbird with a low-drag nose and a high wing on the tail; nearly 2000 of these NASCAR specials were built. Dodge's equivalent was the Charger with a Superbee style and the same engine choice. Ford put the 429 427 cu.in into Galaxies and Fairlanes. The trend continued through to 1972. Any one of these over-engined compacts is a classic today.

America introduced another new breed in 1964 with the Ford Mustang, the American 2+2. It was a trend perhaps started with the Studebaker Golden Hawk with its supercharged 286 cu.in engine in 1957. Ford's 1955 Thunderbird had provided fast personal transport for two with all mod cons and had the option of a supercharged V-8 in 1957. When the T-bird became a four-seater, it lost its elegance and youth appeal.

Ford still wanted a car that looked sporting, but could provide a range of performance; it also had to be affordable for the young and as appealing as the sports car imports.

Developed from the Falcon, the Mustang came in 1964 in open and hard-top four-seater forms with engines that ranged from a 101 bhp 170 cu.in six to the 260 cu.in V-8 with 164 bhp; by the end of the year the 271 bhp 289 cu.in engine was available. Ford had a head start with two years of pony car sales before the arrival of General Motors' Chevrolet Camaro and Pontiac Firebird, Chrysler's Plymouth Barracuda and the Mustang's cousin, the Mercury Cougar.

While NASCAR racing was still the popular outlet for the muscle cars, a new form of road-racing started in 1966 – Trans-Am, a name soon to be annexed by

Pontiac. This rapidly bred the same horsepower race and the big V-8s were soon available in the pony cars.

Last of the performance Mustangs was the 1971 Boss 351 with 347 cu.in; there had earlier been a very limited run of Boss 429s with the 427 cu.in Ford engine. There were Shelby Mustangs too in GT-350 and GT-500 form.

Also worthy of note was the 1963 Buick Riviera – Buick's belated answer to the 4-seater Thunderbird. Initially with the 402 cu.in V-8, it was powered by a 427 cu.in version by 1965 and was capable of nearly 130 mph – it still only had drum brakes though. GM's new styling boss, Bill Mitchell, had removed all the Fifties fins and produced a very elegant 2-door, 4-seater coupe. The lines were carried through to another pair of notable GM classics – the front-wheel-drive Oldsmobile Toronado (1966) and the Cadillac Eldorado (1967) – both two-door luxury coupes with 427 cu.in engines. One of GM's more lasting contribution to the Sixties was the aluminium 213 cu.in V-8 which was only briefly used by Buick, but has been a great success for Rover, who bought the rights to it in 1963.

In the luxury world, the 1961 Lincoln Continental was one of the best ever for its combination of elegance and equipment. Cadillac's 1965 Fleetwood was equally restrained – one of Mitchell's outstanding designs. That was the year when Rolls-Royce brought out the Silver Shadow with the matching T-series Bentley, both powered by revised versions of the Silver Cloud's 378 cu.in V-8. Although these used unitary construction, there was still scope for coachbuilt versions; Mulliner Park Ward produced the 2-door coupe in 1966 and convertible in 1967 – both called Corniche from 1971. Last of the variants before the 1977 Shadow II was the Camargue with Pininfarina bodywork.

Mercedes' response to the Rolls' claim of "Best Car in the World" was the 1964 600 limousine, complete with all possible comforts and a 384 cu.in V-8, but of more lasting classic appeal was the 300SEL 6.3; the 300 bhp engine from the 600 was dropped into the long wheelbase 300 sedan in 1967 to

produce a German muscle car – over 7000 were built.

One of the features of the Sixties was the growth of sedan car racing and rallying as a means of make promotion – works teams rather than enthusiastic amateurs.

Controlling this on an International level was the work of the FIA (Federation Internationale de l'Automobile); they had originally drawn up rules in 1954 which demanded minimum levels of production and listed allowed changes. In 1960 they introduced a system whereby the specifications and production numbers would be confirmed by FIA visits to the factories before homologation forms were issued. So manufacturers had to produce limited numbers for general sale of cars that they wanted to use for competition – the homologation specials.

Following their total performance philosophy, Ford was particularly active through the Sixties and the competition successes of the homologation specials was reflected on all models in the range. In 1962 the Cortina was just another family sedan, but the arrival of the Cortina-Lotus in January 1963 saw the first of the homologation specials, just two months ahead of the Mini Cooper S and the Cortina GT. The Cortina-Lotus engine was one that had been announced for the Lotus Elan in October 1962. The GT engine was also used in the Capri (1961) and the Corsair (1964). In 1967 Ford changed the Cortina body-style and introduced the 97 cu.in cross-flow engine. Cortina 1600GT and Cortina-Lotus continued but an addition to the range was the 1600E, a 1600GT with Cortina-Lotus running gear and Executive luxury fittings.

In 1968 Ford replaced the Anglia with the Escort which had more competition derivatives – 1300GT, Mexico (1600GT engine), Twin-Cam (Lotus engine) and the RS1600 with the Cosworth BDA engine. This was the first of the classic RS (Rallye Sport) models, all of which rate as classics.

Then came the second generation Capri in 1969 as a European Mustang with a large number of options including engines from 79 cu.in to V-6 183 cu.in; competition versions came from Germany with

354-355 Ferrari 250GT Lusso of 1964.

the RS2600 and Britain with the RS3100, both of which recorded many track successes. The last of the Capris rolled off the lines in 1987.

Other contributions to the British classic sedan ranks came from Rover with the 2000 in 1963 and Jaguar who introduced the XJ6 range in 1968, both of which would continue well into the next decade. An unusual rival in this class came from the house of NSU; the German company had launched an open version of the 36 cu.in Sport Prinz with a nominal 61 cu.in single-rotor Wankel engine as the Wankel Spider in 1963 as a pilot exercise. It was interesting but made little impact.

The 1967 launch of a spacious 4-door, front-wheel-drive, aerodynamic sedan was a considerable contrast, given NSU's history of motor cycles and small rear-engined cars. The 122 cu.in twin-rotor Wankel engine made a very good car doubly interesting.
It was a German Citroen DS19 with a wheel at each corner to give a comfortable ride, excellent ZF power steering and semi-automatic transmission.

Sadly, NSU never truly sorted out the lubrication problems of the rotor-tip seals, even after the 1970 introduction of a Mark II, and only 37,000 had been built by 1977.

A number were subsequently converted in the after-market with 103 cu.in Taunus V-4 engines and transmissions. In fact NSU had been absorbed by the VW group in 1969 and NSU's planned K70 intermediate car was launched as a VW K70 in 1969 with a 97 cu.in version of the smaller NSU – another power pack that can replace the rotary unit.

But the major news in Germany was the resurgence of BMW, starting with the four-door 1500 in 1962; its single overhead camshaft 'four' with hemi-head valve disposition was a design that served the company well and with independent suspension all-round it was a very modern car.

An 1800 followed in 1963 together with a limited run of 1800TISA 130 bhp models for racing; a 2000 came in 1966 with the 2000TI and injection 2000tii in 1969. The two door 1600-2 (later 1602) range began in 1966, leading to the 2002 and 2002ti (1968), 2002tii (1971) and 2002 turbo (1973). Meanwhile the old V-8 cars had continued through to the Sixties and the Bertone-styled 3200CS coupe came out in 1962 for a 3-year run of 600 units; and the 700 lasted until 1965.

The first coupe from the new range came in 1965 with the 2000C and more powerful 2000CS; the style of its rear half owed much to the 3200CS, but the front panel with pronounced wrap-round headlights was not a success. In 1968 BMW launched the new 6-cylinder cars, bringing in the 2800CS coupe with a revised front panel that was far more successful than its predecessor. It was an incredible range of cars to launch and produce in a single decade, and many of them have become classics.

From Sweden, Saab had brought in the 38 bhp 52 cu.in engine for the 96 in 1960, then added the GT850 to the range in 1962 with triple carburetors and 55 bhp; this was called the Saab Sport in the UK and the Monte Carlo in the USA. The 96 proved to be a remarkable rally car in the hands of Erik Carlsson, winning the Monte Carlo Rally twice and the RAC Rally three times. A 96 even finished 12th overall at Le Mans in 1959. Emission pressures saw the 2-stroke finally replaced by the 91.5 cu.in Ford V-4 for 1967, but rally victories continued. The old shape continued to be produced in Finland until 1980, but the new 99 had arrived in 1969, still front-wheel-drive but using the inclined 4-cylinder engine from Triumph; this too would have its share of rally successes including some with turbocharged 250 bhp engines. Competition did much to develop and promote the classic sedans of the Sixties.

356-357 Aston Martin DB4 GT Zagato from 1961.

GRAND TOURERS

While Ford's adoption of the term GT to add to their faster Cortina somewhat devalued the initials, the FIA didn't help either. They instituted a GT championship in 1962 for which there were

minimum dimensions specified and a requirement that at least 100 were built per year; thus, many open sports cars also became GTs.

But the market still knew that real Gran Turismos were built to carry two – or two plus two occasional children – far and fast in entertaining comfort.

Some of the Sixties GTs were designed around such racing requirements.

The Ferrari 250GTO (1962) was the lightweight streamlined version of the 250GT SWB, and the Lusso (luxury) was its roadgoing equivalent. Jaguar built

special lightweight versions of its E-type roadster. Aston Martin raced re-bodied versions of the DB4GT. The Ford GT40 (1965) was a mid-engined coupe built to race against Ferrari's 275LM, and the GT40 Mk.III was the road-going version.

Most of the GTs, though, were built as fast tourers and some were genuine four-seaters. Aston Martin changed the DB4 for the DB5 244 cu.in in 1963 and lengthened the chassis for the DB6 in 1965. While the 4-seater DB6 was still in production, Aston Martin brought in the DBS(1967) to provide more back seat space; the DBS V-8 followed in 1969, the start of a range that would run through to 1989.

In search of cheap high performance, four British manufacturers made cars with American engines under

Italian coachwork; the AC 428 had a Ford 427 cu.in under Frua bodywork and Gordon Keeble had a Chevrolet engine under a Bertone skin – a combination that was also used for the Iso Rivolta and its two-seater Grifo version.

The Jensen CV-8 with Chrysler power had replaced the 541 in 1962 and the new Interceptor used the same engine with Vignale bodywork from 1966; the FF version was the first to offer four-wheel-drive in a road car. And from 1961 Bristol used a special Chrysler 311 cu.in V-8 for the 407; the identically-bodied 406 had seen the final 134 cu.in development of the famous 'six'.

Jensen had also been responsible for the assembly of the Saint's Volvo P1800 for its first three years (1961-63) before production was transferred to Sweden as the 1800S. In 1968, it had the 122 cu.in B20 engine and the 1800E (for Einspritz-injection) came in 1969. The sporting estate 1800ES arrived in 1971. Overall nearly 47,500 1800s were produced, of which 8000 were estates, and the majority of production went to the USA.

The sports estate theme had been pursued by Reliant in England. A 3-wheeler manufacturer, they had entered the sports car market in 1962 with the fiberglass-bodied Sabre using a 103 cu.in Ford engine, then the 158 cu.in Ford 'six'. This somewhat ugly car was transformed by Ogle into the Scimitar GT in 1966. The Ford V-6 was available in 1967 and in 1968 the Scimitar GTE was launched as a four-seater estate car. Perhaps the first sports estates were the 12 'shooting brakes' specially built on the Aston Martin DB5 by coachbuilder Harold Radford from 1964.

It was certainly Aston Martin that put the first opening hatch-back, as opposed to a 2-door estate car, into production with the DB2/4 in 1953. Jaguar adopted the same system for the 1961 213 cu.in XKE coupe and continued it on the 2+2 that came in 1966 by which time the 256 cu.in engine was fitted. The V-12 came in 1971.

A scaled down E-type coupe was built by Triumph as the GT6 from 1966 using the 122 cu.in 'six' from the Vitesse and Triumph 2000 in what was basically the Herald chassis, complete with swing axle rear suspension; from 1968 the Mk.II had revised rear suspension and became a nice little car.

Triumph's other sporting GT was the elegant Stag which arrived in 1970; based on the 2000 chassis, but with a single-cam 183 cu.in V-8, it followed the Mercedes 230SL theme of having a removable winter hard-top with a soft-top concealed under a metal cover.

1961 - 1970

Having invented the Gran Turismo breed, Italy continued to make a significant contribution to the GT ranks, encouraged by their coachbuilders who were always ready to produce niche models on sedan platforms. Ghia's 2300 coupe on the six-cylinder Fiat 1800/2100/2300 platform was a wonderfully elegant creation which had power and sound to match, particularly with the 136 bhp Abarth conversion. It lasted from 1961-68, by which time the Fiat 124 Sport had taken over (1967) with a Pininfarina-styled Spider to back it up. Both used twin-cam 87 cu.in versions of the standard 124's pushrod 67 cu.in 'four'; this was increased to 98 cu.in in 1969 and 107 cu.in in 121 cu.in, while the Spider carried on from 1978 with a 122 cu.in engine. Nearly 180,000 Spiders and 280,000 Sport coupes were produced. At the same time, budget sports Fiats were being produced on the rear-engined 850 platform initially with the 51 cu.in unit (1965-68) and then with 55 cu.in (1968-73); Fiat designed the coupe (343,000 produced) and Bertone the Spider (125,000 produced). This was a golden decade for sporting Fiats as the company also produced the Fiat Dino in both Coupe (Bertone) and Spider (Pininfarina) forms – see separate chapter.

Round the corner in Turin, Lancia had replaced the Aurelia with the 152 cu.in Flaminia back in 1956 – this became a 171 cu.in from 1964. From 1958 Pininfarina produced some elegant bodies for the short wheelbase coupe and also for the 109 cu.in flat-four front-wheel drive Flavia, which arrived in 1961 (122 cu.in from 1969).

The narrow V-4 front-wheel-drive 73 cu.in Fulvia came in 1964; the little coupe versions, using 79 and 97 cu.in engines, were very effective rally cars and were still in production in 1975, some time after Fiat's 1969 take-over. All three of these Sixties models were also available with Zagato bodywork.

At the other end of the Turin-Milan autostrada, Alfa Romeo were doing much the same as Fiat, albeit in smaller volumes. The bigger cars continued with the 122 cu.in 'four' exchanged for a 158 cu.in 'six' in 1962, with bodies still from Touring, Bertone and Zagato, the 2600SZ being one of Zagato's finest designs, ranking alongside their Aston Martin DB4 GT. The Giulietta Sprint, Spiders and SS became Giulias with the 97 cu.in engine in 1963 but a new Sprint GT came in with Bertone bodywork – one of his best shapes which would last through 106 cu.in and 122 cu.in versions until the Mid-seventies. Pininfarina's Duetto Spider would continue through to 1993.

Zagato built the competition Giulia TZ (Tubolare Zagato) of which 112 were the TZ1 followed by 12 of the lower and lighter TZ2 (1963-67); they followed this up with 1500 of the Sprint GT Zagato (1969-75) using 79 and 97cu.in engines.

Down the road from all this volume production activity was Modena, the home of Ferrari and Maserati, to be joined in 1963 by de Tomaso and in 1964 by Lamborghini.

Together they were to produce an incredible range of vehicles – all destined to be classics. Vehicle homologation and crash-testing had yet to arrive, so there were no constraints on adding a constant stream of variations on basic themes. All four were able to produce rolling chassis of varying lengths, with different engines, leaving the coachbuilders to finish the cars.

De Tomaso produced the mid-engined Mangusta (Ford 286 cu.in V-8) in 1967 which became the Pantera in 1969, and the following year saw the first of their front-engined road cars – the Ford V-8 powered 4-door Deauville. Lamborghini started with the front-engined 350GT with Touring bodywork in 1964, followed it with the 400GT in 1965, to which was added a 2+2 version; the mid-engined Miura

358-359 Jaguar E-type 3.8 roadster from 1962.

(Bertone) came in 1967 and the Islero (Marazzi) replaced the 400GT 2+2 in 1968. Tubular frames were replaced by sheet steel platforms when the four-seater Espada (Bertone) was launched at the same 1968 show.

Maserati's collection moved on from the 3500 GTI, the first car to use those initials following the adoption of fuel injection in 1962. A short chassis Spider version of this had been bodied by Vignale in 1959; Vignale then added a roof to produce the Sebring in 1963. The same year, the 4-door Quattroporte, using a tamed version of the racing V-8, emerged from the house of Frua, who also produced the two-seater Mistral (open and closed) on a further shortened 3500GTI frame. Vignale made a luxury four-seater Mexico using the V-8 in 256 and 286 cu.in forms from 1965; then Ghia produced the memorable Ghibli (286 and 298 cu.in
V-8) in 1966, which was followed by Vignale's similar-looking fast-back four-seater Indy in 1968.
It was Maserati's most prolific period, brought to gradual rationalisation by the Citroen merger of 1969. The first product of this was the 1970 Citroen SM which used a new Maserati four-cam V-6 164 cu.in engine in a sporting development of the DS.

Like the rest of the Modena group, Ferrari had begun to take their road cars seriously in this decade and produced a remarkable variety, all with Pininfarina bodywork. From the short-wheelbase 250GT, Ferrari moved on to the lighter and faster competition 250GTO, and then developed the luxury (Lusso) equivalent. Using the last development of this engine was the 275GTB and 275GTS (Berlinetta and Spider), Ferrari's first road car with no competition aspiration; the four-cam 275GTB/4 from 1966 was the most desirable of this range. A new 244 cu.in V-12 single-cam engine was used to power the 330 range from that year with 330GTC and 330GTS (Coupe and Spider). An enlarged engine for 1967 brought in the long-wheelbase 365GT 2+2 to which 365GTC and 365GTS were added in 1968.
A year later came the flag-ship 365GTB/4 Daytona coupe with twin-cam heads, followed by the 2+2 version – the 365GTC/4 in 1971.

Meanwhile Ferrari had introduced the mid-engined Dino 206GT in 1968 using the 122 cu.in engine that Fiat had put into production for them, and followed that with the 146 cu.in version that Fiat had developed as more suitable for road use; the beautiful Dino 246GT arrived in 1969 as the

affordable Ferrari to take on Porsche.

The German company had introduced the Porsche 911 to replace the old Beetle-based 356 in 1963. Using a flat-six air-cooled engine mounted in the familiar place at the rear, the 911 was an instant success which has forever remained a sporting icon; more power and controllability have been added over the years. Porsche also designed the mid-engined 914 as a Volkswagen sports car of which 120,000 were produced from 1970-75; their own version, using the 911 engine, was the 914/6 made in much smaller numbers.

Around the corner in Stuttgart, Mercedes-Benz had finished production of the specialized 190SL and 300SL in 1963 and introduced the 140 cu.in 230SL as a sporting version of the new 220 sedan range. The 2-seater was sold as a roadster, but came with a substantial fully-trimmed hard-top, which gave it GT comfort. The 250SL came in 1966 and the 280SL in 1968 with successive enlargements of the six-cylinder engine. Coupe (250C and 280C) and convertible versions of the sedans were further classics from the make.

A further German GT came from the unlikely source of Opel, which, like General Motors' British subsidiary Vauxhall, had steadfastly ignored the sporting scene. Opel's Rallye-Kadett was the first step in 1966. The 2-seater fastback Opel GT followed in 1967, based on the revised Kadett platform.
It was offered with 67 or 116 cu.in engines; over 100,000 were built, of which 60 per cent went to the USA, by the time production finished in 1973. Preceding the Ford Capri, coupe versions of the Rekord (1966) and Commodore (1967) were attractive scaled-down versions of the Oldsmobile Toronado.

On their home territory, General Motors continued to produce the Chevrolet Corvette in gradually increasing numbers – 11,000 in 1961 rising to 38,800 in 1969. The second series gave way to the Sting Ray in 1963, the first with independent rear suspension, and another body change in 1968 gave Targa-top and convertible versions. Gradually losing its battle with the big three, Studebaker took on the Corvette market with the 2+2 Avanti (1962), an amazing piece of sculpture in fiberglass by Raymond Loewy. The company had foreseen the compact market with the 1959 Lark and used a shortened version of this chassis with their own 286 cu.in V-8, offering a Paxton supercharger option; front disc brakes were the first seen on an American car. Financial problems saw the company close its American plant after some 4500 Avantis had been built; however the design was taken over by two dealers who continued to produce the car with Chevrolet power for many years.

SPORTS AND SPECIALIST GT

While many manufacturers were offering GT cars and then making a convertible version, there were still some making roadsters first and then perhaps adding the fixed head model later. Fastest of the true roadsters was undoubtedly the AC Cobra, which emerged from the marriage of the Fifties AC Ace and the 256 cu.in Ford V-8 in 1961. By the time that AC adopted the strengthened chassis that Ford had designed to take 427 cu.in power, the AC 289 had become a very desirable sporting machine.

As recounted in a previous chapter, the Sunbeam Tiger (1964-67) used the same 256 cu.in engine and the Tiger II followed with the 286 cu.in V-8.

Morgan, too, adopted American V-8 power in 1968 with the Plus 8, but this was the ex-Buick 213 cu.in that Rover had acquired. Over thirty years later, they are still using the same engine in 238 cu.in and 280 cu.in forms in almost the same chassis.

Before the V-8, Morgan were still using the Triumph 'four' which had been around since the days of the Standard Vanguard.

Triumph continued to use this engine for their own TR3 and TR3A (1955-61); a handful of TR3As with Michelotti fixed head bodies were built by Vignale and sold as Triumph Italias. When the TR4 arrived in 1961 with new Michelotti bodywork, including a targa-top version, the engine had been enlarged to 130 cu.in. By then the chassis was getting old and uncomfortable, so the TR4A came in 1965 with independent rear suspension which gave some improvement. The TR5 followed in 1967 using the Triumph 2500 six-cylinder engine with fuel injection within the same bodywork. The body was redesigned by Karmann for the 1969 TR6, which proved to be the most popular of all the real TRs as nearly 92,000 were produced over the next 8 years.

From 1962, Triumph were also represented in the small sports car market with the Spitfire, a neat and popular two-seater based on the Herald sedan. With a twin-carburetor 70 cu.in 63 bhp engine, it was fast enough and agile. Successive developments saw the Mk.II in 1964 and the Mk.III with a 79 cu.in 75 bhp engine in 1967. The Mk.IV came in 1971 with the engine changed to the later 1500TC unit in 1975 to overcome the power loss due to emission controls. Its major rival throughout was the MG Midget which initially used the BMC A-series engines (58, 67 and 77 cu.in) through to 1974 until it, too, adopted the same Triumph 1500 engine. By 1979 both had been axed.

MG had replaced the MGA with the MGB in 1962 using an 110 cu.in version of the BMC B-series engine in a new unitary construction sports car; the MGBGT followed in 1965. The MGC came along in 1967 with a new 183 cu.in engine in a vain attempt to replace the big Healey; over half a million MGBs were produced but only 9000 MGCs in 1967-69. The B would continue in production to 1980.

While the MG was a traditional unsophisticated sports car, Lotus set new standards of performance, ride and roadholding with the Lotus Elan which replaced the Elite in 1962. The Elan, with a fiberglass body on a steel backbone chassis, was small and light, which allowed the 95 cu.in Ford twin-cam to give impressive performance. A fixed head coupe joined the range in 1965 and the Elan +2 came in 1967. In between Lotus found time to produce the Europa (1966), a mid-engined GT 2-seater using the Renault 16 drive-train reversed – the first affordable mid-engined production car.

Among Britain's other small specialist producers, TVR produced a new Mk.III chassis in 1962 with wishbone suspension, and adopted the 109 cu.in MGB engine and transmission when that became available in 1963. From 1964 the body was modified to give a cut-off Manx tail for the 1800S. This was displaced in 1967 by the Vixen series with Ford Cortina GT power; the Vixen S2 of 1968 saw a longer wheelbase which was also used for the Tuscan, the 286 cu.in Ford-engined model which had started life in America as the Griffith. By the end of the decade the Tuscan was also available with the 183 cu.in Ford V-6. Marcos had also joined the ranks of the small GT cars. Early cars used wooden chassis and body of questionable beauty, but the 1964 Marcos 1800, styled by Denis Adams, was a very attractive machine. The chassis still used marine quality plywood but the body was fiberglass and a Volvo 110 cu.in engine was used. A 91.5 cu.in Ford Cortina GT engine was also offered and a tuned 100 cu.in version replaced the Volvo unit in 1966. For 1969 a Ford V-6 version became available and a steel space-frame chassis replaced the wooden one. Marcos also tried to enter the luxury

four-seater GT market with the Mantis, using a Triumph 2500 engine, but this was not a success.

Marcos were also responsible for the Mini-Marcos, probably the best of a number of fiberglass monocoque units designed to take the transverse Mini engine and subframes.

While this installed the engine at its customary end, the Unipower GT had its own space-frame chassis and installed the Mini engine and transmission behind the driver; it was an effective little car – forerunner of the Fiat X1/9 – but only some 70 or so were made from 1966-69.

Two other well-engineered and good-looking British GT cars deserved to last longer than they did. The 2-seater Rochdale Olympic was created by the designer of the Lotus Elite in 1960 and used the same fiberglass monocoque principles with Riley 1.5 components under very aerodynamic lines; a Phase II

version came in 1963 using the Cortina GT engine. The Tornado Talisman was a small 4-seater GT which used the 81 cu.in Ford engine from 1961 – an attractive little car which went very well in British sedan car racing.

Small GT cars were not just a British preserve. In Sweden, Saab had introduced the Sonett II using the two-stroke 850GT fwd engine in a small coupe in 1966; a year and 260 cars later, the V-4 engine replaced the two-stroke as it had done for the 96. From 1967-69 1610 of these were produced.

A minor redesign of the fiberglass body accompanied the Sonett III and 8365 were built before the end in 1974.

In France, the Panhard-powered fiberglass-bodied DBs had become Renault-powered Rene Bonnets in 1962; Le Mans and Missile used 67 cu.in R8 and 51 cu.in Dauphine power trains converted to

front wheel drive, while the Djet mounted the R8 engine amidships. Matra took the company over at the end of 1964 and continued with the Djet, gradually improving its performance. A new mid-engined coupe, the Matra MS530, came in 1967 using the 103 cu.in Ford V-4. Alpine continued their Renault association with the A110 coupe and Simca produced a nice coupe on the rear-engined Simca 1000. Italian tuner Abarth was to take this development further with Abarth-Simca 1300GT and 2000 coupes.

And in South Africa, the GSM Delta was another pretty little GT car using fiberglass bodywork on a tubular frame. This was powered by a tuned Ford Anglia 105E engine and proved very effective on the race circuits. The arrival of glassfibre certainly gave small manufacturers the chance to produce properly styled cars at a reasonable price during the Sixties.

360-361 Triumph TR4 of 1962 was shaped by Michelotti.

Jaguar E-type

When it was launched at Geneva in 1961, the Jaguar E-type set new standards for the ideal sports car, just as the XK120 had done 13 years earlier. The engine was a development of the original, but everything else was new. With independent rear suspension from the saloon Mk.X – announced 5 months later – it had good roadholding with ride comfort unmatched in a sports car. Its aerodynamic body shape, developed from the race-winning D-type, ensured that it had effortless high speed performance. And it was considerably cheaper than the Aston Martin DB4 and Ferrari 250GT which were the only cars of similar performance.

Jaguar had actually started work on the new car in 1957 using a development of the center monocoque D-type chassis with aluminium panels and a tuned 146 cu.in XK engine. A major feature of E1A, though, was the independent rear suspension which initially used twin wishbones before the upper one became a fixed length drive-shaft.

TECHNICAL DESCRIPTION OF THE JAGUAR E 3.8

YEARS OF PRODUCTION	1961-1965
MODELS	ROADSTER AND COUPE 2-SEATER
ENGINE	FRONT-MOUNTED IN-LINE 6
BORE X STROKE, CAPACITY	3.4 x 4.1 INCHES, 230 CU.IN
VALVEGEAR	TWIN OVERHEAD CAMSHAFTS
FUEL SYSTEM	THREE SU CARBURETORS
POWER	265 BHP AT 5500 RPM
TRANSMISSION	4-SPEED
BODY/CHASSIS	STEEL MONOCOQUE
SUSPENSION	FRONT, WISHBONES AND TORSION BARS
	REAR, WISHBONE, DRIVE-SHAFT AND COIL SPRINGS
TIRES/WHEELS	6.40 x 15 ON 5K x 15 WIRE WHEELS
WHEELBASE, TRACK (F), TRACK(R)	96 x 50 x 50 INCHES
LENGTH, WIDTH, HEIGHT	175 x 65 x 48 INCHES
MAX SPEED	143 MPH
WHERE BUILT	COVENTRY, ENGLAND

362-363 *The Jaguar E-type, launched in 1961, gave remarkable performance for its price.*

The second level of prototype was E2A which might have been used for Jaguar's return to sports-car racing in 1958/9. Although Jaguar decided not to race, they allowed American Briggs Cunningham to use the car for Le Mans 1960. For this it was fitted with a dry sump D-type unit reduced to 183 cu.in but with fuel injection and an aluminium cylinder block.

The production E-type followed the basic design of E2A closely. The chassis used the D-type's central monocoque but extended it rearwards to be able to carry a separate rubber-mounted cradle for the differential, inboard disc brakes, coil springs and suspension links including the drive-shaft. Fore and aft wheel location was provided by a pressed steel trailing arm with large rubber bushes. At the front, the D-type system of a separate space-frame bolted to the monocoque was continued, as were the torsion bar springs. The body design showed a front section just like that of E2A, but the doors were bigger and the tail section was lower. Both the roadster and the fixed head coupe were developed in the wind tunnel.

The engine was identical to that used in the 3.8 XK150S with 265 bhp (gross) together with the 4-speed gearbox, a Moss unit still with unsynchronised first gear. Since the car weighed only 2520 lb, the performance was good for its day with 0-60 mph in 7.0 sec. This sounds slow now, but the E-type only had four gears and a speed range of 150 mph, so first gear was high. The first E-types to be tested achieved almost 150 mph, but they used higher gearing from racing tires and had a little more power than standard; standard E-types with normal gearing were limited to 144 mph.

Private entrants raced the early E-types with factory assistance and these were a match for the Ferrari 250GT in short races, but could not keep up with the GTO in 1962. Jaguar eventually produced a car for International GT competition in 1963. The original homologation form allowed aluminium or steel for chassis and bodywork, so the competition one used aluminium. However the later extension included bigger Dunlop wheels, Girling brakes, ZF 5-speed gearbox, dry sump lubrication, D-type cylinder head, aluminium cylinder block, Weber carburetors or fuel injection. Although the engine could produce 340 bhp with all the extras, the competition Jaguar E was never as fast as the Ferrari 250GTO or the

AC Cobra that took over. Jaguar built up just 14 of these 'lightweight' E-types for private entrants.

When the E-type 4.2 arrived in 1965, it had improved brakes and the gearbox gained synchromesh on first gear. Although the maximum power was still quoted as 265 bhp, and the top speed of the two models remained the same, the new one had more torque which improved drivability. Up to that point the E-type had always been a two-seater. In 1966, a 2+2 joined the range with its wheelbase increased by 9 inches and the height by 2 inches. Radial tires were fitted and automatic transmission was also offered for the first time.

Series II cars followed in 1968 with exposed headlights, a larger radiator intake to provide extra air for the optional air conditioning, revised bumpers and optional power assistance. Series III cars came in 1971 with the new 323 cu.in V-12, a change which was necessary to overcome the power lost due to emission controls. The final E-type rolled off the lines in 1973 after 56,000 six-cylinder cars and 15,300 with the V-12.

TECHNICAL DESCRIPTION OF THE JAGUAR LIGHTWEIGHT COUPE

YEARS OF PRODUCTION	1961-1965
MODELS	ROADSTER AND COUPE 2-SEATER
ENGINE	FRONT-MOUNTED IN-LINE 6
BORE X STROKE, CAPACITY	3.4 X 4.1 INCHES, 230 CU.IN
VALVEGEAR	TWIN OVERHEAD CAMSHAFTS
FUEL SYSTEM	FUEL INJECTION
POWER	344 BHP AT 6000 RPM
TRANSMISSION	5-SPEED
BODY/CHASSIS	ALUMINIUM MONOCOQUE
SUSPENSION	FRONT, WISHBONES AND TORSION BARS
	REAR, WISHBONE, DRIVE-SHAFT AND COIL
	SPRINGS
TIRES/WHEELS	7.00L & 7.25L X 15 ON 7 & 7.5 IN ALLOYS
WHEELBASE, TRACK (F), TRACK(R)	96 X 53 X 55.5 INCHES
LENGTH, WIDTH, HEIGHT	175 X 65 X 48 INCHES
MAX SPEED	168 MPH
WHERE BUILT	COVENTRY, ENGLAND

N.B FIGURES FOR LIGHTWEIGHT COUPE ARE THOSE FOR THE 1964 LE MANS CAR

AC Cobra

When the Cobra-Ford took the FIA World GT championship in 1965, its chassis design was more than twelve years old. Variously known as a Shelby Cobra or AC Cobra powered by Ford, it was effectively an AC Ace with a big Ford V-8 engine. The Ace story started with a special

chassis that John Tojeiro had designed to take the engine and gearbox from his MG TA. With twin steel tubes and box-section cross members at each end, it carried independent suspension along the lines of the racing Coopers which had used the transverse leaf spring and lower wishbones from the Fiat 500 (Topolino).

Cliff Davis bought a Cooper-MG complete with a Ferrari 166 Barchetta body style and used an identical body for his Tojeiro-Bristol chassis. A similar car with a body style only slightly changed from that of Touring's masterpiece was finally shown to AC in mid-1953. With a few changes to equip it for the road and AC's own 122 cu.in six-cylinder

engine, it was on the AC stand at the Earls Court Motor Show in October. As announced it developed 85 bhp.

One of many enthusiasts who raced their Aces was Ken Rudd, who first used a Bristol engine and gearbox in 1956. AC offered the 102 bhp 100B from October that year and also fitted disc front brakes. The 120 bhp 100D came in 1957, and the 100D2 raised this to 128 bhp. The new Ace-Bristols became very successful race cars too, particularly in American sports car racing. When Bristol engines ceased to be available, Rudd inserted a pushrod 158 cu.in Ford Zephyr unit which AC were happy to adopt as an option from October 1961; Rudd's tuning company

offered this in various states of tune with 100 to 170 bhp.

Meanwhile former racing driver Carroll Shelby wanted to use an American V-8 engine instead of the Bristol units and approached AC in September 1961. With Ford assistance two examples of the new 221 cu.in V-8, which was very little heavier than a Bristol engine, were sent to AC, who completed the installation relatively easily, using a Borg Warner gearbox and Salisbury differential; a modified chassis had thicker main tubes, stronger differential mounting, new hubs and kingpins and various bracing plates, but retained the leaf springs. The first prototype ran in England in January 1962. By the time it arrived in America, Shelby had

366-367 The 1963 AC Cobra 289 retained the original leaf springs of the AC Ace.

decided to call it the Cobra. By the end of February it had been tested with the new 260 cu.in engine and was announced to the US press in April. They were instantly successful on the race track, developing 260 bhp in standard form or up to 330 bhp in full race trim.

The first 75 cars used the 260 cu.in. engine before the 289 cu.in came in mid-1963 with a little more power but usefully greater torque. All the Cobras this far had been sold in America but two cars had been sent to AC; one of these raced at Le Mans, as an AC Cobra Ford, in 1963 and finished 7th, fourth in the GT category behind three Ferrari 250GTOs. It had been homologated at the beginning of 1963.

For 1964, Shelby produced the more aerodynamic Daytona coupe for a serious onslaught on the GT championship. Only six were to be built. Using the rules to advantage, the mountings for the alternative body style considerably stiffened the chassis. Ferrari managed to win that year but the Cobra-Fords won in 1965.

A further development in late 1964 had been a new coil sprung chassis designed by Ford to take the 427 cu.in Ford V-8 with 425 bhp, but Shelby did not build enough over that winter to achieve homologation and continued racing with the old chassis and engine. The 427 was finally homologated for 1966. As Shelby was already involved in

the Ford GT40 programme, the Cobra 427 was never really developed into a racing car, although 480 bhp semi-competition cars were sold, but it was an extremely fast road car. Later cars had the 'softer' 390 bhp 428 engine. However AC acquired surplus chassis in 1966 and installed the 286 cu.in engine, selling this as the AC 289 as Ford had acquired the rights to the Cobra name. It was actually the best of the V-8 engined ACs, but only 27 were built. In all 655 leaf-sprung Cobras were built and, eventually, around 320 of the 427/428.

368-369 Simple chrome bars protected the vulnerable aluminium bodywork.

TECHNICAL DESCRIPTION OF THE AC COBRA 289	
YEARS OF PRODUCTION	1963-1965
MODELS	SPORTS 2-SEATER
ENGINE	FRONT-MOUNTED V-8
BORE X STROKE, CAPACITY	3.9 X 2.8 INCHES , 288 CU.IN
VALVEGEAR	PUSHROD OVERHEAD VALVES
FUEL SYSTEM	HOLLEY CARBURETOR
POWER	271 BHP AT 5750 RPM
TRANSMISSION	4-SPEED
BODY/CHASSIS	TUBULAR CHASSIS, ALUMINIUM BODY
SUSPENSION	FRONT, TRANSVERSE LEAF AND WISHBONE
	REAR, TRANSVERSE LEAF AND WISHBONE
TIRES/WHEELS	6.40 X 15 ON WIRE WHEELS
WHEELBASE, TRACK (F), TRACK(R)	90 X 51.5 X 52.5 INCHES
LENGTH, WIDTH, HEIGHT	151 X 61 X 49 INCHES
MAX SPEED	150 MPH
WHERE BUILT	ABINGDON-ON-THAMES, ENGLAND

Ferrari 250GTO and Lusso

When the 250GTO was first shown in 1962, it was the most beautiful Ferrari yet produced. The Lusso, which was effectively its roadgoing equivalent, was even better even if it lacked the racing charisma. Time has since seen many good looking products of the Pininfarina-Ferrari liaison, but the last two of the long 250GT line have never lost their appeal.

Throughout the Fifties and Sixties, the Le Mans 24-hour race was Mecca for manufacturers. A good performance in the ultimate endurance race brought invaluable prestige to both make and model. Ferrari took it even more seriously than others. When Le Mans brought in a separate GT category in 1959, Ferrari was there; a 250GT won in 1959 and the 250GT SWB won in 1960 and 1961.

In fact, wherever there was a GT race, the SWB usually won it.

For 1962, the FIA turned the World Sports Car Championship of Makes into a Manufacturers GT championship; even though Le Mans and other events continued to run sports cars and, from 1963, GT prototypes, they were not part of an FIA championship. Ferrari was already prepared for this as they had been working on a purpose-built GT car from late

TECHNICAL DESCRIPTION OF THE FERRARI 250GT LUSSO

YEARS OF PRODUCTION	1963-1964
MODELS	2-Seater Coupe
ENGINE	Front-mounted V-12
BORE X STROKE, CAPACITY	2.8 x 2.3 inches, 180 cu.in
VALVEGEAR	Single overhead camshaft per bank
FUEL SYSTEM	3 Weber twin-choke carburetors
POWER	250 bhp at 7500 rpm
TRANSMISSION	4-speed
BODY/CHASSIS	Steel tube with aluminium panels
SUSPENSION	Front, Wishbones and coils Rear, live axle with leaf springs, radius arms
TIRES/WHEELS	185 x 15 on wire wheels
WHEELBASE, TRACK (F), TRACK(R)	94.5 x 54.9 x 54.6 inches
LENGTH, WIDTH, HEIGHT	173.5 x 68.9 x 51 inches
MAX SPEED	150 mph
WHERE BUILT	Modena, Italy

370-371 *The 1963/4 Lusso was a graceful marriage between the front of the 250GT Berlinetta and the rear of the 250GTO to make a luxury 2+2.*

1960. However, the rules required 100 identical models to have been built in 12 months; the FIA would issue a certificate of homologation. Once the model was homologated, special bodies could be used provided the car still weighed within 5 per cent of the weight of the standard model; options could be listed on a separate sheet.

Ferrari took this to the limits. The 1962 car had a new body, 6.5 inches longer and 3 inches lower, which had been developed in a wind tunnel. Two different carburetor set-ups were allowed within the original 100 cars, so six Weber carburetors were used instead of three. Options included a 5-speed gearbox, a transverse Watt linkage for the rear axle and a dry sump for the engine, which enabled a lower bonnet line. The basic chassis remained the same. The standard 250GT had been homologated in June 1960, just before Le Mans that year. Ferrari had to get the new options homologated, so the application form showed the standard 250GT SWB with the option list. When confirmation came back

from the FIA, "250GT Omologato" was written on the papers and the 1962-4 competition cars have been known as 250GTO ever since. Just 36 were built with the 183 cu.in engine. Jaguar went through exactly the same process for the E-type and its evolution, which was always known as the "Lightweight E-type". Aston Martin never quite made 100 of the DB4GT before producing the Zagato and Project 214 variants.

So the 250GTO was aerodynamically better than its predecessor with less lift and less drag. Its roadholding was also better due to the lower center of gravity and the new rear axle linkage which freed the leaf spring from its task of lateral location. That the car was also 250 lb lighter came within the allowed tolerance. With the engine output increased to 300 bhp it was considerably faster and Ferrari won the GT championship in 1962 and 1963. They won in 1964 too with a different body style which allowed wider wheels; it was modelled on the 250LM, a mid-engined GT car which Ferrari had hoped to homologate, but the FIA

would not accept that it was just another 250GT evolution; as Ferrari never made 100 LMs it ran as a prototype with a 201 cu.in engine – usually called a 275LM – before being accepted into the 50-off Sports category in 1966 along with the Ford GT40. By the end of 1964, though, Ferrari's 183 cu.in engine was being outpaced by bigger American V-8s, so development ceased on the 250GTO.

Meanwhile Ferrari continued to build 2+2 road cars based on the earlier 250GT. The two-seater GT market was covered by the steel-bodied 250GT SWB until the end of 1962. A proper road car was then evolved as the 250 GT Berlinetta Lusso, still on the 2.4-metre wheelbase, but with the engine moved forward to gain interior space. By this time all Ferrari road cars were designed by Pininfarina and the Lusso was an appealing mixture of the front of a 250GT SWB married to the rear of a GTO. It was only in production for 18 months but 350 were built. It was the final swan song of the 250GT as the next generation 275 arrived in 1964.

372-373 The GTO was built solely for competition and had no concessions to comfort

Chevrolet Corvette 1963 - 1967

The Sting Ray era produced what was probably the most classic of all the Corvettes with its combination of exciting elegant lines, effective suspension and raw high performance. The range included a coupe for the first time while the roadster had an optional hard top; and there was the usual selection of RPO extras to enable anyone to tailor his own specification.

While the first two generations of America's sports car saw a progression from the two-seater personal tourer to a very fast sporting machine, these early Corvettes lacked the technical sophistication of their European equivalents when it came to the chassis. Although Ferrari was still using a live rear axle with leaf springs, ride comfort was less important in a Ferrari than roadholding. Aston Martin had much

better live axle location. When the Jaguar E-type emerged in 1961 with a simple and effective independent rear suspension, the sporting world had to accept that a comfortable ride need not compromise roadholding.

Chevrolet had evolved a similar principle on experimental cars, so the third generation Corvette, like the Jaguar, used the drive-shaft as an upper link; a lower link controlled the camber angle, and wheel torques were absorbed in a forward extension of the hub carrier. Front suspension and steering continued with adapted Chevrolet parts; the one area where the new Corvette was behind the times was in the retention of drum brakes, however

disc brakes became standard in 1965. These new suspension parts required a new chassis which was a stiffer ladder frame.

Engine choices continued where the old model had stopped with the 327 cu.in. V-8 developing 250-360 bhp. In response to the demands of Corvette racers trying to keep up with the 427 cu.in Cobra, Duntov managed to insert the big-block V-8 into the engine compartment as a 1965 option; a bonnet-top bulge was needed to clear the taller engine, and side exhaust systems became an option. The first big-block unit was the 396 cu.in with a massive 425 bhp; a year later this was increased to 427 cu.in with 390-435 bhp variations. By 1967, the racers could order the L88 engine as an RPO

to make the ultimate Corvette; with aluminium heads, racing camshaft and strengthened bottom end the 427 cu.in unit developed around 560 bhp.

The body continued to be made in GRP and had been styled by Bill Mitchell around an earlier Sting Ray race car. The 1963 coupes had a divided rear window but the division was removed the following year. From almost every angle the production Sting Ray was a superb-looking car, open or closed but the front was too high; with concealed headlights there was no feature to break up the sharp prow. But, beautiful or not, the new Corvette sold 50% more in 1963 than had its predecessor the year before and would keep up a steady growth until it was replaced by an even more successful model in 1968.

Despite a steady rise in sales, Chevrolet brought out a new look Corvette for 1968. Modelled on Mitchell's 1965 Mako Shark II, the new body had a much lower nose still with retractable headlights and Coke-bottle effect in its sills and waistline.

With a vertical rear window set between sail panels, it anticipated Jaguar's similar treatment for the XJS. The roof had a pair of removable panels but a convertible was also available until 1975. From 1978, the rear window returned to conventional fast-back shape. Chrome bumpers had disappeared in favor of soft front and rear panels for 1973.

Underneath the chassis was stiffened for the new car and wider wheel rims were used. Initially engine options continued as before with 327 and 427 cu.in, including the L88 and from 1969 a new racing ZL-1 with an aluminium cylinder block; however the 327 was increased to 350 cu.in for 1969, a stronger but softer engine with hydraulic valve lifters. A similar treatment was applied to the big-block engine option with an increase to 454 cu.in for 1970.

The 4th generation Corvette – Stingray from 1969-1978 – kept its performance image until the 1973 models when emission equipment took its toll on horsepower figures.

This didn't slow demand, though, as production continued to grow and 1979 saw almost 54,000 cars produced. The model ran through to 1983 but it was the pre-1973 cars that provided the classics.

YEARS OF PRODUCTION	1963-1967
MODELS	COUPE AND CONVERTIBLE
ENGINE	FRONT-MOUNTED V-8
BORE X STROKE, CAPACITY	3.9 x 3.2 INCHES, 326 CU.IN
VALVEGEAR	PUSHROD OVERHEAD VALVES
FUEL SYSTEM	CARTER 4-BARREL CARBURETOR
POWER	250 BHP AT 5500 RPM
TRANSMISSION	3-SPEED
BODY/CHASSIS	STEEL CHASSIS, FIBERGLASS BODYWORK
SUSPENSION	FRONT, WISHBONES AND COIL SPRINGS
	REAR, WISHBONES, FIXED LENGTH DRIVE-SHAFTS AND TRANSVERSE LEAF SPRING
TIRES/WHEELS	6.70 x 15 ON STEEL WHEELS
WHEELBASE, TRACK (F), TRACK(R)	98 x 56.3 x 57 INCHES
LENGTH, WIDTH, HEIGHT	175 x 69.6 x 50 INCHES
MAX SPEED	130 MPH
WHERE BUILT	MISSOURI, USA

*376-377 With concealed headlights,
the Sting Ray's sharp prow is set too high.*

MGB

The 7-year production run of over 100,000 MGAs came to an end in 1962. When the MGB took over it was not expected to last another 18 years and over half a million models. While this extended run was largely due to the mergers that took BMC into British Leyland, a contributory factor was the expected American ban on open cars; British Leyland assumed the MGB would come to a natural end when it could no longer be imported into America, and had designed the TR7 coupe as the replacement for the MGB and the TR6. When the open cars were reprieved, the MGB just continued to sell.

However higher production numbers were always expected for the MGB, so the design used unitary construction. Mechanically the car was a developed MGA with the same 4-speed gearbox, independent front suspension and a live rear axle, but the B-series engine was enlarged to 109 cu.in and the wheels were smaller; with 94 bhp, this

was enough to make the MGB a genuine 105 mph car. The major improvements were to comfort with wind-up windows, a better ride, more interior and luggage space. As before, though, a lot of the expected fittings were optional extras – heater, headlamp flasher, anti-roll bar, cigar lighter, wing mirror, folding (rather than removable) roof among them – so don't be surprised if such things are missing if you buy an early one. Original road testers thought the car was a great improvement over the MGA even if the character had become more touring than sporting.

A year later overdrive was offered as an extra. While a factory hard-top was soon available, the B followed the A with a coupe version in 1965; an attractive design created with some help from Pininfarina, the MGB GT had a useful hatchback and rear seat space for 7-year-olds. By this time the B-series engine had been given five main bearings, using the engine that had been revised for the Austin 1800 saloon; the power

output was unchanged.

As the Austin Healey 3000 was about to go out of production because it would no longer pass American safety standards, MG added the MGC in 1967, using an engine from the big Austin 183 cu.in saloon.

The extra length of this unit forced a change to torsion bar front suspension, but the only outward change from the MGB were bulges in the bonnet top to allow for a bigger radiator and the front carburetor. Although, on paper, the engine specification looked almost the same as that for the big Healey – 145 bhp at 5500 rpm and 170 lb.ft at 3500 rpm against 150 bhp at 5250 rpm and 173 lb.ft at 3000 rpm – it was a very poor design; overlarge ports gave it very little low speed torque and it was also very heavy, adding 330 lb to the front end of an MGB. The result was considerable understeer, heavy steering and an unresponsive engine. It lasted just two years with 4542 roadsters and 4457 GTs, the

378-379 The interior of this 1963 roadster has been personalised with a sports steering wheel and a wooden gear lever knob.

380-381 The MGB had much more luggage space than the MGA. Non standard air filters and an alloy rocker cover are more personal touches.

latter being the nicer car.

For 1970, in an attempt to modernize the MGB, the chrome grille gave way to a matte black open version, Rostyle wheels were fitted, the seats were changed and a heater had at last become standard. The biggest change came in 1973 when the MGB GT was available with the 213 cu.in Rover V-8 in 137 bhp Range Rover form; using the stronger MGC gearbox but retaining the MGB front suspension, this was a much better car than the MGC with a 125 mph maximum; it should have been a great success.

However British Leyland stopped it going to America where it might have competed against the Triumph Stag and Jaguars, Europe was beset by petrol price rises and Rover needed their V-8 engines for the SD1, so the car ceased production in 1976 after only 2591 had been built.

Meanwhile the MGB was still being sold in America, for which the output had been stifled to 85 bhp. Legislation also necessitated a change to energy absorbing front and rear bumpers for 1975; while this was cleverly done, classic enthusiasts prefer the chrome bumper MGB.

It was because the MGB had already become a classic that the MG RV8 emerged in October 1992, an updated MGB roadster powered by the 237 cu.in 190 bhp Rover V-8. British Motor Heritage had acquired the tooling for MGB roadster bodyshells for use in restoration; by 1992 over 3000 old MGBs had benefitted. The project was taken further by Rover Special Projects who skilfully modernized the style with flared wings, bigger wheels, soft end panels and a luxury interior; although it was still the old MGB underneath, the RV8 was an appealing car that relaunched MG into the sporting market. By 1995, the planned 2000 had been sold.

TECHNICAL DESCRIPTION OF THE MGB

YEARS OF PRODUCTION	1962-1980
MODELS	SPORTS 2-SEATER
ENGINE	FRONT-MOUNTED IN-LINE 4
BORE X STROKE, CAPACITY	3.1 x 3.5 , 109 CU.IN
VALVEGEAR	PUSHROD OVERHEAD VALVES
FUEL SYSTEM	TWIN SU CARBURETORS
POWER	95 BHP AT 5500 RPM
TRANSMISSION	4-SPEED
BODY/CHASSIS	STEEL MONOCOQUE
SUSPENSION	FRONT, WISHBONES AND COILS
	REAR, LIVE AXLE WITH LEAF SPRINGS
TIRES/WHEELS	5.60 x 14 ON WIRE WHEELS
WHEELBASE, TRACK (F), TRACK(R)	91 x 49 x 49 INCHES
LENGTH, WIDTH, HEIGHT	154 x 60 x 49.5 INCHES
MAX SPEED	106 MPH
WHERE BUILT	ABINGDON-ON-THAMES, ENGLAND

The Giulietta Sprint had been a landmark design as much for its looks as for its place in history, the first in the new line of volume production Alfa Romeos. The same shape had become a Giulia Sprint in 1962 with disc front brakes and the 95 cu.in engine.

A year later came one of Bertone's finest shapes, the Giulia Sprint GT, based on a Giulia chassis shortened by 5 inches to almost the same wheelbase as the Sprint's Giulietta-based chassis. However the overall length was 4.7 inches longer, which allowed the Sprint GT to be a full four-seater with reasonable luggage space. The lines were very similar to those that Bertone had used for the 2000 Sprint in 1960 – very clean, modern and lasting. It was the first car to be built at Alfa Romeo's new Arese factory. In its initial form the engine developed 106 bhp using two twin-choke Weber carburetors. This was enough to give it a maximum speed around 110 mph.

As Alfa Romeo wanted to continue taking part in GT racing, Zagato were asked to produce a Giulia-based competition car. The resulting beautiful Giulia TZ (Tubolare Zagato) used the Giulia engine and gearbox, but the chassis was a space frame which carried independent rear suspension. From 1963, some 120 were built, of which the last 10 were in fiberglass, before a handful of even lower TZ2s were produced

for competition in 1965. Zagato continued their Alfa Romeo involvement by using the Giulia Spider (Duetto) chassis as a base for retro versions of the famed Alfa Romeo 1750 Zagato of 1929-1933; 92 of these neo-classics were built from 1965.

Meanwhile Bertone continued to produce the Giulia Sprint until 1964 when it was also offered with the 79 cu.in engine. The first Sprint GT variant came in March 1965 at the Geneva Show, the Giulia GTC (Cabriolet), which managed to retain all the appeal of the Sprint GT with a well-planned folding roof. Later that year came the Giulia GTA, a GT lightened (Allegerita) for competition with aluminium body panels and a 115 bhp engine. The GTA won the European Touring Car Challenge in 1966 and 1967, and produced further modifications for the GTAm which used an oil pressure driven supercharger.

A Giulia GTV with a little more power came in April 1966 and, as there were tax advantages for smaller engines, a 1300 GT Junior was added to the range in September that year. When Alfa Romeo brought in the 1750 saloon, a name evoking the Thirties sports cars, with a 108 cu.in engine, this was used to create the 1750GTV in 1968. The only noticeable body change was the adoption of four headlights. With 122 bhp, its maximum speed went up to 112 mph. The final version came in

Alfa Romeo Sprint GT

1971 with the 122 cu.in engine (2000GTV) giving 132 bhp and 115 mph. The car still looked as modern as it had in 1963 but its suspension was beginning to show its age. This was eventually rectified with the next generation Alfetta GT (1974) with a new Bertone body style – a new 2000GTV would follow for 1976 using the Alfetta's de Dion rear axle.

Meanwhile Zagato had finished building the TZ series and the limited run of the 1750 GS, so turned their attention to a roadgoing coupe to follow in the steps of the Giulietta SZ. They built road-going equivalents to the TZ with a similar style by Ercole Spada from 1969 – his last for the Milanese coachbuilder. Using the shorter Duetto sports car platform, 1108 Junior Z 1300s were built before the 97 cu.in engine was inserted in 1972 – production ceased in 1975 after 402 had been built. Many were subsequently modified using the bigger engines from the GTVs. Over the 1965-1972 period Zagato also produced some 2900 Fulvia Sports for Lancia.

While the Giulietta launched Alfa Romeo into volume production, the Giulia in all its forms gave the company its well-deserved International reputation. The original Duetto was still being produced by Pininfarina until 1993 as the 2000 Spider Veloce.

382-383 Alfa Romeo Sprint GT was one of Bertone's great designs. With thr famous twin-cam engine, a 5-speed gearbox and a well-located live rear axle, it went as well as it looked.

Lamborghini 350GT

The story of Ferruccio Lamborghini's arrival in the automobile world is well known. Dissatisfied with Ferrari's service to road car owners, and denied the chance to discuss this with Enzo, he resolved to usurp Ferrari as king of the road. With successful businesses in tractors and industrial climate control, he had the necessary backing. Next he needed people. In March 1962, he brought in from Maserati Giampaolo Dallara, to be chief engineer, together with Paulo Stanzani – they would evolve the chassis and running gear.

For the new engine Lamborghini contracted Giotto Bizzarini (former project director for the Ferrari GTO); Bizzarini had his own business and was already working on the forthcoming Iso Rivolta. The engine had to be a V-12 with dry sump lubrication and four cams – Ferrari engines only had two – and had be more powerful than the regular Ferrari 250 series. It is said that Bizzarini had previously designed a 91.5 cu.in V-12 and scaled this into the 213 cu.in; it was certainly a very quick process as the first engine was running in May 1963 producing over 100 bhp per 61 cu.in.

Bizzarini had hoped the programme would also include racing, so the engine was strong enough for even more power, but Lamborghini was never interested in taking on Ferrari at that level. With Bizzarini's task completed, the refinement of the engine became Dallara's responsibility. With ZF gearbox and Salisbury final drive the rolling

tubular chassis was sent to Carrozzeria Sargiotto in Turin to build a two-seater coupe to the design of Franco Scaglione, former head of Bertone styling. This 350GTV was shown at the Turin Show in November 1963. Partly because this was all done in a very short space of time, the result was not pretty; the lines lacked harmony and the show car was poorly made.

With little enthusiasm amongst press and public, Lamborghini cancelled production plans and took the project to Superleggera Touring, who could also build the bodies. The Touring design was very similar but they improved the relationship between side and rear windows, balanced the front and rear with more rounded lines, fitted oval headlights instead of previously concealed ones and had the front wheels moved forward by 3.9 inches. Since the new debut was at Geneva in March 1964, there wasn't time to make major alterations; accordingly, it wasn't one of Touring's more memorable works but it was better than the original 350GTV. Dallara meanwhile had removed the dry sump which raised the engine, requiring side-draft carburetors rather than the original vertical ones. The car was well received by all.

During the next year, a 244 cu.in version became available as the 400GT with 320 bhp; there were 108 350GTs and 23 400GTs, of which 20 had steel body panels. Lamborghini extended the range in 1966 with the 2+2, using the same wheelbase, but converting the padded luggage

bench to two extra seats. This was skilfully achieved by lifting the body (now steel) by 2.6 inches, adjusting the front wheel arch and deepening the sills to lower the floorpan. Reversing the mounting of the rear wishbones gave extra internal width. The 350/400GT had various front intake treatments but the 2+2 adopted the horizontal bars, quarter-bumpers with no over-riders, and the four round headlights that had been required for the American market. Engine power remained the same but Lamborghini now used their own gearboxes and final drives. Over 1966-68, 224 of these were built.

Meanwhile Touring had financial problems due to steel-worker problems in 1962, followed by cancellation of two Rootes Group projects. Receivership in 1964 was followed by closure in early 1967, so the later 400GT 2+2 were built by ex-Touring employees who had moved to previous sub-contractor Mario Marazzi.

To replace the 400GT 2+2, Lamborghini stayed with Marazzi who used a two-door version of a full four-door proposal drawn up by Touring in 1966. The Islero emerged in 1968, an understated design with the concealed headlights of the 350GTV; it was a 2+2 on the previous 400GT 2+2 chassis but slightly shorter. Viewed alongside the full four-seater Espada, a striking Bertone design based on the Marzal show car, it was not exciting in 1968, but, thirty years on, the Islero looks the nicer car. The Islero S came in for 1969 with an improved interior and a more powerful engine with 350 bhp. There were 225 Isleros of which just 100 had the S engine. The Islero did not last long and was replaced in 1970 by the Bertone-designed Jarama which continued until 1976, the last of the front-engined Lamborghinis.

TECHNICAL DESCRIPTION OF THE LAMBORGHINI 350GT

YEARS OF PRODUCTION	1964-1966
MODELS	2-SEATER COUPE
ENGINE	FRONT-MOUNTED V-12
BORE X STROKE, CAPACITY	3 x 2.4 INCHES, 211 CU.IN
VALVEGEAR	TWIN OVERHEAD CAMSHAFT PER BANK
FUEL SYSTEM	6 WEBER TWIN-CHOKE CARBURETORS
POWER	270 BHP AT 6500 RPM
TRANSMISSION	5-SPEED
BODY/CHASSIS	STEEL TUBE WITH ALUMINIUM BODY
SUSPENSION	FRONT, WISHBONES AND COILS
	REAR, WISHBONES AND COILS
TIRES/WHEELS	210 x 15 ON WIRE WHEELS
WHEELBASE, TRACK (F), TRACK(R)	100.4 x 54.3 x 54.3 INCHES
LENGTH, WIDTH, HEIGHT	182 x 68 x 48 INCHES
MAX SPEED	145 MPH
WHERE BUILT	BOLOGNA, ITALY

Lotus Elan

When Colin Chapman's new Lotus Elan appeared at the London Motor Show in October 1962 it seemed just a cleverly designed roadster replacement for the Elite coupe. Like the Elite it was also available in kit form which avoided the British purchase tax at the time. It wasn't until it was tested by the motoring press that it became clear that the Elan was a breath of fresh air in sports car design.

It had independent suspension all round, not just to demonstrate race technology, but to provide a hitherto unmatched combination of sports car ride and roadholding; it was softly comfortable for the bumps but well damped to prevent sudden body movement; and it clung to the road with its suspension designed to keep the tires at optimum angles. It was small and light, so its 105 bhp engine gave good acceleration; although the final drive gearing was too low for effortless motorway cruising, the car was designed to be fun to drive – straight roads are not fun.

As a company, Lotus began producing cars for sale in 1952 but, for the first five years, they were competition cars – trials or racing – which could be used on the road. The first genuine road car was first shown in October 1957; the Lotus Elite (type 14) could also be raced. It used three large fiberglass moldings bonded together to create a monocoque with steel inserts and tubes for mounting the mechanical components. It was powered by a special version of the Coventry Climax FW series which the competition cars had been using; the 74 cu.in FWE developed 75 – 105 bhp in road to race states of tune. Beautifully shaped, it was a remarkable car and proved its effectiveness in the Le Mans 24-hour race by winning its class from 1959-1964, including 8th overall at 99.5 mph in 1962. Exciting though it was, the Elite was not the strongest nor the most reliable of cars; from 1958-1963, they built 1050, but the next car had to be stronger.

While fiberglass was an effective material for the body, it was not appropriate for a load-bearing road-car chassis. So the Elan retained a fiberglass body but used a separate back-bone chassis of deep section to maintain torsional strength. Suspension used a pair of wishbones at the front, while the rear used a MacPherson strut and lower wishbone; rubber couplings in the drive-shaft absorbed plunge and transmission shocks.

By this time Lotus had some recognition within Ford as the Lotus 18, 20, 22 had all been successful in Formula Junior with Ford 105E engines. Chapman wanted a twin-cam engine for

---

TECHNICAL DESCRIPTION OF THE LOTUS ELAN

YEARS OF PRODUCTION	1962-1966
MODELS	2-SEATER SPORTS
ENGINE	FRONT-MOUNTED IN-LINE 4
BORE X STROKE, CAPACITY	3.2 x 2.8 INCHES , 95 CU.IN
VALVEGEAR	TWIN OVERHEAD CAMSHAFTS
FUEL SYSTEM	TWIN WEBER 40DCOE CARBURETORS
POWER	105 BHP AT 5500 RPM
TRANSMISSION	4-SPEED
BODY/CHASSIS	STEEL BACKBONE, FIBERGLASS BODY
SUSPENSION	FRONT, WISHBONES AND COIL SPRING
	REAR, COIL SPRING STRUT AND WISHBONE
TIRES/WHEELS	4.50 x 13 ON 4.5 IN RIMS
WHEELBASE, TRACK (F), TRACK(R)	84 x 47 x 48 INCHES
LENGTH, WIDTH, HEIGHT	145 x 56 x 45.5 INCHES
MAX SPEED	110 MPH
WHERE BUILT	CHESHUNT AND HETHEL, ENGLAND

386-387 Original Lotus Elan had few luxuries but was a very efficient sports car. Headlights were lifted by vacuum control.

the Elan and Harry Munday designed a suitable head for the the 81 cu.in 109E 3-bearing block. Ford heard of the project and offered the 5-bearing 91 cu.in 116E block which was to be announced in September 1962. Lotus used this twin-cam 1500 in the sports-racing Lotus 23 and surprised the bigger cars in the rain at Nurburgring 1000Km in May 1962. The Elan was announced and the first twenty so cars were sold with the 91 cu;in engine giving 100 bhp. All these were converted to the definitive 95 cu.in for which the block was bored out to the maximum replacement piston size.

An Elan S2 came in November 1964 with such refinements as electric windows, wooden fascia and bigger brakes. The S3 arrived a year later in fixed head coupe form (Lotus 36), so the open S2 continued until June

1966. The type 45 Elan (drophead S3 and S4) came in March 1968 continuing through to 1973 by which time some 10,000 had been built. Special Equipment 115 bhp engines were offered from January 1966 and 126 bhp Sprint versions became available at the end of 1970.

Stretching the Elan wheelbase by 12 inches, widening the track by 7 inches and adding nearly two foot to the overall length produced the Lotus 50 Elan +2 four-seater in 1967 using the Special Equipment engine. A +2S with more comfort and no kit-purchase option came in 1968, being replaced by the +2S 130 in 1971 using the Sprint engine. The final +2S 130/5 denoted the 5-speed option offered from October 1972 until the end of the line in 1974 after 5168 of the +2 had been produced.

388-389 With the longer and wider Elan +2, the family man could enjoy Lotus performance and roadholding.

TECHNICAL DESCRIPTION OF THE LOTUS ELAN +2	
YEARS OF PRODUCTION	1967-1974
MODELS	4-SEATER COUPE
ENGINE	FRONT-MOUNTED IN-LINE 4
BORE X STROKE, CAPACITY	3.2 X 2.8 INCHES, 95 CU.IN
VALVEGEAR	TWIN OVERHEAD CAMSHAFTS
FUEL SYSTEM	TWIN WEBER 40DCOE CARBURETORS
POWER	118 BHP AT 6000 RPM
TRANSMISSION	4-SPEED
BODY/CHASSIS	STEEL BACKBONE, FIBERGLASS BODY
SUSPENSION	FRONT, WISHBONES AND COIL SPRING
	REAR, COIL SPRING STRUT AND WISHBONE
TIRES/WHEELS	165 X 13 ON 5.5 IN RIMS
WHEELBASE, TRACK (F), TRACK(R)	96 X 54 X 55 INCHES
LENGTH, WIDTH, HEIGHT	69 X 66 X 47 INCHES
MAX SPEED	115 MPH
WHERE BUILT	CHESHUNT AND HETHEL, ENGLAND

Iso Grifo GL400

When it first appeared at the Turin Show in 1963, the Iso Grifo A3L (Lusso) was a strikingly beautiful car, which had been styled by Giugiaro during his time with Bertone. With Chevrolet's 327 cu.in V-8 producing 365 bhp, it was a high performance machine with a top speed of 161 mph, considerably faster than Aston and Jaguar could manage with their highly tuned six-cylinder engines.

The Iso Grifo was the 2-seater coupe based on a shortened chassis from the Iso Rivolta which had been launched at Geneva in March 1962. Iso had made their name from Isetta scooters and bubble cars in the Fifties when the company was owned by Count Renzo Rivolta. His son, Piero, wanted to return to car manufacture for the Sixties and approached Giotto Bizzarrini to design a chassis for a fast but comfortable 4-seater sports saloon; Bizzarrini had been project director for the Ferrari 250GTO but had set up his own Societa Autostar in 1962.

Facel Vega had started the trend of using American power in European bodies in 1954. Gordon Keeble, Bristol, AC and Jensen would

follow in the early Sixties. In fact the first was the Gordon GT, which might be called the father of the Iso Rivolta. John Gordon had been the Managing Director of Peerless, making four-seater coupes with space-frame chassis, fiberglass bodywork and Triumph engines from 1957-1960. This had been designed by Bernie Rodger, who went on to refine the car further as the Warwick GT (1960-1962) while Gordon went in a different direction – same concept but faster and more luxurious. He had a new chassis designed by Jim Keeble, once more a space frame, but stronger to take a Chevrolet V-8. In 1959 they took this to Bertone, for whom Giugiaro produced his first work; the Gordon GT was shown with steel bodywork at Geneva in March 1960.

Financial problems then delayed its production for four years, after which time it used a fiberglass body and became a Gordon Keeble – some 140 would be built under two different company owners. Bizzarrini and Rivolta were obviously aware of the Gordon GT by the time they started on the Iso Rivolta. It was very close to what they wanted. Bizzarini

390-391 The Iso Grifo was one of Bertone's masterpieces.

TECHNICAL DESCRIPTION OF THE ISO GRIFO GL400

YEARS OF PRODUCTION	1969-1974
MODELS	2-SEATER COUPE
ENGINE	FRONT-MOUNTED V-8
BORE X STROKE, CAPACITY	4.2 X 3.6 INCHES, 425 CU.IN
VALVEGEAR	PUSHROD OVERHEAD VALVES
FUEL SYSTEM	ONE 4-BARREL HOLLEY CARBURETOR
POWER	406 BHP (GROSS) AT 5400 RPM
TRANSMISSION	4-SPEED
BODY/CHASSIS	STEEL PLATFORM, STEEL BODYWORK
SUSPENSION	FRONT, WISHBONES AND COIL SPRINGS
	REAR, DE DION AXLE WITH RADIUS ARMS
	AND PANHARD ROD
TIRES/WHEELS	205 X 15 ON ALLOY WHEELS
WHEELBASE, TRACK (F), TRACK(R)	98.5 X 55.5 X 55.5 INCHES
LENGTH, WIDTH, HEIGHT	174.7 X 69.5 X 47 INCHES
MAX SPEED	161 MPH
WHERE BUILT	MILAN, ITALY

designed a fresh chassis using pressed sheet steel rather than a space frame, fitted wishbone front suspension and a de Dion axle with Panhard rod lateral location rather than the Gordon's Watt linkage. All round disc brakes were inboard at the rear.

The engine was Chevrolet's latest 327 cu.in V-8 in either 300 or 340 bhp form with a Warner 4-speed gearbox, both of which the Gordon Keeble would later adopt. And Giugiaro, for Bertone, provided a body similar to that of the Gordon GT but more modern. In fact, the wheelbase was 4 inches longer for the same overall length, and the roof provided 2 inches more headroom. The result was shown in late 1962 and production started in 1963 – it was a remarkably good car and 800 were built before it gave way to the 2-door Lele and 4-door Fidia in 1969.

For the Turin Show in November 1963, Bizzarrini shortened the Rivolta chassis by 7.8 inches for Giugiaro to create the beautiful Iso Grifo A3L (Lusso). A sleeker more aerodynamic A3C (Corsa) was also shown for which Bizzarrini had moved the engine rearwards; Piero Drogo designed and built the 29 cars bearing the Iso name. Grifo A3C models competed at Le Mans in 1964 (14th) and 1965 (9th).

Bizzarrini returned to his own business in 1964, changing the name to Societa Prototipi Bizzarrini and, with Iso agreement, started to make the A3C as a Bizzarrini 5300GT or Strada as road cars with a little restyling from Giugiaro. By 1969, 155 had been built. Meanwhile production of the Grifo A3L did not start until 1965. The standard A3L would be known as the GL365, as it used the 365 bhp engine with solid valve lifters for more revs and power – the 300 bhp Rivolta engine was an option. The GL400 was added in 1969 with the Corvette's 406 bhp 427 cu.in engine; installing this big block engine required an unsightly hump on the bonnet. The Grifo continued until 1974 when Piero Rivolta sold out to American interests which shortly collapsed. The Grifo was the car that ensures the name will be remembered; Bertone built 411 of them of which 90 were GL400s.

391

The Ghibli was one of Maserati's greatest road cars, the best and almost the last of the real Italian breed. The fastback coupe body, designed by Giugiaro during his three-year period at Ghia, is as elegant today as it was when the world first saw the car at the 1966 Turin Show. Beautifully finished inside too with plenty of leather, deep pile carpet and air conditioning as an option. Further appeal and some noise came with a race-bred 286 cu.in four-cam dry-sump V-8 giving 320 bhp, enough to exceed 160 mph; for later models, the V-8 was increased to 298 cu.in with a little more power and usefully more torque. The usual transmission choice was the manual ZF 5-speed, but an automatic was available.

Supporting all this was still an old-fashioned tubular chassis – like Ferrari – but this one still had a live rear axle mounted on leaf springs. Although the American muscle cars of the period were similarly equipped, most of Europe's supercars had rear wishbones or at least a De Dion axle. Contemporary reports, though, suggest that ride and roadholding were as good as the rivals. Production of the Ghibli started slowly during 1967. A year later it was joined by the lovely slender convertible version. Over a seven year production life, 1150 coupes and just 125 convertibles were built.

For the first 30 years of its life from 1926, the company had existed largely on the sale of single seater and sports racing cars to private competitors, with only a handful of the early post-war A6 cars equipped with coupe bodywork for road use. In 1937, the Maserati brothers had sold out to the Orsi group who moved the factory to Modena in 1941; however the contract retained the brothers' services until 1947, at which point they returned to Bologna and set up OSCA, leaving Omer Orsi to take over the reins.

Before the Maseratis departed they designed a 6-cylinder 122 cu.in engine which was fitted in sports-racing and road coupe models; it then became the basis of the A6GCM which was a strong contender in the 122 cu.in Grand Prix period of 1952-3. When the 152 cu.in GP formula came in 1954, Colombo further developed the six-cylinder unit with a new chassis, and the legendary 250F was born to establish Maserati's racing tradition in the top level during 1954-1957; a further development

Maserati Ghibli

of this engine was used in the 300S, to be joined by the 450S with a new 274 cu.in V-8 engine. The straight six and the V-8 engines were to provide the basis of power units for road cars from then until the arrival of the Biturbo in 1982.

The first of these road cars was the Touring-bodied 3500GT 2+2, announced in 1957 with the six-cylinder engine giving 220 bhp, later 235 bhp in GTi fuel injection form. Vignale made spider versions on a shorter wheelbase, then produced the fixed head 3500GTiS (Sebring) on the Spider chassis; around 2700 of the various 3500 models were produced. The Frua-styled 2-seater Mistrales, open and closed, were the last to use the straight-six engine in 225 cu.in 245 bhp and 244 cu.in 255 bhp forms; with a further shortened chassis, these were the nicest of the six-cylinder cars.

The first road use of the former racing V-8 was for a few 5000GT models, mostly with Allemano fixed-head bodies, which arrived in 1959 using a 350 bhp 298 cu.in version in the longer 3500GT chassis. It was used in the Quattroporte from 1963, and the Vignale Mexico 2+2 from

1966, both using the V-8 in either 260 bhp 256 cu.in or 290 bhp 286 cu.in forms. Ghibli and Spider derivative followed in 1966 and 1968, when the Vignale-bodied Indy 2+2 was added to the range as a slightly stretched Ghibli.

Although Maserati could sell a large number of different models by producing two chassis lengths and various engines and leaving the rest to the coachbuilders, some order was restored when Citroen acquired the company in 1969. Their main interest was in using Maserati to build their new V-6 engine for the SM. Using some Citroen components, they brought in the Bora for 1971, and the Merak for 1972, both with ItalDesign bodies (Giugiaro).The Khamsin 2+2 (Bertone) went into production in 1974 with the 298 cu.in V-8 and was the first front-engined Maserati road car to feature independent rear suspension; effectively replacing both the Indy and the Ghibli, the Khamsin was to continue in production until the new generation arrived.

392-393 Long and low, the Ghibli was the best-looking of all the Sixties Maseratis; here, a 1971 Ghibli SS.

TECHNICAL DESCRIPTION OF THE MASERATI GHIBLI

YEARS OF PRODUCTION	1970-1974
MODELS	2-Seater Coupe and convertible
ENGINE	Front-mounted V-8
BORE X STROKE, CAPACITY	3.7 x 3.5 inches, 300 cu.in
VALVEGEAR	Twin overhead camshafts per bank
FUEL SYSTEM	4 Weber twin-choke carburetors
POWER	355 bhp at 5500 rpm
TRANSMISSION	5-speed
BODY/CHASSIS	Reinforced steel tube chassis with steel body panels
SUSPENSION	Front, wishbones and coils Rear, live axle and leaf springs
TIRES/WHEELS	205 x 15 on 6.5 in. alloy wheels
WHEELBASE, TRACK (F), TRACK(R)	100.3 x 56.6 x 55.9 inches
LENGTH, WIDTH, HEIGHT	180.7 x 70.8 x 45.6 inches
MAX SPEED	160 mph
WHERE BUILT	Modena, Italy

Renault Alpine 1600S

Until the Renault Alpine 1600S started to win International rallies outright at the turn of the decade, few outside France were familiar with this compact two-seater coupe with its Renault engine pushed out behind the rear axle. It was very low with seemingly little space inside for two large people wearing helmets, but it kept on winning. Alpine driver Andruet became European Rally Champion in 1970 and the team won the International championship in 1971.

The Sixties had seen the start of the homologation specials for racing and rallying, the limited edition models produced in just enough numbers to qualify for FIA homologation – Mini Cooper S and Lotus Cortina. Renault 8 Gordini and Lancia Fulvia HF were European replies to the British. Then came the Escort Twin-Cam and RS1600, but the rules also allowed GT cars with fewer seats and smaller numbers. So rallies accepted the front drive Lancia Fulvia coupe and the rear-drive Porsche 911 and the Alpine A110.

The A110 arrived in 1962. John Redele had set up the Societe des Automobiles Alpine in 1955 at the Renault dealership of his father. After several years competing with a Renault 750, including winning his class in the Mille Miglia, Redele produced the A106 in 1956. This used the 750 running gear with a fiberglass 2+2 coupe body; when the Dauphine came out the engine was increased to 51 cu.in. The 1957 A108 was the cabriolet version available. By 1960, Redele had evolved the steel tube backbone chassis that was to characterise all subsequent Alpines. New body styles for the 2+2 GT4 coupe and convertible came in 1961, with the convertible on a shorter wheelbase. The same chassis length was used for the new A110 2-seater coupe for 1962.

As state-owned Renault was still only producing 61 cu.in cars for the people, the Alpine's performance appeal was somewhat limited. The turning point came with the introduction of the Renault 16 in 1965. Although this was a front wheel drive car, the layout was the same as for the Renault 8; the engine was behind the gearbox. The 89 cu.in engine was ideal for the Renault Alpine; with a little tuning the A110 was moving up the rally leader boards. When the 95 cu.in TS engine became available in 1968, Redele returned to rallying with the 1600S and the financial help of Renault. A 3rd place in the 1969 Monte Carlo Rally and 1,2,3 in the 1969 Alpine Rally was the start of an amazing rally career for the little blue cars. By now Renault were 30% shareholders and Alpine was Renault's competition department.

Alpine had started very much like Porsche. Both used humble saloon cars as the base for their first GT cars, but by the time the A110 arrived, Porsche were about to produce the 911. Although there were technically very different, and you could buy two Alpines for a Porsche, both proved ideal for the loose surface roads which were increasingly used for rallies. The rear engine package gave good traction and tight controllable handling, but neither was as successful on the race tracks where greater grip upset the rear suspension. On the road this was not important and the A110 was fun, despite the hard ride and noisy engine.

Although the A110 was to continue through until 1977, Alpine brought in the A310 at Geneva 1971 as a 2+2 using the same Renault 16

running gear under a new distinctive shape. The body was still a fiberglass shell mounted on a tubular back-bone frame, but the rear suspension now featured double wishbones. It was bigger, more comfortable and trimmed to proper GT levels. Alpine had finally become a serious producer of internationally acknowledged performance cars.

By the Mid-seventies Renault owned 87% of Alpine whose production then included A110s, A310s and R5 Alpines – the 1975 total was 4500 vehicles; the A110 ceased in 1977 by which time some 7200 had been built over 14 years. The A310, with the PRV 164 cu.in V-6 from 1980, became the GTA in 1985 with 160 bhp or 200 bhp using a turbocharger. Alpine were still regarded as the French Porsche but they didn't sell enough and the last Alpine was built in 1994.

394-395 Neat and aerodynamically efficient, the 1600S (1969 here) won many International rallies.

TECHNICAL DESCRIPTION OF THE RENAULT ALPINE 1600S

YEARS OF PRODUCTION	1968-1973
MODELS	2-SEATER COUPE
ENGINE	REAR-MOUNTED 4-CYLINDER
BORE X STROKE, CAPACITY	3 x 3.3 INCHES, 95 CU.IN
VALVEGEAR	PUSHROD OVERHEAD VALVES
FUEL SYSTEM	TWIN WEBER CARBURETORS
POWER	138 BHP AT 6000 RPM
TRANSMISSION	4-SPEED
BODY/CHASSIS	BACKBONE STEEL CHASSIS AND FIBERGLASS BODY
SUSPENSION	FRONT, WISHBONES AND COIL SPRINGS REAR, SWING AXLE AND COIL SPRINGS
TIRES/WHEELS	165 x 13 ON ALLOY WHEELS
WHEELBASE, TRACK (F), TRACK(R)	83 x 51.6 x 53.2 INCHES
LENGTH, WIDTH, HEIGHT	151.6 x 61 x 44 INCHES
MAX SPEED	130 MPH
WHERE BUILT	DIEPPE, FRANCE

Ferruccio Lamborghini had achieved the first stage of his Ferrari rivalry in launching the fast and comfortable 350GT in 1964. While Lamborghini had no intention of going racing, engineers Stanzani, Dallara and Wallace evolved the Miura as a road car that might be raced – it never was. They had a superb engine in the V-12 and they could design and build any necessary transmission. Comfort required equal space for both passengers without the intrusion of wheel arches into the foot-well, a problem with the genuine racing Ford GT40 and Ferrari 250LM. To avoid a long wheelbase they turned the engine, through 90 degrees, and then built the transmission into the rear side of the block-cum-crankcase – a very large and complex single casting which could only have been achieved in Italy at that time. The problem of connecting the gear lever to the back of the engine was solved by passing the linkage under the crankshaft. As low engine height was not as important for a mid-engined car, the unusual and efficient downdraft inlet porting of the 400GT could be used to maximum advantage with matching triple-choke Weber carburetors mounted vertically; with a higher compression ratio, output rose to 350 bhp. This mechanical masterpiece was mounted in a pressed steel monocoque chassis liberally pierced for lightness and strength – a plate with flared edges to

holes is stiffer than a flat plate. Engine and front suspension were mounted on square tube sub-frame extensions, the suspension using double wishbone and coil springs all round.

Lamborghini duly gave his approval and the rolling chassis was unveiled at the Turin Show in November 1965. Even without a name or a body it was a sensation. During 1965, Touring was still making bodies for the 350GT; they produced some studies which were unquestionably heralds of the final Miura shape. With Touring still in the hands of the receiver and unable to guarantee future production, these thoughts were taken to Bertone. It was Marcello Gandini, to whom the Miura design is always attributed, who refined the Touring designs.

The definitive shape, a classic mid-engined fastback, was shown at Geneva in March 1966. Features inspired by development included bonnet-top vents to let hot air out of the radiators, ducts in the sills to feed air to the rear tires, scoops in the rear edge of the doors feeding air through the B-posts to the engine intakes and the slatted rear 'window' to let hot air out of the engine compartment; there was a vertical rear window between the sail panels to keep the engine noise out. The 'flatfish' headlights, with black strakes above and below them were the least clever part of a striking design. Lamborghini had only expected to make perhaps

Lamborghini Miura

25 a year, prestige advertisements for the GT cars, but demand was far greater. The first cars were delivered in early 1967 and their performance was sensational with a maximum speed around 170 mph. And they handled very well too with less than 60 per cent of the weight on the rear wheels but, after 125 cars, the chassis was stiffened using sheet steel 10 per cent thicker. After 475 of the P400, the P400S came in 1969 with anti-squat rear suspension and 370 bhp at 7700 rpm with new camshafts and bigger carburetors; there were around 140 of these. The output was further increased to 385 bhp in 1971 for the P400SV, for which the sump was made deeper to lessen the effects of oil surge in fast cornering, and the oil for the gearbox and engine was separated by a partition to allow different oil for a limited slip differential; other SV changes included widened rear bodywork for wider tires, ventilated disc brakes and headlamps which were no longer surrounded by eyelashes. Meanwhile, Ferruccio Lamborghini's businesses were suffering in the general climate and he sold 51 per cent to Swiss interests in 1972, disposing of the remaining 49 per cent a year later to another Swiss. Following the 1971 showing of the Countach, the new owners killed the Miura, but then took another three years to get the Countach into production. After 150 of the SV and a total run of 762, the Miura died too soon.

396-397 The Miura was the first road-going mid-engined supercar.

TECHNICAL DESCRIPTION OF THE LAMBORGHINI MIURA P400	
YEARS OF PRODUCTION	1966-1969
MODELS	2-SEATER COUPE
ENGINE	MID-MOUNTED V-12
BORE X STROKE, CAPACITY	3.2 x 2.4 INCHES, 239 CU.IN
VALVEGEAR	TWIN OVERHEAD CAMSHAFT PER BANK
FUEL SYSTEM	4 WEBER TRIPLE-CHOKE CARBURETORS
POWER	350 BHP AT 7000 RPM
TRANSMISSION	5-SPEED
BODY/CHASSIS	SHEET STEEL WITH ALUMINIUM BODY
SUSPENSION	FRONT, WISHBONES AND COILS
	REAR, WISHBONES AND COILS
TIRES/WHEELS	210 x 15 ON ALLOY WHEELS
WHEELBASE, TRACK (F), TRACK(R)	98.6 x 55.6 x 55.6 INCHES
LENGTH, WIDTH, HEIGHT	172 x 69.3 x 41.3 INCHES
MAX SPEED	170 MPH
WHERE BUILT	BOLOGNA, ITALY

Ferrari 365GTB4 Daytona

In presenting the 365GTB4 Daytona at the Paris Show in October 1968, Ferrari and Pininfarina were making a clear statement to the world in general, and Lamborghini in particular, that, even if the engine was still at the front, Maranello could still make sensational road cars.

Logically, the 365GTB4 should have been just a 365GTC with the 4-camshaft engine.

Fortunately, it wasn't. The mid-engined Miura had stolen Ferrari's prime position for two years, and Ferrari needed a reply.

So the Daytona had a style like no other Ferrari before, an exciting mixture of a long aggressive chisel nose with a flat top and powerful haunches extending all the way from the rear wheels to the top of the front windscreen. It exuded power and it was faster than the Miura.

It looked good, big too, yet its wheelbase was the same as all the Berlinettas from the 250 GT SWB through the 275 series. The 275GTB (Berlinetta)and GTS (Spider), announced at the 1964 Paris Show, were the first Ferraris to be designed purely as road cars. Although the chassis structure followed the familiar tubular principles, its design had finally moved with the times and Lamborghini, and had independent rear suspension; this allowed Ferrari to group the gearbox, now with five speeds, and final drive unit into a single transaxle to keep the weight distribution more even. The body style retained 250GTO lines with pronounced curves above the rear wheels and an inset cabin.

Two years later, the 1966 Paris Show hosted the launch of the 275GTB4 denoting four overhead camshafts; it was Ferrari's first four-cam

road car, three years after Lamborghini's.

With 300 bhp at 8000 rpm it would run to 160 mph. Of the 275 series which ran into 1967, some 450 were GTB, 200 GTS and 350 GTB4. The 275GTB4 launch had extended the life of the 275 by a year, so it overlapped with the new 330 range which had been presented in March 1966. With a new longer block, the 300 bhp 244 cu.in two-cam V-12 was used to power the 330GTC (Coupe) and GTS. The chassis was still very like that of the 275, but the drive-shaft was now enclosed in a torque tube.

Pininfarina's new body style had a lower straight waistline, deeper windows, a tail with a separate trunk and an oval grille more like a Superamerica. Around 600 330GTC and 100 330GTS were built from 1966-68 when the 365 engine came in.

The 330 engine had been used in the sports-racing 330P in 1964; the factory continued to develop this engine for their own team in 1965 but produced a 268 cu.in 365P for the non-works teams.

For 1967 the 330P4 had four cams, three-valve twin-plug heads and fuel injection to generate 450 bhp at 8200 rpm; private entrants made do with 380 bhp at 7300 rpm using carburetors and single-cam 365s. Ferrari used sports car racing to develop designs that could be adapted for road use later. On the way, they won the world sports car championship three times in those four years, including victory at Daytona.

The first production car to use a 268 cu.in single-cam V-12 was the 365GT 2+2, an extremely elegant Pininfarina stretch of the 330GTC. The 330GTC and GTS had to wait another year until late 1968 to be uprated to 365-series. However, the big event of that year was the October arrival of the ultimate two-seater coupe, named Daytona after Ferrari successes there; racing experience dictated the engine specification.

The 365GTB4 engine (268 cu.in) had twin-cams per bank but only

two valves, six carburetors and dry sump lubrication; at 352 bhp it was 30 more than the single-cam cars.

The chassis was basically that of the 330/365GTC. And the style set it off to perfection.

On early cars the headlights were set behind a band of clear plastic running across the nose, but American laws required proper glass, so the plastic was replaced by painted metal and the headlamps were concealed. aOther variants included a convertible – 100 only – and the 365GTC4, a 2+2 Daytona with less horsepower and a revised front end which was available in 1971/2 following the phasing out of the previous 2+2.

But the Daytona stayed in production until 1974; over 1300 were built in that six-year period.

400-401 The Daytona Spyder was just as attractive but lost the brutal appeal of the coupe.

TECHNICAL DESCRIPTION OF THE FERRARI 365GTB4 DAYTONA

YEARS OF PRODUCTION	1968-1974
MODELS	2-SEATER COUPE AND CONVERTIBLE
ENGINE	FRONT-MOUNTED V-12
BORE X STROKE, CAPACITY	3.1 X 2.7 INCHES, 267 CU.IN
VALVEGEAR	TWIN OVERHEAD CAMSHAFTS PER BANK
FUEL SYSTEM	6 WEBER TWIN-CHOKE CARBURETORS
POWER	352 BHP AT 7500 RPM
TRANSMISSION	5-SPEED
BODY/CHASSIS	TUBULAR CHASSIS WITH STEEL AND ALUMINIUM BODY PANELS
SUSPENSION	FRONT, WISHBONES AND COILS REAR, WISHBONES AND COILS
TIRES/WHEELS	205 X 15 ON ALLOY WHEELS
WHEELBASE, TRACK (F), TRACK(R)	94.5 X 56.5 X 56 INCHES
LENGTH, WIDTH, HEIGHT	174 X 69.2 X 49 INCHES
MAX SPEED	175 MPH
WHERE BUILT	MODENA, ITALY

Ferrari Dino 246GT

The Dino 246 was the first to prove that the racing-inspired concept of placing the engine behind the driver could produce a perfect road car. It went fast, cornered well and looked beautiful in its Pininfarina clothes. Mid-engined road cars before it had tail-heavy handling, poor rearward visibility and no storage space. The Dino's handling and stability were superb; the driver's view through glazed sail panels and the neat curved vertical rear window was more than adequate; and there was a good luggage space behind the transverse engine. Its 146 cu.in V-6 would power the car to around 150 mph and reach 60 mph in 7 seconds.

The V-6 engine had an impeccable pedigree. It started life as a Formula Two (F2) engine for the 1957 91 cu.in formula, co-designed by Vittorio Jano and Ferrari's son Alfredino, who sadly died in 1956 before the engine had raced. The 65-degree four-cam V-6 became the Dino in his memory. While it did not do particularly well as an F2 engine, it went on to power Mike Hawthorn to his 1958 Grand Prix world championship in 146 cu.in form.

When GP rules changed to 91.5 cu.in for 1961, the original Dino engine was used before the team switched to a wider angle V-6. When F2 reverted to 91.5 cu.in, the engine had to have a production cylinder block of which 500 had been made. Ferrari persuaded Fiat to produce a limited run of front-engined sports cars in time for Ferrari to use the engine during 1967; the Pininfarina Fiat Dino sports car arrived in November 1966 with the V-6 in 122 cu.in form and the Bertone coupe came in March 1967.

Ferrari had been using the V-6 in sports car racing in 1965/66. Pininfarina used a 206P to show a special concept GT in October 1965, following it with another a year later. Ferrari had been seeking an entry-level car to take on the Porsche 911 market and adopted Pininfarina's GT shape and changed the engine from longitudinal to transverse mounting; this was launched at Turin in November 1967 as the Dino 206GT – not using the Ferrari name. The aluminium bodies were built by Scaglietti and production started in mid 1968 – around 150 were built over the next year.

Meanwhile Fiat had dutifully turned out many more of the Fiat Dino 2.0 than were required for the F2 rules, but had also been developing the version they would have preferred to build if there had not been such a rush to build the first 500. The result was a very much revised chassis and the V-6 aluminium block was exchanged for a quieter and stronger cast iron 146 cu.in. The new Fiat Dino 2.4 was announced at the 1969 Turin Show, where the new (Ferrari) Dino 246GT, with a steel body, was also making its first public appearance. It was to continue in production until 1975, having been joined by the Targa-top 246GTS in 1972, and just over 3000 were built.

402-403 Although created by Ferrari, the Dino 246GT was never called a Ferrari by the factory. This did not stop some owners putting a Ferrari badge on the car.

By the time the 246GT was around, the original purpose of productionising the V-6 had been forgotten. Ferrari eventually used it in mid-1967 F2 races with no success. They had a better year in 1968 with few results until they won the last two European races of the year, and went on to take three out of four of the Argentine Temporada races. In 146 cu.in form, the engine did well for Chris Amon in the 1968 Tasman series and he won the championship in 1969. There was just one more achievement for the same basic power unit; the Dino engine/transmission package was used for the Lancia Stratos which won the World Rally Championship from 1974-1976, 20 years after the original first ran.

But Ferrari moved on from the V-6 to a V-8, two thirds of the 365 V-12, but with its overhead camshafts driven by toothed belt. In 1973, this was installed in the Bertone-designed 308 GT4 which had an extra 8 inches in the wheelbase to carry four people. The 246GT was replaced by the 308GTB in 1975, initially with fiberglass bodies but with steel from 1977 when the 308GTS Spider came along and the cars became Ferraris. The GT4 lasted until 1980, and the 308GTB and 308GTS until 1985 having gathered fuel injection in 1980 and 4-valve heads from 1982.

TECHNICAL DESCRIPTION OF THE DINO 246GT

YEARS OF PRODUCTION	1969-1974
MODELS	246GT AND 246GTS 2-SEATER
ENGINE	MID-MOUNTED V-6
BORE X STROKE, CAPACITY	3.6 X 2.3 INCHES, 147 CU.IN
VALVEGEAR	TWIN OVERHEAD CAMSHAFTS PER BANK
FUEL SYSTEM	THREE WEBER CARBURETORS
POWER	195 BHP AT 7600 RPM
TRANSMISSION	5-SPEED
BODY/CHASSIS	TUBULAR CHASSIS, STEEL BODY
SUSPENSION	FRONT, WISHBONES ANDCOIL SPRINGS
	REAR, WISHBONES AND COIL SPRINGS
TIRES/WHEELS	205/70VR14 ON 6.5 IN ALLOY WHEELS
WHEELBASE, TRACK (F), TRACK(R)	92 X 56 X 55 INCHES
LENGTH, WIDTH, HEIGHT	165 X 67 X 44 INCHES
MAX SPEED	148 MPH
WHERE BUILT	MARANELLO, ITALY

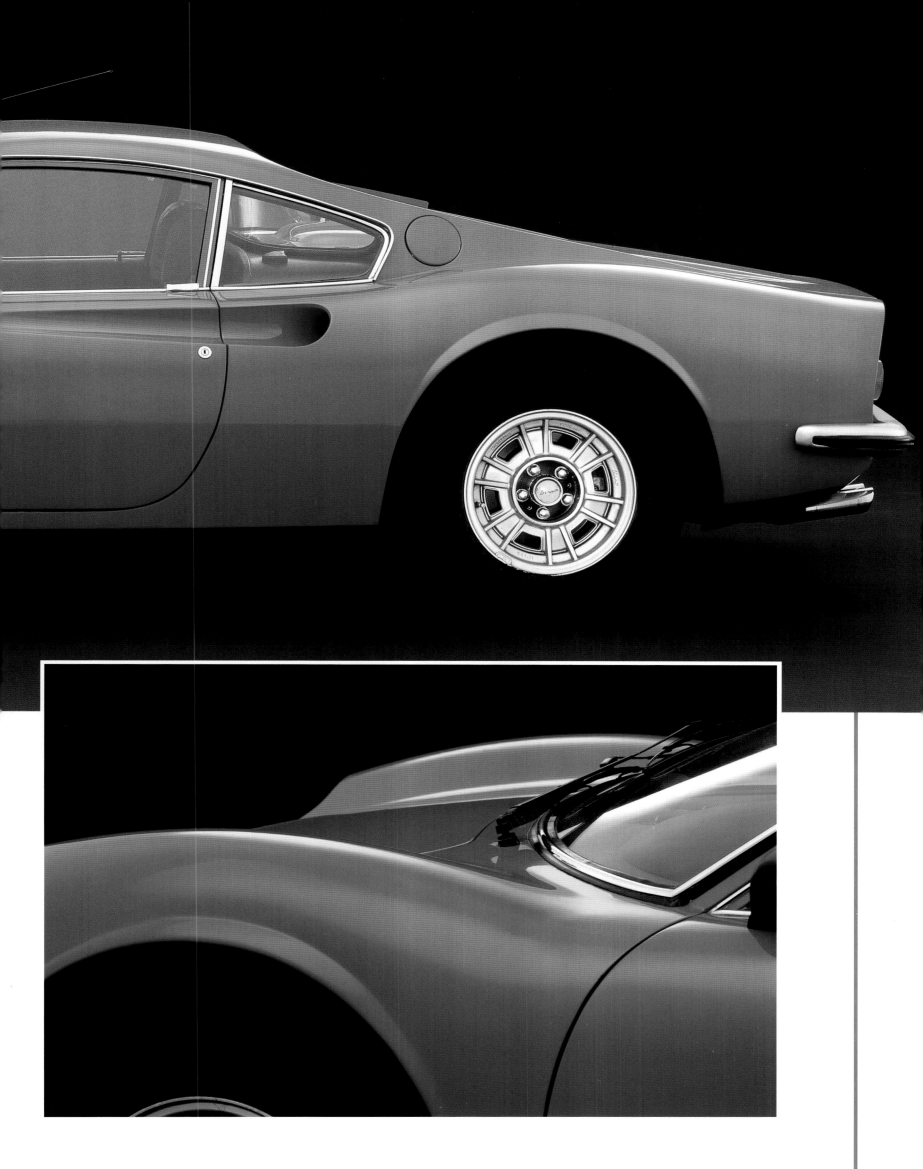

404-405 *The Dino 246GT performed as well as it looked.*

Fiat Dino 2.4 Spider

Through the Fifties Fiat had only dabbled in sports cars. Producing just a handful of the early 1100/1200 and 8V, they missed out on the big post-war American demand. Fiat were not prepared to tool up for lower volumes, so any sports car had to use a saloon platform and have its body built by one of the coachbuilders. It was Pininfarina who produced the 1200/1500/Oscar series of cabriolets from 1959 -66 and built 37,500 of them over the seven year period. It was Ghia who pushed through the 2300S from 1961.

Serious sporting thoughts began with the little rear-engined 850 saloon launched in May 1964. Fiat styled and built the attractive coupe, Bertone styled and built the Spider; both were launched together in March 1965. Fiat had read the market right and they were a success in

America. By 1973, 342,873 coupes and 124,660 Spiders had been made, including the 55 cu.in Sport version from 1968.

The Fiat 124, launched in April 1966, had been scheduled for similar derivatives from its inception. Its engine had been designed by Lampredi (back at Fiat from Ferrari) as a pushrod 73 cu.in unit that could be stretched and fitted with a twin-cam head. The 124 Sport had a 87 cu.in twin-cam unit. The fixed head coupe was built within Fiat and the Spider, on a shortened platform, at Pininfarina.

While this was being planned, Ferrari had persuaded Fiat to produce at least 500 sports cars with the Dino V-6 engine as soon as possible; this would allow Ferrari to use the engine block in their Formula Two racing cars in 1967. So Fiat took over development and production of the 65-

406-407 The Fiat Dino 2.4 (1969 here) was
a much better car than the 1966 2.0 model although fewer
were made.

degree four-cam V-6 for which Lampredi settled on a 122 cu.in capacity, still with the aluminium block. Fiat engineers created a suitable platform from available parts but used a new rear suspension – a live axle on single leaf springs with rear radius arms and telescopic dampers ahead of and behind the axle.

Heavily committed to producing the complete 124 coupe in house, Fiat subcontracted the body building of both Dinos; Bertone made the delightful four-seater coupe and Pininfarina made the shorter and beautifully curvaceous Spider.

Both Spiders were launched at Turin in November 1966, and both coupes at Geneva in March 1967. Although the Fiat Dinos were twice the price of the 124 Sports, they were very well received.

They had style, performance and pedigree with a real race-derived engine. Pininfarina had built 1163 Spiders and Bertone 3670 coupes by 1969, when Fiat launched the Dino they would have built without the rush to build 500. The Dino 2400 was launched in November 1966, alongside Ferrari's Dino 246GT. In mid-1969 Fiat had acquired 50 per cent of Ferrari, and final assembly of the new car was transferred from Turin to an extension of the Maranello factory.

The new 146 cu.in engine retained just the basic design details of the V-6 with 65 degree vee-angle and four chain-driven cams; its 3.6 x 2.3 inches dimensions compare with 3.3 x 2.2 inches for the 122 cu.in and 3.3 x 2.7 inches of the original F1 engine in both its 1958 and 1966 forms. The block was made of cast iron which was heavier but quieter and easier to make without the removable liners; the major virtue was the improved drivability with the peak torque at 4600 rpm rather than

408-409 Although the engine was used by Ferrari, the Dino 2.4 was always a Fiat.

6000 rpm. The extra 20 bhp was also a bonus.

The previous gearbox had been a 2300 4-speed converted to five speeds with an additional casing. The new one was a ZF 5-speed box shared with the new Fiat 130. This car also supplied the new independent rear suspension – a MacPherson strut with, effectively, a lower wishbone. Outwardly there were no changes but the new 2400 was a much better car than its predecessor.

Despite that, sales of both models were lower over a similar production period than for the 122 cu.in. Just 420 Spiders and 2398 coupes were built before the line finished in 1973. Doubtless Ferrari put more effort into selling their own more expensive Dinos. Meanwhile both Fiat 124 Sport models continued to sell well. The engine grew to 98 cu.in in 1969 and 107 cu.in in 1972. The coupe finished in 1975 after nearly 280,000 units, while the Spider (almost 130,00 to 1978) rolled on into a 122 cu.in version to maintain the American sales until 1983.

TECHNICAL DESCRIPTION OF THE FIAT DINO 2.4 SPIDER

YEARS OF PRODUCTION	1969-1973
MODELS	SPIDER AND LWB 4-SEATER COUPE
ENGINE	FRONT-MOUNTED V-6
BORE X STROKE, CAPACITY	3.6 X 2.3 INCHES, 147 CU.IN
VALVEGEAR	TWIN OVERHEAD CAMSHAFTS PER BANK
FUEL SYSTEM	THREE WEBER CARBURETORS
POWER	180 BHP AT 6600 RPM
TRANSMISSION	5-SPEED
BODY/CHASSIS	STEEL MONOCOQUE
SUSPENSION	FRONT, WISHBONES AND COIL SPRINGS
	REAR, MACPHERSON STRUT, TRANSVERSE
	LINK AND TRAILING ARM
TIRES/WHEELS	185 X 14 ON 6.5 IN ALLOY WHEELS
WHEELBASE, TRACK (F), TRACK(R)	90 X 54.5 X 53 INCHES
LENGTH, WIDTH, HEIGHT	162 X 67.4 X 50 INCHES
MAX SPEED	128 MPH
WHERE BUILT	MARANELLO, ITALY

Pontiac Firebird

When Ford introduced the Mustang in April 1964, General Motors hoped their revised Chevrolet Corvair would be more appealing than a rebodied Ford Falcon. By August, when 100,000 Mustangs had been sold, they started work on their Mustang rival, determined to make it faster, more comfortable and more stylish. The Camaro was an all-new car; it used a unitary body chassis but with a rubber-mounted front sub-frame. By the time the Camaro hit the showrooms in September 1966, it had more options available than the Mustang. Ford brought out the Mercury Cougar, with a longer platform, as their high-style Mustang.

Pontiac initially ignored the new compact sports youth market. NASCAR successes still appealed to the young and they used competition names on their big 2-door sports coupes. Tempest Le Mans, Catalina Grand Prix while speed record venue Bonneville was used for the biggest cars – these early Sixties coupes are particularly attractive future classics. Then came the magnificent GTO muscle car for 1963 with a 389 cu.in V-8 in the Le Mans coupe. However, Pontiac finally gave in and joined the Camaro development programme in early 1966; the Firebird used the Camaro's center section and added its own front end and rear panels, but retained the slightly different Pontiac engine range.

The Firebird, named after earlier turbine-powered concept cars, went on sale in February 1967 as a coupe and a convertible. The engine choice ranged from the 165 bhp 230 cu.in. overhead cam six-cylinder through a 250 bhp 326 cu.in V-8 to the 400 cu.in with 325 bhp. By then the Mustang was available with a 390 cu.in. 335 bhp unit and you could get a Shelby Mustang GT-500 with the 428 cu.in with 350 bhp.

Ever since the early days of NASCAR, the American market had responded to racing success – win on Sunday, sell on Monday. With the rise in the pony car market, the SCCA launched the Trans-American Championship in 1966 for cars with 304 cu.in engines and the manufacturers joined in. The Shelby Mustang won comfortably in the first year but had to work harder in 1967 to beat the Mercury Cougar and the new Camaro Z-28. The Camaro beat the Mustang in 1968 with the American Motors Javelin not far behind. The Camaro won again in 1969 from the Mustang Boss 302, but the Firebird had joined in to take third. In 1970 Mustang took the honours from the two Chryslers, Dodge Challenger and Plymouth Cuda, with Camaro and Firebird trailing. By 1971 the major manufacturers had left the scene and Javelin won the final year before the championship switched to private entries.

Entering the Trans-Am championship for 1969 justified a new Firebird model, the Trans-Am which has been the top model ever since. Although the racers used 302 cu.in engines, the Trans-Am model had the 335 bhp 400 cu.in engine, together with sports suspension and a choice of two colors, white with blue stripes or blue with white stripes – American racing colors. The 1969 Firebirds had bumpers replaced by the new plastic front end which was also seen on the Judge derivative of the GTO; Pontiac had pioneered the Endura deformable front panel made from polyurethane.

Firebird and Camaro were both rebodied in 1970 with European-style long bonnet, short fastback tail and dropped the convertible. Firebird

410-411 Pontiac's Firebird (1968 400 illustrated) had smoother style than the sister Chevrolet Camaro.

sales never reached Mustang levels but had been comfortable; 82,000 in 1967 went to 107,000 in 1968, 87,000 in 1969 but only 48,000 in 1970. This reflected the decline in the overall pony car market which had made up 13 per cent of US sales in 1967, 9.2 per cent in 1969 and 3.4 per cent in 1972. The Mustang had peaked at 550,000 in 1967 but was down to 127,000 in 1972.

To maintain the high engine outputs on lower octane fuels, engine sizes were increased in 1971 and the 455 cu.in became the Trans-Am's

standard unit, still with 335 bhp. Production went up to 53,000, but was back to 30,000 in 1972.

Ford also claimed the same power for their 1971 Boss Mustang 351 – the last performance Mustang.

High performance was no longer acceptable. By 1975, the Mustang had become a small car, the Cougar was too big and Chrysler and Javelin had left the market to the Firebird and Camaro, which continued to survive on style before the power resurgence of the Nineties.

TECHNICAL DESCRIPTION OF THE PONTIAC FIREBIRD 400	
YEARS OF PRODUCTION	1967-1968
MODELS	2-DOOR COUPE
ENGINE	FRONT-MOUNTED V-8
BORE X STROKE, CAPACITY	4.1 X 3.7 INCHES, 400 CU.IN
VALVEGEAR	PUSHROD OVERHEAD VALVES
FUEL SYSTEM	SINGLE CARBURETOR
POWER	325 BHP (GROSS) AT 5000 RPM
TRANSMISSION	3-SPEED AUTOMATIC
BODY/CHASSIS	STEEL BODY AND CHASSIS
SUSPENSION	FRONT, WISHBONES AND COIL SPRINGS
	REAR, LIVE AXLE AND LEAF SPRINGS
TIRES/WHEELS	7.75 X 14 ON STEEL WHEELS
WHEELBASE, TRACK (F), TRACK(R)	108 X 60 X 60 INCHES
LENGTH, WIDTH, HEIGHT	189 X 74 X 49.6 INCHES
MAX SPEED	130 MPH
WHERE BUILT	DETROIT, USA

Alfa Romeo Duetto

Few cars remained in production as long as the Alfa Romeo Giulia Spider; the seductively-shaped two-seater was launched at Geneva in 1966 with a 97 cu.in engine and finally retired in 1993 using the 122 cu.in version of an engine that had long ceased to be used in any other Alfa Romeo. With various adjustments over the years, the design looked almost as fresh and modern at the end as it had done 27 years earlier. Over 120,000 of the various models were built by Pininfarina.

Following Alfa Romeo's replacement of the Giulietta with the new boxy Giulia saloon in 1962, Bertone took 6.2 inches out of its platform to create the Giulia Sprint GT; Pininfarina's Giulietta-based Giulia Spider continued rather longer until the new car took over in 1966, with the Sprint GT chassis shortened a further 3.9 inches. The name Duetto was the product of a Europe-wide competition.

The styling theme, which Pininfarina carried forward from an earlier show car, was the principle of oval cross sections decreasing towards each end, with a shallow central scoop running along most of the side of the car. In fact the name didn't last long in Alfa terminology as the 1750 (106 cu.in) engine was introduced a year later and the Duetto became simply a 1750 Spider Veloce. But most people continued to call the car Duetto until the shapely tail was cut short during 1970 – Pininfarina had made some 15,000 cars by then.

Power outputs generally matched those of the equivalent Sprint GT or GTV. In 97 cu.in form, the Alfa engine gave 109 bhp, enough for a maximum speed of 111 mph. It was a good all-round performer. When the Giulia changed into the 106 cu.in, the 108 cu.in GTV engine with 122 bhp powered the Spider to 118 mph. The short-tail 1750 became the 131 bhp Spider 2000 in 1971, but it was still possible to get 97 cu.in and even, for a time, 79 cu.in versions.

The next significant change came in 1983 with a new full width rubber front bumper shaped around the lower half of a new Alfa shield. A large rubber molding was attached to the rear panel, with an aerodynamic lip matching the front chin-spoiler; American market bumpers were 2 inches longer. For 1986, a skirt was added along the sills, finally destroying the original oval section, and a more

412-413 Pininfarina's delightful Duetto shape lasted for 27 years with no major change.

pronounced spoiler was added under the front bumper. By this time, the 1600 still had 104 bhp and the 2000, with fuel injection, gave 128 bhp or 117 bhp to American regulations.

The final change came in 1990 with car colored soft bumpers and a smoother rounder tail. With the familiar scoop along the sides, it looked more like the original Duetto than any of its interim versions. It was finally phased out when it became uneconomical to develop the old engine for modern emission regulations.

TECHNICAL DESCRIPTION OF THE ALFA ROMEO DUETTO (1750 SPIDER)	
YEARS OF PRODUCTION	1966-1967 (1967-1971)
MODELS	SPORTS 2-SEATER
ENGINE	FRONT-MOUNTED IN-LINE 4
BORE X STROKE, CAPACITY	3 X 3.2 INCHES, (3.1 X 3.4) 95 CU.IN (108)
VALVEGEAR	TWIN OVERHEAD CAMSHAFTS
FUEL SYSTEM	TWO WEBER TWIN-CHOKE CARBURETORS
POWER	109 BHP (122) AT 6000 RPM (5500)
TRANSMISSION	5-SPEED
BODY/CHASSIS	STEEL MONOCOQUE
SUSPENSION	FRONT, WISHBONES AND COILS
	REAR, LIVE AXLE, RADIUS ARMS, A-BRACKET, COIL SPRINGS
TIRES/WHEELS	155 X 15 ON 4.5 IN STEEL WHEELS
WHEELBASE, TRACK (F), TRACK(R)	88 X 51.5 X 50 INCHES
LENGTH, WIDTH, HEIGHT	169 X 64 X 51 INCHES
MAX SPEED	111 MPH (118)
WHERE BUILT	TURIN, ITALY

1971 - 1980

SAFETY LEGISLATION AND EMISSIONS CHANGE PERFORMANCE ATTITUDES

The Seventies were expected to continue the expansion of the Sixties, but a world fuel crisis and legislation had other ideas. The Arab-Israeli war of October 1973 restricted fuel supplies and increased costs throughout the world; almost overnight big-engined cars lost credibility and prices of old classic ones fell drastically. America brought in the 55 mph limit to save fuel in 1974. There was a near-repeat when the Shah of Persia was deposed in 1979, but by then manufacturers were working hard to improve efficiency of cars and engines.

Legislation came from America in two forms. Los Angeles air pollution was blamed on the motor car, resulting in lead free fuel and catalytic converters in California from 1975. The American performance market was instantly stifled and all manufacturers started making European-style compacts. There were a few big-engined cars like the 500 cu.in Cadillac Fleetwood or the 457 cu.in Lincoln Continental but they could only generate 200 bhp and had nothing to commend their appearance either. Apart from a few muscle car developments

from the previous decade, hardly a classic emerged from the USA after 1972 – all looks and no go.

Then Nader's safety crusade of the Sixties resulted in a steady flow of crash-test regulations and the convertible was almost banned; US manufacturers were certainly expecting it and stopped designing roadsters. Even European makers stopped making soft top cars for the US, as America had long been their biggest market. However, the ban never came in and convertibles resumed their popularity in the early Eighties.

THE HOT HATCHES

In small cars the Mini influence was spreading, not just for its front wheel drive but also for its transverse engine position. It also bred the supermini, the next size up with cars like the Renault 5 (1972), Ford Fiesta (1976) and the Autobianchi A112 (1969) which acted as the prototype for the Fiat 127 (1971) – all 3-door hatchbacks. The front-wheel-drive theme was developed further in the next size up of which BMC's own 1100/1300 series had been the forerunners from the early Sixties – a little more space and a five-door option. The Simca 1100 (1967) and the Fiat 128 (1969) were in the same mold. But what really made the hatchback breed was the Volkswagen Golf which arrived in 1974. Ford were slow to follow; the rear-drive Mk.2 Escort ran from 1975-80 and it was 1980 before the front-drive Mk.3 arrived.

None of these small cars were classics in their standard forms, but the faster models have already generated a classic following. Front wheel drive cars had such good roadholding that they could easily handle more power, so a mini muscle-car revolution took place. First away was the VW Golf GTI, a year after the standard Golf launch, with a 96 cu.in fuel-injected 110 bhp 'four'.

Ford's XR3 Escort came in 1980 with 96 bhp. Renault brought the 5 into line with the R5 Alpine or Gordini with 85 cu.in and 93 bhp, and added a 5 Turbo in 1979 with the turbocharged 85 cu.in engine mounted in the middle and now producing 160 bhp. This was another homologation special developed for rallying.

Some retained rear wheel drive for their superminis, though. Vauxhall had added the Chevette as their supermini in 1975, but produced a limited run of Chevette HS2300s in 1979 with special 16-valve heads for rallying. Talbot took a different route for the Sunbeam and acquired 134 cu.in Lotus 16-valve engines for the Sunbeam-Lotus which was another rallying success; the Talbot had been designed under Chrysler ownership but Peugeot took over in 1978.

Fiat took a slightly different view. They left International rallying to sports machinery, like the 124 Spider and Lancia Stratos, or the 131 Abarth Rally (1976), so stayed out of the mini-muscle horsepower race and provided extra style instead. While the 128 was available with 67 and 79 cu.in engines, they added a 3-door fastback, the 128 coupe sport, on a shortened platform from 1971-1975 and changed it in 1975 for the 3P (tre porte) to make a hatch-back. Calling in Bertone for a Spider version again, they finished up with the mid-engined X1/9.

Meanwhile Alfa-Romeo opened a new plant in southern Italy to create the remarkable Alfasud, Alfa's first front wheel drive car, which used a flat-four engine of 72 cu.in from 1971. Although the Alfasud would be enlarged to 91.5 cu.in, the model that appealed was the Alfasud Sprint, a fastback 2+2 designed by ItalDesign of which over 100,000 would be built.

Actually, VW had taken a leaf out of the Italian book in producing the Golf-based 3-door fastback Scirocco at the same time (1974) as the standard car; both the Golf and Scirocco were also shaped by ItalDesign.

The arrival of all these hot hatches and coupe derivatives virtually killed the youth sports-car market. They had all the convenience of a family four-seater with plenty of performance; they were far more practical and insurable than an open sports car.

414-415 Star personalization – the overstated grille on Presley's 1973 Cadillac Fleetwood is not quite the way Cadillac built it.

1971 - 1980

FAMILY SEDAN COUPES

Racing and rallying continued to produce sporting and desirable versions of the family sedans. Triumph's 1965 1300 front-wheel-drive car gradually evolved into the rear-drive Dolomite with the 113 cu.in overhead cam slant-four engine that had been used for the 1971 Saab 99; the Dolomite Sprint emerged in 1973 with a 16-valve 122 cu.in 127 bhp version and was highly successful in British sedan car racing.

Vauxhall's Firenza coupe 122 cu.in superseded the Viva GT in 1970 to join the Capri market. The 1972 Firenza Sport SL came with a 140 cu.in version of the belt driven ohc 'four'. Under the guiding hand of tuning expert Bill Blydenstein, this had become a successful sedan racer; lessons learnt were carried through to a new attractive Firenza coupe for 1974. This 'droop-snoot' car had a full width flat front panel with headlights set behind plastic and a deep air-dam; a tuned 131 bhp 140 cu.in was attached to a ZF 5-speed box and sports suspension was fitted. Sadly, it became a limited edition special as Vauxhall only produced 204. The balance of the aerodynamic fronts were used up on 197 Sportshatch models based on the Magnum (big Viva) 2300 estates in 1975 – an equally rare classic.

Until General Motors' first world car arrived in 1974 as the Chevette, Kadett (1976) or Gemini, Opel still had a fair amount of autonomy and were free to develop their own Capri rival; the Manta coupe arrived in late 1970 as a fastback version of the Ascona using 72, 115 cu.in 4-cylinder engines. A Rallye version was available, the SR and the GTE following later. Evolutions of the Ascona and Manta continued for many years.

In 1981 the homologation special Manta 400 arrived with 144 bhp from 146 cu.in; the same specification was available in the Ascona 400 which also had its share of rallying success. Like the Capris and Cortinas, the top end of the Ascona and Manta ranges have their classic following.

Fiat joined the same market through Lancia which they had taken over in 1969. The Lancia Beta came in late 1972 as a fastback sedan using versions of the twin-cam Fiat 125 engine mounted transversely on top of a 5-speed gearbox co-developed with Citroen. The coupe version followed in 1973 on a shortened platform with notchback styling similar to the Fulvia coupe, while 1975 saw the Spider and the High Performance Estate (HPE). The Lancia Gamma, a longer Beta with the 122 cu.in and a further enlarged 146 cu.in engines, came in 1976 using similar styles to those of the Beta, a fast-back sedan and an elegant notch-back coupe. The Beta was a good car in its day, but they all suffered badly from rust due largely to Fiat's use of second-rate steel at the time, so there may not be many still in existence.

Alfa Romeo had phased out the Giulia with the restyled 1750 in 1968 and made it into the 2000 for 1971; the Alfetta came in 1972 with the 1750 engine, but with a rear-mounted gearbox and de Dion rear suspension.

The important derivative was the Bertone-styled Alfetta GT which arrived in 1974 with the 109 cu.in 4-cylinder. By 1977, this had become the 2000GTV finally replacing the Giulia-based GT. When the Alfa 6 came out in 1979 with a new 152 cu.in V-6 engine, this provided an appropriate power plant for the 2000GTV to create the GTV6 2.5 – the last classic sporting Alfa Romeo before Fiat took over the company in 1986.

Toyota continued to produce the Celica as a Carina coupe with 97 cu.in engines, and added a lift-back. Toyota twin-cam engines had dominated formula 3 in this period and a 122 cu.in version of this engine became an option in the new 1977 range.

BIG SEDANS AND COUPES

A few large sedans deserve classic status in their own right, but the coupes that were derived from the rest have also become classics. Typical of classic sedans were the Bristol 411, Aston Martin Lagonda, Ferrari 400, Rover SD1 and Jaguar XJC, while such coupes as the Jaguar XJS, BMW 3.0CS, Fiat 130 all came from less appealing sedan models.

Bristol had moved on from the first Chrysler-engined 407, through the 408 (1963) with mild body differences and improved headroom, the 409 (1965), and the 410 (1967) before the 411 arrived in 1969 with radial tires and its Chrysler engine up to 383 cu.in. The 411 moved through five series from 1969-77 with the Series III (1972) notable for its headlights set within the grille.

The first major change of shape since the 406 came with the 412 convertible in 1975; the body design by Zagato was an enlarged version of the Pininfarina-styled Beta Spider which Zagato were building for Lancia at the time. It had the same style of targa-roof and the same half hard-top at the rear, which could be replaced for summer use with a soft-top, but the B-pillar carried a small window for rear passengers. It was very much a car for all seasons like the Triumph Stag. A turbocharged version came in 1980 as the 412 Beaufighter. Meanwhile Bristol made a major change to their sedans as well when the fast-back 603 replaced the last of the 411s in 1977; this gave way to the bodily similar Brittania and turbocharged Brigand in 1982. Bristol has always been a small company evolving their cars by steady

416-417 Beta Monte Carlo (Scorpion in USA) was Lancia's equivalent to the mid-engined Fiat X1/9 and was later used as the basis for the 037 rally car of the early Eighties.

development; they accomplished a lot in the Seventies.

Aston Martin had been renowned for their high-speed grand tourers from the DB2 onwards; the Lagonda sedans based on that were highly regarded, but four-door versions of the DB4 and DBS Aston Martin under the Lagonda name were less successful. The DB4-based Rapide was also styled by Touring, but only 55 were made from 1961-64 as they were too expensive to make and upset production of the DB4. When a 4-door version of the DBS V-8 finally went into production in 1974 as the V8 Lagonda, the company was going through a change of ownership and only seven of this desirable sedan were built.

Aston Martin's new owners immediately set about creating a new Lagonda, similar underneath to the Aston Martin V-8, but with completely new razor-edged body styling by William Towns; inside were advanced digital instrumentation and touch-sensitive switchgear. Launched in 1976, it was eventually put into production in 1978. Fuel injection replaced the downdraft Weber carburetors in 1986 and the instrumentation was changed to TV screens in 1984. When the body's razor edges were rounded off and a new front was added in 1987, the instruments were changed again to a liquid crystal display; this was the final and best interpretation of the Lagonda. While the Lagonda does not have as much classic appeal as the equivalent Aston Martin, it has very much the same character for considerably less money.

There might have been another big 4-door sedan in the Monica, an Anglo-French project that was to use big Chrysler V-8s in a space-frame chassis under bodywork resembling the Ferrari 365GT4. The two parties were Jean Tastevin of the French railway company CFPM and Chris Lawrence, an engineer well known in the Morgan racing world. Sadly, production never really got under way after various motor show launches, but a number of prototypes were built and tested by the press. If you find one, it is worth keeping, as it was an excellent concept.

Another to use Chrysler engines in low volume production runs was Peter Monteverdi in Switzerland. The first road-car, the High Speed , was launched in 1967 using a 439 cu.in V-8 (or the 427 cu.in Hemi) in a steel frame with Frua building the bodies to Monteverdi's design. The car was so well received that Monteverdi had to find another coachbuilder who could produce more cars. Frua claimed the shape was his, so Monteverdi had to redesign it in 1969 for Fissore to build. The 375S 2+2, 375L 4-seater, 375C convertible (also Palm Beach cabriolet) and a 4-door Limousine (375/4) followed from 1970-75. They were well-built high-class cars, very much in the style of Jensen for whom Monteverdi was the Swiss importer. He also built a handful of the mid-engined Hai 450SS using the Chrysler Hemi engine.

1971 - 1980

Ferrari had originally joined the 4-seater sedan car market with the 330GT 2+2 in 1963 and followed this with the bigger-engined 365GT 2+2 in 1967; these were semi fastback cars with limited rear headroom. Pininfarina produced considerably more headroom for the more formal 365GT4 2+2 in 1972, but only 470 were built before the 292 cu.in 400 appeared in 1975 – the first Ferrari to be sold with automatic transmission, manual optional. It stayed in production for 10 years before being replaced by the 412 in 1985.

Rover may not naturally follow Ferrari in classic thinking, but the 1976 Rover SD1 was quite deliberately styled to look like a 4-door Ferrari Daytona, and successfully too. Four and six-cylinder versions were sold, but the only one with classic pretensions was the 3500 which used the Rover aluminium V-8 engine with 157 bhp. Fuel injection was added to give 193 bhp to the 1982 3500 Vitesse, which was the basis for a successful racing sedan.

Jaguar's coupe based on the Series 2 XJ6 eventually came out in 1975 after a 1973 launch. In XJ6C and XJ12C (XK 256 cu.in 'six' and 323 cu.in V-12) forms, the coupe used the sedan wheelbase, but with only two doors, and the side windows dropped down fully to give a pillarless appearance. By 1977

production had stopped after 6505 XJ6C and only 1873 XJ12C; it wasn't the easiest of cars to produce to Jaguar's high standards of quietness, but it was always destined to be a classic Jaguar.

The XJS V-12 had also been launched in 1975 just as the XJC started production and the V-12 E-type stopped. On a shortened XJ6 platform, it was better suited to the 2+2 GT market than was the coupe, but it was never regarded as a replacement for the E-type. The XJS would continue through until the arrival of the XK8 in 1996. Along the way came the coupe-cabriolet in 1983, together with the option of the 219 cu.in twin-cam AJ6 engine; the true cabriolet followed in 1988, while the engine sizes were increased to 244 cu.in (AJ6) and 366 cu.in (V-12) in 1991. The XJS had all the attributes of a classic car but lacked the elegance of the big sedans or the style of the E-type; the wide headlights ruined the appearance of the front – the American version with twin round lamps was better – and the rear sail-panel with a near vertical rear window may look good on a Dino, but it is clumsy on the XJS. The notchback cabriolet and convertible looked much better and the estate conversion by Lynx was the most elegant of all bodies seen on the XJS.

Fiat took a similar route into the big coupe market in 1971 with the graceful Pininfarina 2-door version of

the Fiat 130, which had been an odd mixture of an ugly body concealing a nice engine (176 cu.in V-6 increased later to 195 cu.in) and good all-round independent suspension; on the same wheelbase as the sedan, the coupe was a spacious four-seater with the elegant lines of a Ferrari. However only 4500 were built between 1971 and 1977.

De Tomaso continued the technical collaboration with Ford and used the 347 cu.in V-8 in the front-engined 1970 Deauville 4-door, and added the Longchamp 2-door on a shortened wheelbase in 1972, both designed by Tom Tjaarda at Ghia. By this time de Tomaso had owned Ghia from 1967 and had also taken over Vignale in 1969 for its production space. Ghia had also produced the styling for the 1968 Iso Fidia 4-door sedan, but Iso went to Bertone for the 1969 Lele 2+2; both cars started with Chevrolet engines but used Ford 347 cu.in by 1973.

In Germany, Mercedes and BMW also produced coupe versions of their big sedans. BMW had started their new coupe range with the 2800CS in 1968. In 1971 they changed the numbering system and

418-419 This 1980 Porsche 911SC Targa has borrowed the whale-tale wing from a Turbo.

brought in the 182 cu.in 3.0CS, CSi and CSL – Coupe Sport with injection or lightness from aluminium panels. A 2500CS was added in 1974 as an economy model. BMW changed the numbering system again in 1972 with the introduction of the 5-series sedans; the 3-series were added in 1975 and 1976 saw the latest coupe, the 6-series, in 630CS/CSi and 633CSi forms; with its wheelbase 3.5 inches longer than the 5-series it was a comfortable 4-seater.

Mercedes had continued the 230SL theme through to the 280SL which ceased in 1971. Meanwhile the new generation Mercedes had been launched in 1968 and had included the 300SEL 6.3. When a new 213 cu.in V-8 was announced in 1971 it became an option for the 280SE/SEL but, more importantly it powered the new 350SL followed within the same year by the 14 inches longer SLC to give fixed head seating for four – perhaps the nicest of the SL range. At last the sporting Mercedes had an engine worthy of its looks and roadholding to match with a redesigned rear suspension. The 450SL and SLC were added in 1973 with an economy 280SL and SLC twin-cam six-cylinder

in 1974; a rather less economical 450SLC 5.0 joined the range in 1977 with 240 bhp. The 450SLC had a resounding success in the 18,500 miles Round South America Rally in 1978 taking the first two places and a 450SL 5.0 took second place in the 1979 Safari rally. For 1980, the range was rationalized with a 204 bhp 231 cu.in V-8 and a 231 bhp 305 cu.in V-8 to produce 380SL and 500SL. The SLC was dropped in favor of the 380 and 500SEC in 1981, an elegant two-door S-class with pillarless side windows.

The American muscle car era was to continue through to 1973. Ford took the Mustang on through Mach 1 and Boss 302 and 429, with the final fling being the 1971 335 bhp Boss 351. Mustang II came in 1974 as a four-seat coupe with just 88 and 100 bhp options; even the 1976 305 cu.in engine only produced 134 bhp. The Pontiac Judge of 1970 was the ultimate GTO with its plastic molded front end, rev counter on the back of the bonnet, a wing on the tail and a 400 cu.in V-8 with 366 bhp. By 1971 the power was on the way down as GM put all its cars onto low-octane fuel in preparation for the arrival of unleaded petrol.

The real GTs

By now anyone could afford a GT as the majority were just sedans with style. But there were still a handful of true Grand Touring 2+2 built for that sole purpose. Porsche continued to develop the 911 and brought out the first of the Turbos in 1975 complete with wide rear wheels and a big wing at the back; by 1977 the 260 bhp 183 cu.in had been exchanged for a 300 bhp 201 cu.in and the car could exceed 155 mph.

In 1971 Porsche had actually thought of replacing the 911 with a new front-engined four-seater, the 928, using a big 274 cu.in V-8 with an automatic transmission option to satisfy the American market. Fortunately the 911 was never replaced and the 928 found its own niche when it finally arrived in 1977; it had been delayed while Porsche decided to put the 924 into production following the withdrawal of VW-Audi from that project.

Porsche's 928 market was then occupied by the Ferrari 400 and the various large sedan coupes mentioned above, plus Aston Martin. While the DB6 Mk.II carried on into 1970, the DBSV-8 was in full production with its 315 bhp 323 cu.in V-8 using fuel injection. The Vantage version with 375 bhp and downdraft Weber carburetors came in 1977, and the

convertible Volante followed a year later.

A worthy newcomer to this scene was the Bitter CD, which had started life as an Opel styling exercise for the 1969 Frankfurt Show; it was based on a short wheelbase version of the Opel Diplomat which used a 232 cu.in Chevrolet V-8 and had de Dion rear suspension. The concept was taken over by former Opel racer, Erich Bitter, who launched the CD (Coupe Diplomat) as a 2+2 in 1973; Baur of Stuttgart built the elegant fast-back bodies. Bitter continued his Opel association and introduced the Bitter SC2 (Senator Coupe) in 1979 using the 183 cu.in engine from the Senator with the 4WD option. A convertible SC2 followed in 1981 and a 231 cu.in option in 1983. Alfa Romeo too put a toe in the exclusive coupe market with the Montreal which had started as Bertone's show car for the Canadian Expo 67. Alfa Romeo took it over and inserted a detuned version of the engine which had powered the company's sports racing Tipo 33, a 158 cu.in all aluminium 4-cam V-8 coupled to a ZF gearbox. It was finally launched in 1971 but fell victim to the 1973 fuel crisis. Lamborghini's striking 4-seater Espada continued through from 1968 to 1978, but they replaced the Islero with the 2+2 Jarama (Bertone) using a shortened Espada platform which now used sheet steel rather than the traditional tubular frames.

These front-engined Lamborghinis are underrated in the classic world; they are mechanically strong but the electrical components can let them down.

The Maserati Mexico, Ghibli and Indy continued through to the Seventies until Citroen's rationalization phased them all out in favor of the Bertone-bodied Khamsin using the 298 cu.in V-8. It was the first front-engined Maserati with independent rear suspension and featured Citroen-style power steering and braking. A practical and good looking 2+2, it was destined for an 8-year production span until de Tomaso's Biturbo took over.

Although Citroen had traditionally produced cars for the people and advanced comfortable sedans, they had ignored the high performance GT market; acquiring access to Maserati technology gave them instant high performance engines and GT market acceptability. Maserati's four-cam V-6 was reduced to 164 cu.in to avoid a steep taxation rise at 170 cu.in and was coupled to Citroen's own gearbox. The rest was pure Citroen with the hydraulic system providing suspension control and power for brakes and steering. It was a remarkable high performance grand tourer with effortlessly quiet cruising ability. Nearly 20,000 were built before Peugeot took over Citroen in 1975 and stopped its production.

THE SPECIALIST SPORTS CARS

Almost any of the limited volume sporting cars has become a classic, although some are more expensive than others. Included here are the two-seater GTs, wherever their engines are situated, and the open two-seaters.

In production numbers, Britain and Italy were probably equal contributors, but Britain made the greater variety. MG continued to produce the MGB and the Midget, but had to add plastic bumpers to both to comply with American regulations in 1974, at which point the Midget became a Mk.III and adopted the 90 cu.in engine from the Triumph Spitfire, the sister company within the Leyland organization. The disappearance of the MGC in 1969 had left a performance gap in the range until the 1972 arrival of the MGB GTV-8; Rover's 213 cu.in V-8 was squeezed into the engine compartment and the aged MGB had instant 125 mph performance. Despite Rover being part of the same group, politics intervened and the V-8 was withdrawn when the Rover SD1 was launched in 1976, so only 2591 GTV-8s were produced. The car did of course make a welcome return in 1992 as the RV8, using new bodyshells from British Motor Heritage; this

time it was a roadster.

Triumph themselves ran the TR6 through until 1976 in both PI (Petrol Injection) form and with carburetors plus rubber bumpers for the US. The various Leyland sports models were all reaching the end of their lives, so the decision was taken to produce a single corporate sports car with the USA remaining the prime market. In the early Seventies it was feared that convertibles would succumb to American roll-over laws, so the TR7 was designed as a monocoque coupe and would use the 122 cu.in 4-cylinder already used in the Dolomite and the Saab. The new car arrived in January 1975 in the USA, but the home market had to wait until May 1976. Eventually the fears of a convertible ban went away and a TR7 convertible came out in 1979. The last of 112,375 TR7s emerged in late 1981.

Part of the corporate strategy had been to build a TR8, using the Rover V-8 in a TR7 with a bonnet bulge and wider tires. Leyland's problems delayed its arrival until 1979 in America only where it had fuel injection for California and carburetors in the other states. The convertible version virtually replaced the coupe at the end of that year. Then came the second OPEC petrol price rise and big engines suddenly lost their appeal; coupled with an adverse exchange rate, this killed the

profitability of the US market and the TR8 ceased in early 1981 after only 2700 had been built, none of them for the home market.

The TR7 styling was not its strong point. It was such a wedge shape that the driver couldn't see anything in front of the screen; separate federal bumpers and the strange crease between the wheels didn't improve its looks – the convertible was far better balanced. It was certainly a modern car in its general behavior but it was a major departure from the high performance TR5 and TR6 that had preceded it. The TR8 was intended to rectify that but market and management combined to prevent that happening.

The TR7 wasn't the only British sports car to suffer from relying too much on the US market. The 1970 Jensen-Healey was supposed to be the replacement for the big Healey 3000 which could no longer pass crash regulations. Jensen were still making the Chrysler-engined Interceptor in its various forms including a convertible and the FF 4WD model. They had also been building the big Healey for British Leyland. Teaming up with Donald Healey to produce a new car was a mutually convenient solution, particularly as Jensen was now largely owned by the Healey's biggest American importer, Kjell Qvale.

Donald Healey already had the basis of a new car on the stocks using Vauxhall running gear under a neat and comfortable two-seater body. By the time of the 1972 announcement, the engine had changed to Lotus' 4-valve 122 cu.in, which had started as a development of the 45 degree slant-four Vauxhall engine, and the gearbox came from Chrysler. It was a nice car but the build quality was not good enough and the engine was unreliable. Most of its problems were cured after the first 800 or so cars with the Mk.2 from August 1973. A 5-speed Getrag box replaced the Chrysler 4-speed in 1974 and a hatch-back Jensen GT was added to the range in July 1975. Not helped by the early engine problems, US sales of the Jensen Healey had not been as good as planned, and there were too many engineering projects being financed as well; in May 1976 Jensen ceased production. Over the four years, 10,926 Jensen Healeys were sold (7709 USA, 1914 UK and 830 other exports), of which 473 were GTs (202 UK). A sad end to a promising design, but a classic nevertheless.

The main beneficiary of the Jensen project was Lotus, for whom Jensen had effectively developed their engine. They had also learnt from their own work with the 1969 racing Lotus 62, outwardly a Europa, using the 122 cu.in engine which was then still called

420-421 Lotus Esprit came in S2 form in 1978 with this new air-dam and rear valance and a change of alloy wheels.

1971 - 1980

the LV (Lotus-Vauxhall) 240. The Europa had been given an S2 designation in 1968, but the Renault engine was replaced by the Lotus twin-cam in 1971. The first production Lotus to use the ex-Jensen 122 cu.in engine was the 1974 Elite, followed in quick succession by the Eclat (1975) and the first of the long-running Esprit (1976). Before these were all given the 134 cu.in version in 1980-1981, Lotus had supplied this engine for the Sunbeam Lotus rally car. If you have an early Jensen-Healey with engine problems, find a Lotus dealer.

The British sports car industry was beset by problems through the Seventies. The Welsh Gilbern had started in 1960 as a fiberglass bodied coupe powered by the BMC A-series engine, followed by the B-series MGA and MGB engines.

A new body accompanied the 1966 Genie which came with Ford V-6 power. The similar Invader came in 1969, with a Mark II and an estate car following in 1971. By then the company ownership had changed several times and the doors were closed in 1973.

Ginetta fared rather better. Like Gilbern and TVR they used a space-frame chassis with fiberglass bodywork. They had made their name with the little road sports racing G4 powered by Ford Anglia 60 and from 1964 Cortina 91.5 cu.in. Over 500 were built between 1961-69; a later version appeared from 1981-84, and it reappeared with independent rear suspension as the G27 in 1985. It is again being made today by subsequent owners of the company. Their next popular road car was the G15 which ran from 1968 to 1974; using the rear-engined 53 cu.in Hillman Imp power train, over 800 were made. TVR continued to develop their models at a remarkable rate of progress despite still only selling around 1000 per year. A heavily revised and stronger chassis came in 1972 with a new longer body to create the M-series for (Ford) 1600M, (Triumph) 2500M and (Ford V-6) 3000M range. A turbocharged version of the 3000M came in 1975, the hatchback Taimar in 1976 and a convertible in 1978. Then 1980 saw the launch of the new TVR Tasmin, part of the story of the next decade.

AC had continued to produce variations on the Cobra theme throughout the Sixties but had little luck with the Frua-bodied AC 428, which had been launched in 1965 as a convertible and 1966 as a coupe. The bodies were built in Italy and Frua had problems producing the required quantity. Then came the 1973 fuel crisis and the market disappeared as did the 428 after only 80 had been built – 29 coupes and 51 convertibles. AC's bread-and-butter was in

making three-wheeled cars for disabled motorists, so the early failure of the 428 was not a major setback. However, seeking an alternative car to make, they made a move into the modern world of mid-engined sports cars with the ME3000. Starting with the privately designed mid-engined prototype Diablo with an Austin Maxi 106 cu.in engine, AC mounted a Ford V-6 transversely behind the driver and Hewland built a special gearbox. The result was a nice looking car but it took a long time to get into production and the first car was finally delivered in 1979; only 82 were made before the design was sold to a Scottish company who built another 30.
A rare classic that should have lasted longer.

Meanwhile in Italy, mid-engined sports machinery was very much in fashion. Fiat made a bigger Fiat X1/9 in the form of the Lancia Beta Monte Carlo, which was launched in 1975, the ex-125 engine increased to 121 cu.in, and placed behind the driver. Also mid-engined, the Lancia Stratos was built for rallying and won the World Championship in 1974-76; with the Ferrari Dino 246 power-train mounted in a space-frame chassis under Bertone bodywork, some 500 were produced from 1972 to 1974. The Stratos ceded the task of Fiat's rallying flagship to the 131 Fiat-Abarth, but it was a development of the Monte Carlo that was to take over from that in the Eighties.

From Modena, Ferrari further developed the Dino 246GT theme with the 308GT4 in 1974 as a Bertone-bodied 2+2 using a 183 cu.in V-8. The 246GT replacement came with the 308GTB in 1975, followed

by GTS (1977) and fuel injection versions in 1980. The final variation came in 1982 with the 4-valve head (QV) versions before the 328 came in 1985. Not to be outdone by Lamborghini and Maserati, Ferrari followed the mid-engined route with the Daytona replacement, the 365GT4/BB. This used a flat-12 with belt-driven camshafts and 387 were built from 1973-76 before the BB512 arrived with a bigger engine.

Lamborghini had produced around 750 Miuras before the Countach arrived in 1973; this now used the 244 cu.in V-12 mounted longitudinally under another breathtaking Bertone body. In various forms it would last for 16 years until the Diablo arrived in 1990. They also produce the little Lamborghini, the mid-engined Urraco, using a transverse V-8 to allow room for +2 seating; the P250 (152 cu.in) and the P300 (183 cu.in) accounted for 700 cars from 1972-1979.

Maserati's first mid-engined road car was the 1971 Bora, using the regular 298 cu.in V-8 in a pressed steel chassis with bodywork by ItalDesign. It was followed a year later by the outwardly similar Merak; with a 183 cu.in version of the Citroen SM V-6 in the back, there was just enough space for two small rear seats. Like the

Khamsin, this featured Citroen power brakes. Although Citroen withdrew from Maserati and De Tomaso took over in 1975, these models would continue until the end of the decade.

The Maserati engine and Citroen gearbox was also seen in the back of the Ligier JS2, a fiberglass-bodied two-seater GT. Former French rugby player Guy Ligier had driven in Formula One but expanded his construction company to produce road cars.

The 1969 JS1 (named after Jo Schlesser) was a competition coupe with a 109 cu.in Cosworth FVC, but the JS2 which emerged in 1971 initially used a 158 cu.in Ford V-6 coupled to a Citroen SM after gearbox, the following year it had the 158 cu.in SM engine. This then grew to the Merak's 183 cu.in capacity for 1974 by which time Ligier was assembling the SMs for Citroen. Around 300 JS2 were made.

France's main constructor of fiberglass coupes was still Alpine who continued to make the A110 until 1977 using Renault 79 and 97 cu.in engines. They added the A310 to the range in 1971 to create a 2+2 using basically the same chassis and 97 cu.in running gear. The engine was still mounted behind the axle like

the Porsche 911. When Renault introduced the R30, the A310 was able to adopt the 164 cu.in V-6 package from 1980 to give the car a performance more suited to its style.

Having taken over Rene Bonnet and produced the Ford-powered M530, Matra formed an association with Chrysler at the end of 1969. In 1973, this resulted in the Matra-Simca Bagheera, a neat little mid-engined fiberglass coupe, powered by an 84 bhp Simca 79 cu.in engine; a notable feature was three seats across the car in a total width of 68 inches. Power rose to 90 bhp when the 88 cu.in Simca engine became available. Peugeot-Citroen took over Chrysler Europe in 1979, so the Bagheera became the 2-seater Talbot Murena using the 97 cu.in Talbot engine, which could produce up to 120 bhp.

In Germany, the only low volume manufacturer was Porsche who introduced the 924 in 1976. Originally an Audi-VW project, the 2+2 924 was powered by a 122 cu.in single cam four-cylinder; the aftermath of the 1973 fuel crisis and a change of VW management in 1975 caused them to cancel the car. Porsche continued with it, developing it through Turbo and Carrera GT into the 1981 944. While the rest of the German coupes were derived from sedans, the exception was to be the mid-engined BMW M1, derived from BMW's 1972 Munich Olympics show car; it finally arrived in 1978, eventually being built by ItalDesign – a separate story.

In Japan Mazda continued their work on the twin-rotor Wankel-powered cars and the 110S coupe

(Cosmo) stayed in production until 1972. Wankel engines, increased to a nominal 140 cu.in, powered the top end of the various model ranges – RX-2 on the Capella 616 (1970), RX-3 on the Grand Familia 808 (1971), RX-4 on the Luce 929 (1972) and RX-5 on the Cosmo 121(1975). But the next classic was the RX-7, or Savanna coupe, which arrived in 1978 with very attractive fast-back lines; the 140 cu.in Wankel produced 130 bhp for Japan but 110-115 bhp for the more emission conscious markets.
In 1983, the turbocharged fuel injected version gave 165 bhp and a serious performance increase.

The first RX-7 came to an end in 1985 with nearly half a million cars produced.

The RX-7 was clearly aimed at the Datsun 240Z which was still going well in the early Seventies, but increasing luxury and stifled power made its successors, the 260Z (1974) and 280Z (1975), rather less sporting – there were also 2+2 versions. The 280ZX (1978) was the first major revision with a new body and independent rear suspension but it was still slower than the original 240Z; this was only rectified when a turbocharger option was added in 1981.

And America's sports car? The Corvette's basic body style remained the same throughout the Seventies, but the chrome bumpers disappeared in favor of a soft front end in 1973 and 1975 was the last year for the roadster.

Power figures are a little confusing as the previous claims had been for gross bhp, but these were net figures from 1973; the combination of emission controls and honesty made the contrast even greater. In 1970, the small block 350 gave 300-370 bhp and the 427 had 390 bhp (the 1969 options had included a high compression 430 bhp). Solid valve lifter engines disappeared for 1973 and the 454 was down to 275 bhp. By 1975 there was just the 350 cu.in engine with 165 bhp or 205 bhp with the optional transistorised ignition – half the power of the real Corvettes. That was the story of the Seventies, safety and emission legislation made a big impact in America, but the rest of the world was not far behind in accepting that high performance had become anti-social.

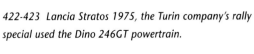

422-423 Lancia Stratos 1975, the Turin company's rally special used the Dino 246GT powertrain.

Maserati Bora

424-425 *First shown at Turin 1971, the Bora was the star of the show.*

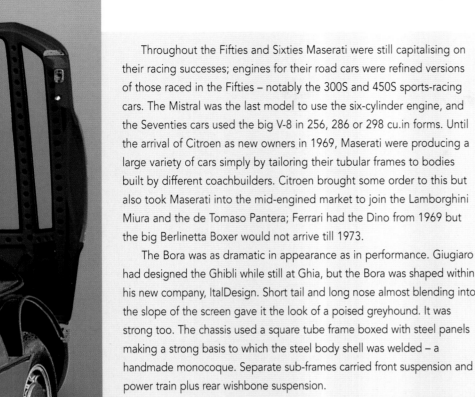

Throughout the Fifties and Sixties Maserati were still capitalising on their racing successes; engines for their road cars were refined versions of those raced in the Fifties – notably the 300S and 450S sports-racing cars. The Mistral was the last model to use the six-cylinder engine, and the Seventies cars used the big V-8 in 256, 286 or 298 cu.in forms. Until the arrival of Citroen as new owners in 1969, Maserati were producing a large variety of cars simply by tailoring their tubular frames to bodies built by different coachbuilders. Citroen brought some order to this but also took Maserati into the mid-engined market to join the Lamborghini Miura and the de Tomaso Pantera; Ferrari had the Dino from 1969 but the big Berlinetta Boxer would not arrive till 1973.

The Bora was as dramatic in appearance as in performance. Giugiaro had designed the Ghibli while still at Ghia, but the Bora was shaped within his new company, ItalDesign. Short tail and long nose almost blending into the slope of the screen gave it the look of a poised greyhound. It was strong too. The chassis used a square tube frame boxed with steel panels making a strong basis to which the steel body shell was welded – a handmade monocoque. Separate sub-frames carried front suspension and power train plus rear wishbone suspension.

The engine was the all-aluminium 286 cu.in V-8 with four downdraft Weber carburetors developing 310 bhp. This was mated to a 5-speed transaxle from ZF, who also supplied the rack and pinion steering. A Citroen touch came with a hydraulic pressure accumulators to power the pop-up headlights, pedal box adjustment, seat vertical movement and the brakes – the least appropriate feature of such a muscle car. There was more luggage space than in most mid-engined cars, because the spare wheel was carried in a cradle above the gearbox, allowing the front compartment to take a number of cases.

It was reasonably quiet too, as the vertical rear window is double-glazed, but very firm suspension transmitted a lot of road noise on coarse surfaces. Some details let it down though; optional air conditioning was poor, headlights did not match the performance, the engine compartment got covered in road dirt and the fuel consumption was heavy.

But the car was designed for performance and it had plenty. It would reach 60 mph in 6.5 seconds, 100 mph in under 15 seconds and go on to a maximum speed around 160 mph. It was well received in the market place and nearly 500 would leave the Modena factory over the next seven years, the later ones with 298 cu.in engines.

Despite the change of Maserati ownership from Citroen to de Tomaso in 1975, the Bora and its SM-powered Merak equivalent continued through till 1978 and 1979 respectively. They have been underrated classics.

TECHNICAL DESCRIPTION OF THE MASERATI BORA

YEARS OF PRODUCTION	1971-1978
MODELS	COUPE 2-SEATER
ENGINE	MID-MOUNTED V-8
BORE X STROKE, CAPACITY	3.6 X 3.3 INCHES, 287 CU.IN
VALVEGEAR	FOUR OVERHEAD CAMSHAFTS
FUEL SYSTEM	4 WEBER TWIN-CHOKE CARBURETORS
POWER	310 BHP AT 6000 RPM
TRANSMISSION	5-SPEED
BODY/CHASSIS	STEEL TUBE FRAME, STEEL BODY
SUSPENSION	FRONT, WISHBONES AND COIL SPRINGS
	REAR, WISHBONES AND COIL SPRINGS
TIRES/WHEELS	215/70 X 15 ON 7.5 IN. ALLOY WHEELS
WHEELBASE, TRACK (F), TRACK(R)	102.4 X 58 X 53 INCHES
LENGTH, WIDTH, HEIGHT	171 X 69.6 X 44.5 INCHES
MAX SPEED	160 MPH
WHERE BUILT	MODENA, ITALY

Lamborghini Countach

Ferruccio Lamborghini was born under the sign of Taurus, the bull in the badge. Miura was a breed of fighting bulls; Countach is what the Piedmontese say when a beautiful woman slinks into view – it was what Bertone said when he first saw Marcello Gandini's design in the flesh. Striking though the Countach is to look at, it had much more than just style when the car was first shown at the 1971 Geneva Show. The Miura was still in production, but as the Countach was expected to be on sale a year later, the Miura was phased out over that period. Unfortunately it took another three years to develop, by which time Automobili Ferruccio Lamborghini had been sold to Swiss partners to enable Lamborghini to return to tractors. It was to go into liquidation and be sold twice again before Countach production finished in 1990; Chrysler took over in 1987.

Countach design started with a clean sheet of paper, just retaining the basic Miura principles of a mid-engined supercar. The Miura's ingenious layout had the V-12 mounted transversely with the gearbox behind; the Countach mounted the same engine fore and aft with the

TECHNICAL DESCRIPTION OF THE LAMBORGHINI COUNTACH LP400	
YEARS OF PRODUCTION	1974-1978
MODELS	COUPE 2-SEATER
ENGINE	MID-MOUNTED V-12
BORE X STROKE, CAPACITY	3.2 X 2.4 INCHES, 239 CU.IN
VALVEGEAR	FOUR OVERHEAD CAMSHAFTS
FUEL SYSTEM	SIX WEBER TWIN-CHOKE CARBURETORS
POWER	375 BHP AT 8000 RPM
TRANSMISSION	5-SPEED
BODY/CHASSIS	STEEL TUBE FRAME, ALUMINIUM BODY
SUSPENSION	FRONT, WISHBONES AND COIL SPRINGS
	REAR, WISHBONES AND COIL SPRINGS
TIRES/WHEELS	FRONT, 205/70 X 14 ON 7.5 IN. ALLOYS
	REAR, 215/70 X 14 ON 9.5 IN. ALLOYS
WHEELBASE, TRACK (F), TRACK(R)	96.5 X 59.1 X 59.8 INCHES
LENGTH, WIDTH, HEIGHT	163 X 74.4 X 42.1 INCHES
MAX SPEED	180 MPH
WHERE BUILT	BOLOGNA, ITALY

426-427 *First of the line, this first prototype was shown at Geneva 1971 before development added ducts and scoops; it is the pure shape that Gandini designed.*

428-429 Last of the line, the 1989 Countach S Anniversary celebrated 25 years of the company's vehicle production. Body changes made it the sleekest of all.

gearbox in front, putting the lever very close to the driver. From drop gears a drive-shaft passed through the sump to a crown wheel and pinion within the sump casting; while this raised the overall center of gravity, there were other benefits. The engine for the prototype LP500 had been stretched to 305 cu.in but the production LP400 retained the Miura's 244 cu.in V-12 with 375 bhp.

The Countach was conceived as a limited run supercar to promote Lamborghini technology, so the prototype was built in a labour-intensive fashion with a space-frame and a steel body welded to it adding strength. The reception at Geneva showed that there would be great demand, so the space-frame was strengthened to carry an unstressed aluminium body.

Following GT40 thinking, the Miura had used a sheet steel tub but this was not as stiff as it could have been and it was liable to corrosion. The Countach frame, ideal for low volume, used a large number of steel tubes over the full length of the chassis.

While the beetle-wing doors were retained for production, the original purity of Gandini's lines was lost during development. Aerodynamic tests deepened the nose and scoops and NACA ducts for the rear mounted radiators replaced the grilles behind the doors. Original tire testing had been with low profile Pirelli tires, but these were slow to get into production and the LP400 used 70% profile Michelins. When the low and wide P7 became available, the clean side of the car

was broken by wheel-arch eyebrows and the front ones were blended into an air dam; with revised suspension, the P400S came out in 1978, still with the same power.

The Countach finally received its 305 cu.in engine in 1982; although this was actually a 289 cu.in, the car was labelled LP500S. The increase had been necessary to restore the power lost through emission equipment. The first true power increase came in 1985 with 455 bhp for the LP5000S QV; new four-valve cylinder heads put the carburetors into the center of the vee and the engine was increased to 315 cu.in.

The American version with catalysts and fuel injection gave 425 bhp. Maximum speed had increased from around 180 mph to nearer 190 mph. Over the 4 years of the LP400 only 150 Countach were produced, with 466 of the LP400S from 1978-82. The LP500S saw 323, but the LP5000S QV was the most long-lived and the most popular with 610 produced. In 1989 the company brought out the Anniversary model to celebrate 25 years of car production.

A 25 year badge was mounted on the rear panel. Underneath, it was still the 5000S QV but various changes had been made to the bodywork by Lamborghini. Although the original designer Gandini had no input, the restyling was very successful. It continued in production for one more year.

Over its 16 years, the Countach remained the iconic supercar.

TECHNICAL DESCRIPTION OF THE LAMBORGHINI COUNTACH LP500S QV

YEARS OF PRODUCTION	1985-1990
MODELS	COUPE 2-SEATER
ENGINE	MID-MOUNTED V-12
BORE X STROKE, CAPACITY	3.3 x 2.9 INCHES, 315 CU.IN
VALVEGEAR	FOUR OVERHEAD CAMSHAFTS
FUEL SYSTEM	SIX WEBER TWIN-CHOKE CARBURETORS
POWER	455 BHP AT 7000 RPM
TRANSMISSION	5-SPEED
BODY/CHASSIS	STEEL TUBE FRAME, ALUMINIUM BODY
SUSPENSION	FRONT, WISHBONES AND COIL SPRINGS
	REAR, WISHBONES AND COIL SPRINGS
TIRES/WHEELS	FRONT, 225/50 x 15 ON 8 IN. ALLOYS
	REAR, 345/35 x 15 ON 12 IN. ALLOYS
WHEELBASE, TRACK (F), TRACK(R)	96.5 x 60.5 x 63.2 INCHES
LENGTH, WIDTH, HEIGHT	163 x 78.1 x 42.1 INCHES
MAX SPEED	191 MPH
WHERE BUILT	BOLOGNA, ITALY

NB LP5000S FOR THE AMERICAN MARKET USED WEBER FUEL INJECTION GIVING 426 BHP

De Tomaso Pantera

When the production Ford GT40 won Le Mans in 1968 and 1969 and Ford then launched the mid-engined Ford-powered de Tomaso Pantera in early 1970, it seemed like there was a link; it was only a very indirect one. Ford had tried to buy Ferrari in the early Sixties as they wanted an Italian sports car maker to take them into racing and production of GT cars. When the bid failed, Ford bought into Eric Broadley's Lola GT project and the Ford GT40 was born in 1964.

However Ford still wanted an Italian involvement and eventually signed an agreement with Alejandro de Tomaso in September 1969 for technical cooperation between Ford of America, Ghia and de Tomaso who would build concept cars and niche vehicles for Ford. The first of these would be the Pantera, to be built at the rate of 5000 a year with de Tomaso retaining the right to non-American sales. If de Tomaso had been able to build as many cars as planned, and if they had been built as well as Ford expected, the Le Mans successes would have been used to promote sales through Ford's Lincoln Mercury dealers. As it was, the Pantera was not fully developed when it was put on the market and the 1973 oil crisis severely restricted demand.

De Tomaso had joined the ranks of Italian sports car builders back in 1963. The first offering was the mid-engined Vallelunga of which 180 were built; this used a backbone chassis to which was bolted a 97 cu.in Ford Cortina engine which took all the rear suspension loads through arms on the transaxle bell-housing. The theme was extended at the 1965 Turin

Show with the display of a sports-racing car using a bigger backbone which carried a 271 bhp Ford Mustang engine; although this was never raced, it formed the basis of the de Tomaso Mangusta for which Giugiaro drew up the body while he was working at Ghia. Production started in 1967 with Ghia building the bodies in Turin and de Tomaso fitting the power train in Modena. Although Ghia had the contract to build the Giugiaro-designed Maserati Ghibli, they were in financial trouble and de Tomaso acquired the company.

Meanwhile, Ford's search for an Italian supercar led them to Ghia, via the Ghibli, and came to look at the Mangusta in 1969, at which time Tom Tjaarda had just completed a scale model of a new Ford-powered sports car. Tom had left Ghia in 1961 but returned as Head of Styling in 1969. Ford didn't like the Mangusta engineering but thought more highly of the Tjaarda car.

Dallara was poached from Lamborghini to redesign the chassis which followed contemporary racing practice with a sheet steel monocoque center section with strong sills; Ford's latest 351 cu.in V-8 was attached to the rear and mated to a ZF transaxle. This acted as a sub-frame under the steel body. The result was a reasonably priced supercar which performed very well. As Ghia didn't have enough space to build the bodies in the required quantity, de Tomaso acquired the nearby Vignale factory in late 1969. Within a year, Ford owned 84% of de Tomaso's Ghia/Vignale/Pantera operation.

TECHNICAL DESCRIPTION OF THE DE TOMASO PANTERA

YEARS OF PRODUCTION	1970-1974
MODELS	2-SEATER COUPE
ENGINE	MID-MOUNTED V-8
BORE X STROKE, CAPACITY	3.9 x 3.4 INCHES, 351 CU.IN
VALVEGEAR	PUSHROD OVERHEAD VALVES
FUEL SYSTEM	AUTOLITE 4-BARREL CARBURETOR
POWER	330 BHP AT 5400 RPM
TRANSMISSION	ZF 5-SPEED
BODY/CHASSIS	UNITARY STEEL CHASSIS AND BODY
SUSPENSION	FRONT, WISHBONES AND COIL SPRINGS
	REAR, WISHBONES AND COIL SPRINGS
TIRES/WHEELS	185/70 & 215/70 x 15
	ON ALLOY WHEELS
WHEELBASE, TRACK (F), TRACK(R)	106 x 57.5 x 57 INCHES
LENGTH, WIDTH, HEIGHT	167.5 x 71 x 43.5 INCHES
MAX SPEED	155 MPH
WHERE BUILT	MODENA, ITALY

430-431 The Pantera was sold through Lioncoln-Mercury dealerships in the USA until 1974 when Ford gave the project back to de Tomaso, who continued to produce variations on the same theme until 1990.

In the first year of production, nearly 300 Panteras were sold in Europe. However Ford had to carry out further development before American approval came 1971. Sales were slower than anticipated, with 1550 in 1972 and 2030 in 1973; and then came the energy crisis. With the prospect of stricter emission laws in 1975, Ford stopped importing the Pantera and closed the Vignale plant in late 1974. De Tomaso had released his minority shareholding to Ford in early 1973 but retained the European sales rights for the Pantera.

European sales had dropped from 508 in 1973 to 78 due to the energy crisis. When Ford closed the Vignale plant de Tomaso collected the work in progress and continued to make the Pantera in Modena for the next 20 years with occasional refinements as new engines or new tires came in.

In 1990, the bodywork was restyled by Gandini and the engine had changed to the Ford 302 cu.in V-8 using fuel injection to give 305 bhp. It was as fast as the original. Although the Pantera never achieved the appeal of a Ferrari or Lamborghini, it remains a very affordable supercar.

Ferrari 308

The Fiat and Ferrari Dinos had stemmed from the desire of Ferrari to run a V-6 engine in 1967 Formula 2 racing. Fiat built some 4830 122 cu.in Dinos from 1966 to 1969 with orders for the Bertone-bodied Fiat Dino Coupe 2+2 being three times greater than those for the Pininfarina-bodied Fiat Dino Spider. Ferrari's own Dino 206GT finally emerged for 1969; at the end of that year Fiat brought out the heavily revised Dino 2.4, and the Ferrari Dino became the 246GT. The same year had seen Ferrari move under Fiat control, one consequence of which was that production of the Fiat Dino 2.4 was moved to an extension of the Ferrari factory.

By then, the V-6 was coming to the end of its days with emission controls becoming tighter, so the Fiat Dinos were scheduled to finish at the beginning of 1973, leaving vacant production space at Maranello. It was logical to combine these events with the desire to pitch a Dino 2+2 against the Porsche 911 as well as the Lamborghini Urraco P250 from the other side of Modena – both with rear seat accommodation; accordingly Ferrari went to Bertone for the new 308GT4. It is probable that Fiat had some influence over this, as the cessation of the Fiat Dino coupe would leave a hole in Bertone's production line; Bertone had also been let down by the failure of the Lamborghini Urraco to reach its planned production levels.

Ferrari needed a more impressive engine than the aged V-6 for the small range, and the heavier body of a 2+2 certainly required more power. Scaling a V-8 from the 268 cu.in V-12 was exactly what Lamborghini should have done for the Urraco; with a change in vee-angle, Ferrari's 90-degree 183 cu.in V-8 had the same bore and stroke dimensions as the 365GT engines and shared many components. The only design change was to adopt the toothed belt drive for the four camshafts as the flat-12 engine was already using. With four downdraft Weber carburetors it produced 250 bhp. Like the Dino 246, the engine was mounted transversely with the gearbox behind it. Italian taxation was responsible for the 208GT4 with 170 bhp.

The chassis followed the Dino principles with a space frame which was stretched by 8.2 inches and widened. Bertone's design was neat and functional and was actually very similar to the Urraco in its proportions, its glazing and the details of the two separate rear deck openings for engine and luggage space.

It has been an underrated car which is really very practical and has most of the feel of a proper sporting Ferrari. Over 3000 308GT4 were made, and some 800 208GT4, before they were replaced by the Pininfarina Mondial in 1980. They were finally allowed to be called Ferrari in 1978.

The next logical step was to install the 308 engine into a new version of the Dino 246GT. In effect this used the wide-track 308GT4 chassis

shortened to the same length as the 246GT. The new 308GTB arrived in 1975 using the GT4 engine fitted with dry sump lubrication for European cars. Pininfarina effected a delightful marriage of the shapes of the previous Dino and the new Berlinetta Boxer. The latter used fiberglass bodywork below its belt line, but the 308GTB used this material for the complete bodyshell until mid-1977 when it was replaced with steel. The Targa-top Spider 308GTS followed in 1977, with all markets using the wet sump engine. Again a 122 cu.in version was available for the Italian market. Demands for increasing emission control brought a change to fuel injection across the Ferrari range, denoted by 308GTBi and 308GTSi in 1980; this lost some power to 214 bhp (205 bhp for the USA), but this was largely recovered by the 1982 adoption of 4-valve heads to give 240 bhp with quattrovalvole written on the rear panels. At this point the Italian version had a turbocharger added to give 220 bhp.

The arrival of fuel injection had also seen the changeover from the GT4 to a new Pininfarina-designed Mondial 8. To give more space for rear passengers the wheelbase was lengthened by 3.9 inches and the roofline raised 3.1 inches. The shape retained some of the GT4 features but the more curved waistline and the pronounced air dam improved the appearance. This also adopted four valve heads in 1982, and in 1984 came the Mondial cabriolet, still with rear seat space. The following year the 308 engine was increased to 195 cu.in for the 328 range.

TECHNICAL DESCRIPTION OF THE FERRARI 308GTB

YEARS OF PRODUCTION	1975-1980
MODELS	COUPE 2-SEATER
ENGINE	MID-MOUNTED V-8
BORE X STROKE, CAPACITY	3.1 x 2.7 INCHES, 180 CU.IN
VALVEGEAR	FOUR OVERHEAD CAMSHAFTS
FUEL SYSTEM	FOUR WEBER CARBURETORS
POWER	255 BHP AT 7600 RPM
TRANSMISSION	5-SPEED
BODY/CHASSIS	STEEL TUBE FRAME, STEEL BODY
SUSPENSION	FRONT, WISHBONES AND COIL SPRINGS
	REAR, WISHBONES AND COIL SPRINGS
TIRES/WHEELS	205/70 x 14 ON 6.5 IN. ALLOY WHEELS
WHEELBASE, TRACK (F), TRACK(R)	92.1 x 57.5 x 57.5 INCHES
LENGTH, WIDTH, HEIGHT	167 x 68 x 44 INCHES
MAX SPEED	154 MPH
WHERE BUILT	MARANELLO, ITALY

NB FOR THE 308, FUEL INJECTION WAS INTRODUCED IN 1980 AND 4-VALVE HEADS IN 1982

432-433 The 308 used a wider version of the Dino 246GT chassis with an even more elegant shape. Early 308GTB bodies were in fiberglass.

Porsche 911 Turbo

When the Porsche 911 Turbo was unveiled at the 1974 Paris Show, it started a new trend of spectacularly powerful road cars. At that time the 911's flat-6 air-cooled engine had been increased to 164 cu.in with the standard car producing 150 bhp, the 911S 175 bhp and the highly tuned Carrera RS had 210 bhp. The Turbo had a 183 cu.in engine and 260 bhp but was just as tractable as the standard car. It proved that turbocharging was a very effective way of increasing performance without having a big engine. Although BMW were the first manufacturer to sell a turbocharged production car with the 1973 2002, they only made 1672 of them as a basis for competition versions . Porsche gave credibility to the cult-following that was to keep growing long after BMW had dropped the idea.

Porsche have always promoted their name through racing, particularly by using their production cars in endurance races and rallies. While the 911 was designed as a road car and then raced and rallied in its various forms, the Porsche Turbo 930 was introduced because the factory wanted to use it and its derivatives for racing. Production was necessary if the model was to take part in the new GT championship which was scheduled to start in 1976.

Porsche customers had already monopolised the existing championship with the 164 cu.in Carrera RSR. By 1973 they had worked out the turbo way ahead.

When the 1969-72 305 cu.in World Sports Car Championship came to an end, Porsche took the successful 917 across the Atlantic to the Can-Am races where rules were less restrictive; they used open versions of the 917 with the 274 or 305 cu.in flat-12 engines of the earlier cars. Competing against the McLarens with big 488 cu.in Chevrolet engines, Porsche engineers closed the power gap by turbocharging the existing engines rather than make bigger ones; for the 917-30, the engine was increases to 329 cu.in and turbocharged to produce 1100 bhp; they won the Can-Am championship in 1973.

Having used the 183 cu.in block in a prototype RSR to win the Targa Florio and come 4th at Le Mans in 1973, the next year's project was to use a turbocharged version running against the 183 cu.in sports prototypes, two-seater Grand Prix cars. Because it was very reliable, the Carrera Turbo finished in the top six in six races, including second at Le Mans. The car thus had a strong racing pedigree by the time it was launched in October that year.

The new GT racing rules were for Group 3 (1000-off road cars), Group 4 (400-off) and Group 5 (Groups 3 and 4 cars with further modifications). By the end of 1975, the necessary 400 of the 930 Turbo road car had been built and Porsche were ready to start the season with the 930 brought up to 934 and 935 racing specifications. Both won their championships and the 934 was equally unbeatable in American racing series.

The racing versions proved that the concept was reliable, despite the engines being developed to over 500 bhp; with only 260 bhp in road trim, the 911 Turbo was going to be as long-lasting as any other Porsche. It still looked like a 911 from the side, but it needed much wider wheel arches to accommodate wider tires, and a big rear wing improved the stability at high speed.

But despite all that power it was very tractable, with so much torque that Porsche only gave it four speeds. Inside, it was more comfortably equipped than any 911.

Porsche rationalized their range for 1978 to produce just two basic models, the 911SC with the 183 cu.in engine, and the Turbo with an increase to 201 cu.in and 300 bhp in European trim, or 280 bhp for America. The car stayed in more or less this form throughout the Eighties, although a Targa-top version was added in 1988. The model came to an end in 1989, but this was only to allow the introduction of the new Carrera 2 and Carrera 4 models.

By 1990, the Turbo was back still with a 201 cu.in engine but with further modifications, the power was raised to 320 bhp. With, finally, a five-speed gearbox it would accelerate even faster, reaching 60 mph in just 4.7 seconds. The original 1975 Turbo took 6.1 seconds. All the 911 designs have been classics, but the Turbo has been just a little more so.

TECHNICAL DESCRIPTION OF THE PORSCHE 911 TURBO 3.0

YEARS OF PRODUCTION	1975-1977
MODELS	COUPE 2 + 2
ENGINE	REAR-MOUNTED FLAT 6
BORE X STROKE, CAPACITY	3.7 X 2.7 INCHES, 182 CU.IN
VALVEGEAR	TWO OVERHEAD CAMSHAFTS
FUEL SYSTEM	BOSCH FUEL INJECTION AND TURBOCHARGER
POWER	260 BHP AT 5500 RPM
TRANSMISSION	4-SPEED
BODY/CHASSIS	STEEL MONOCOQUE
SUSPENSION	FRONT, MACPHERSON STRUTS, COILS REAR, TRAILING ARMS, TORSION BARS
TIRES/WHEELS	FRONT, 205/50 X 15 ON 7 IN. ALLOY WHEELS REAR, 225/50 X 15 ON 8 IN. ALLOY WHEELS
WHEELBASE, TRACK (F), TRACK(R)	89.4 X 56.3 X 59.1 INCHES
LENGTH, WIDTH, HEIGHT	168.9 X 69.7 X 51.2 INCHES
MAX SPEED	155 MPH
WHERE BUILT	STUTTGART, GERMANY

434-435 Although originally announced as the PorscheTurbo, the design type number for this 911 was actually 930.

TVR 3000

Through the early post-war years, Britain was home to a large number of special builders, people who created sporting cars around the running gear or even complete chassis of older cars. Many perished, Lotus and TVR survived. After an early series of cars using their own chassis and Austin A40 parts under proprietary fiberglass body shells, TVR built their own tubular backbone chassis and fiberglass body from 1958; they used Volkswagen front suspension with a choice of engines of which the Coventry Climax was most popular. Having produced around 500 of these Grantura Mk. I, II and IIA, the Blackpool-based company moved on to the Mk.III in 1962 with a new chassis carrying all-round wishbone suspension and the MGA engine.

The 1800S, with the MGB engine, came in 1964. Meanwhile, the company sold the Griffith in America from 1963-1965 using a 286 cu.in Ford V-8; this became the Tuscan V-8 from 1967-1970. Ford engines powered the other models too, the 183 cu.in Tuscan V-6 and the Vixen with the Cortina GT unit. Emission regulations dictated a change from the Ford V-6 to the Triumph 2500 twin carburetor engine for the American market in 1971.

The early Sixties saw TVR go through several changes of ownership but from 1966 this had stabilised under the Lilley family. They had introduced the Tuscans and Vixens including lengthening the very short wheelbase in 1968; but it was not until 1970 that they had sufficient confidence to invest in the next generation of cars and bigger premises in which to build them. By the time the new M-series came in late 1971, some 1800 of the previous chassis had been built over nine years.

The new chassis followed the TVR tubular frame principles but was stronger and easier to make. The new body had a longer nose which allowed the spare wheel to be mounted on top of the sloping radiator instead of taking up internal luggage space. The sharply cut-off Manx tail, introduced in 1964, gave way to a more slender version. All the glass was carried over from the previous model. By the time the changeover had taken effect, TVR produced the 1600M, 2500M and 3000M from late 1972. The 2500M became the export model as the Triumph TR6 had been certified for America; 950 were sold from 1972-77, by which time TVR had certified the 3000M.

In the seven years of the M-series models, 2480 were built from 1972-79, more than had been built in the previous 14 years. TVR were beginning to appeal to the wider market. Although the 1600M was no faster than the Sixties cars, the 3000M was capable of nearly 125 mph and could reach 60 mph in 7.5 seconds. There was little advantage in having the slower car so the 1600M was dropped in 1977; however some wanted even more performance.

Developing 128 bhp at 4750 rpm, the Ford Essex V-6 was not a very sporting engine in the Sixties, but it had been considerably improved (138 bhp at 5000 rpm) by the time the 3000M came along. The revised engine was also better able to withstand more power and Broadspeed developed a suitable turbocharger installation; installed in a TVR, this developed 230 bhp at 5500 rpm – enough to lift the performance to 140 mph and reduce

the 0-60 mph time to 5.8 seconds. The Turbo option was announced at the 1975 London Motor show.

Getting luggage into a TVR was always difficult as there was no direct access to the space behind the seats. For those who wanted to travel, this was finally corrected in 1976 with the hatchback Taimar, which soon outsold the outwardly identical 3000M. The only model missing from the line-up was a convertible. This finally came in 1978 with the body considerably modified. The door tops were changed to take removable sliding glass side-screens, the tail was altered to provide a lockable trunk, and the windscreen was changed to take the quick-action soft-top. It was an instant success and 270 were built in the two years before the M-series changed over to the new Tasmin. The Turbo option was offered on all models but it was expensive and only 63 were sold. While the 3000M was the biggest seller with 654 produced, Taimar and Convertible would have surpassed it given more time.

TECHNICAL DESCRIPTION OF THE TVR 3000

YEARS OF PRODUCTION	1972-1979
MODELS	COUPE 2-SEATER
ENGINE	FRONT-MOUNTED V-6
BORE X STROKE, CAPACITY	3.6 x 2.8 INCHES, 182 CU.IN
VALVEGEAR	PUSHROD OVERHEAD VALVES
FUEL SYSTEM	ONE TWIN-CHOKE WEBER CARBURETOR
POWER	138 BHP AT 5000 RPM
TRANSMISSION	FORD 4-SPEED
BODY/CHASSIS	STEEL TUBE FRAME, FIBERGLASS BODY
SUSPENSION	FRONT, WISHBONES AND COIL SPRINGS
	REAR, WISHBONES AND COIL SPRINGS
TIRES/WHEELS	185 x 14 ON 6 IN. ALLOY WHEELS
WHEELBASE, TRACK (F), TRACK(R)	90 x 54 x 54 INCHES
LENGTH, WIDTH, HEIGHT	134 x 64 x 47 INCHES
MAX SPEED	121 MPH
WHERE BUILT	BLACKPOOL, ENGLAND

436-437 This TVR Convertible (sometimes 3000S)
was only in production from 1978-1979.

Aston Martin Lagonda

Long before it joined forces with Aston Martin, Lagonda had established its own history. Founded in 1905, some 15 years before Aston Martin started to make cars, Lagonda made fast 4-seater tourers and, from the early Thirties, comfortable sedans. Aston Martin generally produced sports cars. When David Brown merged the two in 1947, it was Lagonda's Bentley-designed engine that set Aston Martin on its GT path. In the Fifties Lagondas retained their own comfortable sedan identity, sharing their engine, until 1957.

Making a 4-door Aston Martin sounds a simple procedure in a low volume manufacturing environment, but it was another four years before the first stretched Aston Martin came out as the Lagonda Rapide. It differed from the DB4 in having the 244 cu.in engine that would be used in the DB5, it had a de Dion rear axle and the body, also designed by Touring, was a totally different style. However, it had such a disruptive effect on the DB4 production line that only 55 were built over its three year life. David Brown built a single 4-door DBS V-8 in 1969 but it was left to new owners to return to the project in 1974; although this was a relatively simple stretch, the changing fortunes of the company were against it.

New owners came in 1975 after just seven of this Aston Martin Lagonda had been built.

The new management started on the Lagonda straight away with the brief that a 2-door version would be the next Aston Martin.

Actually Aston designer William Towns drew the 2-door car first, but the owners wanted to start with the 4-door version. Just eight months later, the prototype was on display at the 1976 Earls Court show. It was a remarkable piece of design; long and slender with razor-edge styling, it caught the imagination of luxury car buyers worldwide. It had the Aston Martin virtues of the 323 cu.in V-8 and excellent roadholding, coupled with 4-door 4-seat luxury; it also had electronic switchgear and digital instrumentation, the two areas that would prove major problems throughout the car's life, despite fundamental changes.

However the masterpiece of styling proved less than ideal when it came to fitting everything inside. Aston's talented engineers achieved the task but development took rather longer

than expected and it was mid-1978 before the first car was handed over, only for the computer to fail at the public ceremony. Following an electronic redesign, new cars finally reached customers in early 1979, just in time for the fuel crisis. However, with energetic salesmanship, the Lagondas found ready buyers in the Middle East which did much to keep the company going over a difficult period.

October 1984 saw the switchgear improved and the instrumentation replaced by three TV tubes, computer driven but rather ahead of their time in an automotive environment. They were replaced with vacuum fluorescent screens in 1987, finally successful. Fuel injection had replaced the four Weber carburetors in early 1986 to increase the power for European markets to 300 bhp.

The only major external change came in 1987. In response to safety legislation which declared that its razor edge styling was too sharp for

errant pedestrians, William Towns rounded the edges of his original design, removing also the belt-line crease, and continuing the sill panels below the doors.

With six exposed lights across the front, rather than the pop-up type, the car became somewhat easier to make; it lost its slender grace but it was still a fine-looking car.

At the end of 1987, new owners Ford moved in as the Virage was about to replace the long-running Aston Martin V8; built on a shortened Lagonda chassis this was the final stage of the 1976 plans. Making way for the new Aston, the last Towns Lagonda emerged in 1990, after just 645 had been built over an 11-year period. They were grand cars but never achieved the same acclaim as the Aston Martins. A few bespoke Lagondas have subsequently emerged from the Aston Martin service department as 4-door and estate versions of the Virage and its successor.

438-439 An early production car, this 1979 Lagonda shows the sharp lines of William Towns' creation.

TECHNICAL DESCRIPTION OF THE ASTON MARTIN LAGONDA	
YEARS OF PRODUCTION	1978-1985
MODELS	SEDAN 4-SEATER
ENGINE	FRONT-MOUNTED V-8
BORE X STROKE, CAPACITY	3.9 X 3.3 INCHES, 325 CU.IN
VALVEGEAR	FOUR OVERHEAD CAMSHAFTS
FUEL SYSTEM	FOUR TWIN-CHOKE WEBER CARBURETORS
POWER	260 BHP AT 5500 RPM
TRANSMISSION	CHRYSLER 3-SPEED AUTOMATIC
BODY/CHASSIS	STEEL MONOCOQUE, ALUMINIUM PANELS
SUSPENSION	FRONT, WISHBONES AND COIL SPRINGS
	REAR, DE DION AXLE AND COIL SPRINGS
TIRES/WHEELS	235/70 X 15 ON 6 IN. ALLOY WHEELS
WHEELBASE, TRACK (F), TRACK(R)	115 X 59 X 59 INCHES
LENGTH, WIDTH, HEIGHT	208 X 71.5 X 51.2 INCHES
MAX SPEED	140 MPH
WHERE BUILT	NEWPORT PAGNELL, ENGLAND

BMW M1

The M1 is unique in BMW history as the only car which the company built specifically for racing. BMW had long had a sporting reputation but this had been built on touring cars, tuned for competition, or the success of their engines in racing machinery built by others – including such as the McLaren F1. The M1 was planned to take on Porsche in the long distance sports car races.

It used the production six-cylinder engine increased to 213 cu.in; equipped with 4-valve heads and fuel injection this gave 277 bhp at 6500 rpm for the road. This was mated to a ZF transaxle and fitted in a space-frame chassis for which the fiberglass bodywork had been designed by Giugiaro.

Although Giugiaro had drawn up the M1's final shape, it was based on the Turbo concept car that BMW presented for the Munich Olympics in 1972; designed by BMW's Paul Bracq, this 'experimental safety vehicle' had side impact bars in its gull-wing doors and soft end panels mounted on rams among many safety features, but it was the mid-engined layout that was of particular interest. The familiar four-cylinder 122 cu.in was mounted transversely and fitted with a turbo-charger to give around 200 bhp; it was this engine, in 170 bhp form, that was fitted to the 2002 turbo the following year. The shape also provided styling cues for the M1; the black belt-line and the low slender nose were features that Giugiaro would adopt. The two prototypes were used to assess mid-engined handling advantages, useful knowledge for the new BMW Motorsport division which was founded in 1973; it was from this department that all the M-series cars would come – the M635CSi used the M1's engine.

International sports car racing in the late Seventies was based on production GT cars. For Appendix J Group 3 you had to make 1000 a year, Group 4 demanded 400 over two years, Group 5 was for cars of Groups 1-4 so heavily modified that they only had to retain the basic shape of the car and the standard engine block. Some races, notably Le Mans, had a class for Group 6 which was for full racing two-seaters with restrictions on the different types of engine – race, turbocharged race, stock-block. Initially BMW had built some turbocharged 3.0CSLs for Group 5 and nearly beat the Porsche 935 in the 1976 Manufacturers Championship.

However, the 3.0CSL was really too old for this form of racing, but BMW continued to use it in Group 2 events, winning the European Touring Championship for Makes and Drivers from 1975-1979. They were waiting for the M1. In Group 4 tune this could develop 470 bhp,

TECHNICAL DESCRIPTION OF THE BMW M1

YEARS OF PRODUCTION	1978-1981
MODELS	COUPE 2-SEATER
ENGINE	MID-MOUNTED IN-LINE SIX
BORE X STROKE, CAPACITY	3.6 x 3.3 INCHES, 210 CU.IN
VALVEGEAR	TWO OVERHEAD CAMSHAFTS
FUEL SYSTEM	BOSCH FUEL INJECTION
POWER	277 BHP AT 6500 RPM
TRANSMISSION	ZF 5-SPEED
BODY/CHASSIS	STEEL TUBE FRAME, FIBERGLASS BODY
SUSPENSION	FRONT, WISHBONES AND COIL SPRINGS
	REAR, WISHBONES AND COIL SPRINGS
TIRES/WHEELS	FRONT, 205/55 x 16 ON 7 IN. ALLOYS
	REAR, 225/50 x 16 ON 8 IN. ALLOYS
WHEELBASE, TRACK (F), TRACK(R)	100.8 x 61 x 62 INCHES
LENGTH, WIDTH, HEIGHT	172 x 72 x 45 INCHES
MAX SPEED	160MPH
WHERE BUILT	MUNICH, GERMANY

440-441 The delay in the start of production stopped the M1 challenging the Porsches in GT races.

so it had a theoretical chance against the Porsche 934, and the mid-engined layout gave it potentially better roadholding. And turbocharged versions with up to 850 bhp could challenge for Group 5 victory.

Having decided to build the M1 in late 1976, BMW contracted Lamborghini to develop and produce it, as low volume work was better suited to the Italian company who were looking for outside work. After much useful work in 1977, Lamborghini had financial problems and couldn't build the cars.

Production finally started after a year's delay with Giugiaro's ItalDesign company sub-contracting manufacture of the tubular chassis and fiberglass bodywork, joining the two and trimming the interior. Baur of Stuttgart then installed the mechanical components and completed the trim.

So it wasn't until 1980 that the required 400 were built, by which time the racing rules were set to change for 1982; these no longer suited the M1 which was too heavy for the new formula.

Meanwhile BMW had launched the M1 at the 1978 Paris Show and arranged the Procar series for 1979; Group 4 M1s had their own races at Grands Prix. It certainly gave the M1 instant publicity and justified 50 or so racing versions being built. They had some success in other races, but the loss of those two years meant that the M1 never had the chance to tackle the Porsches seriously in Group 4 racing or the faster Group 5. Despite that, the M1 was a superb 160 mph road car in the supercar mold. It looked the part and it was well built with luxurious trim.

Cadillac Seville

American manufacturers were so beset by emission and safety legislation during the Seventies that few cars of that period generated any lasting classic appeal. The established big cars lost performance and style. And the new smaller ones were slow and functional. It was only towards the end of the decade that any design confidence returned to create possible future classics.

Apart from the rare sports cars, most of the American classics come from the mid-size coupes, Firebirds and Mustangs, or the high performance 2-door sedans like the Sixties muscle cars.

Some achieve classic status because their style sets them apart from others of similar performance, like the early Sixties Buick Riviera. Some have great technical merit, like the Oldsmobile Toronado. Only a few big four-door sedans earn a place in classic lore.

It is a combination of style, technical merit and the high standards of Cadillac production that sets the 1980 Cadillac Seville apart from other big sedan cars. Cadillacs were as near hand-built as possible within a GM production line and the numbers were correspondingly lower, the cars rarer. "Craftsmanship a creed, accuracy a law" was the motto established by the company founder, and this has remained true since 1902.

Cadillac was generally used to lead the way in GM engineering. Perhaps it was to protect the Cadillac name from possible failure that it was left to Oldsmobile to pioneer the use of front-wheel-drive with powerful engines with the 1965 Toronado. A Cadillac Eldorado followed two years later using the same technology and slightly different style. The two cars continued until 1978 before they were replaced by smaller and lighter equivalents bearing the same names. These both retained the same system of front wheel drive with chain drive from the torque converter to the side-mounted gearbox ; following the Toronado success, GM used front wheel drive on many models but mostly with a transverse V-6.

Independent rear suspension was also a new feature for 1978 together with the option of the 347 cu.in V-8 petrol engine converted for diesel fuel. Perhaps because they had been prime targets of the Nader consumerism campaign, GM invoked all manner of technology to reduce emissions and fuel consumption. This had also inspired the 1976 Seville, the shortest Cadillac for many years; it was old technology, though, with a rear drive live axle, drum rear brakes and the 347 cu.in petrol V-8 producing 180 bhp – in 1978 it would produce 105 bhp as a diesel.

Although the wheelbase and overall length remained the same on the Seville's 1980 replacement, it used the latest technology with independent self-levelling rear suspension, the V-8 chain-drive transmission for front wheel drive and disc brakes all round.

It was also fitted with the diesel engine as standard with 350 and 368 cu.in petrol engines as options. The diesel engine was not a success and most people chose petrol engines; by 1982 the diesel engine had become the option alongside a new aluminium 250 cu.in V-8 with 147 bhp for Europe, and 10 bhp less in America where catalytic converters were mandatory.

The diesel engine was also offered with the other GM equivalent cars, Cadillac's own Eldorado, the Oldsmobile Toronado and the Buick Riviera. These three and the Seville shared the same platform, but the Seville was the only one with four doors; the two door cars all used the de ville style with an almost upright rear screen, heavy rear quarter panels and a long trunk deck. The Seville's style was a complete contrast with full side glazing for the rear passengers, a thinner quarter panel and a trunk-back tail where the trunk is narrower than the body after the style of the English coachbuilder Hooper. It was certainly the most elegant of GM's big sedan cars of the period and came in two forms; the standard car used chrome strips and contrasting roof finish to suggest a convertible – faux-cabriolet – while the limited edition Elegante used two tone finish and coachlines for the more formal limousine appearance.

The Seville arrived during the 1979 oil crisis but demand rose steadily throughout its life and nearly 40,000 were built in its final year.

442-443 The Elegante model had two-tone paintwork.
The 1980 model was offered with a diesel engine as standard.

TECHNICAL DESCRIPTION OF THE CADILLAC SEVILLE

YEARS OF PRODUCTION	1980-1985
MODELS	4-DOOR SEDAN
ENGINE	FRONT-MOUNTED V-8
BORE X STROKE, CAPACITY	3.4 x 3.3 INCHES, 249 CU.IN
VALVEGEAR	PUSHROD OVERHEAD VALVES
FUEL SYSTEM	FUEL INJECTION
POWER	137 BHP AT 4400 RPM
TRANSMISSION	4-SPEED AUTO FRONT-DRIVE
BODY/CHASSIS	STEEL FRAME CHASSIS, UNITARY BODY
SUSPENSION	FRONT, WISHBONES AND TORSION BARS
	REAR TRAILING ARMS AND COIL SPRINGS
TIRES/WHEELS	205/75 x 15 ON 6 IN. STEEL WHEELS
WHEELBASE, TRACK (F), TRACK(R)	114 x 59.3 x 60.6 INCHES
LENGTH, WIDTH, HEIGHT	204.7 x 71 x 54.3 INCHES
MAX SPEED	109 MPH
WHERE BUILT	DETROIT, USA

NB FROM 1980-82 A 347 CU.IN 105 BHP DIESEL ENGINE WAS FITTED AS STANDARD WITH 347 CU.IN AND 366 CU.IN PETROL ENGINES AS OPTIONS.

1981 - 1990

MODERN CLASSIC DEFINITIONS

Before going further, we need to return to one of our original definitions of a classic car – a post-1945 car with some feature which set it apart from its peers, and not just the mere fact of its survival. Such is the level of protection and durability in the Eighties car that many more will survive to great ages without restoration; where the Fifties car would be worn out after 80,000 miles, many Eighties cars are mechanically and bodily capable of over 200,000 miles with reasonable care and maintenance along the way. So we have to be more selective. Performance with style is what makes a latter-day classic.

One of the ways of enjoying classic car ownership is to be a member of a car club for that particular make or model. The long-standing classic makes are well represented. World-wide clubs for Aston Martin, Bentley, BMW, Ferrari, Jaguar, Lotus, MG, Mercedes, Porsche, Rolls-Royce and many others are open to all ages of the model. There are more specialized clubs too for such as Ford RS Owners or Fiat Dinos. But can you imagine a group of Vauxhall Cavalier or Nissan Bluebird owners enjoying each other's company in ten years time? Not classics, however long they survive.

A DECADE OF CHANGE

By the Eighties, the global car was becoming a reality. Manufacturers were all heading in the same direction as classifications became an international currency – A-class, B-class, C-class. Many were making the same car in different countries under different names or setting up factories in distant lands to take advantage of local conditions, like Honda, Toyota and Nissan in Britain.

The big three American manufacturers each had factories in every continent and most European countries; all had a stake in Japanese companies. The fourth, American Motors, had joined forces with Renault.

Inter-manufacturer co-operation increased in the search for economies of scale as design and development costs became ever greater. Peugeot, Renault and Volvo had co-built the Douvrin V-6 from 1974. Fiat and Saab shared platforms for the transverse front wheel drive Lancia Thema (1984), Saab 9000 (1985), Fiat Croma (1985), and Alfa Romeo 164 (1987).

Some famous names retained their ability to produce classics but lost their independence. Fiat bought Alfa Romeo from its state ownership in late 1986. Ford took over Aston Martin in 1987 and Jaguar in 1989, to the lasting benefit of both companies. Ford had also taken a majority share in AC in 1987 when the new Ace was under development, but gave it back to Cobra builder Brian Angliss in 1992.

Toyota had a stake in Lotus, but General Motors took over in early 1986 and then acquired control of Saab in 1990.

The outcome of all this rationalization and co-operation was that classics still came from the

444-445 Toyota Supra was the six cylinder derivative of the Celica. This new body style came in 1986; 183 cu.in straight-6 developed 204 bhp or 230 bhp with turbo.

traditional low volume manufacturers, whoever now owned them, or as genuine but expensive coupes or sports cars from the volume producers.

Sedans would only be classics if the model was built for competition – the limited production rally cars like the RS and Cosworth from Ford, or the Lancia Delta Integrale – or from such accepted tuning agents as Mercedes AMG or the BMW M-series. Special editions, merely a different mix of established options under a short-term model name, did not make a classic out of a boring sedan. A few of the chic superminis, like the Peugeot 205GTI or the MG Metro turbo, could survive into classic status.

The trouble with the medium-size sedans was that the Eighties was the era of soap-bar styling and loss of make identity. All began to look the same as they sought to achieve the same object, hatchback 4/5 seaters with low drag factors; they looked as if they came from the same wind-tunnel and were shaped by perpetually squeezing a bar of soap. In the process

the distinctive face of the car – the grille – disappeared into a common radiator intake slot. In the UK these were the repmobiles – company-owned transport for the sales representative – which were as likely to come from Nissan or Toyota as Ford or Vauxhall.

It was the era when all companies expanded their own styling departments and placed offices in important markets around the globe. The traditional Italian styling houses had a difficult time. They could function as styling studios with prototype build facilities like Giugiaro's ItalDesign or IDEA, but any production area had to be capable of producing at least 25,0000 cars a year – supermini cabriolets were a popular product for volume producers to contract out to Pininfarina and Bertone in Italy, Karmann in Germany or Heuliez in France.

Ghia and Vignale were safe as de Tomaso had sold them to Ford back in 1973. It was Zagato who was to suffer, particularly as the company was at the Milan end of Auto Valley and control of such regular customers as

Alfa Romeo and Lancia had passed to Fiat in Turin. With facilities for only 1000 cars a year, Zagato survived the Eighties thanks to de Tomaso reshaping Maserati around a number of variations on a Biturbo theme – the Spider and the 228 were built at Zagato – and to Aston Martin who reopened an old association to create the Vantage Zagato and Volante Zagato from 1985-90. Such supercars were very much a product of the late Eighties.

A new breed of exclusive car came through International rallying which had seen increasing participation from factory teams. The FIA rules laid down minimum production numbers, 500, 400 or 200 over 1975-1986. So factories built these quantities of specialist high performance cars. And since the Audi Quattro had shown the way, most of these Eighties cars used four wheel drive. They were not as comfortable and refined as the supercars, but they had a lot of performance and were very much classics of their period.

The advanced technology that we see in the cars of today was largely born in the Eighties. Not only did engines receive increasing levels of electronics but so too did transmissions and suspensions. Turbochargers were seen regularly in the Seventies (the 1962 Corvair Monza was probably the first) but the Eighties saw their driveability much improved; electronic ignition and injection combined with smaller, lighter rotating parts to cut the turbo-lag. Turbos were seen particularly in hot hatchbacks and as a means of providing petrol levels of power for diesel engines.

Most manufacturers had at least one model in their ranges equipped with twin-cam four-valve cylinder heads. Four wheel drive, spearheaded by the Audi Quattro, moved on from fixed ratios of torque split between front and rear, to more sophisticated limited slip center differentials with viscous couplings or Torsen worm-and-wheel differentials through to electronic control of center differential clutches. Anti-lock braking (ABS) was still the preserve of more expensive cars, but an increasingly widespread option on the rest. Rear wheel steering had long been understood and achieved by controlled suspension movement, but the Japanese introduced electronic control. Power steering and air-conditioning had been around for a long time but these were increasingly fitted lower down the market.

The bi-product of all this technology is that it will be much harder to keep your Eighties classic going through the ages, as any restoration required will be beyond the ability of most home mechanics. Original dealers will have to keep servicing older cars and providing replacement parts for much longer than before.

THE BIG SEDANS

Although the rally world contributed some memorable special sedans, there were a few others to catch the eye as future classics. Inevitably the Rolls-Royce and Bentleys will live on; the Silver Shadow and Bentley T were finally replaced by the Silver Spirit and the Bentley Mulsanne in 1980, but what marked the Eighties was the belated reconition that a Bentley should be a sporting Rolls, not just a Rolls with a Bentley radiator. The Mulsanne Turbo came in 1982, followed by the Bentley 8 with firmer suspension in 1984; a merger of the two came in 1985 with the Turbo R. At last, high performance more suited to a history that includes five victories at Le Mans. And the Continental name returned on the convertible that had been called Corniche from 1971. There was still a Lincoln Continental in Ford's premier range. While the Lincolns possessed a certain Fifties style, like an Austin A135, the mechanical elements were also pretty dated – live rear axles and a pushrod V-8. Far more appealing was the Cadillac range with front wheel drive and independent rear suspension; the Seville 4-door was particularly elegant. The Eldorado coupe and convertible had matching Buick Rivieras with more performance.

Jaguar finally unveiled the XJ40 as the new XJ6 in 1986 using a single-cam 176 cu.in 'six' and the new AJ6 4-valve 219 cu.in, which had already been seen in the XJS. The previous XJ12 models had to continue as the V-12 wouldn't fit into the new car until major changes were made in 1992. At that point Jaguar, Mercedes S-class and BMW 7-series all had 12-cylinder versions and competed for the title of best in the world; good cars maybe, classic perhaps, but not cars that you might cherish in your garage in twenty years time.

Good cars emerged from the Club of Four who had shared a common transverse-engined platform. The top Lancia Thema used a Ferrari 308 4-valve engine for the 8.32 which was announced in 1986 to give 150 mph performance. From Saab, the 9000 Turbo was almost as fast and three of them averaged 132 mph to cover 62,000 miles in 20 days at Talladega, creating a new limited edition model name. Alfa Romeo were the last to introduce their

version as the 164 in 1987; with Pininfarina styling, it was one of the best-looking sedans on the market and, with the 183 cu.in V-6 was a worthy rival to such as the BMW M3.

De Tomaso was still in control of Maserati and the 1976 Quattroporte was to continue to 1988 using a 256 cu.in version of one of the earlier V-8 engines. From 1985 this was increased to 298 cu.in and the car became a Royale in 1987. In the latter half of the Seventies there had been a shorter two-door derivative called the Kyalami. Both cars had exceptionally clean lines, but were little known outside Italy. For the Eighties, de Tomaso developed the entirely new Maserati Biturbo range using different chassis lengths for a rear wheel drive platform with derivatives of a new 4-cam 90-degree V-6 which had three or four valves per cylinder and twin turbochargers. All had variations on the same basic three-volume body style; stylistically they were not the most exciting to look at but the mechanical specification was worthy of the best of Maserati tradition.

But perhaps the most memorable sedan of the Eighties was the Vauxhall Lotus Carlton, also sold as the Opel Lotus Omega, a product of General Motors' ownership of Lotus. The standard 183 cu.in 24-valve 204 bhp engine was increased to 221 cu.in with a new crankshaft and given twin turbochargers to develop 377 bhp. With the Corvette's six-speed gearbox, various aerodynamic additions and much improved suspension, the Lotus Omega/Carlton was capable of over 170 mph, the fastest ever 5-seater sedan car. After a 1989 launch, production started in 1990 but finished in 1992 when Lotus was sold on, so only 950 were built.

THE COUPES

The major manufacturers continued to produce coupe versions of their sedans, or at least use their sedan platforms, and these have traditionally acquired classic status. At the lower end of that market, Volkswagen had introduced the Scirroco in 1974 as a Golf coupe in the Ford Capri market.

It had a revised body in 1981. Giugiaro designed both that and the Isuzu Piazza (rear-drive 122 cu.in coupe) with near identical styling. The Scirroco continued until 1991 but the best addition to the Golf range was the slightly bigger Corrado in 1988, a 2-door hatchback based on the latest Golf GTI; initially offered with the G-Lader supercharged 109 cu.in, as also used in the limited edition 4WD Golf GTI G60 Rallye, the Corrado matured when the VR6 170 cu.in came in 1992. It was VW's sports car, a genuine 2+2, with Porsche 944S2 performance.

As Germany was the only country to allow unrestricted speed on some of its autobahns, sports machinery was an important part of their market; Mercedes took it seriously and used a purpose designed platform, rather than an adapted sedan one, for the new SL300 (183 cu.in 'six') and the SL500 (305 cu.in V-8) in 1989. Like Mercedes, BMW do not change their coupes very often; the 6-series came in 1976 and the 218 bhp BMW 635CSi was added in 1976. It was 1983 before the M-series M635CSi came out with the 286 bhp 24-valve 213 cu.in to make one of BMW's most desirable classics. The replacement 850i arrived in 1989 with a 300 bhp 305 cu.in V-12 as a superb-looking successor; the engine was increased to 341 cu.in in 1992 and a 244 cu.in V-8 made the 840Ci in 1993.

Cadillac tried to take back some of the European coupe market in 1987 by using Italian styling for the Allante convertible. They sent shortened Eldorado chassis to Pininfarina in converted 747 jumbo-jets; the production line was completed when the body-chassis units returned to Detroit for the running gear, which included a 170 bhp 250 cu.in V-8. The power was increased to 200 bhp with a 274 cu.in for 1989, and to 299 bhp with the new 280 cu.in 32-valve V-8 in 1992, but the model was never a major seller.

446-447 Corvette ZR-1 of 1989 brought in the new wheels and convex tail panel with its 380 bhp Lotus-developed engine.

Chrysler tried a similar exercise with Maserati receiving a Le Baron chassis with a turbocharged 134 cu.in 'four'. Although Maserati installed a 16-valve head to get 205 bhp, and a less-stressed 183 cu.in V-6 was offered in 1990, the Chrysler TC by Maserati was not a commercial success.

The one-time kings of the American pony-cars recovered from their disastrous downsizing and power losses of the late Seventies. A new Chevrolet Camaro and sleeker-looking Pontiac Firebird came in 1981 with 88 bhp from a 152 cu.in 'four' or 155 bhp from a 305 cu.in V-8; power was increased steadily throughout the Eighties and by 1990 the range was 142-248 bhp. Ford's Mustang underwent a similar performance transformation, but lacked the style of the GM cars. The Mercury Cougar, which was once a luxury Mustang, became aligned to the Ford Thunderbird; the new styles of 1988 considerably improved both of

them. More striking was the new Ford Probe based on a chassis from the Mazda MX-6 using 'fours' or V-6s; launched in 1988, it might have been a Capri replacement but it never had the same appeal in the European market. The last of 1.9 million Capris was built in 1986, one of the final 1000 Capri 280 Special Editions.

While Vauxhalls were very much Opel-based, from 1988 the two ranges had identical cars, although not all Opels had a Vauxhall equivalent. However, Calibra, launched in 1989, was the name given to the coupe derivatives of both the Opel Vectra and Vauxhall Cavalier shown a year earlier. Initially with 122 cu.in engines in 115 bhp 8-valve and 150 bhp 16-valve forms, both were also offered with four wheel drive; however, when the 204 bhp Turbo 4x4 Calibra arrived in 1991, General Motor's European divisions had a serious 152 mph classic coupe.

BL Cars (British Leyland) had been government

owned from 1975, but at the beginning of the Eighties they had forged technical links with Honda, which revitalized aged technology and production methods. Having lost Triumph production, sold Jaguar and kept the MG badge for faster Austins, the company became the Rover group in 1986. The new Rover 800 range (Sterling in America) was a joint Rover-Honda development based on the Honda Legend using a 122 cu.in 4-cylinder for the 820. A 177 bhp 164 cu.in V-6 engine came in 1988 (827), followed by a fastback coupe; it was the 827 Vitesse coupe, with style changes, which was the potential classic. In 1992, the front was changed to include a pronounced Rover-style grille and this is the most appealing version of the 827 Vitesse. Meanwhile the company had been taken over by British Aerospace in 1988; it was sold on to BMW in 1994 and Honda links were quickly severed.

448-449 Aston Martin Vantage Volante came in 1986 with skirts and spoilers but some retained the original body shape.

Sports and Sporting Coupes

By the end of the Seventies, it seemed as if American emission legislation was going to stifle all sporting machinery, but the engineering challenge was taken up around the world and the Eighties saw a steady performance increase as engines became more and more efficient.

Mid-engined small cars remained a rarity despite the success of Fiat X1/9, but two emerged in the Eighties, the Toyota MR2 and the Pontiac Fiero. The Midship Runabout 2-seater was a product of Toyota's change to a transverse front wheel drive power train for the Corolla, with development through Toyota's early Eighties liaison with Lotus. The MR2 used a monocoque chassis and the Corolla engines, a 16-valve 97 cu.in 130 bhp and an 8-valve 91.5 cu.in 83

bhp unit for the home market. Neat, compact yet spacious, the MR2 did all that was expected of a mid-engined coupe. A supercharged 145 bhp model was available in some markets from 1986 and a T-bar roof variant arrived in 1987.

The Pontiac Fiero was not quite in the same mold. Within General Motors, Chevrolet produced the sports car – the Corvette – so the Fiero was labelled as a commuter car. With a steel sub-frame covered in plastic panels, it was a good design let down by its basic engine, a 152 cu.in 'four' with 92 bhp at its 1983 launch. By 1985, it had a 170 cu.in V-6 option with 140 bhp, a more appealing proposition. Sadly, the American market was not receptive to a mid-engined commuter car and the Fiero ceased production in 1988.

It was Pontiac's former Chief Engineer and General Manager, John De Lorean who was behind the De Lorean DMC-12. When he left General Motors in 1973, he wanted to build an ideal sports coupe with gull-wing doors. Lotus were eventually entrusted with its development. A fuller story is told later, but what finally emerged at the end of 1980 was a Lotus – steel backbone chassis with fiberglass underbody – with stainless steel panels to Giugiaro's design; it was powered by a rear-mounted Douvrin V-6 in its 173 cu.in Volvo form. The ambitious project failed at the end of 1983 after 8583 examples had been built – a classic might-have-been.

For their own models of the Eighties, Lotus increased their engine size to 134 cu.in for the Elite S2 and Eclat S2 in 1980; these only lasted two years before the Excel replaced the Eclat, using a number of Toyota components, and stayed in production until 1992. The Turbo Esprit also arrived in 1980; its original angular shape was modernized in 1987 with rounder lines and various versions were available by the end of the decade, still based on the 134 cu.in engine.

For many years, Lotus had wanted a new small sports car to recapture the old Elan market. While this might have shared engines with the Lotus-developed Toyota MR2, the 1986 take-over by General Motors caused a change to a front-wheel-drive Isuzu package, a 97 cu.in with 132 bhp or, for the SE, 167 bhp with a turbocharger; this delayed the Elan's arrival until late 1989. The power train was used by Isuzu for the Impulse coupe which had replaced the Piazza. Despite an enthusiastic reception, Elan world-wide sales never hit their targets in a recessionary period. When General Motors pulled out and sold Lotus to Bugatti president Romano Artioli in 1992, only 3857 had been built; the new owners had to use up the 800 power trains in stock for the Elan S2 which was completed in 1994-1995. Kia then bought the rights and built the Kia Elan in South Korea from 1995 using their own ex-Mazda engines.

The car that really replaced the old Elan was the Mazda MX-5 Miata, which arrived just before the new Lotus Elan. Conceived by Mazda North America, the MX-5 followed the original Elan concept with a 97 cu.in front engine in a rear-drive chassis with all-independent suspension. A 130 bhp 109 cu.in engine came in 1993; it had all the charm and now most of the performance of the original Elan.

Mazda had heavily revised the RX-7 in 1985 with a new Porsche 944-style body, independent rear suspension and a Wankel engine enlarged to 158 cu.in to give 150 bhp, or 200 bhp with a turbocharger, enough to give it 150 mph performance. Adding a convertible in 1987 for the first time was a classic addition to the RX-7 story. An interesting extension to the Wankel range from 1990 was the Eunos Cosmo coupe on a longer wheelbase and with the option of a 3-rotor engine to make 237 cu.in.

The Japanese companies were very active in the sporting sector. Mitsubishi had introduced the Starion 2+2 coupe into the Nissan Z-car market in 1982 with a 144 cu.in Turbo, and a 4WD Rally version followed a year later. The Starion handed over to the 3000GT with 4WD, four-wheel-steering (4WS) and twin-turbocharged 183 cu.in V-6 in 1990; this was sold in the USA as the Dodge Stealth.

1981 - 1990

Nissan had brought the 240Z concept through to the 300ZX in 1983, but launched an all-new 300ZX 2+2 in 1989 using a 183 cu.in V-6 with twin turbos (280 bhp) or without (230 bhp). Like the Mitsubishi it also had 4WS. It actually became a classic in its own production period which ended in 1996. The smaller 200SX used four-cylinder engines in another attractive little coupe. Meanwhile in 1987, Nissan had started their Skyline GT-R run with 4WD, 4WS and incredible turbocharged performance.

Toyota's 1981 Celica grew into a Supra derivative with a six-cylinder engine of 144 or 170 cu.in in a slightly longer chassis. From this came the even longer Soarer with a 144 cu.in turbo or a 183 cu.in dohc as a more comfortable 2+2 coupe. The Celica changed shape and adopted front wheel drive in 1985; 4WD and a turbocharger followed in late 1986 for the Group A rally team. Supra and Soarer went their own stylistic ways with 144 cu.in or 183 cu.in engines from 1986, presenting attractive alternatives to the equivalent Nissan and Mitsubishi – good Porsche 944 rivals too. For 1989 the Celica changed shape again and still included the Turbo 4WD. The Soarer was not available on all markets but is a particularly handsome coupe.

And then there was Honda who had ignored sports cars after the S800. Their range had long excelled technically but lacked styling flair – an important part of latter day classic appeal. The Prelude 2+2 coupe arrived in 1982 but we had to wait until the 1987 version for style to match the 145 bhp performance – it also brought in mechanical 4WS. Style and performance continued with the 1991 model which had 185 bhp from its 134 cu.in VTEC engine. What really set Honda apart was the 1990 introduction of the superb mid-engined NSX with all-aluminium chassis and bodywork and a powerful 24-valve 274 bhp V-6 183 cu.in. It was such a good user-friendly car that Ferrari and Porsche 911 owners found it almost unexciting. A Targa-top model came in 1995.

Porsche continued to develop the 911 with increasing engine sizes. The 183 cu.in came in 1980 and the Carrera name was reintroduced in 1983 with a 195 cu.in engine. The Speedster name came back too in 1987. A year later came the Carrera 4 with a 219 cu.in engine and four wheel drive – a 959 without the turbocharger – and in 1989 the Carrera 2 also gained the 219 cu.in. The Turbo meanwhile continued with a 201 cu.in engine from 1977 which was

increased from 300 bhp to 320 bhp in the cleaner Carrera 2 shape. But there was also the more affordable front-engined 944 which had taken over from the 924 in 1981; a 16-valve 944S arrived in 1986 and the 183 cu.in S2 came in 1989 together with a Cabriolet while the 152 cu.in Turbo (1985) moved on from 220 bhp to 250 bhp. The 928 had gone through S2, S3 and S4 versions into the 1990 928 GTS with a 305 cu.in V-8 coming in 1987. The front-engined Porsches may not have the iconic appeal of the 911 series, but they are still worthy future classics.

The 911's French rival, the Alpine Renault A310, became the sleeker and more luxurious GTA in 1985 with the Douvrin V-6 now increased to 173 cu.in (160 bhp) or a 152 cu.in Turbo with 200 bhp. The final Alpine A610 Turbo came in 1991 with a wider body, a more aerodynamic front and 250 bhp from the 183 cu.in Turbo but, by 1996, production had ceased – a sad end to a name that had done so much for French racing and rallying prestige.

However a new French make had arrived in 1986 and has continued in business after a change of ownership in 1991. The Venturi 210 had a turbocharged version of the 152 cu.in PRV engine but mounted it amidships in a sleek two-seater coupe

with composite bodywork on a pressed steel chassis. A neat cabriolet came in 1988 and the 1990 260 used the 173 cu.in V-6 with 260 bhp.

From Germany came the BMW Z1 in 1988, a short-lived sports two-seater powered by the 152 cu.in injection six. With quickly removable fiberglass body panels, its major feature was doors that dropped into the sills. Only just over 8000 were built from 1987-91.

Fiberglass continued to be used for America's only sports car, the Corvette. The latest model arrived in 1983, more compact and more aerodynamic, with a 200 bhp 347 cu.in V-8. This was increased to 230 bhp for 1985 and the following year saw a new convertible. When the ZR1 arrived in 1989 using an entirely special Lotus-designed 347 cu.in 4-cam with 380 bhp, the Corvette finally recovered its 1967 performance; there was a new 6-speed gearbox too. While Alfa Romeo's aged 124 Spider continued to be produced by Pininfarina through to the Nineties, and the 164 was a sporting sedan, the make lacked a mid-size sports coupe following the demise of the Alfetta-based GTV6 in 1987. The Sprint 1.3 with the developed AlfaSud engine continued a little longer. The new SZ, called Il Mostro from its 1989 launch,

was based on the 1985 Alfa 75 sedan. The coupe used a 75 platform with shortened overhangs; its plastic composite bodywork was designed within Alfa Romeo and built by Zagato. When Fiat's then chief, Vittorio Ghidella, was satisfied that the SZ roadholding could match a Porsche 944, the project was given the green light; its V-6 183 cu.in (an option in the 75 from 1987) was tuned to 210 bhp for 152 mph performance.

Zagato set up the production process and built 1000 of the SZ before the Alfa Romeo 75 production was stopped in 1993; Zagato continued with their own roadster version, the RZ until 1994. Meanwhile they had shown the Hyena in 1992 based on the Lancia Delta HF Integrale; in the style of a modernized Giulietta SZ, it was a very good car. Sadly only a handful were built before Zagato finally closed its production doors – a fitting farewell to a company that always produced cars in a classic mold.

In England TVR introduced the sleek new Tasmin as a 2-seater coupe on a new tubular chassis in January 1980, following this up later in the year with the convertible and the 2+2. From 1980-1985 this was available with the 170 cu.in German V-6 and, from 1981-1984, as the Tasmin 200 with the Ford Pinto 144

cu.in. Current owner Peter Wheeler took over from Martin Lilley in 1982 and dropped the Tasmin name a year later in favor of engine-related numbers – 280i. A further engine variation began in 1983 with the Rover V-8; initially in 213 cu.in form (350i) for the same body range, this was increased for the 237 390SE and then to 256 cu.in for the 420 in 1986.

This came in 300 bhp SEAC sports form (Special Equipment Aramid Composite) or as a 265 bhp sports sedan with genuine space for two adults in the back. Fearing they were getting out of the enthusiast price range TVR brought back an old shape – the Seventies 3000S – widened it and gave it a new chassis with the 280i engine; this S convertible was half the price of the 420SEAC. By the end of the Eighties, the S2 was using the 176 cu.in Ford V-6, the Speed Eight convertible with 237 cu.in had replaced the rest and the Rover engine had been enlarged to 274 cu.in for the 450SE. And there was the racing Tuscan too, but that belongs to the Griffith story of the Nineties.

After a promising start in the specialist GT world in the Sixties, Marcos hit problems. A factory move, the failure to get cars into America and a UK tax change that affected cars sold in kit form, all conspired to close the company down in 1971.

450-451 This 1988 Porsche Carrera Cabriolet has various non-standard items – new wheels, an intake ahead of the rear wheels and a rear wing – but it is still very much a Porsche.

COMPETITION
IMPROVES THE BREED

However founder, Jem Marsh, continued a business in Marcos spares and gradually reintroduced limited kit-car production of the Ford 1600 and 183 cu.in models from 1981. Then Marcos, too, adopted the Rover V-8 and came up with the Mantula in 1984 in the same basic shape as the original 1800, which was still as striking 20 years later – just flared rear wheel arches for a wider axle – and available in kit form for home assembly. A Spyder convertible followed in 1986 with wishbone independent rear suspension finally available in 1989.

The aim, though, was still to build complete cars for which Type Approval was necessary – the Mantara was finally homologated in 1993 as coupe and Spyder with the 237 cu.in Rover V-8.

In the interim Marcos continued to offer well-made cars in kit form. The Martina used running gear from old Ford Cortina Mk 4 or Mk 5 in a Mantula body/chassis and the Mini-Marcos returned as a Mark V using new molds for Mini components. Not many kit cars deserve classic status, but these were just modernized versions of previous classic production shapes.

Morgan never stopped making classics. They too had continued with Rover power for the Plus 8, with the 237 cu.in in 1990. The 4/4 continued with Ford 97 cu.in engines while the Plus Four returned in 1985 with a Fiat 122 cu.in twin-cam engine; this was replaced by the Rover 16-valve 122 cu.in in 1988.

By now there were many small companies building replicas of some of the more famous shapes of the past. Some, as below, have achieved a classic status of their own, others are just specials. Lynx and Wingfield built Jaguar D-type replicas that were very close to the original designs. GT Developments built the GTD40 looking very like a proper GT40 but with a space-frame and a more modern Ford V-8. AC continued to make the Cobra as a Mark IV – copies from other companies were less desirable.

And Caterham continued to make ever faster variations on the theme of the Lotus 7 to which they had acquired the rights in 1973.

While the rules of the rallying and racing worlds had been responsible for a number of limited edition classic sedans throughout the Seventies, the International rally rules of the Eighties resulted in an amazing collection of specialist machines which were destined to be instant if expensive classics. However, because they were produced in limited numbers and many of them were used in competition, it is not easy to find good standard examples.

Early Seventies rallies were run to FIA Appendix J group 2; 1000 4-seater cars had to be built, but the modifications allowed were considerable, provided enough parts were made to equip 100 cars. Late Seventies rallies were run to Appendix J group 4 which called for cars of at least two seats of which 400 had been produced over 24 months. Modifications allowed were fewer but 400 special editions for rallying was well within the capability of most manufacturers. The Lancia Stratos was one such specialist car; Ford Escort Mk.II RS, Fiat Abarth 131 Rallye, Sunbeam-Lotus, Vauxhall Chevette, Opel Ascona 400 were less specialized but heavily modified. But they were all two-wheel-drive cars as the FIA had banned four wheel drive. For whatever reason, the FIA reinstated four wheel drive for 1979 by which time Audi were already working on the Quattro with intent to go rallying. The rest soon had to follow.

For 1982 new rules came in; Group B only asked for 200 examples. Special Evolutions of these (another

10 per cent production) were allowed for the competitions, but 200 standard road cars had to be built first – all destined to be future classics. Group A (5000-off) ran alongside but didn't challenge for outright victory. By 1986, the Group B cars had become too fast for rallying, so the rules were changed to limit the power to 300 bhp; the World Rally Championship was limited to Group A (5000 examples) or Group B cars with a 97 cu.in limit.

Audi's first Quattro was launched in March 1980; it was based on the two-door fastback Audi GT with a new floorpan and its turbocharged five-cylinder 128 cu.in engine gave 200 bhp. Audi had previously tried to rally the front-drive Audi 80, but, as the engine was mounted ahead of the front axle line, it was ill-suited to rallying on loose surfaces – it needed four wheel drive. Audi duly built 400 Quattros and had an impressive 1981 season.

For the Group B regulations Audi continued their developments and a new model, the A2, arrived in mid-1983 with many lightweight panels and an engine that could produce as much as 340 bhp.

The end of 1983 saw the Sport Quattro with wide wheelarches, a short wheelbase and new cylinder head with four valves per cylinder; in standard turbocharged form it had 306 bhp which could be increased to over 400 bhp for rallying.

In Group A, Audi ran the 200 Quattro Turbo for 1987 with a somewhat more sophisticated torque split arrangement using Torsen differentials. Any of the

Quattros that provided the basis for the rally cars is a likely classic.

Ford were rather left behind in Group B. Having tried to develop the RS1700T within the Escort Mk.III body, following old Escort front-engine rear-drive principles, they decided on the all-new RS200 as a mid-engined four-wheel-drive coupe with a turbocharged 109 cu.it giving 200-350 bhp. The 200 were finally built by January 1986; while the car proved effective, it was only to have one year of International rallying. They went on to develop the 1985 Sierra XR4x4 (176 cu.it V-6 and 4WD) and then the 1987 5000-off Sierra Cosworth using a turbocharged 144 cu.in four-cylinder 16-valve engine with 220 bhp; the RS500 (500-off) Evolution came in 1987 but that could only be used for racing or national rallying. The Sierra Cosworth is a likely classic too. As the competition arm for the Fiat Empire (excluding Ferrari in Grands Prix), Lancia took rallying very seriously throughout the Seventies and

Eighties. The purpose-built Stratos, which won the World Rally Championship from 1974-6, was succeeded by the Fiat-Abarth 131 Rallye, an Escort-type car using the old Fiat 125 twin-cam engine in its 144 cu.in Lancia Beta form. This won the championship in 1977, 1978 and 1980. Their first group B car, the good-looking Rally 037, was loosely based on the mid-engined Lancia Monte Carlo; it used the later 16-valve 131 Rallye engine but with a Volumex supercharger. The necessary 200 were built in time for the 1982 season and the car performed well, but it soon became obvious that four wheel drive was essential to keep up with the Audis and other 4WD machines.

Lancia's response was to take the shape of the normally front-drive 4-door Delta, transfer as many 037 bits as possible to it and add 4WD in its most sophisticated form with three viscous coupling differentials. The engine became a new four-cylinder unit of 107 cu.in but used both a Volumex supercharger

and a turbocharger in series to develop around 400 bhp. This Delta S4 was finally homologated (200 built to a standard specification) for the 1986 season – another Group B car with only a season to run. It won four events, but Peugeot won six and took the cup.

Lancia had introduced the Delta – similar to the Fiat Strada – in 1979. The Delta HF arrived in 1983 with a turbocharged 97 cu.in engine. With an eye to competing in Group A classes before Group B was abandoned, this was developed into the Delta HF 4WD in mid-1986 with a turbocharged 144 cu.in 8-valve engine; following the mid-season announcement 5000 were hurriedly built in time for the first event of 1987. Being best prepared, Lancia duly won the 1987 championship with Sierra Cosworths and BMW M3s as also-rans. For the 1988 season, the second generation HF Integrale came in with flared wheel arches for bigger wheels and brakes and another 5000 were built. A 16-valve version followed in 1989 by which time, 200 bhp was available.

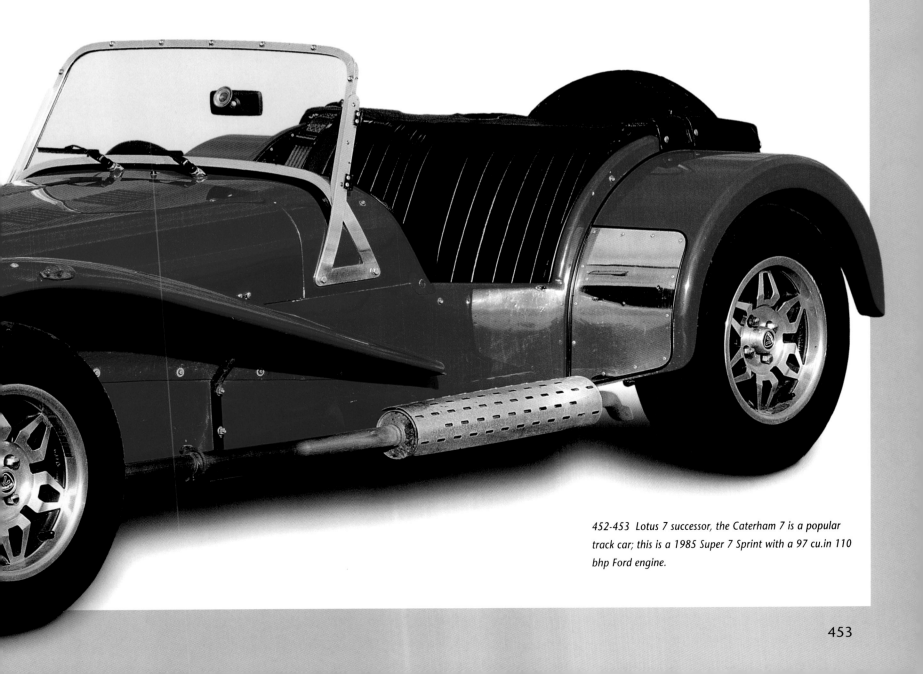

452-453 Lotus 7 successor, the Caterham 7 is a popular track car; this is a 1985 Super 7 Sprint with a 97 cu.in 110 bhp Ford engine.

1981 - 1990

Championship wins continued from 1988-90. More Evolutions followed and Integrales won in 1991 and 1992, six in succession. Production finally ceased in November 1994 after 44,300 had been sold with various special edition models on the way including rally replicas in Martini colors. Any of the Integrale models is a classic worth keeping.

The Peugeot combine had included Citroen from 1974 and Chrysler-Talbot from 1978. Peugeot themselves had taken part in such events as the East African Safari with some success, but left sprint rallying to the Coventry-based Talbot-Sunbeam-Lotus after the take-over. That rewarded them with the Manufacturers championship in 1981, the last year of Group 4. For Group B the operation was run from France and a purpose-built rally machine was designed to fit under a slightly stretched version of the 205 which was launched in 1983. The 205 Turbo 16 was homologated later that year with the 200 cars laid out alongside the extra 20 Evolution specials. Using the strong light-alloy diesel block with a twin-cam 16-valve head on top, the turbocharged 109 cu.in produced a standard 200 bhp or 335 bhp in Evolution 1 form. The engine was mounted transversely at the rear, offset to the right, with a Citroen SM gearbox coupled to four wheel drive.

Successful enough in 1984, the 205 T16 came out for 1985 in Evolution 2 form with front fins and a rear wing with up to 450 bhp and won the Championship in both 1985 and 1986. With no group A car available, Peugeot took wilder versions of the T16 into long distance rally-raids like the Paris-Dakar. In appearance, the 205 Turbo 16 managed to retain the chic charm of the 205 – an attractive and very effective little classic.

Despite being from the same company as Peugeot, Citroen also went into Group B. The Visa 1000 Pistes was built as a class contender for 1984 using a Peugeot 82 cu.in transverse engine and 4WD with 145 bhp in Evolution form. It never achieved success and Citroen switched to the BX 4TC for 1986 using a Peugeot 505 128 cu.in engine, turbocharged with an oversimplified 4WD system that lacked a center differential. That too failed and the cars joined Peugeot in Paris-Dakar

events. A classic pair of failures.

BMC, BMLC, British Leyland, BL Cars had become Austin Rover in 1982. Under its various guises the company had a long tradition of rallying from the big Healeys, through the Minis and into the Triumph TR8, which had its last rally in 1980. For Group B, they eventually chose to use a mid-engined derivative of the MG Metro with four wheel drive. The basic design was carried out in 1982 by the Williams Grand Prix Engineering offshoot of the F1 team. Unlike all its rivals, the car did not use a turbocharged engine as the designers wanted a more user-friendly power delivery; the team elected to develop an entirely new 183 cu.in V-6 engine, having initially used a shortened Rover V-8. In basic 'Clubman' 200-off form this developed 250 bhp with around 400 bhp for the 20-off Evolution model. After considerable development, which included the addition of an ugly front spoiler and rear wing, the MG 6R4 was finally homologated in mid-1985. A succession of minor problems prevented it gaining any great results before the end of Group B, but it became a popular and effective UK rally car from 1987 onwards. Not the most appealing of classics, but still a

significant machine. Among the Japanese, the Nissan 240RS (2-door sedan) and Toyota Celica Turbo had made some impact in the early days of group B, but they were only rear-drive machines.

Mazda aimed at Group A and produced a 323 Turbo 4WD using the 97 cu.in engine with a four valve head and a simple 4WD system; the necessary 5000 were completed by mid-1986. The 323 wasn't a great success in 1987 but had some better outings in 1988 with X-trac transmission; for 1989 the mechanical components were transferred to the new shape 323 and the engine increased to 112 cu.in and 180 bhp. In the same mold as the Integrale, it was a neat compact design.

THE RACING REVOLUTION

When Group B was announced for 1982, it was expected that there would soon be a World Championship for racing GT cars as well as for rallying. In the event, there was only a Group C championship for sports-racing cars which lasted well into the next decade. However Ferrari decided to build a 200-off road car from which 20 Evolution racers would be made

available for private entrants. The 288GTO is more fully described later but the way in which it was announced was to prove significant.

When the car was first shown at Geneva 1984, it was stated that the model was to be a limited edition of only 200 cars and that deposits would be taken from those wishing to reserve a car. As the 1962 Ferrari 250GTO had proved to be an appreciating classic, many buyers appeared and the planned 200 cars became 273 before the end. The principle was subsequently used for all the supercars that followed, the deposits making a useful contribution to the production process.

Porsche too were hoping for a Group B racing championship when they produced their Gruppe B 959 prototype in 1983. And they had a history of rallying too from the Sixties, so it was envisaged as a dual-purpose car.

The 959 was based on the 911, so the flat-six engine was mounted behind the rear axle with the gearbox ahead; like the Audi Quattro in reverse, it needed four wheel drive to improve stability. The 173 cu.in engine used twin turbochargers to develop 450 bhp and the transmission used computer control to vary the torque split of the center differential. A prototype won the 1984 Paris-Dakar rally-raid and a production 959 won it again in 1986, but it was to be 1988 before the 200th car was completed and group B rallying had finished. The model was rarely raced but served as a very effective development car for the four-wheel-drive Porsches that were to follow.

Jaguar too conceived the XJ220 as a Group B contender when it was announced in 1988 with a 500 bhp V-12 and Ferguson-designed four-wheel-drive. Deposits were taken, more than the 200 plus 20 Evolutions, so Jaguar had to build the car. By then Group B racing was not going to displace Group C, so JaguarSport redeveloped it without 4WD and replaced the heavy V-12 with a turbocharged 213 cu.in V-6 based on the Metro 6R4 power unit.

The Supercars

First of the Eighties supercars with no competition pretension was the Aston Martin Vantage Zagato. Aware of Ferrari's success in taking deposits for the 288GTO, Aston Martin took deposits for the proposed 50 cars, based on a Zagato sketch at Geneva 1985 and a scale model at Frankfurt. Working prototypes were shown at Geneva 1986 and deliveries started soon after.

A convertible Volante Zagato followed on. Production of the faithful V-8, Volante and Vantage continued until 1989 when Aston Martin finally replaced them with the Virage, a more modern car with using the existing 323 cu.in V-8 with new 4-valve cylinder heads. After the success of the 288GTO launch, Ferrari found another excuse for a low volume supercar.

The F40 celebrated 40 years of Ferrari in 1988. As there had been no Group B racing available for the 288GTO, the 20-off Evolution model was still-born. The F40 used that as its basis for over 1300 F40s. Meanwhile normal Ferrari production continued with the 512 becoming 512i (for injection) in 1981 and the Testarossa with four valve heads and new style in 1984. The Bertone-bodied 308GT4 was replaced in 1981 by Pininfarina's Mondial 8 with a longer wheelbase to be a more serious 2+2; a year later came the 308 Qv and Mondial Qv with four valve heads to retain the power while improving emissions. A very attractive cabriolet arrived in 1984.

All the smaller cars changed from 308 to 328 in 1985 and 348 in 1989. As the capacity of the V-8 engine rose from 183 to 195 to 207 cu.in, the names changed to 328 or 3.2 Mondial and 348 or Mondial T. With the 348 the chassis changed from tubular to monocoque and the engines were changed from transverse to longitudinal mounting. Lamborghini's Countach grew from LP400S to LP500S in 1982 with the V-12 becoming a 289 cu.in. LP5000S QV came in 1985 with a 317 cu.in and four-valve heads.

Of their smaller cars, the Urraco 2+2 had been joined by the Silhouette 2-seater targa-top in 1976, both bring replaced in 1981 by the Jalpa 350 which continued in production to 1989.

After a difficult period, the company was taken over in 1987 by Chrysler, who were able to bring in the Diablo in 1990. Meanwhile Bugatti and McLaren had started work on their supercars for the next decade.

454-455 The 4-valve 317 cu.in engine arrived for the Countach 5000S in 1985. Rear wings were an option.

Mazda Rx-7

With the RX-7 Mazda achieved two things. They consolidated their faith in the new Wankel rotary engine and produced a sporting car that did much to raise the Mazda profile. Mazda only started producing 4-wheeled cars in 1960 but they learnt fast. Early car production was of small cars for the Japanese market; the new light and compact Wankel power unit looked like an ideal replacement for their existing vee-twins so Mazda signed a licence agreement with NSU.

German manufacturers of motor cycles and small cars, NSU had developed the rotary power unit from a compact supercharger designed for them by Dr. Felix Wankel in 1956. After slow development, they introduced a single rotor unit in the Sport Prinz Spyder in 1963, before going onto their definitive twin-rotor powered Ro80 introduced in 1967 – a superb car even without its fascinating power unit.

Early Wankel power units had suffered from excessive wear of the rotor tip seals and poor combustion, and it took NSU some time to eradicate these problems; however what no-one ever cured was heavy fuel consumption. When the 1973 fuel crisis came, most manufacturers stopped their Wankel work. NSU had been absorbed by Volkswagen in 1969; even they ceased Wankel production in 1977.

Citroen went into limited production in 1969 with 500 Ami 8 coupes using a single rotor, followed by the GS Birotor in 1973, but they too dropped out in 1975.

Mazda were more persistent. Having taken on the licence, they worked faster than NSU and showed their first prototype in 1964, the two seater 110S Cosmo with twin rotors and a 122 cu.in equivalent capacity. This attractive coupe was sold from 1967-1972.

The R100 followed a year later with the same engine installed in a coupe version of the smallest sedan – a good engine in search of a chassis. It was a pattern that Mazda would repeat with the RX-2 (1970 Capella 616), RX-3 (1971 Grand Familia 808), 140 cu.in RX-4 (1972 Luce 929) and 158 cu.in RX-5 (1975 Cosmo 121). In fact, the Cosmo coupes were nicely styled but not available in all markets.

By the time the RX-7 came out in 1978, Mazda had made the Wankel unit as reliable as any conventional engine, so the world could enjoy its real benefits of smooth high performance in a compact package, particularly in America where the high consumption was offset by low fuel costs; America was the first overseas market for the the RX-7 (Savanna), which was very much aimed at the Datsun 240Z.

For the RX-7 the Wankel was a twin-rotor unit of 140 cu.in developing 100 bhp. In other respects, the RX-7 was really just a conventional 2+2 sports coupe with a 5-speed gearbox and a live rear axle with coil springing. But the lightweight engine gave good weight distribution and handling, and its size allowed a low bonnet line, which gave it distinctive styling and a low drag factor. It was a great success and Mazda made over half a million of this model before the second generation came along in 1985. The power output had been increased to 115 bhp in 1981 and a 165 bhp turbocharged version came along in 1983, enough for nearly 140 mph. The turbocharged engine was also offered in the Cosmo.

With the new RX-7 came an increase to 158 cu.in, turbocharged for 185 bhp or normally aspirated at 150 bhp.

It had independent rear suspension too and became a strong rival to the Porsche 944 whose style it also resembled. A convertible became available in 1987 and the output from the turbocharged version was increased to 200 bhp in 1989. That year saw the new Eunos Cosmo, a good-looking 4-seater coupe, with a 3-rotor 237 cu.in Wankel turbocharged to give 280 bhp; it was the family man's sporting RX-7 and continued to be available until 1998. The third generation RX-7 came along in 1991 with its 158 cu.in Wankel fitted with twin turbochargers to gave a remarkable 255 bhp, rising to 280 bhp for the fourth generation RX-7 in 1999.

Over the years, the RX-7 has also been successful on the race-track and the Wankel engines have also been used in sports-racing cars; when they finally won Le Mans in 1991, they were using a 4-rotor 317 cu.in engine developing around 700 bhp at 9000 rpm –
a pair of RX-7 units. Although the Wankel engine has been seen in a number of different models over the years, the popularity of the RX-7 alone has justified Mazda's faith in the rotary engine.

TECHNICAL DESCRIPTION OF THE MAZDA RX-7

YEARS OF PRODUCTION	1978-1985 (1981)
MODELS	COUPE 2-SEATER
ENGINE	FRONT-MOUNTED 2-ROTOR WANKEL
BORE X STROKE, CAPACITY	EQUIVALENT TO 139 CU.IN
VALVEGEAR	PORTS IN CASING
FUEL SYSTEM	ONE 4-BARREL CARBURETOR
POWER	115 BHP AT 6000 RPM
TRANSMISSION	5-SPEED
BODY/CHASSIS	STEEL MONOCOQUE
SUSPENSION	FRONT, WISHBONES AND COIL SPRINGS
	REAR, LIVE AXLE AND COIL SPRINGS
TIRES/WHEELS	185/70 x 13 ON 5 IN. ALLOY WHEELS
WHEELBASE, TRACK (F), TRACK(R)	95 x 56 x 55 INCHES
LENGTH, WIDTH, HEIGHT	169 x 65 x 49 INCHES
MAX SPEED	125 MPH
WHERE BUILT	HIROSHIMA, JAPAN

456-457 In 1981, the RX-7 had a minor face-lift which included the rear spoiler. Turbo version came in 1983 with 165 bhp.

Chevrolet Corvette 1983 - 1996

When the latest Corvette was announced in 1983, it was still America's only home-grown sports car. Although it was the fifth distinct body style, it was arguably only the third chassis design. The previous model had lasted since 1968; despite the anti-performance attitudes of the Seventies, it continued to sell well at its own 40,000 a year level and was still selling 25,000 in 1981-1982, so the planned launch for the 1982 model year was deferred for two years.

Work on the new car started in the late Seventies when the decision was finally taken to maintain the front-engine rear drive configuration. They had been looking at mid-engined designs since 1970, using transverse V-8s, or two and four-rotor Wankel engines in what became the Aerovette show car, but any stylistic advantages were outweighed by the practicality of the conventional layout, which could be made to hold the road just as well. A mid-engined V-8 had actually been given the production go-ahead for 1980 but its main supporters moved on and the project was cancelled.

The philosophy of the new Corvette was to make it the best sports car in performance terms; acceleration, top speed, handling, braking had to

be as good as possible and they were starting with a clean sheet of paper. Good suspension demands a stiff chassis; previous Corvette coupes had a steel cage, bonded to the fiberglass body and rubber-mounted to a simple perimeter frame. The new one united the steel sections to make a single welded sheet steel monocoque running from front to rear, incorporating a substantial roll-over hoop behind the cockpit and a strong windscreen surround section. The whole structure was built of galvanized steel. Fiberglass sections for the rear roof, the sills, scuttle and parts of the underbody were bonded to the frame to add stiffness.

An aluminized steel subframe carried the engine, transmission and front suspension while the final drive and rear suspension were carried on their own cast aluminium sub-frame. The two sub-frames were joined by a 'torque-tube' which was actually a cast aluminium channel-section encasing the aluminium prop-shaft. With the exhaust system also suspended under this channel, the complete running gear could be assembled separately. Keeping weight down, aluminium was also used for fixed length drive shafts, wheel uprights, the forged front wishbones, the rear suspension trailing arms and the transverse lower link; and

TECHNICAL DESCRIPTION OF THE CHEVROLET CORVETTE ZR-1

YEARS OF PRODUCTION	1989-1996
MODELS	2-SEATER TARGA-COUPE AND CONVERTIBLE
ENGINE	FRONT-MOUNTED V-8
BORE X STROKE, CAPACITY	3.8 X 3.6 INCHES, 349 CU.IN
VALVEGEAR	FOUR-CAM, FOUR-VALVE
FUEL SYSTEM	FUEL INJECTION
POWER	1989 380 BHP AT 5800 RPM
TRANSMISSION	4-SPEED + O/D, 6-SPEED, 4-SPEED AUTO
BODY/CHASSIS	STEEL FRAME, FIBERGLASS BODY
SUSPENSION	FRONT, WISHBONES AND LEAF SPRING REAR, WISHBONE, DRIVE-SHAFT AND LEAF SPRING
TIRES/WHEELS	275/40ZR AND 315/35ZR X 17 ON 9.5 AND 11 IN ALLOYS
WHEELBASE, TRACK (F), TRACK(R)	96 X 59 X 60 INCHES
LENGTH, WIDTH, HEIGHT	176 X 71 X 46 INCHES
MAX SPEED	175 MPH
WHERE BUILT	BOWLING GREEN, KENTUCKY, USA

458-459 The ZR-1 (main picture) arrived in 1989 with new wheels with over 50% more horsepower than the best of the rest. Inset, a convertible shows the LCD dashboard.

fiberglass was used for the transverse leaf springs front and rear. The maximum Goodyear Eagle tire size played a considerable part in the car's overall scheme; 255/50VR x 16 tires were mounted on 8.5 and 9.5 in. wide alloy wheels.

For the engine, Chevrolet retained the existing 347 cu.in pushrod V-8 which was producing a very unstressed 205 bhp at 4300 rpm using a pair of single point injectors. The four-speed Borg Warner gearbox was mated to a very high overdrive (0.67:1) whose engagement was electronically selected by the engine's ECU (electronic control unit) according to engine speed and throttle position – a useful device to register good fuel economy for the EPA (environmental protection agency) tests. This would eventually be replaced in 1989 by a six-speed gearbox providing similarly long ratios. A GM 4-speed automatic was always an option.

A superb-looking body style was conceived within GM, still made of fiberglass but with a particularly good finish due to the injection of resin into the mold during the curing process. Early studies showed that the radiator could get enough air from underneath the nose which all helped to produce a good drag factor of 0.34; this was much better than the previous car and enabled a 140 mph maximum on 205 bhp. The original plan had been to continue with the T-bar roof of the previous car but a late change was made to make the roof into a single removable panel; the chassis side members were deepened to compensate for the loss of roof stiffness.

A change to multi-port injection in 1985 boosted the power to 230 bhp at 4000 rpm and in 1986 the full convertible arrived. By the time the 6-speed gearbox arrived in 1989, the standard 347 cu.in was producing 250 bhp, but there was a new all-aluminium 347 cu.in V-8 developed by Lotus using four-valve heads with 380 bhp; this Corvette ZR-1 moved into the supercar category with a 175 mph maximum. By the last year of the 1983 Corvette, the two engines were pushing out 304 and 411 bhp respectively. There was a stylish beauty about those 4th generation Corvettes; it is for sure that the ZR-1 is a collectable classic.

TECHNICAL DESCRIPTION OF THE CHEVROLET CORVETTE

YEARS OF PRODUCTION	1986-1996
MODELS	2-SEATER TARGA-COUPE AND CONVERTIBLE
ENGINE	FRONT-MOUNTED V-8
BORE X STROKE, CAPACITY	3.9 x 3.4 INCHES , 349 CU.IN
VALVEGEAR	PUSHROD OHV
FUEL SYSTEM	FUEL INJECTION
POWER	1986 233 BHP AT 4000 RPM
TRANSMISSION	SPEED + O/D, 6-SPEED, 4-SPEED AUTO
BODY/CHASSIS	STEEL FRAME, FIBERGLASS BODY
SUSPENSION	FRONT, WISHBONES AND LEAF SPRING
	REAR, WISHBONE, DRIVE-SHAFT AND
	LEAF SPRING
TIRES/WHEELS	255/50VR X 16 ON
	8.5 OR 9.5 IN ALLOYS
WHEELBASE, TRACK (F), TRACK(R)	96 X 59 X 60 INCHES
LENGTH, WIDTH, HEIGHT	176 X 71 X 46 INCHES
MAX SPEED	144 MPH
WHERE BUILT	BOWLING GREEN, KENTUCKY, USA

460-461 The convertible arrived in 1986 by which time the power had risen from the 1983 205 bhp to 233 bhp. This is an early example.

Ferrari Testarossa 1984 and BB512

The Testarossa was the last of Ferrari's big mid-engined road cars, finally outclassed in handling by the more nimble V-8 engined F355 and replaced by the front-engined 550 Maranello in 1996 – heavier but more practical, more powerful and faster. In its day, though, the Testarossa was the most exciting looking of all the mid-engined supercars and 182 mph was fast by 1984 standards. It would have had a greater following if Ferrari had not produced even more exciting but considerably less practical cars like the 288GTO, F40 and F50; these were just toys alongside the Testarossa, which was a serious road car.

Its origins stem from 1970. The Daytona had been in production since 1968, but Ferrari never rushed into production just to keep up with such

opposition as the Lamborghini Miura. However the Daytona's replacement had to be a 12-cylinder car; they didn't want to follow the Miura's transverse V-12 arrangement, so chose to use a flat-12 engine to maintain a low center of gravity despite its width. Ferrari had been using 183 cu.in flat-12 engines in the Grand Prix cars from 1970 and the same unit would be used in the 312PB sports-racing car.

To create a road-going flat-12 engine, Ferrari opened out the V-12 Daytona engine into a boxer unit – hence the 365GT4BB (Berlinetta Boxer) – and changed the cam drive from chain to toothed belt. Racing cars have their gearboxes in line with the crankshaft and usually behind the axle line, which would produce a long wheelbase for a road car with the gearbox taking up space required for the transverse silencers. Ferrari mounted the gearbox alongside the engine with the drive to the opposite wheel passing under the penultimate main bearing; for the Countach, Lamborghini turned the engine through 180 degrees and had

462-463 The mid-engined Ferrari Testarossa was a striking Pininfarina design with the theme of the side strakes carried round to the rear of the car.

a conventional gearbox at the front, driving the differential at the rear via a shaft in the sump. Both therefore had to lift their engines above the axle line; the Countach power train mass was further forward than for the BB, but Ferrari had the lower center of gravity. A further benefit of the raised engine was that there was more space to provide an exhaust system for the ports on the underside of the heads; for this engine the spark plugs were on the upper face rather than between the cams. Four Weber triple-choke carburetors sat on top of the engine which produced 344 bhp, enough to match the Daytona's 172 mph top speed.

The BB frame was a conventional Ferrari construction with a tubular frame carrying all-round wishbone independent suspension. The BB's Pininfarina body style was an obvious forerunner to the 308 but lacked the later car's more slender elegance; to break up the depth of the side panels a deep belt line ran the length of the car merging into the tops of the fiberglass front and rear bumpers.

On many cars the lower area was painted matte black but they looked far

464-465 This 1980 BB512 has been mildly tailored for competition with a bigger air dam, a lip on the tail, scoops feeding air to sealed air intakes and wider wheels. Most, but not all, had the fiberglass sill panel and the rear wing painted matte black.

better when the whole car was the same color.

The BB was first shown at the 1971 Turin Show as a concept car to test potential purchaser opinion. Production then started in 1973. After some 380 cars, the first update came in 1976 with the capacity increased to 305 cu.in to overcome the effects of emission controls; the 512BB followed the new system of capacity followed by the number of cylinders and included dry sump lubrication, wider rear tires and a front bumper with an air-dam to counteract high speed lift. Fuel injection was added in 1981 to make the 512i. Then came the Testarossa in 1984 and it was a Pininfarina masterpiece whose major feature was the horizontal strakes leading to the radiator intakes just ahead of the rear wheels. The 305 cu.in engine had been fitted with four-valve heads so the power had increased to 390 bhp; this required bigger radiators for which the side location was better than the previous front mounting. The front intake still fed air to the brake cooling ducts. Rear radiators, plus bigger rear tires, made the car six inches wider than the BB; two inches were added to the wheelbase and five inches to the overall length.

The Testarossa stayed virtually unchanged until 1992 when the 512TR arrived with 428 bhp and anti-lock brakes; a new front showed a family identity that would be carried across to the 355. Only two years later came the 512M, with 440 bhp in slightly less weight, new wheels and a revised front with headlights now visible behind clear plastic, but the overall shape was unchanged from the 512TR. And two years later, 1996 saw the flat-12 Ferrari replaced by the Maranello.

YEARS OF PRODUCTION	1976-1981
MODELS	COUPE 2-SEATER
ENGINE	MID-MOUNTED FLAT-12
BORE X STROKE, CAPACITY	3.2 X 3 INCHES, 301 CU.IN
VALVEGEAR	TWIN OHC PER BANK, 2-VALVES
FUEL SYSTEM	BOSCH K-JETRONIC FUEL INJECTION
POWER	360 BHP AT 6500 RPM
TRANSMISSION	5-SPEED
BODY/CHASSIS	STEEL TUBE FRAME, STEEL BODY
SUSPENSION	FRONT, WISHBONES AND COIL SPRINGS
	REAR, WISHBONES AND COIL SPRINGS
TIRES/WHEELS	FRONT, 215/70 X 15 ON 7.5 IN ALLOYS
	REAR, 225/70 X 15 ON 9 IN ALLOYS
WHEELBASE, TRACK (F), TRACK(R)	98.4 X 59 X 61.5
LENGTH, WIDTH, HEIGHT	173 X 72 X 44
MAX SPEED	172 MPH
WHERE BUILT	MARANELLO, ITALY

Aston Martin Vantage and Volante Zagato

By 1984 Aston Martin had been producing the DBS shape for 17 years through four changes of ownership, and, for 15 of those years, the car had been powered by the same 323 cu.in aluminium four-cam V-8 engine. The Lagonda had finally gone into production but its appeal was limited. The company needed a new product but couldn't afford the major capital investment needed. The answer was a new suit of clothes for the top Vantage model.

David Brown had taken the company through DB1 to DB6 models, from being a maker of small sports cars through to a world-renowned manufacturer of the finest Grand Tourers. The DB4 and DB5 had been

four seaters with a reasonable space in the back for adults.

The DB6 had provided more rear seat space, but David Brown wanted his next model to be a full four-seater and faster than the previous range. The new wider shape was designed by Aston Martin's own William Towns; extra weight and frontal area demanded a new engine, a big V-8 with twin overhead camshafts.

Although work had started on the V-8 engine in 1963, it wasn't ready for production when the DBS was announced in 1967; so this had to use the 6-cylinder DB6 engine until the V-8 was ready in 1969. With 315 bhp, the DBS V-8 was the 160 mph car that David Brown wanted.

Two owners later, the Vantage high performance version arrived in 1977 with 375 bhp and an aerodynamically improved body with a front air-dam, filled-in front grille and a tail spoiler. The convertible Volante followed a year later in response to American demand and remained a very popular model until it was replaced in 1989.

While the Vantage was capable of 170 mph, the new breed of supercar was aiming for even higher speeds. It was the renewal of an old association which brought Aston Martin back into the supercar league. Zagato of Milan had built a limited series of 19 bodies on the DB4GT chassis from 1962-1964. Twenty-five years on, the new owners were looking for an extension to the Vantage range at the time of the 1984 Geneva Motor Show and visited the Zagato stand. Soon afterwards, the general performance criteria for a new Aston Martin Zagato were agreed – a maximum speed of 185 mph and the ability to reach 60 mph in under 5 seconds, with just two seats and a probable production of 50 cars. The engine would be the trusty V-8 developed to produce 435 bhp with bigger carburetors, new camshafts, higher compression and larger exhaust manifolds; as this was to be an after-market conversion, fitted together with a higher axle ratio, not every Vantage Zagato would match the figures.

TECHNICAL DESCRIPTION OF THE ASTON MARTIN VANTAGE ZAGATO	
YEARS OF PRODUCTION	1986-1989
MODELS	COUPE
ENGINE	FRONT-MOUNTED V-8
BORE X STROKE, CAPACITY	3.9 x 3.3 INCHES, 325 CU.IN
VALVEGEAR	TWIN OVERHEAD CAMSHAFT PER BANK
FUEL SYSTEM	4 WEBER 48IDF WEBERS
POWER	432 BHP AT 6000 RPM
TRANSMISSION	ZF 5-SPEED MANUAL
BODY/CHASSIS	STEEL PLATFORM, ALUMINIUM BODY
SUSPENSION	FRONT, WISHBONES AND COILS SPRINGS
	REAR, DE DION AXLE AND COIL SPRINGS
TIRES/WHEELS	255/50VR x 16 ON 8 IN. STEEL WHEELS
WHEELBASE, TRACK (F), TRACK(R)	103 x 59 x 59 INCHES
LENGTH, WIDTH, HEIGHT	173 x 74 x 51 INCHES
MAX SPEED	186 MPH
WHERE BUILT	NEWPORT PAGNELL, ENGLAND

466-477 Vantage Zagato was Aston Martin's supercar challenger and achieved 185 mph. Bonnet hump was needed to hide downdraft carburetors.

The Zagatos could have had a prototype ready for the 1985 Geneva show if Aston Martin had not enforced a 6-month delay in the middle. However a drawing plus the Aston Martin and Zagato reputations were enough to persuade 50 buyers over the next six months to place deposits, a major contribution to the development costs. Three prototypes were shown at Geneva in 1986 and production of the 50 cars began shortly afterwards. Zagato received the working platforms, built new superstructures, fitted the aluminium bodywork, trimmed the interiors, painted the cars and sent them back to Newport Pagnell.

Zagato had originally drawn a flat bonnet around the lower profile of the planned injection system but had to insert a bulge to clear the original downdraft Weber carburetors. Although Zagato introduced a relatively unobtrusive bulge for the production cars, the first press tests were conducted on a factory prototype with a very unsightly hump which the press never forgot. The French magazine Sport Auto was the only one able to find enough road to check the maximum speed – a piece of unopened motorway. They achieved 185 mph – near

468-469 Volante Zagato had less power but used fuel injection to allow a flat bonnet and hid its headlights behind shutters.

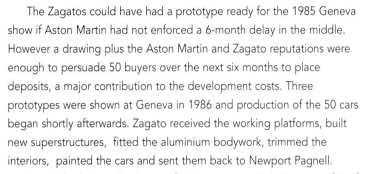

enough – with 0-60 mph in 4.8 seconds. In fact, 51 Vantage Zagatos were built; it might have been 52 but the car assigned to Aston Martin Chairman, Victor Gauntlett, was used as the prototype for another limited series. The convertible Volante Zagato was shown at Geneva in 1987; this time the fuel injection engine was used, so the Volante looked very much as the Vantage should have looked with an almost flat bonnet and concealed headlights.

Although the Zagato-bodied V-8s never achieved the accolades accorded to the DB4GT Zagato, their contribution to the company finances was far greater; without them, Ford's 1987 takeover might never have happened.

TECHNICAL DESCRIPTION OF THE ASTON MARTIN VOLANTE ZAGATO	
YEARS OF PRODUCTION	1988-1990
MODELS	CONVERTIBLE
ENGINE	FRONT-MOUNTED V-8
BORE X STROKE, CAPACITY	3.9 x 3.3 INCHES, 325 CU.IN
VALVEGEAR	TWIN OVERHEAD CAMSHAFT PER BANK
FUEL SYSTEM	FUEL INJECTION
POWER	305 BHP AT 5500 RPM
TRANSMISSION	AUTO OPTION
BODY/CHASSIS	STEEL PLATFORM, ALUMINIUM BODY
SUSPENSION	FRONT, WISHBONES AND COIL SPRINGS
	REAR, DE DION AXLE AND COIL SPRINGS
TIRES/WHEELS	255/50VR x 16 ON 8 IN. STEEL WHEELS
WHEELBASE, TRACK (F), TRACK(R)	103 x 59 x 59 INCHES
LENGTH, WIDTH, HEIGHT	173 x 74 x 51 INCHES
MAX SPEED	150 MPH
WHERE BUILT	NEWPORT PAGNELL, ENGLAND

Ferrari F40

The 288GTO and the F40 were both based on the desire of Ferrari to stem Porsche's domination of GT racing. Ferrari had withdrawn from factory participation in sports car racing at the end of 1973 when FIA sports cars were just two-seater Grand Prix cars. When this was changed in favor of modified GT cars for 1976, some private owners wanted to race their 512BBs; Ferrari produced seven special 512BBs over 1978/9 but none achieved any success. The rules changed again for 1982 with Group B – GT cars – requiring 200 identical units for homologation. While these were not for racing, they had to be produced before the necessary 10 per cent of competition (evolution) models could be used.

As it turned out, Group B racing failed to capture any following. Fortunately Ferrari was well under way with the project and introduced the 288GTO at the 1984 Geneva Show as a Limited Edition of 200. The initials deliberately evoked memories of the 250GTO, where O stood for Omologato. To be sure that 200 such cars could be sold, they started taking deposits at the show, setting a new trend in the process. Inevitably demand exceeded the intended 200 supply and over 270 were finally built.

It wasn't necessary for homologation purposes but Ferrari chose to use the 308GTB as the basis for the new car. A small light car was obviously better for racing than the big Boxer, and Porsche had shown that turbocharging was the way to go for endurance racing. Ferrari were also using a turbocharged 91.5 cu.in engine in the 126C Grand Prix car from 1981 and had chosen to turbocharge the Italian market 2-valve 208 when the 308 was given four-valve heads in 1982 – this raised the 144 cu.in output from 170 bhp to 220 bhp with 0.6 bar pressure. The 308 engine had further development when it was used to power the Lancia LC2 Group C car from 1983-1986; it withstood over 700 bhp when turbocharged to 1.5 bar.

470-471 Ferrari F40 was derived from the Evolution version of the 288GTO but with all-new composite bodywork.

472-473 Small venturis are used at the rear to provide some
downforce. Bodywork was wider than for the 288GTO as the
F40 used the latest Pirelli P Zero tires.

To run the V-8 engine in the 244 cu.in category of a future Group B, the capacity had to be set at 173 cu.in, allowing for the 1.4 turbo equivalence factor. With twin IHI turbochargers the GTO engine produced 400 bhp at 7000 rpm using 0.8 bar with air-to-air intercooling. Using two small turbochargers reduces turbo-lag – the time taken for the turbines to speed up – and leaves scope for bigger ones for more power. For racing, you need to be able to change gear ratios quickly, which is not possible with a transverse gearbox in unit with the final drive, so the engine was swung through 90 degrees to allow a conventional gearbox behind the axle line; this also eased the installation of the twin turbos. As a result, an extra 4 inches was added to the wheelbase, and the rear of the body was flared out by seven inches to accommodate wider wheels and tires. The chassis was just a stretched version of the 308's tubular frame, but the body was a mixture of materials using fiberglass, Kevlar for the bonnet, and carbon/Kevlar for the roof. The homologated weight was 2550 lbs; although production ones with full interior trim were nearer 2860 lbs they were still 110 lbs lighter than the 308GTB. The GTO looked very like the 308, just longer and wider, until you came to the vertical slots behind the 288GTO's rear wheels, classic reminders of those behind the front wheels of the 250GTO twenty years earlier.

In parallel with the design of the 288GTO, Ferrari also developed the Evolution version which would have been used for racing. When the decision was taken to produce a special car to celebrate the 40th anniversary of Ferrari, the Evo was an obvious basis.

The chassis was a similar tubular space-frame but used fibercarbon bonded to the sills, rather than welded sheet steel, to give a lighter stronger structure; body panelling used Kevlar and fibercarbon while the interior displayed a lot of bare fibercarbon and little sound-deadening.

The suspension was modified for Pirelli's latest P Zeros which were considerably wider, adding further to the width of the body, for which Pininfarina created a superbly aggressive style. The power was increased to 478 bhp by adjusting the capacity slightly but with the twin turbos running up to 1.1 bar.

The F40 was duly launched in July 1987, appropriately the last car launched in Enzo Ferrari's presence. The plan was to build around 750 with perhaps a quarter going to the USA which had not been included in GTO sales; the run finally ended in 1992 with 1310 built.

The BMW Z1 marked a turning point in the BMW philosophy, the return of the sports car. Over 1988-1991, 8000 of these neat little two-seaters were built and their success led directly to the launch of the Z3 roadster in late 1995, and the Z3 coupe in 1998.

Although BMW's pre-war reputation was founded on the competition successes of its two-seater sports cars, no open two-seaters had been produced since the 1960 rebirth. Only 252 of the classic 507 had been produced in the Fifties. From then BMW had concentrated on refined sedans and coupes until the launch of the Motorsport division in 1973; the 2002 Turbo wore M-Sport colors but their first product was the mid-engined M1 in 1978.

It wasn't until the 1984 launch of the M635CSi, followed in 1985 by the M3, that the division's activity focussed on producing high performance versions of the sedan cars, taking a leaf from the book of BMW tuning specialists, Alpina. Seeking more creative input from their engineers, BMW set up BMW Technik in 1985 to look at new production processes and vehicle technologies. As a visible product of the new department, they wanted to show a car designed for a new market sector, one that could also be produced if the public response was favorable. The Z1 was the result, Z being the abbreviation for Zentral Entwicklung or Central Development. Based on the 325i, it was a mixture of the old and the new.

The platform used elements from the 3-series, with built-up sill boxes, strong A-pillars for roll-over protection, and an engine compartment revised to allow the engine to be mounted further back in the search for a 50:50 weight distribution. The engine and gearbox came

BMW Z1

from the 170 bhp 325i but an aluminium torque-tube was used between the aluminium casing used for the gearbox and the final drive unit. Strut-type front suspension followed the 3-series but the rear suspension used a geometrical equivalent to a double wishbone set-up; called the Z-axle this would be used by the 1990 3-series cars. This modified chassis was then zinc-coated for maximum corrosion resistance.

Further chassis stiffening was provided by a full-length resin-foam sandwich undertray, shaped to manage underbody air-flow and produce some downforce. Wind-tunnel work also produced a clean overall shape that returned a drag factor of 0.32 with the soft-top erected, and 0.44 without. Air diverters on the top of the screen and a carefully shaped tail minimized wind buffeting for the occupants.

The principle of a stiff monocoque chassis with detachable body panels had been exploited by such as Citroen with the DS19; BMW avoided the usual weight penalty by using lightweight plastic panels. In style, its frontal aspect would appear on the 8-series and the rear panel was adopted for the 3-series. The sills were high enough to provide side impact protection and restrain the driver, so the doors were very shallow and could safely be left open; this was made possible by designing them to drop down between the sill and the outer body, only after the side windows had retracted first.

There was actually little to be gained from such an exercise as it was more difficult to get in and out over the high sill, but it was different from other cars and it proved to the company that they were capable of making appealing two-seaters; from there to the Z3 was a relatively small step.

474-475 BMW made just 8000 of the clever Z1 from 1988 to 1991. Small front grille was copied by the BMW 850.

TECHNICAL DESCRIPTION OF THE BMW Z1

YEARS OF PRODUCTION	1988-1991
MODELS	ROADSTER 2-SEATER
ENGINE	FRONT-MOUNTED IN-LINE SIC
BORE X STROKE, CAPACITY	3.3 x 2.9 INCHES, 152 CU.IN
VALVEGEAR	SINGLE OVERHEAD CAMSHAFT
FUEL SYSTEM	BOSCH MOTRONIC FUEL INJECTION
POWER	170 BHP AT 5800 RPM
TRANSMISSION	5-SPEED
BODY/CHASSIS	STEEL MONOCOQUE, PLASTIC BODY
SUSPENSION	FRONT, STRUTS AND COIL SPRINGS
	REAR, SEMI-TRAILING ARMS AND COILS
TIRES/WHEELS	225/45ZR X 16 ON 7.5 IN. ALLOYS
WHEELBASE, TRACK (F), TRACK(R)	96.3 x 57 x 58 INCHES
LENGTH, WIDTH, HEIGHT	154 x 66 x 50 INCHES
MAX SPEED	135 MPH
WHERE BUILT	MUNICH, GERMANY

476-477 Doors dropped down inside the sill which was deep enough to allow driving with the doors down. Inset shows three door positions, up, down and intermediate.

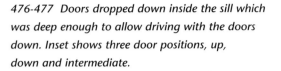

Nissan 300ZX

The second generation 300ZX was a widely respected car, acknowledged as a classic while it was still in production. It had the right combination of performance, handling, practicality and comfort to appeal to a wide range of people.

Nissan had entered the serious sports coupe market in 1969 with the Datsun 240Z, which quickly established a wide USA following and a reputation in Europe as the new Austin-Healey 3000. Over the next twenty years it developed through 260Z, 280ZX and (Nissan) 300ZX, each of these being available as a 2-seater or 2 + 2.

The first Nissan 300ZX had arrived five years after the 280ZX in 1983. The engine this time was a two-cam 183 cu.in V-6 in normally aspirated 170 bhp and turbocharged 225 bhp forms, the American turbo version having 205 bhp while the Japanese market had a 122 cu.in V-6 turbo with 170 bhp (Fairlady Z200). While the 300ZX was essentially a revised 280ZX, the body panels were all new and the shape considerably cleaner – the European cars would reach 140 mph. Japanese market cars had a foretaste of the next model in 1986 when the V-6 gained four-cam four-valve heads to get 190 bhp. The Japanese 122 cu.in reverted to a straight six with turbo for 180 bhp. Further shape revisions took place in 1987 making the final version seem outwardly remarkably similar to its successor, but underneath it was time to start again.

The new 300ZX was launched at the 1989 Chicago Show, the same show that saw the Honda NSX in prototype form, mid-engined versus the conventional front engine rear drive Nissan. Everything was changed for the new generation 300ZX, which was going to be produced as a 2-seater or 2+2 (5-inches longer), with or without turbochargers. Although the T-bar roof was an option, most cars had it. The European markets only had 300ZX Turbo 2+2, while Americans could only have the Turbo as a 2-seater, but could have either body with the non-turbo engine.

The basic 183 cu.in V-6 engine was almost the same as that used in the previous 300ZX but the cylinder block was lightened and stiffened, although still of cast iron. New 4-cam 4-valve cylinder heads were fitted with variable valve timing used for the inlet camshafts. In normal form, the engine developed 230 bhp, but a turbocharger for each cylinder bank produced 280 bhp for the Europeans, or 300 bhp for the USA with higher octane fuel. There was nothing special about the transmission which used either a 5-speed manual or a 4-speed automatic.

Monocoque design too was conventional, with strong box sections surrounding the cockpit and running to each end of the car. It was all steel with most of the inner sections being zinc-nickel plated. Aluminium was used for the large bonnet and inside the polyurethane bumpers. Where the previous model had carried on the old 240Z strut-type front suspension, it had picked up the semi-trailing arm rear suspension from the 280ZX.

The new car used double-wishbone geometry, but with three links at the front and double wishbone plus a track control arm at the rear. The latter was used for the Super HICAS electro-hydraulic rear steering system fitted to the Turbo model – depending on speed and steering angle it countersteers the rear wheels by up to 1 degree to improve the turn-in before settling back to the straight ahead position. Both front and rear brakes use ventilated discs with twin calipers and have ABS control.

The body shape was evolved in house with help from the wind-tunnel to achieve a drag factor of 0.31, giving the Turbo a maximum around 160 mph. The philosophy was to capture the appearance of a Group C sports-racing car with a forward cockpit and short overhangs outside the wheelbase; the designers succeeded in this as the first impression is that it could be a mid-engined car. The sloping bonnet placed a premium on space for the engine and its ancillaries, but the short length of a V-6 made this possible and also served to keep the weight evenly distributed – 55:45 on the 2-seater and 53:47 on the 2+2. The wheelbase was 5 inches longer than before but the overall length was shorter. For access to the luggage space, the 300ZX retained a hatchback.

During its lifetime there were no significant changes, apart from the introduction of a convertible version in 1992. Having become a classic in its own production lifetime the 300ZX was dropped in 1997 after around a quarter million had been built in various forms.

TECHNICAL DESCRIPTION OF THE NISSAN 300ZX TURBO 2+2

YEARS OF PRODUCTION	1989-1996
MODELS	COUPE 2+2
ENGINE	FRONT-MOUNTED V-6, TWIN-TURBO
BORE X STROKE, CAPACITY	3.4 X 3.2 INCHES, 180 CU.IN
VALVEGEAR	DOUBLE OVERHEAD CAMSHAFT
FUEL SYSTEM	FUEL INJECTION
POWER	280 BHP AT 64000 RPM
TRANSMISSION	5-SPEED MANUAL
BODY/CHASSIS	STEEL MONOCOQUE
SUSPENSION	FRONT, WISHBONES AND COILS
	REAR, WISHBONE, LINKS AND COILS
TIRES/WHEELS	FRONT, 225/50 X 16 ON 7.5 IN. ALLOYS
	REAR, 245/45 X 16 ON 8.5 IN. ALLOYS
WHEELBASE, TRACK (F), TRACK(R)	101 X 58.9 X 61.2 INCHES
LENGTH, WIDTH, HEIGHT	178 X 70 X 50 INCHES
MAX SPEED	158 MPH
WHERE BUILT	TOKYO, JAPAN

478-479 Nissan's second generation 300ZX became a classic in its own production life-time; the convertible was added to the range in 1992 and used the shorter wheelbase.

Honda NSX

While Honda developed their sedans and coupes cars to perform better and better, the NSX was the welcome return to the sports car market which they had ignored from 1965-1990. The 1999 S2000 showed they mean to stay there.

Honda built up their engineering reputation through their motorcycles which pushed the British and Italian bikes out of the top positions during the Sixties. Their first cars came in 1962, mini-cars for the Japanese market. They went into Formula One in 1965 with a 91.5 cu.in V-12, and built cars for the 183 cu.in formula, gaining a single Grand Prix success with each. But it was the performance of the 61 cu.in Formula Two engines with which Brabham dominated the class in 1966 that really established their reputation in the car racing world. Once they returned to Grand Prix racing as an engine supplier in 1983, their success became legendary.

Honda, perhaps more than anyone else, understood the science of combustion. The 1971 introduction of CVCC (Compound Vortex

Controlled Combustion) used a pre-combustion chamber to produce a stratified charge and very clean exhaust emissions. Because the rest of the American industry were unable to match this, the adopted solution was to continue to produce inefficient engines and then strangle the exhaust with catalytic converters.

The arrival of V-TEC (Variable Valve Timing and Electronic Control) engines in the Mid-eighties was another demonstration of Honda's engineering superiority which would be copied by all; Honda used four valves per cylinder with one inlet valve inoperative until the driver demanded more power, at which point hydraulic controls brought that valve into use and changed the cam timing giving a pronounced power increase.

With such race and technology backgrounds, it was not surprising that Honda felt able to challenge the established supremacy of Ferrari and Porsche in the ultimate sports car market. The NSX (New Sports eXperimental) was first shown in 1989, with production to start a year

later. The technological triumph of this car was the extensive use of aluminium in the suspension and monocoque chassis-body unit, some 5 years before Audi's much acclaimed A8.

Such a car had to be mid-engined, so Honda mounted a 183 cu.in V-6 transversely with the gearbox on the end, giving a compact unit that gave plenty of cockpit space and also allowed luggage space behind. The engine used Honda's V-TEC variable valve timing (belt drive) and added the VVIS (Variable Volume Intake System). In this form it produced 274 bhp at 7300 rpm; although the peak torque was produced at 5500 rpm, the V-TEC system ensured that it was extremely tractable at low speeds. Transmission choices were a manual 5-speed gearbox or a 4-speed automatic.

Traction control and ABS braking were to be expected in such a design; electrically operated speed-sensitive assistance was provided for the power steering in cars fitted with automatic transmission, but this became a no-cost option for manual transmission cars in 1994. This all

helped to ensure that the NSX was easy to drive and the suspension was well designed to provide superb roadholding with no drama if the limits were exceeded. Early reports suggested that it was so good that it was unexciting, but it was certainly safe.

Although Honda used Pininfarina as a consultant on some of their projects, the NSX was created in-house with wind-tunnel assistance.

It has a longer rear deck than most mid-engined cars, but at least this is used to provide useful space for luggage.

The tail carries a rear wing which blends into the body sides. The resulting shape obviously works as the car achieves 160 mph on its 274 bhp. The NSX is virtually hand-built, so Honda set up a special factory,

480-481 Honda's new sporting flagship used an aluminium body and many of the castings were in aluminium; the NSX was marketed as an Acura in the USA.

capable of producing up to 25 cars a day.

Although the car was not built for racing, Honda produced the lightweight NSX-R in 1992 weighing 2710 lbs instead of 3020 lbs. Three ran in the 1994 Le Mans and all finished. Further appeal had been added with the introduction of the targa-style T-Roof in 1995; at the same time, came the press-button semi-automatic transmission using drive-by-wire connection between engine and accelerator pedal.

For 1997, there were two versions, depending on the transmission chosen. The automatic transmission retained the 183 cu.in engine with a lower compression ratio to give 256 bhp, but manual transmission cars had a 6-speed gearbox with the engine capacity increased to 195 cu.in to bring the power output to 280 bhp with a slight increase in torque.

The NSX will eventually be replaced but it will be a hard act to follow such a perfect classic.

*482-483 The long tail concealed a useful space for luggage.
The 183 cu.in V-6 gave 274 bhp but this was increased to 195 cu.in
and 280 bhp in 1997. The T-roof also came in 1997.*

TECHNICAL DESCRIPTION OF THE HONDA NSX

YEARS OF PRODUCTION	1990-PRESENT
MODELS	TWO-SEATER COUPEAND TARGA
ENGINE	MID-MOUNTED V-6
BORE X STROKE, CAPACITY	3.5 X 3 INCHES, 181 CU.IN
VALVEGEAR	FOUR OVERHEAD CAMSHAFTS
FUEL SYSTEM	HONDA FUEL INJECTION
POWER	274 BHP AT 7300 RPM
TRANSMISSION	5-SPEED MANUAL
BODY/CHASSIS	ALUMINIUM MONOCOQUE
SUSPENSION	FRONT, WISHBONES AND COILS
	REAR, WISHBONES AND COILS
TIRES/WHEELS	FRONT, 205/50 X 15 ON 6.5 IN. ALLOYS
	REAR, 225/50 X 16 ON 8 IN.ALLOYS
WHEELBASE, TRACK (F), TRACK(R)	99.6 X 59.4 X 60.2 INCHES
LENGTH, WIDTH, HEIGHT	174.4 X 71.3 X 46.1 INCHES
MAX SPEED	160 MPH
WHERE BUILT	TOCHIGI, TOKYO, JAPAN

1991 - 2001 and beyond

MORE CARS FEWER MANUFACTURERS

The Nineties saw further rationalization across the global motor industry as manufacturers merged companies and interests to remain competitive in a market that was producing too many cars.

In 1998 Daimler (Mercedes-Benz) merged with Chrysler and bought a 34 per cent stake in Mitsubishi a year later; Chrysler already had an agreement with the Japanese company and various Mitsubishis had been sold under Chrysler/Dodge names in the USA for some time. Renault took a major stake in Nissan in 1999. Fiat Auto acquired Maserati in 1993 and, in 1999, merged technical interests (excluding Ferrari) with General Motors who already had partnership agreements with Isuzu, Suzuki and Subaru as well as major shareholdings in Saab and Holden; GM also signed an engine exchange agreement with Honda in 1999. General Motors tenure of Lotus came to an end in 1992 when the company was bought by Romano Artioli, the Bugatti president, but Malaysian company Proton took over in 1996.

Volkswagen bought several supercar manufacturers in 1998. Lamborghini was owned by Chrysler from 1987-1993, then by MegaTech (an associate company of South Korea's Kia) until 1998. The remains of Bugatti were also acquired in 1998. From England, Volkswagen took Bentley Motors, while being forced to cede Rolls-Royce Motors to BMW from 2003. Rolls-Bentley's previous owners Vickers also sold Cosworth Racing to Ford and Cosworth Engineering to VW-Audi. Seat and Skoda also came under VW control during the Nineties.

BMW's 1994 purchase of Rover went sour towards the end of 1999 when the new Rover 75 sold poorly on its home market and found difficulty overseas through the weakness of the Euro. BMW kept their new Mini project but sold Land Rover to Ford while Rover was taken over by an English consortium.

While such movement guaranteed the continuation of many famous names, it is difficult to extol the classic heritage of, say, an Aston Martin DB7, when it is a Jaguar under the skin or a Rolls Royce Silver Seraph when it owes all its mechanical elements

to a 7-series BMW. But part of the appreciation of classic motoring is an appreciation of style, the ability to turn the heads of bystanders; to them it matters little that the parts underneath do not necessarily match the badge on the car. To the owner too, it is the badge that matters most; provided that the overall behavior of the car still matches the aspirations, sharing platforms and drive-trains with other makes is no deterrent.

Badge engineering was a dirty word when different grilles were put on the same basic car; at least the bodies now tend to be unique to a single make. Classic makes will continue to produce classic cars.

A major technical feature of the Nineties was the rapid increase in the level of computer involvement in every aspect of the car's running gear, interior comfort, vehicle security and infotainment. Engines became ever more efficient with high specific power outputs and low emissions. By the middle of the first decade (2005) new cars will be using 36-volt batteries with 42-volt systems in a bid to reduce fuel consumption still further by using electrical assistance for such as steering, brakes and climate control. While computers have become extremely reliable, they are impossible to restore. We can only wait and see how the classic car owner of the future will be able to replace an ECU in twenty years time; the cars will last but will the systems?

A CLASSIC HICCUP

The dawn of the Nineties saw the temporary bursting of the classic car bubble.

Through the second half of the Eighties, prices had risen dramatically and almost any old car suddenly acquired a value. The enthusiastic classic car owner found himself involved in the investment market as those with money to burn sought new ways of making even more. Any Ferrari became a blue chip investment.

The rarer Aston Martins and Jaguars doubled or tripled in price over five years and the cost of a full restoration was easily recouped in the selling price.

When orders were taken for the Jaguar XJ220, investors rushed to place their deposits, convinced

484-485 Mazda RX-7 was reshaped in 1991; this 1998 version has minor changes to lights and rear wing.

they could make an easy profit.

Jaguar laid down 350; by the time the first cars were coming out in 1992, the bubble had burst. Stock market indices worldwide had fallen steadily from 1989-1992; investors retreated and tried to sell on their deposits. Jaguar finally produced 280.

McLaren had intended to make 300 of their technical masterpiece, the F1, when they planned the project in 1990; but they were too late and built just over 100 of which some 30 cars were special competition versions. Yamaha had tried to join in at the same time with their Grand Prix supercar but stopped development in 1993 when the supercar market had evaporated. The Bugatti name was revived in 1987 to build another hi-tech supercar; the EB110 went into production in 1993, but four years later the factory closed after just 139 cars had been built.

All this had a knock-on effect in the general classic car market and prices dropped back, almost to where they had started in 1985. For the genuine classic car enthusiast it was good news and sense prevailed again on what constituted a classic car.

Sedans

Future classics from the Nineties can only follow past trends. What stands out in a crowd now has a chance of being a future classic. Sedan cars will be appreciated if they have a performance heritage. Inevitably some of the Nineties hot hatchbacks will also reach the level of classic appreciation, such as the Renault Clio Williams (1993-1995). With a 150 bhp 122 cu.in engine, this was produced in three mini-series to celebrate the Williams-Renault Grand Prix partnership. With the next generation Clio, Renault went on to produce the even more powerful Clio 172 (bhp) from 1998. Peugeot's three GTI models – 106, 206, 306 – are also likely to have some future appeal.

Volkswagen's trend-setting Golf GTI had become ever quicker, bigger too; the 1974 Mk.I was replaced by the Mk.II in 1983. With the 1991 Mk.III came a new top of the range 170 cu.in 174 bhp VR6 – a desirable 140 mph small sedan.

The Mk.IV arrived in 1997 and 4WD (4MOTION) became available in 1998; in late 1999 the previous top model 140 cu.in VR5 was displaced by the new 170 cu.in V6 (V6 not VR6 denotes the 24-valve version) with variable valve timing and 204 bhp coupled with a 6-speed gearbox and 4MOTION

transmission – the most classic Golf yet.

As in the Eighties, International rallying was responsible for some desirable cars, but it was getting very expensive for manufacturers to produce a further ten per cent of evolution models on top of 5000 Group A specials. So, in an attempt to keep production costs down, World Rally Championship (WRC) rules changed again in 1997. The production volume required for group A was cut to 2500 cars, provided it was part of a model family of which 25,000 had been produced.

As every WRC car was expected to have 4WD and turbocharger, entrants could then use a Group A car with approved modifications or produce 20 kits of special parts to convert a conventional two-wheel-drive car into a turbocharged 4WD rally car, although

the power limit was still set at 300 bhp for both types.

So Mitsubishi and Subaru continued to run group A cars while others just produced WRC cars for their own use – Ford Focus, Peugeot 206, Seat Cordoba, Toyota Corolla, Hyundai Accent. It is the genuine group A cars and the rally car replicas that are likely to be the future classics.

Mitsubishi's Lancer started as a front wheel drive compact in 1983. By 1991 it had gone through two body revisions and the top version had four-wheel-drive and a 109 cu.in turbo 'four' with 195 bhp. Then they went rallying with the four-door GSR and produced an Evolution version with a 122 cu.in engine and 250 bhp for 1993 – GSR Evo I. Evo II to Evo VI followed from 1994-1999 by which time the four wheel drive systems had been refined, there was

a six-speed gearbox, the 122 cu.in engine was producing 280 bhp and Tommi Makinen had won the world rally championship from 1996-9. Mitsubishi's motorsport arm Ralliart produce various special editions of the Evo models. Evo VII arrived in 2001 Subaru had used four-wheel-drive and flat-four engines from 1979. Nothing classic emerged until 1985 when the neat XT coupe appeared with a flat-four 109 cu.in turbo; for 1987 it had the option of a flat-six 164 cu.in non-turbo version to make an appealing GT package. This was replaced by the attractive SVX coupe in 1991 with the flat-six taken out to 201 cu.in with 240 bhp.

The sedan Impreza came in late 1992 as a shortened Legacy with the flat-four in turbocharged 122 cu.in form with 240 bhp for the rally replica WRX.

Like Mitsubishi they have produced an evolution model each year, won the world championship in 1995 and, by 1998, the twin-turbo WRX had 280 bhp – a Japanese limit for road cars. The first Impreza can not be called beautiful but the rally-derived models, WRX and STI (Subaru Tecnica Industries), are future classics on pure driving appeal. In 2000, Subaru UK produced 1000 Impreza P1 rally replicas – improved versions of the WRX – to pass UK road regulations: P stood for Prodrive who have run the Subaru rally teams in the WRC. A new Impreza is came in 2001.

Ford missed out on rally success in the late Eighties as the Sierra-Cosworth was too big for rallying, but they returned in 1992 with the Escort RS Cosworth equipped with the running gear of the Sierra Cosworth 4x4, a 220 bhp turbo 'four' and four

wheel drive. As this was intended for group A rallying 5000 examples had to be built; once this was completed the ugly rear wings became an option. The RS2000 also returned to the scene in 1991 with a 150 bhp 122 cu.in Zetec engine and 130 mph performance; a 4WD option came in 1993. When the Escort came out in its final form in 1995, 4WD remained as an option with the RS2000 4x4 for another two years to make one of the nicest of all the RS models – already a classic. The rallying mantle has now passed to the Ford Focus WRC, for which a 4WD Cosworth derivative is expected in 2002.

For most of the Nineties, Toyota were also part of the rally scene, using the Celica coupe as a base, winning the WRC in 1993 and 1994. A new shape had come along in 1989, and the 122 cu.in 208 bhp turbo 4WD was added in 1991. When the model was revised again in 1993, the Turbo 4WD had 242 bhp. However the 1999 7th generation Celica just has front-wheel drive and a new 140 bhp 109 cu.in engine as the company has withdrawn from rallying to put its competition effort into Grand Prix racing, but its new-edge wedge styling looks like a future classic.

Nissan were not involved in world championship rallying, but developed a very effective track car with the Skyline GT-R series. Although there had been a limited series of GT-Rs in the late Sixties, the new hi-tech series started in 1987 as a Group A evolution of the 1985 GTS for competition.

The GTS gave 190 bhp from a turbocharged straight six 24-valve 122 cu.in.

When the 8th generation Skyline came in 1989, there was a special GT-R with the engine increased to 158 cu.in and 280 bhp with 4WD and the Nissan rear wheel steering system HICAS; this was R-32. The 9th Skyline included R-33 from 1995 with the same basic specification but many improvements; in 1997, an R-33 took the unofficial production car lap record round the 13-mile Nurburgring circuit. NISMO (Nissan Motorsport) produced an R400 version with 400 bhp. In the 10th Skyline series, the R-34 arrived in 1999 with further technical changes – a stiffer bodyshell, 6-speed gearbox, electronic torque-split on the 4WD and, for the V-spec, underbody aerodynamics.

These competition cars may not be the most elegant of vehicles, but they are such remarkable pieces of engineering that they deserve permanent reconition.

486-487 Jaguar XK8 arrived in 1996 with the new all-aluminium 32-valve 244 cu.in V-8 engine.

1991 - 2001 and beyond

COUPES AND CABRIOLETS

Two door coupe versions of regular sedans will only be appealing if they really look good, like the Peugeot 406 Coupe which was designed and built at Pininfarina; in its top 190 bhp 176 cu.in V-6 form, it goes as well as it looks. But there are more potential classic coupes which use all-new skins on sedan car platforms – Mercedes CLK, Jaguar XK8, Pontiac Firebird, Ford Mustang and Mercury Cougar, Toyota Soarer (Lexus SC in America) Volvo C70. Many of these also have high performance options and most have cabriolet versions.

Starting from smaller platforms, the Coupes and Spiders from Alfa Romeo and Fiat will also find a classic niche – both with interesting styling. The Fiat Coupe (1993) and the shorter Barchetta (1995) are based on the Tipo which became the Bravo in 1995, while the Alfa Romeo GTV (1994) and Spider (1994) stemmed from the same platform using Pininfarina styling with the GTV having the option of the 183 cu.in V-6. Cabriolets created from such sedans as the Saab 9-3 and BMW M3-series will also be worth keeping.

Aston Martin's big V-8s continued throughout the Nineties but the 1993 arrival of the DB7, then heavily based on the Jaguar XJS, put production numbers up to the highest ever at 1000 a year; they added a convertible in 1996 and installed a V-12 for the new-look Vantage in 1999.

Bristol was still an independent and continued to produce a handful of luxury cars per year. The Blenheim, still powered by 366 cu.in Chrysler V-8, replaced the Brittania in 1993; Blenheim 2 had minor revisions for 1997. And at the end of 1999 Bristol revealed plans to build a new coupe due for production in 2001; the Fighter will use the Chrysler Viper 488 cu.in V-10 in a lightweight aluminium chassis – its proportions are reminiscent of the early Fifties Le Mans racing Bristol 450.

Maserati's final variations on the original Biturbo theme were the Ghibli (1992) with the familiar V-6 in 122 cu.in 306 bhp or 170 cu.in 284 bhp forms and the Shamal (1989) using a 326 bhp 195 cu.in V-8. A stretched Biturbo, the Quattroporte, continued with the 170 cu.in V-6. The first model since the Ferrari takeover, the 3200GT 2+2, joined the luxury coupe market in 1998 using the 195 cu.in V-8 with 280 bhp – styled by Giugiaro who had been responsible for the original Ghibli when he was at Bertone.

Mercedes' 1989 SL range continued throughout the Nineties, adding the V-12 SL600 in 1992, and replacing the in-line sixes with 90 degree V-6s in 1998. A new range of SLs is expected for 2001 to be followed by the hi-tech McLaren-Mercedes SLR from 2003.

488-489 Lamborghini Diablo roadster was seen as a prototype in 1993 and went into production in 1995.

THE SUPERCARS

Certainly all Porsches and Ferraris will continue to be revered in the purpose built GT category. In the Mid-nineties, Porsche dropped their front-engined range, the 968 (the 1991 replacement for the 944) and the 928, to produce ever more sophisticated variations of the 911 – the 993 from 1993 and the 996 from 1997. Competition produced its own models; the limited mid-engined GT1 came in 1997, the GT2 in 1998 and the GT3 in 1999.

Ferrari developed the Testarossa into the 512TR in 1992 and 512M in 1994, but reverted to front engines for the 550 Maranello in 1996 as their performance flagship. This followed on from the successful launch of the front-engined 456GT 2+2 in 1992. The 'little' Ferrari became the 355 in 1994 and the 360 Modena in 1999, although the 355 Spider continued for another year until the 360 cabriolet

arrived. After the success of the F40, Ferrari produced the F50 in 1995 – less than ten years later; like its predecessor, the F50 was a road-going racer with all the appropriate technology, but was not designed for racing. An F60 will soon follow.

Honda continued to be the major rival to the Ferrari 355/360 with the NSX; an even lighter limited edition of the aluminium body/chassis unit was used for the NSX-R in 1992, a T-roof came in 1995, and the V-6 engine was increased to 195 cu.in in 1997. With Honda's more active return to formula one in 2000, albeit still only as an engine supplier, we can expect more sporting models – like the type R Integra – and a new NSX is expected in 2001.

Lamborghini had been reduced to a single model when the Diablo replaced the Countach in 1990; various versions followed including the 4WD VT in 1991 and a roadster in 1995. Audi's influence became apparent in 2000 with the Diablo 6.0 VT

brought back to its original smooth shape which was further refined; almost every detail, inside and out , was improved. The Lamborghini is the classic king of the road, which the VW-Audi group will challenge themselves when they eventually bring the Bugatti name to the market. Bugatti had been a classic name from its foundation at Molsheim in 1910. While a few type 101 cars were built after the war, the make was effectively dead from the time of Ettore Bugatti's death in 1947 until it was revived in 1987; Romano Artioli, with moral support from the son of Bugatti's second marriage, set up a brand new hi-tech factory near Modena in Italy. The EB110 (110 years from Bugatti's birth in 1881) was launched in 1991 as an engineering masterpiece; the body was in aluminium but fibercarbon was used for the chassis, which carried a mid-mounted 213 cu.in V-12 with four turbochargers, coupled to a six-speed gearbox and a four-wheel drive system. It would

1991 - 2001 and beyond

comfortably exceedut the failure of the supercar market killed the project and the company by 1997.

Inevitably the McLaren F1 has to be considered a classic, a rare and expensive one. With its central driver seat, all fibercarbon body and chassis, and mid-mounted BMW V-12 engine it was very much a road-going Grand Prix car, but with some very sophisticated refinement. A racing version was also built. Production had started in 1993 but stopped in 1997 after just 100 of the planned 300 had been built.

Venturi too were still active in the luxury mid-engined category; they produced the twin-turbo 408 bhp 400GT for a one-make racing series in 1992 and the 3183 cu.in Douvrin V-6 came in 1994 for the Atlantique. Lotus finally became a serious rival when they added the twin turbo 354 bhp 213 cu.in V-8 to the long-running Esprit in 1996; the 243 bhp 122 cu.in turbo 'four' was still offered in the more sporting GT3. Lotus will finally replace the Esprit in 2002 with what is currently (2000) called the M250

using Elise chassis technology.

Another English rival will be the Spectre R45. This started as the GTD R42 in 1993; GTD had made some 350 GTD40s as steel-framed fiberglass-bodied replicas of the famous GT40 from 1985-1992, and they were very good cars in their own right, usable on road or track. Seeking a move into the world of homologated production road cars, they evolved the mid-engined R42 using an aluminium and steel monocoque with the 280 cu.in quad-cam Ford V-8 with their own gearbox. As with the GT40 the number reflected the height in inches. GTD never reached the production stage and the company was reformed as Spectre Cars. The restyled Spectre R45 was shown in 1997 and production is expected to start in 2000. As a roadgoing evolution of the classic GT40 it deserves to succeed.

Another classic name of the Fifties returned when Osca was revived in 1998 by the heirs of Touring, Zagato and Maserati with Japanese

backing. The Osca 2500 uses a steel frame chassis with a mid-mounted Subaru 190 bhp 152 cu.in flat-four under neat-looking two-seater aluminium bodywork. Production was scheduled for late 2000. Of a similar specification is the Vemac RD180 which uses a 180 bhp 109 cu.in Honda V-TEC; with engineering by Tokyo R&D, it will be developed and built in England by the company that produced the Yamaha-powered tandem-seater Rocket of the early Nineties, designed by McLaren's Gordon Murray. Subsequently the only supercars have been those built to take part in World Championship Sports car racing which demanded a production of 25 for the GT1 category. Mercedes and Porsche were the only major manufacturers to get involved. Porsche produced the 911 GT1 in 1997 but made it mid-engined and Mercedes made the CLK-GTR using fibercarbon chassis and bodywork with a mid-mounted 421 cu.in V-12 developing over 600 bhp – the 25 were built in 1998-1999.

Two small companies that were also involved in

490-491 Porsche Boxster started production in 1996 with the 204 bhp 152 cu.in flat six

Sports 2-seaters, open and closed

sports-car racing of the Nineties were Lister and Panoz. Panoz had built old-style roadsters from 1996 but made a new front-engined design for racing. Engineering company Lister had produced successful sports-racing cars in the Fifties; although the engineering side has continued throughout, the Lister make was revived in the Eighties using highly modified Jaguar XJS V-12 with enlarged engines, improved handling and revised bodywork. The 1994 Lister Storm took the Jaguar V-12 several stages further with a supercharged 427 cu.in derivative in an all-new chassis and body with luxury interior at a high price. Racing versions followed.

In Germany Isdera, which started to make cars in 1981, continued to make a handful of mid-engined Imperators and Commendatores using Mercedes V-8s and V-12s. Mercedes V-12 power was also used for the Italian Pagani Zonta announced in 1999 while a new French company, Mega, had joined the scene in 1998 also using Mercedes V-12 power for the mid-engined Montecarlo.

Despite increasing restrictions on using performance, sports cars have regained popularity and there are many more on the roads now. Although many sporting drivers prefer the practicality of a closed roof, the near-universal speed limits have brought the open car back into favor. Necessarily owned by driving enthusiasts, they are all likely to become classics in time.

Most sports cars continued to use the classic front engine rear drive principle, although greater attention was paid to keeping the weight distribution evenly balanced for better handling. Mazda redesigned the MX-5 Miata in 1998 and continued to show their faith in the Wankel engine with a new RX-7 coupe in 1999. After many years, Honda finally returned to this market with the S2000 in 1999 using a variable cam 122 cu.in engine and 6-speed gearbox in a classic two-seater; with 240 bhp available it is impressively quick.

Mercedes surprised the market by joining the small sports-car sector with the SLK roadster in 1996; initially with only four cylinders (136 bhp or 192 bhp with a supercharger) it became a serious performer when the 195 cu.in V-6 was installed for 2000.

Audi continued to make high performance S versions of their A sedans but finally turned their TT concept sports coupe into the production 2-seater TT in 1998, following this with the roadster a year later. Using the 5-cylinder turbocharged 109 cu.in (180 or 225 bhp), it broke new ground in offering Audi's highly-developed 4WD in a small sporting car. It is not the most beautiful future classic being based on the lines of the retro VW Beetle, but it is a classic piece of engineering.

Morgan only produce classics. Even the new Aero 8 announced in 2000 looks like a traditional Morgan, but underneath all is new. New extruded aluminium chassis, wishbone suspension and a BMW 268 cu.in V-8 are covered by the first Morgan body to visit a wind-tunnel.

BMW, themselves, had joined the sports car fraternity with the Z3 roadster in 1995 using a

1991 - 2001 and beyond

shortened 3-series chassis; within a year the basic 109 cu.in 'four' was joined by the 170 cu.in 'six' from which came a 195 cu.in M version with 320 bhp in 1997. A coupe model was added in 1998, together with a more extreme-looking M coupe.

While the Z3 was just a classic style, BMW's Fifties 507 gave the 1999 Z8 some more evident design cues and the Nineties M5 305 cu.in V-8 with 394 bhp gave it remarkable performance – a real classic of the future.

Ford continued to be a major engine supplier to specialist manufacturers, the 280 cu.in aluminium quad-cam V-8 being particularly well suited. The classic Jensen name reappeared in 1998 with the prototype SV8, a traditional looking comfortable two-seater; production is still awaited. Earlier Jensens were Chrysler powered but the new sports car used the Ford V-8 producing 330 bhp.

The same engine was also used for the de Tomaso (now Qvale) Mangusta, a similar style of car now being produced through an association with California based BMCD which once had a major shareholding in the original Jensen firm; the de Tomaso Guara, previously using BMW V-8 power, also used the Ford quad-cam V-8 from 1998. And yet another similar car to use that power plant was the AC Ace from 1997; the old Cobra shape came back into production in 1997 and from 1999 was available with fibercarbon bodywork. And finally, Marcos made further revisions to the original shape for the Mantis and Manta Ray using the Ford quad-cam with the 237 cu.in Rover V-8 remaining as an option.

Still from the UK, TVR restyled their range around the Griffith in 1990 using Rover V-8 power in 237 cu.in and 262 cu.in forms with the softer Chimaera arriving in 1992. TVR finally increased the Rover unit to 305 cu.in before bringing in their own 256 cu.in V-8 for the Cerbera 2+2 in 1995. Their own 244 cu.in straight six was used for the 1996 Tuscan Speed Six which was further restyled in 1999. Through the Nineties TVR became a performance icon well able to accelerate faster than many more established

supercars.

From Japan, Mitsubishi's 4WD 3000 GT with up to 280 bhp remained in production through the Nineties and was joined by a spyder in 1995. Toyota's Supra changed shape in 1993, gaining an aggressive rear wing, with in-line six-cylinder engine options of 152 and 183 cu.in with twin turbos and 280 or 324 bhp giving remarkable performance.

And after many years of solo representation the Chevrolet Corvette finally found an American rival in the Dodge Viper. Starting life as a 1989 show car, the Viper was conceived by Chrysler chief Bob Lutz with Cobra creator Carroll Shelby in the original AC mold – tubular steel chassis but fiberglass bodywork and a big engine, an 488 cu.in V-10 Chrysler commercial unit. By the time the Viper went into production in 1992, the V-10 had been reworked in aluminium by Lamborghini to give 400 bhp at 4600 rpm. A coupe version came in 1996 with V-10 power up to 455 bhp. Successful also in International GT racing, the Viper has become an a classic in its own time. Chrysler's other classic offerings of the Nineties were the sports two-seater Plymouth Prowler based on Thirties American hotrods with separate front wings and the four-door coupe PT Cruiser; both are more retro than classic now, but will become future classics.

The Corvette itself moved on to its fifth generation in 1997 with restyled bodywork, still using a small-block Chevrolet engine but now increased to 347 cu.in with 350 bhp. The use of a rear transaxle was the major mechanical change. With a cabriolet in 1998 and a targa-style roof in 1999, the latest Corvette will continue well into the new millenium – as classic as ever. And from 2003 the world is hoping to see a new Jaguar sports car, the F-type, nearly 30 years after the final E-type. The XJS and XK8 were aimed at E-type owners who wanted more comfort, but they did not replace the E-type.

The F-type concept car, shown by Jaguar at the 2000 Detroit show, was based on the running gear from the S-type sedan which had been introduced in

1998. If the production car looks as good as the concept, the F-type will be an instant classic.

While the Morgan had long ruled as the traditional minimalist sports car – all performance and few comforts – a new breed has taken over. The Caterham 7 continues to provide exciting dynamic behavior but is really more at home on the race track. Westfield and Donkevoort (Holland) followed the same theme but without the original Lotus blessing. The Rocket was even less of a road car, looking more like a Late-fifties Cooper GP car; designed by McLaren's Gordon Murray, it had tandem seating for two and a 143 bhp 61 cu.in Yamaha 4-cylinder unit

492-493 BMW Z-8 Roadster has an aluminium space frame and 400 bhp; limited production started in 2000.

ahead of the rear axle. Renault joined the fray with the Sport Spider in 1996 using a mid-mounted 122 cu.in 'four' with 150 or 175 bhp and a race championship was organized for them. And 1999 saw the Lotus 340R, Elise with cycle front wings and skimpy bodywork.

At the end of 2000 a new name entered the ring – Strathcarron – on a lightweight two-seater powered by a Triumph 73 cu.in motorcycle 'four' producing up to 140 bhp. Low volume cars built for enthusiasts usually become classics in time.

Mid-engined sports cars were still a rarity. MG returned to the market in 1995 with the MGF using the Rover K-series engine and transmission mounted behind the driver. Lotus used the same power unit when they presented the Elise in 1995; this pioneered new extruded aluminium technology in the chassis, which has also been adopted by Vauxhall and Opel for the VX220. Toyota too still had faith in mid-mounted engines for sports cars and redesigned the MR-2 for 2000. Having dropped the 968, Porsche created a new entry-level sports car in the Boxster (1996) with the 152 cu.in flat-six engine mounted amidships, another classic Porsche destined for a long life.Still the home of the low-volume sports car, England produced the Noble M10

V6 in 1998. Designer Lee Noble had been familiar to racing enthusiasts for his Ultima, Prosport and Ascari track cars. The M10 was his road car; using a mid-mounted Ford Duratec 152 cu.in aluminium V-6 in a steel chassis with fiberglass composite bodywork, it is built to a remarkably high standard: Based on past experience, all the cars from the Nineties that we have mentioned are likely to become future classics.

However, many of them are still in production and will depreciate in value like any new car. Classic reconition can take up to 15 years, so catch them before the prices go up.

Lamborghini Diablo 5.7

By the time the Countach ceased production, it had been around for 16 years. It may not have been the most beautiful of supercars but it was unquestionably the most dramatic. Two changes of ownership had slowed the funds available for its replacement, but Chrysler's takeover in 1987 contributed considerably to the birth of the Diablo, finally launched in January 1990.

The Countach had been drawn by Bertone's Marcello Gandini. It was Gandini who styled the Diablo, long, low and with none of the sharp edges of the Countach.Where the Countach grew scoops and airducts during its development, the Diablo used the wind-tunnel to get the air flowing where it was wanted.

During the Diablo's gestation period, four-wheel-drive had become fashionable for supercars, starting with the Porsche 959; the prototype Jaguar XJ220 and the Bugatti EB110 followed. The Countach layout was particularly suitable for this; the gearbox was ahead of the engine with the shaft to the final drive running via drop-gears through the sump; the

shaft could easily be extended forward to drive the front wheels through a center differential. The Diablo had an extra six inches in the Countach-style chassis to allow the four-wheel-drive option – the Diablo VT (Viscous Traction).

Inevitably the new car had to produce more power. The Countach's V-12 was increased from 315 to 347 cu.in, and 455 bhp to 492 bhp. With the smoother body shape, this took the Diablo to 205 mph at the Nardo test track in southern Italy. The VT, launched a year later, recorded 202 mph; some power is lost through the four-wheel-drive system.

By mid-1992 the recession was biting and Lamborghini were suffering from a lack of orders. By the end of the year Chrysler were ready to sell. But it was a year before the company was taken over by Megatech, a Bermuda-based company under Indonesian control. Meanwhile Lamborghini were trying to boost sales with limited editions; the factory could build 650 cars a year but had only produced 300 in 1992.

The SE30, shown in September 1993, was a Special Edition of 150 cars

494-495 Gandini and the wind tunnel ensured that the Diablo did not requite wings and ugly scoops. The shape is almost a single volume.

only to celebrate 30 years of production in 1994. It used two-wheel-drive with a traction control system to manage power increased to 525 bhp; strategic use of magnesium castings and fibercarbon reduced the weight from 3470 lbs to 3220 lbs. Externally, the spoiler under the nose had been reshaped to provide an air intake, and a slatted fibercarbon engine cover filled the hollow behind the rear window. A rear wing had an adjuster flap in the center; Lamborghini claimed 207 mph.

Then in 1995 came the Jota, a Diablo for private entrants in GT racing with 590 bhp available from the 347 cu.in engine. Engine air scoops over the cabin were the most obvious sign that this wasn't just an SE30. At the end of 1995, the Bologna Motor Show saw the first production Roadster; the open Diablo, with four-wheel-drive, had first been shown as a prototype at the 1993 Geneva Show.

In 1998, Lamborghini standardized the output at 530 bhp for all models, the VT, the Roadster and the SV (originally the Jota); by 1998 the SV was available in GT2 form with 640 bhp. Audi acquired the company during that year. For the following year, the Diablo VT was mildly restyled with air intakes cut into the front spoiler, exposed headlights while the track was widened front and rear. At the Frankfurt Show in September 1999, they launched the evolution of the SV into the limited edition 366 cu.in GT (80 cars) and GT-R (30 cars).

The 366 cu.in unit became standard with 550 bhp for the Diablo 6.0 (ex-VT) for 2000, while the Roadster retained the 530 bhp 347 cu.in. Production of the Roadster and GT are scheduled to finish in 2001, leaving the single model Diablo to evolve into the next generation.

TECHNICAL DESCRIPTION OF THE LAMBORGHINI DIABLO 5.7	
YEARS OF PRODUCTION	1991-2000
MODELS	COUPE AND ROADSTER
ENGINE	MID-ENGINED V-12
BORE X STROKE, CAPACITY	3.4 x 3.1 INCHES, 348 CU.IN
VALVEGEAR	FOUR OVERHEAD CAMSHAFTS
FUEL SYSTEM	FUEL INJECTION
POWER	492-530 BHP AT 7100 RPM
TRANSMISSION	5-SPEED (SV MODEL WITH 4WD)
BODY/CHASSIS	STEEL FRAME, ALUMINIUM AND COMPOSITE BODY
SUSPENSION	FRONT, WISHBONES AND COIL SPRINGS REAR, WISHBONES AND COIL SPRINGS
TIRES/WHEELS	FRONT 235/35 x 18 ON 8.5 IN. ALLOYS REAR 335/30 x 18 ON 13 IN. ALLOYS
WHEELBASE, TRACK (F), TRACK(R)	104.3 x 60.6 x 64.6 INCHES
LENGTH, WIDTH, HEIGHT	175.6 x 80.3 x 43.3 INCHES
MAX SPEED	205 MPH
WHERE BUILT	MODENA, ITALY

496-497 Additional side window allows better visibility than many mid-engined cars. Diablo continues the Countach's beetle-wing door system.

Bugatti EB110

The mid-engined four-wheel-drive Bugatti EB110 came from the short and sweet period of the neo-classic supercars of the late Eighties. Sadly, it arrived too late and never achieved the sales needed to cover the massive investment in the car's design and development, or the all-new factory near Modena. The project had started in 1988 and the EB110 was launched in September 1991; by the end of 1995 the company had collapsed after just 95 of the EB110GT and 31 EB110SS had been built.

Everything on the EB110 was designed to the highest available standards. The fibercarbon chassis was designed by Aerospatiale; Messier Bugatti, aircraft undercarriage specialists, developed the racing style adaptive suspension; Bosch collaborated on the anti-lock brakes; Weber provided the fuel injection and Michelin built special tires for the car. Engine and transmission were the products of Bugatti's own engineers, led by former Lamborghini designer Paolo Stanzani.

To provide the power to achieve at least 200 mph, Bugatti chose to use a relatively small 213 cu.in V-12 engine with turbocharging to 1 bar pressure which produced 560 bhp for the 110GT and, with 1.2 bar, 610 bhp for the 110SS. To minimize turbo-lag and provide good low down performance they chose to use four small IHI turbochargers, one for each trio of cylinders. Helping to maintain a low center of gravity, the engine had a very short stroke of just 2.2 inches; the 3.1 inches bore allowed the use of five valves per cylinder, three inlet and two exhaust.

Having worked at Lamborghini from the beginning, Stanzani had considerable experience of making compact mid-engined packages. The V-12 engine was mounted longitudinally but offset to the left – the driver's side – to allow a two-shaft 6-speed gearbox on the right, such that the main-shaft provided drive to the front wheels through a torque tube in the center of the car. The main-shaft also carried the epicyclic center differential and the Torsen differential for the rear wheels. The two block-crankcase castings, split across the centers of crankshaft and gearbox shafts, were works of art on their own.

Clothing all these mechanical marvels was largely the work of Lamborghini sculptor Marcello Gandini with adjustments by Giampaolo Benedini, who had designed the new factory. Not beautiful, it was certainly dramatic and contained such original Bugatti styling cues as the little horseshoe intake set within the grille and the style of the aluminium wheels. The fibercarbon chassis was further reinforced by a steel roof section, but the aluminium body panels were bolted into position. Scissor-action doors were chosen to keep the open-door width down and ease payment of motorway tolls.

At Bugatti's last Geneva Show in 1995, the company displayed three examples of the EB110, each proclaiming a world record.

The EB110SS had achieved 218 mph during its official ministry testing at the Nardo test-track in southern Italy; another claimed to be the fastest

498-499 In the later shade of Bugatti
blue, the EB110 was launched 110 years
after the birth of Ettore Bugatti.

car using methane gas as a fuel – 214.2 mph. And the third claimed the fastest speed ever recorded on ice – 184.1 mph. The Bugatti EB110 was a very fast car of exceptional stability.

The Bugatti name had a long history. Italian-born Ettore Bugatti set up his factory in Molsheim in 1909; over the next thirty years he produced a selection of delectable motor cars for competition and road use. After WW2, with Ettore's health failing, the company failed to regain its former glories and it was finally taken over by Messier. While attempts to revive the name included the Grand Prix type 251 in 1956 and a sports car in 1960, the name passed into history for nearly 30 years.

Its revival was due to a consortium of businessmen led by Romano Artioli, with Bugatti's son Michel (by his second marriage) as the family connection. In 1988, a new factory was set up at Campogalliano near Modena, the home of Ferrari and Lamborghini. The EB110 was announced in 1991, 110 years after the birth of Ettore. Following its extravagant series of launches in September 1991 in Paris and Molsheim, it moved into slow production. Two years later, the 4-seater sedan EB112 was shown, but it never reached the production stage.

Artioli took over Lotus in mid-1993 to promote the image of an engineering group capable of working for others, but it did nothing to change the overall post-recession situation. The final end came with the auction of the factory and its contents in April 1997. A large fortune had been spent with litle return.

Subsequently the VW group gathered the remains and intend to use the name, together with those of Bentley and Lamborghini, on a new generation of supercars.

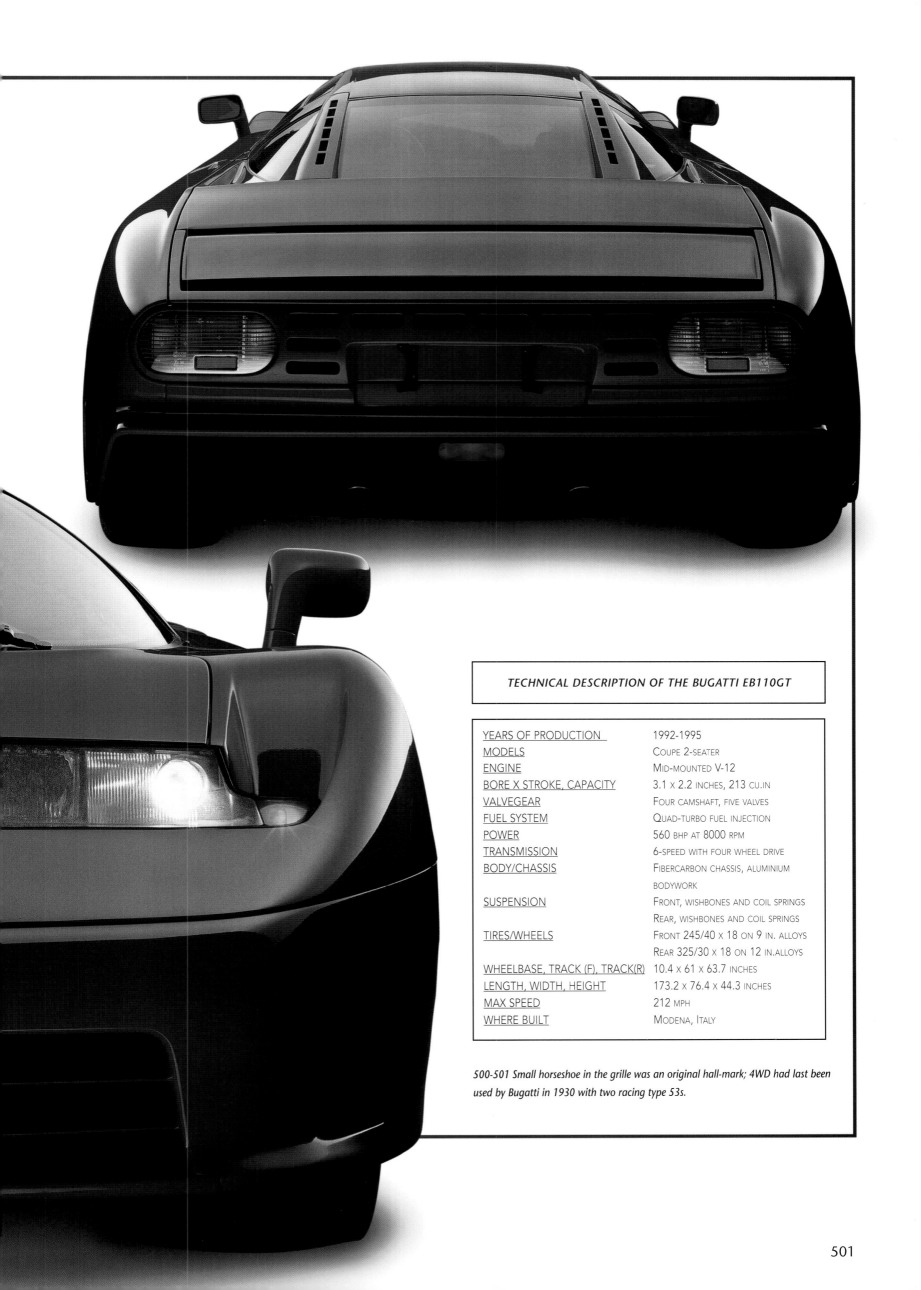

TECHNICAL DESCRIPTION OF THE BUGATTI EB110GT

YEARS OF PRODUCTION	1992-1995
MODELS	COUPE 2-SEATER
ENGINE	MID-MOUNTED V-12
BORE X STROKE, CAPACITY	3.1 x 2.2 INCHES, 213 CU.IN
VALVEGEAR	FOUR CAMSHAFT, FIVE VALVES
FUEL SYSTEM	QUAD-TURBO FUEL INJECTION
POWER	560 BHP AT 8000 RPM
TRANSMISSION	6-SPEED WITH FOUR WHEEL DRIVE
BODY/CHASSIS	FIBERCARBON CHASSIS, ALUMINIUM BODYWORK
SUSPENSION	FRONT, WISHBONES AND COIL SPRINGS
	REAR, WISHBONES AND COIL SPRINGS
TIRES/WHEELS	FRONT 245/40 x 18 ON 9 IN. ALLOYS
	REAR 325/30 x 18 ON 12 IN.ALLOYS
WHEELBASE, TRACK (F), TRACK(R)	10.4 x 61 x 63.7 INCHES
LENGTH, WIDTH, HEIGHT	173.2 x 76.4 x 44.3 INCHES
MAX SPEED	212 MPH
WHERE BUILT	MODENA, ITALY

500-501 Small horseshoe in the grille was an original hall-mark; 4WD had last been used by Bugatti in 1930 with two racing type 53s.

Jaguar XJ220

When the mid-engined Jaguar XJ220 was first shown at the 1988 Birmingham Show, it instantly attracted a flock of people trying to place orders. It was the height of the classic and supercar boom.
As first shown it had a 500 bhp 4-cam 378 cu.in V-12 mated to a 5-speed four-wheel-drive transmission. When deliveries finally started in 1991, it looked much the same but it had rear wheel drive only and a turbocharged 213 cu.in V-6 engine with 542 bhp.

Although this was an engine that Jaguar had used in sports-car racing, many people felt it was not a real Jaguar engine and tried to reclaim their deposits. It was the depth of the trough after the boom. They needed their money back and were prepared to give up their $70,000 deposits as long as they did not have to pay the rest of the money. In the end fewer than 300 of the projected 350 cars were built.

The design of the XJ220 started some four years before its first showing. It was planned for International GT racing (Group B) for which only 200 had to be built. Porsche had announced their 959 but had not built any, and Ferrari had started producing the 288 GTO. Jaguar had already allowed the American Group 44 team to fly the flag in the American IMSA version of Group C and Tom Walkinshaw Racing (TWR) was going to take Jaguar back on the world's tracks in Group C during 1985.

The XJ220 would be a useful addition to the Jaguar armoury should Group B replace Group C, and it would be a flagship road car.

The first prototype was built away from Jaguar after working hours by a few dedicated employees, with a lot of help from suppliers around

502-503 XJ220 was very long and wide but beautifully styled.

Coventry, particularly FF Developments who designed the transmission and provided the secret assembly area. With this part-time work, it was not surprising that it took three years to produce. It was finished a week before the 1988 show and that was the first time that the Jaguar chairman, John Egan, had seen it, but he was happy to allow it to be shown.

After the successful reception, Jaguar wanted to give the green light to the production of at least 200, but they had nowhere to build it. So the project was given to JaguarSport, which Jaguar had set up with TWR to make niche-market versions of Jaguar road cars and to go racing.

While Group B had been adopted by the rally world, it never became a force in racing, so TWR simplified the design; they removed the 4WD and changed the engine to the turbocharged 213 cu.in V-6, which was to be used in Group C racing for 1989/90. It had been the power unit for the MG Metro 6RV rally car. The XJ220 was shortened but it still looked much the same, had even more power and was 606 lbs lighter than the original.

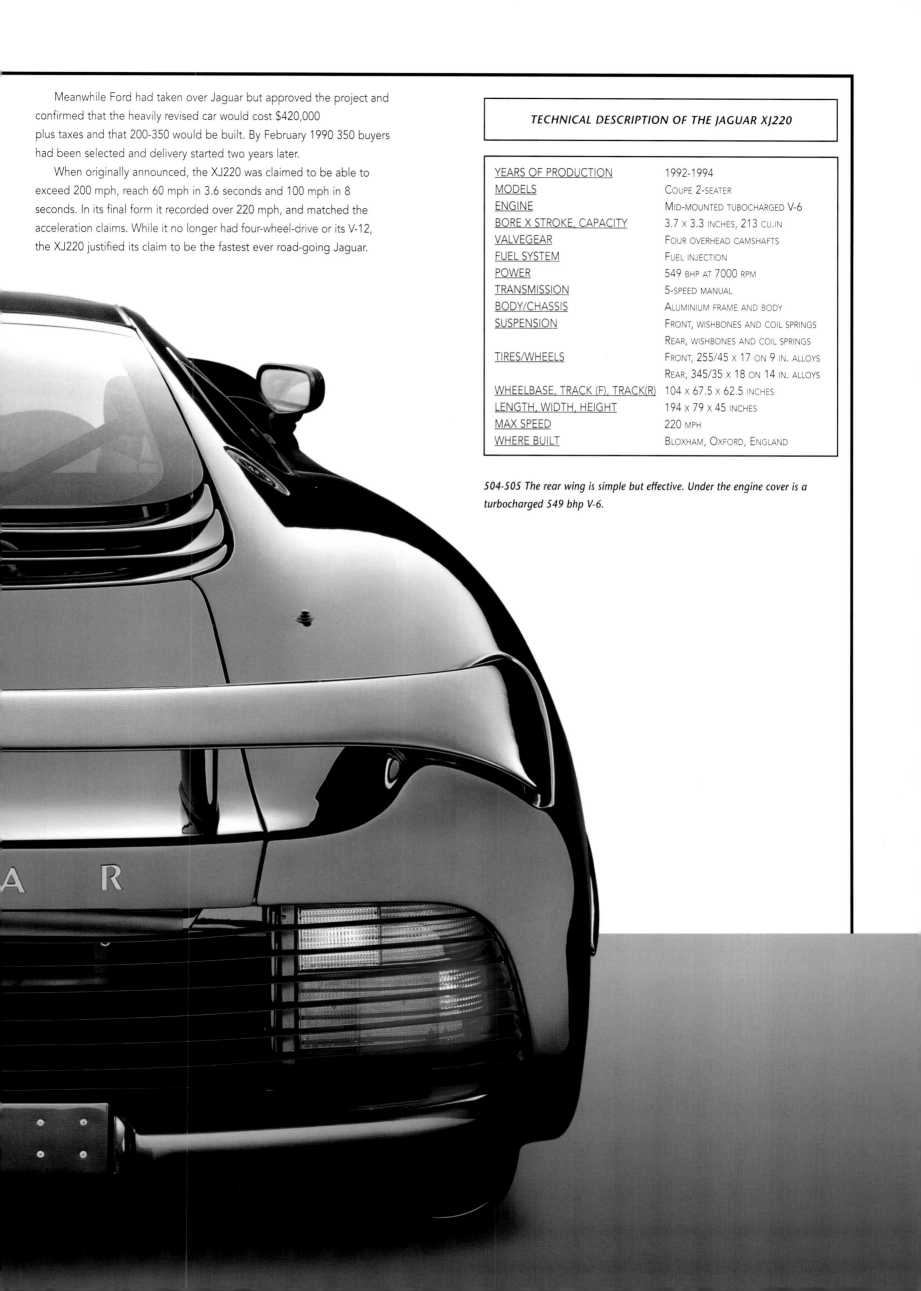

Meanwhile Ford had taken over Jaguar but approved the project and confirmed that the heavily revised car would cost $420,000 plus taxes and that 200-350 would be built. By February 1990 350 buyers had been selected and delivery started two years later.

When originally announced, the XJ220 was claimed to be able to exceed 200 mph, reach 60 mph in 3.6 seconds and 100 mph in 8 seconds. In its final form it recorded over 220 mph, and matched the acceleration claims. While it no longer had four-wheel-drive or its V-12, the XJ220 justified its claim to be the fastest ever road-going Jaguar.

TECHNICAL DESCRIPTION OF THE JAGUAR XJ220

YEARS OF PRODUCTION	1992-1994
MODELS	COUPE 2-SEATER
ENGINE	MID-MOUNTED TUBOCHARGED V-6
BORE X STROKE, CAPACITY	3.7 X 3.3 INCHES, 213 CU.IN
VALVEGEAR	FOUR OVERHEAD CAMSHAFTS
FUEL SYSTEM	FUEL INJECTION
POWER	549 BHP AT 7000 RPM
TRANSMISSION	5-SPEED MANUAL
BODY/CHASSIS	ALUMINIUM FRAME AND BODY
SUSPENSION	FRONT, WISHBONES AND COIL SPRINGS
	REAR, WISHBONES AND COIL SPRINGS
TIRES/WHEELS	FRONT, 255/45 X 17 ON 9 IN. ALLOYS
	REAR, 345/35 X 18 ON 14 IN. ALLOYS
WHEELBASE, TRACK (F), TRACK(R)	104 X 67.5 X 62.5 INCHES
LENGTH, WIDTH, HEIGHT	194 X 79 X 45 INCHES
MAX SPEED	220 MPH
WHERE BUILT	BLOXHAM, OXFORD, ENGLAND

504-505 The rear wing is simple but effective. Under the engine cover is a turbocharged 549 bhp V-6.

European sports cars have always sold well in the USA but Americans like their home-grown sports cars big. Once the Corvette gained V-8 muscle-power, it could outperform any other American product – until the Cobra came along in the Mid-sixties. The Corvette almost kept pace with the Cobra until the latter retired in the face of safety legislation, leaving the Corvette to regain its place as King of the American Road – until the Viper came along. Once more a snake. And behind it was the man who created the Cobra, Carroll Shelby, encouraged by Chrysler's President at the time, Bob Lutz. The roadster first appeared in public as the Dodge Viper concept car at the 1989 Detroit Show. It was 5 inches lower and 7 inches wider than the Cobra. Like the Cobra it had a separate chassis, side exhausts and a big lazy engine, an 488 cu.in V-10 from a Chrysler truck; the chassis is made of sheet steel with strong box section in the sills and around the transmission tunnel. By the time the production Viper arrived in 1992, the engine had been transformed by Lamborghini – owned by Chrysler at the time – with aluminium castings replacing the cast iron cylinder block and heads; it still only had two valves per cylinder but was able to produce over 400 bhp. Although the car is heavy at over 3300 lbs, it has good performance, reaching 100 mph in just over ten seconds, a match for a tuned Cobra 427. And there are six gears with the highest ratio

Chrysler Viper

allowing 70 mph cruising at just 1400 rpm – it reaches its maximum speed in fifth gear. On the road, cornering power is very high due to its massive tires and low center of gravity, but the roadster's ride is very harsh and uncomfortable. It is a fair weather sports car as it only had removable side-screens and a simple soft-top. But despite that, it is a great sporting machine for the serious enthusiast. The GTS, which was added in 1996, was

506-507 Viper RT-10 is the Roadster, here. The 488 cu.in V-10 was a truck engine transformed by Lamborghini.

modelled on the Cobra Daytona coupe, the car that gave Ford the FIA Manufacturer's GT Championship in 1965, even down to its blue paintwork with twin white stripes – American racing colors.

It is a two-seater fixed head coupe with a separate hatchback luggage area and it has roll-up side windows. Improvements in the chassis, together with the stiffer body, have allowed the ride to be improved and there is even more power available, if you live in America.

The American market gets 455 bhp, but the Europeans aren't allowed side exhaust outlets and also have to be quieter. The result is just 384 bhp; this is still enough to make the European GTS faster than the roadster, thanks to a more slippery shape, but the 0-100 mph time has slipped from 10.7 to 11.7 seconds.

Where the roadster was impractical for anything but fine days or the race track, the GTS is an all-weather car which can even be used for commuting.

TECHNICAL DESCRIPTION OF THE CHRYSLER VIPER RT-10 (1992)

YEARS OF PRODUCTION	1992-2002
MODELS	2-SEATER ROADSTER AND COUPE
ENGINE	FRONT-MOUNTED V-10
BORE X STROKE, CAPACITY	3.9 x 3.8 INCHES, 487 CU.IN
VALVEGEAR	PUSHROD OHV
FUEL SYSTEM	ELECTRONIC FUEL INJECTION
POWER	406 BHP AT 4600 RPM
TRANSMISSION	6-SPEED MANUAL
BODY/CHASSIS	SHEET STEEL CHASSIS, ACRYLIC BODY PANELS
SUSPENSION	WISHBONES AND COIL SPRINGS, FRONT AND REAR
TIRES/WHEELS	FRONT 275/40 X 17 AND ON 10 IN ALLOY WHEELS REAR 335/35 x 17 ON 13 IN ALLOY WHEELS
WHEELBASE, TRACK (F), TRACK(R)	96.2 x 59.5 x 60.6 INCHES
LENGTH, WIDTH, HEIGHT	176.7 x 77.7 x 47 INCHES
MAX SPEED	167 MPH
WHERE BUILT	DETROIT, USA

508-509 US side exhausts had to be replaced by power-robbing longer quieter pipes for Europe.

Being attractive little GT cars produced in small numbers, TVRs have always had a following among dedicated classic enthusiasts, but it was only in the Nineties that they reached the level of instant reconition by the man in the street, even though the company had been producing cars for 40 years. The modern TVRs are instantly eye-catching even before the raucous sound of a powerful engine turns the heads. They are very fast but usable every-day cars that are seen in increasing numbers in Europe and around the world, except in America.

Ironically, it was American importer, Jack Griffith, who first installed a big V-8 in a TVR – a 1962 Mk.IIA with Ford power. From this came the Griffith 200, a Mark III TVR using a strengthened chassis with the 286 cu.in Ford V-8. The Griffith 400 followed in early 1964. Although few Griffiths were sold outside America, the replacement Tuscan V-8, the first of the new Lilley management, was a success and gave over 150 mph in 1967. Tuscan V-6s, Vixens, M-series and Taimars took the company through the Seventies without recapturing that performance level.

The design for the Eighties was the wedge-shaped Tasmin, initially with Ford V-6 power which also temporarily returned the cars to the US market. Current owner Peter Wheeler had taken charge from 1981.The Tasmin name was dropped when the Rover unit arrived in 1983 for the 350i convertible. By the Mid-eighties the Rover engine had grown further to extend the range, providing the 145 mph 390SE (1984) and the 150 mph 420SEAC (Special Edition with Aramid Composite bodywork) in

1986; by 1989 these were 400SE and 450SE and a new Speed Eight came in, a longer more aerodynamic cabriolet, with 3.9 and 262 cu.in Rover engines.

Motor Show 1986 had seen the launch of the TVR S as a low cost alternative. While the chassis used the familiar steel tubes, it was powered again by the Ford V-6, and clad in a body more reminiscent of the Seventies cars. The Tuscan name returned when the Rover unit was inserted into the S3 as a basis for the one-make TVR-sponsored Tuscan Challenge for 1989; the body was changed, the chassis uprated and the engines reworked to develop 350 bhp from 268 cu.in. The equivalent road-car became the TVR S3C V8 (or SV8) in 1991 using a 240 bhp 244 cu.in Rover V-8. By now TVR had developed their own engine shop, TVR Power, to work on the Rover engines and develop their own new AJP V-8.

When the new Griffith finally arrived in mid-1992, it had a 262 cu.in Rover unit with 280 bhp installed in a chassis that had learnt the lessons of Tuscan racing; its curvaceous body had an extremely effective quick-action soft-top. The Chimaera followed a year later, a little longer for more luggage space and a little softer for more comfort, with similar lines carrying different detailing. As this was given the option of 244 and 262 cu.in units, the Griffith moved up to a 305 cu.in Rover developing a massive 340 bhp; the acceleration of the Griffith 500 is brutally quick with 0-100 mph in just over 10 seconds.

TVR Griffith 500

Griffith and Chimaera have continued through 2000, Chimaera with a choice of the 244, 280 and 305 cu.in Rover-based engines, Griffith with the 305 cu.in.

The first sign of TVR's own engine came with the long-wheelbase Cerbera 2+2 first shown in 1994; production started two years later. Engineer Al Melling designed a compact 256 cu.in 75-degree V-8 using single overhead cams and only two valves per cylinder to develop 350 bhp at 6500 rpm, proving that complication was not an essential part of efficiency.

A 274 cu.in version came in 1996 for which the Cerbera chassis was uprated with bigger brake discs and tires.

Melling followed up his V-8 with a new straight six 244 cu.in engine with twin-cam four valve heads developing 355 bhp; this was an optional engine for the Cerbera, but it was also installed in yet another new model, the Tuscan Speed Six, which went into production in 1999.

In concept it is a shortened Cerbera with a clever two-piece detachable hard-top giving coupe, Targa-top and roadster in one design. The new style has the rounded sides of the Griffith but very striking detail in its front and rear panels; the interior is pretty striking too with nothing conventional in switchgear or instrumentation.

It is the best looking TVR so far and the performance is amazing, with 0-100 mph in 9.3 seconds and a maximum speed towards 180 mph. TVR will continue to produce classics for many years.

TECHNICAL DESCRIPTION OF THE TVR GRIFFITH 5.0

YEARS OF PRODUCTION	1992-PRESENT
MODELS	TWO-SEATER ROADSTER
ENGINE	FRONT-MOUNTED V-8
BORE X STROKE, CAPACITY	3.7 X 3.5 INCHES, 304 CU.IN
VALVEGEAR	PUSHROD OVERHEAD VALVES
FUEL SYSTEM	LUCAS FUEL INJECTION
POWER	326 BHP AT 5250 RPM
TRANSMISSION	5-SPEED MANUAL
BODY/CHASSIS	STEEL TUBE FRAME, FIBERGLASS BODY
SUSPENSION	FRONT, WISHBONES AND COILS
	REAR, WISHBONES AND COILS
TIRES/WHEELS	FRONT, 205/55x 15 ON 7 IN. ALLOYS
	REAR, 245/45 x 16 ON 7.5 IN.ALLOYS
WHEELBASE, TRACK (F), TRACK(R)	90 X 57.5 X 57.5 INCHES
LENGTH, WIDTH, HEIGHT	153 X 76 X 47.6 INCHES
MAX SPEED	160 MPH
WHERE BUILT	BLACKPOOL, ENGLAND

510-511 The Griffith grew from the Tuscan racing car and was made with Rover engines of 244, 262 and 305 cu.in.

Aston Martin DB7

Aston Martins are like Ferraris; every one is a classic. In fact, Aston Martins are rarer. Over the past decade Ferrari has produced around 3000 cars a year; Aston Martin have only recently reached 1000 cars a year, of which perhaps 100 have been based on the old V-8, built by hand at Newport Pagnell. The balance has been the DB7, made possible by Ford's acquisition of Aston Martin in 1987 and of Jaguar in 1989. Without Ford and Jaguar, Aston Martin would have died. Ten years on Ford use the company as the prototype for new technologies. In the old days this would have spelled a reversion to development by customer, but Aston Martin compete for sales with Porsche and Mercedes, so new model development is just as thorough as these, but is considerably assisted by the availability of all the Ford facilities.

The old V-8 range had been somewhat revitalized with the Virage in 1988, for which the 323 cu.in V-8 had four valves per cylinder and electronic fuel injection, but the construction was no lighter; Volante (1990) and Vantage (1992) followed before the Virage name was quietly dropped in 1994, but the old cars continued, still in low numbers. Throughout the Eighties, Aston Martin's owners – Victor Gauntlett and Peter Livanos – were well aware that a new smaller car was needed to increase production levels, and knew that this would require considerable contributions from other manufacturers. While Jaguar had supplied Aston Martin with parts over the years, they were not prepared to help if Aston

Martin were going to produce a rival in their own market. The Ford take-over changed all that.

Initially, Ford had left Aston Martin management alone to get the Virage into production but they finally assumed full control in 1991, by which time they had also taken control at Jaguar, who happened to have the ideal basis for a new Aston Martin. Jaguar had taken a long time to put the 1986 XJ6 – XJ40 – into production and had been working on XJ41, the replacement for the XJS. After several XJ41 prototypes had been built, Jaguar decided that it was not a viable proposition in terms of the probable numbers and attempted to salvage the situation by marrying the new car with the old XJS platform. With Ford in charge, one of these became the prototype for the new small Aston, starting in 1991; it became the DB7 when Sir David Brown was invited to be patron of the company.

With the project came the six-cylinder four-valve AJ-6 engine which would form a logical extension to the DB2-6 range of cars with six-cylinder engines. It had to be an engine unique to Aston Martin, so a 195 cu.in version was chosen and supercharged to give the 335 bhp necessary to take on the 500SL and Porsche 928. The body was reworked and given a distinctive Aston appearance that reflected the earlier DB cars – its designer Ian Callum is now the design chief at Jaguar. The DB7 was duly launched in 1993 and received high acclaim.

Meanwhile Jaguar had developed the next XJ-6 (X300) which was launched in October 1994 as an evolution of the previous model, but with revised rear suspension.

It had taken a long time but the XJS replacement, the XK8 (X100), finally came in March 1996. It still used much of the XJS floorpan which meant that it fitted neatly under the DB7. Although this had previously used its own rear suspension, it now shares more components with the XK8. The convertible DB7 Volante had followed on in January 1996.

The lines of the DB7 and XK8 were very similar, they had the same interior space, but the XK8 had a new four-valve V-8 engine; as it developed 284 bhp against the 335 bhp of the DB7 and was only available with automatic transmission, the two models were not in conflict. But when the supercharged XKR appeared in 1998 with 363 bhp and 5-speed manual transmission, the DB7 needed to restore its superiority.

The answer appeared in 1999; the DB7 Vantage had a new 366 cu.in V-12 engine with 420 bhp and a 6-speed gearbox, as used in the latest Chevrolet Corvette. Developed from Ford's modular engine series by Cosworth, the new V-12 is a remarkably compact piece of machinery weighing very little more than the six-cylinder unit. Brakes, tires and suspension were also uprated to make the Vantage a truly modern supercar with 180 mph performance. It will be worth keeping.

TECHNICAL DESCRIPTION OF THE ASTON MARTIN DB7

YEARS OF PRODUCTION	1993-PRESENT
MODELS	COUPE AND CONVERTIBLE 2+2
ENGINE	FRONT-MOUNTED STRAIGHT-6, SUPERCHARGED
BORE X STROKE, CAPACITY	3.5 X 3.2 INCHES, 197 CU.IN
VALVEGEAR	TWIN CAMSHAFT, FOUR VALVES
FUEL SYSTEM	FUEL INJECTION
POWER	335 BHP AT 6000 RPM
TRANSMISSION	5-SPEED
BODY/CHASSIS	STEEL MONOCOQUE
SUSPENSION	FRONT, WISHBONES AND COIL SPRINGS REAR, WISHBONES AND COIL SPRINGS
TIRES/WHEELS	245/40ZR X 16 ON 8 IN. ALLOYS
WHEELBASE, TRACK (F), TRACK(R)	102 X 60 X 60 INCHES
LENGTH, WIDTH, HEIGHT	182 X 71.5 X 50 INCHES
MAX SPEED	160 MPH
WHERE BUILT	BLOXHAM, ENGLAND

512-513 Aston Martin DB7 used a prototype XJS replacement as its starting point, but developed a very different style and character.

Ferrari 355

With the 1999 arrival of the 360 Modena, Ferrari's small car grew up. The Testarossa line had ceased in 1996, so the new car had to outperform the old by such a margin that it would appeal to those who wanted their mid-engined Ferraris to have twelve cylinders. In fact, the 360 is just as big as the Testarossa – a big car.

The range had started with the V-6 Dino 246GT in 1969. The replacement 308 – 183 cu.in V-8 – stayed in production for ten years in various forms, which included changes to fuel injection and four-valve cylinder heads. Increasing the capacity to 195 cu.in in 1985 brought a significant power increase from 240 to 270 bhp for the 328, which only had a few body detail changes to distinguish it from its predecessor. However it had moved with the times and had such details as air conditioning and ABS brakes.

The 308 and 328 were among Pininfarina's finest shapes, taken to

their ultimate in the 288GTO.

The first major change came with the 348 in 1989. The engine was further enlarged to 207 cu.in to produce 300 bhp, but mounted fore-and-aft. Behind it, the transmission unit contained a transverse gearbox under the limited slip differential with the clutch at the rear. With a dry sump system, this allowed the mass of the engine to be set lower to give better roadholding. As a result the wheelbase was lengthened by 4 inches. There were important changes to the chassis as well. The 348 was the first Ferrari to have a pressed steel welded chassis rather than the tubular frame designs that had served the company for so long.

The 308 had been styled to look like a scaled down 365GT4/BB but the lines were far better balanced in the smaller car.

The 348 followed the Testarossa and also used side radiators with strakes lining the intakes, but it lacked the fluid curves of its big brother

and was not as appealing. Both coupe and spider (targa-roof) versions were launched in 1989 as 348 tb and 348 ts with the 't' referring to the transverse gearbox. The 2+2 Mondial was uprated at the same time with the 348 layout, but retained the tubular chassis and its existing bodywork; the Mondial T cabriolet came in 1991. When the open and better-looking 348 Spider arrived in early 1993, the other models became 348GTB and GTS; a few months later the engine output was increased to 320 bhp across the range.

The 348 Spider stayed in production until May 1995, by which time the new F355 Berlinetta and GTS had been on sale for a year. The number this time referred to 213 cu.in 5-valve.

Ferrari lifted the performance of the new car considerably. The five-valve head design, three inlet and two exhaust, was part of an improved efficiency which included titanium connecting rods to allow higher engine

speeds. As a result, the 355 developed 380 bhp at 8250 rpm, compared with 320 bhp at 7200 rpm; with the latest Bosch engine management system it still retained surprising tractability, but it needed six speeds squeezed into the transverse gearbox to make the best use of the higher rev range. Although the car looked quite different, the body was unchanged above the waistline; new front and rear lower sections were deeper to include underbody venturis and the side radiator intake shape was changed with the strakes removed. Bigger tires and electronic damper control were among the changes to the chassis.

All these gave the 355 a quite different character, almost a racing car for the road. This impression was further heightened by the option in 1997 of F1-style two-pedal control with clutch and gear selection operated electro-hydraulically via levers each side of the steering column. As with the 348, the Spider had followed in 1995 and continued in production alongside the 360 which came in 1999.

The new 360 set out to be even faster with its 219 cu.in V-8 engine using variable-length inlet tracts, variable exhaust cam timing to produce 400 bhp at 8500 rpm.

The chassis uses extruded aluminium sections for stiffness and light weight while the outer skin has more extreme underbody venturis for greater downforce; the radiators have been moved to the front where the intakes help to create the front end of a GP car.

This time there was no GTS equivalent. The 360 Modena is a spectacularly fast car capable of 180 mph and reaching 100 mph in under 9 seconds.

Sooner or later, they will all be classics, but you can still have a very good and practical Ferrari for less money with a Mondial; they were dropped when the F355 came out.

TECHNICAL DESCRIPTION OF THE FERRARI F355	
YEARS OF PRODUCTION	1994-1999
MODELS	COUPE AND SPIDER 2-SEATER
ENGINE	MID-MOUNTED V-8
BORE X STROKE, CAPACITY	3.3 X 3 INCHES, 213 CU.IN
VALVEGEAR	FOUR CAMSHAFT, FIVE VALVES
FUEL SYSTEM	BOSCH MONO-MOTRONIC M5.2 INJECTION
POWER	381 BHP AT 8250 RPM
TRANSMISSION	6-SPEED
BODY/CHASSIS	STEEL MONOCOQUE
SUSPENSION	FRONT, WISHBONES AND COIL SPRINGS
	REAR, WISHBONES AND COIL SPRINGS
TIRES/WHEELS	FRONT 225/40 X 18 ON 7.5 IN. ALLOYS
	REAR 265/50 X 18 ON 10 IN.ALLOYS
WHEELBASE, TRACK (F), TRACK(R)	926.5 X 59.6 X 63.6 INCHES
LENGTH, WIDTH, HEIGHT	167.3 X 74.8 X 46.1 INCHES
MAX SPEED	183 MPH
WHERE BUILT	MARANELLO, ITALY

516-517 355 came in three forms, Berlinetta, GTS Targa and Spider, seen here.

The Venturi is a French sporting car that deserved to succeed, and may still do so. When such respected names as Bugatti, Delage, Delahaye, and Talbot died as a result of post-war luxury taxes, France lost its performance heritage. Since then small bands of enthusiasts have tried to keep the sporting flag flying. Alpine lasted from 1956-1994, having been absorbed into Renault during the Seventies; Ligier road cars came and went in the Seventies; Matra lasted a little longer before being absorbed into Peugeot-Citroen in 1979. And the latest to try and resuscitate a tradition that stretched back to the beginning of motor racing was Venturi. By 1996 it had changed hands for the second time but the new owners had run out of money by 1999; it has now been taken on by a group in Monaco who have yet to revive production or development. Around 1000 cars have been built over the 15 years.

Venturi was founded in 1984 by two racing enthusiasts, Claude Poiraud and Gerard Godfroy; the first prototype was shown later that year but it was not until the 1986 Paris Show that the first of the high quality mid-engined sports cars was launched. As they were doing for Alpine, Renault provided turbo-charged V-6 engines and transmissions for which Venturi increased the power output with higher boost pressures. Unlike Alpine, though, Venturi mounted the engine ahead of the rear wheels in the classic racing position, like the equivalent Ferrari 308. The chassis was well designed with a full length pressed steel frame and racing-style wishbone geometry front and rear. This was clothed in composite bodywork of an effective yet simple low-drag shape. It was luxuriously trimmed inside with all the care that goes into hand-made bespoke cars with leather upholstery and polished wood veneers. Although it didn't have the design skills of Ferrari behind it, the Venturi was arguably better built and certainly had appropriate performance.

The first model, which became the 210, used the 152 cu.in PRV V-6 with a single Garrett T3 turbocharger at 0.85 bar pressure to give 210 bhp with a maximum speed around 150 mph. The 260 used the 173 cu.in V-6 with 1 bar of boost pressure to give 260 bhp and a maximum over 160 mph; the Atlantique was a lightweight 260 without such heavyweight luxuries as air conditioning, electric seat adjustment and radio/cassette system, thereby saving 320 lbs. By 1988, both 210 and 260 were available in coupe and "Transcoupe" form – removable roof panels and a rear window assembly that swings forward, down and back to hide partly under the rear deck.

Over 1992 and 1993, Venturi organized the Gentleman Drivers Trophy, a one-make series to promote the name of Venturi. For this they prepared and maintained a number of identical 400 GTs; these used

Venturi 210

twin turbos with the 183 cu.in V-6 producing 408 bhp attached to a racing style gearbox. The chassis was 4 inches longer and the rear body section adopted a full width rear wing; the whole body was widened to accept bigger wheels and provide scoops for brakes and the rear radiators. They had two seasons of successful racing for the two seasons before producing a road-going equivalent 400GT. Some of the 400's features were carried across to the 1995 Atlantique 300, which used Peugeot's new all aluminium 183 cu.in single-cam V-6 with a single turbo to generate 270 bhp; this had the longer wheelbase but narrower rear tires than the 400, so the it was only 5.5 inches wider than the 210/260.

By 1998, the cars had been restyled at the front and the Atlantique came in two forms both using Peugeot's latest 4-cam, 4-valve V-6. The standard one had 210 bhp without the turbocharger, and was mated to a ZF 4-speed automatic transmission. The 300 had twin turbochargers for 302 bhp and still used a 5-speed manual gearbox. The 400GT continued with the two-valve heads and twin turbos. While the same basic car has been around for over ten years, the engines have been progressively updated and the specification is still modern. Inevitably there are very few dealers but many of the components come from other cars, or can be obtained from original suppliers. As a classic, the Venturi is a good Ferrari substitute and very much more rare.

TECHNICAL DESCRIPTION OF THE VENTURI 210	
YEARS OF PRODUCTION	1998-PRESENT
MODELS	COUPE 2-SEATER
ENGINE	MID-MOUNTED V-6
BORE X STROKE, CAPACITY	3.4 X 3.2 INCHES, 179 CU.IN
VALVEGEAR	FOUR OVERHEAD CAMS, 24 VALVES
FUEL SYSTEM	BOSCH FUEL INJECTION
POWER	207 BHP AT 5500 RPM
TRANSMISSION	4-SPEED
BODY/CHASSIS	STEEL MONOCOQUE, COMPOSITE BODY
SUSPENSION	FRONT, WISHBONES AND COILS
	REAR, WISHBONES AND COILS
TIRES/WHEELS	FRONT, 205/50 X 17 ON 7.5 IN. ALLOYS
	REAR, 255/40 X 17 ON 9 IN.ALLOYS
WHEELBASE, TRACK (F), TRACK(R)	98.4 X 59 X 62.6 INCHES
LENGTH, WIDTH, HEIGHT	167 X 72.4 X 46.4 INCHES
MAX SPEED	150 MPH
WHERE BUILT	NANTES, FRANCE

518-519 The French Ferrari. With the revised shape of 1997 came a longer and wider car to give more space and comfort.

McLaren F1

While the McLaren F1 was and is unattainable by all but a few, it stands as the ultimate classic supercar. Designed and built regardless of cost, it was superbly engineered to be perfect in every detail. Despite the fact that it was not designed to be a track car, a privately-entered McLaren F1 won Le Mans in 1995. That fully justified its claim to be a true Grand Prix car for the road. While the Ferrari F50 can lay the same claim, it was not a road car in the McLaren sense of comfort and practicality alongside tremendous performance. While McLaren intended to build 350 F1s over seven years, the market had gone by the time the first cars were delivered in 1994; just 100 were built and the unamortised engineering costs had to be written down to advertising the company's ability for future projects. The F1 was a first class advertisement.

Most classics started their lives as cars with a price that reflected the costs involved in their production, whether it was a sports-racing Ferrari or a Jaguar E-type, and their prices then depreciated. The market decreed that they had become classics when the prices rose. Prices for the rarer and more desirable classic cars rose very rapidly during the Eighties, such that a number of specialist manufacturers built their own instant classics, whatever the cost. Ferrari started it with the 288GTO when they launched the concept in 1984; Aston Martin Vantage Zagato (1985), Porsche 959 (1987), Ferrari F40 (1988), Jaguar XJ220 (1989), McLaren and the TWR Jaguar XJR-15 (1990) followed on while the old

name of Bugatti had been relaunched in 1987 to produce supercars from 1991 but only lasted until 1997.

Although the McLaren F1 became the fastest ever road car with a recorded speed of 240 mph, high speed wasn't the main purpose behind the concept of the McLaren. Designer Gordon Murray wanted to make the best possible car to his own ideals; as he had designed so many successful Grand Prix cars in the past, the ultimate road car was bound to be interesting. It had to be agile, easy to drive, practical, comfortable and be able to out-corner and out-accelerate anything else on the road.

Extensive use of Grand Prix-style fibercarbon in the construction of the chassis and body kept it small and light. A 372 cu.in V-12, purpose-built by BMW, gave it plenty of torque throughout the rev range and 627 bhp for a car weight of around a ton ensured electrifying performance. It was a 3-seater with a central driver seat set ahead of two passengers; luggage could be stored in special compartments behind its upward-hinging doors and it was quiet enough to hear the stereo.

520-521 Fastest production car ever, the McLaren F1 achieved 240 mph. Chassis and body are made of fibercarbon composites.

A comfortable ride without loss of high speed stability was achieved with firm springing, special absorption-mounted sub-frames, and high speed aerodynamic control – a wing-shaped under-body gave negative lift. A small rear wing lifted under high speed braking to maintain braking balance, and a suction fan controlled the under-body air for optimum aerodynamic downforce.

Only after everything was packaged around the chassis in the best possible position was the body shrink-wrapped around the hard points with no wasted space. Style engineer Peter Stevens controlled the wind-tunnel tests and had a little freedom to create a shape that is supremely functional. To an engineer, that is also beautiful.

Unfortunately all this technology is necessarily expensive. Fibercarbon is a very costly material before you start to mold it in high temperature ovens over long periods, and there were nearly 100 separate fibercarbon components, ranging from large chassis components to little door trims. All the metal components like suspension links are made to Grand Prix standards. And the F1 took some 700 man-hours spread over 4 months per car. It wasn't difficult to see where a large part of the £530,000 asking price went.

The result was a very fine car which fulfilled all its designer's aspirations. What else can reach 60 mph in just 3.2 seconds and go on to clock 100 mph three seconds later? It is more a work of art than mere transport.

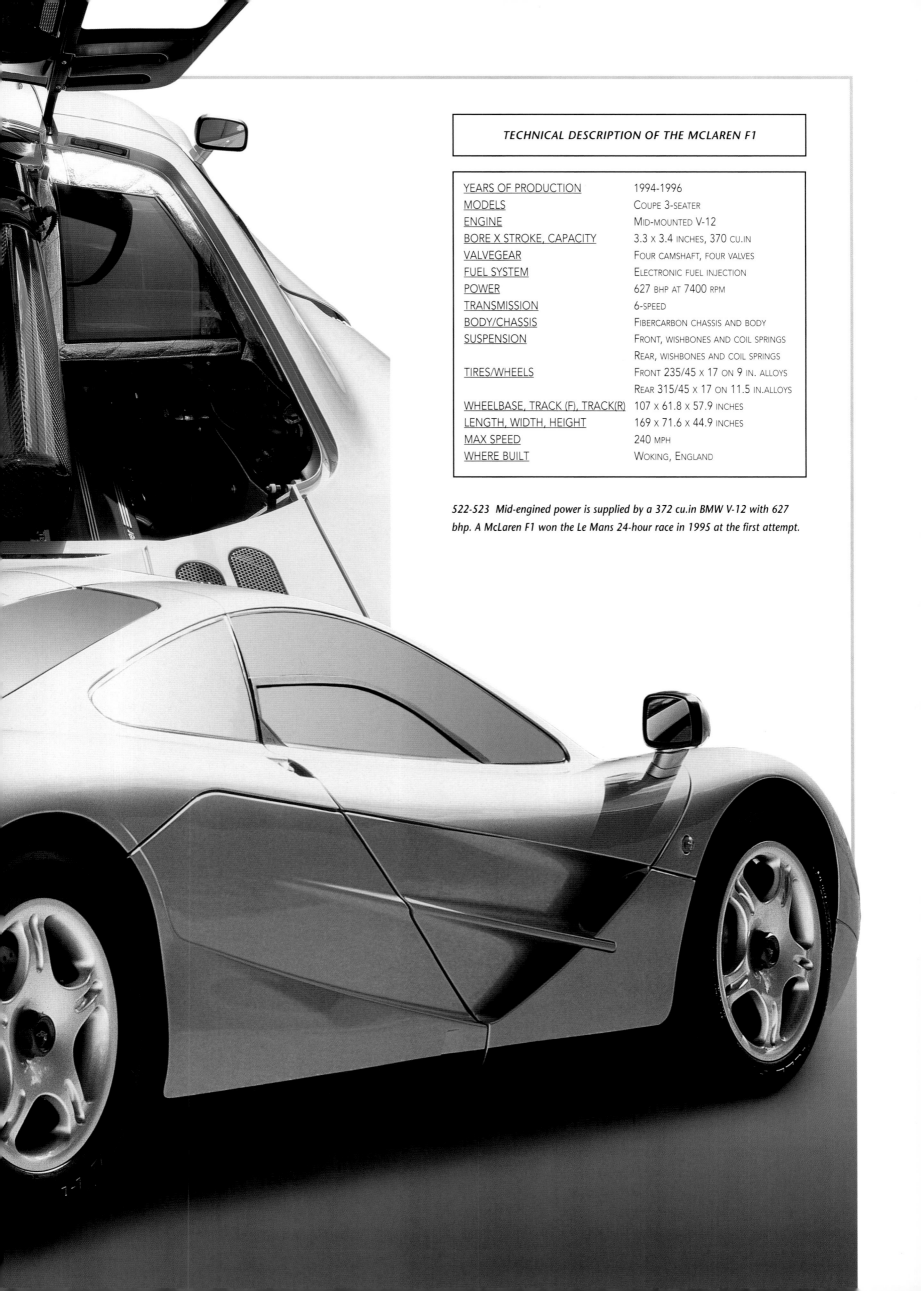

TECHNICAL DESCRIPTION OF THE MCLAREN F1

YEARS OF PRODUCTION	1994-1996
MODELS	COUPE 3-SEATER
ENGINE	MID-MOUNTED V-12
BORE X STROKE, CAPACITY	3.3 X 3.4 INCHES, 370 CU.IN
VALVEGEAR	FOUR CAMSHAFT, FOUR VALVES
FUEL SYSTEM	ELECTRONIC FUEL INJECTION
POWER	627 BHP AT 7400 RPM
TRANSMISSION	6-SPEED
BODY/CHASSIS	FIBERCARBON CHASSIS AND BODY
SUSPENSION	FRONT, WISHBONES AND COIL SPRINGS
	REAR, WISHBONES AND COIL SPRINGS
TIRES/WHEELS	FRONT 235/45 X 17 ON 9 IN. ALLOYS
	REAR 315/45 X 17 ON 11.5 IN.ALLOYS
WHEELBASE, TRACK (F), TRACK(R)	107 X 61.8 X 57.9 INCHES
LENGTH, WIDTH, HEIGHT	169 X 71.6 X 44.9 INCHES
MAX SPEED	240 MPH
WHERE BUILT	WOKING, ENGLAND

522-523 Mid-engined power is supplied by a 372 cu.in BMW V-12 with 627 bhp. A McLaren F1 won the Le Mans 24-hour race in 1995 at the first attempt.

Throughout the Seventies and Eighties, the major European manufacturers virtually ignored the open two-seater sports car.

They left that niche market to the specialists and made convertible versions of their high volume cars. But by the Mid-nineties the demand for sports cars had returned and BMW had already put a toe in the water by making 8000 of the Z1. The Z1 was a low volume product of BMW's own specialist department, but its success led to the introduction of the 2-seater Z3; it was a pleasantly practical two-seater with normal doors, comfortable and with an electrically powered soft-top.

Using a conventional BMW-style platform with the same wheelbase as the Z1, it was built in their South Carolina factory. Initially it was offered with two four-cylinder engines, the 2-valve 116 bhp 109 cu.in and a new 4-valve 140 bhp 115 cu.in, but the car could take more power and the Z3 2.8 followed in March 1996 with the six-cylinder 192 bhp engine. That raised the top speed from 123 mph with 140 bhp to 136 mph. In early 1997 came the M roadster, a Z3 with the 321 bhp 195 cu.in six cylinder which BMW's M-Sport division produced for the M3. This was accompanied by

some frontal restyling and outlet vents behind the front wheels. Suspension was reworked too with wider wheels under flared arches.

This all transformed the Z3 into a fast sporting machine, capable of reaching 100 mph in just 12 seconds and going on to a maximum speed limited to 155 mph.

Later in 1997, BMW showed the Z07 design study; although it appeared to be based on the Z3, it had an aluminium space frame and aluminium bodywork, and was powered by the 400 bhp 298 cu.in V-8 that would later be used in the M5.

It appeared in production form as the 193 bhp Z3 and 321 bhp M coupes in late 1998; the coupe was only available with the six-cylinder engines. In 1998, the roadsters had a minor restyle at the rear with the now typical flat panel, and the 2.8 engine adopted the variable valve timing which improved the performance.

Over the next two years engine options increased; the 4-cylinder 115 cu.in engine remained, but there were no fewer than four 24-valve six-cylinder versions available – 134 cu.in 170 bhp, 152 cu.in 187 bhp, 183 cu.in 231 bhp

BMW Z3

with the 195 cu.in M giving 325 bhp; only the latter two were offered in the coupe.

While the Z07 concept car provided a shape for the coupe, it went on to provide a chassis for the new Z8 in 2000. This retained the aluminium space-frame and the 400 bhp V-8 engine. In style, it is like a Z3 with such classic cues from the Fifties BMW 507 as the twin wide radiator intakes.

The wheelbase is slightly longer than that of a Z3 and the car is some 585 lbs heavier, but it is more sophisticated, and faster than even the M Roadster with 0-100 mph in 11 seconds before going on to the same 155 mph limited top speed. The Z8 is hand-built and only a few will be made, just like the Z1.

524-525 The BMW M Roadster is a Z3 with a revised front spoiler, wider wheels and the M5 engine.

TECHNICAL DESCRIPTION OF THE BMW Z3 M ROADSTER

YEARS OF PRODUCTION	1997-DATE
MODELS	ROADSTER AND COUPE
ENGINE	FRONT-MOUNTED IN-LINE SIX
BORE X STROKE, CAPACITY	3.4 x 3.5 INCHES, 195 CU.IN
VALVEGEAR	TWIN OVERHEAD CAMSHAFTS
FUEL SYSTEM	SIEMENS MOTRONIC FUEL INJECTION
POWER	321 BHP AT 7400 RPM
TRANSMISSION	5-SPEED
BODY/CHASSIS	STEEL MONOCOQUE
SUSPENSION	FRONT, MACPHERSON STRUTS AND COIL SPRING
	REAR, SEMI-TRAILING ARMS AND COIL SPRINGS
FRONT TIRES/WHEELS	225/45 x 17 ON 7.5 IN. ALLOYS
REAR TIRES/WHEELS	245/40 x 17 ON 9 IN. ALLOYS
WHEELBASE, TRACK (F), TRACK(R)	96.3 x 55.9 x 58.7 INCHES
LENGTH, WIDTH, HEIGHT	158.5 x 68.5 x 50 INCHES
MAX SPEED	155 MPH (LIMITED)
WHERE BUILT	NORTH CAROLINA, AMERICA

Ferrari F50

With the F50, Ferrari set out to build the ultimate two-seater, a Grand Prix supercar for the road, including passing worldwide emission and noise tests . Where the F40 had been a development of the 'evolution' version of the 288 GTO Group B car, and was then used to celebrate 40 years of Ferrari production, the F50, launched at Geneva in 1995, celebrated nothing more than Ferrari technology. Production of the 1311 F40s had been completed over 1988-1992 and the engineers needed a fresh challenge.

The heart of any Ferrari is the engine. Much was made of the fact that this was a copy of the 1990 Grand Prix engine, but you can't turn a short stroke 213 cu.in F1 engine with gear-driven cams and four main bearings into a long-stroke 286 cu.in engine with chain-driven cams and seven main bearings. Sure, the cylinder block was made of the same nodular cast-iron, the cylinders were inclined at the same 65-degree angle, the bore was very close to that for the F1 engine, and the cylinder heads had five valves, but this was just F1 technology applied to a new engine. It wasn't even a prototype for the 456GT engine, as that used an aluminium block, four-valve-heads and belt-driven cams. However, it is a very powerful engine, developing 520 bhp at 8500 rpm from 286 cu.in, a higher specific output than the Ferrari 355. Thanks to the Bosch Motronic engine management system, it remains very tractable at low engine speeds, although the peak torque comes at 6500 rpm. Some of this tractability is due to the variable geometry inlet tracts, and a computer choice of two tuned exhaust system lengths before the gases reach the silencers and catalysts. Five valves per cylinder, three inlet and two exhaust, allow 10,000 rpm to be reached, despite chain-driven camshafts and spring-operated valve closure.

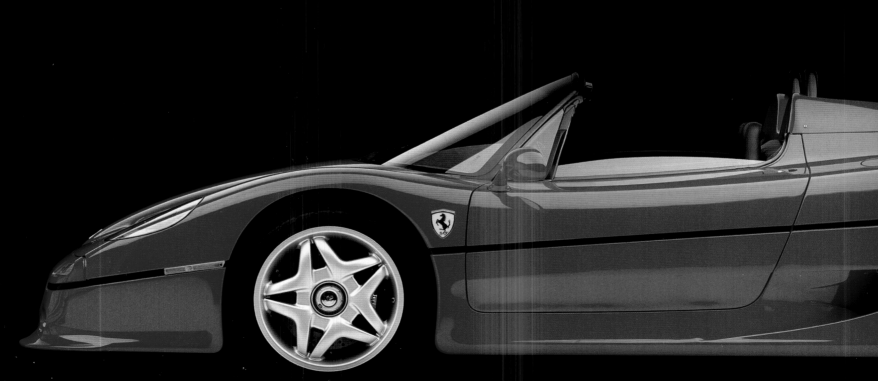

As with a Grand Prix car, this unique engine was bolted directly to the fibercarbon monocoque which contains an F1-style rubberised fuel tank; the 6-speed synchronised gearbox is attached to the bell-housing which incorporates a dry-sump oil tank. The rear suspension followed F1 principles with long wishbones and push-rods operating inboard electronically adjustable dampers with coil springs around them; the same system was used at the front, attached directly to aluminium inserts bonded into the monocoque. Inevitably, with no rubber in the mounting system, a lot of engine noise is transmitted to the interior, but Ferrari made a virtue out of this by arguing that it was part of the car's appeal. Similarly the only elements to absorb road shocks were the low profile tires, Goodyear Fioranos specially designed for this car, but the electronic damping works well and the ride is better than that of the F40. Maintaining the purity of feedback, there is no servo-assistance for the steering or the brakes.

Inside the car, composite seats are trimmed in leather but most of the

526-527 The black belt-line and the rear wing were design cues taken from the F40, but the tightly curved windscreen echoes Group C racing practice.

527

fibercarbon surfaces are left bare although the rear bulkhead is covered in sound-deadening panels. The LCD instruments are computer controlled to display analogue rev counter and speedometer with bar graphs for the other instruments. There is even a gear selection indicator which the computer works out according to revs and road speed. Inevitably, Pininfarina designed the body, a mixture of curves evocative of both the F40 and racing Group C designs. It also adopted Grand Prix car technology in its aerodynamic solutions; the raised section under the nose, later adopted for the 360, allows the air to flow along a flat underbody until it reaches the venturis each side of the gearbox. The downforce created at each end is balanced by a rear wing sweeping across the car from curved sides, just like the F40. It is this increased downforce and the electronically controlled suspension that justifies the creation of the F50. It was designed to be faster than the F40 in its ability to go round a race circuit. It came in two forms, open Barchetta or closed Berlinetta. The front section of the engine cover is interchangeable between a roof and a faring, which also includes twin roll bars to be bolted to the monocoque. Both the 288GTO and the F40 exceeded their planned production numbers. This time it was a strictly Limited Edition; 349 were built, many of which went to the USA – a worldwide classic.

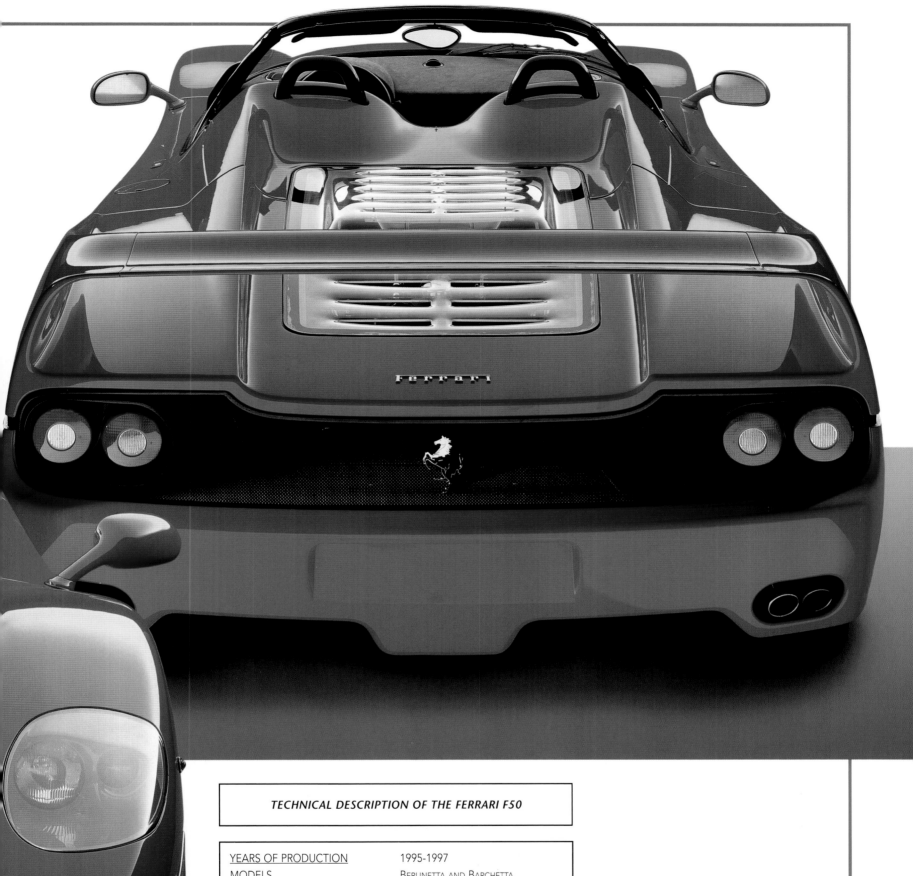

TECHNICAL DESCRIPTION OF THE FERRARI F50

YEARS OF PRODUCTION	1995-1997
MODELS	BERLINETTA AND BARCHETTA
ENGINE	MID-MOUNTED V-12
BORE X STROKE, CAPACITY	3.3 X 2.7 INCHES, 238 CU.IN
VALVEGEAR	FOUR OVERHEAD CAMSHAFTS
FUEL SYSTEM	BOSCH MOTRONIC 2.7 FUEL INJECTION
POWER	520 BHP AT 8500 RPM
TRANSMISSION	6-SPEED
BODY/CHASSIS	COMPOSITE MONOCOQUE AND BODY
SUSPENSION	FRONT, WISHBONES, PUSHRODS AND COILS
	REAR, WISHBONES, PUSHRODS AND COILS
TIRES/WHEELS	FRONT, 245/35ZR X 18 ON 8.5 IN. ALLOYS
	REAR, 335/30ZR X 18 ON 13 IN. ALLOYS
WHEELBASE, TRACK (F), TRACK(R)	101.6 X 63.8 X 63.1 INCHES
LENGTH, WIDTH, HEIGHT	176.4 X 78.2 X 44.1 INCHES
MAX SPEED	202 MPH
WHERE BUILT	MARANELLO, ITALY

528-529 For the Berlinetta, the twin roll-hoops and the faring around them are replaced by a fixed roof. The raised section under the front intake allows air to flow smoothly to the rear venturis.

Chevrolet Corvette 5th Generation

The latest Corvette, launched at Detroit in 1997, is once again a much more refined car than its predecessor. There is more space inside and the ride is more comfortable. Its faster too. With automatic transmission it will reach 100 mph in 13 seconds, or 11.5 seconds with the manual gearbox. The coupe will go on to over 170 mph, and the convertible, in production from 1998, is only 5 mph slower.

It always takes a long time to develop a new Corvette. Given that its production rate is around 40,000 a year it doesn't justify a large design and development team. They say it took seven years to bring C5 to production, the fifth generation Corvette – 1953, 1963, 1968 and 1983 being the start points for previous generations. Like its predecessor, it is all new apart from some drive-train elements.

But this time even the major components are different. The 347 cu.in V-8 may look like a continuation of previous engines, as it is near enough the same capacity as the previous LT1 (349 cu.in) or the Lotus-designed LT5 for the ZR1(350 cu.in), but the new LS1 (345 cu.in) is a cross between the two; the Lotus-style aluminium block has the same 3.8 inches bore as the LT5 but retains a central camshaft, pushrods and two valves per cylinder in the aluminium head. With sequential fuel injection and a new composite intake manifold, power was increased to 350 bhp, midway between the LT1 at 304 bhp and the LT5 at 411; given that the new car is 3% lighter and has a 15% lower drag factor, that gives a useful performance increase over the previous standard car.

The gearbox too is different. The 6-speed manual version now comes from Borg Warner; while the 4-speed automatic is still GM-Hydramatic, both types are now mounted in unit with the rear transaxle. This improves the weight distribution and reduces the transmission hump in the cockpit. They've made the car wider and the wheelbase longer, further increasing interior space; as intended, this has made the handling more user friendly.

The suspension has received considerable attention. To start with, the new chassis frame is much stiffer than the previous one, so the suspension can work more effectively. At the front there are still twin wishbones but the rear suspension now uses the same system, rather than making the drive-shaft act as a transverse link – the principle used since 1963. The latest Goodyear Eagle Tires have a run-flat capability which saves carrying a spare wheel.

Like most high performance cars, the Corvette has anti-lock brakes and the associated traction and stability controls.

There is a choice of suspension options too from comfortable to adaptive to sport modes. Its rack and pinion steering is servo-assisted and the steering wheel position is adjustable.

Since the launch, a hard-top coupe was added to the range in 1999, together with head-up display for some of the information; although the facia now has dials with needles, a projection onto the bottom of the screen shows engine speed and oil pressure as bar graphs and a digital road speed.

A little more power was added in 2001 with improved fuel consumption, and it is now possible to get a Corvette C06, a hard-top coupe with 390 bhp, 110 lbs less and wider wheels. Meanwhile the Corvette has also been out on the International GT race-tracks, taking on the Vipers and Porsches; the C5-R won the 2001 Daytona 24-hour race outright. Impressive as previous Corvettes have been in their day, this one is equally sure to become a future classic, worth the seven-year wait.

TECHNICAL DESCRIPTION OF THE CHEVROLET CORVETTE

YEARS OF PRODUCTION	1997-PRESENT
MODELS	COUPE AND CONVERTIBLE 2-SEATER
ENGINE	FRONT-MOUNTED V-8
BORE X STROKE, CAPACITY	3.8 X 3.6 INCHES, 345 CU.IN
VALVEGEAR	CENTRAL CAMSHAFT
FUEL SYSTEM	BOSCH SEQUENTIAL INJECTION
POWER	350 BHP AT 5600 RPM
TRANSMISSION	4-SPEED AUTO OR 6-SPEED MANUAL
BODY/CHASSIS	STEEL FRAME, FIBERGLASS BODY
SUSPENSION	FRONT, WISHBONES AND LEAF SPRING
	REAR, WISHBONES AND LEAF SPRING
TIRES/WHEELS	FRONT, 245/45 X 17 ON 8.5 IN. ALLOYS
	REAR, 275/40 X 17 ON 9.5 IN. ALLOYS
WHEELBASE, TRACK (F), TRACK(R)	104.5 X 62 X 62.2 INCHES
LENGTH, WIDTH, HEIGHT	179.7 X 73.6 X 47.6 INCHES
MAX SPEED	171 MPH
WHERE BUILT	KENTUCKY, USA

530-531 The latest generation Corvette was launched in 1997, followed a year later by the Cabriolet.

Porsche Boxster

From the time that the mid-engined Boxster was shown as a concept car at Detroit in 1993, the front-engined 968's days were numbered. This was the new entry-level Porsche, a real sports car packed with all the latest Porsche technology including a new version of Porsche's hallmark engine, the flat-6 'boxer'. Boxer roadster produced Boxster. Although the concept car was styled after the fashion of the mid-engined 550 Spyder of 1953, with no luggage space and little room for crash absorption, the mechanical elements stayed with the design through the next three years of development.

The Boxster will inevitably become a classic one day; like all Porsches, the relatively low production rate ensures some rarity.

Just before the Boxster went into production in Finland, the millionth Porsche was produced covering a period of exactly 50 years; a quarter

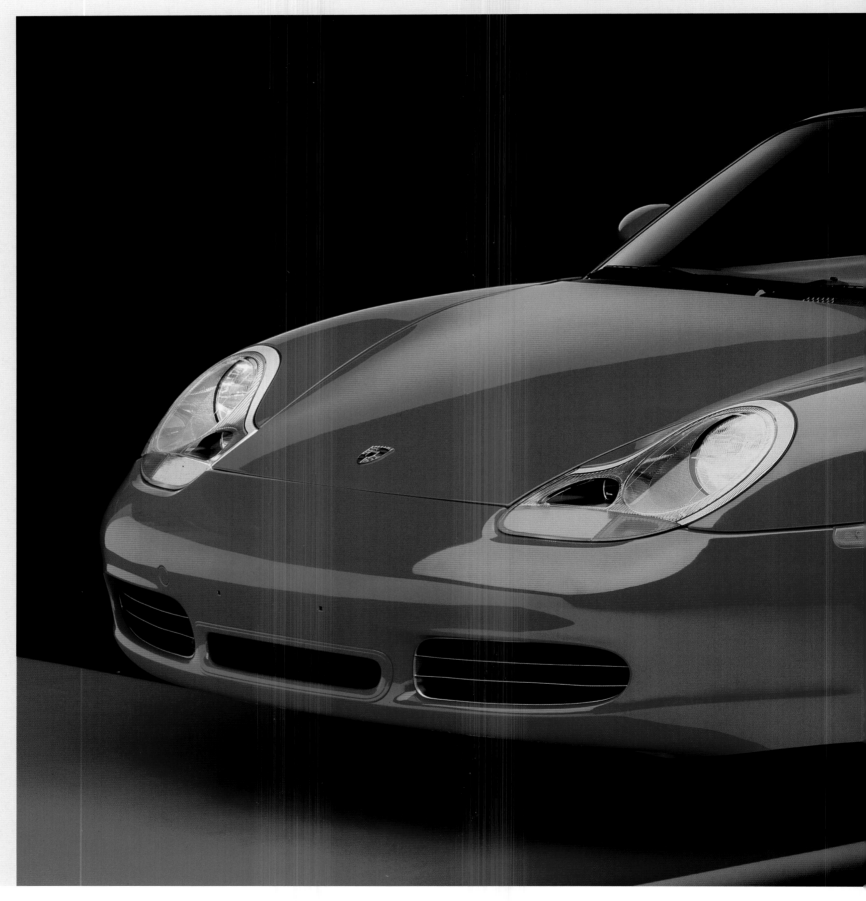

have been open cars. In round figures, there have been 77,000 of the 356, 118,000 of the 914/916, 325,000 of the 924/944/968, 61,000 of the 928 with the 911 still running after 419,000 had been produced by July 15, 1996. That average rate of 20,000 per year has now been almost doubled to around 40,000, with the Boxster contributing approximately half.

The heart of any car is the engine, particularly with a Porsche.

The Boxster has a new flat-6 with full water-cooling, integral dry sump lubrication and four-valve heads.

The two-piece alloy crankcase clamps a central cast-iron bearing bridge, containing the seven main bearings and a layshaft which takes the drive to the camshafts; chain wheels are mounted at each end of the layshaft to drive the exhaust camshafts. These drive the inlet

camshafts through separate chains via Porsche's Variocam system which alters the inlet timing. Aluminium cylinder blocks use Silumin cylinder coating, and the heads too are aluminium castings.

Ignition and the sequential injection are controlled by the latest Bosch Motronic system.

As launched the engine was a 152 cu.in developing 204 bhp at 6000 rpm with maximum torque of 181 lb.ft at 4500 rpm but it maintained over 80 per cent of that between 1750 and 6500 rpm. The Boxster S

532-533 With the 1999 Boxster S came the 195 cu.in engine and wider wheels and tires.

TECHNICAL DESCRIPTION OF THE PORSCHE BOXSTER S

YEARS OF PRODUCTION	1999-PRESENT
MODELS	ROADSTER 2-SEATER
ENGINE	MID-MOUNTED FLAT-6
BORE X STROKE, CAPACITY	3.6 X 3 INCHES, 193 CU.IN
VALVEGEAR	FOUR CAMSHAFT, FOUR VALVES
FUEL SYSTEM	BOSCH MOTRONIC FUEL INJECTION
POWER	252 BHP AT 6250 RPM
TRANSMISSION	6-SPEED
BODY/CHASSIS	STEEL MONOCOQUE
SUSPENSION	FRONT, STRUTS AND COIL SPRINGS
	REAR, STRUTS AND COIL SPRINGS
TIRES/WHEELS	FRONT 205/50 X 17 ON 7 IN. ALLOYS
	REAR 255/40 X 17 ON 8.5 IN.ALLOYS
WHEELBASE, TRACK (F), TRACK(R)	95.1 X 57.7 X 60.2 INCHES
LENGTH, WIDTH, HEIGHT	170 X 70 X 50.8 INCHES
MAX SPEED	164 MPH
WHERE BUILT	STUTTGART, GERMANY

came in early 1999 with the engine increased to 195 cu.in, 252 bhp and 225 lb.ft at 4500 rpm; and later the same year, the standard engine was increased to 164 cu.in in 1999, increasing the power to 220 bhp and torque to 192 lb.ft at 4750 rpm. The standard transmission is a 5-speed manual gearbox but Porsche's 5-speed Tiptronic box allows manual override by push-buttons on the steering wheel. The 195 cu.in S has a six-speed gearbox.

Galvanized steel is used for the unitary chassis; this carries MacPherson strut suspension front and rear, chosen for its compactness, while the brakes use 4-piston calipers.

Features of the body include a rear aerofoil that rises at over 50 mph and a remarkable electrically-operated folding roof that can be raised or lowered in just 12 seconds. There are also two luggage compartments, one under the bonnet and another over the gearbox. The style retains the traditional broad sloping front which produces a very low 0.31 drag factor with the hood raised; a hard-top is one of the many options available.

There are many other features both standard and optional which add together to make the Boxster such an exceptional car.

It is above all a driver's car providing maximum enjoyment in safety; top speeds of the three versions range from 145 mph to 160 mph and the acceleration is very quick thanks to an overall weight of only 2750 lbs. Early reports praised the handling and roadholding and said that the chassis could easily handle more power.

The 252 bhp Boxster S is just the first of probably many higher power derivatives – the more power the more classic.

534-535 Styling is simple and effective and is unlikely to show signs of age in the future.

A CENTURY OF COMPETITION
AND HUMAN CHALLENGES

MOTOR RACING

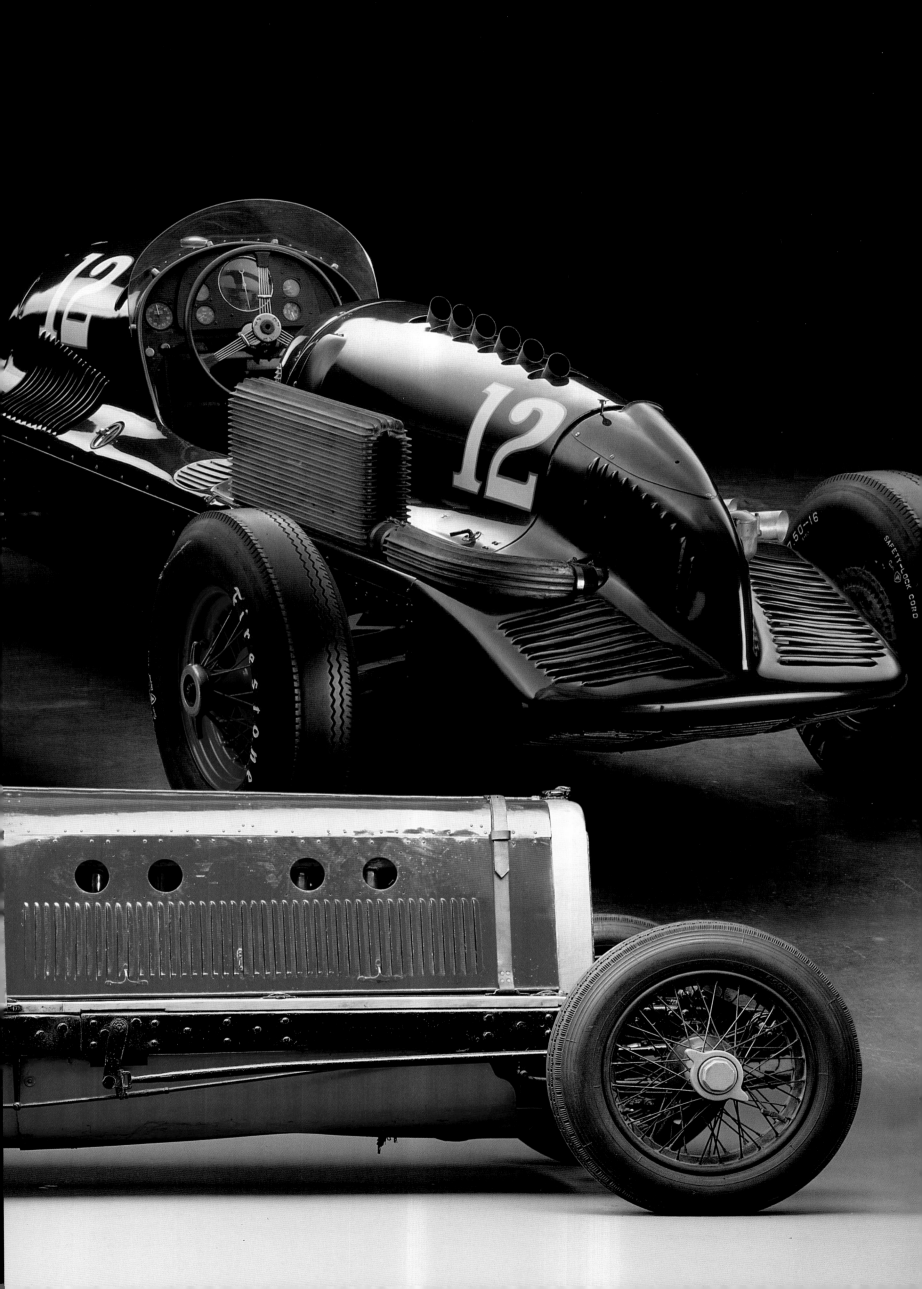

537 The red shadows of Formula 1: the Italian national livery has, over the years, become Ferrari's symbol.

538 top left The Italian driver Materassi, at the wheel of a Bugatti, tackling the Ponticello curve during the XVIII Targa Florio.

538-539 bottom Mephistopheles, a Fiat F.B.4 racer, never passed unobserved in early 20th century races.

539 top right Millers were protagonists on the Indianapolis oval from the Twenties to the Forties.

540-541 Olivier Panis at the wheel of the Prost AP01 during the 1998 World Championship. The Frenchman drove the Professor's car to 11th place in the 1998 San Marino GP.

542 top left The culminating moment of a race is when the first car crosses the finish line with the race official waving the checkered flag.

542 bottom left The racing driver par excellence, the champion of champions, a man who treated his steeds with kid gloves: Juan Manuel Fangio.

542 right The Ferrari 158 F1 and John Surtees, two Formula 1 legends. The Italian manufacturer is the only one to have participated in every edition of the World Championship while the English driver is the only man to have won world titles on both two wheels (seven) and four (one).

542-543 The Kaiser of Formula 1 is Michael Schumacher, the only driver worthy of taking on the mantle of the late, great Ayrton Senna.

CONTENTS

Preface

It is said that humans were created from dust of the earth. While this may be true, in the case of racing drivers the Creator surely added a dose of engine oil.

Racing drivers are, without doubt, strange creatures, finding their raison d'être, fulfillment, and exaltation within an invisible tunnel tangible only when maximum speed is achieved. Then, and only then, do they detach themselves from the terrestrial world in a process something like what happens to an aircraft pilot—although in the latter case the detachment takes place in an immense soap bubble rather than a viscous tunnel.

It is probable that no one can effectively describe the sensations experienced by top drivers at the wheel—not even the drivers themselves. Those fortunate enough to have accompanied a true racing driver on a demonstration lap will know how far removed are the thought processes of even the most skillful ordinary driver from those of a pure racer, for whom the road is wider, the car is narrower, the curves are straighter and even the most anonymous of vehicles is transformed into a road-burner.

On the other hand, those who have had the experience of completing a flying lap on a racing circuit themselves will have gained at least a vague idea of the energy that courses through every nerve-end, that weakens and sets the knees trembling but strengthens and stills the hands, confuses the survival instinct but hones the projection of the vehicle along the Racing Line.

Over the course of more than a century of motor racing, much of the spirit and substance of the sport has changed, except for the drivers' desire to experience that extreme emotion at all costs. And, up until recent times, those costs were often perilously high—there were few pioneer racers who died of natural causes. Today, technology and strict regulations have reduced the risks for drivers and spectators, and this is without doubt a good thing. At the same time, however, racing has lost something of its original purity.

This is unfortunately a phenomenon found in all sports. No longer spontaneous manifestations of the competitive spirit, they have become products of televised entertainment. In this sense motor racing, and especially Formula 1, CART and NASCAR, has led the way, bending to the whims and schedules of television before any other discipline.

The history of motor racing, however, remains rich in statistics, episodes, personalities and legends. It would be presumptuous of us to attempt to document it all and thus we shall restrict ourselves to a presentation of the essential historical framework of the principal competitions. We shall attempt, in moderation, to satisfy the thirst for dates and numbers and we shall try to describe the prerogatives, characteristics and salient aspects of the various championships.

Not so much a dedication but rather an honorable mention goes to all those enthusiasts with speed in their DNA who have never had the opportunity to display their suspected dexterity behind the wheel. We hope that they will always bear in mind the difference between racing circuits and everyday roads.

We also ask our readers to forgive our inevitable errors and omissions.—The Authors

544 The cars that have taken part in the various sports-prototype championships are often hard to recognize. This photo shows a Ferrari 333SP that participated in the 1998 Le Mans 24 Hours.

545 Michael Schumacher in the cockpit of his Ferrari. It is 2001: the helmet he wore at the Gran Prix in the United States was auctioned off along with those of the other 21 drivers. Over 200,000 dollars were raised -- 60,000 of which were paid for Schumacher's helmet alone -- which went to the victims of the terrorist attacks in New York.

The plaything of bored gentlemen

The birth of motor racing virtually coincided with that of the car itself, in the last decade of the 19th century. The earliest events were exhibitions that, rather than rewarding a driver and car faster and stronger than others, aimed to demonstrate the reliability of the motorized carriage. The triumph of one model over another was not what was at stake so much as the success of the automobile itself.

The first drivers were often the men who actually designed and built the cars. Technical pioneers obsessed with the idea of combining the nascent technology of applied thermodynamics (thanks to which an engine miraculously transformed fuel into motion) with contemporary running gear and chassis, they battled the vibrations and stresses from which those strange quadricycles powered by steam, electricity or with increasing frequency internal-combustion

546 top Felice Nazzaro, one of the most famous and daring of the pioneer drivers, seen tackling the Targa Florio. The Sicilian race snaked through the Madonie mountains behind Palermo. The photo was taken during the second edition held in 1907 and won by Nazzaro at the wheel of a Fiat.

546-547 Cars ready for the off. Races were started in various ways, but in some cases, as at Indianapolis or Brooklands (seen here), the cars were already lined up on grids. Note the smoke generated by the cars' screaming engines as the starter hurries to the edge of the track.

The origins

engines suffered.

Shortly afterward, however, cars came of age, becoming profitable, entertaining to drive and interesting to watch. Racing developed as a consequence of three needs: to improve the reliability of engines and ancillary components (brakes, suspension, transmissions); to distinguish individual models; to set the commercial wheels rolling by portraying the motor car heroically.

Our account will begin with this last factor. The young gentleman of the late nineteenth century, devoted to romantic success and challenge as an end in itself, immediately seized the opportunities offered by the new plaything. As happened at the same time for the athletic and gymnastic disciplines (the accounts of the New Olympic Games are full of enterprises of an exhibitory rather than sporting nature), the car soon proved to be an ideal means of proving one's manhood: Strength, stamina, skill, courage, recklessness and, even then, substantial financial resources were all required. In peacetime there was nothing better for releasing pent-up aggression and relieving boredom. Death? Since that of others served to feed the climate of risk and emotive tension that developed within the circus of speed, one's own was a

risk worth running. Thus did the aristocracy and well-to-do of the time lend (and frequently donate) the flower of their youth to motor sport. With regards to technological development it is clear that in the early decades the room for improvement was vast, and manufacturers with racing programs enjoyed alternating advantages. Today things are very different, and motor sport has become a very limited test bench due to restrictions imposed by the regulations, especially in the field of electronics. Experimentation takes place elsewhere, and any reference to the importance of racing for improving the breed smacks of hypocrisy or naiveté. What instead has developed and taken on a primary role is the commercial and promotional aspect. At the dawn of motor racing history the great patriarchs of the automobile were unwilling to allow their vehicles to be used in those insane, useless and dangerous competitions. Nonetheless, virtually all manufacturers, past and present, eventually became involved in competition in one form or another. Which were the first races and how and where were they held? There were many events on both sides of the Atlantic, spontaneous or carefully organized, before the first trophies were awarded and the first Grand Prix disputed. In the following chapters we shall look at a number of examples, while some of the great events that were born in this period (Indianapolis, Le Mans, the Targa Florio) will be discussed later.

Lack of space prevents us from recounting the stories and results of events that were not part of a championship program. In this book devoted to auto racing, Formula 1 naturally occupies the highest step of the podium, to use an expression dear to the world of the race track. Ever since the first World Championship was held at Silverstone, UK on May 13, 1950, manufacturers and drivers alike have seen the annual event as the absolute pinnacle in terms of technology, investment, popularity and fame throughout the world. Since 1950, the championship has been contested every year, and it has now successfully entered the third millennium.

Two great champions have won undisputed positions at the head of the honor roll. Juan Manuel Fangio has won lasting fame as a five-time winner, capturing the trophy in 1951, 1954, 1955, 1956 and 1957, while Michael Schumacher recently matched the Argentinean by winning his own fifth title in 2002. Ferrari cars have carried Fangio (once) and the German Schumi (three times) to no fewer than four of those titles.

Formula 1,
The Circus of Speed

The birth of the Formula 1 World Championship splits the automotive century in two: the colorful saga, rich in characters and roles curiously similar to those of adventures stories, in fact began in 1950.

We have a "gray eminence," Bernie Ecclestone, who following the death of Enzo Ferrari—a charismatic figure not inclined to overt subjection—transformed from a Cardinal Mazzarino-type figure into the championship's absolute monarch. We have the baronies, the fiefdoms of ancient lineage or recent investiture, represented by the teams who submit to the decisions of the organizing bodies with heads bowed, despite frequently harboring dreams of rebellion. We also have the emergent economic potentates, the sponsors—initially the teams' financiers but later increasingly active and decisive in the selection of drivers and managers. Then of course we have the knights on horseback—the drivers themselves, who as in serial novels are apparently protagonists but in reality unwitting

548 top This photograph reveals the absolute concentration of the modern racing driver awaiting the green light that signals the start of his high-speed challenge.

548 bottom This black and white picture shows two great Formula 1 protagonists, the Ferrari 158 F1 and John Surtees.

Formula 1

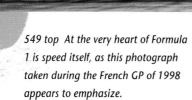

549 top At the very heart of Formula 1 is speed itself, as this photograph taken during the French GP of 1998 appears to emphasize.

549 bottom left Juan Manuel Fangio and Mercedes, an invincible combination in the Formula 1 of the 1950s. The Argentine driver conquered two of his five world titles at the wheel of the Silver Arrows, here seen without the streamlined bodywork covering the wheels.

549 bottom right Looking like astronauts invading Earth from some other planet, the mechanics in the pits can make the difference between winning and losing a Grand Prix. During split-second pit stops they load hundreds of liters of fuel into the tanks and change all four wheels.

551 top left A line-up of nose cones: this frontal element of the bodywork—in the picture can be seen those of the 1998 Sauber C17—is of fundamental importance to the car's aerodynamics and frequently the main difference between one model and another.

550 left Sitting in his car, elbow resting on the bodywork, Ayrton Senna appears more intent on a Sunday drive around the countryside rather than the last checks on his Lotus prior to the start.

550 top The drivers "parading" in front of the celebrities and enthusiastic admirers that have always accompanied the world of motor racing. This photograph shows the unmistakable lines of the celebrated Bugatti Type 35 driven by Tazio Nuvolari.

550 center Teamwork has its place in Formula 1, and not only when one of the two drivers administers or controls the race on behalf of his teammate: Pit-stops are perfectly choreographed with 40 hands moving around the car for just a few seconds.

550 bottom Prior to the birth of the World Championship, many Grands Prix, including the Italian GP seen here, were held on street circuits. This image shows the 1948 edition held on the Valentino circuit in Turin, won by Wimille in the Alfa Romeo Tipo 158, the first on the left in car number 52.

pawns in the hands of the powers that be. And then we have the cars, perfect transcriptions of the noble steeds of the past, with the mechanics their faithful handlers. As for beautiful maidens, Formula 1 has never been lacking in ideal candidates.

By 1950 motor racing had already long been subjected to the laws of big business. From this moment on there was however a slow but inexorable mutation from sporting events to spectacles, with many other sports following on behind as they adapted to suit the demands of television and entertainment in general. Take, for example, basketball, tennis, volleyball and even the Olympic Games.

The basic elements of the sport have apparently remained the same: cars and drivers. But in reality the true protagonist of modern racing is the spectacle itself, stripped of its atmosphere and excitement and crudely channeled into television

colored by passion and fired by emotions.

The story of these 50 years of single-seater racing is a fabric woven with threads of different kinds and colors: the "eras" of the great drivers, Fangio, Clark, Stewart, Lauda, Prost and Senna; the technological innovations comprising an infinite series of mechanical, structural and aerodynamic modifications that began with the momentary end of the supercharged era and includes the advent of telemetry (which extinguished like a light the value of the human factor); the changes in the regulations, frequently dictated by lobbyists or demagogic impositions; the historic races and the strategies of the various teams, some of which represent solid pillars of the establishment while others are of the second rank or merely bit players.

We would like to remain imprisoned within the logic of the plot and watch from above as this enthralling story fast-forwards before our eyes. The Formula 1 World Championship remains, albeit with its highs and lows, the world's greatest motor racing series—although to call it a "world" championship is perhaps stretching a point. Not only has Bernie Ecclestone, the true ringmaster, never succeeded in distracting the great American public from its Indy championship, but neither has he managed to establish a permanent bridgehead in the States by organizing attractive Grands Prix.

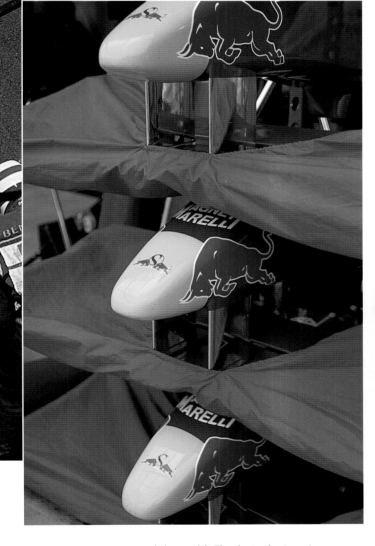

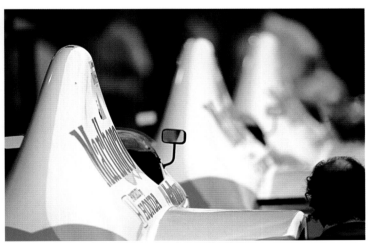

sets around the world. Thanks to the invasive presence of television, which changes the very nature of everything that passes in front of a camera, the interests revolving around the Formula 1 championship are such that it is legitimate to ask whether today the Grands Prix are anything but motor races.

We shall leave this question unanswered until the end of this chapter, which concludes at the threshold to a new century. For the moment we shall continue to enjoy motor racing as a sport, a contest revisited in a mechanical key but nonetheless fed by courage,

The Formula 1 story officially began on the 13th of June, 1950, at the former military airfield of Silverstone. With the pain and damage of the war slowly healing, motor racing had returned to thrill the public. There were endurance races, legendary road races, city-to-city raids and sporadic rallies. Above all the open-wheeled single-seaters began to roar again, even though their technological flywheel had yet to pick up speed: the cars were frequently those developed in the late 1930s and it was actually one of these, the Alfetta Tipo 158 and subsequently the Tipo 159 that was to dominate the first two editions of the World Championship, carrying Nino Farina and Juan Manuel Fangio to

consecutive titles. During the German occupation of Italy the 158s designed by Gioacchino Colombo had been hidden in a cheese factory.

The formula used to assign the new championship title was less abstruse than previous systems and was based on decreasing points from eight to two. At the end of the season the driver with the most points was crowned World Champion. A clause in the regulations rendered the races even more interesting: an extra point was assigned to the driver recording the fastest lap. This clause was eliminated in 1961, the point being added to those given to the winner of each race. The first championship was composed of the British Grand Prix (that first race

would never again see on the starting grid aces of the caliber of Varzi, Rosemeyer and the debilitated Nuvolari. One of those new drivers, however—Juan Manuel Fangio—was to win no fewer than five World Championships, a record to this day.

Alfa Romeo's superiority was crushing thanks to the Alfetta 158 which won all 11 races for which it was entered in 1950. The first three places in the final championship table were filled by the *Alfisti*: Farina, Fangio and Fagioli. This domination was repeated in 1951, although the Ferrari was now competitive enough to challenge Fangio's leadership. Certainly the 13-year-old Alfetta was by now aging, but it was still very reliable; the 158 had

552 left Fangio and Farina are saluted by King George VI before the start of the 1950 British Grand Prix at Silverstone, the very first Formula 1 race.

552 right Fangio (top) arriving in the pits with the Alfa Tipo 158 Alfetta at the Italian GP, the last round of the 1950 championship. His race was curtailed by a broken gearbox on the 24th lap, thus putting an end to his championship hopes. The race was won by Farina who also became the first Formula 1 World Champion. In the photo below Farina is seen with the second Alfetta behind Ascari in the Ferrari. Ascari later took over Serafini's car (on the third lap after his own engine failed) and finished second.

was attended by the Royal Family), and those of Monaco, Switzerland, Belgium, France and Italy. Up until 1960 the Indianapolis 500 was also valid for the World Championship, although in practice only local drivers competed in the American race.

The races were disputed by cars with 1.5-liter supercharged or 4.5-liter naturally aspirated engines. There were no restrictions on weight or power output.

Five main teams took part in that first championship season: Alfa Romeo, Ferrari, Maserati, Talbot and Gordini. Among the 19 drivers there were interesting newcomers such as the Italians, Farina and Alberto Ascari; two red-hot Argentines, Fangio and Gonzales; and two Britons, Parnell and Moss. Then there was the old guard composed of the likes of Fagioli, Chiron and Lang, and regrets that we

also evolved into the 159, the power output of which reached 470 hp with a specific output of 278 hp/liter (the engine had a total displacement of just 1479 cc).

In those years there was a custom that today appears curious but at the time added to the spectacle: the "stealing" of cars. It was in fact within the rules for the teams to move a driver from one car to another in the middle of a race. A classic example of this took place in the ACF Grand Prix of 1951. Ascari at the wheel of a Ferrari overtook Fangio but broke down on the 10th lap while the Argentine slowed with engine problems. Farina, the reigning champion, thus found himself in the lead. Fangio took over Fagioli's car while Ascari in turn took the place of Gonzales. Farina in the meantime lost a wheel but there were no more cars available. Victory went to Fangio, the Alfetta's 27th consecutive win.

1950 - 1951

In the following GP at Silverstone, Ascari broke with this tradition: he was let down by his own car but recognized that Gonzales had the opportunity not only to beat his fellow countryman Fangio but also to interrupt the Alfetta's winning streak. Ascari could have demanded Gonzales' car but refrained from doing so and the *simpatico* Gaucho Gonzales went on to win the race. It was a noble gesture but an error as far as the championship was concerned. By the last race held at Barcelona, Ascari was two points behind Fangio (he would have had a clear lead had he won at Silverstone) and was obliged to chase. The team got its tire strategy completely wrong and the dream was over: Fangio the *Chueco* (crooked-leg) won and was crowned champion.

Fangio was to be the undisputed king of 1950s Grand Prix racing, winning a further four championships from 1954 to 1957 when driving for Mercedes, Maserati and Ferrari. His last race was the 1958 French GP at the wheel of a Maserati, a race that unfortunately will be remembered for the death of his great friend Luigi Musso: the Argentine's pain was so great he announced his definitive retirement.

His adieu was one of those that leave a vacuum.

Apart from his five world titles, a feat yet to be equaled, he took with him a record of 51 Grands Prix disputed, nearly half of which he won (24), 28 pole positions and 23 fastest laps.

The Spanish GP of 1951 was the Alfetta's last great victory: at the height of its power Alfa Romeo realized that it could no longer squeeze anything more from its magnificent single-seater and decided to abandon GP racing. Forty-eight years later the firm returned to Formula 1 from 1979 to 1987, but with disappointing results.

553 top On the extremely long (over 22 km/ 13.7 mi.) and difficult Nürburgring circuit, Fangio could only manage second place in the 1951 German GP. He was beaten by a Ferrari which thus scored its second Formula 1 win.

553 center left Fangio with the Alfa Tipo 159 Alfetta dominated in Spain the last Grands Prix of 1951: he held pole position, got the fatest lap and, of course, won.

553 center Alfa Romeo against Ferrari, a duel that was to last two seasons and which was to see Alfa prevail. In this photograph Farina with the Tipo 159 is seen leading Taruffi with the Ferrari at the Italian GP of 1951: the two finished third and fifth, respectively.

553 center right Juan Manuel Fangio is applauded following his victory in the Swiss GP of 1951.

553 bottom Farina borne aloft in triumph following his victory in the Belgian GP held at the Spa-Francorchamps circuit.

FORMULA 2 CARS WHILE AWAITING NEW REGULATIONS

554 top Alberto Ascari at the wheel of a Ferrari during the 1952 British Grand Prix.

554 center Two Ferrari drivers racing almost side by side during the 1952 Italian GP. The two, Ascari and Villoresi, were to cross the line in first and third places, respectively. With this win Ascari celebrated his sixth consecutive victory and his first World Championship title.

554 bottom The great absentee from the '52 championship was Fangio, who only returned to the circus the

following year. In the meantime he continued racing and taking risks: he crashed at the Monaco GP and suffered a concussion. Here he is seen on a stretcher while being loaded onto the ambulance.

555 top Farina, Ascari and Fangio during the 1953 Italian GP: the Argentine driver at the wheel of a Maserati took the race. Giuseppe "Nino" Farina was second, 1.4 seconds behind. Ascari was out of luck as he collided with slow-moving Fairman in the HWM coming out of the parabolica on the last lap.

Alfa's withdrawal was almost fatal for the World Championship. Lack of serious opposition meant that Ferrari's domination was so evident and absolute that it was hardly worth racing. The British teams were working hard and had some good ideas but were still well behind in terms of research and development. The most advanced of them was the youthful BRM (British Racing Motors), a concern born out of the collaboration between around a hundred different manufacturers. The team had presented the Formula 1 field's most powerful car in 1951, the Type 15 Mark 1 producing 525 hp. The Germans had the know-how and the experience, but did not yet have sufficient resources to enter the fray. Making up numbers on the grid were models such as Maserati, Simca-Gordini and Talbot.

There were many who believed that the FIA's attempt to run an organized championship was doomed, like its predecessors, to failure after just two editions. The solution that was found was valid and providential: in order to give the constructors time to design new Formula 1 cars, for two years the World Championship was reserved for Formula 2 cars, i.e., those with 2-liter naturally aspirated or 500-cc supercharged engines. (Supercharging was thus impractical, since it could not overcome such a severe disadvantage). Formula 1 was to return in 1954 with naturally aspirated engines of up to 2.5 liters or supercharged units of 750 cc.

The use of Formula 2 cars opened the Championship to new constructors that had previously been absent due to the exorbitant costs of developing Formula 1 cars. New and unknown models thus found themselves on the starting grids for the Grands Prix: Cooper, Connaught, AFM,

Veritas and OSCA to name some of them. The Cooper developed by Moss's mechanic Francis is worthy of particular mention as it was presented at the 1953 Italian GP with disc brakes, a novelty that was to be adopted on nearly all racing cars during the course of the 1950s, and fuel injection in place of carburetors.

The spectacle however was penalized by the new regulations: the earlier Formula 1 cars had boasted power outputs of well over 400 hp thanks to supercharging and reached extremely high maximum speeds on the order of 300 kph (186 mph). In acoustic terms, too, the roar of their engines was undoubtedly more thrilling. Nonetheless, the Formula 2 machines had the advantage of being lighter than the 1.5-liter supercharged cars and were thus themselves very fast (up to 260 kph/ 161 mph) despite power outputs of under 200 hp. Moreover, the races were

more straightforward as there were fewer refueling stops.

The two-year period was nonetheless dominated by Ferrari who won every round of the 1952 championship and six out of seven of the 1953 Grands Prix (excepting Indy in both cases, of course). Alberto Ascari, son of the great Antonio, who had died during the French GP in 1925, won all the 1952 championship races in which he participated (six out of seven, having missed the opening round in Switzerland because he was driving for Ferrari in the Indianapolis 500) and five of the seven rounds in 1953.

Fangio had moved to Maserati but missed the whole of the 1952 season. He crashed in the nonchampionship Monza GP, suffering the first and only serious injuries of his career. The accident was due to the Argentine's state of fatigue as he had presented himself for the start of the Milanese

555 bottom left *Ascari aboard a Ferrari 500 (number 10) and de Graffenried (in a Maserati) passing the pits at Reims. The race was the French GP of 1953: the Englishman Hawthorn won, his first victory for Ferrari.*

555 bottom right *The 1953 German GP with Fangio at the wheel of a Maserati. After 18 laps of the Nürburgring the Argentine champion finished over a minute behind the winner, Giuseppe Farina in a Ferrari 500.*

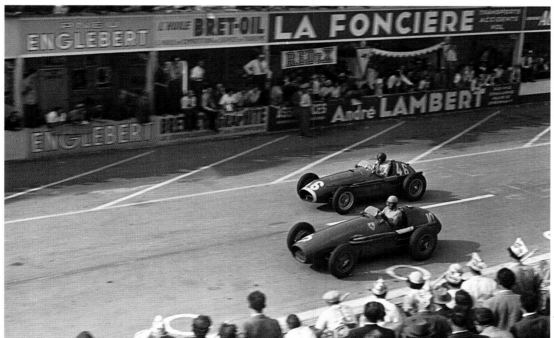

race just an hour and a half beforehand, after having raced a BRM the day before in Ireland and undergoing an exhausting journey by plane to Paris and then by car to Italy. He started the race from the back of the grid, not having participated in the qualifying sessions, completed two laps and then crashed.

Even though he had completed only 6 km (3.8 mi.), they were sufficient to demonstrate the potential of the new A6CM from *Ingegnere* Colombo, who had recently joined Maserati after his success with Alfa Romeo and Ferrari.

Motor racing lost one of its all-time greats that year as Tazio Nuvolari died after a lengthy illness. He was buried with his leather helmet, yellow shirt and blue trousers.

1952 - 1953

The return of Formula 1 power

Maserati, Fangio (who won his second World Championship), and Mercedes (who poached the Argentine driver), were the protagonists of the 1954 season, an important year for the World Championship as it was the first to run to the new regulations specifying 2.5-liter naturally aspirated or 750-cc supercharged engines, a formula that remained unchanged until 1960. The reduced cylinder capacity for supercharged engines was a clear signal to the constructors from the FIA that they should concentrate their technical and economic resources on the development of naturally aspirated units.

Mercedes returned to the formula with the introduction of the new regulations and launched a series of mechanical and stylistic innovations that were to leave their mark not only on the world of competition but on automotive production in general. The German firm's participation in Formula

them to gain a second a lap over the agile Ferraris and the powerful Maseratis. The technological innovations were equally surprising: the W196 entranced both humble racing fans and enthusiasts of advanced mechanical engineering.

On its debut the Mercedes was the car to beat despite its weight: 680 kg (1,500 lb.) the streamlined version and 640 (1,411 lb.) for the open-wheeler. The W196 won straight out of the box in France with Fangio. The Argentine driver's remarkable results were due to the respect with which he treated his car as well as to his own undisputed talent: his was the Mercedes works car that suffered the least mechanical problems and wear over the season.

556 top and 557 center left
Streamlined styling that would be the envy of the single-seaters of the 1990s, a full width body with covered wheels finished in the unmistakable silver unpolished metal livery. These are the characteristics of the Mercedes W196, the undisputed protagonist of the 1954 season. At the 1954 British GP (top) Fangio was obliged to chase the Ferraris and a Maserati that finished in the first three places. The Argentine finished fourth after a minor accident in which he struck a track marker, damaging the front part of his Mercedes W196's right-hand flank.

1 was to last only two seasons, however. At the end of 1955 the Silver Arrows (as the fearsome Mercedes race cars were known) were withdrawn. While it's generally assumed that this followed the tragic Levegh crash at Le Mans, in fact Mercedes-Benz was eager to concentrate its resources on its more profitable production models. This policy was also dear to Lancia, another debutante in the 1954 season but one which, like Mercedes, was to withdraw at the end of 1955.

When the Silver Arrows—the Mercedes W196s—took to the track at Reims, they catalyzed the attention of spectators and technicians alike with their streamlined full-width bodywork: the wheels were covered by flowing torpedo-like wings, lending the cars a degree of class and elegance that rendered the others obsolete. This was a lesson in design that Mercedes preached to the entire world, demonstrating that extreme performance and beauty could coexist. The streamlined bodywork worn by the W196s on fast circuits to improve the cars' aerodynamics allowed

556 center and 556-557 bottom After 15 years absence from the tracks, Mercedes returned with the W196 in 1954 when the championship was already under way: its first race was the French GP, in which it finished first and second. This photographs show the German car driven by Fangio: note the supplementary air intake integrated into the right-hand flank of the car to augment the flow of cooling air from the shark-like mouth at the front. The bodywork in this case left the wheels exposed and was used as an alternative to the full-width body on slow circuits such as that at

Monaco in which handling was all-important. The weight of the car in this form was 40 kg lighter at 640 kg, but it was still heavier than its rivals. The W196 nonetheless proved to be unbeatable. Fortunately for the other teams the German manufacturer's involvement in Formula 1 lasted for only two seasons, 1954-'55, during which it scored nine victories out of 12 Grands Prix disputed. The team's withdrawal came as a result of the manufacturer's decision to concentrate its resources on its production models. Mercedes returned to Formula 1 in 1994 as an engine supplier, firstly to Sauber and then to McLaren, with whom it won the championship in 1998.

557 top left The Mercedes were futuristic compared with the other cars seen here at the start of the 1954 Italian GP. They finished first and fourth in the race driven by Fangio and Hermann.

557 top right A Mercedes 1-2 at the French GP in 1954: the W196s lapped the rest of the field and finished first and second with just a tenth of a second separating Fangio from Kling, seen here with car number 20.

557 center right and bottom Posters are mementos of the races of the past. Like those of the 1954 French GP (center) held at Reims, or that of Pau (bottom), a French circuit, venue of a non-championship Grand Prix.

1954 - 1955

THE FIRST WORLD CHAMPIONSHIP VICTIMS

Nineteen fifty-four was unfortunately also the year of the Formula 1 World Championship's first fatality. The Argentine driver Marimon was killed at the wheel of a Maserati during practice for the German GP. The tragedies continued into 1955: the worst accident in motor racing history happened at Le Mans when Pierre Levegh's Mercedes collided with Lance Macklin's Austin-Healey and plunged into the crowd, killing its driver and 83 spectators. The obituary columns also recorded the deaths of Ascari and the two-time winner of the Indianapolis 500, Vukovich. As a mark of respect, the Swiss, German and French Grands Prix were canceled, while the AAA (American Automobile Association) withdrew as an organizer of motor racing in America.

"Ciccio" Ascari died like his father Antonio: a terrible premonitory sign had struck the Italian at the Monaco GP where he crashed at the chicane on the sea-front (at the same point where Bandini was to die 12 years later) but survived unscathed. Four days later while testing Castellotti's Ferrari 750 Ciccio failed to negotiate the Vialone curve at Monza, later renamed the Ascari curve. His friend Villoresi was devastated and Gianni Lancia, patron

of the team that had just signed Ascari, decided that enough was more than enough: he sold the company and ceded his racing cars, the D50s, to Ferrari.

The drivers' World Championship of 1955 was composed of just six races: Mercedes had signed the English driver Stirling Moss who, together with Fangio, formed an unbeatable duo. The car, the W196, presented a number of modifications to the chassis (shorter wheelbase) and the braking system (the front drums were moved outboard), while power had been increased to 290 hp, greater than that of the Ferraris and Maseratis. The new Silver Arrows won five of the six rounds that season, four of which were conquered by Fangio, the fifth by Moss.

558 top left The Italian GP of 1955 featured a modified circuit, including a high-speed section with 38° banked curves. The Mercedes of Fangio, in the foreground, and Taruffi, behind the Argentine ace, were in their element, reaching 260 kph (161 mph) and finishing first and second.

558 top right The heart of the Maserati 250 F was its longitudinal six-cylinder engine. The Trident's new single-seater made its debut in 1955 but it was in 1957 that it proved unbeatable when it carried Fangio to his fifth World Championship title and Stirling Moss to second place behind the Argentine.

558 center left Stirling Moss' Mercedes tackling a sharp corner at the Monaco GP of 1955. The English driver was forced to withdraw, as were his teammates Fangio and Simon—a black day for the Stuttgart firm, but one enjoyed by Trintignant with the Ferrari, who won after starting from ninth place on the grid.

558 center right At the start of the 1955 British GP held at Aintree, Jean Behra with the Maserati, first on the right, attempts to take the lead by out-sprinting the Mercedes of Fangio (center) and Moss (left). It was to be the latter who won the race.

558 bottom The remains of the Ferrari 750 driven by "Ciccio" Ascari at the Vialone Curve, later renamed after him, at Monza on the 26th of May, 1955. Thus passed one of the greats of the early days of Formula 1, the only Italian to have won two World Championships.

558-559 The 1957 Monaco GP on the Monte Carlo street circuit was the second race of the season and the first in Europe following the one in Argentina. It was won by Fangio with the Maserati 250F number 10; behind the Argentine were the Ferraris of Musso and Collins.

1955

BRITISH ARRIVALS, MERCEDES FAREWELL

An English driver's victory in the British GP was a result of Mercedes' desire to improve its image on the other side of the Channel: an Englishman victorious at the wheel of a German car could only have had a positive effect on sales. Thus during the race Fangio was comfortably in the lead, his third World Championship title already in the bag, when he let Moss through and finished in second, two-tenths behind. In the meantime, the British Vanwall had made its debut for bearing magnate Tony Vandervell. The car's engine was built in collaboration with the engineers of the Norton motorcycle firm. That first season was not particularly successful but things picked up in 1956 with the cars designed by Frank Costin—brother of Mike, who founded Cosworth in 1960 together with Keith

559 top During the 1956 season Fangio raced for Ferrari after Mercedes had withdrawn from competition: in this photograph the Argentine is seen during the British GP which he won from the Ferrari of de Portago/Collins and Behra's Maserati.

559 center right Stirling Moss at the wheel of the Maserati 250F crosses the line first in the 1956 Italian GP, the last round of the Championship. Fangio finished behind him after taking over his team mate Collins' Ferrari on the 20th lap (his own car's engine had failed). The Argentinean's second-place finish earned him his fourth championship title.

559 bottom right Eternal runner-up Stirling Moss made his Formula 1 debut in 1951 at the Swiss GP. He finished second in the World Championships from 1955 to '58. A 1962 accident at Goodwood in

England brought an end to his career after disputing 66 Grands Prix, winning 16 overall and recording 16 pole positions. Here he is pushed to the pits at the 1957 Italian GP at the wheel of a British Vanwall.

Duckworth—and Colin Chapman, the father of Lotus. Jack Brabham also made his debut and in 1958 was to found his own famous team. He took part in the British GP with a Bristol-powered Cooper T40. This car, which retired with engine problems, was a forerunner of the cars of the 1960s with its lightweight construction and mid-mounted engine.

There were also innovations with regards to the circuits and at Monza the high speed oval with 38° banked curves was inaugurated—a project that was intended to provide spectacular racing but which actually proved to be an error. The uneven paving of the *parabolica* proved very hard on the cars, and over the years structural faults rendered the racing surface too dangerous to use.

Mercedes abandoned Formula 1 at the end of the 1955 season; Fangio, however, was still able to

celebrate because his Mercedes had carried him to his third title. The fourth he was to conquer the following year with Ferrari after a close-fought season with Moss in the Maserati. To clinch it, Fangio again took advantage of the rule allowing him to take over a teammate's car: in Argentina his Ferrari-Lancia betrayed him on the 43rd lap and Musso gave way. At Monaco and Italy it was Collins who ceded his mount to the Argentine. (The Englishman himself, meanwhile, had been having a fine season and was currently leading the championship table—a third place in Italy would have been sufficient for him to win the title had he not been obliged to cede to his team leader.)

In the late 1950s, only Ferrari was left to defend the Italian colors that up until then had been so well represented. The Prancing Horse had insufficient

resources, however, to contain the numerous ambitious British teams with their innovative cars for 1957. The new era of British motor racing—returning to greatness after over 30 years on the sidelines—dawned at the British GP which was won by the Vanwall of Moss, a driver destined to inherit the sceptre of the king of the track from his friend and former teammate Fangio.

COOPER AND VANWALL, NEW FORCES IN FORMULA 1

The Constructors' Championship came into being in 1958, and there was also a changing of the guard among the drivers and cars. The retirement of the champion of champions, Fangio was a tangible sign of this change and was unfortunately accompanied by the deaths of Musso, Collins, Lewis-Evans and Hawthorn. They were all killed in cars, whether it was on the track or on the road, in races or in practice. It was actually Musso's death that persuaded the 46-year-old Fangio to retire.

The British teams and drivers took it upon themselves to enliven the championship, overshadowing the Italian constructors. They were, however, pipped at the post by Ferrari thanks to the points system: Stirling Moss at the wheel of the

560 top left Peter Collins during the 1958 British Grand Prix. Ferrari's English driver won at Silverstone despite starting from the last row of the grid, leading home Mike Hawthorn by 24 seconds.

560 bottom left The cars are still in the pits for the last checks prior to the start of the Italian GP of 1958, the penultimate round of the World Championship. In the foreground is the Vanwall of Stirling Moss who was

560 top right The cover of La Domenica del Corriere recording the terrible accident at Monza during a non-points race in 1959. Tinazzo and Crivellari collided at 160 kph (99 mph).

forced to retire during the race with a broken gearbox. The British team was the first to win the Constructors' Championship introduced in 1958.

1958 - 1959

Vanwall lost the title to Mike Hawthorn and the Ferrari despite having won four races outright to his rival's single victory in France.

These bare statistics do not, however, have much to say about an episode that, especially when compared with the attitudes of drivers in the 1990s, is surprising if not literally incredible.

On the eve of the last World Championship round, the Casablanca GP in Morocco, Moss had won three races to Hawthorn's one but the latter had recorded five second-place finishes. In the race he was lying second behind Moss, a placing that would have been sufficient to give him the world title. However, he spun off in his Ferrari, got out of the car, pushed it back onto the track and restarted. He was later disqualified because according to the officials he had pushed his car against the direction of traffic. Moss was thus the World Champion.

Sporting to a fault, Moss testified that his rival had in fact acted within the regulations. This allowed Hawthorn and Ferrari to take the title and Moss to gain a reputation for absolute sporting integrity.

The British superiority was now manifest, and Vanwall deservedly won the first Constructors' Championship. The reasons behind this superiority were principally technical: the new had the legs on the old.

There was a veritable revolution in regards to engine location, the Cooper being powered by an engine mounted just ahead of the rear axle. Enzo Ferrari long held this to be a conceptual error: the "oxen should stay in front of the cart." He was later obliged to revise this opinion, but for the moment the two whippings given to the Dino 246 in Argentina and Monaco were insufficient evidence. Anglo-Saxon supremacy ran deeper than the

successes of the Championship-winning Vanwall and Cooper: in 1958 the surprising Lotus 16 designed by Colin Chapman made its debut in the hands of Allison and the then-unknown Graham Hill.

It appeared that success in the World Championship was a form of deadly disease: at the end of the season Vanwall too retired from Formula 1. Tony Vandervell's team nonetheless had the merit of kick-starting the British motor racing revival which was continued thanks to the feats of the Cooper.

In a curious coincidence, John Cooper's British team which won the Constructors' Championship in 1959 signed two unknown drivers, both from the southern hemisphere, the Australian Jack Brabham who immediately won the championship, and the New Zealander Bruce McLaren who in winning the United states Grand Prix at just 22 years old became the youngest driver to win a Grand Prix. The coincidence lies not only in the fact that both came from distant former British

560 right center Women were not immune to the appeal of motor racing and the most courageous of them joined in. In 1958 the Italian Maria Teresa de Filippis drove a Maserati in the Belgian, Portuguese and Italian Grands Prix. She finished 10th at Spa but was forced to retire at Oporto and Monza.

560 bottom right Jack Brabham at the wheel of a Cooper-Climax passing the BRM driven by Harry Schell during the 1959 Italian GP. The Australian driver finished the race in third place, earning sufficient points to clinch the Formula 1 World Championship. The American finished the race in seventh place and the championship in tenth.

561 top The Englishman Hawthorn was the protagonist of 1958 season: he conquered his first World Championship

at the wheel of a Ferrari. He won only one Grand Prix, in France, but scored numerous placings that allowed Maranello to dominate the Constructors' Championship.

561 center left In 1958 Fangio competed in his last Grands Prix in Argentina and France. He finished both races in fourth place at the wheel of a Maserati 250F. "El chueco" withdrew from racing at 47 years of age after having won a record five World Championship titles, a feat yet to be matched.

561 center right The Lotus Mark 16 made its debut in 1958 driven by the unknown Graham Hill and by Cliff Allison. Here Hill is seen at the wheel of the Climax-powered Lotus as he attempts to make an impression in the British Grand Prix of 1959. He was to finish no better than ninth, nine laps down on the winner Jack Brabham in a Cooper-Climax.

561 bottom The Lotus Mark 16 was the genial Colin Chapman's first single-seater and made its debut at the Monaco GP in 1958.

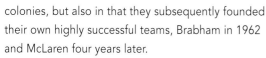

colonies, but also in that they subsequently founded their own highly successful teams, Brabham in 1962 and McLaren four years later.

British celebrations were completed by the presence of competitive teams such as Lotus and BRM and by the somewhat uninspiring debut of Aston Martin, one of whose drivers, Carroll Shelby, was to become famous for his fabulous Shelby Cobra sports cars. In contrast, the British motor racing world was saddened by the loss of Mike Hawthorn, killed in a car accident in Surrey.

Another great champion also passed away, Rudolf Caracciola, finally defeated by liver disease.

The early years of the new decade were marked by the ferocious criticism that for the first time was levelled at constructors regarding the fragility of their cars. At the center of this controversy was Colin Chapman (not for the last time) who was held responsible for the fatal accident involving Stacey in the Belgian GP; the bloody feathers found on the front of the car led to the accident being attributed to an unfortunate and unidentified bird. Shortly before at the same circuit Bristow had also lost his life when he crashed into a fence at the wheel of a Cooper. The Belgian GP took place immediately after a race in Holland that had also been marred by tragedy when the brakes on Dan Gurney's BRM

Formula 1 World Championship.

In spite of the number of drivers who lost their lives, 1960 was notable for the debut of two other all-time greats, Jim Clark and John Surtees, the latter a World Champion motorcycle racer. Along with Brabham, McLaren and Moss (who changed teams all too frequently), Phil and Graham Hill were also challenging for the title. Although they were almost always off the pace, the Ferraris won at Monza in a race deserted by the British teams because the unevenness of the surface of the parabolica made it dangerous for their extremely lightweight cars.

The world titles remained firmly in the hands of Brabham and Cooper and the British run of

working for some years on a 1.5-liter V6, while a similar unit was dominating Formula 2. Ferrari found itself handed the 1961 World Championship on a silver platter, while the new formula also favored Porsche's participation in the series as the company already had an air-cooled four-cylinder boxer engine used successfully in sports car racing.

It goes without saying that there were many complaints of clear favoritism on the part of the CSI toward the Italian and German teams, but the boycott attempted by the British teams came to nothing. As predicted, the championship season was a monotonous Ferrari cavalcade with five wins out of eight. The team conquered the Constructors'

failed, causing him to plough into the crowd and kill a spectator.

The funereal 1960 was also the last season of the 2.5-liter formula (having lasted a record seven seasons), and the last with creditable front-engined cars. The central engine location represented the new technological frontier and was championed and perfected by the British teams, Lotus and Cooper leading the way. It was also the last year that the Indianapolis 500 was valid as a round of the

successes extended into 1961. However, the Commission Sportive Internationale (CSI) took it upon itself to shuffle the cards, introducing the 1.5-liter formula. This was a body-blow for Cooper, Lotus and BRM as they had invested heavily in the preceding 2.5-liter formula and now had to dust off Formula 2 engine designs while Ferrari—surprise, surprise—already had excellent engines up and running.

The Italian manufacturer had, in effect, been

562 top left Rain beating down on the Aintree circuit, the venue for the 1961 British Grand Prix. The weather did not slow the American driver Richie Ginther who finished third with the Dino 156/61, completing a Ferrari 1-2-3 behind the winner Von Trips and Phil Hill in second.

562 top right The start of the 1961 Dutch Grand Prix saw the three Ferraris of Von Trips, Hill and Ginther on the front row of the grid. They were to finish first, second and fifth. The race earned its place in the record books because there were no retirements: fifteen drivers started, 15 finished.

Championship for the first time while Phil Hill became the first American to win a Formula 1 championship title. The Ferrari's scarce international popularity was worsened by the Maranello team's attitude in refusing to withdraw from the Italian GP even though on the second lap Von Trips had collided with Clark's Lotus and his Ferrari had cartwheeled into the crowd killing 14 spectators as well as Von Trips himself.

In the light of the accidents of the previous year, the new regulations introduced by the CSI included new safety norms and minimum weight limits for the cars which also had to be fitted with an automatic starter that prevented push starts, an electrical cut-off switch for use in emergencies and a twin-circuit braking system. Among the innovations there was also the roll-bar—a tubular structure placed behind the driver's head designed to protect him should his car roll over. Unfortunately, there were no technical specifications regarding this feature and thus the constructors simply welded an ineffective semi-circular tube to the bodywork.

562 center left The indispensable work of the mechanics constantly searching for the optimal set up: the photograph shows the BRM (British Racing Motors) pits. Like Ferrari, the British team founded in 1947 built its own chassis and engines.

562 center right and 562 bottom Porsche cars participated in Formula 1 from 1957 to 1964, although mainly in the hands of privateers given that the Zuffenhausen company only officially participated in the World Championship in '61 and '62. In 1959 the Dutchman de Beaufort and the American Blanchard raced the RSK in the Dutch and United States Grands Prix: the first finished tenth at Zandvoort, the second seventh at Sebring.

562-563 and 563 center right Phil Hill waves to the crowd as he crosses the line at the 1961 Italian GP at the wheel of a Ferrari. The race had to be interrupted on the second lap when Von Trips' car (right) collided with Clark's Lotus and

careened into the crowd, killing 14 before sliding to a halt on the track. The German driver also lost his life, bringing a tragic conclusion to a Formula 1 career that had lasted just four years; he debuted at the 1957 Argentine GP with a Ferrari, won two out of the 27 Grands Prix he disputed and conquered one pole.

563 top right This poster publicized the 46th French Grand Prix held at Reims, a race dominated by the British contingent. In fact ten British cars filled the first ten places, mainly Coopers with Climax and Maserati engines. The race would be Vanwall's last.

563 bottom left The new regulations introduced by the FIA for 1961 specified maximum cylinder capacities of no more that 1500 cc, which favoured Porsche, officially returning to the championship in 1961 with a four-cylinder boxer engine and in 1962 with a flat-Eight. Jo Bonnier, seen here, was a Porsche works driver together with Gurney, Hermann and de Beaufort in the 1961 season.

563 bottom right An American in Italy: Phil Hill triumphed at Monza, winning the 32nd edition of the Italian GP in 1961 with a Ferrari.

THE INTRODUCTION OF MONOCOQUES

The British teams were determined to extract their revenge both in 1962 and 1963. The early favorite Ferrari reached the end of the season bloodied, battered and no higher than fifth out of six in the final Constructors' Championship table, while Phil Hill could manage no better than sixth in the Driver's Championship.

Formula 1 lost another of its leading lights in 1962, Stirling Moss, the eternal runner-up who was always so close to taking the championship title. He crashed in a nonchampionship race and the effects of the accident on his sight and reflexes persuaded him to retire from racing.

The British teams' successful innovations, with Chapman in the forefront as usual, were light monocoque chassis and super-smooth eight-cylinder engines of an efficiency that outclassed the Maranello V6. For the monocoque chassis the Lotus chief had drawn inspiration from aeronautical technology, creating a container in riveted light alloy that to some resembled the hull of a speedboat, to others a bathtub. The box sections of the lateral elements were occupied by rubber fuel tanks while steel bulkheads at the front and rear stiffened the structure. The main advantage of this new concept was increased torsional stiffness. The "bathtub," equipped with wheels, suspension, brakes and an eight-cylinder engine, became the Lotus 25 and was entrusted to Jim Clark. He won the Belgian, British and United States Grands Prix but missed out on the World Championship, which went to another Briton, Graham Hill with the BRM.

The season's technical innovations were not restricted to the historically important integrated structure: the frontal sections of the cars were reduced by up to 30% in some cases, carburetors were replaced by fuel injection (which allowed more precise dosing of fuel and thus smoother power delivery at all engine speeds), wire wheels disappeared (replaced by those in light alloy), and steering wheels were reduced in diameter and trimmed in leather, not wood. The cars were, in fact, radically transformed and had never been so different to the pioneering horseless carriages, being closer to four-wheeled horizontal rockets.

The Clark/Lotus pairing took a handsome revenge in 1963, winning seven of the ten World Championship rounds. The talent of the driver, the perfection of Chapman's monocoque Lotus 25 and the power of the fuel-injected Coventry-Climax V8 formed an explosive mixture that was capable only of winning.

Ferrari made its comeback in 1964. Where any other team would have crumbled in the face of the British onslaught, Ferrari held firm, ably dictating a season in which it was the only continental manufacturer in a field dominated by Lotus, BRM, Cooper and Brabham. The championship was up for grabs until the last three laps of the last round in Mexico: Clark with the Lotus, Graham Hill with the BRM and Surtees with the Ferrari had shared the victories during the season. In the final phase of the race the British cars were obliged to retire (Hill being rammed by Bandini's Ferrari); Surtees finished second and Ferrari took both the Constructors' and Drivers' titles. This was the first time a former World Motorcycling Champion had repeated the feat in the automotive Formula 1 Championship.

564 top left The work of the mechanics in the pits is always frenetic and the space available always restricted. In the foreground Graham Hill's BRM is being prepared for the 1962 German GP. The labours were not in vain, as the Englishman went on to win the race.

564 top center The starting grid for the Belgian GP of 1962 saw Graham Hill in pole position at the wheel of a BRM; McLaren with a Cooper-Climax and Trevor Taylor with a Lotus completed the front row. Nineteen cars started the race while 11 finished.

564 top right Baghetti's Ferrari leads a quartet composed of de Beaufort, who is tackling this Nürburgring corner in his Porsche with plenty of opposite lock, Clark in a Lotus and Maggs in a Cooper-Climax hard on his heels. The race was the 1962 German GP.

564 center Jim Clark out on his own at Spa as he prepared to win the 1962 Belgian GP with the Lotus-Climax. The English cars proved to be unbeatable. BRM, Lotus, Cooper and Lola conquered the first four places in the Constructors' Championship.

564 bottom Graham Hill with a BRM passing Dan Gurney in a Porsche during the 1962 German GP held on the difficult but enthralling 22.722 km Nürburgring. Hill went on to win the race while Gurney finished third behind Surtees in a Lola-Climax.

AUTORACES ZANDVOORT om de
GROTE PRIJS VAN EUROPA
GROTE PRIJS VAN NEDERLAND
zondag 20 mei 1962

565 top right This poster publicized the Dutch GP of 1962 which was also run as the Grand Prix of Europe. This was the first round of the championship season and was won by Hill in a BRM with Taylor in a Lotus-Climax 27 seconds behind. The fastest lap was recorded by Bruce McLaren in a Cooper-Climax.

565 center The crowded start of the 1962 British GP at Aintree saw the Lotus-Climax of Innes Ireland start from pole position. Victory went to another of Chapman's cars driven by Jim Clark.

565 bottom The podium at the Belgian GP at Spa-Francorchamps in 1962 was an all-star affair with Clark after his first victory with the Lotus 25 saluting the crowd together with the English and American Hills, Graham and Phil.

1962 - 1963

1963 - 1964

566 top left Tired after having covered 32 laps of the Zandvoort circuit for a total of 450 km, but happy to have won the race, Jim Clark celebrates with the trophy in hand following his victory in the 1963 Belgian GP, the second round in the World Championship.

566 top right The start of the 1963 French GP held at Reims. The starting grid, with four cars abreast rather than the two normal today, saw Clark (the eventual winner with the Lotus) fighting for the lead with Hill in a BRM, Gurney in a Brabham and Surtees in a Ferrari.

566 center left Jim Clark in his Lotus-Climax with the laurels, is acclaimed by his team: as well as having won the 1963 Italian GP and recorded the fastest lap, he was crowned as World Champion three races from the end of the season. He was to repeat the feat two years later, again with a Lotus-Climax.

566 center right The two Formula 1 greats who dominated the 1963 season: on the left Chapman, the man who revolutionized Formula 1 on a number of occasions with technological innovations, seen here using a stop-watch; on the right Clark, the British team's number one driver.

566 bottom left Surtees attempted to counter the domination of the Clark-Lotus pairing in 1963 with the Ferrari Dino 156. Clark won seven out of ten Grands Prix and Surtees had to submit to the British team's superiority as at Silverstone, where he finished second behind Clark.

566 bottom Open-face helmet with no sponsor's decals, plus goggles, gloves and a mini-windshield: this was racing in the 1960s. Only the determination and the will to win have remained over time. Surtees showed all these qualities as he raced to fourth place in the Monaco GP.

566-567 center left Jim Clark racing toward victory in the 1963 Dutch GP aboard his Lotus 25. Green was the British national racing color, red that of Italy, blue that of France and gray that of Germany.

567 top left Hill at the wheel of his BRM passing the grandstands erected against the buildings of the exclusive Monégasque capital. The 100 laps of the 1963 Monaco GP were completed on a fine spring afternoon. The British driver won the race from Ginther in the second BRM.

567 top right Hill loses his traditional British aplomb, spraying trophy and laurel wreath with champagne at the 1962 South African GP. He needed no justification as victory in the East London race gave him his first World Championship.

567 bottom Graham Hill concentrating in his BRM while Jim Clark has been distracted by something or someone. Both are waiting to start from the front row of the grid for the 1963 Dutch GP, which Clark went on to win with Hill finishing fourth.

HONDA, FORMULA 1'S FIRST JAPANESE CONSTRUCTOR

1965 - 1966

In a championship that had temporarily shifted its center of gravity to the continent, technical innovations were very conspicuous as they were provoked by changes in tire technology: tires had become wider and lower thanks to the use of nylon rather than cotton fibers in the carcass, and grip had been improved by the use of synthetic rubber for the tread.

The American manufacturer Firestone was the first company to introduce the new tires, supplying them to Honda. The highly successful Japanese motorcycle firm had decided to compete in Formula 1 as well, presenting a car powered by a 12-cylinder engine mounted transversely behind the driver.

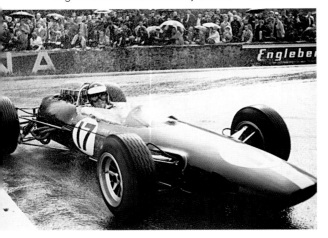

BRM instead tested a four-wheel drive car with the engine rotated through 180° behind the driver. Drive was controlled via a special shaft mounted inside the cockpit to the left of the driver. Technical complexity meant that the first four-wheel drive Formula 1 car was never raced, and it remains an historical oddity.

Clark and Lotus had time to win the title again in 1965 before the 1.5-liter formula was abandoned. The great British driver, who captured the affection of racing enthusiasts as perhaps only Fangio had managed to do, won six of the ten championship races, took his second world title and brought the Constructors' Championship to Lotus. He was even able to desert Monaco in favor of traveling to the United States to become the first European in 48 years to win the Indianapolis 500. This was also the first time that a mid-engined car had taken the prestigious trophy.

While Jim Clark was simply unbeatable, his rivals were by no means also-rans. Graham Hill was joined by a young rookie, a certain Jackie Stewart, an extremely promising Scotsman who was to continue the fine tradition of drivers with names beginning with "J": Juan Manuel Fangio, Jack Brabham, John Surtees and Jim Clark. Evidently J is a lucky letter for Formula 1 drivers, and in the years to follow the Formula 1 honor roll was to be graced by others of the caliber of Jo Siffert, Jochen Rindt, Jacky Ickx, James Hunt, Jody Scheckter and Jacques Villeneuve.

568 top The Japanese proved to be hard workers in Formula 1: these mechanics are making Ginther's Honda ready for the 1966 Italian GP. The American driver was forced to retire on the 17th lap after an accident.

568 left Absent from the 1965 Monaco GP because he was in America winning the Indianapolis 500, Jim Clark, seen here in his Lotus with race number 17, returned to his Formula 1 day job in time for the Belgian GP which he won easily in the rain.

568 center Jim Clark chasing the leading group composed of Jack Brabham, Denny Hulme and Graham Hill in the 1966 British GP at Brands Hatch. He eventually finished in fourth place, a lap behind the winner Jack Brabham.

568-569 The 17 cars have just started the 1965 French GP, moved that year to the Clermont Ferrand circuit. The track was, however, poorly maintained, and the roughness of the surface caused 10 cars to retire. Clark won with the Lotus and also recorded the fastest lap.

568 bottom The starting grid for the 1966 German GP saw a front row composed of, from left to right, Scarfiotti with the Ferrari, Stewart with the BRM, Surtees with a Cooper-Maserati and Clark with the Lotus-Climax. Surtees recorded the fastest lap but the race was won by Jack Brabham, first right on the second row.

BRABHAM WINS HIS THIRD TITLE

In the second half of the decade, with the advent of the three-liter engines that were to last until 1986, Formula 1 was transformed. A minimum weight limit of 500 kg (1,103 lb.; with oil and water but not fuel) was introduced while cylinder capacities were restricted to 3000 cc for naturally aspirated and 1500 cc for supercharged units.

These new engine sizes had been discussed since 1963, with the British constructors attempting to maintain the status quo—as with the old formula they had proved to be virtually unbeatable. The nascent American constructors were instead in favor, as they already had suitable three-liter engines available, while Ferrari could count on many years' experience with 12-cylinder units well suited to the new maximum displacement.

As in 1961, the new regulations appeared to have been introduced due to pressure from certain quarters rather than designed to prompt new technical developments. Coventry-Climax, which had in truth been in decline for the previous two years, announced that it was pulling out of Formula 1, leaving Lotus, Cooper and Brabham without engines. Of the 47 races disputed in those years

with the 1.5-liter formula, no fewer than 34 had been won with Climax engines.

Only Brabham (with the Australian V8 Repco engine), Cooper (with a Maserati unit) and Ferrari (with its own V12) were ready for the new Formula 1 season. Lotus and BRM had to fall back on provisional solutions, boring out the old 1.5-liter engines to a full two liters. McLaren instead opted for the Indianapolis Ford V8. Honda started out with its old V12, postponing the presentation of a new engine with similar architecture until the end of the season. The 1966 World Championship also saw the debut of the Eagle team founded by Dan Gurney's new All-American Racers, a California-based firm that would go on to brilliant success in Indy- and sports-car racing.

However, during the course of the year the pre-season favorite Ferrari was unable to exploit its advantage due to Surtees' desertion in France (provoked by internal disputes) and the strike of Italian engineering workers which caused the firm to miss the British GP. (In effect, Maranello has frequently been an unsettled place: firstly the strong, despotic character of Enzo Ferrari and then the infighting amongst too many "prima donnas" for decades have had serious effects on the sporting side of the company.)

The list of competitors for that year's World Championship was one to gladden the heart of any racing enthusiast: Clark, Hill, Bandini, Scarfiotti, Surtees, McLaren, Rindt, Stewart... And the title? In the end it went to Brabham for the third time: Jack remains the only driver to win the title at the wheel of a car bearing his own name, his team also winning the Constructors' Championship.

569 The Australian Jack Brabham dominated the 1966 season. The image bottom right shows him close to the table full of bottles of champagne ready to be uncorked in his honor as winner of the British GP. Brabham was nicknamed Black Jack for his hardness and determination at the wheel. Driver and owner of the team carrying his name, he scored the four wins that gave his team the Drivers' Championship and, together with the points collected by Denny Hulme, the Constructors' title. The Australian's season, both as a driver and as a team manager, did not get off to the best of starts as he was forced to retire from the first race with mechanical problems. His desolate expression while gazing at his car as he sits on the pit wall in the photograph above says it all.

THE DAWN OF THE FORD-COSWORTH ERA

570 top left The Silverstone circuit here is crowded—and not only with drivers—as preparations are completed for the start of the 1967 British GP. The Lotus-Ford in the foreground was driven by Clark who took both pole position and the race.

570 top right Hulme exploits all the power of his Brabham-Repco, the front wheels leaving the ground after a hump at the Nürburgring. The New Zealander won the race (the 1967 German GP) and the world title.

570-571 Clark at the wheel of the Lotus-Ford in the 1967 Italian GP. This was a difficult race for the Scot: starting from pole position, he was obliged to make a pit stop to change a tire. He restarted in 15th place but, one by one, he managed to pick off his rivals and regain the lead by the 59th lap. Exiting the parabolica on the last lap he ran out of fuel, but managed to coast home in third place.

570 bottom Jack Brabham in the Brabham pits talking to one of the Australian team's mechanics. This was the 1967 Italian GP won by Clark with the Lotus.

Chapman and his Lotus, deprived of a competitive engine, were overshadowed. BRM had no intention of ceding the V12 it was working on to its great rival and Coventry-Climax had ruled itself out of the picture. The old fox Colin Chapman then showed his true entrepreneurial colors and arranged an agreement between the giant Ford Motor Company and the tiny British engineering firm Cosworth for the production of Formula 1 engines: the £100,000 put up by the American carmaker allowed Cosworth to produce the first Cosworth V8, an engine that was to dominate the next 16 years from 1967 to 1983, winning no fewer than 155 Grands Prix, a record no other engine in the history of Formula 1 has ever matched.

The engine designers became obsessed with the figure 400—the power output asked of the new three-liter engines, be they eight-cylinder,

12-cylinder or even 16-cylinder units (as in the case of the BRM). Ferrari won the horsepower race, achieving 408 hp with its 48-valve V12 which was initially available as a 36-valve variant developing 390 hp. The Honda V12 and the new Ford-Cosworth V8 fitted to the Lotus followed with 405 hp while the Eagle's Weslake V12, the BRM H-16 and the 36-valve Maserati V12 managed a round 400 hp. The BRM V12 and the 36-valve Maserati V12 trailed with 375 and 365 hp, respectively.

The world of motor racing lost one of its leading figures that year in Tony Vandervell, the founder of the Vanwall team that had given Ferrari and Maserati so much trouble in the early 1950s, thus stimulating the United Kingdom's prolific small specialist manufacturers. As for Maserati, the firm took its final bow after having ceased supplying engines to Cooper.

One young driver decided that his future lay in team management and branched out on his own. His name was Frank Williams.

The tragic death of Lorenzo Bandini was the key event of the 1967 championship and led to the adoption of stricter safety norms. The tragedy occurred at the Monaco GP. The Italian driver started the race from the front row of the grid with his Ferrari 312 and was confident he could score only his second Formula 1 victory (his first had come in the 1964 Austrian GP, again at the wheel of a *Rossa*). On the 82nd lap, at the entrance to the chicane after the tunnel, his car hit a barrier, overturned and caught fire. Bandini was extracted from the wreck with severe burns and died in agony the following Wednesday.

The causes of that accident were never fully explained. Fatigue due to the 100 laps traditionally covered in the Monaco GP was blamed, as was the inadequacy of the rescue services provided by the organizers. From the following year, the Monaco GP was run over 80 laps, while firefighters and extinguishers were installed in the pits and around the tracks immediately after Bandini's accident. Shortly afterward, the drivers began wearing fireproof overalls made of Nomex, a fabric made by DuPont.

In spite of Clark's four victories and Brabham's pair, it was Hulme who took the championship thanks to his numerous placings.

571 top Jim Clark triumphed in the Dutch Grand Prix of 1967, a race that entered the history books as the debut of the Ford-Cosworth eight-cylinder engine that was to dominate the Formula 1 circus until 1983, collecting 155 victories along the way.

571 center and bottom This mass of scorched wreckage can be recognized as the remains of Lorenzo Bandini's Ferrari 312 that crashed into the barriers coming out of the chicane during the 1967 Monaco Grand Prix and burst into flames. Nothing could be done for the driver who died of his burns three days later.

IT'S TIME FOR SPOILERS, WINGS AND SPONSORS

At the 1967 Belgian GP Clark was the center of attention when he took to the track in a Lotus 49 fitted with an unusual appendage at the front designed to generate negative lift—a.k.a. "downforce"—that would press the car to the ground. Similar devices were quickly tested and adopted by the other teams but, once again, it was Colin Chapman who led the way.

By the following year's Belgian GP, virtually all contenders tried spoilers or wings in order to keep the car—for better or worse—more firmly on the ground. These aerodynamic appendages often resembled nothing so much as ironing boards above the cars, and they flexed dangerously with the risk of breakage at every corner. Another innovation was the full-face helmet, first popularized by Dan Gurney.

However, the key feature of the 1968 season was not technical. From that year on the teams began to carry advertising on their cars, which thus became multicolored high-speed billboards. Sponsors were essential to the survival of the World Championship in the light of the delicate economic situation that arose at the end of 1967, wherein suppliers such as Firestone, BP, and Esso asked to be paid for their products, rather than providing them *gratis*.

In that season AAR-Eagle, Honda and Cooper abandoned Formula 1 and the sport lost the great Jim Clark, Schlesser, Spence and Scarfiotti.

The Clark tragedy occurred in a Formula 2 race at Hockenheim after he had begun the new World

with the Ford-Cosworth powered Lotus 49. This engine was also fitted to the new Matra and the McLaren and won 11 of the 12 rounds, an exceptional performance given that this was only its second year of competition.

Formula 1 ended the 1960s with the success of Matra International and Jackie Stewart who won six of the 11 championship races. Matra's debut in Formula 1 had been a result of Ken Tyrrell's need to find a chassis suitable for the Ford-Cosworth engine that he had purchased—and one worthy of Jackie Stewart's talent. Matra, an aeronautical engineering firm supported by the French government and Elf-Aquitaine, was designing its own engine (the introduction of which was to be a fiasco) and was more than happy to co-operate with Tyrrell and lend its name to the enterprise. The company was

572 top Grace Kelly and Prince Ranier alongside Graham Hill, who had just won the Monaco GP for the fifth time in his career. This was in 1969 and the record number of wins on the Monte Carlo circuit set by the Englishman remained until 1993 when Ayrton Senna won his sixth.

572 bottom left The Lotus-Fords in the pits. The Dutch GP of 1968 was not a happy one for Colin Chapman's team as its cars could do no better than Graham Hill's ninth place. Siffert with the Rob Walker Lotus was obliged to retire with gearbox problems.

1968 - 1969

Championship season with a win in the first Grand Prix in South Africa, thus breaking Fangio's record with his 25th victory. Schlesser lost his life during the French GP, the first F1 race of his career (this was actually the first time the French race had been run under that name, the glorious ACF GP having finally been abandoned). Scarfiotti and Spence, on the other hand, were the victims of fatal accidents in a hillclimb event with a Porsche and during practice at Indianapolis, respectively. Ironically, Spence had taken Jim Clark's place at Lotus and died exactly a month after the great British champion.

The season concluded with Hill taking the title

delighted to win the title only a year after its debut.

The Ford-Cosworth V8 engine that in the 1969 season powered the Lotus, Brabham and McLaren cars as well as the French cars, won every World Championship round and conquered all three places on the podium in every race with the exception of the Dutch and United States Grands Prix (third place for Amon with the Ferrari and third for Surtees with the BRM, respectively). The supremacy of the British V8 was thus undisputed: the Ferrari and BRM V12s appeared lightyears away from the performance provided by their rival.

Another statistic may help to comprehend the

efficiency, versatility and longevity of the Ford-Cosworth DFV. From 1968 to 1982, with the exception of 1975, 1977, and 1979, it powered the car driven by every World Champion driver.

In 1969 new wing regulations were introduced, as too many accidents had been caused by spoilers breaking; under these conditions the cars became uncontrollable and thus extremely dangerous for both drivers and spectators. Another question resolved at the end of the 1960s was four-wheel drive: such chassis were all built by Lotus, McLaren, Matra and Cosworth, but each proved too heavy, complex and expensive in the end.

572 bottom center Siffert's Lotus attempting to keep Surtees' Honda at bay. Neither driver was to finish the 1968 Monaco GP, Siffert retiring on the 11th lap with a broken transmission, the Englishman lasting another six laps before he too was forced out with gearbox problems.

572 bottom right and 573 bottom The Brabham-Repco stripped down by the mechanics of the Australian team: note the eight-cylinder engine, the small spoiler and the grooved tires.

573 top Matra International made its debut in 1968. The team was managed by Ken Tyrrell with cars powered by the Ford-Cosworth V8 and driven by Jackie Stewart. The MS10 single-seater is seen here in the pits at the British GP, in which Stewart finished sixth.

573 center In the late 1960s the constructors tackled the problem of aerodynamics by fitting towering wings such as those of the Lola T102, which were very similar to ironing boards.

573 bottom left The Lotus touching down with its rear wheels on the Nürburgring asphalt. The demanding 1968 German GP with its apparently modest 14 laps (totalling 320 km) saw Hill finish second behind Stewart in the Matra-Ford. This was the French team's second F1 victory.

573 bottom right Graham Hill is extracted from his Lotus-Ford after the frightening accident caused by the loss of the car's wings in the 1969 Spanish GP. Fortunately the English driver escaped with his life. This was not the only accident caused by wings: Rindt's Lotus also crashed after losing its spoilers.

ENZO FERRARI GOES HALVES

June, 1969 was an important month for Ferrari, albeit not in terms of results. As his Formula 1 cars continued to be dominated by their British Cosworth-powered rivals, 50% of the Modenese firm, forever in financial difficulties, was sold to Fiat. The Fiat buyout was the final movement in a dance which had actually begun between Ferrari and Ford at the dawn of the decade. This dance had ended in acrimony on both sides, and in Ford's intense commitment to racing—or at least to beating Ferrari.

Thus, Formula 1 celebrated its first 20 years—a period in which the changes and revolutions had been such that it would have been difficult for similar mutations to have taken place in the 20 years that followed. Much had, of course, changed since 1950. For the manufacturers, it had been Italy (with Alfa Romeo and then Ferrari), then Germany with Mercedes-Benz, then Italy again. Later the Union Jack reigned supreme. As for the drivers, between 1958 and 1969 the World Champion's flag was British on no fewer than seven occasions.

Would someone, or something, be able to dent the supremacy of British drivers, technicians and teams in the years ahead?

RINDT, THE POSTHUMOUSLY CROWNED CHAMPION

The answer to the question at the end of the last paragraph has to be yes, because Ferrari staged a magnificent comeback—at least in terms of the Constructors' Championship, which was won by Maranello four times (Lotus also won four titles, Tyrrell and McLaren one each). The team enjoyed less success in the Drivers' Championship as on seven occasions the champion's car was powered by the Ford-Cosworth engine and on each occasion the team was British. It was a decade of doubles for the drivers: Stewart won two titles (his second and third, thus equaling Brabham's record), as did the Brazilian, Fittipaldi (the first South American champion after Fangio), and Lauda, the Ferrari team's number one.

Although his grip on his company may have been weakened, Enzo Ferrari stubbornly resisted the British domination and never despaired. He retained Ickx and signed Regazzoni. The moustachioed Swiss driver, much later confined to a wheelchair after a

574 top The start of the 1970 British GP with Rindt in the Lotus (left), Brabham in a Brabham (center) and Ickx in a Ferrari (right) immediately in the thick of things. Rindt went on to win with Brabham second; Ickx retired on the seventh lap.

574 bottom left Enzo Ferrari on the pit wall at Monza timing one of his drivers. They were to give him partial satisfaction in that in 1970 the Italian Grand Prix was won by Regazzoni but Ickx and Giunti both retired.

574 bottom right Ferrari managed to record four victories in the 1970 championship, all coming in the last part of the season. Three went to Ickx, one (the Italian GP) to Regazzoni, seen here.

574-575 and 575 bottom right Tyrrell and Jackie Stewart were the protagonists of the 1971 season: the driver and the car formed an unbeatable pairing, as had happened the previous decade with Lotus and Jim Clark. After his experience with March and Matra late in 1970 Ken Tyrrell presented his own Ford-powered car that proved unbeatable the following season. Jackie scored no fewer than seven wins including the British (left) and Monaco (right) Grands Prix.

serious accident, was to be remembered for his audacity and the good luck that, up until that final crash, had always seen him emerge unscathed from wrecked Formula 1 and sports cars. Regazzoni was joined by other names new to the highest level of the sport: Emerson Fittipaldi, Ronnie Peterson, Rolf Stommelen and Henri Pescarolo.

Ferrari finally enjoyed some long-overdue success in the Austrian GP and this was to be repeated in Italy, Canada and Mexico, which was sufficient for the team to finish second in both the Constructors' and the Drivers' Championships with Ickx. The title, however, again went to Lotus, and it was once more Chapman who was in the forefront

of technological innovation with the wedge-shaped structure of his Lotus Type 72 and its chisel-like nose and side-mounted radiators.

There was unfortunately a macabre note to this season as the champion was crowned posthumously, Jochen Rindt having been killed during practice for the Italian GP. Death also came to Bruce McLaren who, like Jack Brabham, John Surtees and Dan Gurney (team Eagle), raced in Formula 1 with cars belonging to his own team. McLaren was killed while testing a McLaren-Chevrolet M8D Can-Am: the car's engine cover opened suddenly and the driver crashed into a wall. Piers Courage, at the wheel of a de Tomaso—a new team competing in

the colors of Frank Williams' British effort with Ford power and a chassis by Dallara (a young but very talented engineer with experience at Ferrari, Lamborghini and Maserati)—fell in Holland. On the other hand, François Szisz, the winner of the very first French Grand Prix in 1906, died in his own bed at the age of 97.

Monocoques, aerodynamic appendages, fire-proof overalls, sponsors: the World Championship circus was gradually being modernized. Another element first appeared in the Grand Prix in 1971, although it had already become common in the US: slick tires for maximum grip on dry tracks. (Grooved tires were still required in the wet, of course).

The second World Championship won by Stewart and Tyrrell could hardly have been predicted at the start of the year. Ferrari won the opening race in South Africa with its new driver Mario Andretti. Maranello had not, however, taken into account the Ford Cosworth engine and the Stewart-Tyrrell pairing which won six of the season's 11 Grands Prix. And to think that the V8 engine layout—which was used by all teams but BRM, Ferrari and Matra—was considered by many to have reached the end of its lifespan, about to be eclipsed by more powerful V12s! Nothing could in fact be further from the truth: the latest version of the DFV produced 440 hp, equaling the outputs of the BRM and Matra units and only slightly trailing the Ferrari's 480. Alfa continued its attempts to regain respect in Formula 1, in 1971 its V8 engines powering the March, not the McLaren. The results were again unsatisfactory, as were those of the curious gas-turbine Lotus.

Giunti was killed at Buenos Aires in January at the wheel of a Ferrari 312P. Pedro Rodriguez, the Mexican idol, also competed in his last race at the wheel of a Ferrari, in this case an Interseries event at Nuremberg in Germany.

As a result of the 31-year-old driver's death, the Mexican GP was canceled. The CSI's justification for this was that the circuit was unsafe, as it allowed the crowd to line the track as if it were a road race. In reality, however, it was a purely commercial decision: in the absence of Mexico's local hero there would be less interest in the event, and it would thus be less profitable. In the end fate intervened, playing a cruel trick on poor Jo Siffert. The Mexican GP was in fact replaced by a "Race of Champions" at Brands Hatch, a nonpoints contest in which Siffert lost his life due to the delay of the rescue services (he was trapped in his blazing car after having struck an earth bank and overturned).

1970 - 1971

575 top left Jochen Rindt scored his second victory of the season in the 1970 Dutch GP at the wheel of the Lotus-Ford. The Lotus 72, with its unusual wedge shape, was very fast and the German finished 30 seconds ahead of Stewart.

575 top right The remains of Rindt's Lotus after his crash at the parabolica during the 1970 Italian GP. Jochen was killed, and thus became the sport's first and only posthumous World Champion.

575 center right In 1971 the Italo-American Mario Andretti met his dream of driving for Ferrari. This was not a good season for Maranello and after his first victory in South Africa, Mario's best result was fourth place in Germany.

SINGLE-SEATS AND ADVERTISING: BRINGING FORMULA 1 BACK TO LIFE

The world of Formula 1 revealed its total economic dependency on its sponsors in 1972 when the name of the company or relative products to be promoted was adopted as an integral or even principal part of the name of the team (Marlboro-BRM, for example). In the extreme case of Lotus, the name of the team became that of a brand of cigarettes, John Player Special, and the cars were finished in black with gold pin-striping like the cigarette packaging.

Depailler, Lauda, Pace, Scheckter, de Adamich, Bell and Reutemann were the new generation of drivers of whom much was to be heard in the future. In the meantime the Brazilian Emerson Fittipaldi, in his third Formula 1 season, conquered the World Championship with the Lotus-Ford, alias John Player Special, winning five of the 12 Grands Prix.

Every time that a great driver, a leading team or

576 top right Beltoise took the BRM to victory at Monaco. This was the British team's sole win in the 1972 championship. Its next best placing was Ganley's fourth in Germany.

576 center right Emerson Fittipaldi spraying the crowd below the podium with champagne as he celebrates victory in the 1972 British GP. This was the Brazilian's third win of the season at the wheel of the Lotus, and he went on to take the title.

a previously unbeatable car has left the stage after a period of domination a cycle draws to a close. A vacuum is created, and there is increasing anxiety that the roughly blended cocktail of potent emotions, intense fears and unforgettable joy—or at least its former intensity—has been lost forever. These fears are stilled in front of the podium on which a new laurel wreath is placed around the neck of a new champion.

The vacuum created in 1973 was a result of the departure of Jackie Stewart, fortunately not in tragic circumstances. The Scottish driver retired at the top as reigning champion after winning his third title and with a record of 99 Grands Prix disputed, 17 pole positions and 27 victories, thus overtaking Fangio (24) and Clark (25).

Lotus continued to play a leading role, winning its sixth Constructors' Championship (Ferrari and Brabham were well behind with two each). During the season Chapman's designers continued working on the aerodynamic appendages and the shape and position of the air intakes, above all the one for the engine intake air that was located above and behind

the driver and resembled some kind of rocket launcher ready to blast away all rivals.

In terms of accidents, the most confused was the one provoked by the impulsive South African Jody Scheckter at the start of the British GP that involved the entire field. Over an hour was needed to clean up the track and de Adamich spent interminable minutes trapped in his car with his legs fractured. As a result of his injuries the Italian driver was forced to retire from the sport prematurely. At Zandvoort in Holland, Roger Williamson burned to death in his car, the trackside rescue services criminally slow in responding to the emergency. The tragic and frightening spectacle was witnessed by helpless millions as the television images were transmitted throughout the world.

Racing fans everywhere were anxiously awaiting the renaissance of the Prancing Horse. The miracle took place in 1974, thanks to the 312B3 12-cylinder, the fulcrum around which rotated Maranello's hopes and plans. Regazzoni and Lauda, fresh from a season with BRM, were the new drivers.

The team was now under the wing of Fiat with

576 bottom Emerson Fittipaldi sewed up the Championship title with two races to go: in the 1972 Italian GP he won easily with the black and gold Lotus 72, more properly known as the John Player Special.

the solid backing of the Agnelli family which led to a significant injection of capital and a complete revision of the organizational side: there were new chief race technicians, while Luca Cordero di Montezemolo, Giovanni Agnelli's protégé, was appointed as team manager. A dual team of mechanics was also assembled, one for each car.

Such attention to detail paid off, even though the Italian team had to settle for second place in both the Drivers' (52 points for Regazzoni against Fittipaldi's 55, the Brazilian now at McLaren) and the Constructors' Championships (65 points, seven behind McLaren). The reasons for this partial success are to be found in the psychological collapse of the team and the heated rivalry between the two drivers.

McLaren and Fittipaldi earned respect as an unbeatable pairing. The M23 proved to be reliable and competitive, the World Champion's car having a widened lower cockpit and an offset steering wheel to accommodate Fittipaldi and his Brazilian hips. This was also a year of glory for the American rubber giant Goodyear, whose tires equipped all the year's Grand Prix winners.

After the first two races of the 1975 season, the Argentine and Brazilian GPs, in which the 312 B3s could manage no better than a fourth place with Regazzoni, Ferrari seemed to have sunk back into oblivion. For the following race in South Africa the Maranello team decided to introduce the new 312T.

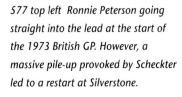

577 top left Ronnie Peterson going straight into the lead at the start of the 1973 British GP. However, a massive pile-up provoked by Scheckter led to a restart at Silverstone.

577 top right Chris Amon with the Matra-Simca made a very good start at the 1972 French GP but the ill-luck that dogged him struck again at Clermont-Ferrand when a stone damaged his car and he dropped back to finish third.

577 center right Clay Regazzoni's BRM caught fire after crashing into the barriers during the 1973 South African GP. Hailwood stopped to lend assistance and dragged Clay out of the car, burning his hands in the process.

577 bottom McLaren won the Constructors' Championship in 1974 thanks to the points accumulated by Hulme, Hailwood and Fittipaldi. The latter is seen here at the French GP, where he was forced to retire on Lap 26.

NIKI LAUDA, THE PERFECTIONIST

The T stood for "trasversale," referring to the transverse location of the gearbox—a feature that allowed for better weight distribution and consequently better handling.

The new car came good on its third outing at the Monaco GP where Lauda led home Fittipaldi in the McLaren-Ford by almost three seconds. The meticulous Austrian driver, capable of painstakingly testing until he had found an optimum set-up, reaped further reward by winning in Belgium, Sweden, France and the United States, thus conquering his first World Championship. Regazzoni won in Italy, Ferrari's total of six wins bringing the Constructors' Championship home to Maranello.

A tragic destiny awaited Graham Hill, a hero of the 1960s who had recently retired from racing to found his own team. He was killed in a plane crash, along with his driver Brise and five colleagues. The moustachioed driver earned his place in the record books with two World Championships, 176 Grands Prix disputed, 14 victories and 13 pole positions.

Hill's death was not the only tragedy that season. The Spanish GP started badly and finished worse. At Barcelona's Montjuich circuit the drivers, led by

1975 - 1976

578 top Carlos Reutemann raced at the wheel of a Brabham-Ford in 1975. He scored his first and only win of the season in Germany in a race in which tire problems caused the retirement of no fewer than 12 cars.

Fittipaldi, were unwilling to race because they claimed that the armco barriers had been erected incorrectly. The organizers threatened to confiscate all the teams' equipment in a partial compensation for the lost revenue should the race be canceled. The drivers were thus obliged by their teams to take part in practice and to race: Fittipaldi protested by completing just two deliberately slow practice laps that were sufficient for McLaren to reclaim its expenses. Clearly the Brazilian did not make the grid and did not take part in a race that lasted just 29 laps. Immediately after the start there was an accident involving the two Ferraris and Andretti's Parnelli. Then, on the 26th lap Stommelen with the Hill-Ford lost his rear wing while holding a clear lead. His car went out of control and crashed into the barriers, causing the deaths of a track marshal, two fire fighters and a journalist. On the 29th lap the race was abandoned with victory being assigned to Jochen Mass in the McLaren. Lella Lombardi became the first, and so far only, woman to score points in a World Championship race.

578 left and bottom Lauda won the 1975 World Championship at the wheel of a Ferrari 312T. The photo on the left shows him in mid-corner during the Italian GP, a race in which the Austrian had to settle for third place behind Regazzoni and Fittipaldi. Things went better in France (bottom): Niki dominated at the Paul Ricard circuit where he started from pole and was first across the line.

578-579 and 579 top left Concentration and tension can be seen in the gaze of Niki Lauda who, before his frightening accident in the 1976 German GP (right), had collected five wins and had the championship all but won. Forty days after the crash Niki was back fighting for the title. However, he retired from the last race in Japan after just three laps due to a rainstorm that was beating down on the Fujiyama circuit.

579 bottom left The English aristocrat, the moustache of Formula 1, Graham Hill was killed in a plane crash in 1975. The great driver left a record of 14 victories from 176 Grands Prix and two World Championship titles.

The debut of the Tyrrell six-wheeler

579 top right A car that all Formula 1 enthusiasts will remember: the Tyrrell P34 six-wheeler; with four small wheels at the front and two standard wheels at the back.

A six-wheeled car, the Argentine GP canceled because of the coup d'état, victories canceled and then reinstated...the 1976 championship was really a controversial affair!

While the no-holds-barred duels between Lauda, Regazzoni and Hunt were spectacular, an equally fascinating moment came at the Spanish GP when the Tyrrell P34 six-wheeler took to the track with four 10-inch wheels on two front axles. The narrow front track and largely faired tires were meant to reduce drag, but this aerodynamic advantage was compromised by the standard-width rear axle. In its first season the P34 scored a 1-2 victory in Sweden, but in the end the benefits of six wheels did not compensate for their added cost and complexity.

The struggle for the 1976 title eventually became a private affair between Lauda and Hunt, with Lauda dominating the early part of the season, Hunt in the second. New safety norms were introduced at the Spanish GP that specified that the cars should be fitted with a supplementary rollbar

surprise verdict the CSI probably intended to right the wrong suffered by Ferrari in Spain, but to many this decision only cast further doubts on the impartiality of the authorities.

The German GP was marred by a dramatic accident. On the second lap, Lauda crashed into the barriers and his car burst into flames. He was rescued by Merzario, Ertl and Lunger who stopped at the side of the track to pull him from his blazing Ferrari before the rescue services arrived. The Austrian driver suffered severe burns to his head, hands and arms and his life was in danger for days because he had inhaled toxic fumes during the fire.

The team signed Carlos Reutemann, who the following season would replace Regazzoni. Forty days after his accident, however, Lauda was back on for the Italian GP. The bandaging on his face and hands did not prevent him from finishing fourth and retaining his lead in the championship, although Hunt was just a few points behind.

The finale to the season seemed to hold the promise of a titanic struggle between Hunt and the

for the cockpit and deformable structures in front of the driver to protect his lower limbs. A tangible result was the moving of the air intakes, which were now almost concealed beneath the rollbar rather than towering above the driver.

In accordance with the new regulations, checks made at the end of the Spanish GP revealed that Hunt's winning McLaren was wider than permitted. The victory thus passed to Lauda, but McLaren appealed and Hunt's win was later reinstated.

At the start of the British GP, on the other hand, Regazzoni collided with Lauda, who had not given way to his teammate. The Swiss driver spun and collided with a series of cars including Hunt's. The race was stopped, and when it restarted Hunt was back on the track. Under way Lauda kept a firm grip on the lead until gearbox problems obliged him to let Hunt past, and the Englishman went on to win. Then Ferrari appealed, claiming that Hunt had used his spare car rather than the repaired race chassis. The CSI accepted this claim, largely on the evidence of two Italian journalists who had photographed the English driver running toward the pits. With this

revitalized Lauda. Hunt pulled off a scorching start and shot into the lead, and on the second lap the unthinkable happened: Lauda pulled out of the race. The Ferrari organization at first tried to cover up this embarrassing situation by attributing Lauda's retirement to mechanical problems, but the Austrian soon released a brief but firm statement to the press: "My life is my own, and it is more important than the World Championship."

The Championship was won by James Hunt. Enzo Ferrari never forgave Niki Lauda.

579 bottom right James Hunt was forced to retire from the 1976 Monaco GP after the engine of his McLaren broke. The Englishman made up for this disappointment by winning six of the season's 16 Grands Prix and snatching the World Championship title.

TURBOS AND GROUND EFFECTS WIN THE DAY

After a season poisoned by disputes, it was the genial Lotus chief who revitalized Formula 1 by launching the era of the first "wing," or ground effects, cars, the Lotus 78-79, featuring an innovative technical package that glued the cars to the track and thus improved overall performance and handling.

The Lotus 78 scored its first victory at the United States West GP, although the spectators and the technicians attributed the success to the presence of a new Getrag differential rather than to ground effects. The 1977 World Championship was nonetheless dominated by Lauda at the wheel of the Ferrari with wins in South Africa, Germany and Holland as well as a series of top three and points-scoring placings.

The Maranello team denied the Austrian driver total commitment, no longer trusting him after his dramatic retirement in the Japanese GP the previous season. In Brazil, in fact, a new rear wing was fitted to Reutemann's car but not to Lauda's. The relationship between Lauda and Ferrari deteriorated to such an extent over the course of the season that the day after Niki won in Holland and consolidated his lead in the Drivers' Championship, Ferrari announced that the young Austrian driver's contract would not be renewed at the end of the season. Lauda gained the point he required to make sure of the World Championship title at the United States West GP and took his revenge on Ferrari by deserting the last two races in Canada and Japan.

During this edition of the World Championship

580 top right Niki Lauda had to settle for second place in the 1977 British Grand Prix. The Austrian was forced to follow in James Hunt's dust but gained handsome revenge elsewhere and won the championship that year.

580 center right Gilles Villeneuve made his Formula 1 debut in 1977 at the wheel of a McLaren. His performance so impressed Enzo Ferrari that he was signed to drive for Maranello by the Canadian GP.

580 bottom right On paper and in the metal, entrusted to the care of its mechanics, the engine that represented at the 1977 British GP the introduction of turbocharging to Formula 1: the 1500 cc Renault V6 that powered Jabouille's car. The same race also saw the debuts of Gilles Villeneuve with the McLaren-Ford and the return of Michelin tires.

1977 - 1978

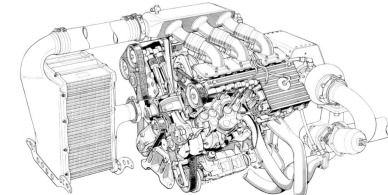

580 top left Andretti scored consecutive wins in Belgium and Spain in 1978. The two victories were added to the one he scored in the first race in South Africa and another three he scored in France, Germany and Holland as he went on to win the title.

580 bottom left The yellow Renault RS01 Turbo of Jean Pierre Jabouille struggling for a decent result in the 1978 British GP. The Frenchman was forced to retire on the 46th lap with a broken engine.

580-581 The 1977 Ford-powered McLaren M23 that the team prepared for James Hunt, winner of the 1976 World Championship. The square-cut air intake in the center of the nose characterized a car that carried the reigning champion to a meagre total of eight points, a third place in the French GP being his best placing. The team also underwent a financial crisis in 1978 that was only resolved in 1980, when McLaren passed into the hands of Ron Dennis. The new organization brought renewed stability and success (eight Drivers' and seven Constructors' Championships) to a team that had struggled to achieve equilibrium in the '70s despite winning championships in 1974 and '76.

581 top right James Hunt tackling one of the straights at Brands Hatch, venue for the 1978 British Grand Prix. The driver had to retire on the seventh lap, after a very short race.

581 bottom right The large rear fan designed to improve ground effects earned the 1978 Brabham BT46B the nickname of "Hoover." This efficient solution gave Lauda victory in the Swedish GP.

the legendary Ford-Cosworth V8 engine recorded its 100th GP win at Monaco. The season was also marked by the return in revolutionary form of the Renault team which had been missing from the Grand Prix circus since 1908 and which ushered in the turbo era. The RS01 was powered by a mighty 1.5-liter V6 that developed 500 hp but was dogged by the delayed throttle response typical of turbocharged engines. Another return was that of Michelin, which supplied tires for the RS01 and thus interrupted the rule of Goodyear and Firestone. Gilles Villeneuve made such a convincing debut at Silverstone that he was signed by Ferrari the following week.

Tragically, Carlos Pace was killed in a plane accident and Tom Pryce ran into and killed a track marshal who had unthinkingly strayed into the middle of the track with a fire extinguisher to lend assistance to Zorzi in the Shadow. The extinguisher struck Pryce who was killed instantly. The glorious BRM model took its leave of the Grand Prix scene due to severe financial problems.

The year spent fine-tuning the ground effects Lotus paid off in 1978. The type 78 was replaced by the 79, which in terms of negative lift was very similar to its predecessor but offered 15% less drag. The creativity of Chapman and his team appeared to be inexhaustible in the late 1970s, light years ahead of their rivals. While in 1978 the other constructors were only just beginning to comprehend the advantages of the wing cars and hurriedly preparing similar models (the exceptions to the rule were the flat 12-cylinder Ferraris and Alfa-powered Brabhams; the packaging difficulties with this type of engine architecture restricted the area of low pressure below the car), Lotus was already tackling the first experiments into aerodynamic aids that were soon to become ubiquitous: side-skirts or lateral seals between the bodywork and the asphalt.

In the meantime, the Lotuses triumphed in eight of the 16 Grands Prix in 1978: six won by Andretti and two by Petersen. Chapman's team scored 1-2s in the Belgian, Spanish, French and Dutch Grands Prix.

Another team in the late 1970s technological avant-garde was Brabham. At the Swedish GP the team presented the BT46-Alfa Romeo equipped with a large fan in the tail that generated a low pressure zone beneath the car (the underbody was sealed with side skirts), thus allowing higher cornering speeds. Despite its "Hoover" nickname, the BT46 proved to be extremely quick and Lauda, who had moved to the Australian team from Ferrari, drove the car to victory on its debut. This was a historic win both for Brabham—its first in three years—and for Alfa Romeo, who tasted Grand Prix success again after 27 years, albeit only as an engine supplier. However, the fan car was immediately outlawed because the extractor fan sucked up gravel and other particles and spat them into the path of the following cars. Moreover, the regulations had clearly stated since 1969 that moveable aerodynamic aids were prohibited, and the fan was classified as such.

"GILLES," HEIR TO CLARK IN THE ENTHUSIASTS' HEARTS

582 top left An extremely rapid Jean Pierre Jabouille conquered pole position at the 1979 German GP, relegating Alan Jones in the Williams to second place on the grid. The Australian driver gained revenge in the race by taking the lead at the first corner and retaining it to the finish.

582 top right The 1979 Austrian GP saw the same Franco-Australian front row as the previous race in Germany: Arnoux took pole at the wheel of the Renault bi-turbo, while Jones was René's closest rival. It was Alan who went on to win the race, his second successive triumph of the season.

582 left The 1979 Spanish GP was one to remember for the Ligier team: the French équipe placed two cars on the front row and Patrick Depailler went on to win the race. Lafitte was instead obliged to retire on the 18th lap with a broken engine.

582-583 The Ford-powered McLarens suffered at the 1979 Monaco GP. The Englishman John Watson conquered an honorable fourth place after starting from the seventh row with the 14th fastest time. Patrick Tambay, in the image, did not even manage to qualify.

582 bottom left In spite of recording the fastest lap and starting from the second row, Gilles Villeneuve in the Ferrari finished only seventh in the 1979 Spanish GP—a disappointing result after two consecutive victories.

582 bottom right An historic 1-2 for the Ferraris in the 1979 Italian Grand Prix: Jody Scheckter and Gilles Villeneuve finished first and second. The following 1-2 for the "Reds" at Monza will be achieved only 9 years later.

1979

The 1970s were left behind but the wing cars and the ground effects technology introduced by Lotus remained. Renault, who in previous years had invested heavily and believed firmly in the turbo, successfully reintroduced boosted engines as the way forward, much in the same way as happened in the 1950s, when supercharged engines—the Alfas above all—enjoyed their heyday. The Renault RS01, powered by a twin-turbo, 1.5-liter V6 won in France with Jean Pierre Jabouille at the wheel, thus earning the company its first turbocharged Grand Prix victory.

The championship title returned to Maranello in 1979 thanks to the 312 T4 and Jody Scheckter, the South African replacement for Reutemann (who had moved to Lotus and who, like Andretti, failed to score a single victory that season). Williams (with Jones and Regazzoni) and Ligier (Laffite, Depailler and Ickx) scored five and three wins respectively, thus taking their places among the circus' leading teams. Similar ambitions were harbored by Alfa Romeo, who had decided to build its own car. The Tipo 177 was, however, conceptually dated and proved to be uncompetitive. The Tipo 179 wing car was instead introduced for the Italian GP powered by a 60° narrow-angle V12 that was also successfully fitted to the Brabham BT48 and allowed modern aerodynamics to be employed.

Ferrari conquered the world title thanks to the reliability of its 12-cylinder engines rather than its chassis, which did not benefit from ground effects. Scheckter scored points in no fewer than 12 of the 15 scheduled Grands Prix, collecting three wins; Villeneuve won another three races.

The audacity of the Canadian driver endeared him to the Italian fans: his duel with René Arnoux in the Renault is the stuff of legends. The pair were fighting for second place, given that Jabouille in the other Renault could not be caught. The last few laps were heart-stopping, an unforgettable show for the millions of people in Dijon and glued to their television screens (it was in these years that the television audience expanded exponentially and became Formula 1's major player). The Ferrari and

the Renault touched at every corner as the drivers attempted to barge their way through, the wheels of one scraping the flanks of the other. In the end Villeneuve had the last word, but the duel was to remain one of the greatest episodes of modern Formula 1, a sport that generally lacks the battles, the overtaking and the explosive laps the Grands Prix of the 1930s and 1950s had offered.

Thirty years had passed since the days of the Alfetta 158 and Giuseppe Farina—30 years alternately marked by on-track rivalries, political infighting, technological innovations and the rising economic influence of firstly sponsors and then television. In spite of moments of intense drama such as those recounted above, it can be said that the cars and drivers have passed gradually, inexorably and perhaps unwittingly into the background.

In the 1980s the actual racing, already corrupted by outside interests, came up against

another powerful enemy in the form of electronics. The new technology began to be applied throughout the cars and tended to unify performance levels, making the figure of the driver increasingly less important.

The situation that arose was somewhat akin to Enzo Ferrari's position, so jealous was he of the glory earned by the drivers at the wheel of his cars. In spite of the commercial vicissitudes, in spite of the fact that his team never succeeded in anticipating the technological innovations introduced by his Anglo-Saxon rivals, the great Enzo was alone in battling on for three decades against the domination of the small but fearsome British teams.

583 left In the 1979 German GP, Emerson Fittipaldi at the wheel of a Type F6/A completed just five laps after which he was betrayed by his Ford engine. He conquered third place— among the retirees!

583 top right Arrows, backed by the Warsteiner Brewery for 1979, employed a chassis design very similar to the French Renault's. No surprise: Renault, achieved all its objectives at that year French GP, earning pole position, fastest lap, and overall victory in the race. Jabouille started from the pole and went on for the win; Arnoux scored fastest lap.

583 bottom right The Ferrari team ready to give their all in their home GP. In 1979 Villeneuve performed well early in the season, collecting three important victories for Maranello. He failed to repeat that feat in Italy, however, yielding first to teammate Scheckter.

A CROWD OF TEAMS IN FORMULA 1

The 1980s opened to violent arguments between the FISA and the FOCA regarding the adoption or banning of side-skirts.

The Fédération Internationale du Sport Automobile (FISA) had been founded at the end of 1978 within the CSI and was supposedly subordinate to the FIA. In reality, it had succeeded in acquiring increasing autonomy and campaigned against the adoption of side-skirts. The Formula One Constructors' Association (FOCA), on the other hand, defended side-skirts at all costs and its members—with the exception of Ferrari, Alfa Romeo

and Renault—threatened to organize their own championship. This and other political struggles, plots and boycotts had the effect of alienating the public, keeping people away from the circuits and their television screens. This was enough to set the sponsors' alarm bells ringing and the teams, for whom the future looked bleak without sufficient funds to plan for a full season, saved face by pretending to engage in serious and constructive attempts to reach a mutually satisfactory solution.

Why did side-skirts cause so much stubborn controversy? The answer is that without the skirts the

British teams could not hope to compete against the turbo-charged units that had already broken the 600 hp barrier. Side-skirts, the fruit of Anglo-Saxon invention, were partially able to compensate for the power differential. The presence of the skirts allowed lap times to be reduced a lot, though in some cases the drivers were subjected to dangerous lateral g forces.

584 top Nineteen-eighty was a season to forget for Jody Scheckter: after winning the championship the previous year, the South-African's best result was a fifth place in the United States. In Canada he even failed to qualify. The nose is slightly protruding, the wheels are set forward and there are no spoilers: the 1981 Ligier-Matra driven by our French drivers, Lafitte, seen here, Jarier, Jabouille and Tambay.

584 center left The first of the two Formula 1 GPs held in the USA in 1980 was the United States West at Long Beach, which proved to be a disaster for Regazzoni: his Ensign's brakes failed and he crashed into a retaining wall. The accident has confined him to a wheelchair ever since.

Nonetheless, racing continued for better or for worse, with Jones in the Williams and Piquet with the Brabham dominating the 1980 season in which no fewer than 20 teams took part. Jones took the title with five victories and a total of 67 points: the Brazilian finished 13 points behind.

Ferrari and Lotus had indifferent seasons in spite of new engines, and absent from the circus was Niki Lauda, who at the end of the '79 season had announced he was retiring to devote himself to his new airline. Clay Regazzoni started the season with Ensign but he too was forced to withdraw after just four Grands Prix—an accident at the United States West GP would confine him to a wheelchair for life. Depailler was even less fortunate, perishing while testing at Hockenheim.

The Italian GP was held at Imola rather than Monza, on the circuit dedicated by Enzo Ferrari to his son Dino who had died at age 24. The following year the race returned to Monza, Imola becoming the San Marino GP.

The most up-to-date engines were turbocharged, with Renault, the technology's chief advocate, scoring three wins in 1980: two with Arnoux (in Brazil and South Africa) and one with Jabouille, in Austria. However, in spite of its prodigious power output the Renault engine was fragile, failures conditioning the outcome of a number of races.

Key players in the 1981 season were the watch manufacturer Longines and Olivetti computers—not as might be imagined in the role of sponsors or racing teams, but involved in the timing of the races. Ten cars were fitted with a micro-transmitter that communicated with a receiver composed of an aluminum strip located on the finishing line. Each car transmitted a different signal that was picked up by the receiver and then decoded by an Olivetti computer which provided lap times to the nearest thousandth of a second, the gaps between cars and the race positions, information which could be superimposed over the television images and which added to the event's interest.

In 1981 FISA banned sliding side-skirts but the designers were cleverly able to overcome the obstacle. The regulations stated that the cars should have a minimum ground clearance of 60 mm. This ground clearance could, however, only be verified with the car stationary, and so hydropneumatic systems were successfully employed that slowly lowered the car until the skirts were grazing the asphalt. Grip was guaranteed, but very rigid suspension had to be used to avoid even the slightest bump nullifying the ground effects for even a fraction of a second. The driver thus had to put up with extremely violent blows to his spine and neck as well as g-forces similar to those experienced by a fighter pilot in a tight turn. Some adopted orthopedic supports. The hydraulic trickery was firstly contested and then adopted by the majority of the teams, tolerated by the FISA and subsequently legalized for the San Marino GP, the fourth race of the season.

Nineteen eighty-one saw the debut of another of the sport's greats, the only driver to threaten Fangio's record of five World Championship titles: Alain Prost, who that season drove for Renault. During his career he took the title four times and was second in the final table on a further three occasions. Fittipaldi instead retired to devote himself to his own team.

The 1981 champion was Nelson Piquet who won the Argentine, San Marino and German GPs at the wheel of a Brabham.

584 bottom right Jean Pierre Jabouille partnered with René Arnoux at Renault in 1980, scoring a single victory in the Austrian GP at the Osterreichring and finishing in eighth place in the championship.

585 top Nelson Piquet with the Brabham-Ford was one of the protagonists of the 1980 season: three wins, two second places, a third and a fastest lap. These results placed him second in the championship behind Australia's Alan Jones.

585 center Jacques Lafitte and Didier Pironi took Ligier to second place in the 1980 Constructors' Championship, a result better than their respective fourth and fifth places in the Drivers' Championship.

585 bottom right By 1980 Gilles Villeneuve was into his fourth season with Ferrari: he scored the last two victories of his career at Monaco and in Spain as well as the highest number of accidents, four.

584 center right The 1980 Monaco GP provided thrills at the start when Derek Daly in the Tyrrell took off, involving his team mate Jarier, Prost in the McLaren and Giacomelli in the Alfa Romeo in a multiple pile-up without serious consequences.

584 bottom left and 585 bottom left These photographs show the Renault (left) and Ferrari (right) pits at the 1980 United States West GP held at Long Beach. The race was an indifferent one for both Maranello, with a fifth place and a retirement, and for the French team, with a ninth and a DNQ.

1980 - 1981

THE LOSS OF COLIN CHAPMAN AND VILLENEUVE

Following the polemics between the FISA and the FOCA that had been suppressed so as not to preoccupy the sponsors, it was thought that Formula 1 might finally be able to put on a show composed solely of competition and speed. This was not to be the case, however, as 1982 was also marred by disputes and, just for a change, cheating. This was the verdict passed on measures adopted by certain teams to overcome the new FISA ruling whereby the

586 left The Finn Keke Rosberg took the 1982 World Championship at the wheel of a Williams-Ford, winning only one GP (Switzerland) but accumulating a long series of priceless points-scoring finishes.

minimum weight of the cars, without fuel but including oil and water, was set at 580 kg (1,279 lb.).

With this system the FISA attempted to favor the smaller teams that did not yet have access to turbocharged engines, encouraging technological research. On the other hand, the turbocharged cars were much lighter than the prescribed minimum, and in order to get round this problem Williams, Brabham, Lotus, Arrows and McLaren invented a fake liquid-cooling circuit for the braking system. The reservoirs were filled prior to the weighing of the car so as to reach the 580 kg (1,279 lb.) minimum and then emptied during the race. The trick was discovered as early as the Brazilian GP, the second race of the '82 season, with a protest being presented by Ferrari and Renault. Piquet in the Brabham and Rosberg with the Williams were disqualified. The situation went critical again two races later at San Marino: the British teams within the FOCA decided not to race unless the Brazilian disqualifications were revoked. The entertainment value of the racing undoubtedly suffered with only 14 drivers taking part. Dispute led to dispute.

Next it was the two Ferrari drivers who were involved as Pironi had failed to respect team orders and allow Villeneuve to win the race. The two refused to speak even on the podium and unfortunately they never had time to make their peace. During the second qualifying session for the successive Belgian Grand Prix, Villeneuve was pressing hard to snatch pole position from his team-mate/rival when he collided violently with the March

that Jochen Mass was driving slowly toward the pits after having completed his qualifying laps. Gilles died that evening and Ferrari withdrew Pironi from the race as a mark of respect.

Fate seemed determined to persecute the Ferrari driver who was involved in an accident similar to that of his former teammate. Pironi started from pole position in Canada but his engine died as the lights changed. All the other drivers managed to avoid him but Paletti, at the wheel of the Osella-Alfa

1982

586 top right After winning the World Championship in 1981, Piquet again drove a Brabham but did not enjoy the same success. He finished 11th in the final table.

586-587 Frenchman Patrick Tambay was signed by Ferrari in 1982 and he drove car number 27, formerly belonging to Villeneuve, to his first victory for the team at Hockenheim in Germany. He finished seventh in the final table whilst his teammate Didier Pironi was second: Ferrari took the Constructors' title.

586 center right At the first of the three GPs held in the United States in 1982—the first time that this had happened in Formula 1, which generally held only one race per country—Bruno Giacomelli with the Alfa Romeo started well from the third row but crashed out on the fifth lap.

586 bottom right Alain Prost with the Renault seen overtaking Riccardo Patrese in the Brabham-Ford. The French driver had the better of the Italian also in the final table as they finished fourth and tenth respectively.

Romeo and starting from the last row of the grid. He never saw the stationary Ferrari: there were no signs of braking, no attempt to avoid the obstacle; the young Italian driver was killed instantly. Pironi instead climbed from his burning car miraculously unscathed.

Formula 1 was about to lose another of its leading figures: in the close of the season, while working on his team's cars for 1983, Colin Bruce Chapman died of a heart attack on the 16th of December. One of the greats had been taken from us—the Fangio of the constructors, a genial, astute and daring man who on a number of occasions changed the face of the sport.

The death of the Lotus chief, together with those of the two drivers and the polemics and subterfuge with regards to the fake water tanks, made 1982 a rather depressing year. The tragedies overshadowed innovations in the field of chassis technology involving the use of composite materials in the

construction of monocoques rather than the sheet aluminum that had characterized the cars of the previous 20 years. A Nomex and aluminum honeycomb sandwich was bonded on both sides to rigid sheets of aluminum and composite materials (Kevlar, carbon-fiber). This type of monocoque was 40% lighter than aluminum equivalents but was exorbitantly expensive to produce. Carbon-fiber and Kevlar were subsequently also used for other components such as wings and brake discs.

Another innovation was that of the "fast tank": the car started the race with soft tires and sufficient fuel to complete half the race, then made a pit-stop during which the tires were changed and fuel for the remainder was provided.

The 1982 World Championship was won by the Finnish driver Keke Rosberg: despite winning only one Grand Prix (the Swiss) he nonetheless finished in the points on numerous occasions.

587 Gilles Villeneuve competed in Formula 1 for just six seasons (1977-1982), almost always at the wheel of a Ferrari: following his debut with the McLaren-Ford at the British GP in 1977 he was signed by the Italian manufacturer and was driving a Ferrari by the Canadian GP. Gilles' brief career at the very top was sufficient to earn him a place in the hearts of the tifosi. His boldness and tenacity and above all his generosity captured the public, but during practice for the Belgian GP in 1982 he ran full tilt into the March being driven slowly back to the pits by Jochen Mass. The Ferrari was launched into the air and when it came crashing back to earth Gilles was thrown out still strapped into his seat. He hit the back of his head against one of the safety fence uprights and died of his injuries.

THE RETIREMENT
OF ANOTHER GREAT

588 top left In 1983 Nelson Piquet conquered his second world title. His BMW-powered Brabham was triumphant in Brazil, Italy and in the Grand Prix of Europe held at Brands Hatch.

588 center left Alain Prost, seen here during the 1983 French GP, missed out on the '83 championship by two points, while Renault finished runner-up to Ferrari in the Constructors' Championship. This scenario was repeated in 1984 when Alain, who had in the meantime moved to McLaren-Porsche, was second to Lauda by just half a point.

The year 1983 marked the end of an era, of a period in the history of Formula 1 that had lasted no less than 16 years. In this case it was not a driver, a team or a manager that left the stage but an engine. The Ford-Cosworth V8, mounted in a Tyrrell, scored its 155th and last Formula 1 win since its debut in 1967.

In little more than six months Grand Prix racing had lost both Chapman and the Ford-Cosworth engine that Colin himself had helped make great. Another quirk of fate had it that the year of the turbocharged engine's definitive consecration was also marked by Renault's last Formula 1 win, at the Austrian GP: the French team abandoned the F1 circus at the end of 1985 without having managed to repeat this feat, and instead concentrated on supplying its V6 engines to Lotus, Ligier and Tyrrell.

The turbo's success also coincided with the abandonment of the ground effects sidepods and the rigid suspension that had been so hard on the drivers. The wing cars were replaced by those with flat underbodies while sufficient downforce was provided by aerodynamic appendages regulated in size by the FISA.

The widespread use of carbon-fiber and composite materials in chassis as well as brake discs allowed closed monocoques to be constructed that required no external bodywork. While these tubs were excellent in terms of torsional stiffness and lightness (the one produced by ATS weighed just 18 kg! [40 lb.]), they were prohibitively expensive. Moreover, the integral monocoque did not allow the suspension geometry to be modified, as the various elements could not be bolted directly to the panel-work but rather to aluminum plates buried deep in the carbon-fiber.

The McLaren-TAG-Porsche made its debut at the

588 bottom and center right Prost, seen below during the Belgian GP, thought he was going to win the 1984 Championship at the wheel of the McLaren but had to settle for second place in spite of scoring seven wins, two more than his teammate and eventual champion Niki Lauda.

FROZEN FUEL

Dutch GP driven by Niki Lauda, who had returned to racing in 1982 to resolve his airline's severe financial difficulties. TAG (Techniques d'Avant Garde) was a company owned by the Arab financier Mansour Ojjeh that presented a turbocharged 80° V6 engine designed and built by Porsche. Another debut toward the end of the season was that of the new Honda V6 powering the Williams.

The 1983 title went to Piquet with the Brabham-BMW: this was his second since 1981 and was again conquered by a handful of points from Alain Prost.

In order to curb the escalating power outputs of the turbo engines (which were approaching the 1000 hp threshold), the FISA fell back on the old system of restricting the amount of fuel that could be carried. In 1984 cars were thus allowed to take on board no more than 220 liters (58 gal.). The teams worked on legal and quasi-legal systems of getting round the new regulations including super-chilling the fuel. A tank that held just 220 liters of standard fuel held roughly 235 liters (62 gal.) of fuel at -50°—enough for five extra laps.

Serious problems would arise, however, in the

1983 - 1984

case of a delayed or repeated start as the fuel would return to its normal liquid state and burst the tanks. Fortunately this situation never occurred.

The 220-liter (58 gal.) limit modified the way the drivers approached the races, as they would ease off the pace toward the end to the detriment of the spectacle. Late charges, desperate overtaking and chases were abandoned in favor of conserving fuel. Some races were more akin to regularity trials.

Nineteen eighty-four was the year of the McLaren-TAG-Porsches. Lauda and Prost formed an unbeatable pair, taking the Constructors' title and the first two places in the Drivers' Championship. It was Lauda who took the title—the third of his career—despite the fact that his teammate won more races.

The record books show that an Italian, in this case Michele Alboreto, drove a Formula 1 Ferrari for the first time in years, but the most important event of the year was the step up from the ranks of the British Formula 3 championship of the young Brazilian driver Ayrton Senna, a phenomenal wet-weather performer.

589 center Ayrton Senna made his Formula 1 debut in 1984. Leap-frogging F2, he reached the F1 circus via the British Formula 3 series with Toleman (top photograph) being the first team to offer him an F1 drive for the Brazilian GP. It was a difficult debut with Senna starting from 16th place on the grid and retiring on the 8th lap with a broken turbo. In the 1984 German GP (center photograph) held at Hockenheim, Ayrton was involved in an accident that had no serious consequences but put him out of the race on the 4th lap. The photograph below, again from the 1984 German GP, shows Tambay's Renault, fifth despite these flames.

589 bottom left The podium at the 1983 San Marino GP was all French: from the left, René Arnoux, third with the Ferrari; Patrick Tambay, the winner with the other Ferrari; and Alain Prost, second with the Renault.

588-589 Piquet was the first champion of the turbo era and brought success to BMW. The three-time champion of the world is closely associated with Brabham: for 15 seasons he drove for the Australian team using three different engines (Alfa, Ford and turbo BMW). He also

drove for Ensign, McLaren, Williams, Lotus and Benetton in a career that concluded in 1991.

589 top left Rain curtailed the entertainment at the 1984 Monaco GP: only 31 of the scheduled 77 laps were completed. Prost won, but Ayrton Senna

was breathing down his neck when the race was interrupted.

589 top right An Italian car and driver excited the Ferrari tifosi in 1984, but Michele Alboreto managed only one win (Belgian GP) and finished fourth in the final table.

589 bottom center and right Lauda (in the photograph on the right with Frank Williams) won his third title in 1984 at the wheel of the McLaren-Porsche that also won the Constructors' Championship.

Lauda, farewell and Prost joins the greats

The 1985 season saw the confirmation of the 220-liter (58 gal.) limit on fuel, but this was to be reduced to 195 in 1986/87 and again to 185 liters (49 gal.) in '88/89, while frozen fuel was outlawed. FISA thus confirmed its wish to control power outputs while the constructors were faced with the conundrum of combining high power outputs with low fuel consumption. The engineers concentrated on ever more sophisticated injection systems and introduced a wastegate control to the cockpit, which the driver could use to temporarily increase turbo boost and therefore horsepower.

The season revealed the talent and daring of Ayrton Senna, with the Brazilian driver scoring his first Formula 1 victory in the Portuguese GP in torrential rain. On the eve of the Austrian GP, Niki Lauda again announced his retirement from racing in spite of the lavish offer of 6.5 million dollars from Bernie Ecclestone, boss of Brabham, to compete in the 1986 season.

Renault and Alfa Romeo also withdrew at the end of the year, due to financial problems. The 1985 title went to Alain Prost, the first Frenchman to win a Formula championship, after two successive seasons in which he had finished second.

Fourteen-hundred hp: this was the awe-inspiring new power output record achieved by a number of cars during practice for the 1986 races. Given that there were no fuel consumption problems during qualifying as the fuel limits did not apply, the teams used special qualifying engines and extremely soft tire compounds in order to pare away fractions of a second per lap—fractions that were vital to the conquest of pole position.

Nineteen eighty-six was a close-fought season and by the last race, the Australian GP at the Adelaide circuit, Mansell, Piquet and Prost were all well placed to win the title. Rosberg took the lead at the start of the race and held it until the 57th lap, when he was forced to retire. Piquet then took up the running, followed by Mansell. That second place would have been enough to guarantee the British driver the championship, but six laps later he was forced to retire when a tire blew. The World Championship thus appeared to be Piquet's, until he was passed by Prost while in the pits. The

590 first photograph top Niki Lauda scored his last Formula 1 victory in 1985 with the McLaren-Porsche number 7. This was the Dutch GP won by two-tenths of a second from his teammate Prost.

590 second photograph The Brazilian Nelson Piquet, at the wheel of car number 6, finished third in the final table in 1986, behind his teammate

Nigel Mansell by a single point (69 against 70) and with a single win less (four against five, with two successive victories in Germany and Hungary).

590 third photograph Ayrton Senna talking with Elio de Angelis: the two Lotus drivers finished the 1985 season fourth and fifth, respectively, separated by just five points.

590 fourth photograph Senna's first Formula 1 victory came in the rain-drenched 1985 Portuguese GP. In such conditions Ayrton was truly unbeatable.

590 fifth photograph Alain Prost keeping things under control as he goes on to win the 1985 Monaco GP. This was an unforgettable season for Alain as he won the first of his four titles.

590-591 Victories in Canada and Germany and numerous points-scoring placings were not enough to allow Michele Alboreto to take the championship title in 1985. The Italian driver nonetheless finished runner-up.

Frenchman retained the lead to win both the race and the title, thus joining that select band of drivers to have won at least two consecutive titles: Alberto Ascari (1952-53), Juan Manuel Fangio (1954-57) and Jack Brabham (1959-60). He also broke Fangio's record and matched that of Jim Clark with 25 Grand Prix victories. The following year he was to overtake even Stewart, and would to record a remarkable career total of 51 victories.

Meanwhile, the floundering Toleman team was bought by Italian clothing manufacturer Benetton—with results that would surprise everyone....

1985 - 1986

591 top Riccardo Patrese had a poor season at the wheel of the Benetton-sponsored Alfa Romeo in 1985: ninth place was his best result, achieved in the British GP and the GP of Europe held at Brands Hatch. Ill-luck persecuted the Italian driver: in this photograph his car is seen as it catches fire in the dramatic accident at the Monaco GP that also involved Nelson Piquet, fortunately without further consequences.

591 center The Englishman Nigel Mansell (left) heading for victory in the Williams-Honda, lapping all his rivals still in the race with the exception of Piquet. This was the 1986 British GP. Nicknamed "Lionheart", Mansell raced for Williams from 1985 to 1988, in 1991-1992 and four Grand Prix in 1994, winning 13 Grands Prix and conquering 11 pole positions. In the picture in the middle Piquet (left) jokes with Mansell (right) while an amused Prost looks on. The three drivers were the protagonists of the 1986 season which finished with Prost champion, Mansell second and Piquet third. This was the fourth season in which Williams used V6 turbocharged Honda engines.

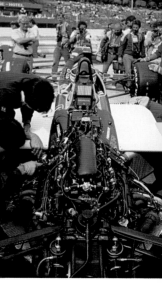

591 bottom Thanks to the Pirellis that allowed him to complete the race without a single pit stop, Gerhard Berger scored his first Formula 1 victory in Mexico in 1986.

The rush to exploit the power of turbocharging had been expensive, and in 1987 the FISA introduced regulations designed to penalize their use: naturally aspirated 12-cylinder engines with total displacements of 3.5 liters (0.9 gal.) fitted to cars with a minimum weight of 500 kg (1,103 lb.) were allowed to compete against turbocharged cars weighing at least 540 kg (1,191 lb.) and with maximum boost pressures of four bar.

In 1988 the restriction on the total amount of fuel that the naturally aspirated cars could carry was to be removed, while the turbo cars would be restricted to 150 liters (40 gal.) and boost pressure

and during the championship as well as for the French GP. While returning from a test session in March, Frank Williams had a serious road accident that has confined him to a wheelchair ever since. Two months later the Italian driver de Angelis crashed at the Verriere corner after his car lost its rear wing. He died as a result of the delayed arrival of the rescue services. After the organizers came in for heavy criticism the circuit was halved in length and the Verriere esses were eliminated.

With the reintroduction of naturally aspirated engines in 1987 the Colin Chapman Cup and the Jim Clark Cup were awarded to constructors and

board computer transmitted data during the race regarding the engine, suspension, chassis, bodywork and tires, allowing appropriate strategies to be devised and adopted. Telemetry equipment was very expensive and thus only Honda, Brabham and Ferrari were able to take immediate advantage of the system.

The Williams-Honda proved to be extremely rapid. The turbocharged Japanese 80° V6 was peerless, and at the British GP it demonstrated crushing superiority with the two Williams and the two Honda-powered Lotuses finishing in the first four places. It was a memorable race. Although Mansell and Piquet were teammates, there was no love lost between them and they battled tooth and claw from the very first corner. Mansell was forced into the pits with a vibrating wheel but then stormed back in a seemingly impossible chase given that 17 laps from the end Piquet had a lead of 16.8 seconds. With two laps to go Mansell had narrowed that gap to 1.6 seconds and, with his fuel running dangerously low and the race all but over, he caught his teammate at Stowe Corner, overtook in a bold thrust, and won by two seconds. During his lap of honor he stopped at the point where he

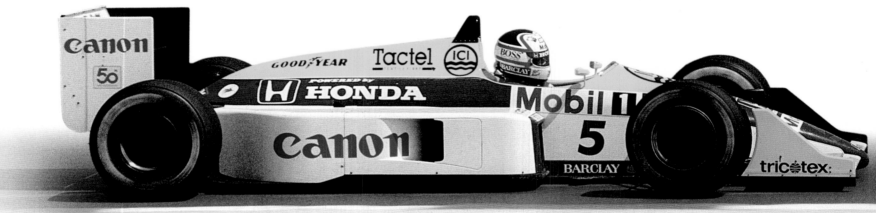

would be restricted to 2.5 bar. In 1989 turbocharging would be definitively outlawed.

In short, at every turn the regulations were modified without the slightest respect for technological progress, while innovations were a result not of logical development but of the FIA's desire to manipulate the World Championship as it saw fit. Officially, the Federation was attempting to lighten the teams' financial burden, but in reality it was favoring Ferrari (which that year celebrated its 400th Grand Prix): the admission of 12-cylinder naturally aspirated engines clearly favored Maranello—the firm had always favored this architecture—but it killed stone-dead the new V8s under development by Ford and Honda. Honda was nonetheless the protagonist of the 1987 season with its 80° V6 powering the mighty Williams.

The season's anti-hero was instead the Paul Ricard circuit at Le Castellet, used for testing before

drivers respectively. Even though Lotus had been orphaned it demonstrated that it had not lost its ability to be innovative with the presentation of self-levelling hydraulic suspension allowing the car's ride height to remain constant, to the benefit of grip.

Before the season got under way, new regulations were defined that would be valid for the next five years: the television revenue was divided between the FIA (30%), the FOCA (24%) and the teams (46%); the technical specifications of the cars (engines, gearbox, weight) were to remain unchanged until 1991; the number of races was fixed at 16; in those countries where the Grand Prix was held alternately at two different tracks (Le Castellet and Dijon in France, Brands Hatch and Silverstone in Great Britain and the Nürburgring and Hockenheim in Germany) the rotation was to be on a five-year basis.

The great novelty of 1987 was telemetry: an on-

592 top left and top center The daring, exuberant Mansell collected six wins in 1987, three fastest laps and eight pole positions. This last achievement was particularly impressive given the presence of the pole position king Ayrton Senna. Here Mansell is seen at the start of the Brazilian GP (left) and engaged in a duel with his team mate Piquet (right).

had overtaken, got out of the car and kissed the asphalt.

Piquet nonetheless won the World Championship laurels, with Williams of course taking the Constructors' title. Meanwhile the Lotus 99T introduced another significant novelty: an electronically controlled suspension that, via fast-acting solenoids, continually optimized the suspension settings. The season was also marked by a violent argument that broke out between Mansell and Senna, eventually leading the furious Englishman to be escorted from the Brazilian's pits.

592 bottom Satoru Nakajima made his Formula 1 debut in 1987 at the wheel of a Lotus-Honda. His presence was determined by Honda's habit of imposing its own drivers on the teams using its engines.

592 top right Nigel Mansell enjoyed a fine season in 1987 with the Williams-Honda, even though he was unable to crown it with the Championship title that went to his teammate Nelson Piquet. Here the Englishman celebrates his victory in the French GP.

592 center In 1987 Mansell had to settle for second overall in the championship, just as the previous season when he was beaten by Alain Prost. His first championship title was only postponed, however, until 1992, when he triumphed with the unbeatable Renault-powered Williams.

593 left and top right Nigel Mansell retired again from Formula 1 after 1995, but rather than abandon motor sport he moved to CART and the British Touring Car Championship (BTCC). He left his mark on the Grand Prix circus with a total of

31 victories placing him fourth in the list of the most successful drivers, behind Prost, Senna and Schumacher.

593 bottom Nigel Mansell's face reveals the pain caused by the crash during the warm-up lap for the 1987 Japanese GP.

The McLaren-Honda was in a league of its own in 1988, and never in the history of modern Formula 1 had a team so convincingly dominated the Championship. The results were 15 wins out of 16 Grands Prix disputed, eight going to Senna and seven to Prost; ten 1-2s; 13 pole positions; the Drivers' Championship won by Senna, with Prost runner-up for the third time; and the Constructors'

more say in Ferrari following the death of the 90-year-old Enzo on the 14th of August. According to the agreement drawn up between the Agnelli family and Ferrari in 1969 that saw 50% of the Modena company sold to Fiat, on the death of the Drake the Turin group's share would increase to 90%, Piero Lardi Ferrari retaining the remaining 10%. Ferrari's death, the corporate changes and the new

Championship won with 199 points—no fewer than 134 ahead of the second-place team, Ferrari. Ayrton Senna confirmed the talent of the Brazilian drivers, the latest South American champion joining his fellow countrymen Piquet and Fittipaldi.

The McLaren-Honda combination was thus one of the most successful of all time. While McLaren proved capable of exploiting its turbocharged performance advantage over the naturally aspirated units to the full, the other teams were hurriedly turning to new engines. Williams, Ligier and March opted for the Judd units, Benetton chose Ford and Arrows Megatron (in effect, revised BMW units). Brabham had instead dropped out of the championship, Ecclestone selling out to Italy's Fiat concern.

The Italian mass manufacturer also had even

organizational structure conditioned the team's performance that season—Maranello won only a single race, but at least this came at the Italian GP, where Berger and Alboreto finished 1-2.

The 1988 World Championship was also characterized by the introduction of pre-qualifying on the previous Friday, together with untimed practice. The 18 teams participating in the championship had entered 31 drivers but the FISA provided only 26 places on the grid and thus a number of hopefuls had to be eliminated before each race. For the first half of the season the drivers recording the slowest times were eliminated while in the second half the results achieved in the first part of the championship were used to decide who would be allowed to start.

594 top and bottom Alain Prost salutes the crowd at "his" French GP of 1988 (bottom). The Professor started from the pole (top) and finished the race over 30 seconds ahead of teammate Ayrton Senna with the two Ferraris of Alboreto and Berger in third and fourth. Alain's victory interrupted Senna's winning streak: two successive wins prior to this race and four in a row afterward.

594 center A line-up of drivers of this calibre would be the envy of any team. In 1988 McLaren had both Ayrton Senna and Alain Prost on its books, the pair finishing first and second in the championship.

594-595 and 595 top left The two aces Alain Prost and Ayrton Senna between them won all the 1988 Grands Prix with the exception of the Italian GP at Monza, which went to Gerhard Berger in the Ferrari. On that occasion Prost (bottom) was forced to retire with mechanical problems (the first of the season for McLaren) while Senna (top, in the pits) could finish no better than tenth after problems with fuel.

595 top right Ayrton Senna, Alain Prost and Nelson Piquet on the podium, a scene repeated twice during the course of the 1988 season at San Marino (in the photograph) and in Australia. Down Under it was Prost who won with Senna second.

1988

The late Eighties and early 1990s were characterized by the monopoly enjoyed by McLaren-Honda and its drivers Ayrton Senna and Alain Prost. As had occurred at Williams between Mansell and Piquet, the rivalry at McLaren between Senna and Prost was fierce and at times extremely personal. Ayrton's talent was now undisputed, as was his exceptional bravura in wet conditions—an authentic champion in continual conflict with his teammate, another of Formula 1's undisputed greats. On a number of occasions Prost accused the McLaren team of favoring the Brazilian by providing

1989

596 top and center left Nineteen eighty-nine was a year to forget for Gerhard Berger: the start to the season was disastrous with an accident in the opening round in Brazil involving Senna immediately after the start. In the next race at San Marino things went from bad to worse because on the third lap Berger lost a front wing and his Ferrari crashed into a retaining wall; the car caught fire but the rapid response of the rescue services avoided a tragedy. Gerhard escaped with burns to his hands and arms.

him with better equipment and manipulating the telemetry data. An end was in sight to the arguments, however, as at the Italian GP Prost announced that he would be driving for Ferrari the following season.

McLaren started the 1989 season as the clear favorite but a surprise was sprung in the first race as Nigel Mansell won with the Ferrari. The Italians, however, were not among the teams tipped for the title because the innovative seven-speed semiautomatic gearbox had not proved its reliability during winter testing. The new transmission system featured two paddles, mounted on either side of the steering wheel, with which the driver engaged gears without having to use the clutch pedal, which only came into play at the start. The Tipo 640 was the first and only Ferrari to be developed and built in England at Ferrari's Guildford premises set up at the behest of John Barnard; final assembly and the building of the mechanical components were still carried out at Maranello.

The 1989 Drivers' and Constructors' Championship tables were in effect photocopies of those of the previous year with the exception of the order of the drivers: first was Alain Prost, taking his third title, with Senna second. Prost left McLaren as champion and helped the team to win its second successive Constructors' Championship. Senna, even though he actually won more races, had to settle for second place. It is curious that the Brazilian

covered no fewer than 2295 km in the lead during the 16 races, almost twice Prost's total of 1217 km.

The 1989 season, the 40th since the birth of Formula 1, saw the banning of the turbocharger and the return of 3.5-liter naturally aspirated engines. The problem faced by all the teams was that of deciding on the optimum engine layout, a decision complicated by the FISA's praiseworthy decision to oblige the constructors to place the pedal-box behind the front axle, thus ensuring greater safety for the drivers.

This measure created packaging difficulties, as with the cockpit set further back the space available for the engine and fuel tanks had to be revised. Would an eight-, ten-, or 12-cylinder engine be better? From the point of view of compactness the former was undoubtedly the best, especially with the cylinders in V-formation. However, an Eight would struggle to match the piston speed of a Twelve. On the other hand, a 12-cylinder engine was bulky, and with the cylinders in V-formation subtracted space from the fuel tanks (that with this type of unit had to be capacious). The solution, as ever, was a compromise: a V10 layout solved all the problems of space.

This type of engine was adopted by Renault (Williams) and Honda (McLaren); Ford (Benetton), Cosworth (AGS, Arrows, Coloni, Dallara, Ligier, Minardi, Onyx, Osella, Rial and Tyrrell), Judd (Brabham, Euro-Brun, Lotus, March), whereas Yamaha (Zakspeed) preferred the V8 while Ferrari and Lamborghini (Lola) stuck with the V12.

596 bottom and 597 top Turbo engines were outlawed in 1989 and the teams returned to naturally aspirated units. Their dilemma was whether to go for 8 or 12 cylinders. Honda found the ideal compromise and fitted a V10 to the McLarens that proved to be powerful, fast and reliable, allowing Prost to win the Drivers' Championship (Senna with the second McLaren was runner-up) and McLaren the Constructors' title.

597 center left Alain Prost started the 1990 season as reigning champion at the wheel of the Ferrari. The duel with Senna was repeated this season, too: the Brazilian took the title by five points.

597 center right In 1989 Nigel Mansell temporarily abandoned Williams (he returned in 1991) to drive for Ferrari. He got off to a fantastic start by winning the first race of the season in Brazil.

597 bottom Jean Alesi made his debut with the Tyrrell-Ford in 1989 and was unfortunate not to achieve better than fourth place. He had to wait until 1995 for his first Formula 1 victory, at the wheel of a Ferrari in the Canadian GP.

596 center right Rain ruined the last race of the 1989 season in Australia: no fewer than 18 drivers retired whilst the champion Prost did not even start after completing a warm-up lap. Boutsen won at the wheel of a Williams.

596-597 Alain Prost won his third title in 1989, and his third for McLaren. The Professor still had time to win his fourth in 1993, this time with Williams, at the venerable age of 38.

UNDER THE SIGN OF SENNA AND THE JAPANESE TEAM

1990 - 1991

Formula 1 was powered toward the end of the century by the Japanese, who proved to be major players in the sport, at least in the early 1990s, from both the technological and economic points of view. The pride of the Land of the Rising Sun was Honda, a company that thanks to its powerful technological and financial resources seemed ready to dominate the decade.

From 1986 the Japanese firm, having found a niche as an engine supplier rather than as a constructor of complete cars, entered a cycle of remarkable success that concluded in 1991 with a record of six consecutive Constructors' titles. The firm's absence from the GP circus from 1992 has proved to be unsupportable for the powers-that-be, and thus in 1998 it was announced that it would be

wins to Prost's five and made sure of the title with one race still to be run. He was in fact crowned as champion at the Japanese Grand Prix, a race that revealed the intensity of his rivalry with Prost: the two had both made claims of favoritism on the part of the FISA and their teams in previous championships. The situation seemed to have been defused at the 1990 Italian GP, when the pair shook hands at a press conference. This was merely a cease-fire, however, not lasting peace. At Suzuka, with both drivers in the running for the title, the Brazilian needed just seven seconds to settle the matter and re-ignite the polemics: he rammed Prost at the first corner, thus gaining revenge for the incident at Suzuka the previous year in which it had been the Professor who sent Senna crashing out and

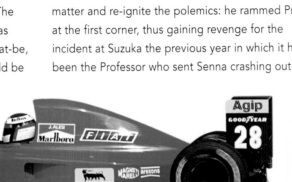

returning to the sport in the year 2000 with the help of *Ingegnere* Dallara, a fount of motor racing expertise in general who has never fully embraced Formula 1, preferring to consolidate his reputation in the United States. Dallara will work on the production of the new car and will lend his know-how to the firm as it attempts to regain a leading role in Grand Prix racing. It is not only Honda that has revealed nostalgia for Formula 1 either: the comeback of BMW is also planned for the new millennium, as is the debut of Toyota.

The wave of Japanese success and its inebriating, beneficial effects involved the Williams and McLaren teams and drivers such as Alain Prost, who won two of his four titles with Honda engines, Nelson Piquet and above all Ayrton Senna. In the Honda-McLaren combination Senna found the ideal conditions in which to express his talent to the full, to confirm his reputation as the undisputed Rain King and to conquer his second and third World Championships in 1990 and '91. He won 13 of the 32 Grands Prix staged in the period.

The conquest of those two titles was by no means easy for Senna: in 1990 Alain Prost was the thorn in his side. Early in the season the Professor led the Championship table with four wins to the Brazilian's three. In the second half, at the German GP, the ninth round, Senna finally regained the podium, and faith in his own abilities, following the Frenchman's three successive wins in Mexico, France and Great Britain. Senna finished the season with six

598 top left Jean Alesi joined Ferrari in 1991, the Maranello firm thus finding itself with prevalently French drivers (there was also Prost) apart from the Italian Morbidelli. Jean's best result was third in Germany, Monaco and Portugal.

598 center left bottom and bottom right Prost and Senna continued their ongoing duel in 1990. The Frenchman, having joined Ferrari,

challenged the Brazilian for the title up to the penultimate round in Japan (right). Here the duel lasted just seven seconds, as Senna rammed the Professor on the first lap, preventing him from continuing and thus conquering the title with a race still to run. With this move Ayrton settled a score with Alain: the previous year Prost had done the same to Senna, again at Suzuka.

took the World Championship title.

In 1991 the threat posed by Alain Prost diminished in that the Ferrari he was now driving was inconsistent: he failed to score a single win, obtaining just three second-place finishes in the USA, France and Spain. Senna's chief rival was instead Nigel Mansell, who had moved from Ferrari to Williams. Following a start to the season which had seen Senna register four consecutive victories

598-599 and 599 top left Nigel Mansell's Williams-Renault took pole position at the 1991 British Grand Prix. Here shortly before the start the car is on the grid with covers still on the tires. The British Lion won the race and set fastest lap: this was the second of three consecutive wins together with those in France and Germany.

599 center Two titles, 174 World Championship points, 23 pole positions, 13 victories, four fastest laps: the statistics whereby Ayrton Senna with highs and lows allowed McLaren to conquer two Constructors' Championships in the 1990 and '91 seasons.

599 bottom left At the start of the 1991 Belgian GP Alain Prost in the Ferrari (in the foreground turning into the corner) is second behind Ayrton Senna. He was to retire on the second lap with a broken fuel pump.

599 bottom right Michael Schumacher in the 1991 Italian GP, his second Formula 1 race. The German driver finished fifth at the wheel of a Benetton-Ford (on his debut he drove a Jordan).

in the first four Grands Prix, including the one held in his home city of Sao Paolo—where he reached the podium so exhausted he was unable to hold the trophy and with his shoulders bruised by over-tight safety belts—Mansell began his fight back. After a win in France where he succeeded in overtaking Prost after a duel lasting 53 laps, the Englishman arrived at his national Grand Prix in dominant form, taking pole position, setting the fastest lap and winning the race. He repeated the exploit in Germany with the exception of the fastest lap which fell to his teammate Riccardo Patrese. As was becoming customary, the rivalry between Senna and Mansell was settled at the penultimate race in Japan: the Englishman attempted to slip past Senna into second place (Berger was leading in the McLaren and went on to win the race), but on the ninth lap finished in the sand and had to abandon the race and all hopes of the title. However, the impulsive Mansell's first World Championship triumph was only postponed by a year. In 1992, thanks in part to the superb chassis developed by the Williams technicians and a Renault engine in sparkling form, Mansell achieved the most important objective of his career, scoring nine Grand Prix wins along the way. Senna and Berger had to settle for the crumbs, winning three and two GPs respectively. Patrese finished in second place in the World Championship thanks to his consistency and excellent series of placings (one victory, six seconds).

598 top right and 599 top right The first part of the 1991 season was totally dominated by Ayrton Senna. The Championship became almost monotonous as he won the first four races and started from the pole in all four, including his national GP in

Brazil. At the Sao Paolo Interlagos circuit Ayrton won for the first time in front of his home crowd. Although this brought Senna immense joy he was exhausted at the finish and struggled to hold the trophy due to pains in his shoulders caused by over-tight safety belts.

ALAIN PROST, SECOND ONLY TO FANGIO

Even though the Professor had had to give way to the Brazilian in the early 1990s, he was by no means a spent force. Not satisfied with the three World Championship titles he had conquered with McLaren in 1985, '86 and '89, Prost wanted to match Juan Manuel Fangio's record of five championship victories. The Frenchman eventually finished up with four titles, a remarkable haul nonetheless—and an honorable second place that he is unlikely to have to share for some time. His fourth came in 1993 at the venerable age (for a Formula 1 driver) of 38. He had spent 1992 away from the tracks following his divorce from Ferrari at the last race of the 1991 season in Australia. The Professor returned at the wheel of a Williams-Renault, taking the place of reigning champion Mansell, who had decided to race in America's CART/Indy series. Prost's teammate would instead be Damon Hill, son of the late, great Graham.

The Williams once again proved to be the car to beat and allowed Hill to record three victories. Combined with the talent of Alain Prost it formed

an exceptional cocktail that Senna and his McLaren-Ford was able to oppose on only four occasions. The only other Grand Prix not to fall to Williams was won by Michael Schumacher, who thus scored his second Formula 1 victory. Prost was crowned World Champion two races from the end of the season at Estoril in Portugal. Twenty-four hours later he announced his retirement (once again) from racing.

As with Honda, however, Formula 1 was Alain Prost's drug of choice, and he returned to the circus in 1997 with his own team. The Professor's fourth title confirmed the French *grandeur* in the sport, with Honda being replaced by Renault as the leading engine supplier. Between 1992 and 1997 the firm powered to six consecutive Constructors' Championships. This success was the French company's return on the massive investment it had made in the sport since 1977, during which time it had competed with its own cars up until 1985 and had had the merit of introducing turbocharging. The firm's wisest decision was that of devoting itself to engines: success followed success from when it began supplying its power units to Williams and Benetton. Renault thus proved to be a worthy successor to Honda and confirmed its position as a major player in the Formula 1 of the 1990s.

1992 - 1993

601 top Shortly after the start of the 1992 French GP Senna and Schumacher found themselves in trouble. The race was won by Nigel Mansell.

601 center Michael Schumacher was the most promising young Formula 1 driver in 1993. After his first victory in the Belgian GP the previous year he repeated the feat in the Portuguese GP after having started sixth on the grid and conquered six second-place finishes over the course of the season. He came to the fore in 1994, winning his first World Championship title.

601 bottom left Prost won his fourth World Championship in 1993 with the Williams. That season the Professor yet again had to battle against Ayrton Senna who finished runner-up: the Frenchman won seven GPs, of which four came in succession, while the Brazilian won five, all concentrated in the second half of the season.

601 bottom right The last 1992 podium with Gerhard Berger preparing to spray Michael Schumacher with champagne: in the Australian GP the Austrian driver crossed the line just seven-tenths of a second ahead of the German.

600 top left Ayrton Senna, portrayed here in his McLaren-Ford, was, with Alain Prost and Michael Schumacher, one of the key figures in the Formula 1 of the Nineties.

600 top center Ayrton Senna (seen here in the pits) went through a transitional period in 1992, not shining with his McLaren as in previous seasons. However, he still managed three wins and interrupted the domination of Nigel Mansell, heading toward the title with the Williams-Renault. Senna concluded the season in fourth place, bettering teammate Berger by a single point.

600 top right Eddie Irvine joined the F1 circus in 1993 at the Japanese GP. At the wheel of a Jordan-Hart, the driver finished sixth—a good start that kept him at Jordan for three seasons before he moved to Ferrari.

600 center Prost leaving the pits and preparing to join battle. His last Grand Prix came in Australia in 1993: having won his fourth World Championship with two races to go, he retired from competition.

600 bottom Riccardo Patrese enjoyed a fine season in 1992 at the wheel of the Williams-Renault, with which he finished runner-up in the championship to teammate Nigel Mansell.

1994

Ayrton Senna

602 *Tragedy struck at the 1994 San Marino Grand Prix at Imola. Ayrton Senna started from pole position but never completed the first lap, the last of his life: at the Tamburello Corner his Williams crashed into the retaining wall (bottom left) and a suspension arm perforated his helmet's visor and his skull. Worse still, Senna's was not the only death that May weekend. At the start of the race itself Lahmy's Lotus and Lehto's Benetton collided (bottom center) causing a number of injuries among the spectators. During practice Ratzenberger crashed his Simtek at the Villeneuve Corner at 314 kph (195 mph), and was killed instantly (bottom right).*

603 top *The 1994 season was also to be the last for another of the sport's greats, albeit in this case not as a result of an accident: Nigel Mansell announced he would be retiring from motor racing at the end of the season (although he was to be seen in a McLaren in 1995).*

603 center *The 1994 Monaco GP was the first race after Senna's death and his colleagues commemorated him at a circuit where he had triumphed no fewer than six times with a banner bearing his portrait. The Monte Carlo race was itself not without incident: in practice Wendlinger (left) exited the tunnel and crashed into the barriers. The Austrian driver was left in a coma but gradually recovered. Mika Hakkinen with the McLaren and Damon Hill in a Williams collided at the Sainte Dévote corner; the Finnish driver spun (right) out of the race together with the Englishman.*

Adieu Ayrton

While Renault took over the reins from Honda in the field of engines, Michael Schumacher became the sport's new star driver, filling the vacuum left by Ayrton Senna, whose brilliant career was cut short at the 1994 San Marino Grand Prix. At 2:17 on Sunday, the first of March, at the Dino and Enzo Ferrari Circuit of Imola, Senna was killed in an accident shortly after the start when he crashed into the retaining wall at the Tamburello Curve. In the massive impact a suspension arm perforated his visor. A cruel destiny: had the suspension arm struck a few millimeters higher he would have survived—and he would have won the 1994 and '95 titles; of this Frank Williams was convinced after having managed to woo Senna away from McLaren. The Brazilian had won three titles and brought three Constructors' titles to the team. Ayrton passed away, and still today the responsibilities for his death have yet to be ascertained. His thrilling Formula 1 career lasted ten years, from his debut with the Toleman at the Brazilian GP in 1984 after having arrived directly from Formula 3—leap-frogging the intermediate categories like his fiercest rival, Professor Alain Prost—through to his last GP victory in Australia in 1993. In that period he won three championships and 41 Grands Prix, claiming 65 pole positions in the bargain. Senna was the latest driver to die in his car, perhaps—as was death on the battlefield for a warrior—the most honorable fate for a racing driver, although in this case it was particularly brutal and premature.

Schumacher gives nothing away to Senna in terms of driving ability in the wet, courage, daring or technique.

Benetton, the team owned by the well known Italian clothing concern and born out of the ashes of Toleman in the Eighties, was ably managed by Flavio Briatore and had the merit of bringing Michael Schumacher's talent to the fore. On his Formula 1 debut in 1991 Schumacher had immediately impressed and moved directly from Jordan to the Italian team, which managed to retain his services until 1995.

Schumy's first World Championship title came in 1994, snatched by a single point from Damon Hill. Of the year's 16 races, eight were won by the German (four in succession at the start of the season) and six by the Englishman, the crumbs being picked up by Gerhard Berger and Nigel Mansell. Michael's talent was shown by the fact that he won the title in a car that was competitive but not dominant like the Williams, and with a Ford V8 engine that was not on the same level as its highly successful Ford-Cosworth

603 bottom Eleven cars were involved in two different accidents immediately after the start and seven retired during the race at the 1994 German GP: this was not the brightest of starts to the Hockenheim race, in which only eight cars managed to finish. Gerhard Berger won for Ferrari, a triumph for the Prancing Horse which thus returned to the winner's enclosure after an absence of four years.

predecessors—and no real match for the Renault unit.

In spite of the abolition of turbos, the French manufacturer still in fact retained its leadership in the field, a position unaffected by the shift to naturally aspirated 3.5- (and subsequently three-) liter engines. The naturally aspirated power units fitted to the Formula 1 cars of the early 1990s were developing in the order of 700 hp in qualifying and 670-680 hp in race tune. The precise power outputs, like the other technical specifications of the cars, were not released by the constructors—a policy adopted by Honda and subsequently by all the other teams.

INCREASED DRIVER SAFETY

The FISA introduced new regulations for the new decade that further addressed driver safety: the cars were now to be subjected to frontal crash tests and had to be fitted with cockpit structures that allowed the driver to climb out of the car unaided in five seconds.

From a stylistic point of view, the Tyrrells

services. Many of his fellow Germans hoped to see him at the wheel of the McLaren, which from 1995 was powered by a Mercedes engine. The first German World Champion at the wheel of a car powered by an engine bearing the three-pointed star would have been a very popular combination in his homeland.

caught the eye with their raised noses resembling that of Concorde. There was finally a degree of originality to the lines of the cars, rather than anonymous tubes dressed up in wings, spoilers and side-skirts. The British car boasted exceptional aerodynamics: drag had been considerably reduced while the ground effects were optimal, the result of hundreds of hours in the wind tunnel.

In 1995 Schumacher revealed all his driving talent and took his second Championship title, again at the wheel of a Benetton but this time powered by Renault. The Italian team could thus count on the best driver in the field and the best engine, and used these advantages to best effect in taking the Constructors' Championship. The conquest of the title seemed to repeat the previous season's script with Damon Hill again second, albeit further behind, and Jean Alesi again finishing fifth in the Ferrari. David Coulthard and Johnny Herbert finished in well-earned third and fourth places, respectively.

With two titles to his name Schumy was red hot and assiduously courted by all the leading teams, who made multimillion-dollar offers for his

604 top The British Lion returned to Formula 1 in 1995, but results were very disappointing. At the San Marino GP Nigel could manage no better than tenth with his McLaren-Mercedes.

604 center The 1995 German Grand Prix was held at Hockenheim and was won by Michael Schumacher with the Benetton-Ford, his fifth victory of the season.

605 top right Dramatic moments in the pits at the 1995 Belgian GP as the fuel filler leaks petrol over Irvine's car, which bursts into flames. Fortunately there were no consequences for the mechanics or driver.

605 center right David Coulthard in the pits to change tires and refuel. After his F1 debut in 1994 the Scot was into his second season with Williams and finished third in the Championship behind Schumacher and Hill.

604 bottom Hill finished in the gravel together with Schumacher on the 23rd lap of the Italian GP. Damon had rammed Schumy's Benetton and the furious German demanded an explanation. He was held back by the marshals, allowing the Englishman to get out of his car.

604-605 There was the usual crowding at the Sainte Dévote corner immediately after the start of the 1995 Monaco GP and the two Ferraris, together with Coulthard's Williams, provoked a multiple pile-up. The race had to be restarted.

605 bottom right Michael Schumacher and Flavio Briatore, the Benetton chief, celebrating the conquest of the Drivers' and Constructors' titles. This was in 1995 and the German had won nine of the 17 scheduled Grands Prix.

1995

SCHUMY ATTEMPTS TO REVIVE FERRARI'S FORTUNES

The Prancing Horse has an undeniable appeal, however, even for a cold, calculating champion like Schumacher: the opportunity to race with the only team to be an ever-present in the Formula 1 circus and the only team to have retained its national racing color in spite of the best efforts of wealthy

sponsors persuaded Michael to move to Maranello in 1996. The Italian constructor was looking to Schumacher to restore it to what it saw as its rightful position; its last Drivers' World Championship title dated back to 1979 with Jody Scheckter, the last Constructors' Championship to 1983.

It was love at first sight between Schumacher and the Ferrari team. The German conquered everyone at Maranello, and not only through his driving: Giorgio Ascanelli, Ferrari pits chief, who has seen plenty of fine drivers pass within range of his spanners and screwdrivers, happily recounts that Schumy is one of the very few drivers able to describe exactly how a racing gearbox is put together. An ace driver, therefore, with the technical knowledge to back up his talent, who is so meticulous, conscientious and precise as to remind one of Lauda.

607 top left Four wins, three pole positions, six fastest laps and second place overall in the 1996 Championship for the young Jacques Villeneuve, seen here at the wheel of his Williams-Renault duelling with Schumacher's Ferrari.

607 center Berger hitches a lift with Alesi: this was the 1996 German GP held at Hockenheim where the Austrian was betrayed by his Benetton's engine two laps from the finish. Jean instead came second to Hill in the Williams.

607 bottom left Making his debut in 1996, the son of the impetuous but shy Gilles (who had been killed 14 years earlier), drove like an authentic veteran. This photo shows the celebrations for his victory at the Hungarian GP.

607 bottom right Damon Hill was World Champion in 1996 with eight victories, nine pole positions and five fastest laps. Williams was thus repaid for the faith it had shown in the Englishman signed to flank Prost in 1993. In this photograph the driver is celebrating victory in the Argentine GP.

606-607 Signed by Ferrari to win the team's first championship since 1979, Michael Schumacher, seen here during the German GP at Hockenheim, was beaten into third place overall by Damon Hill and Jacques Villeneuve.

606 bottom Eddie Irvine joined Ferrari in 1996. The Irishman appeared to settle in well as Schumacher's number two. He collected 11 points with a best placing of third in Australia.

THE FUTURE OF FORMULA 1
LIES WITH THE FATHERS' SONS

Since 1996 the spotlights have been trained on Maranello and its long awaited revival and on Schumacher, a driver who had inherited the mantle of Ayrton Senna and appeared destined to match the number of championships won by Prost or even Fangio.

However, as is frequently the case when expectations are allowed a free rein, the results were disappointing. Ferrari undoubtedly made progress with Schumacher, but in 1996 came up against the Williams-Renault and Damon Hill (the son of Graham, the 1962 and 1968 World Champion) who finished in the top three in 12 of the 16 Grands Prix, with eight victories, three second places and a third. In 1997 it was the turn of Jacques Villeneuve, son of the dashing Gilles who was killed in 1982 before he had the chance to translate his great natural talent into trophies and titles.

In 1996 Schumacher could finish no better than third and Damon Hill gained revenge for having twice finished second to the German when he won his World Championships with Benetton. In second place was Jacques Villeneuve, a fine performance given that he was finishing in front of the driver of the moment.

The following year Schumy improved, but the title was lost during the last race when the German attempted to run Villeneuve off the track as the Canadian tried to overtake in a corner. The German came off the worse in the fight, as following the collision he was forced to retire, thus losing any hope of taking the title.

When in 1998 it appeared that Schumacher would have a clear run at the championship, McLaren-Mercedes arrived from nowhere with an innovative car that appeared to corner as if on rails. Schumy's excellent form and a well prepared car nonetheless allowed him to challenge for the title up to the last race in Japan. At Suzuka, however, the 29-year-old from Hürth-Hermühlheim had to start from the back of the grid after stalling on the starting line, and after staging a thrilling comeback that saw him reach as high as third place, had to retire with a blown tire on the 32nd lap.

The talented Mika Hakkinen of Finland thus won his first World Championship after a fantastic season in which he won eight Grands Prix and collected 100 points—14 more than Schumacher—and dominated the World Championship scene from the first race to the last.

608 top Alexander Würz in the Benetton started from the fifth row of the grid and finished in fifth place in the 1998 French GP. His teammate Fisichella started alongside Würz but could only manage ninth place at the finish.

608 bottom They can win or lose a Grand Prix, are fundamental elements in race strategy, determinant in pit-stops and are prepared for the race by being heated in electric covers: The importance of tires is thus evident.

608-609 The Ferrari faithful celebrate a 1-2 triumph in the 1998 Italian GP, something that had not happened for ten years. Schumacher thus joined Hakkinen at the top of the championship table, something that until then had seemed impossible.

609 top Eighth place for "Fisico" Fisichella and the retirement of Würz on the 24th lap with a broken gearbox was all the Benetton B198s could manage at the 1998 Italian GP. This was nonetheless better than the previous GP in Belgium, where both drivers failed to finish.

609 center right The Argentine GP was Michael Schumacher and Ferrari's first win of the 1998 season. The rain and Hakkinen's errors after two consecutive victories took the German to the highest step of the podium.

609 bottom left The Finnish driver Mika Hakkinen started from pole position in the 1998 Brazilian GP with his extremely rapid McLaren-Mercedes: this was the first of a total of nine poles during the season.

609 bottom right Hakkinen, Coulthard and Schumacher made up the podium at the Brazilian GP, a lineup repeated in Spain and Austria. At the Luxembourg GP the order of first and second place was inverted.

The race for the 1999 title opened with Eddie Irvine's victory in Australia, the Irish driver's first Grand Prix win. Those who thought that the McLarens were a spent force had to think again, however, following Hakkinen's success at Interlagos. The gap between the Rosse of Maranello and the Silver Arrows nonetheless appeared to have narrowed to almost nothing especially after Michael Schumacher's triumph at Imola and the Ferraris' remarkable 1-2 victory at Monte Carlo.

The turning point came at Silverstone where brake failure caused Michael Schumacher to crash head-on into the barriers at the fourth corner. The accident was dramatic and although Schumacher came away with nothing worse than a badly broken leg, his championship chances had evaporated. Eddie Irvine assumed the mantle of the team's number one driver and, flanked by Mika Salo, won in Austria and Germany. The McLaren response was swift and uncompromising: consecutive 1-2 wins in Hungary and Belgium which could have been a hat-trick had a nervous Mika Hakkinen not thrown away a race seemingly won at Monza. Three races from the end of the season the Finn and Irvine were equal on points, followed by Frentzen. The Grand Prix of Europe at the Nürburgring was one of the most thrilling races of recent years: the intermittent rain played havoc with race strategies, favouring the outsiders. Hakkinen mistimed his tyre change but Ferrari failed to take advantage.

A three-way summit meeting between Schumi, Montezemolo and Avvocato Agnelli convinced Michael to return for the last two races of the season. The brand-new track at Sepang was the setting for the Malaysian Grand Prix: a dazzling Michael Schumacher in magnificent form dominated the race from the outset but, respecting team orders, he allowed his team-mate Irvine to pass twice during the race and score a victory that could have meant the difference between winning and losing the title. Post-race, however, the two Ferraris, which had finished first and second, were

disqualified on technical grounds due to oversized barge-boards. The FIA appeals commission, however, accepted Ferrari's defence and restored the original finishing order. The Maranello cars made the trip to Suzuka for the last race of the season with a 4-point lead over their rivals. Michael Schumacher claimed pole position, but it was Mika Hakkinen who took advantage of the German's chronically slow starting to streak away to victory in both race and championship. Irvine finished third on the day and second overall, placings that there not good enough to keep him at Ferrari: in 2000 he was to become the number one driver for the new Jaguar Formula 1 team.

Maranello took temporary consolation from the fact that it won its first Constructors' Championship for sixteen years, an excellent appetizer for the main course that was to follow seventeen Grands Prix and almost 5,000 racing kilometres later. In 2000, in fact, the team went on to win both the drivers' and constructors' championships. A season, that from the point of view of the podium was somewhat

monotonous, with either Ruben Barrichello or one of the McLaren drivers almost always alongside Kaiser Schumacher. The exceptions were Fisichella, Frentzen and Ralf Schumacher: the Italian Benetton driver was second in Brazil and third in Monte Carlo and Canada, the Jordan driver was third in the United States while Michael's brother, driving for Williams, snatched a third placed at Monza in a race that was to be remembered not so much for Schumacher's sixth win or Ferrari's home-turf triumph, but for the death of a marshal struck by a wheel detached in a pile-up triggered by Frentzen at the second chicane. The race should perhaps have been interrupted, but the show must go on...

David Coulthard had a miraculous escape from an air crash. Those who thought that the fright would keep him away from racing were making a big mistake: he subsequently finished third in the Grand Prix of Europe and first in Monte Carlo and France. The season had, however, been tinged red from the outset: an incandescent Ferrari won the first three races with Michael Schumacher, the first time

Maranello had managed such a feat. McLaren was on the ropes, with engines blowing (Australia), other mechanical failures afflicting Hakkinen's car and Coulthard's disqualification for having a rear wing that was too low (Brazil). The Anglo-German team was competitive at San Marino but pit stop strategy favored Schumacher and penalised Barrichello who had to cede third place to Coulthard. The McLaren renaissance got underway in England: Hakkinen won at Silverstone and dominated in Spain. Then in Belgium came the Finn's crowning moment with a majestic overtaking maneuver that swept him past Schumacher and on to victory and the lead in the championship. However, Ron Dennis' team then proceeded to undo all the good work in the revived United States Grand Prix: Schumi paid back Hakkinen in kind, overtaking him on the track and the points table, while Coulthard was immediately penalised for jumping the start.

Ferrari now held all the aces: at the penultimate Grand Prix in Japan Schumacher claimed the drivers' title while at the last in Malaysia, the Prancing Horse

made sure of the constructors' championship, the tenth for the Drake's team. Barrichello also finished well, taking second place in the final table.

This was a remarkable season for Ferrari: ten victories of which nine were scored by the Kaiser, three 1-2 finishes, ten pole positions. Twenty-one years of waiting was finally rewarded and the team celebrated long and hard: shaved heads and red wigs were the order of the day for engineers, mechanics and managers at Maranello, Luca Cordero di Montezemolo included.

Racing year 2001 began exactly where 2000 had left off, namely, with a victory by Michael Schumacher, who dominated that season and also established new racing records. He became World Champion for the fourth time, with four races in hand. The world title event then took place in Melbourne: the German driver gained the highest step on the podium and began to accumulate a large number of points. Schumacher's win in the Australian Grand Prix was his fifth consecutive victory, counting four wins at the end of the 2000 season. However, the joy of victory was diminished by the death of a track official struck by Jacques Villeneuve's car when it took to the air after grazing Ralf Schumacher's car.

In Malaysia the Ferrari's built in Maranello cars continued to dominate with Schumacher achieving his second victory of the season and his sixth consecutive win; right behind him came Barrichello, giving Ferrari their 50th one-two placing.

The wet surface of Brazil's Interlagos track brought changes to the situation that had seemed to focus on just one color: red. This time Schumacher came second behind Mika Hakkinen's McLaren-Mercedes, making it a sad return home to Europe for Ferrari fans. On home ground, at Imola, the Ferraris had to accept Ralf Schumacher's domination of the entire race, which gave him and his first Formula 1 win and also brought Williams-BMW one after almost four years; it their first triumph since 1986. In the listing, Scotland's David Coulthard joined Schumacher, with 26 points.

In Spain, Ferrari's difficult period seemed to be continuing but the last five bends proved treacherous for Mika Hakkinen: with his clutch gone, he saw Michael Schumacher snatch victory from his grasp. If Lady Luck was kissing the German while on Spanish soil, she continued to spurn him in Austria, despite his starting from pole position. Coulthard was first, in front of the two Ferraris, and closed up on the German in the classification.

The presence of Luca Cordero di Montezemolo, Ferrari's president, brought good fortune to the Ferrari drivers at the Monaco Grand Prix; they took another one-two. Schumacher's victory lifted him 12 points above Coulthard.

612 2001 Monaco G.P.: Ferraris race together towards the finish line, an outcome that up till the evening before had not been expected. In the trials, McLaren had dominated, but Coulthard, who started in pole position, came to a stop during the reconaissance lap whereas Hakkinen pulled back just as he was about to attack Schumacher.

612-613 Michael Schumacher's Ferrari chases Juan Pablo Montoya's Williams-

BMW: at the 2001 Austrian GP, the German started from pole for the first time, but during the race was forced to follow the Colombian; both drivers went off the track in the 10th lap but Schumi eventually finished third.

613 top A troubled Ralf Schumacher explains to the Williams-BMW technicians the reasons for his crash on the 20th lap, when he was lying in 4th place. This was the 2001

Spanish GP; Schumi Jr. started from the third row but it was his brother who was to cross the finishing line and gain the highest step on the podium.

613 bottom left The Ferrari mechanics fine-tuning the F2001 during the 2001 Brazilian GP, a thrilling race for the rosse: Barrichello was immediately eliminated along with Ralf Schumacher after the two collided. Michael Schumacher was leading when it began to rain, but made two

mistakes: he had to settle for second place behind Coulthard.

613 bottom right Michael Schumacher celebrates victory and a 12-point lead in the championship table: Ferrari has just scored a fine one-two victory in the Monaco GP in the presence of company president Luca Cordero di Montezemolo, who had traveled to the principality to bring his team luck. Mission accomplished!

2001

614-615 A spectacular accident in the 2001 German GP, without serious consequences: Michael shoots away but his car slows and all but stops after just a few meters. Luciano Burti is unable to avoid him destroying his car. The Brazilian driver had already been involved in a frightening crash during practice.

614 bottom left The highlight of 2001 European GP at the Nürburgring was the duel between the Schumacher brothers. Michael is seen here leading after the first few corners immediately after the start, hounded by his brother Ralf who was, however, to lose the battle after being hit with a stop-and-go penalty.

614 bottom right Michael crosses the line in the 2001 French GP, placing the championship within his grasp. The German dominated a race that initially seemed destined to be won by his brother Ralf. Everything was to change after the first pit stop when his Williams-BMW was unable to maintain decent lap times.

2001

In Canada, the race turned into a duel between the Schumacher brothers: Ralf won, thanks partly to the superiority of the Michelin tires, thus bringing joy to Ralf and Michael's father, who had long dreamed of this double triumph.

At the Nürburgring, the family duel continued but Ralf infringed the rules, which forced him to accept a stop-and-go. Schumacher and his Ferrari won and he took a 24-point lead in the classification, which allowed him to set his sights on the world champion title once again. At Magny Cours in France, Schumacher won his fiftieth Grand Prix, leaving him just one victory away from Alain Prost's all-time record. But this was a short-lived situation because in Hungary, on August 19 (just one week later), the German won his 41st pole position, his 51st Grand Prix and his 4th World Championship.

Next, at Silverstone, Mika Hakkinen regained the top of the podium for the first time in 11 months, while at Hockenheim it was Ralf Schumacher's turn once more. Ferrari could hope to achieve second place with Barrichello, but this wasn't to be the case. In Belgium Michael Schumacher won again; however, this race was not remembered as his record 52nd Grand Prix victory. Instead, the Brazilian Luciano Burti's accident, with his rival Alain Prost finishing up against the tires (against the barriier?), seized the racing community's attention. Fortunately Burti was only slightly injured.

However, this seemed to be just a preview for the sad and politicized atmosphere of the Italian Grand Prix in Monza, just five days after the Twin Towers attack and one day after Zanardi had both legs amputated following a horrific crash in Formula Cart. At first the

drivers at first did not want to race, then they agreed to a soft start to avoid incidents on the track's first bends. Montoya won the first GP of his career, ahead of Rubens Barrichello. On 30 September the event moved to a shocked United States, where to everyone's surprise Mika Hakkinen took first place, having just announced his (temporary) retirement from racing. Michael Schumacher, in second place, was unsparing in his applause for Mika: he will miss his duels with the old Finnish lion.

The season came to an end in Japan, where Michael Schumacher returned to victory with a masterful race on the Suzuka circuit, bringing the curtain down on this unusual season. It was his 53rd personal victory and the 144th for Ferrari. With this success, the world champion matched Nigel Mansell's 1992 record for the highest number of wins in a single season, which Schumacher himself matched in 2000. He also became the Formula 1 driver who won highest number of points in a season – 123.

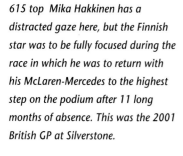

615 top Mika Hakkinen has a distracted gaze here, but the Finnish star was to be fully focused during the race in which he was to return with his McLaren-Mercedes to the highest step on the podium after 11 long months of absence. This was the 2001 British GP at Silverstone.

615 center Ralf Schumacher on track during the 2001 Italian GP: he was to finish third, behind Montoya and Barrichello, in one of the saddest races in the history of Formula 1. This was just nine days after the attack on the Twin Towers and the day after Alex Zanardi's tragic Formula Cart accident, after which he underwent amputation of both his legs.

615 bottom Celebrations on the podium for the Schumacher family: the two brothers triumphed in the 2001 French GP on the Magny Cours. Michael celebrated his 50th victory, just one fewer than Alain Prost's record: it was only a matter of weeks however, as in the Hungarian GP…

616 top The 2002 Hungarian GP was tinted with red: Rubens Barrichello started from pole ahead of his teammate Michael Schumacher, the Brazilian took the checkered flag, followed by Michael and his brother Ralf and the two McLaren-Mercedes of Raikkonen and Coulthard.

616-617 Rubens Barrichello crosses the line: the Brazilian scored points in 11 races in the 2002 World Championship as he finished runner-up to the peerless Michael Schumacher. His 4 wins, 5 second places and single third and fourth place finishes accounted for a total of 77 points.

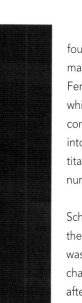

While Kaiser Michael had won the 2001 title with four races in hand, in 2002 he the put his seal on the matter with six in hand before the end of the season. Ferrari established further records thanks to the F2002, which had already garnered itself a bouquet of compliments on the day of its introduction. Its entry into the history books was due to its revolutionary cast titanium gearbox, completely new aerodynamics, and numerous other innovations that made it unbeatable.

The combination of this amazing vehicle and Schumacher's driving ability was devastating as far as the competition was concerned, and the championship was wrapped up at Magny Cours after just 11 of the 17 championship races. Schumacher was first as usual, after taking advantage of a mistake by Raikonnen just

In Monaco the competition heated up and Michael could only come in second behind Coulthard, though in front of his brother, but then in Canada he returned to the winner's rostrum.

Michael Schumacher then took second place in the European Grand Prix at the Nürburgring, behind Barrichello. In Austria, he overcame his bad luck to take first place. He repeated this win at Silverstone and then again at Magny Cours, where he won his fifth world title. Throughout the 2002 season, Schumacher never finished lower than in third place: 11 events, 8 victories, 2 second places and 1 third place. And this was without considering Ferrari's 221 manufacturer's championship points --equal to those of all the other car-builders' points added together.

five laps from the finish. Until then, Raikonnen had driven impeccably. Thanks to Juan Pablo Montoya coming in only fourth, Michael won his fifth World Championship, thereby equaling Juan Manuel Fangio's record.

It all began in Australia when the German driver crossed the line in front of Montoya and Raikonnen. At the second GP in Malaysia he had to be content with third place and with four points, behind his brother Ralf in first place and Montoya in second.

At this point Michael gritted his teeth and won four Grand Prix in a row, extending his lead in the table: they were Brazil, San Marino, Spain, and Austria, giving him 40 solid and decisive points toward the title. His victory in Austria, however, was won among violent arguments: Barrichello, who was leading at the end, allowed Schumacher to overtake him and take the race. Much ado about nothing: Ferrari was fined and that was the end of it.

2002

The rules were changed in 2003: there were two days of official trials (Friday and Saturday) with a single lap to be timed. In the first Grand Prix the cars came onto the track one at a time, following the driver's placement in the 2002 world championship classification. In the second GP, the order was set by the times obtained the day before -- and only the times achieved on the Saturday were used to decide the starting order. Points won on the track were designated as 10 to the winner, 8 to second place, 6 to third, and so on down to the 8th-placed driver, who received 1 point. Teams were strictly forbidden to "engineer" the result of a race; this was to prevent a repetition of what happened in Austria in 2002. And in 2003 there was to be no Grand Prix in Belgium because the host country was unable to reach an agreement with the drivers over

and the television public); and finally, limiting spare-car use when the track car was damaged.

For 2005, the use of a single engine for two races is planned (for six races in 2006), the extension of the "working life" span of most car parts, and new sanctions for substitution of the engine or other parts outside of the fixed times.

Whether races are held under new or old rules, Ferrari remains the team to beat. It opened the new season with the F2003-GA, in which the letters GA represent a salute to Giovanni Agnelli, Ferrari's No. 1 fan, who died early in the year.

The F2003-GA is the 49th car built by Ferrari for the Formula 1 championships. This car reflects the design philosophy of the winning F2002; Ferrari has improved the F2002's aerodynamic efficiency and given it improved handling by lowering the center of

the ban on the advertising of tobacco. In consequence, the championship was to be reduced from 17 events to 16.

The FIA decided to postpone until the first GP of the 2004 season its ban on Formula 1 driver-aid systems (antispin, automatic gearbox, and automatic starting), which was supposed to take effect after the British Grand Prix. The technical procedures required for implementing controls entails large investments by the FIA, and so it naturally preferred to put the moment off.

Another FIA's cost-cutting move included four elements. These were: prohibition of active telemetry (box to car); partial restriction of passive telemetry (car to box); authorization of team-to-driver communication (provided it could be heard by the FIA

gravity. It is a completely redesigned race car: the chassis is new from both a design and construction standpoint, and the bodywork, radiators, exhaust, rear end, and steering have been redesigned; and the suspension has been enhanced. All these modifications have been made to improve the car's streamlining and therefore its performance. The F2003-GA uses new materials to reduce weight and size, and, as with the F2002, the new engine is load-bearing and mounted longitudinally. The cast titanium gearbox has sequential electro-hydraulic control and 7 gears (plus reverse). Finally, in line with a Formula 1 tradition begun by Ferrari, the exhausts are high. In short, everything is set to continue Maranello factory's success, including a Michael Schumacher who remains the unquestioned king of modern Formula 1.

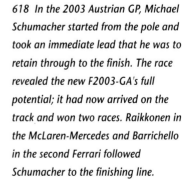

618 In the 2003 Austrian GP, Michael Schumacher started from the pole and took an immediate lead that he was to retain through to the finish. The race revealed the new F2003-GA's full potential; it had now arrived on the track and won two races. Raikkonen in the McLaren-Mercedes and Barrichello in the second Ferrari followed Schumacher to the finishing line.

618-619 In the 2003 Malaysian GP, Michael Schumacher collided with Jarno Trulli a few hundred meters after the start: he was to finish only sixth, allowing Kimi Raikkonen to take the highest step on the podium, the McLaren-Mercedes driver scoring his maiden Formula 1 victory.

619 top A joyous Michael Schumacher celebrating victory in the 2003 Austrian GP at the A-1 Ring. This win was all the more deserved as Schumacher had had to face a potential inferno while making his refueling stop. As the flames were dealt with the German sat absolutely impassive in the cockpit.

619 bottom left A dramatic shot inside the Williams-BMW pits. The team lined up for the 2003 season with the FW25 powered by a V10 BMW engine producing over 850 hp and drivers Juan Pablo Montoya and Ralf Schumacher (seen here in the cockpit ready for the start) and the tester Mark Genè.

619 bottom right The young German driver Nick Heidfeld (born 1977) passes his team's timekeepers: 2003 is his fourth World Championship season. During the last three seasons, he has driven a Sauber (he was with Prost for his debut year in 2000), and he has competed in 50 Grands Prix.

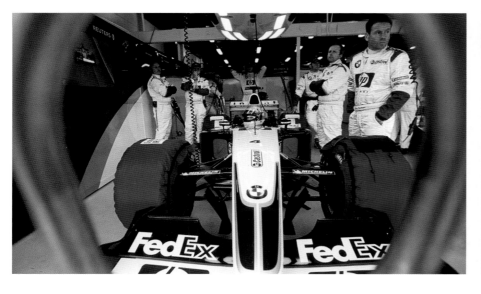

HONOR ROLL

The Gran Prix from 1950 to 2002

Year	Champion Driver	Nationality	Car	Champion Constructor
1950	Giuseppe Farina	Italian	Alfa Romeo 158/159	-
1951	Juan Manuel Fangio	Argentine	Alfa Romeo 159	-
1952	Alberto Ascari	Italian	Ferrari 500	-
1953	Alberto Ascari	Italian	Ferrari 500	-
1954	Juan Manuel Fangio	Argentine	Merc.-Benz W196/Maserati 250F	
1955	Juan Manuel Fangio	Argentine	Mercedes-Benz W196	-
1956	Juan Manuel Fangio	Argentine	Lancia-Ferrari D50	-
1957	Juan Manuel Fangio	Argentine	Maserati 250F	-
1958	Mike Hawthorn	British	Ferrari Dino 246	Vanwall
1959	Jack Brabham	Australian	Cooper T51-Climax	Cooper-Climax
1960	Jack Brabham	Australian	Cooper T53-Climax	Cooper-Climax
1961	Phil Hill	USA	Ferrari Dino 156	Ferrari
1962	Graham Hill	British	BRM P57	BRM
1963	Jim Clark	British	Lotus 25-Climax	Lotus-Climax
1964	John Surtees	British	Ferrari 158	Ferrari
1965	Jim Clark	British	Lotus 33-Climax	Lotus-Climax
1966	Jack Brabham	Australian	Brabham-Repco Bt19/Bt20	Brabham-Repco
1967	Denny Hulme	New Zealand	Brabham-Repco Bt20/Bt24	Brabham-Repco
1968	Graham Hill	British	Lotus-Ford 49/49B	Lotus-Ford
1969	Jackie Stewart	British	Matra-Ford MS10/MS80	Matra-Ford
1970	Jochen Rindt	Austrian	Lotus-Ford 49C/72	Lotus-Ford
1971	Jackie Stewart	British	Tyrrell-Ford 001/003	Tyrrell-Ford
1972	Emerson Fittipaldi	Brazilian	Lotus 72-Ford	Lotus-Ford
1973	Jackie Stewart	British	Tyrrell-Ford 005/006	Lotus-Ford
1974	Emerson Fittipaldi	Brazilian	McLaren M23-Ford	McLaren-Ford
1975	Niki Lauda	Austrian	Ferrari 312T	Ferrari
1976	James Hunt	British	McLaren M23-Ford	Ferrari
1977	Niki Lauda	Austrian	Ferrari 312T2	Ferrari
1978	Mario Andretti	USA	Lotus-Ford 78/79	Lotus-Ford
1979	Jody Scheckter	South African	Ferrari 312T3/T4	Ferrari
1980	Alan Jones	Australian	Williams FW07B-Ford	Williams-Ford
1981	Nelson Piquet	Brazilian	Brabham BT49C-Ford	Williams-Ford
1982	Keke Rosberg	Finnish	Williams-Ford FW07C/FW08	Ferrari
1983	Nelson Piquet	Brazilian	Brabham-BMW BT52/52B	Ferrari
1984	Niki Lauda	Austrian	McLaren MP4/2-TAG Porsche	McLaren-TAG
1985	Alain Prost	French	McLaren MP4/2B-TAG Porsche	McLaren-TAG
1986	Alain Prost	French	McLaren MP4/2C-TAG Porsche	Williams-Honda
1987	Nelson Piquet	Brazilian	Williams Fw11B-Honda	Williams-Honda
1988	Ayrton Senna	Brazilian	McLaren MP4/4-Honda	McLaren-Honda
1989	Alain Prost	French	McLaren MP4/5-Honda	McLaren-Honda
1990	Ayrton Senna	Brazilian	McLaren MP4/5B-Honda	McLaren-Honda
1991	Ayrton Senna	Brazilian	McLaren MP4/6-Honda	McLaren-Honda
1992	Nigel Mansell	British	Williams FW14B-Renault	Williams-Renault
1993	Alain Prost	French	Williams FW15C-Renault	Williams-Renault
1994	Michael Schumacher	German	Benetton B194-Ford	Williams-Renault
1995	Michael Schumacher	German	Benetton B195-Renault	Benetton-Renault
1996	Damon Hill	British	Williams FW18-Renault	Williams-Renault
1997	Jacques Villeneuve	Canadian	Williams FW19-Renault	Williams-Renault
1998	Mika Hakkinen	Finnish	McLaren MP4/13-Mercedes	McLaren-Mercedes
1999	Mika Hakkinen	Finnish	McLaren MP4/14-Mercedes	Ferrari
2000	Michael Schumacher	German	Ferrari F1-2000	Ferrari
2001	Michael Schumacher	German	Ferrari F1-2001	Ferrari
2002	Michael Schumacher	German	Ferrari F1-2002	Ferrari

620 Jacques Villeneuve prepares to restart after a pit stop at Interlagos (San Paulo). The 1997 World Champion started from the fifth row of the grid in 1998's Brazilian GP and eventually finished in seventh place.

621 top 1998 was a truly fantastic season for Mika Hakkinen; the Finnish driver at the wheel of the silvery McLaren-Mercedes conquered the World Championship title by winning no fewer than eight Grands Prix and accumulating 100 points.

621 bottom Ferrari and Williams were, apart from the McLaren-Mercedes of course, the protagonists of the 1998 season. The red cars had the unenviable task of chasing the silver McLarens. This photograph from the Brazilian GP shows Michael Schumacher trailing a Williams. The German driver finished the race third behind the McLaren-Mercedes of Hakkinen and Coulthard.

Drivers to Have Won the Most Championship Titles

Driver	Titles	Years
Juan Manuel Fangio	5	1951, 54-5-6-7
Alain Prost	4	1985-6, 89, 93
Jack Brabham	3	1959-60, 66
Niki Lauda	3	1975, 77, 84
Nelson Piquet	3	1981, 83, 87
Ayrton Senna	3	1988, 90-1
Jackie Stewart	3	1969, 71, 73
Michael Schumacher	3	1994-95-2000-01-02
Alberto Ascari	2	1952-3
Jim Clark	2	1963, 65
Emerson Fittipaldi	2	1972, 74
Mika Hakkinen	2	1998-9
Graham Hill	2	1962, 68

Drivers to Have Won the Most Grands Prix

Driver	Victories
Alain Prost	51
Michael Schumacher	61
Ayrton Senna	41
Nigel Mansell	31
Jackie Stewart	27
Jim Clark	25
Niki Lauda	25
Juan Manuel Fangio	24
Nelson Piquet	23
Damon Hill	22
Mika Hakkinen	18

Manufacturers to Have Won the Most Titles

Team	Titles	Years
Ferrari	8	1961, 64, 75-6-7, 79-82-83-99-2000-01-02
Williams	9	1980-1, 86-7, 92-3-4, 96-7
McLaren	9	1974, 1984-85, 1988-9-90-91, 1998-9
Lotus	7	1963, 65, 68, 70, 72-3, 78
Brabham	2	1966-7
Cooper	2	1959-60

Teams to Have Won the Most Grands Prix

Team	Victories
Ferrari	135
McLaren	130
Williams	103
Lotus	79
Brabham	35
Benetton	27
Tyrrell	23
BRM	17
Cooper	16
Renault	15
Alfa Romeo	10

Engine Suppliers to Have Won the Most Championship Titles

Maker	Titles	Years
Ferrari	12	1961-64-75-76-77-79 82-83-99-2000-01-02
Ford	10	1968-69-70-71 72-73-74-78 80-81
Honda	6	1986-87-88 89-90-91
Renault	6	1992-93-94 95-96-97
Climax	4	1959-60-63-65

GLOSSARY

- ***ABS*** - Anti-Block System, the original term for Anti-lock Brakes.
- ***Air dam (bib)*** - A transverse lip or bib, mounted under the nose of the car, which diverts air around the car and reduces the flow under the body.
- ***Ballooning*** - The aerodynamic effect which forces the rear part of the top to swell when the car is traveling at high speed. The effect is caused by the drop in air pressure resulting from the direction of the airflow over the convex shape of the windshield/roof. It is as if the top were being sucked up by the air above.
- ***Baquet*** - Literally "bath tub". It refers to cars at the beginning of the century in Europe with two rows of raised seats (single seats or divans) similar to those used in turn of the century horse-drawn carriages. Baquets were generally without front doors, a top or a windshield. The motor usually had four cylinders and displaced 3-4 liters. In the United States the term "touring" was often used. See Phaéton.
- ***Barchetta*** - An open top dedicated to racing without doors or a top and with uniform and streamlined bodywork. It had either one or two separate seats.
- ***Bateau*** - The shape of the rear end of open-topped racers at the beginning of the century which looked like the hull of a boat.
- ***Bellows*** - A part of the soft top, made from leather, plastic or canvas.
- ***Berlina*** - After the horse-drawn Berlin coach, Berline (Fr) or Berlina (It) is a closed car capable of carrying at least four people. Saloon (Eng) and Sedan (US) are the equivalent terms.
- ***Berlinetta*** - A little saloon, therefore a two-seater fixed head coupé. The equivalent Salonette was only ever used by MG.
- ***BHP*** - Brake Horsepower, or the rate at which an engine can work. One brake horsepower is 550 pounds-feet per second. Pounds-feet is a measure of torque; the time per cycle is shorter so the power is greater as engine speed rises. It is called Brake Horsepower because it is measured against a braking torque on a dynamometer.
- ***Boattail*** - The tapered form of the rear end. The term literally describes the shape of the vehicle's tail which resembled the bow of a boat. It was much used in racing.
- ***Break*** - A motorized carriage without side protection but with a fixed, non-rigid cover held up by rods like a canopy. Breaks were very basic vehicles in use at the turn of the century.
- ***Brougham*** - Coachwork term referring to a size half way between a limousine and a saloon, but with an open section over the front seats and a relatively small rear compartment for two.
- ***Bullnose*** - A term in use in Great Britain during the 1920's to indicate a type of radiator which resembled the nose of a bull.
- ***Cabriolet*** - This term has changed meaning significantly over the years and in different countries. During the 1920's and 30's in continental Europe it meant an open top with a top, two doors and four seats which was often derived from a sedan. The equivalent in Great Britain was called a Drophead Coupé while the English used the term cabriolet to mean a four-door open top. Concurrently in the United States, the term used was Convertible Coupé. Today a cabriolet describes open-topped cars derived from a sedan or coupé (i.e. from a hard top). It could also be understood to mean an open top with two rows of seats (4-5 seats) with just two doors.
- ***Chummy*** - In Great Britain from the 1920's and later, a chummy was an open-topped car. The vehicle was usually a 2+2, i.e. two full-size seats in front and two very small seats behind.
- ***Convertible*** - In the US from 1927 on, the term was used to mean a car with a soft, retractable top provided the top was hooked permanently to the bodywork, and therefore not removeable like for some roadsters. Other requisites were side windows (that opened) and the absence of lateral uprights and any framework above the waist of the car apart from the windshield. The most common and exact type had two doors and was therefore called a Convertible Coupé: those with four doors were called Convertible Sedans. In both cases, four or five people could be seated.
- ***Convertible Coupé*** - A two seater convertible. In the US in the 1930's the term was often synonymous with cabriolet though not with the modern usage of the word.
- ***Convertible Sedan*** - A four door convertible.
- ***Coupé*** - Pronounced "coupay", this is a French term for a shortened saloon, now much used by English-speaking manufacturers; American speech ignores the acute accent on the 'e' and refers to it as a 'coop'. Since the Sixties it has become the 2-door sporting version of a 4-seater saloon car. Before that the coupé was usually a 2-seater, or 2+2; drop-head coupés (dhc) had soft tops that folded down (as cabriolets) and fixed-head coupés (fhc) were the solid roof equivalent of a dhc. Drophead coupés, cabriolets and convertibles all have roll-up side windows - Roadsters did not in the Fifties.
- ***De Ville*** - A town carriage with the front seats covered by a removable panel, giving rise to Coupé de Ville or Limousine de Ville.
- ***Downforce*** - The overall downward force exerted by aerodynamic attachments on the upper surface of the car.
- ***Drag*** - The overall aerodynamic force encountered by the body as it goes through the air. The drag coefficient gives the measure of efficiency of the shape compared with a vertical flat plate of coefficient 1.
- ***Drophead Coupé*** - A drophead coupé was the British term for the equivalent of the American term 'Convertible Coupé' and continental European 'Cabriolet' from the 1930's on.
- ***Dual Cowl*** - A design of car which saw the cab divided into two compartments - front and back - and separated by metal panels and a supplementary windshield. It was a typical configuration of luxury cabriolets during the 1930's, 40's and 50's.
- ***Eddy*** - The turbulent air created in the wake of the car as it moves through the air. Eddies increase drag.
- ***ESP*** - Electronic Stability Programme. Porsche's term for the overall computer control that can apply individual brakes or decrease the power to maintain traction on slippery roads, or to recover a potentially dangerous cornering situation. Other manufacturers use different initials for the same functions.
- ***Facia*** - The complete padded panel with instruments, and controls for heating, radio etc. The old dashboard just carried instruments and switches.
- ***Fairing*** - A panel added to lessen aerodynamic drag as in the covering of rear wheel arches or in the head-fairing behind the seats of some open two-seaters.
- ***Fastback*** - A body with a rear section that slopes from roof to tail in a straight or convex line - as the pre-war Airline designs.
- ***Fencer's Mask*** - The term describes a type of radiator grill designed from the 1930's which resembled a fencer's mask for its shape and the tight weave of the grill.
- ***GT*** - Gran Turismo or Grand Touring was a fixed-head coupé with, probably, a fast-back, giving sports car performance in comfort for two people and luggage. The initials have been abused over the years to imply high performance without style.
- ***Hard Top*** - A removable top to replace the soft top. It is made from plastic and usually of the same color as the car body. It has a Plexiglas or glass rear window. In Targa models, the hard top fits between the windshield and a central upright.
- ***Hatchback*** - A body with an opening rear panel.
- ***Homologated*** - FIA-recognized
- ***Kamm tail*** - A sharp vertical cut-off at the rear of the car. This retains the streamlining effect of a long shapely tail but provides quick separation from the drag-inducing eddies created by a conventional notchback.
- ***Landau*** - A partially open limousine. The open part was usually the front where the driver sat.
- ***Landaulet*** - A Landau with the rear part of the roof (hard or soft) which could be opened or folded down.
- ***Lift*** - Air flowing over surfaces creates a pressure. If the pressure below a body is greater than above, the result is lift. The opposite is usually referred to as negative lift. The pressure difference multiplied by the surface area gives the overall upwards or downwards force.
- ***Limousine*** - Originally a six-light large saloon - three windows per side - now any large car capable of carrying six or more people.
- ***Notchback*** - A body with separate rear luggage compartment
- ***Oversteer*** - Handling term to denote that the tire slip angle is greater at the rear than at the front. The car tightens its line in a corner and less steering lock is required.
- ***Phaéton*** - A French term taken from the name of the son of Helios, Greek god of the sun. It means an open-topped car with four seats. At the beginning of the century the term was often used instead of baquet. During the 1930's, it was synonymous in the US with Convertible Sedan and Convertible Phaéton. The term Double Phaéton was also used.
- ***Ragtop*** - the same as soft top.
- ***Rear wing*** - A wing across the rear of the car, shaped to give some downforce and straighten the air-flow to reduce the turbulence behind the car.
- ***Rib*** - A rigid arc of metal or wood which makes up part of the rigid or semi-rigid frame of the top.
- ***Roadster*** - The term 'roadster' has had several meanings depending on the origin and the period. In the US and sometimes in Europe at the start of the century, it meant models that were successors to, and sometimes contemporary with, Runabouts but which were more powerful and fitted with a jump seat. They did not have a top. More recently, the term has meant 'sports car' in Anglo Saxon countries. Generally it is a two seater sports car, small and powerful.
- ***Roll bar*** - A metal bar to protect the car in case it rolls over. If located in the center of the cab in place of the central upright, it may be a single piece in the form of an arc or it may be a 'pop-up' bar which appears when the car overturns. If placed behind the headrests, it may be composed of two pieces, either fixed or 'pop-up'.
- ***Runabout*** - A small, light two-seater. Runabout was a term used mainly in the United States to indicate a small open car, generally without a top. It was basic, cheap and generally had a single cylinder motor.
- ***Saloon*** - English equivalent to Sedan (US) and Berlina (It), derived from the room in a house.
- ***Sedan*** - American name for Saloon.
- ***Sedanca*** - A type of early body design in which the top extended for a quarter of a circle and covered only the passengers in the rear seats.
- ***Sill*** - The boxed panel below the bottom of the door opening. Called the rocker panel in America.
- ***Skirt*** - Technically this refers to plastic sheet hanging down under the sills to ensure that underbody air is directed to the rear of the car. On road cars, the skirt refers to any moulding mounted below the sills and is usually only for cosmetic purposes.
- ***Slip angle*** - When a tire is subjected to a cornering force it runs at an angle to the direction it is pointing. This is known as the slip angle.
- ***Spider*** - The continental European equivalent of the English term Roadster. It was first used to describe small, fast horse-drawn carriages but came to describe open-topped two seaters or 2+2's. From a commercial point of view, in Europe the term Spider is used when talking about an open top that is an independent design, i.e. not derived from a sedan (unlike a cabriolet).
- ***Spoiler*** - Usually fitted at the rear of the car, this acts like a Kamm tail and interrupts the air flow; by its shape it also acts to provide downforce. Front spoilers are shaped to provide front downforce, rather than just act as air diverters.
- ***Strake*** - a curved strip on the side of the bodywork. This comes from the full-length wooden planks used on in boat-building.
- ***Streamlined*** - A term which simply means aerodynamic. It was predominantly used to describe convertibles during the 1950's and 60's but its origin is drawn from futuristic American models from the 1930's based on airplane design. The coachwork is uniform with all features designed to offer least wind resistance.
- ***Supercharger*** - Engine-driven air-pump or compressor which supplies air under pressure to the engine's intake system.
- ***Tank*** - Denotes open tops with completely closed and uniform bodywork except for the opening of the cab. See Barchetta.
- ***Targa*** - An open-topped car with a hard top provided. It is a halfway house between a spider and a coupé. It sometimes has a longitudinal crosspiece. In this case the hard top is made up of two pieces.
- ***Tonneau*** - The rear part of the cab (see Phaéton).
- ***Tonneau Cover*** - Soft cover used on parked roadsters to protect the cab from the rain when the top is down.
- ***Top*** - Soft covering laid over a framework, generally made of metal, with joints and a rib to hold it taut both crossways and lengthways. Tops were for a long time made from waxed canvas, and occasionally still are, although today plastic materials are usually used. They often have two layers and sometimes are made from two separate pieces. The tops on modern convertibles are partially or totally opened and closed electrically taking approximately 25 seconds depending on the complexity of the mechanism.
- ***Torpedo*** - Long wheelbase open tops from the top to the bottom end of the market. They succeeded Tourers and Phaétons. The coachwork was made of flat panels, the doors were low and the sides offered no protection from the weather. The soft top turned around a pin placed in the center of the body. It was held taut by ribs and fixed in place by uprights or tie-rods. With the top down, the metallic upper part of the torpedo seemed very flat; with the top up, there was a huge expanse between the pin and the front fastener.
- ***Tourer*** - An open 2-door car with four seats and a cabriolet top. Twenties Tourers often had smaller doors for the rear compartment.
- ***Touring/tourer*** - Used in the USA at the start of the century to mean the equivalent of a European baquet. During the 1920's in the US, it came to mean a four-seater open top with four doors, generally in the medium-low segment of the market.
- ***Traction Control*** - Original form of ESP where braking or power can be adjusted to maintain traction, but not to correct cornering problems.

- **Turbo(charger)** - Compressor, driven by a turbine which is powered by the engine's exhaust gases.
- **Understeer** - Handling term to denote that the tire slip angle is greater at the front than at the rear. The car runs wide in a corner and more steering lock is required.
- **Venturi** - Underbody ducts at the rear of the car which are shaped to create negative pressure and therefore downforce.

- **Vis a vis** - A very early type of car, almost always open-topped, in which the two rows of passengers sat face to face.
- **4-cam** - Term used to show that a vee-engine has twin overhead camshafts for each bank of cylinders. Also quad-cam.
- **4-choke** - Each intake hole in a carburetter is called a choke because the air-flow is choked to create the low pressure to suck the fuel out of the jets. With

big V-8s, a single carburetter with four chokes is a very efficient means of supplying the mixture. Most have progressive later opening of the larger pair of chokes.
- **4WD** - Four-wheel-drive. FWD means Front-wheel-drive.
- **4WS** - Four wheel steering, the computer-controlled system. that actively steers the rear wheels by small amounts to improve handling.

BIBLIOGRAPHY

PART ONE

AA. VV., *Daimler 1896-1996*, Jaguar Italia SpA, 1996
AA. VV., *Der Unschützbare Cabrio*, Hamr Verlag Gmbh, 1995
AA. VV., *Detroit style automotive form 1925-1950*, Detroit Institute of Arts, 1985
AA. VV., *Ferrari 1946-1990 Opera Omnia*, Automobilia, 1990
AA. VV., *Museo Vincenzo Lancia*, Lancia, 1972
AA. VV., *Peugeot 60 ans de cabriolets*, Automobiles Peugeot, 1987
AA. VV., *Pininfarina catalogue raisonné 1930-1990*, Automobilia, 1990
AA. VV., *Tempi di mobilità*, Audi Ag, 1992
AA. VV., *The Great American Convertibles*, Beekman House, 1991
AA. VV., *Tutte le Alfa Romeo 1910-1995*, Editoriale Domus, 1995
AA. VV., *Tutte le Fiat*, Editoriale Domus, 1970
AA. VV., *Volvo 1927-1996*, Volvo Car Corporation, 1996
Adcock, I., *The birth of the MG F*, Bloomsbury Publishing, 1996
Alfieri, B., *Form Mercedes Benz*, Automobilia, 1995
Alfieri, B., Casucci, P., *Ferrari Spider 1949-1990*, Automobilia, 1989
Altieri, P., Lurani, G., *Alfa Romeo catalogue raisonné 1910-1989*, Automobilia, 1988
Amatori, F., *Storia della Lancia 1906-1969*, Fabbri Editori, 1992
Burgess Wise, D., *Tutta la storia della Ford*, Automobilia, 1982
Cancellieri, G., De Agostini, C., *La storia della Maserati*, Automobilia, 1995
Cherret, A., *Alfa Romeo Tipo 6C 1500, 1750, 1900*, Giorgio Nada Editore, 1990
De Serres, O., *Cabriolets Français 1945-1995*, Epa Editions, 1995
Dumont, P., *Tutta la storia della Renault*, Automobilia, 1982
Flammang, J., *Chronicle of the American Automobile*, Publications International, 1994
Flammang, J., *Chrysler Chronicle*, Publications International, 1995
Fusi, L., *Alfa Romeo, tutte le vetture dal 1910*, Emmeti Grafica Editrice, 1978
Lewandowski, J., *Mercedes Benz catalogue raisonné 1886-1990*, Automobilia, 1990
Lewandowski, J., *Opel*, Sudwest, 1995
Lorieux, G., Wolgensinger, J., *Genealogie*, Citroën, 1988
Madaro, G., *Alfa Romeo Duetto*, Giorgio Nada Editore, 1990
Moretti, V., *Ghia*, Automobilia, 1991
Newbery, J., *Classic Convertibles*, Grange Books, 1994
Norris, I., *Jaguar catalogue raisonné 1922-1992*, Automobilia, 1991
Pasini S., Solieri, S., *Porsche 356*, Edizioni Rebecchi, 1987
Schrader, H., *BMW Automobili*, Editoriale Semelfin, 1992
Schrader, H., *Klassische Cabriolets*, Blv, 1986
Turinetto, M., *Automobile: le forme del design*, Progetto Leonardo, 1991
Wolgensinger, J., *André Citroën*, Flammarion, 1991

• **Specialized magazines and periodicals**
Auto, Conti Editore SpA
AutoCapital, Editoriale Motori srl
La Manovella e ruote a raggi, Giorgio Nada Editore
Le Grandi Automobili, Automobilia
Ruoteclassiche, Editoriale Internazionale Milano SpA
Guida all'acquisto di tutto, Edizioni Errezeta
Radar Coupé & Spider, Studio Zeta Editore

PART TWO

Alfa Romeo Tradition, Griffith Borgeson, Haynes Publishing, Somerset, UK, 1990.
Alfa Romeo, Le Vetture dal 1910, Luigi Fusi, Editrice Adiemme, Milan, Italy, 1965.
America, Great Marques of, Jonathan Wood, Octopus Books, London, UK, 1986.
American Automobile, Art of, Nick Georgano, Cadogan Publishing, London, UK, 1985.

Austin Healey, Original, Anders Clausager, Bay View Books, Devon, UK, 1990.
BMW, A History, Halwart Schrader, Osprey Publishing, London, UK, 1979.
Boss Wheels, Robert C.Bowden, TAB Books, Pennsylvania, USA, 1979.
Bristol Cars and Engines, L.J.K.Setright, Motor Racing Publications, Surrey, UK, 1974.
Bristol Cars Gold Portfolio, Various Road Tests, Brooklands Books, Surrey, UK, 1988.
British Post-war Classic Cars, Jonathan Wood, Osprey Publishing, London, UK, 1980.
Camaro (Chevrolet), The Great, Michael Lamm, Lamm-Morada Publishing, California, USA, 1978.
Cars of the Fifties & Sixties, Michael Sedgwick, Grange Books, London, UK, 1983.
Cars of the Seventies & Eighties, Nick Georgano, Grange Books, London, UK, 1990.
Classic Cars around the world, Michael Bowler, Parragon, Bristol, UK, 1995.
Corvette (Chevrolet), Karl Ludvigsen, Automobile Quarterly, New Jersey, USA, 1977.
Corvette, Cream of the Crop, Henry Rasmussen, Top Ten Publishing, California, USA, 1991.
Corvette, The Newest, Michael Lamm, Lamm-Morada Publishing, California, USA, 1984.
Corvettes (Chevrolet) 1953-88, Richard Langworth, Motor Racing Publications, Surrey, UK, 1988.
De Tomaso Pantera Gold Portfolio, Various Road Tests, Brooklands Books, Surrey, UK, 1992.
Decade of Dazzle, Fifties America, Henry Rasmussen, Motorbooks International, Wisconsin, USA, 1987.
Encyclopaedia of Motorcars, N. Georgano et al, Ebury Press, London, UK, 1973.
Fastest Cars around the world, Michael Bowler, Parragon, Bristol, UK, 1995.
Ferrari, the Complete, Godfrey Eaton, Cadogan Books, London, UK, 1986.
Ferrari, The Machines and the Man, Pete Lyons, Foulis, Somerset, UK, 1989.
Fiat Sports Cars, Graham Robson, Osprey Publishing, London, UK, 1984.
Fifty years of classic Cars, Jonathan Wood, Colour Library Books, Surrey, UK, 1994.
Ghia, Ford's Carrozzeria, David Burgess-Wise, Osprey Publishing, London UK, 1985.
Giugiaro and Ital Design, Akira Fujimoto, Car Styling Publishing, Tokyo, Japan, 1981.
Jaguar Saloon Cars, Paul Skilleter, Haynes Publishing, Somerset, UK, 1988.
Jaguar Sports Cars, Paul Skilleter, Haynes Publishing, Somerset, UK, 1983.
Japanese Car, Complete History, Marco Ruiz, Foulis, Somerset, UK, 1988.
Jensen and Healey Stories, Browning & Blunsden, Motor Racing Publications, Surrey, UK 1974.
Lamborghini, Stefano Pasini, Automobilia, Milan, Italy, 1985.
Lamborghini, the Complete Book, Pete Lyons, Foulis, Somerset, UK, 1988.
Lotus Book, The, William Taylor, Coterie Press, London UK, 1998.
Maserati 1965-75, Various Road Tests, Brooklands Books, Surrey, UK, 1985.
Maserati from 1926, Richard Crump, Foulis, Somerset, UK, 1983.
Mercedes-Benz Motor..Engines, Anon, Daimler-Benz Ag, Stuttgart, Germany, 1973.
MG - Britain's Favourite Sports Car, Malcolm Green, Haynes Publishing, Somerset, UK, 1998.
MG by McComb, Wilson McComb, Osprey Publishing, London, UK, 1990.
Mille Miglia, la storia della, Giovanni Lurani, I G de Agostini, Novara, Italy, 1979.
Nissan 300ZX, Ray Hutton, Motor Racing Publications, Surrey, UK, 1990.
On Four Wheels, Anon - part work, Orbis Publishing, London, UK, 1975.
Pininfarina, Cinquantanni, Anon, Industrie Pininfarina SpA, Turin, Italy, 1980.
Porsche 911 Turbo, Various Road Tests, Brooklands Books, Surrey, UK, 1988.
Porsche Catalogues, Malcolm Toogood, Apple Press, London, UK, 1991.
Porsche Specials, Boschen & Barth, Patrick Stephens, Northants, UK, 1986.

Renault, Romance of, Edouard Seidler, Edita SA, Lausanne, Switzerland, 1973.
Rootes Group, Cars of the, Graham Robson, Motor Racing Publications, Surrey, UK, 1990.
RS, The Faster Fords, Jeremy Walton, Motor Racing Publications, Surrey, UK, 1987.
Saab, The Innovator, Mark Chatterton, David & Charles, London, UK, 1980.
Touring Superleggera, Anderloni & Anselmi, Autocritica srl, Rome, Italy, 1983.
Triumph TRs, The Complete Story, Graham Robson, Crowood Press, Wiltshire, UK, 1991.
TVR Collectors Guide, Graham Robson, Motor Racing Publications, Surrey, UK, 1987.
TVR Portfolios 1959-94, Various Road Tests, Brooklands Books, Surrey, UK, 1996.
World Car Catalogue 1975-2001, Anon, Hallwag AG, Berne, Switzerland, Annual.
Zagato, Settant'anni, Michele Marchiano, Giorgio Nada Editore, Milan, Italy, 1989.

• **Magazines**
Autocar, Iliffe - IPC Business Press - Haymarket, UK.
Autosport, Autosport - Haymarket, UK.
Classic Car, IPC Business Press - EMAP, UK.
Motor, Temple Press - IPC Business Press, UK.
Autocritica srl, Rome, Italy.
Motor Sport, Teesdale Press - Haymarket, UK.
Crowood Press, Wiltshire, UK.
Road and Track, CBS Publications, California, USA.

PART THREE

AA. VV., *Grand Prix Story*, Hellwag, 1990
AA. VV., *Daimler 1896-1996*, Jaguar Italia SpA, 1996
AA. VV., *Ferrari 1946-1990 Opera Omnia*, Automobilia, 1990
AA. VV., *Official Historical Championship Car Record Book*, CART Ind, 1998
AA. VV., *Tutte le Alfa Romeo 1910-1995*, Editoriale Domus, 1995
AA. VV., *Tutte le Fiat*, Editoriale Domus, 1970
AA.VV., *Le macchine Sport e Prototipo 1923-82*, Automobilia, 1982
Altieri, P., Lurani, G., *Alfa Romeo Catalogue Raisonné 1910-1989*, Automobilia, 1988
Amatori, F., *Storia della Lancia 1906-1969*, Fabbri Editori, 1992
Brown, D, *Monaco Grand Prix*, Motor Racing Publications, 1989
Casamassima, P, *Storia della Formula 1*, Edizioni Calder, 1996
Demaus, A. B., *Motor Sport in the 20s*, Alan Sutton, 1989
Flammang, J., *Chronicle of the American Automobile*, Publications International, 1994
Fusi, L., *Alfa Romeo, tutte le vetture dal 1910*, Emmeti Grafica Editrice, 1978
Lewandowski, J., *Mercedes Benz Catologue Raisonné 1886-1990*, Automobilia, 1990
Norris, I., *Jaguar Catologue Raisonné 1922-1992*, Automobilia, 1991
Raffaelli, F. & F., *Terra di piloti e di motori*, Artioli Editore, 1994
Rendall, I., *Bandiera a scacchi*, Vallardi & Associati, 1993
Schrader, H., *BMW Automobili*, Editoriale Semelfin, 1992

• **Annuals**
AA. VV, *Annuari Autosprint*, Conti Editore
Deschenaux, J., *Marlboro Grand Prix Guide*, Charles Stewart & Co Ltc
Higham, P., *The Guinness Guide to International Motor Racing*, Guinness Publishing

• **Specialist magazines and periodicals**
Auto, Conti Editore SpA
AutoCapital, Editoriale Motori srl
Autosprint, Conti Editore
La Manovella e ruote a raggi, Giorgio Nada Editore
Le Grandi Automobili, Automobilia
Ruoteclassiche, Editoriale Internazionale Milano SpA
Guida all'acquisto di tutto, Edizioni Errezeta
Radar Coupé & Spider, Studio Zeta Editore

625

PHOTOGRAPHIC CREDITS

Pages 392-393: Neill Bruce Automobile Photolibrary
Pages 394-395: Maggi & Maggi
Pages 396-397, 398-399, 400-401: Ron Kimball Stock
Pages 402 and 403, 404 and 405: Maggi & Maggi
Pages 406 and 407, 408-409, 410 and 411: Midsummer Books LTD
Pages 412 and 413: Maggi & Maggi
Pages 414-415: Fotostudio Zumbrunn
Pages 416-417: Midsummer Books LTD
Pages 418-419: Ron Kimball Stock Photography
Pages 420-421, 422-423: Neill Bruce Automobile Photolibrary
Pages 424 and 425: Maggi & Maggi
Pages 426 and 427: Giorgio Nada Editore
Pages 428 and 429: Maggi & Maggi
Pages 430 and 431: Ron Kimball Stock Photography
Pages 432-433: René Staud Studios
Pages 434-435: Ron Kimball Stock Photography
Pages 436 and 437, 438-439: Midsummer Books LTD
Pages 440-441: Neill Bruce Automobile Photolibrary
Pages 442-443: Ron Kimball Stock Photography
Pages 444-445: Neill Bruce Automobile Photolibrary
Pages 446-447, 448-449: Fotostudio Zumbrunn
Pages 450-451: Ron Kimball Stock Photography
Pages 452-453: Neill Bruce Automobile Photolibrary
Pages 454-455: Fotostudio Zumbrunn
Pages 456-457: Midsummer Books LTD
Pages 458 and 459, 460 and 461: Fotostudio Zumbrunn
Pages 462-463 top: René Staud Studios
Page 462 bottom, 464-465: Fotostudio Zumbrunn
Pages 466 and 467: Neill Bruce Automobile Photolibrary
Pages 468 and 469: Midsummer Books LTD
Pages 470 and 471, 472 top: Fotostudio Zumbrunn
Pages 472-473: René Staud Studios
Pages 474-475, 476 and 477: Fotostudio Zumbrunn
Pages 478-479: Ron Kimball Stock Photography
Pages 480-481: Jim Fets
Pages 482-483: Ron Kimball Stock Photography
Pages 484-485: Maggi & Maggi
Pages 486-487: Archivio White Star
Pages 488-489, 490-491: Ron Kimball Stock Photography
Pages 492-493: Atelier Schlegelmilch
Pages 494 and 495: Maggi & Maggi
Pages 496 and 497, 498 and 499, 500 and 501: Fotostudio Zumbrunn
Pages 502 and 503: René Staud Studios
Pages 504-505, 506-507: Fotostudio Zumbrunn
Page 507 top: Neill Bruce Automobile Photolibrary
Pages 508 and 509: Fotostudio Zumbrunn
Pages 510-511, 512-513: Neill Bruce Automobile Photolibrary
Pages 514-515, 516 and 517, 518-519: Midsummer Books LTD
Pages 520 and 521, 522 and 523: Neill Bruce Automobile Photolibrary
Pages 524-525, 526 and 527: Ron Kimball Stock Photography
Pages 528 and 529: Fotostudio Zumbrunn
Pages 530-531: Jim Fets;
Pages 532-533, 534-535: Ron Kimball Stock Photography
Page 537 top: Photo 4
Page 538 left: Farabolafoto
Pages 538-539 bottom and 539: Fotostudio Zumbrunn
Pages 540-541: Atelier Schlegelmilch
Page 542 top left: Daimler Benz Archives
Page 542 bottom left: Collezione Privata
Pages 542-543 bottom: GP Library
Page 542 center: Archivio Ferrari
Page 544: Photo 4
Page 545: Paul Henri Cahier
Pages 546 top and 547 center: The National Motor Museum Bealieau

Pages 546-547 and 547 bottom: The Peter Roberts Collection c/o Neill Bruce
Pages 548, 548-549, 549 bottom right: Atelier Schlegelmilch
Page 548 bottom left: GP Library
Page 550 top: Actualfoto
Page 550 bottom: The Peter Roberts Collection c/o Neill Bruce
Pages 550 center left and 551 right: Photo 4
Pages 550-551, 551 left and bottom: Atelier Schlegelmilch
Pages 552 left, top right, 553 center right and left and bottom: Archivio Storico Alfa Romeo
Page 552 bottom right: Actualfoto
Page 553 top: The Peter Roberts Collection c/o Neill Bruce
Pages 554 center and 555 top: Actualfoto
Page 554 bottom: Farabolafoto
Pages 555 bottom, 556 top and 557 bottom left, center right and bottom: The Peter Roberts Collection c/o Neill Bruce
Pages 556 center and 556-557: Sporting Pictures
Page 557 top left: Daimler Benz Archives
Page 557 top right: Neill Bruce
Page 558 top left and center right: Daimler Benz Archives
Pages 558-559 and 559 right: Farabolafoto
Page 558 center left: The Peter Roberts Collection c/o Neill Bruce
Page 558 bottom and 559 bottom: Actualfoto
Page 558 top right: Neill Bruce
Page 559 top: GP Library
Page 560 top left and center, center right and bottom: Actualfoto
Page 560 top right: Farabolafoto
Page 561 top and center: GP Library
Page 561 bottom left: Neill Bruce
Page 561 bottom right: The Peter Roberts Collection c/o Neill Bruce
Page 562: Neill Bruce
Pages 562-563: Farabolafoto
Page 563 top: The Peter Roberts Collection c/o Neill Bruce
Page 563 center right: Photo 4
Page 563 bottom: Upi Corbis
Page 563 bottom right: Actualfoto
Pages 564 top center, center right and bottom and 565 bottom: Atelier Schlegelmilch
Pages 564 left and top right, 564-565, 565 top: The Peter Roberts Collection c/o Neill Bruce
Pages 566 top and 567 bottom: Atelier Schlegelmilch
Page 566 center top left: Photo 4
Pages 566 center right and bottom, 566-567: GP Library
Page 566 center left: Neill Bruce
Page 567 top: Farabolafoto
Page 568 top and center right: GP Library
Pages 568 center left, bottom, 568-569, 569, 570 top, bottom, 571 top and bottom: Atelier Schlegelmilch
Pages 570-571 and 571 center: Actualfoto
Page 572 top: Farabolafoto
Page 572 left: The National Motor Museum Bealieau
Pages 572-573 and 573 top: GP Library
Pages 572 center, 573 bottom right: Actualfoto
Page 573 bottom: Atelier Schlegelmilch
Pages 574 top and 574-575: Neill Bruce
Page 574 bottom left: Farabolafoto
Pages 574 bottom right, 575 top left and bottom: GP Library
Page 575 top right: Actualfoto
Page 576 top and bottom: GP Library

Page 576 right: Actualfoto
Page 576 center: Farabolafoto
Pages 576-577, 577 top: Atelier Schlegelmilch
Pages 578 top, left, bottom, 579 top right and bottom: GP Library
Pages 578-579, 579 top left and bottom: Actualfoto
Page 579 center left: Sporting Pictures
Pages 580 center right, 581 bottom: Actualfoto
Pages 580 top left, 581 top: GP Library
Pages 580-581: Foto Zumbrunn
Page 580 bottom: The Peter Roberts Collection c/o Neill Bruce
Page 581 bottom right: Sporting Pictures
Pages 582, 583: Atelier Schlegelmilch
Pages 584 top, center left, bottom, 585 top, center and bottom left: Sporting Pictures
Pages 584-585: Actualfoto
Page 584 bottom right: Farabolafoto
Pages 586 top left, 587 top left: Sporting Pictures
Page 586 center right: Actualfoto
Pages 586 top right, 586-587: GP Library
Pages 586 bottom right, 587 center left: Photo 4
Page 587 top left and bottom: Atelier Schlegelmilch
Pages 588 top left and bottom, right, 588-589, 589 top right, 589: Photo 4
Pages 588 center left, 589 top left: Sporting Pictures
Pages 590 first, second and fourth picture from above, 591 bottom left: Sporting Pictures
Pages 590 third picture from above, 591 top, 590-591, 591 bottom right: Photo 4
Page 590 fifth picture from above: GP Library
Page 592: Photo 4
Pages 592 bottom right, 593 bottom: Sporting Pictures
Page 593 center: The National Motor Museum Bealieu
Pages 594, 595 top right: Photo 4
Pages 594-595: Sporting Pictures
Page 595 top left: Farabolafoto
Pages 596 top, center and bottom, 597 top and bottom: GP Library
Page 596 top left: GP Library
Pages 596 top right, 597 center: Photo 4
Page 597 top and bottom: Sporting Pictures
Page 598 center left and bottom: Farabolafoto
Pages 598-599, 599 center right, bottom right: Photo 4
Pages 598 top right and bottom, top left, 599 top, center left, bottom left: Sporting Pictures
Pages 600 top left and right, 600-601, 601 top: Photo 4
Page 601 bottom left: Atelier Schlegelmilch
Pages 600 center left and right, 601 bottom right: Sporting Pictures
Page 600 bottom: Farabolafoto
Pages 602, 602-603, 603, 604, 604-605, 605 center and bottom: Photo 4
Page 605 top: Atelier Schlegelmilch
Pages 606-607, 607 center and bottom: Photo 4
Pages 606 bottom and 607 top : Sporting Pictures
Pages 608, 608-609, 609 top and center: Atelier Schlegelmilch
Page 609 bottom: Corbis
Pages 610, 611, 612, 613, 614, 615: Atelier Schlegelmilch
Pages 616 top, 617 center, 617 bottom: Paul-Henri Cahier and Bernard Cahier
Pages 616-617, 616 bottom, 617 top: Atelier Schlegelmilch
Page 618: Paul-Henri Cahier and Bernard Cahier
Pages 618-619, 619 bottom left, 619 bottom right: Atelier Schlegelmilch
Page 619 top: Archivio Ferrari
Pages 620 bottom, 621: Corbis

ACKNOWLEDGMENTS

The Publisher would like to thank:

FOR PART ONE
Press Offices:
Augerma; BMW Italia; Chrysler Italia; Citroën Italia; De Tomaso; Ford Italia; Jaguar Italia; Mercedes Italia; Nissan Italia; Peugeot Italia; Porsche Italia; Renault Italia; Rover Italia; Sidauto; Suzuki Italiaa; Toyota Italia
Petra Nemeth and Karin Ammach BMW Mobile Tradition,
Massimo Castagnola Archivio Storico Fiat,
Robert Denham Studebaker National Museum,
John Emery Auburn Cord Duesenberg Museum,
Mrs. Figini Quattroruote,
Cathy Latendresse and Alene Soloway Henry Ford Museum & Greenfield Village,
Isotta Fraschini Fabbrica Automobili S.p.A.,
Philip Hall The Sir Henry Royce Memorial Foundation,
Thomas A. Kayser Gilmore CCCA Museum,
Leo W. Lincourt Corvette Americana Hall of Fame,
Lotus
Laura Mancini GM Media Archives,
Aston Martin Lagonda Limited,
Stefano Mazza,
Charles Morgan,

Francesco Pagni Pininfarina Collection,
Klaus Stekkönig and Jens Torner Porsche,
Elvira Ruocco Archivio Storico Alfa Romeo,
The Triumph Sports Six Club,
Loris Tryon Blackhawk Automotive Museum,
Weimper Mercedes-Benz Classic Archives Team

FOR PART TWO
The foundation of all research is the contemporary report. I would like to thank all the motoring journalists, including many former colleagues, for their dedicated work in getting their stories whether it be from the manufacturers for new cars and road tests or by recording motor sport events. Following the absorption of my original employer, Motor, into Autocar, the latter has been my modern bible. I would also like to thank all the fellow motoring historians who have combed through these magazines and whose works now grace my reference library;I hope they are all included in the Bibliography. Some thanks are also due to those club secretaries who have unwittingly helped me by setting up useful web-sites. But my main thanks have to be reserved for my father, who brought me up to appreciate the finer points of vintage and classic

motoring, and my family who have allowed me to maintain that interest.

Michael Bowler

Archivio Storico Alfa Romeo;
Vittorio Berzero;
Archivio Ferrari;
Porsche Archives, Germany;
Maserati S.P.A.;
Stefano Mazza;
Mercedes-Benz Classic Archives Team;
TR Register Italy

FOR PART THREE
The Press Offices PPG CART, IRL, CSAI, Professional Sportcars;
The Archives of the Companies; the colleagues Giorgio Angeletti, Franco Carmignani, Guido Daelli, Marco Ragazzoni.
A special acknowledgment Anna Giudice.
The Publisher would like to thank: the Historical Archives of BMW, Ferrari, Fiat, Mercedes, Porsche, Indianapolis Motor Speedway;
Elvira Ruocco of Archivio Storico Alfa Romeo; Laura Mancini of GM Media Archives; Ken Breslauer and Bob Tronolone.